T0214628

Lecture Notes in Computer Science 12399

More information about this series at http://www.springer.com/series/7408

Jyotirmoy Deshmukh · Dejan Ničković (Eds.)

Runtime Verification

20th International Conference, RV 2020
Los Angeles, CA, USA, October 6–9, 2020
Proceedings

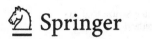 Springer

Editors
Jyotirmoy Deshmukh (iD)
University of Southern California
Los Angeles, CA, USA

Dejan Ničković (iD)
AIT Austrian Institute of Technology GmbH
Vienna, Austria

ISSN 0302-9743   ISSN 1611-3349   (electronic)
Lecture Notes in Computer Science
ISBN 978-3-030-60507-0   ISBN 978-3-030-60508-7   (eBook)
https://doi.org/10.1007/978-3-030-60508-7

LNCS Sublibrary: SL2 – Programming and Software Engineering

This Springer imprint is published by the registered company Springer Nature Switzerland AG
The registered company address is: Gewerbestrasse 11, 6330 Cham, Switzerland

Preface

This volume contains the refereed proceedings of the 20th International Conference on Runtime Verification (RV 2020), held virtually October 6–9, 2020.

The RV series is a sequence of annual meetings that brings together scientists from both academia and industry interested in investigating novel lightweight formal methods to monitor, analyze, and guide the runtime behavior of software and hardware systems. Runtime verification techniques are crucial for system correctness, reliability, and robustness; they provide an additional level of rigor and effectiveness compared to conventional testing, and are generally more practical than exhaustive formal verification. Runtime verification can be used prior to deployment, for testing, verification, and debugging purposes, and after deployment for ensuring reliability, safety, and security, for providing fault containment and recovery, as well as online system repair.

RV started in 2001 as an annual workshop and turned into a conference in 2010. The workshops were organized as satellite events of established forums, including the Conference on Computer-Aided Verification and ETAPS. The proceedings of RV from 2001 to 2005 were published in the *Electronic Notes in Theoretical Computer Science*. Since 2006, the RV proceedings have been published in Springer's *Lecture Notes in Computer Science*. Previous RV conferences took place in Istanbul, Turkey (2012); Rennes, France (2013); Toronto, Canada (2014); Vienna, Austria (2015); Madrid, Spain (2016); Seattle, USA (2017); Limassol, Cyprus (2018); and Porto, Portugal (2019).

In 2020, RV celebrated its 20th edition, and to mark this occasion, the conference had a couple of new initiatives. The first initiative was to invite researchers from a special focus area to submit papers; the focus area for RV 2020 was "Runtime Verification for Autonomy." The second initiative was a panel discussion on RV for Autonomy, which invited selected prominent researchers from academia and practitioners from industry to serve as panelists. The panel focused on the role of runtime verification in the emerging field of autonomous systems, highlighting the theoretical and technical challenges and presenting potential opportunities.

This year we received 43 submissions, 27 as regular contributions, and 16 as short, tool, or benchmark papers. Each of these submissions went through a rigorous single-blind review process, as a result of which most papers received four reviews and all papers received at least three review reports. The committee selected 23 contributions, 14 regular and 9 short/tool/benchmark papers for presentation during the conference and inclusion in these proceedings. The evaluation and selection process involved thorough discussions among the members of the Program Committee and external reviewers through the EasyChair conference manager, before reaching a consensus on the final decisions.

The conference featured three keynote speakers:

- Katherine Driggs-Campbell, University of Illinois at Urbana-Champaign, USA
- Lane Desborough, Nudge BG, Inc., USA
- Thomas Henzinger, IST Austria, Austria

The conference included five tutorials on the first day, including one invited tutorial and four other tutorials selected to cover a variety of topics relevant to RV:

- Laura Nenzi, Ezio Bartocci, Luca Bortolussi, Michele Loreti, and Ennio Visconti presented the invited tutorial on "Monitoring Spatio-Temporal Properties"
- Yanhong A. Liu and Scott D. Stoller presented a tutorial on "Assurance of Distributed Algorithms and Systems: Runtime Checking of Safety and Liveness"
- Joshua Heneage Dawes, Marta Han, Omar Javed, Giles Reger, Giovanni Franzoni, and Andreas Pfeiffer presented a tutorial on "Analysing the Performance of Python-based Web Services with the VyPR Framework"
- Maximilian Schwenger presented a tutorial on "Monitoring Cyber-Physical Systems: From Design to Integration"
- Klaus Havelund and Doron Peled presented a tutorial on "BDDs for Representing Data in Runtime Verification"

The 2020 RV Test of Timed Award was given to Nicholas Nethercote and Julian Seward for their RV 2003 seminal paper "Valgrind: A Program Supervision Framework" on the dynamic analysis of programs.

RV 2020 is the result of the combined efforts of many individuals to whom we are deeply grateful. In particular, we thank the Program Committee members and sub-reviewers for their accurate and timely reviewing, all authors for their submissions, and all attendees of the conference for their participation. We thank Houssam Abbas for helping us organize the poster session. We are very grateful to RV sponsor Toyota Research Institute, USA, and Springer who provided an award for the best RV paper. We thank the RV Steering Committee for their support.

October 2020   Jyotirmoy Deshmukh
                                                               Dejan Ničković

Organization

RV Program Chairs

Jyotirmoy Deshmukh   University of Southern California, USA
Dejan Ničković   Austrian Institute of Technology (AIT), Austria

RV Poster and Demo Chair

Houssam Abbas   Oregon State University, USA

RV Program Committee

Houssam Abbas   Oregon State University, USA
Wolfgang Ahrendt   Chalmers University of Technology, Sweden
Ezio Bartocci   Vienna University of Technology, Austria
Nicolas Basset   Verimag, France
Domenico Bianculli   University of Luxembourg, Luxembourg
Borzoo Bonakdarpour   Michigan State University, USA
Chih-Hong Cheng   Denso, Germany
Katherine Driggs Campbell   University of Illinois at Urbana-Champaign, USA
Georgios Fainekos   Arizona State University, USA
Ylies Falcone   University of Grenoble Alpes, Inria, France
Chuchu Fan   Massachusetts Institute of Technology, USA
Lu Feng   University of Virginia, USA
Thomas Ferrère   Imagination Technologies, UK
Bernd Finkbeiner   Saarland University, Germany
Sebastian Fischmeister   University of Waterloo, Canada
Dana Fisman   Ben-Gurion University, Israel
Adrian Francalanza   University of Malta, Malta
Radu Grosu   Vienna University of Technology, Austria
Sylvain Hallè   Universitè du Quèbec à Chicoutimi, Canada
Klaus Havelund   NASA JPL, USA
Stefan Jakšić   Austrian Institute of Technology (AIT), Austria
Violet Ka I. Pun   Western Norway University of Applied Sciences, Norway
Jim Kapinski   Amazon, USA
Safraz Khurshid   The University of Texas at Austin, USA
Bettina Könighofer   TU Graz, Austria
Martin Leucker   University of Lübeck, Germany
Chung-Wei Lin   National Taiwan University, Taiwan

David Lo	Singapore Management University, Singapore
Leonardo Mariani	University of Milano-Bicocca, Italy
Nicolas Markey	Inria, Irisa, France
Laura Nenzi	University of Trieste, Italy
Gordon Pace	University of Malta, Malta
Nicola Paoletti	University of London, UK
Doron Peled	Bar-Ilan University, Israel
Giles Reger	The University of Manchester, UK
Kristin Yvonne Rozier	Iowa State University, USA
César Sánchez	IMDEA, Spain
Gerardo Schneider	Chalmers University of Technology, Sweden
Julien Signoles	CEA LIST, France
Oleg Sokolsky	University of Pennsylvania, USA
Bernhard Steffen	Technical University Dortmund, Germany
Stefano Tonetta	Fondazione Bruno Kessler, Italy
Hazem Torfah	University of California, Berkeley, USA
Dmitriy Traytel	ETH Zurich, Switzerland
Dogan Ulus	Samsung, USA

Additional Reviewers

Daniel Aldam	Shaun Azzopardi
Alexey Bakhirkin	François Bobot
Jesus Mauricio Chimento	Norine Coenen
Alexandre Donzé	Antoine El-Hokayem
Felipe Gorostiaga	Sophie Gruenbacher
Ramin Hasani	Ludovic Henrio
Einar Broch Johnsen	Hannes Kallwies
Eunsuk Kang	Brian Kempa
Srdan Krstić	Thomas Letan
Meiyi Ma	Niklas Metzger
Chi Mai Nguyen	Dung Phan
Jose Ignacio Requeno	Torben Scheffel
Malte Schmitz	Joshua Schneider
Maximilian Schwenger	Simone Silvetti
Daniel Thoma	Ennio Visconti

RV Steering Committee

Howard Barringer	The University of Manchester, UK
Ezio Bartocci	Technical University of Vienna, Austria
Saddek Bensalem	Verimag, University of Grenoble Alpes, France
Ylies Falcone	University of Grenoble Alpes, Inria, France
Klaus Havelund	NASA JPL, USA

Abstracts of Invited Presentations

Fantastic Failures and Where to Find Them: Designing Trustworthy Autonomy

Katherine Driggs-Campbell

University of Illinois at Urbana-Champaign, USA

Abstract. Autonomous robots are becoming tangible technologies that will soon impact the human experience. However, the desirable impacts of autonomy are only achievable if the underlying algorithms are robust to real-world conditions and are effective in (near) failure modes. This is often challenging in practice, as the scenarios in which general robots fail are often difficult to identify and characterize. In this talk, we'll discuss how to learn from failures to design robust interactive systems and how we can exploit structure in different applications to efficiently find and classify failures. We'll showcase both our failures and successes on autonomous vehicles and agricultural robots in real-world settings.

The Physical Side of Cyber-Physical Systems

Lane Desborough

Nudge BG, Inc., USA

Abstract. When our commercial reach exceeds our technical grasp, it is imperative that we advance our knowledge, that we embrace approaches to manage complexity, lest that complexity introduce undesired emergent properties. These complexity management approaches may seem new or novel, yet they rarely are. As science fiction author William Gibson is wont to say, "The future is already here, it just hasn't been evenly distributed yet."

Chemical engineering process control has afforded me a career spanning five continents and five industries. Although my current focus is the "artificial pancreas" – automated insulin delivery for people living with insulin-requiring diabetes – I have been privileged to be exposed to some of the most complex and challenging cyber-physical systems in the world; systems upon which society depends.

Most industries exist within their own bubble; exclusionary languages and pedagogy successfully defend their domains from new ideas. As one who has traversed many industries and worked on scores of industrial systems, a variety of personal, visceral experiences have allowed me to identify patterns and lessons applicable more broadly, perhaps even to your domain. Using examples drawn from petrochemical production, oil refining, power generation, industrial automation, and chronic disease management, I hope to demonstrate the need for, and value of, real-time verification.

Monitorability Under Assumptions

Thomas A. Henzinger and N. Ege Saraç

IST Austria, Klosterneuburg, Austria
{tah,ege.sarac}@ist.ac.at

Abstract. We introduce the monitoring of trace properties under assumptions. An assumption limits the space of possible traces that the monitor may encounter. An assumption may result from knowledge about the system that is being monitored, about the environment, or about another, connected monitor. We define monitorability under assumptions and study its theoretical properties. In particular, we show that for every assumption A, the boolean combinations of properties that are safe or co-safe relative to A are monitorable under A. We give several examples and constructions on how an assumption can make a non-monitorable property monitorable, and how an assumption can make a monitorable property monitorable with fewer resources, such as integer registers.

This research was supported in part by the Austrian Science Fund (FWF) under grant Z211-N23 (Wittgenstein Award).

Contents

Runtime Verification for Software

Runtime Verification with Temporal Logic Specifications

Stream-Based Monitoring

Runtime Verification for Cyber-Physical Systems

Invited Presentation

Monitorability Under Assumptions

Thomas A. Henzinger and N. Ege Saraç[✉]

IST Austria, Klosterneuburg, Austria
{tah,ege.sarac}@ist.ac.at

Abstract. We introduce the monitoring of trace properties under assumptions. An assumption limits the space of possible traces that the monitor may encounter. An assumption may result from knowledge about the system that is being monitored, about the environment, or about another, connected monitor. We define monitorability under assumptions and study its theoretical properties. In particular, we show that for every assumption A, the boolean combinations of properties that are safe or co-safe relative to A are monitorable under A. We give several examples and constructions on how an assumption can make a non-monitorable property monitorable, and how an assumption can make a monitorable property monitorable with fewer resources, such as integer registers.

1 Introduction

Monitoring is a run-time verification technique that checks, on-line, if a given trace of a system satisfies a given property [3]. The trace is an infinite sequence of observations, and the property defines a set of "good" traces. The monitor watches the trace, observation by observation, and issues a positive verdict as soon as all infinite extensions of the current prefix are good, and a negative verdict as soon as all infinite extensions of the current prefix are bad. The property is *monitorable* if every prefix of every trace has a finite extension that allows a verdict, positive or negative [17]. All safety and co-safety properties, and their boolean combinations, are monitorable [5,10].

The above definition of monitorability assumes that the system may generate any trace. Often a stronger assumption is possible: in predictive monitoring, the monitor has partial knowledge of the system and, therefore, can partly predict the future of a trace [7,8,16,18]; in real-time monitoring, the monitor can be certain that every trace contains infinitely many clock ticks [12]; in composite monitoring, a secondary monitor can rely on the result of a primary monitor. In all these scenarios, the monitor can assume that the observed trace comes from a limited set A of admissible traces. We say that the given property is *monitorable under assumption A* if every prefix of every trace in A has a finite extension in A

This research was supported in part by the Austrian Science Fund (FWF) under grant Z211-N23 (Wittgenstein Award).

J. Deshmukh and D. Ničković (Eds.): RV 2020, LNCS 12399, pp. 3–18, 2020.
https://doi.org/10.1007/978-3-030-60508-7_1

that allows a verdict relative to A, that is, either all further, infinite extensions in A are good, or they all are bad.

Assumptions can make non-monitorable properties monitorable. Consider the finite alphabet $\{req, ack, other\}$ of observations, and the response property

$$P = \Box(req \to \Diamond ack)$$

that "every req is followed by ack." The property P is not monitorable because every finite trace can be extended in two ways: by the infinite extension ack^ω which makes the property true, and by the infinite extension req^ω which makes the property false. Now suppose that the monitor can assume that "if any req is followed by another req without an intervening ack, then there will not be another ack," or formally:

$$A = \Box(req \to \bigcirc((\neg req) \, \mathcal{W} \, (ack \lor \Box(\neg ack)))).$$

The property P is monitorable under A because every finite prefix in A has the admissible extension $req \cdot req$ which makes the property false[1].

In Sect. 2, we study the boolean closure and entailment properties of monitoring under assumptions. In Sect. 3, we study safety and co-safety under assumptions, following [12]. We show that for every assumption A, every property that is safe relative to A, every property that is co-safe relative to A, and all their boolean combinations are monitorable under A. The results of both sections hold also if the universe of properties and assumptions is limited to the ω-regular or the counter-free ω-regular languages, i.e., those properties which can be specified using finite automata over infinite words or linear temporal logic, respectively.

In Sect. 4, we show that assumptions can reduce the resources needed for monitoring. Following [11], we define k-register monitorability for monitors that use a fixed number k of integer registers. A register that is operated by increments, decrements, and tests against zero is called a $counter$. It is known that the k-counter monitorability hierarchy is strict, that is, strictly more properties are $(k + 1)$-counter monitorable than are k-counter monitorable, for all $k \geq 0$ [11]. We present a property which requires k counters for monitoring, but can be monitored with $k - \ell$ counters under an assumption that can be monitored with ℓ counters.

Finally, in Sect. 5, we construct for every property P three assumptions that make P monitorable: first, a liveness assumption A_S that makes P safe relative to A_S, and therefore monitorable under A_S; second, a liveness assumption A_C that makes P co-safe relative to A_C, and therefore monitorable under A_C; and third, a co-safety assumption A_M so that P is monitorable under A_M. We use topological tools for our constructions, most notably the characterization of monitorable properties as those sets, in the Cantor topology on infinite words, whose boundary is nowhere dense [9].

---

[1] We follow the notation of [13] for temporal logic, where $\mathcal{U}$ is the (strong) *until* operator, and $\mathcal{W}$ is the *unless* (or weak until) operator.

2 Monitorability and Assumptions

Let $\Sigma = \{a, b, \ldots\}$ be a finite alphabet of observations. A *trace* is a finite or infinite sequence of observations. We usually denote finite traces by $s, r, t, u \in \Sigma^*$, and infinite traces by $f \in \Sigma^\omega$. A *property* $P \subseteq \Sigma^\omega$ is a set of infinite traces, and so is an *assumption* $A \subseteq \Sigma^\omega$. For traces $f \in \Sigma^\omega$ and $s \in \Sigma^*$, we write $s \prec f$ iff s is a finite prefix of f, and denote by $pref(f)$ the set of finite prefixes of f. For trace sets $P \subseteq \Sigma^\omega$, we define $Pref(P) = \bigcup_{f \in P} pref(f)$. We denote by $\overline{P}$ the complement of P in Σ^ω.

Intuitively, an assumption limits the universe of possible traces. When there are no assumptions, the system can produce any trace in Σ^ω. However, under an assumption A, all observed traces come from the set A. We extend the classical definition of monitorability [17] to account for assumptions as follows.

Definition 1. *Let P be a property, A an assumption, and $s \in Pref(A)$ a finite trace. The property P is positively determined under A by s iff, for all f, if $sf \in A$, then $sf \in P$. Similarly, P is negatively determined under A by s iff, for all f, if $sf \in A$, then $sf \notin P$.*

Definition 2. *The property P is s-monitorable under the assumption A, where $s \in Pref(A)$ is a finite trace, iff there is a finite continuation r such that $sr \in Pref(A)$ positively or negatively determines P under A. The property P is monitorable under A iff it is s-monitorable under A for all finite traces $s \in Pref(A)$. We denote the set of properties that are monitorable under A by* Mon(A).

For a property P and an assumption A, if $P \cap A \neq \emptyset$, we say that P *specifies under A* the set $P \cap A$. The monitorability of P under A may seem related to the monitorability of $P \cap A$. However, the two concepts are independent as we show in the following remark.

Remark 1. In general, $P \in$ Mon(A) does not imply $P \cap A \in$ Mon(Σ^ω). Consider $A = \Box\Diamond c$ and $P = a \vee ((\neg b)\,\mathcal{U}\,(a \wedge \Box\Diamond c))$. The property P specifies $((\neg b)\,\mathcal{U}\,a) \wedge \Box\Diamond c$ under A. Observe that every finite trace $s \in Pref(A)$ can be extended to $sr \in Pref(A)$ which satisfies or violates $((\neg b)\,\mathcal{U}\,a)$. Then, since every infinite extension of sr in A satisfies $\Box\Diamond c$, the finite trace sr positively or negatively determines P under A. Therefore, $P \in$ Mon(A). However, $P \cap A$ is not s-monitorable under Σ^ω for $s = a$ because for every finite extension r we have $src^\omega \in P \cap A$ and $sra^\omega \notin P \cap A$.

Conversely, $P \cap A \in$ Mon(Σ^ω) does not imply $P \in$ Mon(A) either. Consider $A = \Box\neg a$ and $P = \Diamond\Box c$. We have $P \cap A \in$ Mon(Σ^ω) because, for every $s \in \Sigma^*$, the finite trace sa negatively determines P. However, $P \notin$ Mon(A) because for every finite trace $s \in Pref(A)$, we have $sc^\omega \in P$ and $sb^\omega \notin P$. We will discuss the upward and downward preservation of monitorability later in this section.

As in the case of monitorability in Σ^ω, the set of monitorable properties under a fixed assumption enjoy the following closure properties.

Theorem 1. *For every assumption A, the set* $\mathsf{Mon}(A)$ *is closed under boolean operations.*

Proof. Let $P, Q \in \mathsf{Mon}(A)$ be two monitorable properties under assumption A.

- $\overline{P} \in \mathsf{Mon}(A)$: If P is positively (resp. negatively) determined under A by a finite trace $s \in Pref(A)$, then s negatively (resp. positively) determines $\overline{P}$ under A.
- $P \cap Q \in \mathsf{Mon}(A)$: Let $s \in Pref(A)$ be a finite trace. Since $P \in \mathsf{Mon}(A)$, there is an extension r such that $sr \in Pref(A)$ positively or negatively determines P under A. Moreover, since $Q \in \mathsf{Mon}(A)$, there exists t such that $srt \in Pref(A)$ positively or negatively determines Q under A. If both properties are positively determined under A by given finite traces, then $P \cap Q$ is positively determined under A by srt. Otherwise, the intersection is negatively determined under A by srt.
- $P \cup Q \in \mathsf{Mon}(A)$: Follows from above points since $P \cup Q = \overline{\overline{P} \cap \overline{Q}}$. ☐

Next, we switch our focus from boolean operations on properties to boolean operations on assumptions. The following examples demonstrate that monitorability is not preserved under complementation, intersection, nor under union of assumptions.

Example 1. Let $A = \Box\Diamond b$ be an assumption, and $P = \Box\Diamond a \vee (\Box\Diamond b \wedge \Diamond c)$ be a property. Under assumption A, the property P specifies $(\Box\Diamond a \vee \Diamond c) \wedge \Box\Diamond b$. For every $s \in Pref(A)$, the finite trace sc positively determines P under A because every infinite extension of sc in A satisfies the property. Therefore, we have $P \in \mathsf{Mon}(A)$. However, under assumption $\overline{A}$, the property P specifies $\Box\Diamond a \wedge (\neg\Box\Diamond b)$, and $P \notin \mathsf{Mon}(\overline{A})$. This is because every finite trace $s \in Pref(\overline{A})$ can be extended to either satisfy or violate P under $\overline{A}$, as illustrated by $sa^\omega \in P$ and $sc^\omega \notin P$.

Example 2. Let $A = \Box\neg a$ and $B = \Box\neg b$ be assumptions, and $P = \Box a \vee \Box b \vee (\Box(\neg a) \wedge \Box(\neg b) \wedge \Diamond\Box d)$ be a property. We have $P \in \mathsf{Mon}(A)$ because for every finite prefix $s \in Pref(A)$, the finite trace sbc negatively determines P under A. Similarly, $P \in \mathsf{Mon}(B)$ because for every $s \in Pref(B)$, the finite trace sac negatively determines P under B. However, $P \notin \mathsf{Mon}(A \cap B)$. If it were, then for every finite $s \in Pref(A \cap B)$ there would exist a finite continuation r such that $sr \in Pref(A \cap B)$ positively or negatively determines P under $A \cap B$. In either case, consider $src^\omega \notin P$ and $srd^\omega \in P$ to reach a contradiction.

Example 3. Let $A = \Box(c \rightarrow \Box\Diamond a)$ and $B = (\neg\Box\Diamond b) \wedge \Box(c \rightarrow (\neg\Box\Diamond a))$ be assumptions, and $P = \Box\Diamond a \vee \Box\Diamond b$ be a property. We have $P \in \mathsf{Mon}(A)$ because for every $s \in Pref(A)$, the finite trace sc positively determines P under A. Similarly, $P \in \mathsf{Mon}(B)$ because for every $s \in Pref(B)$, the finite trace sc negatively determines P under B. Consider the assumption $A \cup B$, and let $s \in Pref(A \cup B)$ be a finite trace containing c. We know that for each continuation f, either (i) sf has infinitely many a's by assumption A, or (ii) sf has finitely many a's and finitely many b's by assumption B. If (i) holds, the trace s positively determines P under $A \cup B$. If (ii) holds, the trace s negatively determines P under $A \cup B$. However, we cannot distinguish between the two cases by looking at finite prefixes. Therefore, for every $s \in Pref(A \cup B)$ that contains c, property P is not s-monitorable under $A \cup B$, which implies $P \notin \mathsf{Mon}(A \cup B)$.

The union is arguably the most interesting boolean operation on assumptions. It is relatively easy to discover strong assumptions that make a given property monitorable. However, in practice, we are interested in assumptions that are as weak as possible, and taking the union of assumptions can be a way to construct such assumptions. Next, we define a relation between two assumptions and a property, in order to capture a special case in which monitorability is preserved under the union of assumptions.

Definition 3. *Let A and B be two assumptions, and P be a property such that $P \in \mathsf{Mon}(A)$ and $P \in \mathsf{Mon}(B)$. The assumptions A and B are compatible with respect to P iff for every finite trace $s \in Pref(A)$ that positively (resp. negatively) determines P under A, there is no finite extension r such that $sr \in Pref(B)$ and sr negatively (resp. positively) determines P under B, and vice versa.*

Intuitively, the notion of compatibility prevents contradictory verdicts as in Example 3. Under the supposition of compatibility with respect to a given property, we show that monitorability is preserved under the union of assumptions.

Theorem 2. *Let A and B be assumptions, and P be a property such that $P \in \mathsf{Mon}(A)$ and $P \in \mathsf{Mon}(B)$. If A and B are compatible with respect to P, then $P \in \mathsf{Mon}(A \cup B)$.*

Proof. Let $s \in Pref(A \cup B)$. We want to show that P is s-monitorable under $A \cup B$. Observe that either $s \in Pref(A)$ or $s \in Pref(B)$. Suppose $s \in Pref(A)$. Since $P \in \mathsf{Mon}(A)$, there is an extension r such that $sr \in Pref(A)$ positively or negatively determines P under A. Suppose sr positively determines P under A.

Observe that either $sr \in Pref(A) \backslash Pref(B)$ or $sr \in Pref(A) \cap Pref(B)$. If $sr \in Pref(A) \setminus Pref(B)$, then sr also positively determines P under $A \cup B$ because all possible continuations of sr come from assumption A. If $sr \in Pref(A) \cap Pref(B)$, since $P \in \mathsf{Mon}(B)$ and the two assumptions are compatible with respect to P, there is an extension t such that srt positively determines P under B, and either $srt \in Pref(B) \setminus Pref(A)$ or $srt \in Pref(A) \cap Pref(B)$. If $srt \in Pref(B) \setminus Pref(A)$, then srt also positively determines P under $A \cup B$ because all possible continuations of srt come from B. If $srt \in Pref(A) \cap Pref(B)$, since sr and srt positively determine P under A and under B, respectively, srt also positively determines P under $A \cup B$.

Cases for $s \in Pref(B)$ and negative determinacy follow from similar arguments. Therefore, $P \in \mathsf{Mon}(A \cup B)$ since P is s-monitorable under $A \cup B$ for every finite trace $s \in Pref(A \cup B)$. $\square$

Next, we explore the preservation of monitorability under the strengthening and weakening of assumptions. We show that, in general, monitorability is neither downward nor upward preserved. However, for each direction, we identify a special case in which monitorability is preserved. The following is an example of a property that is monitorable under an assumption, but becomes non-monitorable under a stronger assumption.

Example 4. Let $A = \Sigma^\omega$ and $B = \Box\neg a$ be assumptions, and $P = \Box(\neg a) \wedge \Diamond\Box c$ be a property. Observe that $P \subseteq B \subseteq A$. We have $P \in \mathsf{Mon}(A)$ because for every finite prefix $s \in Pref(A)$, the finite trace sa negatively determines P under A. We claim that $P \notin \mathsf{Mon}(B)$. If it were, then for every finite $s \in Pref(B)$ there would exist a finite continuation r such that $sr \in Pref(B)$ positively or negatively determines P under B. Consider $srb^\omega \notin P$ and $src^\omega \in P$ to reach a contradiction in either case.

In the example above, the stronger assumption removes all prefixes that enable us to reach a verdict. We formulate a condition to avoid this problem, and enable downward preservation as follows.

Theorem 3. *Let A and B be assumptions, and P be a property such that $B \subseteq A$ and $P \cap A = P \cap B$. If $P \in \mathsf{Mon}(A)$ and $B \in \mathsf{Mon}(A)$ such that every prefix that negatively determines B under A has a proper prefix that negatively determines P under A, then $P \in \mathsf{Mon}(B)$.*

Proof. Let $s \in Pref(A)$ be a finite trace and $r, t \in \Sigma^*$ be extensions such that $sr, srt \in Pref(A)$ positively or negatively determine P or B under A.

- Suppose sr positively determines P under A. Then, sr also positively determines P under B since $B \subseteq A$ and $P \cap A = P \cap B$.
- Suppose sr positively determines B under A, and srt positively determines P under A. Then, srt positively determines P under B.
- Suppose sr positively determines B under A, and srt negatively determines P under A. Then, srt negatively determines P under B.
- Suppose sr negatively determines P under A, and srt positively determines B under A. Then, sr negatively determines P under B.
- Suppose sr negatively determines P under A, and srt negatively determines B under A. If we have $t \neq \varepsilon$, then we have $sr \in Pref(B)$ and therefore negatively determines P under B. Otherwise, there is a shortest proper prefix u of sr that negatively determines P under A, and $u \in Pref(B)$, therefore u negatively determines P under B.
- Suppose sr negatively determines B under A, then there is a proper prefix of sr that negatively determines P under A. We can resolve this case as above.

These imply that P is s-monitorable under B for every finite trace $s \in Pref(B)$. Therefore, $P \in \mathsf{Mon}(B)$.   □

Next, we move on to the upward preservation of monitorability. We give an example of a property that is monitorable under an assumption, but becomes non-monitorable under a weaker assumption.

Example 5. Let $A = \Sigma^\omega$ and $B = \Box(b \to \Diamond c)$ be assumptions, and $P = \Diamond a \wedge \Box(b \to \Diamond c)$ be a property. Observe that $P \subseteq B \subseteq A$. We have $P \in \mathsf{Mon}(\mathsf{B})$ because for each finite prefix $s \in Pref(B)$, the finite trace sa positively determines P under B. One can verify that $P \notin \mathsf{Mon}(\mathsf{A})$ by supposing that a finite trace $s \in Pref(A)$ positively or negatively determines P under A, and considering $sb^\omega \notin P$ and $sa(bc)^\omega \in P$.

Intuitively, the weaker assumption in the previous example introduces prefixes that prevents us from reaching a verdict. The following theorem provides a condition to ensure that all new prefixes can be extended to reach a verdict.

Theorem 4. *Let A and B be assumptions, and P be a property such that $B \subseteq A$ and $P \cap A = P \cap B$. If $P \in \mathsf{Mon}(\mathsf{B})$ and $B \in \mathsf{Mon}(\mathsf{A})$, then $P \in \mathsf{Mon}(\mathsf{A})$.*

Proof. Let s be a finite trace and r be a finite continuation such that $sr \in Pref(A)$ positively or negatively determines B under A. If sr negatively determines B under A, then it also negatively determines P under A because $B \subseteq A$ and $P \cap A = P \cap B$. Suppose sr positively determines B under A. Since $P \in \mathsf{Mon}(\mathsf{B})$, there is a finite extension t such that $srt \in Pref(B)$ positively or negatively determines P under B. Then, srt also positively or negatively determines P under A. It yields that P is s-monitorable under A for every finite trace $s \in Pref(A)$, hence $P \in \mathsf{Mon}(\mathsf{A})$. $\qquad\Box$

For many problems in runtime verification, the set of ω-regular and LTL-expressible properties deserve special attention due to their prevalence in specification languages. Therefore, we remark that the results presented in this section still hold true if we limit ourselves to ω-regular or to LTL-expressible properties and assumptions.

3 Safety and Co-safety Properties Under Assumptions

In this section, we extend the notion of relative safety from [12] to co-safety properties, and to general boolean combinations of safety properties, with a focus on monitorability.

Definition 4. *A property P is a safety property under assumption A iff there is a set $S \subseteq \Sigma^*$ of finite traces such that, for every trace $f \in A$, we have $f \in P$ iff every finite prefix of f is contained in S. Formally,*

$$\exists S \subseteq \Sigma^* : \forall f \in A : f \in P \iff pref(f) \subseteq S.$$

Equivalently, P is a safety property under assumption A iff every $f \notin P$ has a finite prefix $s \prec f$ that negatively determines P under A. We denote by $\mathsf{Safe}(\mathsf{A})$ the set of safety properties under assumption A.

Definition 5. *A property P is a* co-safety *property under assumption A iff there is a set $S \subseteq \Sigma^*$ of finite traces such that, for every trace $f \in A$, we have $f \in P$ iff some finite prefix of f is contained in S. Formally,*

$$\exists S \subseteq \Sigma^* : \forall f \in A : f \in P \iff pref(f) \cap S \neq \emptyset.$$

Equivalently, P is a co-safety *property under assumption A iff every $f \in P$ has a finite prefix $s \prec f$ that positively determines P under A. We denote by* CoSafe(A) *the set of co-safety properties under assumption A.*

One can observe from these definitions that, for every assumption A and property P, we have $P \in$ Safe(A) iff $\overline{P} \in$ CoSafe(A).

Definition 6. *A property P is an* obligation *property under assumption A iff $P = \bigcap_{i=1}^{k}(S_i \cup C_i)$ for some finite $k \geq 0$, where $S_i \in$ Safe(A) and $C_i \in$ CoSafe(A) for all $1 \leq i \leq k$. We denote by* Obl(A) *the set of obligation properties under assumption A.*

The set Obl(A) is exactly the boolean combinations of properties from Safe(A) and CoSafe(A). Therefore, we have Safe(A) $\subseteq$ Obl(A) and CoSafe(A) $\subseteq$ Obl(A) for every assumption A. Note also that when $A = \Sigma^\omega$, our definitions are equivalent to the classical definitions of safety, co-safety, and obligation properties. Next, we present examples of non-monitorable properties that become safe or co-safe under an assumption.

Example 6. Let $P = ((\neg a)\, \mathcal{U}\, b) \vee \Box\Diamond c$. The property P is not monitorable, thus not safe, because the finite trace a has no extension that positively or negatively determines P. Let $A = \neg\Box\Diamond c$. Then, P specifies $((\neg a)\, \mathcal{U}\, b) \wedge \neg\Box\Diamond c$ under A. Observe that every $f \notin P$ has a finite prefix $s \prec f$ that negatively determines P under A because every such infinite trace in A must have a finite prefix that violates $((\neg a)\, \mathcal{U}\, b)$. Therefore, we get $P \in$ Safe(A).

Example 7. Let $P = (\neg\Box\Diamond a) \wedge \Diamond b$. The property P is not monitorable, thus not co-safe, because the finite trace b has no extension that positively or negatively determines P. Let $A = \neg\Box\Diamond a$. Then, every $f \in P$ has a finite prefix $s \prec f$ that contains b, which positively determines P under A. Therefore, $P \in$ CoSafe(A).

For the sets of safety and co-safety properties relative to a given assumption, the following closure properties hold.

Theorem 5. *For every assumption A, the set* Safe(A) *is closed under positive boolean operations.*

Proof. Let $P, Q \in$ Safe(A) be two safety properties under assumption A. Let $f \notin (P \cup Q)$ be a trace. Since we also have $f \notin P$, there is a finite prefix $s \prec f$ that negatively determines P under A. Similarly, we have $r \prec f$ that negatively determines Q under A. Assume without loss of generality that s is a prefix of r. Then, r negatively determines $P \cup Q$ under A, and thus $P \cup Q \in$ Safe(A).

Now, let $f \notin (P \cap Q)$. By a similar argument, we have a prefix $s \prec f$ that negatively determines P under A or Q under A. Then, one can verify that s also negatively determines $P \cap Q$ under A. Therefore, $P \cap Q \in$ Safe(A). $\square$

Theorem 6. *For every assumption* A, *the set* CoSafe(A) *is closed under positive boolean operations.*

Proof. Let $P, Q \in$ CoSafe(A) be two co-safety properties under assumption A. Observe that $P \cup Q = \overline{\overline{P} \cap \overline{Q}}$ and $P \cap Q = \overline{\overline{P} \cup \overline{Q}}$ where $\overline{P}, \overline{Q} \in$ Safe(A), and apply Theorem 5.   □

By combining Theorems 5 and 6 with the definition of Obl(A), we obtain the following corollary.

Corollary 1. *For every assumption* A, *the set* Obl(A) *is closed under all boolean operations.*

Next, we show that relative safety, co-safety, and obligation properties enjoy downward preservation. In other words, if P is a safety, co-safety, or obligation property under an assumption, then it remains a safety, co-safety, or obligation property under all stronger assumptions.

Theorem 7 [12]. *Let* A *and* B *be assumptions such that* $B \subseteq A$. *For every property* P, *if* $P \in$ Safe(A), *then* $P \in$ Safe(B).

Theorem 8. *Let* A *and* B *be assumptions such that* $B \subseteq A$. *For every property* P, *if* $P \in$ CoSafe(A), *then* $P \in$ CoSafe(B).

Proof. Since $P \in$ CoSafe(A), we have $\overline{P} \in$ Safe(A). Then, by Theorem 7, we get $\overline{P} \in$ Safe(B), which implies that $P \in$ CoSafe(B).   □

Theorem 9. *Let* A *and* B *be assumptions such that* $B \subseteq A$. *For every property* P, *if* $P \in$ Obl(A), *then* $P \in$ Obl(B).

Proof. By definition, $P = \bigcap_{i=1}^{k}(S_i \cup C_i)$ for some finite $k > 1$, where $S_i \in$ Safe(A) and $C_i \in$ CoSafe(A) for each $1 \leq i \leq k$. Theorems 7 and 8 imply that $S_i \in$ Safe(B) and $C_i \in$ CoSafe(B) for every $1 \leq i \leq k$. Therefore, $P \in$ Obl(B).   □

Finally, we show that every safety, co-safety, and obligation property relative an assumption A is monitorable under A.

Theorem 10. *For every assumption* A, *we have* Safe(A) $\subseteq$ Mon(A).

Proof. Let $P \in$ Safe(A) be a property and $s \in Pref(A)$ be a finite trace. If there is a continuation f such that $sf \notin P$, then there is a finite prefix $r \prec sf$ that negatively determines P under A. Otherwise, s itself positively determines P under A. In either case, P is s-monitorable under A for an arbitrary finite trace $s \in Pref(A)$, and thus $P \in$ Mon(A).   □

Theorem 11. *For every assumption* A, *we have* CoSafe(A) $\subseteq$ Mon(A).

Proof. The proof idea is the same as in Theorem 10. Let $P \in \mathsf{CoSafe(A)}$ be a property and $s \in Pref(A)$ be a finite trace. If there is a continuation f such that $sf \in P$, then there is a finite prefix $r \prec sf$ that positively determines P under A. Otherwise, s itself negatively determines P under A. In either case, P is s-monitorable under A for an arbitrary finite trace $s \in Pref(A)$, and thus $P \in \mathsf{Mon(A)}$.

Theorem 12. *For every assumption A, we have $\mathsf{Obl(A)} \subseteq \mathsf{Mon(A)}$.*

Proof. Let $P \in \mathsf{Obl(A)}$ be a property. We can rewrite P as $\bigcap_{i=1}^{k}(S_i \cup C_i)$ for some finite $k > 0$ such that $S_i \in \mathsf{Safe(A)}$ and $C_i \in \mathsf{CoSafe(A)}$. By Theorems 10 and 11, each S_i and C_i is in $\mathsf{Mon(A)}$. By Theorem 1, each $S_i \cap C_i$ and their union is in $\mathsf{Mon(A)}$. Therefore, $P \in \mathsf{Mon(A)}$. □

We note that, as in Sect. 2, the results of this section still hold when restricted to the ω-regular or to the LTL-expressible properties and assumptions.

4   Register Monitorability

In this section, we study monitorability under assumptions for an operational class of monitors, namely, register machines. We follow [11] to define register machines. Let X be a set of *registers* storing integer variables, and consider an *instruction set* of integer-valued and boolean-valued expressions over X. An *update* is a mapping from registers to integer-valued expressions, and a *test* is a boolean-valued expression. We denote the set of updates and tests over the set X of registers by $\Gamma(X)$ and $\Phi(X)$, respectively. We define a *valuation* as a mapping $v : X \to \mathbb{Z}$ from the set of registers to integers. For every update $\gamma \in \Gamma(X)$, we define the *updated valuation* $v[\gamma] : X \to \mathbb{Z}$ by letting $v[\gamma](x) = v(\gamma(x))$ for every $x \in X$. A test $\phi \in \Phi(X)$ is true under the valuation v iff $v \models \phi$.

Definition 7. *A register machine is a tuple $M = (X, Q, \Sigma, \Delta, q_0, \Omega)$ where X is a finite set of registers, Q is a finite set of states, Σ is a finite alphabet, $\Delta \subseteq Q \times \Sigma \times \Phi(X) \times \Gamma(X) \times Q$ is a set of edges, $q_0 \in Q$ is the initial state, and $\Omega \subseteq Q^{\omega}$ is a set of accepting runs, such that for every state $q \in Q$, letter $\sigma \in \Sigma$, and valuation v, there is one and only one outgoing edge $(q, \sigma, \phi, \gamma, r) \in \Delta$ with $v \models \phi$, i.e., the machine is deterministic.*

Let $M = (X, Q, \Sigma, \Delta, q_0, \Omega)$ be a register machine. A *configuration* of M is a pair (q, v) consisting of a state $q \in Q$ and a valuation $v : X \to \mathbb{Z}$. A *transition* $\xrightarrow{\sigma}$ between two configurations of M is defined by the relation $(q, v) \xrightarrow{\sigma} (q', v')$ iff $v' = v[\gamma]$ and $v \models \phi$ for some edge $(q, \sigma, \phi, \gamma, q') \in \Delta$. A *run* of M over a word $w = \sigma_1\sigma_2\ldots$ is an infinite sequence of transitions $(q_0, v_0) \xrightarrow{\sigma_1} (q_1, v_1) \xrightarrow{\sigma_2} \cdots$ where $v_0(x) = 0$ for all $x \in X$. The word $w \in \Sigma^{\omega}$ is *accepted* by M iff its (unique) run over w yields an infinite sequence $q_0 q_1 q_2 \ldots$ of states which belongs to Ω. The set of infinite words accepted by M is called the *language* of M, and denoted $\mathcal{L}(M)$.

Register machines are a more powerful specification language for traces than finite-state monitors. Even when confined to safety, this model can specify many interesting properties beyond ω-regular, as explored in [11]. Formally, we can limit our model to safety properties as follows: let $q_{sink} \in Q$ be a *rejecting state* such that there are no edges from q_{sink} to any state in $Q \setminus \{q_{sink}\}$, and let Ω be the set of infinite state sequences that do not contain q_{sink}. Under these conditions, $\mathcal{L}(M)$ is a safety property monitored by M. Next, we introduce assumptions to register monitorability.

Definition 8. *Let P be a property, A an assumption, and $s \in Pref(A)$ a finite trace. The property P is* positively k-register determined *under A by s iff there is a register machine M with k registers such that, for all $f \in \Sigma^\omega$, if $sf \in \mathcal{L}(M) \cap A$, then $sf \in P$. Similarly, P is* negatively k-register determined *under A by s iff there is a register machine M with k registers such that, for all $f \in \Sigma^\omega$, if $sf \in A \setminus \mathcal{L}(M)$, then $sf \notin P$.*

Definition 9. *A property P is* k-register monitorable *under assumption A iff for every finite trace $s \in Pref(A)$ there is a finite extension r such that P is positively or negatively k-register determined under A by $sr \in Pref(A)$. We denote the set of properties that are k-register monitorable under A by* k-RegMon(A).

In the following, we restrict ourselves to a simple form of register machines in order to demonstrate how assumptions help for monitoring non-regular properties.

Definition 10. *A* counter machine *is a register machine with the instructions $x+1$, $x-1$, and $x = 0$ for all registers $x \in X$. We write* k-CtrMon(A) *for the set of properties that are monitorable by k-counter machines under assumption A.*

Computational resources play an important role in register monitorability. As proved in [11], for every $k \geq 0$ there is a safety property that can be monitored with k counters but not with $k - 1$ counters, that is, the set k-CtrMon$(\Sigma^\omega) \setminus$ $(k - 1)$-CtrMon(Σ^ω) is non-empty. We now show that assumptions can be used to reduce the number of counters needed for monitoring.

Theorem 13. *Let $\Sigma_k = \{0, 1, \ldots, k\}$. For every $k \geq 1$ and $1 \leq \ell \leq k$, there exist a safety property $P_k \in$ k-CtrMon$(\Sigma^\omega) \setminus (k - 1)$-CtrMon$(\Sigma^\omega)$ and a safety assumption $A_\ell \in \ell$-CtrMon(Σ_k^ω) such that $P_k \in (k - \ell)$-CtrMon(A_ℓ).*

Proof. For every letter $\sigma \in \Sigma$ and finite trace $s \in \Sigma^*$, let $|s|_\sigma$ denote the number of occurrences of σ in s. Let $P_k = \{f \in \Sigma_k^\omega \mid \forall 0 \leq i < k : \forall s \prec f : |s|_i \leq |s|_{i+1}\}$. We can construct a k-counter machine M that recognizes P_k as follows. For each $0 \leq i < k$, the counter x_i of M tracks the difference between $|s|_i$ and $|s|_{i+1}$ by decrementing with letter i and incrementing with $i + 1$. The machine keeps running as long as every counter value is non-negative, and rejects otherwise. Notice that we can rewrite $P_k = \bigcap_{i=0}^{k-1} S_i$ where $S_i = \{f \in \Sigma_k^\omega \mid \forall s \prec f : |s|_i \leq |s|_{i+1}\}$ and $S_i \in$ 1-CtrMon(Σ_k^ω). Then, for each $1 \leq \ell \leq k$, we can construct an assumption $A_\ell = \bigcap_{i=0}^{\ell-1} S_i$ where $A_\ell \in \ell\text{-CtrMon}(\Sigma_k^\omega)$. Since the properties S_0 to $S_{\ell-1}$ are true under assumption A_ℓ, we only need to monitor the remaining conditions S_ℓ to S_{k-1}. Therefore, it is not hard to verify that $P_k \in (k-\ell)\text{-CtrMon}(A_\ell)$. $\qquad\square$

5   Using Topology to Construct Assumptions

Let X be a topological space, and $S \subseteq X$ be a set. The set S is *closed* iff it contains all of its limit points. The complement of a closed set is *open*. The *closure* of S is the smallest closed set containing S, denoted $cl(S)$. Similarly, the *interior* of S is the largest open set contained in S, denoted $int(S)$. The *boundary* of S contains those points in the closure of S that do not belong to the interior of S, that is, $bd(P) = cl(P) \setminus int(P)$. The set S is *dense* iff every point in X is either in S or a limit point of S, that is, $cl(S) = X$. Similarly, S is *nowhere dense* iff $int(cl(S)) = \emptyset$. For the operations in relative topology induced by X on a subspace $Y \subseteq X$, we use $cl_Y(S)$, $int_Y(S)$, and $bd_Y(S)$ where $S \subseteq Y$.

The safety properties correspond to the closed sets in the Cantor topology on Σ^ω, and the liveness properties correspond to the dense sets [1]. Moreover, the co-safety properties are the open sets [6], and the monitorable properties are the sets whose boundary is nowhere dense [9]. Since these topological characterizations extend to subsets of Σ^ω through relativization [9,12], we use them to construct assumptions under which properties become safe, co-safe, or monitorable.

Theorem 14. *For every property P, there is a liveness assumption A such that $P \in \mathsf{Safe}(A)$ [12]. Moreover, if P is not live, then $P \subset A$; and if P is not safe, then for every assumption B such that $A \subset B$, we have $P \notin \mathsf{Safe}(B)$.*

Proof. Using the standard construction, we can rewrite P as an intersection of a safety property and a liveness property. Formally, $P = P_S \cap P_L$ where $P_S = cl(P)$ is the smallest safety property that contains P, and $P_L = \overline{P_S} \setminus P$ is a liveness property [1]. Let $A = P_L$. We know by Theorem 7 that $P_S \in \mathsf{Safe}(A)$. Since $P_S \cap A = P \cap A$, we also have $P \in \mathsf{Safe}(A)$. Also, if P is not live, we have $P_S \subset \Sigma^\omega$, and $A = \overline{P_S} \cup P$ strictly contains P.

Now, let B be an assumption such that $A \subset B$. Then,

$$cl_B(P \cap B) = cl(P) \cap B = P_S \cap B$$

strictly contains $P \cap B$ because there is a trace $f \in (P_S \setminus P) \cap B$ by construction. It implies that $P \cap B$ is not closed in B, therefore $P \notin \mathsf{Safe}(B)$. $\qquad\square$

Intuitively, the construction in the proof of Theorem 14 removes all traces in $\overline{P}$ which have no prefix that negatively determines P. We can alternatively exclude the traces in P which have no prefix that positively determine P, in order to turn P into a relative co-safety property.

Theorem 15. *For every property P, there is a liveness assumption A such that $P \in \mathsf{CoSafe}(A)$. Moreover, if $\overline{P}$ is not live, then $P \cap A \neq \emptyset$; and if P is not co-safe, then for every assumption B such that $A \subset B$, we have $P \notin \mathsf{CoSafe}(B)$.*

Proof. Let $P_C = int(P)$ be the largest co-safety property contained in P, and $A = \overline{P \setminus P_C}$ be an assumption. The assumption A is live since $int(P \setminus P_C) \subseteq int(P) \setminus int(P_C) = \emptyset$. We know by Theorem 8 that $P_C \in \mathsf{CoSafe}(A)$. Then, because $P_C \cap A = P \cap A$, we also have $P \in \mathsf{CoSafe}(A)$. Also, if $\overline{P}$ is not live, we have $P_C \neq \emptyset$, and thus $P \cap A \neq \emptyset$ by construction.

Now, let B be an assumption such that $A \subset B$. Then,

$$int_B(P \cap B) = int((P \cap B) \cup \overline{B}) \cap B = int(P) \cap B = P_C$$

is strictly contained in $P \cap B$ since there is a trace $f \in (P \setminus P_C) \cap B$ by construction. It implies that $P \cap B$ is not open in B, therefore $P \notin \mathsf{CoSafe}(\mathsf{B})$. $\square$

Notice that we removed elements from $cl(P) \setminus P$ and $P \setminus int(P)$ in the above constructions. The union of these two regions corresponds to $bd(P)$, and a property P is monitorable iff $bd(P)$ is nowhere dense [9], that is, $int(cl(bd(P))) = \emptyset$. Since boundary sets are closed in general, and $cl(S) = S$ for every closed set S, this condition is equivalent to $int(bd(P)) = \emptyset$. Now, we describe a construction to make any property monitorable by removing a subset of $bd(P)$ from Σ^ω.

Theorem 16. *For every property P, there is a co-safety assumption A such that $P \in \mathsf{Mon}(A)$. Moreover, if $\overline{P}$ is not live, then $P \cap A \neq \emptyset$.*

Proof. We want to construct a subspace $A \subseteq \Sigma^\omega$ such that $int_A(bd_A(P \cap A)) = \emptyset$. Note that $bd_A(P \cap A) \subseteq bd(P \cap A) \cap A$ and $int_A(P \cap A) = int((P \cap A) \cup \overline{A}) \cap A$. Then, we have

$$int_A(bd_A(P \cap A)) \subseteq int((bd(P \cap A) \cap A) \cup \overline{A}) \cap A.$$

Since union of interiors is contained in interior of unions and we want the expression on the right-hand side to be empty, we have

$$int(bd(P \cap A) \cap A) \cup int(\overline{A}) \subseteq int((bd(P \cap A) \cap A) \cup \overline{A}) \subseteq int(\overline{A}).$$

It implies that $int(bd(P \cap A) \cap A) \subseteq int(\overline{A})$, and since $bd(P \cap A) \cap A$ and $\overline{A}$ are disjoint, we get $int(bd(P \cap A) \cap A) = \emptyset$. Then,

$$int(bd(P \cap A) \cap A) \subseteq int((bd(P) \cup bd(A)) \cap A)$$
$$= int((bd(P) \cap A) \cup (bd(A) \cap A)).$$

Now, we can pick A to be open to have $bd(A) \cap A = \emptyset$, which yields

$$int((bd(P) \cap A) \cup (bd(A) \cap A)) = int(bd(P) \cap A)$$
$$= int(bd(P)) \cap A$$

since interior of finite intersection equals intersection of interiors and A is open. At this point, we want $int(bd(P)) \cap A = \emptyset$ such that A is open. It is equivalent to choosing A such that $\overline{A}$ is a closed set containing $int(bd(P))$, for which the smallest such choice is $\overline{A} = cl(int(bd(P)))$. Therefore, we let $\overline{A} = cl(int(bd(P)))$.

Observe that A is indeed open, i.e., a co-safety assumption. Since we obtained that $int_A(bd_A(P \cap A)) = \emptyset$ if $int(bd(P)) \cap A = \emptyset$ and A is open, we have $P \in \mathsf{Mon}(A)$.

Finally, given that $\overline{P}$ is not live, we get $int(P) \neq \emptyset$. It implies that $bd(P) \subset \Sigma^\omega$. Then, since $int(P) \subseteq \overline{bd(P)} \subseteq A$ and $int(P) \subseteq P$, we obtain that $P \cap A \neq \emptyset$. $\qquad\square$

Since both ω-regular and LTL-definable languages are closed under the topological closure [2, 15], the constructions presented in this section can be performed within the restricted universe of ω-regular or LTL-definable languages. In other words, given an ω-regular (resp. LTL-definable) property, the constructions from the proofs of Theorems 14, 15 and 16 produce ω-regular (resp. LTL-definable) assumptions. Note also that, if P is safe, co-safe, or monitorable under Σ^ω, respectively, then all three constructions yield $A = \Sigma^\omega$.

As pointed out in the previous theorems, the constructions are useful only for certain classes of properties. To demonstrate this, consider a liveness property P such that $\overline{P}$ is also live, that is, P is both live and co-live. Such properties are said to have zero monitoring information [14]. For example, $P = \Box \Diamond a$ is a property with zero monitoring information because there is no finite prefix s such that P is s-monitorable under Σ^ω. Since P is live, we have $cl(P) = \Sigma^\omega$, and since $\overline{P}$ is live, we have $int(P) = \emptyset$. It follows that $bd(P) = \Sigma^\omega$. Therefore, if we let A_S, A_C, and A_M be assumptions as constructed in Theorems 14, 15, and 16, respectively, we obtain $A_S = P$, $A_C = \Sigma^\omega \setminus P$, and $A_M = \emptyset$.

Next, we present an example of a non-monitorable property that is neither live nor co-live, and apply the constructions described in this section.

Example 8. Let $P = (a \vee \Box \Diamond a) \wedge \bigcirc b$. One can verify that $cl(P) = \bigcirc b$ and $int(P) = a \wedge \bigcirc b$ by constructing the corresponding Büchi automata. Then, we also get $bd(P) = (\neg a) \wedge \bigcirc b$. We now apply the constructions described above. If we let $A_S = \overline{cl(P)} \cup P$, we get $P \in \mathsf{Safe}(A_S)$ because every finite trace in A_S that satisfies $\bigcirc \neg b$ negatively determines P under A_S. If we let $A_C = \overline{P} \cup int(P)$, we get $P \in \mathsf{CoSafe}(A_C)$ because every finite trace in A_C that satisfies $a \wedge \bigcirc b$ positively determines P under A_C. Now, observe that $cl(int(bd(P))) = bd(P)$. Then, we have $A_M = a \vee \bigcirc(\neg b)$, which yields that P specifies $a \wedge \bigcirc b$ under A_M, and therefore $P \in \mathsf{Mon}(A_M)$. Note that both A_S and A_C are live, while A_M is co-safe.

Finally, we apply the construction from the proof of Theorem 16 to make a non-monitorable liveness property monitorable.

Example 9. Let $\Sigma = \{req, ack, reboot, other\}$ be a finite set of observations, and consider the property

$$P = (\Box(req \rightarrow \Diamond ack) \vee (\neg ack)\,\mathcal{U}\,req) \wedge \Diamond reboot.$$

The property P is live because $cl(P) = \Sigma^\omega$. We can compute its boundary as $bd(P) = \overline{int(P)} = cl(\overline{P})$. Constructing the Büchi automaton for $\overline{P}$ and taking its closure gives us $bd(P) = (ack\,\mathcal{R}\,(\neg req)) \vee \Box\neg reboot$. One can similarly compute $int(bd(P)) = ack\,\mathcal{R}\,(\neg req)$, and observe that $cl(int(bd(P))) = int(bd(P))$. Therefore, we have $A = (\neg ack)\,\mathcal{U}\,req$, which is indeed a co-safety assumption. The property P specifies $((\neg ack)\mathcal{U}\,req) \wedge \Diamond reboot$ under A, therefore $P \in \mathsf{Mon}(\mathsf{A})$.

Since the assumption A constructed in the proof of Theorem 16 is co-safe, we get by Theorem 4 that $P \cap A$ is also monitorable. However, as explained in Sect. 2, this is not necessarily the case in general for monitorability under assumptions. We can look for other ways of constructing an assumption A such that P is monitorable under A, but $P \cap A$ is not necessarily monitorable. For this, Theorem 4 may prove useful, and we aim to explore it in future work.

6   Conclusion

Inspired by the notion of relative safety [12], we defined the concepts of co-safety and monitorability relative to an assumption. Assumptions may result from knowledge about the system that is being monitored (as in *predictive* monitoring [18]), knowledge about the environment (e.g., time always advances), or knowledge about other, connected monitors. In further work, we plan to develop a theory of composition and refinement for monitors that use assumptions, including assume-guarantee monitoring, where two or more monitors are connected and provide information to each other (as in *decentralized* monitoring [4]). We gave several examples and constructions on how an assumption can make a non-monitorable property monitorable. In the future, we intend to study the structure of the *weakest* assumptions that make a given property monitorable, particularly the conditions under which such assumptions are unique. Finally, we showed how an assumption can make a monitorable property monitorable with fewer integer registers. More generally, carefully chosen assumptions can make monitors less costly (use fewer resources), more timely (reach verdicts quicker), and more precise (in the case of quantitative verdicts). In further work, we will study all of these dimensions to provide a theoretical foundation for the practical design of a network of monitors with assumptions.

References

1. Alpern, B., Schneider, F.B.: Defining liveness. Inf. Process. Lett. **21**(4), 181–185 (1985). https://doi.org/10.1016/0020-0190(85)90056-0. http://www.sciencedirect.com/science/article/pii/0020019085900560
2. Alpern, B., Schneider, F.B.: Recognizing safety and liveness. Distrib. Comput. **2**(3), 117–126 (1987). https://doi.org/10.1007/BF01782772
3. Bartocci, E., Falcone, Y., Francalanza, A., Reger, G.: Introduction to runtime verification. In: Bartocci, E., Falcone, Y. (eds.) Lectures on Runtime Verification. LNCS, vol. 10457, pp. 1–33. Springer, Cham (2018). https://doi.org/10.1007/978-3-319-75632-5_1
4. Bauer, A., Falcone, Y.: Decentralised LTL monitoring. In: Giannakopoulou, D., Méry, D. (eds.) FM 2012. LNCS, vol. 7436, pp. 85–100. Springer, Heidelberg (2012). https://doi.org/10.1007/978-3-642-32759-9_10

5. Bauer, A., Leucker, M., Schallhart, C.: Runtime verification for LTL and TLTL. ACM Trans. Softw. Eng. Methodol. **20**(4) (2011). https://doi.org/10.1145/2000799.2000800

6. Chang, E., Manna, Z., Pnueli, A.: The safety-progress classification. In: Bauer, F.L., Brauer, W., Schwichtenberg, H. (eds.) Logic and Algebra of Specification. NATO ASI Series, vol. 94, pp. 143–202. Springer, Heidelberg (1993). https://doi.org/10.1007/978-3-642-58041-3_5

7. Chen, F., Serbanuta, T., Rosu, G.: Jpredictor. In: 2008 ACM/IEEE 30th International Conference on Software Engineering, pp. 221–230 (2008). https://doi.org/10.1145/1368088.1368119

8. Cimatti, A., Tian, C., Tonetta, S.: Assumption-based runtime verification with partial observability and resets. In: Finkbeiner, B., Mariani, L. (eds.) RV 2019. LNCS, vol. 11757, pp. 165–184. Springer, Cham (2019). https://doi.org/10.1007/978-3-030-32079-9_10

9. Diekert, V., Leucker, M.: Topology, monitorable properties and runtime verification. Theoret. Comput. Sci. **537**, 29–41 (2014). https://doi.org/10.1016/j.tcs.2014.02.052

10. Falcone, Y., Fernandez, J.C., Mounier, L.: What can you verify and enforce at runtime? Sotfw. Tools Technol. Transf. (2011). https://hal.archives-ouvertes.fr/hal-00497350

11. Ferrère, T., Henzinger, T.A., Saraç, N.E.: A theory of register monitors. In: Proceedings of the 33rd Annual ACM/IEEE Symposium on Logic in Computer Science, pp. 394–403 (2018). https://doi.org/10.1145/3209108.3209194

12. Henzinger, T.A.: Sooner is safer than later. Inf. Process. Lett. **43**(3), 135–141 (1992). https://doi.org/10.1016/0020-0190(92)90005-G. http://www.sciencedirect.com/science/article/pii/002001909290005G

13. Manna, Z., Pnueli, A.: The Temporal Logic of Reactive and Concurrent Systems - Specification. Springer, Heidelberg (1992). https://doi.org/10.1007/978-1-4612-0931-7

14. Peled, D., Havelund, K.: Refining the safety–liveness classification of temporal properties according to monitorability. In: Margaria, T., Graf, S., Larsen, K.G. (eds.) Models, Mindsets, Meta: The What, the How, and the Why Not?. LNCS, vol. 11200, pp. 218–234. Springer, Cham (2019). https://doi.org/10.1007/978-3-030-22348-9_14

15. Petric Maretić, G., Torabi Dashti, M., Basin, D.: LTL is closed under topological closure. Inf. Process. Lett. **114**(8), 408–413 (2014). https://doi.org/10.1016/j.ipl.2014.03.001. http://www.sciencedirect.com/science/article/pii/S0020019014000386

16. Pinisetty, S., Jéron, T., Tripakis, S., Falcone, Y., Marchand, H., Preoteasa, V.: Predictive runtime verification of timed properties. J. Syst. Softw. **132**, 353–365 (2017). https://doi.org/10.1016/j.jss.2017.06.060. http://www.sciencedirect.com/science/article/pii/S0164121217301310

17. Pnueli, A., Zaks, A.: PSL model checking and run-time verification via testers. In: Misra, J., Nipkow, T., Sekerinski, E. (eds.) FM 2006. LNCS, vol. 4085, pp. 573–586. Springer, Heidelberg (2006). https://doi.org/10.1007/11813040_38

18. Zhang, X., Leucker, M., Dong, W.: Runtime verification with predictive semantics. In: Goodloe, A.E., Person, S. (eds.) NFM 2012. LNCS, vol. 7226, pp. 418–432. Springer, Heidelberg (2012). https://doi.org/10.1007/978-3-642-28891-3_37

Tutorials

Monitoring Spatio-Temporal Properties (Invited Tutorial)

Laura Nenzi[1,2(✉)], Ezio Bartocci[1], Luca Bortolussi[2], Michele Loreti[3], and Ennio Visconti[1]

[1] TU Wien, Vienna, Austria
laura.nenzi@tuwien.ac.at
[2] DMG, University of Trieste, Trieste, Italy
[3] University of Camerino, Camerino, Italy

Abstract. From the formation of traffic jams to the development of troublesome, whirlpool-like spirals in the heart's electrical activity, spatio-temporal patterns are key in understanding how complex behaviors can emerge in a network of locally interacting dynamical systems. One of the most important and intriguing questions is how to specify spatio-temporal behaviors in a formal and human-understandable specification language and how to monitor their onset efficiently. In this tutorial, we present the spatio-temporal logic STREL and its expressivity to specify and monitor spatio-temporal behaviors over complex dynamical and spatially distributed systems. We demonstrate our formalism's applicability to different scenarios considering static or dynamic spatial configurations and systems with deterministic or stochastic dynamics.

1 Introduction

Spatio-temporal patterns are central to the understanding of how complex behaviors can emerge in a network of locally interacting dynamical systems.

A prominent example is the electrical currents that regularly traverse the cardiac tissue and are responsible for the heart's muscle fibers to contract. These electrical impulses travel as a planar wave smoothly and unobstructed in a healthy heart. In certain circumstances, myocytes can partially or entirely lose excitability [46,47,60], that is their ability to propagate and reinforce an electric stimulus. Lack of excitability can cause the formation of whirlpool-like spirals (see Fig. 1) of electrical activity that are a precursor to a variety of cardiac arrhythmias, including atrial fibrillation (AF), an abnormal rhythm originating in the upper chambers of the heart [11]. This type of behavior is called *emergent* because it emerges as the result of the local interactions of several (potentially heterogeneous) entities. Thus, these behaviors cannot be studied analyzing the individual entities, but they can be reproduced only by simulating/observing

This research has been partially supported by the Austrian FWF projects ZK-35 and W1255-N23, by the Italian PRIN project "SEDUCE" n. 2017TWRCNB and by the Italian PRIN project "IT-MaTTerS" n, 2017FTXR7S.

© Springer Nature Switzerland AG 2020
J. Deshmukh and D. Ničković (Eds.): RV 2020, LNCS 12399, pp. 21–46, 2020.
https://doi.org/10.1007/978-3-030-60508-7_2

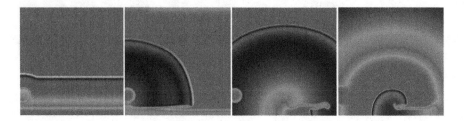

Fig. 1. Tachycardic spiral wave induced by the left hand side disc of unexcitable myocytes.

their collective behavior. A typical mechanism responsible for the onset of emergent behaviors is the change in space and time of the concentration of one or more chemical substances. In the cardiac tissue example, the electrical polarization results from a complex interplay between ion pumps and ionic channels embedded in the cell membrane that are responsible for the inward/outward flows of different ionic species (e.g., sodium, potassium, calcium).

Turing's reaction–diffusion systems [71] are suitable mathematical tools commonly used to model and simulate such physical phenomena. Mathematically, they consist of semi-linear parabolic partial differential equations (PDEs) with two terms that sum to each other: (a) a *reaction term* that describes, via nonlinear ordinary differential equations (ODEs), how the chemical species are transformed into each other in time; (b) a *diffusion term* modeling the flow/the spread of species in space.

Turing's reaction–diffusion systems can be employed to model a wide range of dynamical processes (not necessary chemical) ranging from wave-like phenomena in excitable media to the formation of other spatio-temporal self-organized patterns that are at the very origin of morphogenesis (e.g., the stripes of a zebra, the spots on a leopard and the filaments in Anabaena [45]) and developmental biology [14]. They are also at the core of self-assembly technologies, tissue engineering [72], and amorphous computing [2,21]. Such patterns are also known as "Turing's patterns".

Spatio-temporal patterns are not only pervasively present in nature, but they can arise also in human engineered artefacts such as Collective Adaptive Systems [54] (CAS) and Cyber-Physical Systems [64] (CPS).

CAS consist of a large number of heterogeneous components featuring complex interactions among themselves, with humans and other systems. Each component in the system may exhibit autonomic behavior and operates in open and non-deterministic environments where entities may enter or leave the CAS at any time. Decision-making in CAS is very challenging because the local interactions among components may introduce novel and sometimes undesired emergent behaviors. A typical example of CAS is a bike sharing system (BSS) [42], a service that allows people to borrow bicycles on a short term basis either for a price or for free. Users can pick-up and return bikes in special stations (spatially distributed in a city) equipped with bike racks. In such case the undesired behavior is to have the pick-up stations completely full or empty.

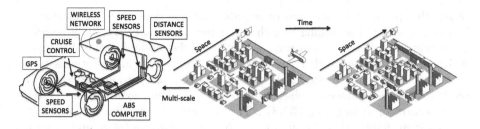

Fig. 2. An example of Cyber-Physical Systems in the automotive scenario.

Cyber Physical Systems (CPS) share similar characteristics with CAS. The term CPS was first coined in 2006 by Helen Gill [53], the Program Director for the Embedded & Hybrid Systems at US National Science Foundation. She defined CPS as "engineering, physical and biological systems whose operations are integrated, monitored, and/or controlled by a computational core. Components are networked at every scale. Computing is deeply embedded into every physical component, possibly even into materials. The computational core is an embedded system, usually demands real-time response, and is most often distributed. The behavior of a cyber-physical system is a fully-integrated hybridisation of computational (logical) and physical action."

Examples of CPS include contact tracing devices, self-driving cars, robotics teams, mobile ad-hoc sensor networks and smart cities. CPS behavior is characterised by the evolution in time of physical quantities measured by sensors and discrete states of computational, connected and spatially arranged entities.

Figure 2 shows an instance of CPS in the automotive scenario where the extensive integration of sensor networks and computational cores into automotive systems has led to the development of various driving assistance features that facilitate the driver during monotonous maneuvers and protect the passengers from hazardous situations. Furthermore, the advent of 5G mobile-network technology will support Vehicle To Vehicle (V2V) and Vehicle To Infrastructure (V2I) communication technologies very soon. These technologies will enable the exchange of information between vehicles and roadside units about position and speed of vehicles, driving conditions on a particular road, accidents, or traffic jams. This will allow to distribute the traffic load among several roads during rush hour and to prevent accidents.

The safety-critical nature of these systems [64] requires the engineers to check their correct execution with respect to rigorously defined spatial and temporal requirements. However, the complexity of these large scale systems often limits the possibility to analyze them using exhaustive verification techniques. A common approach consists instead in simulating their design with different initial conditions, parameters and inputs. The generated traces (e.g., mixed-analog signals) are then monitored [10,15] with respect to a formal specification of the behavioral property to satisfy. The verdict of such specification-based monitoring approach can return either a Boolean value specifying whether the traces satisfy or not the specification or a real value indicating how much the specification is satisfied or violated according to a chosen notion of distance [12,39,49,50,65].

Specification-based monitoring is nowadays the basic functionality upon which are built several other computer-aided verification and synthesis techniques such as statistical model checking [24,33,75], falsification analysis [1,67, 68,73], failure explanation/debugging [16–18], parameter synthesis for system identification or design [9,23,35,37]. The majority of specification languages and tools available for CPS supports only the monitoring of temporal properties. Examples are Metric Temporal Logic (MTL) [52], Signal Temporal Logic (STL) [57,58] and Timed Regular Expressions (TRE) [6].

However, one of the most important and intriguing questions in monitoring these systems is how to formally specify in a human-understandable language also spatio-temporal emergent behaviour, and how to efficiently monitor its onset.

In this tutorial, we present the Spatio-Temporal Reach and Escape Logic (STREL), a spatio-temporal specification language originally introduced in [13]. STREL enables the specification of spatio-temporal requirements and their monitoring over the execution of mobile and spatially distributed components. In this framework, space is represented as a weighted graph, describing the topological configurations in which the single components (nodes of the graph) are arranged. Both nodes and edges have attributes modelling physical and logical quantities that can change in time. STREL extends the Signal Temporal Logic [57] with two spatial operators *reach* and *escape* from which is possible to derive other spatial modalities such as *everywhere, somewhere* and *surround*. These operators enable a monitoring procedure where the satisfaction of the property at each location depends only on the satisfaction of its neighbours. Furthermore, we show how STREL can be interpreted according different semantics (Boolean, real-valued) semantics based on constraint semirings, an algebraic structure suitable for constraint satisfaction and optimisation.

The rest of this paper is organized as follows. Section 2 introduces the model we consider to represent the spatio-temporal signals, while Sect. 3 provides the syntax and the semantics of STREL. In Sects. 4, 5 and 6, we demonstrate the applicability of our formalism to different scenarios considering static (Sect. 4 and Sect. 5) or dynamic (Sect. 6) spatial configurations and systems with deterministic or stochastic dynamics. Section 7 discusses the related work, while Sect. 8 draws our conclusions and discusses future works.

2   Space Model, Signals and Traces

In this section we introduce some preliminary notions, including the model of space we consider and the related concept of spatio-temporal signal, illustrating them through a working example.

Sensor Network. As a running example, let us consider a network [4] of n devices, equipped with a sensor to monitor for example the temperature. Two nodes can communicate with each other if their Euclidean distance is within their communication range.

2.1 Discrete Space as a Graph

The design of a spatial logic is strictly related to the description of *space* in which the dynamics takes place. In this tutorial, we consider a discrete space, described as a weighted direct graph (undirect graphs can be treated as direct graph with a symmetric relation). The reason why we focus our attention on discrete space is that many applications, like bike sharing systems, smart grid and sensor networks are naturally framed in a discrete spatial structure. Moreover, in many circumstances continuous space is abstracted as a grid or as a mesh. This is the case, for instance, of many numerical methods that simulate the spatio-temporal dynamics using partial differential equations (PDEs). Hence, this class of models can be dealt with by checking properties on such a discretization.

Definition 1 (Space Model). *We define the spatial model S as a pair $\langle L, \mathbf{W} \rangle$ where:*

- *L is a set of nodes that we call* locations;
- *$\mathbf{W} \subseteq L \times \mathbb{R} \times L$ is a* proximity function *associating a label $w \in \mathbb{R}$ to distinct pair $\ell_1, \ell_2 \in L$. If $(\ell_1, w, \ell_2) \in \mathbf{W}$ it means that there is an edge from ℓ_1 to ℓ_2 with weight $w \in \mathbb{R}$, i.e. $\ell_1 \overset{w}{\mapsto} \ell_2$.*

Considering our running example, let us define a sensor space model. L is given by the set of devices, i.e. each device represents a location. As proximity function $\mathbf{W}_C$, we can consider the connectivity graph, i.e. a location ℓ_i is next to a location ℓ_j if and only if they are within their communication range. Another possibility as proximity function is the dual graph of the Voronoi diagram [7] which partitions the plane into set of n regions, one per location, assigning each point of the plane to the region corresponding to the closest location. These two examples of graphs can be seen in Fig. 3.

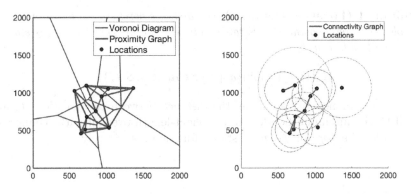

Fig. 3. Proximity graph (left) and connectivity graph (right)

Given a spatial model we can define *routes*.

Definition 2 (Route). *Let $\mathcal{S} = \langle L, \mathbf{W} \rangle$, a route τ is an infinite sequence $\ell_0 \ell_1 \cdots \ell_k \cdots$ in $\mathcal{S}$ such that for any $i \geq 0$, $\ell_i \overset{w}{\mapsto} \ell_{i+1}$.*

Let $\tau = \ell_0 \ell_1 \cdots \ell_k \cdots$ be a route, $i \in \mathbb{N}$ and $\ell \in L$, we use: $\tau[i]$ to denote the i-th node ℓ_i in τ, $\tau[i..]$ to indicate the suffix route $\ell_i \ell_{i+1} \cdots$, and $\tau(\ell)$ to denote the first occurrence of ℓ in τ:

$$\tau(\ell) = \begin{cases} \min\{i | \tau[i] = \ell\} & \text{if } \ell \in \tau \\ \infty & \text{otherwise} \end{cases}$$

We also use $Routes(\mathcal{S})$ to denote the set of routes in $\mathcal{S}$, while $Routes(\mathcal{S}, \ell)$ denotes the set of routes starting from $\ell \in L$.

We can use routes to define the *distance* among two locations in a *spatial model*. This distance is computed via an appropriate function f that combines all the weights in a route into a value.

Definition 3 (Route Distance). *Let $\mathcal{S} = \langle L, \mathbf{W} \rangle$, τ a route in $\mathcal{S}$, the distance $d_\tau^f[i]$ up-to index i is:*

$$d_\tau^f[i] = \begin{cases} 0 & i = 0 \\ f(d_{\tau[1..]}^f[i-1], w) & (i > 0) \text{ and } \tau[0] \overset{w}{\mapsto} \tau[1] \end{cases}$$

Given a location $\ell \in L$, the distance over τ up-to ℓ is then $d_\tau[\ell] = d_\tau^f[\tau(\ell)]$ if $\ell \in \tau$, or ∞ otherwise[1].

Considering again the sensor example, we can be interested in different types of distance. For example we can count the number of *hops*, simply using the function *hops* defined as $hops(v, w) := v + 1$ and in this case $d_\tau^{hops}[i] = i$. We can also consider the distances with respect the weighted label w in the edges, in that case we have $weight(v, w) = v + w$ and $d_\tau^{weight}[i]$ is the sum the weights in the edges of the route until the i-th node ℓ_i.

Definition 4 (Location Distance) *The distance between two locations ℓ_1 and ℓ_2 is obtained by choosing the distance values along all possible routes starting from ℓ_1 and ending in ℓ_2:*

$$d_\mathcal{S}[\ell_1, \ell_2] = \min\{d_\tau[\ell_2] | \tau \in Routes(\mathcal{S}, \ell_1)\}.$$

In the sensor network example, the distance between two locations ℓ_1 and ℓ_2, will be the minimum hop-length or weight-length over all paths connecting ℓ_1 and ℓ_2 for the *hops* or *weight* distance function respectively.

---

[1] We restrict here only to the tropical semiring, a more general definition can be found in [13].

2.2   Signal, Trace and Dynamic Models

We assume to have *piecewise constant temporal signal* $\nu = [(t_0, d_0), \ldots, (t_n, d_n)]$ with $t_i \in \mathbb{T} = [0, T] \subseteq \mathbb{R}_{\geq 0}$ a time domain and $d_i \in D$. Different kinds of signals can be considered: signals with $D = \{true, false\}$ are called *Boolean signals*; with $D = \mathbb{R}^\infty$ are called real-valued or *quantitative signals*, signal with $D = \mathbb{Z}$ are integer signals. We use $\mathcal{T}(\nu)$ to denote the sequence of $(t_0, \ldots, t_n)$ of *time steps* in ν.

Definition 5 (Spatio-temporal signal) *Let $\mathcal{S} = \langle L, \mathbf{W} \rangle$ be a space model and $\mathbb{T} = [0, T]$ a time domain, a spatio-temporal signal is a function*

$$\sigma : L \rightarrow \mathbb{T} \rightarrow D$$

that associates a temporal signal $\sigma(\ell) = \nu$ at each location. We use $\sigma@t$ to denote the spatial signal at time t, i.e. the signal $\mathbf{s}$ such that $\mathbf{s}(\ell) = \sigma(\ell)(t)$, for any $\ell \in L$.

Definition 6 (Spatio-Temporal Trace) *Let $\mathcal{S} = \langle L, \mathbf{W} \rangle$ be a space model, a spatio-temporal trace is a function*

$$\mathbf{x} : L \rightarrow \mathbb{T} \rightarrow D^n$$

such that for any $\ell \in L$ yields a vector of temporal signals $\mathbf{x}(\ell) = (\nu_1, \ldots, \nu_n)$. Note that this means that a spatio-temporal trace is composed by a set of spatio-temporal signals. In the rest of the paper we will use $\mathbf{x}(\ell, t)$ to denote $\mathbf{x}(\ell)(t)$.

We can consider a spatio-temporal trace of our sensor network as $\mathbf{x} : L \rightarrow \mathbb{T} \rightarrow \mathbb{R} \times \mathbb{R}$ that associates a set of temporal signals $\mathbf{x}(\ell) = (\nu_B, \nu_T)$ at each location, where ν_B and ν_T correspond for example to the temporal signals of the battery and the temperature respectively in location ℓ.

We also consider spatial models that can dynamically change their configurations. For example, the devices can move in space and change their position and connectivity pattern. For this reason, we need to define a structure that returns the spatial configuration at each time.

Definition 7 (Dynamic Spatial Model) *Let L be a set of locations and $(t_0, \ldots, t_n)$ a set of time step with $t_i \in \mathbb{T} = [0, T] \subseteq \mathbb{R}_{\geq 0}$, a Dynamic Spatial Model is a function associating each element t_i with a space model $\mathcal{S}_i$ that describes the spatial configuration at that time step, i.e. $(t_i, \mathcal{S}_i)$ for $i + 1, \ldots, n$ and $\mathcal{S}(t) = \mathcal{S}_i$ for all $t \in [t_i, t_{i+1})$.*

In case of a static spatial model we assume that $\mathcal{S}(t) = \mathcal{S}$ for all t.

3   Logic and Monitoring Procedures

Here we consider the specification of spatio-temporal properties by the *Spatio-Temporal Reach and Escape Logic* (STREL). STREL is an extension of the *Signal Temporal Logic* (STL) [34, 36, 57], with a number of spatial modal operators. Signal Temporal Logic is a linear-time temporal logic, it integrates the dense-semantics of the *Metric Interval Temporal Logic* (MITL) [5] with a set of parametrised numerical predicates playing the role of atomic proposition μ, these are inequality of the form $(g(\nu_1,\ldots,\nu_n) \geq 0)$, for $g : \mathbb{R}^n \to \mathbb{R}$. Considering our wireless sensor network, example of atomic propositions are: $v_B > 0.5$, i.e. the level of the battery should be greater than 0.5, or $v_T < 30$, i.e. the value of temperature should be less than $30°$.

The syntax of STREL is given by

Definition 8 (STREL Syntax)

$$\varphi := true \mid \mu \mid \neg\varphi \mid \varphi_1 \wedge \varphi_2 \mid \varphi_1 \, \mathrm{U}_I \, \varphi_2 \mid \varphi_1 \, \mathrm{S}_I \, \varphi_2 \mid \varphi_1 \, \mathcal{R}_d^f \, \varphi_2 \mid \mathcal{E}_d^f \, \varphi$$

where *true* is the Boolean *true* constant, μ is an *atomic predicate (AP)*, *negation* $\neg$ and *conjunction* $\wedge$ are the standard Boolean connectives, the temporal modalities are the *until* (U_I) and the *since* (S_I), where I is a non singular positive real interval, while *reachability* ($\mathcal{R}_d^f$) and the *escape* ($\mathcal{E}_d^f$) are the spatial operators, with f a *Distance Function* described in the previous section (e.g. the *hops* function) and d a non singular positive real interval. Both I and d can be infinite intervals, in case of using all $\mathbb{R}_{\geq 0}^\infty$ the interval can be omitted. In addition, we can derive the *disjunction* operator ($\vee$), the future *eventually* (F_I) and *always* (G_I) operators and the past *once* (O_I) and *historically* (H_I). We can derive also three other spatial operators: the *somewhere*, the *everywhere* and the *surround*. Below, we describe in detail the semantics of the spatial operators, we will see the temporal operators directly in the next Sections within the case studies, for more detail about temporal operators of STL we refer the reader to [34,36,57].

3.1 Boolean and Quantitative Semantics

The logic presents two semantics: a Boolean semantics, $(\mathcal{S}, \boldsymbol{x}, \ell, t) \vDash \varphi$, with the meaning that the spatio-temporal trace $\boldsymbol{x}$ in location ℓ at time t with spatial model $\mathcal{S}$, satisfies the formula φ and a quantitative semantics, $\rho(\varphi, \mathcal{S}, \boldsymbol{x}, \ell, t)$, that can be used to measure the quantitative level of satisfaction of a formula for a given trajectory. The function ρ is also called the *robustness* function. The robustness is compatible with the Boolean semantics since it satisfies the soundness property: if $\rho(\varphi, \mathcal{S}, \boldsymbol{x}, \ell, t) > 0$ then $(\mathcal{S}, \boldsymbol{x}, \ell, t) \vDash \varphi$; if $\rho(\varphi, \mathcal{S}, \boldsymbol{x}, \ell, t) < 0$ then $(\mathcal{S}, \boldsymbol{x}, \ell, t) \nvDash \varphi$. Furthermore it satisfies also the correctness property, which shows that $\boldsymbol{x}$ measures how robust is the satisfaction of a trajectory with respect to perturbations. We refer the reader to [36] for more details.

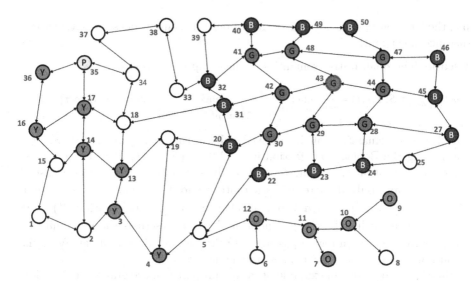

Fig. 4. Example of spatial properties. ℓ_3 satisfies $yellow \mathcal{R}^{hops}_{[1,4]} pink$ while ℓ_4 does not. ℓ_9 satisfies $\mathcal{E}^{hops}_{[3,\infty]} orange$ while ℓ_{10} does not. ℓ_1 satisfies $\Diamond^{hops}_{[3,5]} pink$ and $\Box^{hops}_{[2,3]} yellow$. All green points satisfy $green \circledcirc^{hops}_{[0,100]} blue$. ℓ_{43} (the green point in the middle with a boild red circle) is the only location that satisfies $green \circledcirc^{hops}_{[2,3]} blue$. The letters inside the nodes indicate the color and the numbers indicate the enumeration of the locations. (Color figure online)

Reach. The quantitative semantics of the reach operator is:
$$\rho(\varphi_1 \, \mathcal{R}^{f}_{[d_1,d_2]} \, \varphi_2, \mathcal{S}, x, \ell, t) =$$

$$= \max_{\tau \in Routes(\mathcal{S}(t),\ell)} \; \max_{\ell' \in \tau : \left(d^{f}_{\tau}[\ell'] \in [d_1,d_2]\right)} \left(\min(\rho(\varphi_2, \mathcal{S}, x, \ell', t), \min_{j < \tau(\ell')} \rho(\varphi_1, \mathcal{S}, x, \tau[j], t)\right)$$

The Boolean semantics can be derived substituting min, max with $\vee, \wedge$ and considering the Boolean satisfaction instead or ρ. $(\mathcal{S}, x, \ell, t)$, a spatio-temporal trace x, in location ℓ, at time t, with a (dynamic) spatial model $\mathcal{S}$, satisfies $\varphi_1 \mathcal{R}^{f}_{[d_1,d_2]} \varphi_2$ iff it satisfies φ_2 in a location ℓ' reachable from ℓ through a route τ, with a length $d^{f}_{\tau}[\ell'] \in [d_1, d_2]$, and such that $\tau[0] = \ell$ and all its elements with index less than $\tau(\ell')$ satisfy φ_1. Practically, the reach operator $\phi_1 \mathcal{R}^{f}_{[d_1,d_2]} \phi_2$ describes the behaviour of reaching a location satisfying property ϕ_2 passing only through locations that satisfy ϕ_1, and such that the distance from the initial location and the final one is greater than d_1 and less than d_2. In Fig. 4, we report an example of reachability property, considering f as the *hops* function described in the previous section. In the graph, the location ℓ_3 (meaning the trajectory x at time t in position ℓ_3 with spatial model $\mathcal{S}(t)$ as in the figure) satisfies $yellow \mathcal{R}^{hops}_{[1,4]} pink$. Indeed, there exists a route $\tau = \ell_3 \ell_{13} \ell_{14} \ell_{17} \ell_{35}$ such that $d^{hops}_{\tau}[\ell_{35}] = 4$, where $\tau[0] = \ell_3$, ℓ_{35} satisfies the pink property (i.e. it is pink) and all the other elements of the route satisfy the yellow property. Instead, for example, the location ℓ_4 does not satisfy the property because it does not satisfies the distance constraint.

Escape. The quantitative semantics of the escape operator is:

$$\rho(\mathcal{E}^f_{[d_1,d_2]}\,\varphi, \mathcal{S}, \boldsymbol{x}, \ell, t) = \max_{\tau \in Routes(\mathcal{S}(t),\ell)} \max_{\ell' \in \tau:\left(d^f_{\mathcal{S}(t)}[\ell,\ell'] \in [d_1,d_2]\right)} \min_{i \le \tau(\ell')} \rho(\varphi, \mathcal{S}, \boldsymbol{x}, \tau[i], t).$$

The Boolean semantics can be derived substituting $\min, \max$ with $\vee, \wedge$, and considering the Boolean satisfaction instead of ρ. $(\mathcal{S}, \boldsymbol{x}, \ell, t)$, a spatio-temporal trace $\boldsymbol{x}$, in location ℓ, at time t, with a (dynamic) spatial model $\mathcal{S}$, satisfies $\mathcal{E}^f_{[d_1,d_2]}\,\varphi$ if and only if there exists a route τ and a location $\ell' \in \tau$ such that $\tau[0] = \ell$, $d_{\mathcal{S}}[\tau[0], \ell'] \in [d_1, d_2]$ and all elements $\tau[0], ...\tau[k]$ (with $\tau(\ell') = k$) satisfy φ. Practically, the escape operator $\mathcal{E}^f_{[d_1,d_2]}\phi$ describes the possibility of escaping from a certain region passing only through locations that satisfy ϕ, via a route with a distance that belongs to the interval d.

In Fig. 4, we report an example of escape property. In the graph, the location ℓ_9 satisfies $\mathcal{E}^{hops}_{[3,\infty]}orange$. Indeed, there exists a route $\tau = \ell_9\ell_{10}\ell_{11}\ell_{12}$ such that $\tau[0] = \ell_9$, $\tau[3] = \ell_{12}$, $d^{hops}_{\mathcal{S}}[\ell_9, \ell_{12}] = 3$ and all elements $\tau[0], \tau[1], \tau[2], \tau[3]$ satisfy the orange property. Note that the route $\ell_{10}\ell_{11}\ell_{12}$ is not a good route to satisfy the property because the distance $d^{hops}_{\mathcal{S}}[\ell_{10}, \ell_{12}] = 2$.

Now we describe the other three derived operators.

Somewhere. $\Diamond^f_{[d_1,d_2]}\varphi := true\,\mathcal{R}^f_{[d_1,d_2]}\varphi$ holds for $(\mathcal{S}, \boldsymbol{x}, \ell, t)$ iff there exists a location ℓ' in $\mathcal{S}(t)$ such that $(\mathcal{S}, \boldsymbol{x}, \ell', t)$ satisfies φ and ℓ' is reachable from ℓ via a route τ with length $d^f_\tau[\ell'] \in [d_1, d_2]$. In Fig. 4, ℓ_1 satisfies the property $\Diamond^{hops}_{[3,5]}pink$ because there is a path $\tau = \ell_1 ... \ell_{35}$ with a length $d^{hops}_\tau(k) \in [3, 5]$, where $\tau[0] = \ell_1$, $\tau[k] = \ell_{35}$, and ℓ_{35} satisfies the pink property.

Everywhere. $\Box^f_{[d_1,d_2]}\varphi := \neg \Diamond^f_{[d_1,d_2]}\neg\varphi$ holds for $(\mathcal{S}, \boldsymbol{x}, \ell, t)$ iff all the locations ℓ' reachable from ℓ via a path, with length $d^f_\tau[\ell'] \in [d_1, d_2]$, satisfy φ. In Fig. 4, ℓ_1 satisfies $\Box^{hops}_{[2,3]}yellow$ because all the locations at a distance between 2 and 3 from ℓ_1 satisfy the yellow property, while ℓ_2 does not satisfies because ℓ_{18} is at a distance less than 3 but does not satisfy the yellow property.

Surround. $\varphi_1 \circledS^f_{[d_1,d_2]}\varphi_2 := \varphi_1 \wedge \neg(\varphi_1\mathcal{R}^f_{[d_1,d_2]}\neg(\varphi_1 \vee \varphi_2) \wedge \neg(\mathcal{E}^f_{[d_2,\infty]}(\varphi_1))$ holds for $(\mathcal{S}, \boldsymbol{x}, \ell, t)$ iff there exists a φ_1-region that contains ℓ, all locations in that region satisfies φ_1 and are reachable from ℓ via a path with length less than d_2. Furthermore, all the locations that do not belong to the φ_1-region but are directly connected to a location in φ_1-region must satisfy φ_2 and be reached from ℓ via a path with length in the interval $[d_1, d_2]$. Practically, the surround operator expresses the topological notion of being surrounded by a φ_2-region, while being in a φ_1-region, with additional metric constraints. The idea is that one cannot escape from a φ_1-region without passing from a node that satisfies φ_2 and, in any case, one has to reach a φ_2-node at a distance between d_1 and d_2. In Fig. 4, the green points satisfy $green \circledS^{hops}_{[0,100]} blue$. Indeed, for each green point we can find a region that contains the point, such that all its points are green and all the points connected with an element that belongs to the region are blue and satisfy the metric constraint. Instead, the property $green \; \textcircled{\tiny s}^{hops}_{[2,3]} \; blue$ is satisfied only by location ℓ_{43} (the location with a bold red circle), indeed ℓ_{43} is the only location for which there exists a region (the green region) such that all its elements are at a distance less than 3 from ℓ_{43} and satisfy the green property; and all the locations directly connected with the green region are at a distance between 2 and 3 from ℓ_{43} and satisfy the blue property.

3.2   Offline Monitoring Algorithm

At the moment the logic supports only offline monitoring. The monitor takes as inputs a static or dynamic spatial model $\mathcal{S}$, a trace x and a formula ϕ and returns the spatio-temporal signal σ representing the monitoring of ϕ, a Boolean spatio-temporal signal for the Boolean Semantics and a real-value spatio-temporal signal for the quantitative one. The monitor of the whole trace corresponds to $\sigma@0$, i.e. the spatial Boolean or real-value signal at time zero. This means that the monitor of the whole trace corresponds to the evaluation at time $t = 0$ in each point in space: $(\mathcal{S}, x, \ell) \models \varphi$ iff $(\mathcal{S}, x, \ell, 0) \models \varphi$ and $\rho(\varphi, \mathcal{S}, x, \ell) := \rho(\varphi, \mathcal{S}, x, \ell, 0)$. We made this choice because we assume no privilege direction or location so we cannot consider a zero location as for the time.

Like in STL, monitoring of temporal operators is linear in the length of the signal times the number of locations in the spatial model. This because the monitoring procedure is performed at each location by using the same (linear) algorithm proposed in [36]. Monitoring of spatial properties is more expensive. These algorithms, formally described in [13], are based on a variations of the classical Floyd-Warshall algorithm. The number of operations to perform is polynomial on the size of the model times the length of the signal.

3.3   Application to Stochastic Systems

The analysis of spatio-temporal properties can be applied also on stochastic systems considering methodologies as Statistical Model Checking [74] (SMC). SMC combines simulation of the stochastic model (i.e. an algorithm that samples traces according to the probability distribution of the model in the Skorokhod space) with a monitoring routine for the property ϕ. Stochastic systems induce a probability measure on the space of all possible traces (i.e. on the so-called Skorokhod space, the space of càdlàg functions, which are piecewise continuous functions of time, taking real values). If we define a *stochastic process* $\mathcal{M} = (\mathcal{T}, \mathcal{A}, \mu)$, where $\mathcal{T}$ is a trajectory space and μ is a probability measure on a σ-algebra $\mathcal{A}$ of $\mathcal{T}$, a quantity for measuring how a certain STREL formula φ is satisfied by $\mathcal{M}$ is the *satisfaction probability* $S(\varphi, t)$, i.e. the probability that a trajectory generated by the stochastic process $\mathcal{M}$ satisfies the formula φ at the time t: $\mathbb{E}[s(\varphi, \xi, t)] = \int_{\xi \in \mathcal{T}} s(\varphi, \xi, t) d\mu(\xi)$ where $s(\varphi, \xi, t) = 1$ if $(\xi, t) \models \varphi$ and 0 otherwise. The quantitative counterpart of the satisfaction probability is the *expected robustness*, defined as $\langle \rho(\varphi, t) \rangle := \mathbb{E}[\rho(\varphi, \xi, t)] = \int_{\xi \in \mathcal{T}} \rho(\varphi, \xi, t) d\mu(\xi)$ that is the expectation of the robustness computed over the trajectories of $\mathcal{M}$.

More specifically, SMC for satisfaction probability works by pipelining the generation of traces and their monitoring: every time a trace is generated by the simulator, it is passed to the Boolean monitor, which returns either 0 (false) or 1 (true). Probabilistically, this can be seen as a sample of a Bernoulli random variable, having probability $p(\phi)$ of observing 1. From a finite sample of such values, we can rely on standard statistical tools to estimate $p(\phi)$ and to compute the confidence level of such an estimate. Estimation of average robustness works in a similar way. Examples of spatio-temporal model checking to compute the approximated probabilistic satisfaction can be found in [14]. Analyzing these systems through the computation of satisfaction probability and/or average robustness, can therefore bring key insights in assessing and evaluating the design choices being made. The combination of Statistical Model Checking with quantitative semantics has been explored earlier for STL in [9] and applied to tasks like system design and parameter synthesis [9,25].

4 Static Space and Regular Grid: The Formation of Patterns

We consider here the simplest scenario, a regular grid, with only hop distance function and a deterministic model. In particular, in this example, we show how to exploit the surround operator to specify the formation of patterns and some other spatio-temporal related properties.

Model and Trace. The space model is a $K \times K$ grid treated as a weighted undirected graph, where each cell $(i, j) \in \{1, \ldots, K\} \times \{1, \ldots, K\}$ is a location, edges connect each pairs of neighbouring nodes along four directions and they have only one label which corresponds to the hop distance function, i.e. if two cells are neighbors the distance is equal to one.

The spatio-temporal trace describes the concentration of two proteins A and B in each cell of the grid at each time step. It is generated by a reaction-diffusion system, discretised according to a Finite Difference scheme [63], as a system of ODEs whose variables are organised in the $K \times K$ rectangular grid. Figure 5 reports the concentration of A for a number of time steps. It can be seen that from time $t = 20$ the shape of the pattern is apparent and remains stable; the pattern consists in a almost equidistant distribution of (blue) spots which have a low concentration of A surrounded by regions with a high concentration of A. For protein B (not shown) happens the opposite (high density regions surrounded by low density regions). More details about the model can be found here [62].

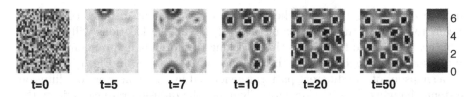

Fig. 5. Concentration of protein A for the reaction-diffusion system for the frames with $t = 0, 5, 7, 12, 20, 50$ time units. The initial conditions (i.e. the initial concentration of A and B) are set randomly. The colour map for the concentration is specified in the legend on the right. (Color figure online)

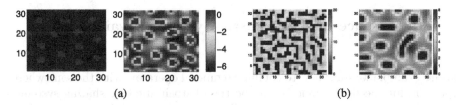

Fig. 6. (a) Boolean (left) and quantitative (right) satisfaction of the (spot formation) property; in the Boolean case the cells that satisfy the formula are in red; (b) Snapshots at time $t = 50$ of protein A for the reaction-diffusion model with different diffusion rates for which we have the formation of different patterns. (Color figure online)

4.1 Properties

Spot. ($\phi_{\text{spot}} := (A <= h) \circledcirc_{[d_1,d_2]}^{hops} (A > h)$) holds in sub-regions that have low concentration of A, surrounded by a high concentrations of A. In detail, this property holds in the location ℓ that belongs to a region L' of the grid where all elements satisfy the atomic proposition $A <= h$ and their distance from ℓ belong to the interval is less than d_2. Furthermore, each element directly connected with L' satisfy $A > 0$, and its distance from ℓ belongs to $[d_1 d_2]$. The elements in the boundary correspond to all elements directly connected to a location of L'. Note that the use of distance bounds in the surround operator allows one to constrain the size/ diameter of the spot to $[d_1 d_2]$. If we have only one type of distance function, the name in the formula can be even omitted.

Spot Formation. ($F_{[T,T+\delta]} G(spot)$) means that from a point in the future between T and $T + \delta$ the *spot* property should always hold. In Fig. 6(a) we can see the Boolean and quantitative satisfaction of the Spot Formation formula with $h = 0.5, T = 19, \delta = 1, d_1 = 1, d_2 = 6$ for the trajectory reported in Fig. 5.

Pattern. ($\boxdot \lozenge_{[0,d_{spot}]} spot formation$) means that each node in the grid should be connected to a node at a distance less than d_{spot} where the *spot* property holds, where d_{spot} represent the maximum distance between spots. This property permits to describe a global behaviour. As we pointed in the description of the logic the monitor is done in each location, differently from the temporal part where we define the satisfaction of the whole trajectory as the satisfaction at time zero. Using the everywhere operator (⊡) without distance constraints means to cover all the locations of the grid, i.e. all the locations will have the same evaluation and this means that checking this formula in a random location of our space is enough to verify the presence of the pattern. In Fig. 6(b), we can see a snapshot of two different patterns generated by the same reaction-diffusion system, changing the diffusion rate. Changing the diffusion rate can affects the shape and size of the spots or even disrupts them. Trajectories generating patterns as in Fig. 6(b) do not satisfy the pattern formula (and the quantitative semantics returns a value around 0.5) while trajectory generating pattern as in Fig. 5 satisfy it.

5   Static Space and Stochastic Systems: Availability of Bikes

In this example we show how to combine temporal operators with the somewhere operator, for specifying some key properties of stochastic bike sharing systems. In particular, we observe how spatio-temporal properties can be used to analyse the availability of bikes or free slots in proximity of users.

Model and Trace. We consider the London Santander Cycles Hire network, modelled as a Population Continuous Time Markov Chain (PCTMC) with time-dependent rates [40]. We set the model parameters using historic journey and bike availability data from January 2015 to March 2015.

The Bike-Sharing System (BSS) is composed of a number of bike stations, distributed over a geographic area. Each station has a fixed number of bike slots. The users can pick up a bike, use it for a while, and then return it to another station in the area. The model, given the number of bikes/free slots in a station at time t, computes the probability distribution of the number of bikes/free slots in that station at time $t + h$ with $h \in [0, 40]$ min. We can describe the model as a transition system where B_i (respectively S_i) represents the bike agent (respectively the slot agent) in the ith station, T_j^i is the bike agent travelling from pick-up station i to return station j, while N is the total number of stations. Each transition describes a possible event changing the state of the system. A transition rule like $B_i \rightarrow S_i + T_j^i$ models that an agent B_i is removed from the system (a bike leaves station i), while new agents S_i and T_j^i are added to the system (a free slot is added to station i, while the bike is set to travel towards station j). The rate of each transition encodes the mean frequency with which it happens, considering historic journey data. For a detailed understanding of the model, the interested reader can refer to [62].

We consider a model with 733 bike stations (each with 20–40 slots) and a total population of 57,713 agents (users) picking up and returning bikes. We simulate the model using Simhya [22], a Java tool for the simulation of stochastic and hybrid systems, using the Gibson-Bruck (GB) algorithm. We are considering in particular the trajectories only of the bike (B) and slot (S) agents, in each station. Our spatio-temporal trace is then $\boldsymbol{x}(i,t) = (B_i(t), S_i(t))$, associating at each station i the number of bikes and free slots at each time. The space is represented by a weighted graph, where the nodes are the bike stations and the edges describe the connection between each station. Two nodes are connected if they are at a distance less or equal than 1 km.

5.1 Properties

We use STREL to study spatio-temporal properties of the system and to explore their robustness considering a set of parameter values for the formulas. In the following, we will consider the distance induced by the function $\Delta(v, (x, y)) = v + \|(x, y)\|_2$, where (x, y) are the coordinates of the distance vector between two adjacent nodes, while v is the distance incrementally computed by Δ.

Local Availability. One of the main problems of these systems consists in the availability of bikes or free slots in each station. The most interesting question related to this issue from a user's point of view is "If I don't find a bike (free slot, resp.) here, can I find another station close enough where there is an available bike (resp. free slot)?" This concern can be expressed by the STREL property described below:

$$\phi_1 = G_{[0,T_{end}]}\{\diamondsuit_{[0,d]}^{\Delta}(B > 0) \wedge \diamondsuit_{[0,d]}^{\Delta}(S > 0)\} \tag{1}$$

A station ℓ satisfies ϕ_1 if and only if it is always true that, between 0 and T_{end} minutes, there exists a station at a distance less than or equal to d, that has at least one bike and a station at a distance less or equal to d that has at least one free slot.

In the analysis, we investigate the value of parameter $d \in [0, 1]$ kilometres to see how the satisfaction of the property changes in each location. Figure 7 shows the approximate satisfaction probability p_{ϕ_1} for 1000 runs for all the stations, for (a) $d = 0$, and (b) $d = 0.3$ For $d = 0$, we can see that many stations have a high probability to be full or empty (indicated by red points), i.e. low values of satisfaction probability, with standard deviation of all the locations in the range $[0, 0.0158]$ and mean standard deviation 0.0053. However, increasing d to $d = 0.3$ km, i.e. allowing a search area of up to 300 metres from the station that currently has no bikes, or no slots respectively, we greatly increase the satisfaction probability of ϕ_1, with a standard deviation that remains in the same range and mean standard deviation of 0.0039. For $d = 0.5$, the probability of p_{ϕ_1} is greater than 0.5 for all the stations; standard deviation is in the range $[0, 0.0142]$ and mean stdv is 0.0002. Figure 8 (a) shows the satisfaction probability of some BBS stations vs distance d=[0,1.0].

Timed Availability. The property we analyzed previously did not consider that a user will need some time to reach a nearby station. Property φ_1 can be refined to take this aspect into consideration by considering a nested spatio-temporal property:

$$\psi_1 = G_{[0,T_{end}]}\{\diamondsuit_{[0,d]}^{\Delta}(F_{[t_w,t_w]}B > 0) \wedge \diamondsuit_{[0,d]}^{\Delta}(F_{[t_w,t_w]}S > 0)\} \tag{2}$$

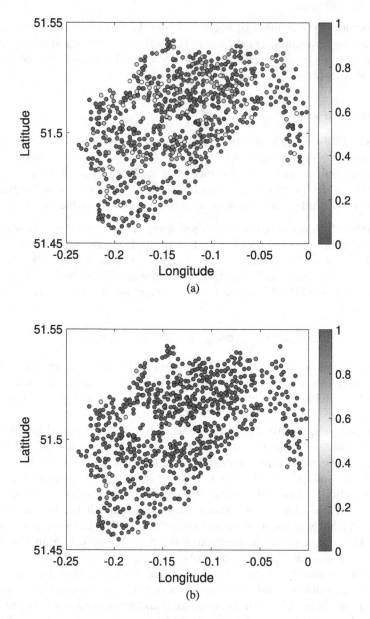

Fig. 7. Approximate satisfaction probability of formula ϕ_1 for 1000 runs for each BSS station for (a) $d = 0$, and (c) $d = 0.3$. The value of the probability is given by the color legend. (Color figure online)

A station ℓ satisfies ψ_1 if and only if it is always true between 0 and T_{end} minutes that there exists a station at a distance less than or equal to d, that, eventually in a time equal to t_w (the walking time), has at least one bike and a station at

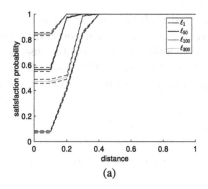 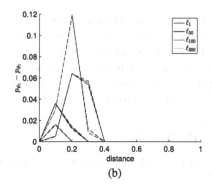

(a)   (b)

Fig. 8. Approximate satisfaction probability for property ϕ_1 (a). (b) $p_{\psi_1} - p_{\phi_1}$ vs the distance d = [0,1.0]. Both evaluated over 1000 runs of BSS stations $\ell_1, \ell_{50}, \ell_{100}$, and ℓ_{300}.

a distance less than or equal to d, that, eventually in a time equal to t_w has at least one free slot.

We consider an average walking speed of 6.0 km/h, this means for example that if we evaluate a distance $d = 0.5$ km, we consider a walking time $t_w = 6$ min. The results of ψ_1 are very similar to the results of ϕ_1. This means that there is not much difference between looking at $t = 0$ or after the walking time. Figure 8(b) shows the difference between the satisfaction probability of properties ψ_1, ϕ_1 for the same locations.

6   Dynamic Space: Connectivity and Reliability in a MANET

In the previous sections we have considered two scenarios where the structure of the space does not change in time. Differently, in this section, we consider a scenario where the structure of the space is dynamic.

Model and Trace. We consider a mobile ad-hoc sensor network (MANET). This kind of systems can consist of up ten thousands of mobile devices connected wirelessly, usually deployed to monitor environmental changes such as pollution, humidity, light and temperature.

Each sensor node is equipped with a sensing transducer, data processor, a radio transceiver and an embedded battery. A node can move independently in any direction and indeed can change its links to other devices frequently. Two nodes can communicate each other if their Euclidean distance is at most their communication range as depicted in Fig. 3. Moreover, the nodes can be of different type and their behaviour and communication can depend on their types.

In this scenario, the spatial model of time t is obtained by considering the graph where each device represents a node/location of the network. Edges are labelled with both their Euclidean distance and with the integer value 1. This last value is used to compute the hop (shortest path) count between two nodes, that is the number of intermediate network nodes through which data must pass between source node and target one. The signal associated with each location contains three values: the type of node (coordinator, router, end-device), the level of battery, and the temperature.

6.1   Properties

We can use STREL to specify, and monitor, properties related to connectivity of the network.

Connectivity. The first property one is interested to monitor is the *connectivity*. That is, each node that is an *end device* is directly connected either to a *router* or to a *coordinator*:

$$\psi_1 = end\_dev \; \mathcal{R}_{[0,1]}^{hops} \, (router \vee coord)$$

The formula above holds if from a node satisfying the atomic proposition *end_dev* (indicating an *end device*), we can reach a node satisfying either *router* or *coord* (that are the atomic proposition satisfied by *coordinators* or a *routers*), following a path in the spatial graph such that the *hops* distance along this path (i.e. its number of edges) is not bigger than 1.

More sophisticated properties can be specified with STREL. For instance, the following property can be used to specify that an *end device* is either connected to the *coordinator* or can reach it via a chain of at most of 5 routers:

$$\psi_2 = end\_dev \; \mathcal{R}_{[0,1]}^{hops} \, (router \mathcal{R}_{[0,5]}^{hops} coord)$$

Delivery. Another property that one could be interested in monitoring is the ability of the system to forward a message at a given distance. The ability of a component to forward a message is related to its battery level. To express this property, we can use the escape operator:

$$\psi_3 = \mathcal{E}_{[5,\infty]}^{hops}(battery > 0.5)$$

This property states that from a given location, we can find a path of (hops) length at least 5 such that all nodes along the path have a battery level greater than 0.5, i.e. that a message will be forwarded along a connection with no risk of power failure.

Reliability. Spatial and temporal operators can be mixed to specify properties regarding the evolution of the space in time. For instance, the following property is satisfied by the nodes with a battery level less than 0.5 that can reach in less than 10 hops another component that will eventually have a the battery level greater than 0.5:

$$\psi_4 = (battery < 0.5) \; \mathcal{R}_{[0,10]}^{hops} \, F(battery > 0.5)$$

Moreover, the following property can be used to state that the correct spatial configuration is preserved in each time step:

$$\psi_5 = G\psi_2$$

where ψ_2 is the formula defined above.

7   Related Work

Machine Learning vs Specification Languages. Pattern recognition is a well-established research area in machine learning. A typical approach consists in using a classifier trained with a labeled data set that assigns each data item to one class. Once the classifier is built from data using one of the several machine learning (ML) techniques [66] available, it can be used to detect/monitor whether a new data "most likely" matching to the classes. An important step is the choice and the extraction of the distinctive features [19,32,51,55] with relevant information from a set of input data representing the pattern of interest. Although extremely powerful, ML techniques lack generally of interpretability: they typically provide black-box data descriptors (e.g., deep neural networks) that are generally far from the human comprehension and ability to reason. Our approach to specify spatio-temporal patterns is instead based on a logic-based specification language. The declarative nature of the language offers an high-level and abstract framework enabling generalisation. STREL specifications are re-usable, compositional and generally closer to the human understanding.

Spatio-Temporal Models. In [69], Talcott introduced the notion of spatial-temporal event-based model to monitor spatial-temporal properties over CPS executions. In this model, actions (e.g. the exchange of messages, or a physical changes) are labeled with time and space stamps and they trigger events that are further processed by a monitor. In [70] the model was further extended to enable different space representations. Although the approaches in [69,70] provide a valuable algorithmic framework, they lack a specification language and the monitors cannot be automatically generated.

Other mathematical structures such as *topological spaces, closure spaces, quasi-discrete closure spaces* and *finite graphs* [61] have been investigated to reason about spatial relations (e.g. *closeness* and *neighborhood*) in the context of *collective adaptive systems* [31]. *Quad-trees* spatial structures [41] have been proposed in [44,47,48] to reason about fractal-like spatial patterns or spatial superposition properties in a grid, such as electrical spiral formation in cardiac tissues [47] or power management requirements in a smart grid [48]. Despite these models are suitable for offline and centralised monitoring of model-based simulations, they do not scale well for the runtime monitoring of spatially distributed CPS.

Spatial and Spatio-Temporal Logics. Spatial logics have been the subject of theoretically investigation since at least almost a couple of decades [3]. The work in [3] focuses on theoretically investigation, expressivity and decidability, often in continuous space. Less attention has been placed on more practical aspects, especially in the verification procedures. In particular, model checking techniques for spatial models have been introduced more recently. In [29], the authors introduce a *Spatial Logic for Closure Spaces* (SLCS) that leverages a discrete and topological notion of space, based on closure spaces [43]. An extension of the SLCS with temporal aspects, as "snapshot" models, was proposed later in [30]. This extends SLCS with the temporal modality of the branching logic *Computation Tree Logic* [38]. However, the algorithms to check snapshot models are very computational expensive and are susceptible to state-space explosion problems because the spatial formulae need to be recomputed at every state.

Relevant works are also those on spatial logics for process algebra with locations such as in [27,28], or spatial logic for rewrite theories [8]. Other logic-based formalisms have been introduced to reason about the topological [20] or directional [26] aspects of locally interacting components. In the topological approach [20], the entities are sets of points in the space and the relation between them is preserved under translation, scaling and rotation. If the relation between objects depends on their relative position then the spatial model supports the directional reasoning. These logics are highly computationally complex [26] or even undecidable [59] and indeed impractical to use.

Table 1. Table comparing the main features of different spatio-temporal logics.

Specification language	Temporal logic	Spatial model	Static/dynamic space
STREL [13]	STL [57]	Weighted graph	Static/dynamic
SpaTeL [48]	STL [57]	Quad-trees	Static
STLCS [30]	CTL [38]	Closure spaces	Static
SaSTL [56]	STL [57]	Weighted graph	Static
SSTL [61]	STL [57]	Weighted graph	Static

Monitoring spatial-temporal behaviors has recently started to receive more attention with *Spatial-Temporal Logic* (SpaTeL) [48], *Signal Spatio-Temporal Logic* SSTL [61], *Spatial Aggregation Signal Temporal Logic* (SaSTL) [56] and *Spatio-Temporal Reach and Escape Logic* STREL [13]. SpaTeL is the unification of *Signal Temporal Logic* [57] (STL) and *Tree Spatial Superposition Logic* (TSSL) introduced in [44] to classify and detect spatial patterns. Spatial properties are expressed using ideas from image processing, namely *quad trees* [41]. This allows one to capture very complex spatial structures, but at the price of a complex formulation of spatial properties, which are in practice only learned from some template images. SSTL combines STL with two spatial modalities, one expressing that something is true *somewhere* nearby and the other capturing the notion of being *surrounded* by a region that satisfies a given spatio-temporal property. SSTL has two possible semantics a Boolean and a real-valued one. SSTL [62] operates over a static topological space while STREL on the contrary can monitor entities over a dynamic topological space. Furthermore, STREL generalizes

SSTL spatial modalities with the *reach* and *escape* operators, simplifying the monitoring that can be computed locally with respect to each node. Finally, SaSTL [56] is recently proposed specification language that augment STL with two new logical operators for expressing spatial aggregation and spatial counting characteristics that are typical in monitoring spatio-temporal requirements in a smart city. Similarly to SSTL, also SaSTL operates on a static topological space. We summarize the main characteristics of the different spatio-temporal logics discussed in section in Table 1.

8   Conclusion

Spatio-temporal logics are high level languages that permit us to specify complex behaviours of dynamical systems distributed in space. In this tutorial paper we presented STREL, a modal logic which permits to specify spatio-temporal requirements and to monitor them automatically over a spatio-temporal trace. We discuss how STREL is suitable to capture behaviours of different scenarios: emergent Turing patterns, bike sharing systems, mobile sensor networks. These scenarios have both static and dynamic spatial structure and deterministic or stochastic dynamics. This flexibility of the logic, however, does not result in a high computational complexity of monitoring algorithms. This is a consequence of endowing the logic with spatial operators which are existential modal operators. Currently, STREL supports only offline monitoring. In order to properly apply STREL to real-time scenarios, we are designing dedicated online and distributed monitoring algorithms. Future work also includes the use of STREL within design and control loops of cyber-physical systems, leveraging the work done with STL in this respect [68].

References

1. Abbas, H., Fainekos, G.E., Sankaranarayanan, S., Ivancic, F., Gupta, A.: Probabilistic temporal logic falsification of cyber-physical systems. ACM Trans. Embed. Comput. Syst. **12**(s2), 95:1–95:30 (2013). https://doi.org/10.1145/2465787.2465797
2. Abelson, H., et al.: Amorphous computing. Commun. ACM **43**(5), 74–82 (2000). https://doi.org/10.1145/332833.332842
3. Aiello, M., Pratt-Hartmann, I., van Benthem, J. (eds.): Handbook of Spatial Logics. Springer, Heidelberg (2007). https://doi.org/10.1007/978-1-4020-5587-4
4. Akyildiz, I.F., Su, W., Sankarasubramaniam, Y., Cayirci, E.: A survey on sensor networks. IEEE Commun. Mag. **40**(8), 102–114 (2002). https://doi.org/10.1109/MCOM.2002.1024422
5. Alur, R., Feder, T., Henzinger, T.: The benefits of relaxing punctuality. J. ACM **43**, 116–146 (1996)
6. Asarin, E., Caspi, P., Maler, O.: Timed regular expressions. J. ACM **49**(2), 172–206 (2002). https://doi.org/10.1145/506147.506151
7. Aurenhammer, F.: Voronoi diagrams—a survey of a fundamental geometric data structure. ACM Comput. Surv. **23**(3), 345–405 (1991). https://doi.org/10.1145/116873.116880

8. Bae, K., Meseguer, J.: A rewriting-based model checker for the linear temporal logic of rewriting. Electron. Notes Theoret. Comput. Sci. **290**, 19–36 (2012). https://doi.org/10.1016/j.entcs.2012.11.009

9. Bartocci, E., Bortolussi, L., Nenzi, L., Sanguinetti, G.: System design of stochastic models using robustness of temporal properties. Theoret. Comp. Sci. **587**, 3–25 (2015). https://doi.org/10.1016/j.tcs.2015.02.046

10. Bartocci, E., et al.: Specification-based monitoring of cyber-physical systems: a survey on theory, tools and applications. In: Bartocci, E., Falcone, Y. (eds.) Lectures on Runtime Verification. LNCS, vol. 10457, pp. 135–175. Springer, Cham (2018). https://doi.org/10.1007/978-3-319-75632-5_5

11. Bartocci, E., Fenton, F.H.: Teaching cardiac electrophysiology modeling to undergraduate students: laboratory exercises and GPU programming for the study of arrhythmias and spiral wave dynamics. Adv. Physiol. Educ. **35**(4), 427–437 (2011). https://doi.org/10.1152/advan.00034.2011

12. Bartocci, E., Bloem, R., Nickovic, D., Roeck, F.: A counting semantics for monitoring LTL specifications over finite traces. In: Chockler, H., Weissenbacher, G. (eds.) CAV 2018. LNCS, vol. 10981, pp. 547–564. Springer, Cham (2018). https://doi.org/10.1007/978-3-319-96145-3_29

13. Bartocci, E., Bortolussi, L., Loreti, M., Nenzi, L.: Monitoring mobile and spatially distributed cyber-physical systems. In: Proceedings of MEMOCODE 2017: The 15th ACM-IEEE International Conference on Formal Methods and Models for System Design, pp. 146–155. ACM (2017). https://doi.org/10.1145/3127041.3127050

14. Bartocci, E., Bortolussi, L., Milios, D., Nenzi, L., Sanguinetti, G.: Studying emergent behaviours in morphogenesis using signal spatio-temporal logic. In: Abate, A., Šafránek, D. (eds.) HSB 2015. LNCS, vol. 9271, pp. 156–172. Springer, Cham (2015). https://doi.org/10.1007/978-3-319-26916-0_9

15. Bartocci, E., Falcone, Y., Francalanza, A., Reger, G.: Introduction to runtime verification. In: Bartocci, E., Falcone, Y. (eds.) Lectures on Runtime Verification. LNCS, vol. 10457, pp. 1–33. Springer, Cham (2018). https://doi.org/10.1007/978-3-319-75632-5_1

16. Bartocci, E., Ferrère, T., Manjunath, N., Nickovic, D.: Localizing faults in simulink/stateflow models with STL. In: Proceedings of HSCC 2018: The 21st International Conference on Hybrid Systems: Computation and Control (part of CPS Week), pp. 197–206. ACM (2018). https://doi.org/10.1145/3178126

17. Bartocci, E., Manjunath, N., Mariani, L., Mateis, C., Ničković, D.: Automatic failure explanation in CPS models. In: Ölveczky, P.C., Salaün, G. (eds.) SEFM 2019. LNCS, vol. 11724, pp. 69–86. Springer, Cham (2019). https://doi.org/10.1007/978-3-030-30446-1_4

18. Bartocci, E., Manjunath, N., Mariani, L., Mateis, C., Nickovic, D., Pastore, F.: CPSDebug: a tool for explanation of failures in cyber-physical systems. In: Proceedings of ISSTA 2020: 29th ACM SIGSOFT International Symposium on Software Testing and Analysis, Virtual Event, USA, 18–22 July 2020, pp. 569–572. ACM (2020). https://doi.org/10.1145/3395363

19. Belongie, S., Malik, J., Puzicha, J.: Shape matching and object recognition using shape contexts. IEEE Trans. Pattern Anal. Mach. Intell. **24**(4), 509–522 (2002). https://doi.org/10.1109/34.993558

20. Bennett, B., Cohn, A.G., Wolter, F., Zakharyaschev, M.: Multi-dimensional modal logic as a framework for spatio-temporal reasoning. Appl. Intell. **17**(3), 239–251 (2002). https://doi.org/10.1023/A:1020083231504

21. Bhattacharyya, A.: Morphogenesis as an amorphous computation. In: Proceedings of the Third Conference on Computing Frontiers, 2006, Ischia, Italy, 3–5 May 2006, pp. 53–64. ACM (2006). https://doi.org/10.1145/1128022.1128032
22. Bortolussi, L., Galpin, V., Hillston, J.: Hybrid performance modelling of opportunistic networks. In: Proceedings of QAPL 2012: The 10th Workshop on Quantitative Aspects of Programming Languages and Systems, pp. 106–121 (2012). https://doi.org/10.4204/EPTCS.85.8
23. Bortolussi, L., Milios, D., Sanguinetti, G.: U-check: model checking and parameter synthesis under uncertainty. In: Campos, J., Haverkort, B.R. (eds.) QEST 2015. LNCS, vol. 9259, pp. 89–104. Springer, Cham (2015). https://doi.org/10.1007/978-3-319-22264-6_6
24. Bortolussi, L., Milios, D., Sanguinetti, G.: Smoothed model checking for uncertain continuous-time markov chains. Inf. Comput. **247**, 235–253 (2016)
25. Bortolussi, L., Silvetti, S.: Bayesian statistical parameter synthesis for linear temporal properties of stochastic models. In: Beyer, D., Huisman, M. (eds.) TACAS 2018. LNCS, vol. 10806, pp. 396–413. Springer, Cham (2018). https://doi.org/10.1007/978-3-319-89963-3_23
26. Bresolin, D., Sala, P., Monica, D.D., Montanari, A., Sciavicco, G.: A decidable spatial generalization of metric interval temporal logic. In: 2010 17th International Symposium on Temporal Representation and Reasoning, pp. 95–102 (2010). https://doi.org/10.1109/TIME.2010.22
27. Caires, L., Cardelli, L.: A spatial logic for concurrency (part I). Inf. Comput. **186**(2), 194–235 (2003). https://doi.org/10.1016/S0890-5401(03)00137-8
28. Cardelli, L., Gordon, A.D.: Anytime, anywhere: modal logics for mobile ambients. In: Proceedings of POPL 2000: the 27th ACM SIGPLAN-SIGACT Symposium on Principles of Programming Languages, pp. 365–377. ACM, New York (2000). https://doi.org/10.1145/325694.325742
29. Ciancia, V., Latella, D., Loreti, M., Massink, M.: Specifying and verifying properties of space. In: Diaz, J., Lanese, I., Sangiorgi, D. (eds.) TCS 2014. LNCS, vol. 8705, pp. 222–235. Springer, Heidelberg (2014). https://doi.org/10.1007/978-3-662-44602-7_18
30. Ciancia, V., Gilmore, S., Grilletti, G., Latella, D., Loreti, M., Massink, M.: Spatio-temporal model-checking of vehicular movement in public transport systems (2015, Submitted)
31. Ciancia, V., Latella, D., Loreti, M., Massink, M.: Spatial logic and spatial model checking for closure spaces. In: Bernardo, M., De Nicola, R., Hillston, J. (eds.) SFM 2016. LNCS, vol. 9700, pp. 156–201. Springer, Cham (2016). https://doi.org/10.1007/978-3-319-34096-8_6
32. Dalal, N., Triggs, B.: Histograms of oriented gradients for human detection. In: Proceedings of CVPR 2005: The IEEE Computer Society Conference on Computer Vision and Pattern Recognition, vol. 1, pp. 886–893, June 2005
33. David, A., Larsen, K.G., Legay, A., Mikučionis, M., Wang, Z.: Time for statistical model checking of real-time systems. In: Gopalakrishnan, G., Qadeer, S. (eds.) CAV 2011. LNCS, vol. 6806, pp. 349–355. Springer, Heidelberg (2011). https://doi.org/10.1007/978-3-642-22110-1_27
34. Donzé, A., Maler, O.: Robust satisfaction of temporal logic over real-valued signals. In: Chatterjee, K., Henzinger, T.A. (eds.) FORMATS 2010. LNCS, vol. 6246, pp. 92–106. Springer, Heidelberg (2010). https://doi.org/10.1007/978-3-642-15297-9_9

35. Donzé, A., Clermont, G., Legay, A., Langmead, C.J.: Parameter synthesis in nonlinear dynamical systems: application to systems biology. In: Batzoglou, S. (ed.) RECOMB 2009. LNCS, vol. 5541, pp. 155–169. Springer, Heidelberg (2009). https://doi.org/10.1007/978-3-642-02008-7_11

36. Donzé, A., Ferrère, T., Maler, O.: Efficient robust monitoring for STL. In: Sharygina, N., Veith, H. (eds.) CAV 2013. LNCS, vol. 8044, pp. 264–279. Springer, Heidelberg (2013). https://doi.org/10.1007/978-3-642-39799-8_19

37. Donzé, A., Krogh, B., Rajhans, A.: Parameter synthesis for hybrid systems with an application to simulink models. In: Majumdar, R., Tabuada, P. (eds.) HSCC 2009. LNCS, vol. 5469, pp. 165–179. Springer, Heidelberg (2009). https://doi.org/10.1007/978-3-642-00602-9_12

38. Emerson, E.A., Halpern, J.Y.: "Sometimes" and "not never" revisited: on branching versus linear time. In: Wright, J.R., Landweber, L., Demers, A.J., Teitelbaum, T. (eds.) Proceedings of POPL 83: The Tenth Annual ACM Symposium on Principles of Programming Languages, pp. 127–140. ACM Press (1983). https://doi.org/10.1145/567067.567081

39. Fainekos, G.E., Pappas, G.J.: Robustness of temporal logic specifications for continuous-time signals. Theoret. Comput. Sci. 410(42), 4262–4291 (2009). https://doi.org/10.1016/j.tcs.2009.06.021

40. Feng, C., Hillston, J., Reijsbergen, D.: Moment-based probabilistic prediction of bike availability for bike-sharing systems. In: Agha, G., Van Houdt, B. (eds.) QEST 2016. LNCS, vol. 9826, pp. 139–155. Springer, Cham (2016). https://doi.org/10.1007/978-3-319-43425-4_9

41. Finkel, R.A., Bentley, J.L.: Quad trees: a data structure for retrieval on composite keys. Acta Informatica 4, 1–9 (1974). https://doi.org/10.1007/BF00288933

42. Fishman, E.: Bikeshare: a review of recent literature. Transp. Rev. 36(1), 92–113 (2016). https://doi.org/10.1080/01441647.2015.1033036

43. Galton, A.: The mereotopology of discrete space. In: Freksa, C., Mark, D.M. (eds.) COSIT 1999. LNCS, vol. 1661, pp. 251–266. Springer, Heidelberg (1999). https://doi.org/10.1007/3-540-48384-5_17

44. Gol, E.A., Bartocci, E., Belta, C.: A formal methods approach to pattern synthesis in reaction diffusion systems. In: Proceedings of CDC 2014: The 53rd IEEE Conference on Decision and Control, pp. 108–113. IEEE (2014). https://doi.org/10.1109/CDC.2014.7039367

45. Golden, J.W., Yoon, H.S.: Heterocyst formation in anabaena. Curr. Opin. Microbiol. 1(6), 623–629 (1998). https://doi.org/10.1016/S1369-5274(98)80106-9

46. Grosu, R., et al.: From cardiac cells to genetic regulatory networks. In: Gopalakrishnan, G., Qadeer, S. (eds.) CAV 2011. LNCS, vol. 6806, pp. 396–411. Springer, Heidelberg (2011). https://doi.org/10.1007/978-3-642-22110-1_31

47. Grosu, R., Smolka, S.A., Corradini, F., Wasilewska, A., Entcheva, E., Bartocci, E.: Learning and detecting emergent behavior in networks of cardiac myocytes. Commun. ACM 52(3), 97–105 (2009). https://doi.org/10.1145/1467247.1467271

48. Haghighi, I., Jones, A., Kong, Z., Bartocci, E., Grosu, R., Belta, C.: SpaTeL: a novel spatial-temporal logic and its applications to networked systems. In: Proceedings of HSCC 2015: The 18th International Conference on Hybrid Systems: Computation and Control, pp. 189–198. IEEE (2015). https://doi.org/10.1145/2728606.2728633

49. Jaksic, S., Bartocci, E., Grosu, R., Nguyen, T., Nickovic, D.: Quantitative monitoring of STL with edit distance. Formal Methods Syst. Des. 53(1), 83–112 (2018). https://doi.org/10.1007/s10703-018-0319-x

50. Jaksic, S., Bartocci, E., Grosu, R., Nickovic, D.: An algebraic framework for runtime verification. IEEE Trans. CAD Integr. Circuits Syst. **37**(11), 2233–2243 (2018). https://doi.org/10.1109/TCAD.2018.2858460

51. Julesz, B.: Textons, the elements of texture perception, and their interactions. Nature **290**, 91–97 (1981)

52. Koymans, R.: Specifying real-time properties with metric temporal logic. Real-Time Syst. **2**(4), 255–299 (1990). https://doi.org/10.1007/BF01995674

53. Lee, E.A., Seshia, S.A.: Introduction to Embedded Systems, A Cyber-Physical Systems Approach, 2nd edn. MIT Press, Berlin (2017)

54. Loreti, M., Hillston, J.: Modelling and analysis of collective adaptive systems with CARMA and its tools. In: Bernardo, M., De Nicola, R., Hillston, J. (eds.) SFM 2016. LNCS, vol. 9700, pp. 83–119. Springer, Cham (2016). https://doi.org/10.1007/978-3-319-34096-8_4

55. Lowe, D.G.: Object recognition from local scale-invariant features. In: Proceedings of the International Conference on Computer Vision, vol. 2, pp. 1150–1157 (1999)

56. Ma, M., Bartocci, E., Lifland, E., Stankovic, J.A., Feng, L.: SaSTL: spatial aggregation signal temporal logic for runtime monitoring in smart cities. In: Proceedings of ICCPS 2020: The 11th ACM/IEEE International Conference on Cyber-Physical Systems, pp. 51–62. IEEE (2020). https://doi.org/10.1109/ICCPS48487.2020.00013

57. Maler, O., Nickovic, D.: Monitoring temporal properties of continuous signals. In: Lakhnech, Y., Yovine, S. (eds.) FORMATS/FTRTFT -2004. LNCS, vol. 3253, pp. 152–166. Springer, Heidelberg (2004). https://doi.org/10.1007/978-3-540-30206-3_12

58. Maler, O., Ničković, D.: Monitoring properties of analog and mixed-signal circuits. STTT **15**(3), 247–268 (2013)

59. Marx, M., Reynolds, M.: Undecidability of compass logic. J. Logic Comput. **9**(6), 897–914 (1999). https://doi.org/10.1093/logcom/9.6.897

60. Murthy, A., et al.: Curvature analysis of cardiac excitation wavefronts. IEEE/ACM Trans. Comput. Biol. Bioinform. **10**(2), 323–336 (2013). https://doi.org/10.1109/TCBB.2012.125

61. Nenzi, L., Bortolussi, L., Ciancia, V., Loreti, M., Massink, M.: Qualitative and quantitative monitoring of spatio-temporal properties. In: Bartocci, E., Majumdar, R. (eds.) RV 2015. LNCS, vol. 9333, pp. 21–37. Springer, Cham (2015). https://doi.org/10.1007/978-3-319-23820-3_2

62. Nenzi, L., Bortolussi, L., Ciancia, V., Loreti, M., Massink, M.: Qualitative and quantitative monitoring of spatio-temporal properties with SSTL. Log. Methods Comput. Sci. **14**(4) (2018). https://doi.org/10.23638/LMCS-14(4:2)2018

63. Olver, P.J.: Finite differences. Introduction to Partial Differential Equations. UTM, pp. 181–214. Springer, Cham (2014). https://doi.org/10.1007/978-3-319-02099-0_5

64. Ratasich, D., Khalid, F., Geissler, F., Grosu, R., Shafique, M., Bartocci, E.: A roadmap toward the resilient Internet of Things for cyber-physical systems. IEEE Access **7**, 13260–13283 (2019). https://doi.org/10.1109/ACCESS.2019.2891969

65. Rodionova, A., Bartocci, E., Ničković, D., Grosu, R.: Temporal logic as filtering. In: Proceedings of HSCC 2016, pp. 11–20. ACM (2016). https://doi.org/10.1145/2883817.2883839

66. Russell, S.J., Norvig, P.: Artificial Intelligence: A Modern Approach. Prentice Hall, Upper Saddle River (2002)

67. Sankaranarayanan, S., Kumar, S.A., Cameron, F., Bequette, B.W., Fainekos, G., Maahs, D.M.: Model-based falsification of an artificial pancreas control system. SIGBED Rev. **14**(2), 24–33 (2017). https://doi.org/10.1145/3076125.3076128

68. Silvetti, S., Policriti, A., Bortolussi, L.: An active learning approach to the falsification of black box cyber-physical systems. In: Polikarpova, N., Schneider, S. (eds.) IFM 2017. LNCS, vol. 10510, pp. 3–17. Springer, Cham (2017). https://doi.org/10.1007/978-3-319-66845-1_1

69. Talcott, C.: Cyber-physical systems and events. In: Wirsing, M., Banâtre, J.-P., Hölzl, M., Rauschmayer, A. (eds.) Software-Intensive Systems and New Computing Paradigms. LNCS, vol. 5380, pp. 101–115. Springer, Heidelberg (2008). https://doi.org/10.1007/978-3-540-89437-7_6

70. Tan, Y., Vuran, M.C., Goddard, S.: Spatio-temporal event model for cyber-physical systems. In: 2009 29th IEEE International Conference on Distributed Computing Systems Workshops, pp. 44–50. IEEE (2009). https://doi.org/10.1109/ICDCSW.2009.82

71. Turing, A.M.: The chemical basis of morphogenesis. Philos. Trans. R. So. London B: Biol. Sci. **237**, 37–72 (1952)

72. Weiss, R.: Synthetic biology: from modules to systems. In: Proceedings of the 20th ACM Great Lakes Symposium on VLSI 2009, Providence, Rhode Island, USA, 16–18 May 2010, pp. 171–172. ACM (2010). https://doi.org/10.1145/1785481

73. Yaghoubi, S., Fainekos, G.: Hybrid approximate gradient and stochastic descent for falsification of nonlinear systems. In: Proceedings of ACC 2017: The 2017 American Control Conference, pp. 529–534. IEEE (2017). https://doi.org/10.23919/ACC.2017.7963007

74. Younes, H.L.S., Kwiatkowska, M., Norman, G., Parker, D.: Numerical vs. statistical probabilistic model checking: an empirical study. In: Jensen, K., Podelski, A. (eds.) TACAS 2004. LNCS, vol. 2988, pp. 46–60. Springer, Heidelberg (2004). https://doi.org/10.1007/978-3-540-24730-2_4

75. Younes, H.L.S., Simmons, R.G.: Statistical probabilistic model checking with a focus on time-bounded properties. Inf. Comput. **204**(9), 1368–1409 (2006). https://doi.org/10.1016/j.ic.2006.05.002

Assurance of Distributed Algorithms and Systems: Runtime Checking of Safety and Liveness

Yanhong A. Liu$^{(\boxtimes)}$ and Scott D. Stoller

Computer Science Department, Stony Brook University, Stony Brook, NY, USA
{liu,stoller}@cs.stonybrook.edu

Abstract. This paper presents a general framework and methods for complete programming and checking of distributed algorithms at a high-level, as in pseudocode languages, but precisely specified and directly executable, as in formal specification languages and practical programming languages, respectively. The checking framework, as well as the writing of distributed algorithms and specification of their safety and liveness properties, use DistAlgo, a high-level language for distributed algorithms. We give a complete executable specification of the checking framework, with a complete example algorithm and example safety and liveness properties.

1 Introduction

Distributed systems are increasingly important in our increasingly connected world. Whether for distributed control and coordination or distributed data storage and processing, at the core are distributed algorithms.

It is well known that distributed algorithms are difficult to understand. That has led to significant effort in specifying these algorithms and verifying their properties, e.g., [5,13,36], as well as in developing specification languages and verification tools, e.g., TLA and TLA+ Toolbox [18,20,34], I/O Automata [31], and Ivy [33]. However, challenges remain for automated verification of practical distributed algorithms using theorem proving or model checking techniques, due to exorbitant manual effort and expertise required or prohibitive state-space explosion.

Runtime verification allows information to be extracted from a running system and used to check whether observed system behaviors satisfy certain properties, and to react based on the results of checking. It is the most effective complement to theorem proving and model checking for sophisticated algorithms and implementations. For routinely checking real distributed applications written in general-purpose programming languages, it is so far the only feasible practical solution.

This work was supported in part by NSF under grants CCF-1414078, CCF-1954837, CNS-1421893, and IIS-1447549, and ONR under grant N00014-20-1-2751.

© Springer Nature Switzerland AG 2020
J. Deshmukh and D. Ničković (Eds.): RV 2020, LNCS 12399, pp. 47–66, 2020.
https://doi.org/10.1007/978-3-030-60508-7_3

Many methods and related issues for doing such runtime checking have been studied, as discussed in Sect. 8. Such checking and all kinds of variations have also long been used extensively in practical program development, testing, debugging, and simulation for distributed algorithms. However, these studies and uses of runtime checking are either more abstract methods, not presented as executable programs, or involving significant programming using commonly-used programming languages, too large to present in complete and exact forms on paper.

This paper presents a general framework and methods for complete programming and checking of distributed algorithms at a high-level, as in pseudocode languages, but precisely specified and directly executable, as in formal specification languages and practical programming languages, respectively. The checking framework, as well as the writing of distributed algorithms and specification of their safety and liveness properties, use DistAlgo, a high-level language for distributed algorithms [21,29]. We give a complete executable specification of the checking framework, with a complete example algorithm and example safety and liveness properties.

The framework can check any desired properties against observed system behavior. Note that since any execution of a practical system is finite, the liveness properties we check are bounded liveness, that is, the desired properties hold within specified time bounds. The framework requires no change to the algorithm code to be checked. It puts the algorithm code, property specification, as well as fault simulation together with small configurations, thanks to the power of the DistAlgo language and compiler. The complete checking program then automatically intercepts messages sent and received by the distributed processes to be checked, with both logical and real times, and checks the specified properties at desired points as written.

This framework has been used in implementing, testing, debugging, simulation, and analysis of many well-known distributed algorithms, and in teaching. Our experiences included discovering improvements to both correctness and efficiency of some well-known algorithms, e.g., [23,25,28].

2   Distributed Algorithms and Their Safety and Liveness

Distributed algorithms are algorithms that run in distributed systems. Understanding and verifying their properties are central challenges for distributed computing.

Distributed Systems and Distributed Algorithms. A distributed system is a set of distributed processes. Each process has its own private memory that only it can access. Processes execute concurrently and communicate with each other by sending and receiving messages.

Distributed processes and communications are prone to various kinds of failures, depending on the underlying infrastructures. Processes may be slow, may crash, may later recover, and may even behave arbitrarily. Messages may be lost, delayed, duplicated, reordered, and even be arbitrarily changed.

Distributed algorithms are for solving problems that involve coordination, negotiation, etc. among distributed processes in the presence of possible failures. Due to nondeterminism from concurrency and uncertainty from failures, distributed algorithms are notoriously difficult to design, understand, and verify. Even as an algorithm executes in a distributed system, the state of the system is not fully observable, and the order of events cannot be fully determined. This led to Lamport's creation of logical clocks, which are fundamental in distributed systems [17].

Distributed computing problems are of an extremely wide variety, and a great number of distributed algorithms have been studied. e.g., [7,9,31]. Well-known problems range from distributed clock synchronization to distributed snapshot, from leader election to distributed mutual exclusion, from atomic commit to distributed consensus, and many more. We give two examples here:

- Distributed mutual exclusion. Distributed mutual exclusion is for multiple processes to access a shared resource mutually exclusively, in what is called a critical section, i.e., there can be at most one process in a critical section at a time.

  It is one of the most studied problems, e.g., [15,37], with at least dozens if not hundreds or more of proposed algorithms and variants. For example, Lamport's algorithm [17], introduced to show the use of logical clocks, was designed to guarantee that access to the resource is granted in the order of logical clock values of the requests.

- Distributed consensus. Distributed consensus is for a set of processes to agree on a single value or a continuing sequence of values, called single-value consensus or multi-value consensus, respectively.

  It is essential in any important service that maintains a state, including services provided by companies like Google and Amazon. This is because such services must use replication to tolerate failures caused by machine crashes, network outages, etc. Replicated processes must agree on the state of the service or the sequence of operations that have been performed, e.g., that a customer order has been placed and paid but not yet shipped, so that when some processes become unavailable, the remaining processes can continue to provide the service correctly.

  Even well-known algorithms and variants number at least dozens, starting from virtual synchrony [1–3], viewstamped replication [22,35], and Paxos [19].

These problems are at the core of distributed file systems, distributed databases, and fault-tolerant distributed services in general. New algorithms and variants for them are developed constantly, not to mention a vast number of other distributed algorithms, such as network protocols, distributed graph algorithms, and security protocols.

Safety and Liveness. Lamport [16] first formulated two types of properties of a distributed system: safety and liveness. Informally, a safety property states that some bad things will not happen, and a liveness property states that some good things will happen. We continue the two examples discussed earlier:

- For distributed mutual exclusion, a most important safety property is that at most one process is in a critical session at a time. A liveness property is that some requests are eventually served, and a stronger liveness property is that all requests are eventually served.

  For example, Lamport's algorithm [17] is designed to guarantee all these, and in fact, as mentioned above, to guarantee a stronger property—that all requests are served in the order of logical clock values. This stronger property can be interpreted and formulated as either a safety property, to mean that no requests are served out of the order of logical clock values, or a liveness property, to include that all requests are eventually served.

- For distributed consensus, there are two important safety properties: (1) agreement on the decided single value, in single-value consensus, or on the sequence of values, in multi-value consensus, by nonfaulty processes, and (2) validity of the decided value or values to be among allowed values. A liveness property for single-value consensus is that nonfaulty processes eventually decide on a value. A liveness property for multi-value consensus is that nonfaulty processes repeatedly decide on additional values in the sequence.

  Good distributed consensus algorithms, such as Paxos [19], guarantee the two safety properties, but they cannot guarantee the liveness property due to the well-known impossibility of consensus in asynchronous distributed systems even with only one faulty process subject to crash failures [6].

Specifying safety and liveness properties is nontrivial, especially liveness properties, even informally. For example, liveness for many consensus algorithms and variants has been left unspecified, or specified too weakly to be useful or too strongly to be possible [4].

Safety and liveness are, in general, global properties about multiple processes. Checking them requires knowing the states of multiple processes. However, the state of a process is private to that process and cannot be accessed directly by any other process. The best one can do is to observe a process by intercepting messages sent and received by that process, and determine the state of the system and desired properties conservatively or approximately, and with a delay.

We use checker to refer to a process that observes the sending and receiving of messages by a set of processes and checks desired properties.

3   A Powerful Language for Distributed Programming

A powerful language for distributed programming must allow (1) easy creation of distributed processes and communication channels for sending messages, (2) easy handling of received messages, both synchronously (with waiting) and asynchronously (without waiting), (3) easy processing of all information communicated as well as a process's own data, and (4) easy configuration of basic elements for real execution on distributed machines.

Running Example: The Polling Problem. We introduce a simple but essential problem, which we call the polling problem, as a running example:

A poller process sends a question to a set of pollee processes, waits to receive answers to the question from all of them, and then sends an outcome message to them.

Small variations of this problem include waiting to receive replies from a subset of the pollee processes, such as a majority or a quorum, instead of all of them.

This problem is essential because any process working with a set of other processes requires talking to and hearing back from those processes one way or another. This problem manifests widely in well-known distributed algorithms, including algorithms for distributed mutual exclusion, atomic commit, and distributed consensus. This problem also manifests itself in everyday life, such as an instructor giving assignments to students, a chairperson soliciting suggestions from committee members, or a campaign organizer sending a poll to voters.

The problem appears simple, but is nontrivial, even without process failures or message delays or losses, because processes are generally communicating with multiple processes and doing other things at the same time. Consider some examples:

- When the poller receives a message from a pollee, how does the poller know it is replying to a particular question? The pollee might happen to send something to the poller with the same format as an expected reply, and send it shortly after the question was sent.
- How does the poller know it has received replies from all pollees? It could compare the number of replies to the number of pollees, but a pollee might send multiple replies, or a communication channel might duplicate messages.

The problem becomes even harder if processes can fail and messages may be lost or delayed. It becomes even more challenging if processes can fake identities and messages can be altered or counterfeited. In the latter cases, processes need to use security protocols for authentication and secure communication. Although we do not consider those problems further in this tutorial, we have extended DistAlgo with a high-level cryptographic API for expressing such security protocols [14].

Figure 1 shows a complete polling program written in DistAlgo. Process classes P and R specify the poller and responder (i.e., pollee) processes, respectively. Definitions run and receive specify the main algorithm. The core of the algorithm is on lines 4–6, 8, 13, and 15–16. The rest puts all together, plus setting up processes, starting them, and outputting about replies and outcomes of the polling. The details are explained in examples as we describe next the DistAlgo language used.

DistAlgo, a Language for Distributed Algorithms. DistAlgo supports easy distributed programming by building on an object-oriented programming language, with a formal operational semantics [29], and with an open-source implementation [21] that extends Python.

Because the implementation uses the Python parser, it uses Python syntax such as send(m, to=p) instead of the ideal send m to p for sending message m to process p. For the same reason, it uses from_ in place of the ideal from because

```
1  class P (process):              # define poller process class
2     def setup(rs): pass          # take a set of responder processes
3     def run():
4        self.t = logical_clock()   # get logical clock time as question id
5        send(('question', question(), t), to= rs)
6        await each(r in rs, has= some(received(('reply',_,_t), from_=_r)))
7        output('-- received Y from:', setof(r, received(('reply','Y',_t), from_= r)))
8        send(('outcome', outcome()), to= rs)

9     def question(): return 'Did you attend RV (Y/N)?' # create question
10    def outcome(): return countof(r, received(('reply','Y',_t), from_= r))

11 class R (process):              # define responder (i.e., pollee) process class
12    def run():
13       await some(received(('outcome', o)))
14       output('== received outcome:', o)
15    def receive(msg=('question', q, t), from_= p):
16       send(('reply', reply(q), t), to= p)

17    def reply(q): import random; return random.choice(['Y','N']) # create reply

18 def main():
19    config(clock = lamport)       # use Lamport clock
20    config(channel = reliable)    # use reliable channels
21    rs = new(R, [], num= 10)      # create and set up 10 responders
22    p = new(P, [rs])              # create and set up poller process p
23    start(rs)                     # start responders
24    start(p)                      # start poller
25
```

Fig. 1. Polling program in DistAlgo.

the latter is a keyword in Python. A final quirk is that we indicate a previously bound variable in patterns with prefix _ in place of the ideal = because _ is the only symbol allowed besides letters and numbers in identifiers. Besides the language constructs explained, commonly used constructs in Python are used, for no operation (pass), assignments $(v = e)$, etc.

Distributed Processes That Can Send Messages. A type P of distributed processes is defined by class P (process): *body*, e.g., lines 1–10 in Fig. 1. The body may contain

- a setup definition for taking in and setting up the values used by a type P process, e.g., line 2,
- a run definition for running the main control flow of the process, e.g., lines 3–8,
- other helper definitions, e.g., lines 9–10, and
- receive definitions for handling received messages, e.g., lines 15–16.

A process can refer to itself as self. Expression self.*attr* (or *attr* when there is no ambiguity) refers to the value of *attr* in the process. ps = new(P, *args*, *num*) creates *num* (default to 1) new processes of type P, optionally passing in the values of *args* to setup, and assigns the set of new processes to *ps*, e.g., lines 21 and 22. start(*ps*) starts run() of processes *ps*, e.g., lines 23 and 24. A separate setup(*ps*, *args*) can also set up processes *ps* with the values of *args*.

Processes can send messages: send(m, to=*ps*) sends message m to processes *ps*, e.g., line 5.

Control Flow for Handling Received Messages. Received messages can be handled both asynchronously, using `receive` definitions, and synchronously, using `await` statements.

- A `receive` definition, `def receive (msg=m, from_=p)`, handles, at yield points, un-handled messages that match m from p, e.g., lines 15–16. There is a yield point before each `await` statement, e.g., line 6, for handling messages while waiting. The `from_` clause is optional.
- An `await` statement, `await` *cond*, waits for *cond* to be true, e.g., line 6. A more general statement, `if await` $cond_1$: $stmt_1$ `elif` ... `elif` $cond_k$: $stmt_k$ `elif timeout`(t) : $stmt$, waits for one of $cond_1$, ..., $cond_k$ to be true or a timeout after t seconds, and then nondeterministically selects one of $stmt_1$, ..., $stmt_k$, $stmt$ whose conditions are true to execute.

High-Level Queries for Synchronization Conditions. High-level queries can be used over message histories, and patterns can be used for matching messages.

- Histories of messages sent and received by a process are automatically kept in variables `sent` and `received`, respectively. `sent` is updated at each `send` statement, by adding each message sent. `received` is updated at yield points, by adding un-handled messages before executing all matching `receive` definitions.

  Expression `sent(m, to=p)` is equivalent to (m,p) in `sent`. It returns true iff a message that matches (m,p) is in `sent`. The `to` clause is optional. `received(m, from_=p)` is similar.
- A pattern can be used to match a message, in `sent` and `received`, and by a `receive` definition. A constant value, such as `'respond'`, or a previously bound variable, indicated with prefix `_`, in the pattern must match the corresponding components of the message. An underscore `_` by itself matches anything. Previously unbound variables in the pattern are bound to the corresponding components in the matched message.

  For example, `received(('reply','Y',_t), from_=r)` on line 7 matches in `received` every message that is a 3-tuple with components `'reply'`, `'Y'`, and the value of `t`, and binds `r` to the sender.

A query can be a comprehension, aggregation, or quantification over sets or sequences.

- A comprehension, `setof(e, `v_1` in `s_1`, ..., `v_k` in `s_k`, `*cond*`)`, where each v_i can be a pattern, returns the set of values of e for all combinations of values of variables that satisfy all v_i in s_i clauses and satisfy condition *cond*, e.g., the comprehension on line 7.
- An aggregation, similar to a comprehension but with an aggregation operator such as `countof` or `maxof`, returns the value of applying the aggregation operator to the collection argument, e.g., the `countof` query on line 10.

– A universal quantification, each(v_1 in s_1, ..., v_k in s_k has=*cond*), returns true iff, for all combinations of values of variables that satisfy all v_i in s_i clauses, *cond* holds, e.g., the each query on line 6.

– An existential quantification, some(v_1 in s_1, ..., v_k in s_k has= *cond*), returns true iff, for some combinations of values of variables that satisfy all v_i in s_i clauses, *cond* holds, e.g., the some query on line 13. When the query returns true, all variables in the query are bound to a combination of satisfying values, called a witness, e.g., o on line 13.

Configuration for Setting Up and Running. Configuration for requirements such as use of logical clocks and reliable channels can be specified in a main definition, e.g., lines 19–20. When Lamport's logical clocks are used, DistAlgo configures sending and receiving of a message to update the clock value, and defines a function logical_clock() that returns the clock value. Processes can then be created, setup, and started. In general, new can have an additional argument, specifying remote nodes where the newly created processes will run; the default is the local node.

4   Formal Specification of Safety and Liveness

When specifying properties about multiple distributed processes, we refer to the sent and received of a process p as p.sent and p.received. We will use ideal syntax in this section in presenting the safety and liveness properties, e.g., p.received m from p at t instead of p.received(m, from_=p, clk=t).

Specifying Safety. Despite being a small and seemingly simple example, a wide variety of safety properties can be desired for polling. We consider two of them:

(S1) *The poller has received a reply to the question from each pollee when sending the outcome.*

This property does not require checking multiple distributed processes, because it uses information about only one process, the poller. In fact, in the program in Fig. 1, it is easy to see that this property is implemented clearly in the poller's run method.

We use this as an example for three reasons: (1) it allows the reader to contrast how this is specified and checked by the checker compared with by the poller, (2) such checks can be important when we do not have access to the internals of a process but can observe messages sent to and from the process, and (3) even if we have access to the internals, it may be unclear whether the implementation ensures the desired property and thus we still need to check it.

(S2) *Each pollee has received the same outcome when the program ends.*

This property requires checking multiple distributed processes, because the needed information is not available at a single process.

We use this example to show such properties can be specified and checked easily at the checker, conservatively ensuring safety despite the general impossibility results due to message delays, etc.

Consider property (S1). The checker will be informed about all processes and all messages sent and received by each process. Also, it can use universal and existential quantifications, just as in line 6 of the poller's code in Fig. 1. However, there are two issues:

1) How does the checker know "the" question? Inside the poller, "the" question is identified by the timestamp in variable t, which is used in the subsequent tests of the replies. To check from outside, the checker needs to observe the question and its id first, yielding a partial specification for (S1):

```
some p.sent ('question', _, t) has
  each r in rs has some =p.received ('reply', _, =t) from =r
```

If one knows that the poller sent only one question, then the some above binds exactly that question. Otherwise, one could easily check this by adding a conjunct count {t: p.sent ('question', _, t)} == 1.

2) How does the checker know that all replies had been received when the outcome was sent (Note that a similar question about identifying "the" outcome can be handled the same way as for "the" question.) Inside the poller, it is easy to see that tests of the replies occur before the sending of the 'outcome' message. Outside the poller, we cannot count on the order that the checker receives messages to determine the order of events. The checker needs to use the timestamps from the logical clocks.

```
some p.sent ('question', _, t), p.sent ('outcome', _) at t1 has
  each r in rs has some =p.received('reply',_,=t) from =r at t2 has t1>t2
```

Note the added p.sent ('outcome', _) at t1 on the first line and at t2 has t1 > t2 on the second line.

Note that when the receiver or logical time of a sent message is not used, it is omitted from the property specification; it could also be included and matched with an underscore, e.g., p.sent m to _ at _.

Consider property (S2), which is now easy, using the same idea to identify "the" outcome o based on the outcome message sent by the poller:

```
some p.sent ('outcome', o) has
  each r in rs has some =r.received ('outcome', =o)
```

The checker just needs to check this at the end.

Specifying Liveness. Specifying liveness requires language features not used in the algorithm description. We use the same specification language we introduced earlier [4]. In particular,

```
evt cond
```

where evt is read as "eventually", denotes that cond holds at some time in the duration that starts from the time under discussion, i.e., eventually, cond holds.

Many different liveness properties can be desired. We consider two of them:

(L1) *The poller eventually receives a reply to the question.*
   This assumes that a question was sent and covers the duration from then to receiving the first reply.
   We use this example because it is the first indication to the poller that the polling really started. We also use receiving the first reply to show a small variation from receiving all replies.

(L2) *Eventually each pollee receives the outcome.*
   This assumes that an outcome was sent and covers the entire duration of the polling.
   We use this example because it expresses the completion of the entire algorithm.

For (L1), one can simply specify it as an `evt` followed by the partial specification for (S1) except with `each r in rs` replaced with `some r in rs`:

```
evt some p.sent ('question', _, t) has
    some r in rs has some =p.received ('reply', _, =t) from =r
```

In practice, one always estimates an upper bound for message passing time and poll filling time. So one can calculate an upper bound on the expected time from sending the question to receiving the first reply, and be alerted by a timeout if this bound is not met.

For (L2), one can see that this just needs an `evt` before the property specified for (S2):

```
evt some p.sent ('outcome', o) has
      each r in rs has some =r.received ('outcome', =o)
```

In practical terms, (L2) means that the program terminates and (S2) holds when the program ends. Thus, with (S2) checked as a safety property, (L2) boils down to checking that the program terminates.

Conceptually, `evt` properties are checked against infinite executions. In practice, they are checked against finite executions by imposing a bound on when the property should hold, and reporting a violation if the property does not hold by then. From a formal perspective, imposing this time bound changes the liveness property to a safety property.

5   Checking Safety

We describe a general framework for checking safety through observation by a checker external to all original processes in the system. The checker observes all processes and the messages they send and receive. We then discuss variations and optimizations.

Extending Original Processes to Be Checked. The basic idea is: each process p, when sending or receiving a message, sends information about the sending or receiving to the checker. The checker uses this information to check properties of the original processes.

The information sent to the checker may include (1) whether the message is being sent or received by p, indicated by 'sent' and 'rcvd', respectively, (2) the message content, (3) the receiver or receivers (for a message sent) and sender (for a message received), and (4) the logical timestamp of the sending or receiving, if a logical clock is used. In general, it may include any subset of these, or add any other information that is available and useful for checking properties of interest.

With ideal channels to send such information to the checker, the checker can extract all the information using the following correspondence:

```
p.sent m to qs at t      ⟺ checker received('sent' m to qs at t) from p
p.received m from q at t ⟺ checker received('rcvd' m from q at t) from p
```

Sending the information can be done by extending the original processes, so the original program is unchanged. The extended processes just need to (1) extend the send operation to send information about the sending to the checker, and (2) add a receive handler for all messages received to send information about the receiving to the checker. A checker process can then specify the safety conditions and check them any time it desires; to check at the end, it needs to specify a condition to detect the end.

Figure 2 shows safety checking for the polling example. It imports the original program polling.da as a module, and extends processes P and R to take checker as an argument at setup. In extended P, it extends send and adds receive to send all 4 kinds of information listed to checker (lines 4–8). In extended R, it sends 3 kinds of information, omitting logical times (lines 12–16). It then defines process Checker that takes in p and rs at setup, waits for a condition to detect the end of the polling (line 20), and checks safety properties (S1) and (S2) (lines 22–31). The main method is the same as in Fig. 1 except for the new and updated lines for adding the checker process, as noted in the comments.

Variations and Optimizations. When checking systems with many processes, a single checker process would be a bottleneck. The single checker framework can easily be extended to use a hierarchy of checkers, in which each checker observes a subset of original processes and/or child checkers and reports to a parent checker.

As an optimization, information not needed for the properties being checked can be omitted from messages sent to the checker, leading to more efficient executions and simpler patterns in specifying the conditions to be checked. In Fig. 2, process R already omits logical times from all messages to the checker. More information can be omitted. For example, process P can omit target processes, the 3rd component of the message, in information about sending. Additionally, process R can omit all information about sending and all but the second component about receiving. Furthermore, more refined patterns can be used when extending send to omit unused parts inside the message content, the second component. For example, the specific question in 'question' messages can be omitted.

Instead of extending the original processes to be checked, an alternative is to let the original processes extend a checker process. While the former approach

```
1  import polling  # import the module, polling.da, to be checked

2  class P (process, polling.P):  # extend process P in module polling
3    def setup(checker,rs): super().setup(rs)  # set up checker and original rs
4    def send(m, to):              # override send to send information to checker
5      super().send(m, to)        # do original send
6      super().send(('sent', m, to, logical_clock()), to= checker) # send to checker
7    def receive(msg= m, from_= fr):  # add a receive matching any message received
8      super().send(('rcvd', m, fr, logical_clock()), to= checker) # send to checker
9
10 class R (process, polling.R):  # as above but extend process R instead
11   def setup(checker): super().setup()  # as above but set up only checker
12   def send(m, to):              # as above but not send logical time to checker
13     super().send(m, to)
14     super().send(('sent', m, to), to= checker)
15   def receive(msg= m, from_= fr):  # as above but not send logical time to checker
16     super().send(('rcvd', m, fr), to= checker)

17 class Checker (process):
18   def setup(p,rs): pass        # pass in processes p and rs
19   def run():
20     await each(r in rs, has= some(received(('rcvd', ('outcome',_), _), from_=_r)))
21     output('~~ polling ended. checking safety:', S1(), S2())
22   def S1():
23     return some(received(('sent', ('question',_,_,t), _, _), from_=_p),
24                 received(('sent', ('outcome',_), _, t1), from_=_p), has=
25                 each(r in rs, has=
26                   some(received(('rcvd', ('reply',_,_,t), _r, t2),from_=_p),
27                        has= t1 > t2)))
28   def S2():
29     return some(received(('sent', ('outcome',o), _, _), from_=_p), has=
30                 each(r in rs, has=
31                   some(received(('rcvd', ('outcome',_o), _), from_=_r))))
32 def main():
33   config(clock = lamport)
34   config(channel = reliable)
35   checker = new(Checker)        # create checker
36   rs = new(R, [checker], num= 10)  # as in polling but add checker
37   p = new(P, [checker, rs])     # as in polling but add checker
38   setup(checker, [p,rs])        # setup checker with p and rs
39   start(checker)                # start checker
40   start(rs)
41   start(p)
```

Fig. 2. Checking safety for the polling program.

requires no change at all to the original processes, the latter approach requires small changes: (1) to each original process class, (a) add the checker process class as a base class and (b) add a setup parameter to pass in the checker process, and (2) in main, (a) create, setup, and start the checker process and (b) in the call to new or setup for each original process, add the checker process as an additional argument. The advantage of this alternative approach is that the same checker class can be used for checking different programs when the same checking is desired. An example use is for benchmarking the run method of different programs[1].

While checking safety using our framework is already relatively easy, higher-level declarative languages can be designed for specifying the desired checks, and specifications in such languages can be compiled into optimized checking programs that require no manual changes to the original programs.

---

[1] http://github.com/DistAlgo/distalgo/blob/master/benchmarks/controller.da.

6   Checking Liveness

As discussed in Sect. 4, in finite executions, checking liveness boils down to safety checking plus use of timeouts to check that properties hold within an expected amount of time. For the polling example, checking timeouts plus the same or similar conditions as (S1) and (S2) corresponds to what can be checked for (L1) and (L2). We describe a general framework for easily checking timeouts during program execution based on elapsed real time at the checker process. Using real time at the checker avoids assumptions about clock synchronization. We then discuss variations and optimizations.

Extending Original Processes to Be Checked. The same framework to extend original processes for safety checking can be used for liveness checking. One only needs to specify checks for timeouts instead of or in addition to safety checks. We show how timeouts between observations of any two sending or receiving events, as well as a timeout for the entire execution, can easily be checked, even with multiple timeout checks running concurrently.

Given any two sending or receiving events e1 and e2, we check that after e1 is observed by the checker, e2 is observed within a specified time bound. There are two steps:

1) When the checker receives e1, it starts a timer for the specified time bound. Each timer runs in a separate thread and, when it times out, it sends a timeout message to the checker.
2) When the checker receives a timeout message, it checks whether the expected event e2 has been observed. If yes, it does nothing. Otherwise, it reports a violation of the time bound requirement.

All time bounds are specified in a map, which maps a name for a pair of events to the required time bound from observing the first event until observing the second event.

This framework can easily be generalized to check conditions involving any number of events. When the timeout happens, instead of checking whether one specific event e2 has been observed, the checker can check whether several expected events have all been observed, or whether any other desired condition on the set of observed events holds.

A time bound for the entire execution of the algorithm can be set and checked separately, in addition to checking any other safety and liveness properties, to directly check overall termination, using an appropriate condition to detect whether the algorithm has completed successfully.

Figure 3 shows timeout checking for the polling example. To check liveness instead of safety, one could use exactly the same program as for safety check except for the added import's and TIMEOUT map at the top and a rewritten Checker process. To check timeouts in addition to safety, the Checker process in Fig. 3 can extend the Checker process in Fig. 2, and just add the function calls super().S1() and super().S2() at the end of the run method here.

Modules `threading` and `time` are imported in order to run each timer in a separate thread. A dictionary `TIMEOUTS` holds the map of time bounds (in seconds) for different pairs of events: `'q-r'` is for the poller sending the question and the poller receiving the first reply, corresponding to (L1), and `'q-o'` is for the poller sending the question and all pollees receiving the outcome, corresponding to (L2). The dictionary also includes an entry `'total'` with a time bound for the entire execution of the algorithm.

The `Checker` process waits for the same condition, as for safety checking, to detect the end of the polling (line 8–9), but with a timeout for `'total'` (line 10) while waiting. It starts two timers corresponding to (L1) and (L2) when observing the question was sent (lines 13–15), and checks and reports timeouts when any timer times out (lines 22–28).

```
 1  import threading
 2  import time
 3  TIMEOUTS = {'q-r':0.00001, 'q-o':0.0001, 'total':1}
 4                              # map of timeout names to time bounds
 5  class Checker (process):
 6    def setup(p,rs): pass
 7    def run():
 8      if await each(r in rs, has=
 9                    some(received(('rcvd', ('outcome',_), _), from_=_r))): pass
10      elif timeout(TIMEOUTS['total']):  # entire execution times out
11        output('!! total timeout receiving outcome by all pollees')
12      output('~~ polling ended. timeouts checked')

13    def receive(msg=('sent', ('question',_,_,t), ps, _)):  # at 1st of two events
14      runtimer('q-r',t,ps)  # start timer 'q-r' that starts at this event
15      runtimer('q-o',t,ps)  # start timer 'q-o' that starts at this event
16
17    def runtimer(*args):   # run timer in a separate thread passing in all args
18      threading.Thread(target=timer, args=args).start()
19    def timer(name, *rest):  # timer, taking timer name and rest of arguments
20      time.sleep(TIMEOUTS[name])  # sleep the time bound for the timer name
21      send(('timeout', name, *rest), to= self)  # send timeout to chcker itself

22    def receive(msg=('timeout', 'q-r', t, ps)):  # at timeout for 'q-r'
23      if not some(received(('rcvd', ('reply',_,_,t), _, _), from_=_)):  # check 2nd event
24        output('!! L1 timeout receiving the first reply by the poller', t, ps)
25    def receive(msg=('timeout', 'q-o', t, ps)):  # at timoeout for 'q-o'
26      if not each(r in rs, has=  # check 2nd event
27                  some(received(('rcvd', ('outcome',_), _), from_=_r))):
28        output('!! L2 timeout receiving outcome by all pollees', t, ps, r)
```

Fig. 3. Checking timeouts for the polling program.

Variations and Optimizations. Variations and optimizations for checking safety can also be used for checking liveness. Checking timeouts using real time is the additional challenge.

In the program in Fig. 3, the timeout `'q-o'` for (L2) waits for the same condition as for detecting the end of polling in `run`, and covers almost the entire execution. Therefore, the test for detecting the end of polling in `run` is unnecessary in this case, and the entire body of `run` may simply be `await (timeout('total'))`. When a timeout `'q-o'` is received, the checker could terminate itself by importing `sys` and calling `sys.exit()`. Of course after either timeout for `'q-o'` or timeout in `run`, the checker process could also do anything else helpful instead of terminating itself.

Instead of or in addition using real time at the checker, one could use real time at the original processes. A clock synchronization algorithm can be used to improve the precision of clocks at different original processes and the overall precision and time bounds. Even without clock synchronization, using real time at the original processes can improve the precision and bounds for liveness properties involving multiple events at the same process, such as (L1).

Note that observing the start and end of an operation or entire program is also how performance measurements can be performed, as mentioned for benchmarking at the end of Sect. 5.

7   Implementation and Experiments

DistAlgo has been implemented as an extension of the Python programming language and used extensively in studying and teaching of distributed algorithms [29]. The framework discussed for checking safety and liveness properties has also been used extensively, in both ad hoc and more systematic ways. We describe using the DistAlgo implementation and our framework for execution and runtime checking.

Execution and Fault Simulation. DistAlgo is open source and available on github [21]. One can simply add it to the Python path after downloading, and run the da module in Python, e.g., running the program polling.da in Fig. 1 as python -m da polling.da.

For runtime checking, a checking program, such as the program in Fig. 2 can be run in the same way. More generally, implementations of three conceptual components are needed:

1) A distributed algorithm, plus input taken by the algorithm. This needs a complete executable program, such as polling.da in Fig. 1.
2) Safety and liveness requirements to be checked. These are expressed as executable functions that can be called at required points during the execution, such as functions S1 and S2 in Fig. 2 and the receive handlers in Fig. 3.
3) Process and communication failures to be considered. These correspond to executable configurations that can be executed for fault simulation, as described below.

Our framework puts these together naturally, with small configurations to observe processes and communications, with both logical and real times, thanks to the power of the DistAlgo language and compiler.

Fault simulation is essential for checking safety and liveness of complex algorithms in simulation of real distributed systems that are fault-prone. Both process and communication failures may happen, but the latter are much more frequent. Also, the former can be simulated with the latter, because a process interacts with other processes only through communication. For example, a crashed process is indistinguishable from one that stops sending messages to other processes.

With our existing framework for checking, we can simply use **send** to simulate all possible communication failures, including message

- loss: drop messages without sending;
- delay: delay messages before sending;
- duplication: send messages multiple times;
- reordering: delay sending messages until after sending later messages; and
- corruption for simulating Byzantine failures: change message before sending.

For example, to simulate a 1% chance of dropping a message sent by a **P** process, in the **send** method in Fig. 2, we can put `super().send(m,to)` inside a conditional:

```
if random.random() < 0.99: super().send(m,to)
```

and add `import random` before it.

Similarly, one may add fixed or random delays, duplications, reorderings, or a combination of them. A main issue to note is that, in general, one would want to send a delayed or duplicated message using a separate thread, to avoid delaying the execution of the algorithm.

Configuration options and values can be provided through command-line arguments and external files, as well as built-in language constructs. All these kinds have been provided in the DistAlgo language and compiler and used in DistAlgo programs. Similar mechanisms have been used in all kinds of system configurations for decades. A challenge is to design and implement a powerful, commonly accepted language for such configurations.

Experiments and Experience. For the running example, checking both safety and liveness, with the **Checker** process in Fig. 3 extending that in Fig. 2 but replacing the last line in **run** in Fig. 3 with the last line in **run** in Fig. 2 and adding `super().` before S1() and S2(), an example output is as shown below:

```
> python -m da .\polling_check_live.da
[54] da.api<MainProcess>:INFO: <Node_:75001> initialized at 127.0.0.1:(UdpTransport=37786, T
cpTransport=45837).
[54] da.api<MainProcess>:INFO: Starting program <module 'polling_check_live' from '.\\pollin
g_check_live.da'>...
[55] da.api<MainProcess>:INFO: Running iteration 1 ...
[56] da.api<MainProcess>:INFO: Waiting for remaining child processes to terminate...(Press "
Ctrl-Brk" to force kill)
[1446] da.api<MainProcess>:INFO: Main process terminated.
[160] polling_check.P<P:a900d>:OUTPUT: -- received Y from: {<R:a9007>, <R:a900b>, <R:a900c>,
 <R:a9004>}
[618] polling_check.R<R:a9009>:OUTPUT: == received outcome: 4
[1303] polling_check.R<R:a9003>:OUTPUT: == received outcome: 4
[400] polling_check.R<R:a900b>:OUTPUT: == received outcome: 4
[1082] polling_check.R<R:a9005>:OUTPUT: == received outcome: 4
[1194] polling_check.R<R:a9004>:OUTPUT: == received outcome: 4
[860] polling_check.R<R:a9007>:OUTPUT: == received outcome: 4
[1417] polling_check_live.Checker<Checker:a9002>:OUTPUT: !! L2 timeout receiving outcome by
all pollees 0 {<R:a9004>, <R:a900a>, <R:a9007>, <R:a9009>, <R:a9003>, <R:a9005>, <R:a900c>,
<R:a9006>, <R:a900b>, <R:a9008>} <R:a9008>
[511] polling_check.R<R:a900a>:OUTPUT: == received outcome: 4
[974] polling_check.R<R:a9006>:OUTPUT: == received outcome: 4
[733] polling_check.R<R:a9008>:OUTPUT: == received outcome: 4
[291] polling_check.R<R:a900c>:OUTPUT: == received outcome: 4
[1438] polling_check_live.Checker<Checker:a9002>:OUTPUT: ~~ polling ended. checking safety:
True True
```

Notice the last process, <R:a9008>, printed in the 3 lines reporting (L2) timeout; it shows a witness for violation of the **each** check on lines 25–27 in Fig. 3, printed at the end of line 28. When we increased the timeout for 'q-o' to 0.01 s, no (L2) timeout was reported in all dozens of runs checked. When we added message loss rate of 10%, we saw some runs reporting total timeout, and some runs reporting even all three timeouts.

Overall, we have used the checking framework in implementation, testing, debugging, simulation, and analysis of many well-known distributed algorithms, and in developing their high-level executable specifications. This includes a variety of algorithms for distributed mutual exclusion and distributed consensus written in DistAlgo [23,25,28,30], especially including over a dozen well-known algorithms and variants for classical consensus and blockchain consensus [26]. Use of DistAlgo has helped us find improvements to both correctness and efficiency of well-known distributed algorithms, e.g., [23,25,28].

We have also used the framework in other research, e.g., [24], and in teaching distributed algorithms and distributed systems to help study and implement many more algorithms. DistAlgo has been used by hundreds of students in graduate and undergraduate courses in over 100 different course projects, implementing and checking the core of network protocols, distributed graph algorithms, distributed coordination services, distributed hash tables, distributed file systems, distributed databases, parallel processing platforms, security protocols, and more [29].

The algorithms and systems can be programmed much more easily and clearly compared to using conventional programming languages, e.g., in 20 lines instead of 200 lines, or 300 lines instead of 3000 lines or many more. Systematic methods for checking these algorithms and implementations has been a continual effort.

Additional information is available at http://distalgo.cs.stonybrook.edu/tutorial.

8 Related Work

Francalanza et al. broadly surveyed runtime verification research related to distributed systems [8]. Here, we focus on aspects related to DistAlgo.

Global Property Detection. Many algorithms have been developed to detect global properties in distributed systems, e.g., [9,15]. These algorithms vary along several dimensions. For example, many consider only the happened-before ordering [17]; others also exploit orderings from approximately-synchronized real-time clocks [38]. Some can detect arbitrary predicates; other are specialized to check a class of properties efficiently. Many use a single checker process (as in our example); others use a hierarchy of checker processes, or are decentralized, with the locus of control moving among the monitored processes. DistAlgo's high-level nature makes it very well-suited for specifying and implementing all such algorithms.

Efficient Invariant Checking. Runtime checking of invariants, in centralized or distributed systems, requires evaluating them repeatedly. This can be expensive for complex invariants, especially invariants that involve nested quantifiers. We used incrementalization for efficient repeated evaluation of predicates in the contexts of runtime invariant checking and query-based debugging for Python programs [10, 11]. We later extended our incrementalization techniques to handle quantifications in DistAlgo programs [29].

Centralization. Due to the difficulty of runtime checking of truly distributed systems, some approaches create centralized versions of them. We have developed a source-level centralization transformation for DistAlgo that produces a non-deterministic sequential program, well-suited to simulation and verification. In prior work, we developed bytecode-level transformations that transform a distributed Java program using Remote Method Invocation (RMI) into a centralized Java program using simulated RMI [39]. Minha [32] takes another approach to centralization of distributed Java programs, by virtualizing multiple Java Virtual Machine (JVM) instances in a single JVM and providing a library that simulates network communication.

DistAlgo Translators. Grall et al. developed an automatic translation from Event-B models of distributed algorithms to DistAlgo [12]. Event-B is a modeling language adapted to verification of distributed algorithms. They chose DistAlgo as the target language because "Its high-levelness makes DistAlgo closer to the mathematical notations of Event-B and improves the clarity of DistAlgo programs." We developed a translator from DistAlgo to TLA+, allowing verification tools for TLA+ to be applied to the translations [27].

Conclusion. We have presented a general, simple, and complete framework for runtime checking of distributed algorithms. The framework, as well as the algorithms and properties to be checked, are written in a high-level language that is both completely precise and directly executable. A challenging problem for future work is a powerful, commonly accepted language for higher-level, declarative configurations for checking distributed algorithms and systems.

References

1. Birman, K., Joseph, T.: Exploiting virtual synchrony in distributed systems. In: Proceedings of the 11th ACM Symposium on Operating Systems Principles, pp. 123–138. ACM Press, November 1987
2. Birman, K., Malkhi, D., Renesse, R.V.: Virtually synchronous methodology for dynamic service replication. Technical report MSR-TR-2010-151, Microsoft Research (2010)
3. Birman, K.P., Joseph, T.A.: Reliable communication in the presence of failures. ACM Trans. Comput. Syst. (TOCS) 5(1), 47–76 (1987)
4. Chand, S., Liu, Y.A.: What's live? Understanding distributed consensus. Computing Research Repository arXiv:2001.04787 [cs.DC], January 2020. http://arxiv.org/abs/2001.04787

5. Chand, S., Liu, Y.A., Stoller, S.D.: Formal verification of multi-Paxos for distributed consensus. In: Fitzgerald, J., Heitmeyer, C., Gnesi, S., Philippou, A. (eds.) FM 2016. LNCS, vol. 9995, pp. 119–136. Springer, Cham (2016). https://doi.org/10.1007/978-3-319-48989-6_8

6. Fischer, M.J., Lynch, N.A., Paterson, M.S.: Impossibility of distributed consensus with one faulty process. J. ACM **32**(2), 374–382 (1985)

7. Fokkink, W.: Distributed Algorithms: An Intuitive Approach. MIT Press, Cambridge (2013)

8. Francalanza, A., Pérez, J.A., Sánchez, C.: Runtime verification for decentralised and distributed systems. In: Bartocci, E., Falcone, Y. (eds.) Lectures on Runtime Verification. LNCS, vol. 10457, pp. 176–210. Springer, Cham (2018). https://doi.org/10.1007/978-3-319-75632-5_6

9. Garg, V.K.: Elements of Distributed Computing. Wiley, New York (2002)

10. Gorbovitski, M., Rothamel, T., Liu, Y.A., Stoller, S.D.: Efficient runtime invariant checking: a framework and case study. In: Proceedings of the 6th International Workshop on Dynamic Analysis, pp. 43–49. ACM Press (2008)

11. Gorbovitski, M., Tekle, K.T., Rothamel, T., Stoller, S.D., Liu, Y.A.: Analysis and transformations for efficient query-based debugging. In: Proceedings of the 8th IEEE International Working Conference on Source Code Analysis and Manipulation, pp. 174–183. IEEE CS Press (2008)

12. Grall, A.: Automatic generation of DistAlgo programs from Event-B models. In: Raschke, A., Méry, D., Houdek, F. (eds.) ABZ 2020. LNCS, vol. 12071, pp. 414–417. Springer, Cham (2020). https://doi.org/10.1007/978-3-030-48077-6_34

13. Hawblitzel, C., et al.: IronFleet: proving practical distributed systems correct. In: Proceedings of the 25th Symposium on Operating Systems Principles, pp. 1–17. ACM Press (2015)

14. Kane, C., Lin, B., Chand, S., Stoller, S.D., Liu, Y.A.: High-level cryptographic abstractions. In: Proceedings of the ACM SIGSAC 14th Workshop on Programming Languages and Analysis for Security. ACM Press, London, November 2019

15. Kshemkalyani, A., Singhal, M.: Distributed Computing: Principles, Algorithms, and Systems. Cambridge University Press, Cambridge (2008)

16. Lamport, L.: Proving the correctness of multiprocess programs. IEEE Trans. Softw. Eng. **3**(2), 125–143 (1977)

17. Lamport, L.: Time, clocks, and the ordering of events in a distributed system. Commun. ACM **21**(7), 558–565 (1978)

18. Lamport, L.: The temporal logic of actions. ACM Trans. Program. Lang. Syst. **16**(3), 872–923 (1994)

19. Lamport, L.: The part-time parliament. ACM Trans. Comput. Syst. **16**(2), 133–169 (1998)

20. Lamport, L.: Specifying Systems: The TLA+ Language and Tools for Hardware and Software Engineers. Addison-Wesley, Boston (2002)

21. Lin, B., Liu, Y.A.: DistAlgo: a language for distributed algorithms (2014). http://github.com/DistAlgo. Accessed March 2020

22. Liskov, B., Cowling, J.: Viewstamped replication revisited. Technical report MIT-CSAIL-TR-2012-021, Computer Science and Artificial Intelligence Laboratory, Massachusetts Institute of Technology, Cambridge (2012)

23. Liu, Y.A.: Logical clocks are not fair: what is fair? A case study of high-level language and optimization. In: Proceedings of the Workshop on Advanced Tools, Programming Languages, and Platforms for Implementing and Evaluating Algorithms for Distributed Systems, pp. 21–27. ACM Press (2018)

24. Liu, Y.A., Brandvein, J., Stoller, S.D., Lin, B.: Demand-driven incremental object queries. In: Proceedings of the 18th International Symposium on Principles and Practice of Declarative Programming, pp. 228–241. ACM Press (2016)

25. Liu, Y.A., Chand, S., Stoller, S.D.: Moderately complex Paxos made simple: high-level executable specification of distributed algorithm. In: Proceedings of the 21st International Symposium on Principles and Practice of Declarative Programming, pp. 15:1–15:15. ACM Press, October 2019

26. Liu, Y.A., Stoller, S.D.: From classical to blockchain consensus: what are the exact algorithms? In: Proceedings of the 2019 ACM Symposium on Principles of Distributed Computing, July–August 2019, pp. 544–545. ACM Press (2019)

27. Liu, Y.A., Stoller, S.D., Chand, S., Weng, X.: Invariants in distributed algorithms. In: Proceedings of the TLA+ Community Meeting, Oxford, U.K. (2018). http://www.cs.stonybrook.edu/~liu/papers/DistInv-TLA18.pdf

28. Liu, Y.A., Stoller, S.D., Lin, B.: High-level executable specifications of distributed algorithms. In: Richa, A.W., Scheideler, C. (eds.) SSS 2012. LNCS, vol. 7596, pp. 95–110. Springer, Heidelberg (2012). https://doi.org/10.1007/978-3-642-33536-5_11

29. Liu, Y.A., Stoller, S.D., Lin, B.: From clarity to efficiency for distributed algorithms. ACM Trans. Program. Lang. Syst. **39**(3), 12:1–12:41 (2017)

30. Liu, Y.A., Stoller, S.D., Lin, B., Gorbovitski, M.: From clarity to efficiency for distributed algorithms. In: Proceedings of the 27th ACM SIGPLAN Conference on Object-Oriented Programming, Systems, Languages and Applications, pp. 395–410. ACM Press (2012)

31. Lynch, N.A.: Distributed Algorithms. Morgan Kaufman, San Francisco (1996)

32. Machado, N., Maia, F., Neves, F., Coelho, F., Pereira, J.: Minha: large-scale distributed systems testing made practical. In: Felber, P., Friedman, R., Gilbert, S., Miller, A. (eds.) 23rd International Conference on Principles of Distributed Systems (OPODIS 2019). LIPIcs, vol. 153, pp. 11:1–11:17. Schloss Dagstuhl - Leibniz-Zentrum für Informatik (2019)

33. McMillan, K.L., Padon, O.: Ivy: a multi-modal verification tool for distributed algorithms. In: Lahiri, S.K., Wang, C. (eds.) CAV 2020. LNCS, vol. 12225, pp. 190–202. Springer, Cham (2020). https://doi.org/10.1007/978-3-030-53291-8_12

34. Microsoft Research: the TLA toolbox. http://lamport.azurewebsites.net/tla/toolbox.html. Accessed 27 Apr 2020

35. Oki, B.M., Liskov, B.H.: Viewstamped replication: a new primary copy method to support highly-available distributed systems. In: Proceedings of the 7th Annual ACM Symposium on Principles of Distributed Computing, pp. 8–17. ACM Press (1988)

36. Padon, O., Losa, G., Sagiv, M., Shoham, S.: Paxos made EPR: decidable reasoning about distributed protocols. Proc. ACM Program. Lang. **1**(OOPSLA), 108:1–108:31 (2017). Article no. 108

37. Raynal, M.: Algorithms for Mutual Exclusion. MIT Press, Cambridge (1986)

38. Stoller, S.D.: Detecting global predicates in distributed systems with clocks. Distrib. Comput. **13**(2), 85–98 (2000). https://doi.org/10.1007/s004460050069

39. Stoller, S.D., Liu, Y.A.: Transformations for model checking distributed java programs. In: Dwyer, M. (ed.) SPIN 2001. LNCS, vol. 2057, pp. 192–199. Springer, Heidelberg (2001). https://doi.org/10.1007/3-540-45139-0_12

Analysing the Performance of Python-Based Web Services with the VyPR Framework

Joshua Heneage Dawes[1,2(✉)], Marta Han[2,3], Omar Javed[4], Giles Reger[1],
Giovanni Franzoni[2], and Andreas Pfeiffer[2]

[1] University of Manchester, Manchester, UK
[2] CERN, Geneva, Switzerland
joshua.dawes@cern.ch
[3] University of Zagreb, Zagreb, Croatia
[4] Università della svizzera italiana, Lugano, Switzerland

Abstract. In this tutorial paper, we present the current state of VyPR, a framework for the performance analysis of Python-based web services. We begin by summarising our theoretical contributions which take the form of an engineer-friendly specification language; instrumentation and monitoring algorithms; and an approach for explanation of property violations. We then summarise the VyPR ecosystem, which includes an intuitive library for writing specifications and powerful tools for analysing monitoring results. We conclude with a brief description of how VyPR was used to improve our understanding of the performance of a critical web service at the CMS Experiment at CERN.

1   Making a Start with Performance Analysis

Understanding a program's performance precisely is vital, especially when the program performs critical activities or fulfils a wide range of use cases. Analysing the performance of a program involves two key steps: *determination of expected performance*, and *investigation when performance deviates from expectation*.

To address the first step, we must construct an appropriate definition of the *performance* of a program. Such a definition usually depends on the category into which the program fits. For example, the program may perform a lot of computation with heavy memory operations and complex control-flow. In this case, performance may be characterised by the time taken to compute a result, along with paths taken through control-flow. Alternatively, the program in question may communicate frequently over a network, in which case a characterisation of its performance may be in terms of the network's stability and the latency experienced with respect to the data being transferred.

In this work, the outcome of the first step is a specification of the performance expectations, based on a combination of data from previous program runs and engineers' intuition, that can be checked during future program runs. Further, the systems with which we concern ourselves are Python-based web services.

© Springer Nature Switzerland AG 2020
J. Deshmukh and D. Ničković (Eds.): RV 2020, LNCS 12399, pp. 67–86, 2020.
https://doi.org/10.1007/978-3-030-60508-7_4

This allows us to investigate the performance of critical services employed at the CMS Experiment at CERN. We remark that we do not currently consider performance in the context of parallelism.

To address the second step, we need a way to determine what caused deviations from expected performance. In this work we call this process *explanation*, the definition of which also depends on the type of program being analysed and the domain in which it operates.

This paper summarises our efforts so far to introduce 1) a new body of theoretical work for performance analysis of programs that is based on Runtime Verification and 2) the implementation of a framework based on this theoretical work. The summary is as follows:

- In Sect. 2, we review existing work to frame our contributions to both the Software Engineering and Runtime Verification (RV) communities.
- In Sect. 3, we describe our theoretical body of work. We begin with an introduction to our specification language along with efficient instrumentation and monitoring algorithms that it admits [32]. We then introduce our approach for explaining violations of properties written in our specification language [31].
- In Sect. 4, we present VYPR [30,33], a framework for the performance analysis of Python web services. We developed VYPR at the CMS Experiment at CERN based on our theoretical contributions. VYPR marks a significant effort to establish RV as a software development tool.
- In Sect. 5, we give details of VYPR's analysis tools [30], which consist of a web application and a Python-based library.
- In Sect. 6, we give a step-by-step reproduction of an investigation that found interesting performance of critical software at the CMS Experiment.

This paper accompanies a tutorial delivered at the International Conference on Runtime Verification 2020, the materials for which can be found at http:// pyvypr.github.io/home/rv2020-tutorial/.

2   Existing Techniques for Performance Analysis

We review well-established profiling techniques, work from the RV community that considers timing behaviour and work from the Software Engineering community on performance data visualisation.

2.1   Profiling

One of the most popular performance analysis techniques for Python, as for most languages, is *profiling*. Profilers record a quantity in which a software engineer is interested, which is usually the time taken by some operation. For example, if a software engineer wanted to understand the behaviour of a function f in a Python program, a profiling tool such as cProfiler [2] (a *deterministic profiler* [14]) could be attached. The engineer would then have the task of finding the data relevant to the function f in the pile of data generated by the profiler. While this search is not too much of a problem (in fact there are tools to help with this [1]), the overhead often is. This is mainly because naive profiling of entire Python programs often relies on *tracing* [13], which involves attaching a function with a specific signature to the Python interpreter and collecting data each time a relevant event is observed. To counter this overhead, *statistical profilers* [5] are sometimes used.

While these approaches are commonly used and well catered for by the standard Python interpreter (CPython [12]), they suffer from drawbacks when one needs to analyse anything other than the time taken by a function each time it is called. If one needs to check whether a constraint holds that relates multiple quantities, offline analysis quickly becomes more difficult and error-prone.

This is one of the first advantages that VYPR brings. That is, VYPR's rich specification language allows measurement and comparison of multiple quantities at runtime, including the time taken by various operations and (properties of) values held by variables. Further, rather than using tracing, VYPR instruments code based on specifications which reduces overhead. Finally, VYPR's offline analysis tools allow engineers to carry out detailed analyses, including inter-procedural analysis, inter-machine analysis and path comparison for determination of root causes of performance problems.

2.2   Runtime Verification for Performance Analysis

The existing work in RV that could be used in performance analysis is necessarily that which considers the timing behaviour of the system being monitored. Since approaches in RV can be characterised, at least in part, by their specification language, we focus on the languages which can reason about time [34].

The collection of specification languages introduced or adapted by the RV community includes temporal logics [15,20,38,40], rule systems [18], stream logics [29], event-processing logics [36] and automata [17,23]. The situations in which each can be used depend on their semantics and expressiveness.

As a first example that can reason about time, we take Metric Temporal Logic (MTL) [38], which extends Linear Temporal Logic (LTL) [40] with intervals attached to modal operators. In MTL one can write a formula such as $\phi \, \mathcal{U}_{[0,5]} \, \psi$ to mean that ϕ should hold for at most 5 units of time until ψ holds. There is also Timed Linear Temporal Logic (TLTL) [20], which extends LTL with operators that allow one to place constraints on how long *since* or *until* some observation was or will be made. Automata are used in settings both with [17] and without [23] time. In other RV work, automata are used only in the synthesis of monitors for specifications written in timed logics [20]. Stream logics, rule systems and event-processing systems are all capable of reasoning about time [18,29,36].

Despite the existing work on timed specification languages, we highlight that those which can reason about time (and are intended for the same setting as our work) tend to have a high level of abstraction with respect to the code being monitored. While this allows specification languages to be more expressive, it creates two problems. First, the software engineer becomes responsible for maintaining a mapping from the program being monitored to the symbols in the specification. Second, it makes interpretation of specifications difficult because a mapping must be considered at the same time.

We have previously called the combination of these problems the *separation problem* [32]. In the same work, we introduced a new specification language, Control-Flow Temporal Logic (CFTL). CFTL formulas are low-level, meaning that they require only the source code of the monitored program to make sense. While formulas must then be changed with the program source code, we remark that this has faced no resistance in practice. Further, we highlight that this fits in with RV's role as a complement to testing in the software development process.

Explanation of property violations has received little attention, though there has been some interest in recent years (our work on explanation of CFTL violations [31]; work on trace edit-distances [41]; explanation in Cyber-Physical Systems [19] and the use of *temporal implicants* [35]). Outside of RV the Fault Localisation [24,25,43,45,46] and Model Checking [16,22,28,44] communities have made significant contributions.

2.3   Performance Data Visualisation

Our experience has shown that effective presentation of data obtained by monitoring at runtime is as important as the specification and monitoring processes themselves. However most existing work on visualising performance data and runtime analytics is done outside RV and focuses on data obtained by methods other than formal verification [21,26,27].

Despite the lack of integration with formal verification, a key trend is the display of performance data in the context of the source code that generated it. The web-based analysis environment that we provide visualises data recorded by VyPR alongside the source code, similarly to contributions from the Software Engineering community. The key difference is that we have not yet looked at displaying performance data directly in the IDE because we have not yet needed to.

3   An Engineer-Friendly Specification Language

Our main goal is to provide a framework with which software engineers can easily analyse the performance of their programs with minimal disruption to their existing development process. This gives rise to the requirement that, if we use a formal specification language, such a language should make the transition from natural language to formal specification as smooth as possible. Here, we give a brief description of our language (Control-Flow Temporal Logic (CFTL)) with its semantics; and our instrumentation, monitoring and explanation approaches. For full details, the reader can refer to [31–33].

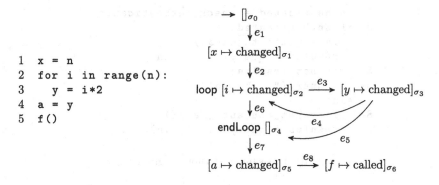

```
1  x = n
2  for i in range(n):
3      y = i*2
4      a = y
5      f()
```

Fig. 1. A Python program with a for-loop with its symbolic control-flow graph.

3.1   A Representation of Programs

We consider a program P whose performance we want to analyse, written in a subset of the Python language defined in [32]. Our first step is to introduce a representation of the program P on which both the CFTL semantics and our instrumentation approach are based. We would like engineers to be able to reason about 1) the *states* created during a run of P by instructions such as assignments and function calls; and 2) the *transitions* that occur to move between such states. Since we need to consider instrumentation, which in this work we assume happens strictly before runtime, we need pre-runtime analogues of these states. We call these *symbolic states*. A symbolic state σ is a pair $\langle \rho, m \rangle$ for ρ a unique identifier of the statement in the source code that generated the symbolic state and m a map from each program variable/function to a *status* in {undefined, changed, unchanged, called}.

We then represent a program P as a directed graph whose vertices are these symbolic states, with edges representing instructions that could move the program from one state to another. We call such a graph a *symbolic control-flow graph*, denote it by $\mathsf{SCFG}(P)$ and give an example in Fig. 1.

3.2   A Representation of Program Runs

We now introduce the structures over which CFTL semantics are defined, that is, our representations of program runs. To help us later with instrumentation, a representation of a run of our program P should be seen as a path through $\mathsf{SCFG}(P)$, the symbolic control-flow graph of P. To this path, we can add information from runtime, such as variable values and timestamps. We do this by augmenting symbolic states to give their runtime analogue, *concrete states*. A concrete state is a triple $\langle \sigma, v, t \rangle$ for σ a symbolic state, v a map from each program variable/function to a value and t a real-numbered timestamp. We can now represent a program run by a sequence of concrete states, which we call a *dynamic run* and denote by $\mathcal{D}$. Further, these dynamic runs have the required

```
1  authenticated = check_authentication()
2  if authenticated:
3    in = get_auth_data()
4    results = query("...", in)
5    if not results:
6      query("...", in)
7  else:
8    in = get_non_auth_data()
9    results = query("...", in)
```

Fig. 2. A sample Python program.

property that each concrete state can be associated with a symbolic state, meaning that each dynamic run forms a path through a symbolic control-flow graph.

3.3   Control-Flow Temporal Logic

Control-Flow Temporal Logic (CFTL) is a linear time, temporal logic designed for writing specifications over low-level program behaviour (at the line-of-code level). We achieve this by defining its semantics over dynamic runs, which are detailed representations of program runs. CFTL formulas are in prenex normal-form, so consist of two parts: the quantifiers, and the inner-most quantifier-free formula. Finally, when a dynamic run $\mathcal{D}$ satisfies a CFTL formula φ, we write $\mathcal{D} \models \varphi$.

For brevity, instead of giving the full syntax, which can be found in [32], we consider the sample program in Fig. 2 and give examples of CFTL formulas that express properties over this program.

A Simple Constraint over Call Durations. We can express the constraint that no call to **query** should ever take more than 2 s by writing

$$\forall c \in \mathsf{calls}(\mathsf{query}) : \mathsf{duration}(c) \le 2$$

In this case, the quantifier $\forall c \in \mathsf{calls}(\mathsf{query})$ identifies all pairs of concrete states in a dynamic run such that, in the second concrete state, the function **query** has just been called. We call c a *variable* and $\mathsf{calls}(\mathsf{query})$ a *predicate*. The quantifier-free part of the formula then uses CFTL's $\mathsf{duration}$ operator. This operator takes the difference of the timestamps associated with the pair of concrete states identified by the quantifier. The final step is to assert that the observed duration is less than or equal to 2.

Place a Constraint, But Only in a Certain Case. One might want to constrain the time taken by every call to **query** in the future, but *only* if **authenticated** was set to **True**. To capture this property, one could write

$$\forall s \in \mathsf{changes}(\mathtt{authenticated}) : \forall c \in \mathsf{future}(s, \mathsf{calls}(\mathsf{query})) :$$
$$s(\mathtt{authenticated}) = \mathtt{True} \implies \mathsf{duration}(c) < 2$$

To form the second quantifier, we use CFTL's future operator to identify all occurrences of an event after whatever is identified by the preceding quantifier. In this case, for each change of the variable `authenticated`, every future call of the function `query` after that will be identified. Then, for each pair formed by this process, the quantifier-free part of the formula will be evaluated.

Place a Constraint on the Time Between Points. Consider the constraint that the time taken to reach the next state in which `results` has been changed after the change of `authenticated` should be less than a certain value. With CFTL, one could write

$$\forall s \in \text{changes}(\texttt{authenticated}) : \text{timeBetween}(s, \text{next}(s, \text{changes}(\texttt{results}))) < 1$$

In this formula, we quantify over changes of `authenticated` and then, in the quantifier-free part, we introduce two new features of CFTL. The first is the next operator, which takes a variable along with a predicate and gives the next part of the dynamic run being considered which satisfies the predicate. The second new idea is the timeBetween operator, which takes two parts of the dynamic run and measures the time between them.

Place a Constraint Relating Two Measurements. Often, the time taken by some function call relates to the size of its input. For example, one might want to express the requirement that each call of the function `query` takes no more than 0.8 times the length of its input variable `in`. Then this could be expressed in CFTL by

$$\forall c \in \text{calls}(\texttt{query}) : \text{duration}(c) \leq \text{length}(\text{source}(c)(\texttt{in})) \times 0.8$$

3.4 Instrumentation

Consider the situation in which a monitoring algorithm must decide whether the formula $\forall c \in \text{calls}(\texttt{query}) : \text{duration}(c) \leq 2$ holds or not, given a dynamic run generated by the program in Fig. 2. Such a dynamic run would contain much more information than is needed to decide whether this formula holds. Hence, when the monitoring algorithm tries to process the dynamic run, it would first have to decide whether each concrete state was useful. In this case, most of the information in the dynamic run would be useless, and a large amount of the work done by the monitoring algorithm would be to conclude as such.

Our instrumentation approach involves 1) ensuring that the dynamic run extracted from the running program includes only the concrete states relevant to a formula by determining a subset of *critical symbolic states* before runtime; and 2) speeding up certain lookup processes that monitoring must perform when it *has* observed something that it needs.

Ensuring extraction of a conservative dynamic run is achieved with two steps. First, we inspect the quantifiers to determine *points of interest* in the program, and then we inspect the quantifier-free part of the formula to determine where measurements need to be taken. As an example, consider again the specification

$$\forall s \in \text{changes}(\texttt{authenticated}) : \text{timeBetween}(s, \text{next}(s, \text{changes}(\texttt{results}))) < 1$$

Determining Points of Interest. We first inspect the quantifiers and see that, based on $\forall s \in$ changes(authenticated), we need to find all symbolic states in the symbolic control-flow graph in which the variable authenticated has just been changed. In this case, we treat authenticated as a local primitive-type variable, so we do not consider side-effects from impure functions.

Determining Instrumentation Points. Once the set of points of interest has been derived, we inspect the quantifier-free part of the formula. In this case, we have a single constraint over multiple quantities that must be measured at runtime. In inspecting the timeBetween operator, we see that the first argument is the variable s, which refers to a concrete state in which the variable authenticated has just been changed. Hence, s refers directly to the points of interest that we have already determined, so we include these in our set of critical symbolic states.

Next, we have next(s, changes(results)), which refers to the next concrete state in which results was changed after authenticated was changed. Since when we perform instrumentation we often cannot be sure of the branches taken at runtime, we must follow the symbolic control-flow graph from each of the points of interest to determine each *possible* next change of results.

Correctness. Informally, instrumentation is correct when the dynamic run without instrumentation satisfies a CFTL formula if and only if the dynamic run with only concrete states included by instrumentation also satisfies it [32].

3.5 Monitoring

The problem that we must solve in monitoring is that of determining whether a dynamic run satisfies a CFTL formula, given incremental updates to the dynamic run (otherwise known as online monitoring).

Our monitoring approach is helped significantly by instrumentation, in that the input dynamic run is both reduced and structured by it. In particular, our instrumentation approach involves constructing a tree that allows our monitoring algorithm to quickly determine in what way some information from a dynamic run with instrumentation is relevant to the property being monitored [33].

When checking a dynamic run for satisfaction of a formula, our monitoring algorithm maintains an and-or formula tree (with extra structure to cope with CFTL formulas) for every part of the dynamic run that is identified by the formula's quantifiers. As more of the dynamic run is processed, the relevant formula trees are updated until they collapse to a truth value. The result of monitoring is then, as expected, the conjunction of these truth values. In the case that a formula tree was not collapsed because the dynamic run did not contain enough information, a number of policies could be implemented, though in practice we opt for discarding such formula trees.

3.6 Explanation by Path Comparison

We now summarise the extension of our work on CFTL to explaining why runs of a program did not satisfy a property, addressing the need identified in [42]. The full details are given in [31].

In that work, we first highlighted that dynamic runs with instrumentation applied may have the problem that their precise path through a symbolic control-flow graph can no longer be determined. Our solution to this was to modify our instrumentation process to ensure that enough concrete states are included in dynamic runs to allow the precise path taken to be reconstructed.

Once we can obtain the exact program path taken by a dynamic run in the form of a sequence of edges from a symbolic control-flow graph, our key contribution is a formalism for comparison of multiple paths. We assume that these dynamic runs generated different verdicts with respect to a CFTL property.

To enable comparison, we introduced a new technique that identifies points of disagreement in sets of paths and enables comparison of how the paths disagreed. To achieve this, we represent the regions over which paths disagree by *path parameters* and say that each path gives each of these parameters a *value* with the sub-path that it took in that region.

Finally, we extended this comparison of paths to take full advantage of CFTL's semantics. This extension enables analyses such as comparison of paths between two statements at which measurements were taken for a specification. Ultimately, this paves the way for identification of problematic regions of code based on monitoring results.

4 Translation into a Software Development Tool

The theory summarised in Sect. 3 has been used to implement VyPR, a framework for the performance analysis of Python programs (most often, web services) along with an ecosystem of supporting tools. VyPR provides facilities for specification of program performance, automatic instrumentation with respect to specifications, efficient online monitoring and in-depth offline analysis. More information, along with documentation, can be found at http://pyvypr.github.io/home/.

The discussion in this section draws on experience from addressing the challenges encountered when implementing VyPR. These challenges can be divided into two categories:

- Determining how to implement a tool based on the theory given so far that enables specification and then performs instrumentation and monitoring automatically.
- Determining how to enable software engineers to benefit as much as possible from the resulting tool.

4.1   A Python Library for CFTL

The first step a software engineer takes when using VYPR is writing their specifications. The process of a software engineer writing a formal specification is that of translation from a natural language specification to its equivalent in the specification language. To facilitate this process, we opted to build a Python library, PyCFTL, with which engineers can write their specifications and supply them to VYPR. To demonstrate PyCFTL, we consider the CFTL specification

$$\forall s \in \mathsf{changes}(x) : \mathsf{timeBetween}(s, \mathsf{dest}(\mathsf{next}(s, \mathsf{calls}(\mathsf{query})))) < 1$$

and construct it in Python code using the PyCFTL library

```
1  Forall(s = changes("x")).\
2  Check(lambda s : (
3    timeBetween(s, s.next_call("query").result()) < 1
4  ))
```

Here, we see two key translations:

Quantifiers. The single quantifier is built at line 1 by instantiating the `Forall` class using Python's keyword argument feature to introduce the variable `s`. The predicates implemented in the PyCFTL library match those defined in the CFTL semantics, namely `changes` and `calls`.

Constraints. The constraint to be checked at each point of interest identified by the quantifier is defined between lines 2 and 4 by passing a *lambda* expression to the method `Check` defined on the `Forall` instance. The arguments of this lambda expression must match the variables bound by the quantifiers. Hence, in this case, our lambda has the single argument `s`.

The constraint definition also includes one of the key features of PyCFTL: variables bound by quantifiers contain objects that can be treated like the events they represent. For example, using the variable `s` that holds a state, we can refer to the next call along using the method `next_call`. We can then get the state immediately after that call using the method `result`.

In Fig. 3 we give a further example, which demonstrates more of the PyCFTL library. Once a specification is written, the next concern to address is how to deal with Python software that contains multiple modules and classes. In the current implementation of VYPR, we wrap PyCFTL in a layer that allows software engineers to indicate to which *individual functions* in their code a given specification should apply. Figure 4 gives an example.

In Fig. 4, lines 2–8 give an example of *explicit indication* and lines 10–14 give an example of *indication using compilation*. *Explicit indication* involves the software engineer manually telling VYPR which package, module and then either 1) function or 2) class/method to instrument and monitor.

This approach to specification gives rise to the problem that software engineers may not know precisely where in their system they would like to measure something. To ease the situation, we have begun development of a set of helper

$$\forall s \in \text{changes}(\texttt{auth}):$$
$$\forall c \in \text{future}(s, \text{calls}(\texttt{query})):$$
$$s(\textbf{authenticated}) = \textbf{True} \implies \text{duration}(c) < 2$$

```
Forall(s = changes("auth")).\
Forall(c = calls("query", after="s")).\
Check(lambda s, c : (
  If(s("auth").equals(True)).then(c.duration() < 2)
))
```

Fig. 3. Another example of the PyCFTL specification library.

```
 1  {
 2    "package.module": {  # explicit indication
 3      "class.method": [
 4        Forall(c = calls("func")).Check(
 5          lambda c : c.duration() < 1
 6        )
 7      ]
 8    },
 9    # indication using compilation
10    Functions(containing_change_of="threshold"): [
11      Forall(s = changes("threshold")).Check(
12        lambda s : s("threshold") < 10
13      )
14    ]
15  }
```

Fig. 4. An example of how to tell VyPR where to instrument and monitor for a specification.

classes to enable *indication using compilation*. In practice, this means that, when a software engineer uses a helper class such as Functions, VyPR will inspect the symbolic control-flow graph of each function in a system and select it for monitoring if it fulfils the criteria given as an argument. Since system-wide static analysis is an obvious source of inefficiency, part of our development efforts involve caching results to mitigate the situation.

4.2   Instrumentation and Monitoring

The instrumentation and monitoring algorithms implemented by VyPR are those described in Sects. 3.4 and 3.5 respectively, extended to the setting of a system with multiple functions written across multiple files.

Instrumentation. This algorithm consists of inserting code in places appropriate for the specification given so that a dynamic run can be generated at runtime. To achieve this, a specification built using PyCFTL generates a structure in memory that VYPR can use, along with the symbolic control-flow graph of each relevant function in a system, to determine where to place new code. Placement of the code is performed statically by 1) adding new entries to the abstract syntax tree (easily obtained via Python's standard library) for each instrumentation point; 2) compiling to bytecode and 3) renaming the original source code file. This renaming prevents Python's default behaviour of recompiling bytecode when disparities between it and source code are detected.

The exact instrumentation code placed depends on the specification given. For example, if the specification calls for the measurement of a duration, VYPR will place code that records timestamps and computes their difference. The communication between instrumentation code and the monitoring algorithm is performed via a queue, since the monitoring algorithm runs asynchronously from the monitored program. For more information on how VYPR performs instrumentation, see our previous work [33].

Monitoring. This algorithm is responsible for processing the dynamic runs generated by instrumentation code, generating verdicts and sending the data to a central server for later analysis. So far, we have not needed our monitoring algorithm to feed verdict information back into the running program, so our implementation is asynchronous.

Since we work with Python, we face the challenge of the Global Interpreter Lock (GIL) [6], the mechanism used to make the Python interpreter thread-safe. Its major disadvantage is that threads running code that is not IO-heavy are not run asynchronously because the GIL is based on mutual exclusion. However, threads with IO activity can run asynchronously because the GIL is released for IO. Since we developed VYPR primarily for web services, the significant IO activity required for reading incoming requests, writing outgoing responses and performing database queries release the GIL to allow VYPR to run.

If one were to consider applying VYPR elsewhere, we have already highlighted that the current implementation of VYPR can generate high overhead if there is more work being done by monitoring than by the monitored program [32]. However, either by using multiprocessing or existing techniques for bypassing the GIL [3], we can remove this problem.

4.3   Storing Verdicts

Once our monitoring implementation generates verdicts, it sends them, along with a collection of other data, to a central repository to be stored in a relational database schema. This central repository of data, called the *verdict server*, is a separate system in itself with which VYPR communicates via HTTP. The server is responsible for:

- Storing verdicts, along with the measurements taken to reach those verdicts and paths taken by monitored functions.
- Providing an API that VYPR uses to send all of the data collected during instrumentation and monitoring.

- Providing APIs for our analysis tools (see Sects. 5.1 and 5.2).
- Serving our web-based analysis environment (see Sect. 5.1).

The server is implemented in Python using the Flask [10] framework with SQLite [8] as a backend database. The relational database is designed to store the data generated by VyPR at runtime compactly, meaning that our analysis tools are designed to enable straightforward access of data stored in a non-trivial schema. Finally, while we have plans to move away from SQLite to use a more robust database system, SQLite has met our needs so far.

5 Analysing Monitoring Results

An area that has received little attention from the RV community is the analysis of results of program monitoring. Our experience with VyPR has shown that the analysis tools provided by a program analysis framework are as important as the specification tools.

This is especially true when one is attempting to help software engineers explain violations of their specifications. In this direction, we have found that the way in which the results of our explanation work described in Sect. 3.6 are presented is just as important as the way in which the explanations are derived.

We now describe the analysis tools in the VyPR ecosystem, which include 1) a web-based environment for visual inspection of monitoring results; and 2) a Python library for writing analysis scripts. The aim of these tools is to make investigation of monitoring data straightforward and facilitate engineers in finding explanations of violations of their specifications. Details on usage can be found at https://pyvypr.github.io/home/use-vypr.html.

5.1 A Web-Based Analysis Environment

Since inspection of some data generated by VyPR lends itself best to a graphical user interface, part of the VyPR ecosystem is a web application. The application enables sophisticated, in-depth inspection to be performed with just a few clicks in the web browser. We now present key features.

Explicit Links Between Specifications and Source Code. In our analysis environment, we allow engineers to select parts of their specifications to focus on relevant parts of their source code. This allows understanding from the engineer of precisely which part of their code they are analysing.

The Performance of Individual Statements. Similarly to existing work on performance data visualisation performed by the Software Engineering community [21, 26, 27], our analysis environment displays the data from monitoring in the context of the relevant code. In fact, results from monitoring for specifications written in CFTL lend themselves easily to such a representation because of CFTL's low-level nature, meaning measurements can be linked directly to lines of source code.

Separating Performance Data by Verdict. When viewing a plot of measurements taken during monitoring, it is reasonable for an engineer to want to see only the measurements that generated either satisfaction or violation. With the analysis environment, engineers can plot measurements and then filter them by whether the specification being monitored was satisfied or violated.

Program Path Highlighting. Given the path reconstruction approach described in Sect. 3.6, the analysis environment can highlight paths in code up to and between measurements. It can also highlight paths taken by whole function calls.

Since it is expected that performance data is visualised across many function calls, we use colour-coding to highlight source code based on how well a specification was satisfied or how severely it was violated on average.

Without the analysis environment, these tasks would require in-depth knowledge of the schema in which data is stored and non-trivial post-processing.

5.2   A Python Analysis Library

For the cases in which the analysis environment is not suitable, we built a Python library. This library helps software engineers to automate their inspection of performance data by writing scripts.

In order to make writing scripts as intuitive as possible, the library is designed similarly to an Object-Relational Mapping (ORM) [7,39]. That is, the library provides classes that mirror tables in a relational schema so that each row in a table becomes an instance of the table's class. Methods defined on these instances then reflect either foreign key relationships between tables, or perform more complex queries. In practice, rather than operating directly on a database, the library communicates with the verdict server via the server's analysis API.

In addition to the ORM, the analysis library provides facilities for post-processing of data generated by VYPR. These facilities greatly simplify otherwise complex tasks, which we now describe.

Comparison of Program Paths. Each time a function monitored by VYPR is executed, program path information is generated by additional instrumentation. It is then coupled with the set of verdicts. Each measurement taken during monitoring is mapped to this path information, so paths up to and between measurements can be reconstructed.

The program path information generated is a sequence of integers, each of which being the unique ID of a more complex path condition. Measurements are mapped into this sequence of integers via a pair consisting of an *offset* and a *reaching path length*, both also integers. The offset identifies the prefix of the sequence whose path conditions lead to the branch on which the measurement was taken. The reaching path length tells us how far along this branch to traverse before the precise statement at which the measurement was taken is reached.

The algorithm that performs this transformation (described in [31]) is integrated with the ORM. The result is that 1) objects representing *function calls* define methods to reconstruct the entire path taken by those calls; and 2) objects representing *measurements* define methods that reconstruct paths up to those measurements. Classes are also provided to help identify where paths disagree and how, using the notion of *path parameters* described in Sect. 3.6.

Construction of Call Trees. If multiple functions in a system are monitored by VʏPR, enough information about each function call is stored that the call tree can be partially reconstructed (it will be missing calls of any function that is not monitored). Since VʏPR associates measurements with the function call during which they were taken, it is also possible to reconstruct the call tree occurring *during* a measurement (if the measurement is over a function call).

Path Comparison with Call Trees. Suppose that a function f calls a function g, both of which are monitored by VʏPR. Suppose further that one of the specifications written over f is the following

```
Forall(c = calls("g")).Check(lambda c : c.duration() < 1)
```

Then, since path information exists for g, we can use comparison of the paths taken through g to explain the verdicts generated by f. The analysis library makes this straightforward again by implementing the notion of *path parameters*.

Call Trees over Multiple Machines. If programs on multiple machines are monitored by VʏPR, with both instances of VʏPR pointing to the same verdict server and synchronised via some global clock such as NTP [4], monitoring results from each machine can be combined. In particular, the analysis library's call tree reconstruction algorithm can detect when a function call from one machine took place during a function call on another. The advantage of this that we have so far used is that one can use comparison of the paths traversed on one machine to explain measurements on another.

6   VyPR in Practice

We conclude with a description of our operational experience with VʏPR at the CMS Experiment [9] at the LHC [11] at CERN. We discuss our experience analysing a system to which VʏPR has been applied extensively, resulting in a detailed understanding of its performance. More detail on the investigations presented here can be found in our tutorial material.

6.1   Finding Performance Problems

Our case study is a web service used at the CMS Experiment for uploading certain data needed in physics analyses to a central database. The service consists of a client program and a server; the client is responsible for reading in and performing some initial checks on data, and the server is responsible for final checks and all database operations. The investigation that we describe here is purely on the server-side, but we have used VʏPR's analysis facilities to see how the two components of the service behave together. To generate the data that we use here, we replayed 4000 instances of data upload from a repository that we have been building up over the past 3 years of data collection at the LHC.

Defining Specifications. We consider a function that is responsible for performing some checks which vary depending on the existing state of the target database. Hence, there are two branches that can be taken and then a final database query. We need to investigate the time taken to get from the start of these branches, to the return of the database query at the end. Our specification for this is

```
Forall(q = changes("tag")).\
Forall(c = calls("commit", after="q")).\
Check(lambda q, c : timeBetween(q, c.result()) < 1.2)
```

This specification will actually lead to VyPR recording more data than we need because of the structure of the monitored code. In our analysis script, we deal with this.

We also need to measure the time taken by some key functions that are called on the paths of interest. VyPR associates measurements with the statements in code from which they were taken, so we write a specification placing an arbitrary constraint over the function calls that we care about. It is then easy to get the measurements that were taken along relevant paths in our monitored function.

Analysing Results. We give a brief description of how we used our analysis library to write a script which generated the plot shown in Fig. 5. The script contains the following steps:

1. Select the function in the system that we need to analyse. For that function, choose the specifications.
2. Since our main specification contains two quantifiers, select the two statements in code between which we will be comparing paths.
3. Get all measurements of the time taken for runs of the function to get between the two statements that we have selected, such that the specification was violated. Additionally get all measurements of function call durations taken on the relevant paths.

Once all measurements have been obtained, we still need to separate them by which path was taken. To do this, we use the analysis library's implementation of *path parameters*. This involves:

1. *Intersecting* all of the paths that we obtain between the two statements we selected.
2. Finding the single point (in this case) where the paths disagree, which is represented by a *path parameter*.
3. Finding the *value* given to this path parameter by each path, ie, the sub-path taken in the region of disagreement.

It is then straightforward to group the measurements by the path that was taken, allowing Fig. 5 to be divided with respect to the two possible sub-paths found. It is clear from these plots that one path taken in the region of disagreement resulted in far worse performance. Further, from the inclusion of the times taken by the two key function calls on those paths, we see that one of the two tends to be to blame for the peaks.

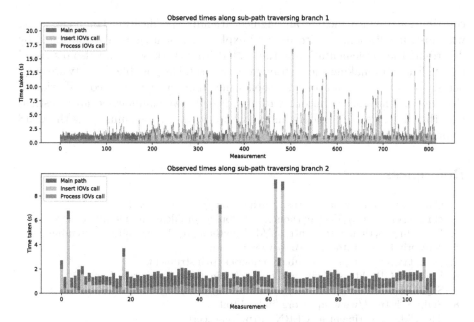

Fig. 5. The plot we built with our analysis library to show the range of time measurements for violations along two distinct paths through some source code.

Ultimately, the results of this investigation and others will be fed into the development process at CMS to help consolidate the service. This will be helped by our work on applying VyPR during Continuous Integration [37].

7   Future Work

There are many directions for future work, which we divide into the following categories:

- *Instrumentation.* There are clear opportunities for improvement of VyPR's instrumentation process.
- *Analysis environment improvements.* We aim to minimise the need for the analysis library.
- *More expressive specifications.* Classes of properties such as those written over multiple functions currently cannot be expressed directly in CFTL.
- *Performance analysis in Continuous Integration.* Work is ongoing on extending VyPR to combine functional testing with performance analysis [37].

8   Conclusion

In this paper, we described the current state of VyPR, a framework for the performance analysis of Python web services. We summarised our theoretical contributions, which include an engineer-friendly specification language, along with instrumentation, monitoring and explanation strategies. We continued by describing the implementation of the VyPR framework, while we also discussed the challenges of making such a framework as useful as possible for software engineers. We introduced our analysis tools which mark a significant contribution to the area of analysing monitoring results. Finally, we summarised an investigation that improved our understanding of a critical service running at the CMS Experiment at CERN.

References

1. Call Graphs for Python. https://github.com/jrfonseca/gprof2dot
2. cProfiler. https://docs.python.org/2/library/profile.html#module-cProfile
3. Extending Python with C. https://docs.python.org/2.7/extending/extending.html
4. Network Time Protocol. http://www.ntp.org
5. pyinstrument. https://github.com/joerick/pyinstrument
6. Python's GIL. https://wiki.python.org/moin/GlobalInterpreterLock
7. SQLAlchemy for Python. https://www.sqlalchemy.org
8. SQLite. https://www.sqlite.org/index.html
9. The CMS Experiment at CERN. http://cms.cern
10. The Flask Framework. https://flask.palletsprojects.com/en/1.1.x/
11. The LHC. https://home.cern/science/accelerators/large-hadron-collider
12. The Python Programming Language. https://github.com/python/cpython
13. trace - the Python tracing tool. https://docs.python.org/2/library/trace.html
14. What is Deterministic Profiling? https://docs.python.org/2.4/lib/node453.html
15. Alur, R., Etessami, K., Madhusudan, P.: A temporal logic of nested calls and returns. In: Jensen, K., Podelski, A. (eds.) TACAS 2004. LNCS, vol. 2988, pp. 467–481. Springer, Heidelberg (2004). https://doi.org/10.1007/978-3-540-24730-2_35
16. Ball, T., Naik, M., Rajamani, S.K.: From symptom to cause: localizing errors in counterexample traces. In: Proceedings of the 30th ACM SIGPLAN-SIGACT Symposium on Principles of Programming Languages, POPL 2003, pp. 97–105. Association for Computing Machinery, New York (2003). https://doi.org/10.1145/604131.604140
17. Bensalem, S., Bozga, M., Krichen, M., Tripakis, S.: Testing conformance of real-time applications by automatic generation of observers. Electron. Notes Theor. Comput. Sci. **113**, 23–43 (2005). Proceedings of the Fourth Workshop on Runtime Verification (RV 2004). https://doi.org/10.1016/j.entcs.2004.01.036. http://www.sciencedirect.com/science/article/pii/S157106610405251X
18. Barringer, H., Goldberg, A., Havelund, K., Sen, K.: Rule-based runtime verification. In: Steffen, B., Levi, G. (eds.) VMCAI 2004. LNCS, vol. 2937, pp. 44–57. Springer, Heidelberg (2004). https://doi.org/10.1007/978-3-540-24622-0_5
19. Bartocci, E., Manjunath, N., Mariani, L., Mateis, C., Ničković, D.: Automatic failure explanation in CPS models. In: Ölveczky, P.C., Salaün, G. (eds.) SEFM 2019. LNCS, vol. 11724, pp. 69–86. Springer, Cham (2019). https://doi.org/10.1007/978-3-030-30446-1_4
20. Bauer, A., Leucker, M., Schallhart, C.: Runtime verification for LTL and TLTL. ACM Trans. Softw. Eng. Methodol. **20**(4), 14:1–14:64 (2011). https://doi.org/10.1145/2000799.2000800

21. Beck, F., Moseler, O., Diehl, S., Rey, G.D.: In situ understanding of performance bottlenecks through visually augmented code. In: 2013 21st International Conference on Program Comprehension (ICPC), pp. 63–72 (2013)
22. Beer, I., Ben-David, S., Chockler, H., Orni, A., Trefler, R.: Explaining counterexamples using causality. Formal Methods Syst. Des. **40**(1), 20–40 (2012). https://doi.org/10.1007/s10703-011-0132-2
23. Barringer, H., Falcone, Y., Havelund, K., Reger, G., Rydeheard, D.: Quantified event automata: towards expressive and efficient runtime monitors. In: Giannakopoulou, D., Méry, D. (eds.) FM 2012. LNCS, vol. 7436, pp. 68–84. Springer, Heidelberg (2012). https://doi.org/10.1007/978-3-642-32759-9_9
24. Birch, G., Fischer, B., Poppleton, M.R.: Fast model-based fault localisation with test suites. In: Blanchette, J.C., Kosmatov, N. (eds.) TAP 2015. LNCS, vol. 9154, pp. 38–57. Springer, Cham (2015). https://doi.org/10.1007/978-3-319-21215-9_3
25. Christakis, M., Heizmann, M., Mansur, M.N., Schilling, C., Wüstholz, V.: Semantic fault localization and suspiciousness ranking. In: Vojnar, T., Zhang, L. (eds.) TACAS 2019. LNCS, vol. 11427, pp. 226–243. Springer, Cham (2019). https://doi.org/10.1007/978-3-030-17462-0_13
26. Cito, J., Leitner, P., Rinard, M., Gall, H.C.: Interactive production performance feedback in the IDE. In: 2019 IEEE/ACM 41st International Conference on Software Engineering (ICSE), pp. 971–981 (2019)
27. Cito, J., Oliveira, F., Leitner, P., Nagpurkar, P., Gall, H.C.: Context-based analytics - establishing explicit links between runtime traces and source code. In: 2017 IEEE/ACM 39th International Conference on Software Engineering: Software Engineering in Practice Track (ICSE-SEIP), pp. 193–202 (2017)
28. Clarke, E., Jha, S., Lu, Y., Veith, H.: Tree-like counterexamples in model checking, pp. 19–29, February 2002. https://doi.org/10.1109/LICS.2002.1029814
29. D'Angelo, B., et al.: LOLA: runtime monitoring of synchronous systems. In: 12th International Symposium on Temporal Representation and Reasoning (TIME 2005), pp. 166–174. IEEE Computer Society Press, June 2005
30. Dawes, J.H., Han, M., Reger, G., Franzoni, G., Pfeiffer, A.: Analysis tools for the VyPR framework for Python. In: 2019 International Conference on Computing in High Energy and Nuclear Physics, Adelaide, Australia (2019)
31. Dawes, J.H., Reger, G.: Explaining violations of properties in Control-Flow Temporal Logic. In: Finkbeiner, B., Mariani, L. (eds.) RV 2019. LNCS, vol. 11757, pp. 202–220. Springer, Cham (2019). https://doi.org/10.1007/978-3-030-32079-9_12
32. Dawes, J.H., Reger, G.: Specification of temporal properties of functions for runtime verification. In: Proceedings of the 34th ACM/SIGAPP Symposium on Applied Computing, SAC 2019, Limassol, Cyprus, 8–12 April 2019, pp. 2206–2214 (2019). https://doi.org/10.1145/3297280.3297497
33. Dawes, J.H., Reger, G., Franzoni, G., Pfeiffer, A., Govi, G.: VyPR2: a framework for runtime verification of Python web services. In: Vojnar, T., Zhang, L. (eds.) TACAS 2019. LNCS, vol. 11428, pp. 98–114. Springer, Cham (2019). https://doi.org/10.1007/978-3-030-17465-1_6
34. Falcone, Y., Krstić, S., Reger, G., Traytel, D.: A taxonomy for classifying runtime verification tools. In: Colombo, C., Leucker, M. (eds.) RV 2018. LNCS, vol. 11237, pp. 241–262. Springer, Cham (2018). https://doi.org/10.1007/978-3-030-03769-7_14
35. Ferrère, T., Maler, O., Ničković, D.: Trace diagnostics using temporal implicants. In: Finkbeiner, B., Pu, G., Zhang, L. (eds.) ATVA 2015. LNCS, vol. 9364, pp. 241–258. Springer, Cham (2015). https://doi.org/10.1007/978-3-319-24953-7_20

36. Hallé, S., Varvaressos, S.: A formalization of complex event stream processing, vol. 2014, pp. 2–11, September 2014. https://doi.org/10.1109/EDOC.2014.12
37. Javed, O., et al.: PerfCI: a toolchain for automated performance testing during continuous integration of Python projects. In: 2020 International Conference on Automated Software Engineering (2020, to appear)
38. Koymans, R.: Specifying real-time properties with metric temporal logic. Real-Time Syst. 2(4), 255–299 (1990). https://doi.org/10.1007/BF01995674
39. Papadopoulos, I., Chytracek, R., Duellmann, D., Govi, G., Shapiro, Y., Xie, Z.: CORAL, a software system for vendor-neutral access to relational databases, pp. 495–499, April 2006. https://doi.org/10.1142/9789812773678_0082
40. Pnueli, A.: The temporal logic of programs. In: 18th Annual Symposium on Foundations of Computer Science (SFCS 1977), pp. 46–57, October 1977. https://doi.org/10.1109/SFCS.1977.32
41. Reger, G.: Suggesting edits to explain failing traces. In: Bartocci, E., Majumdar, R. (eds.) RV 2015. LNCS, vol. 9333, pp. 287–293. Springer, Cham (2015). https://doi.org/10.1007/978-3-319-23820-3_20
42. Reger, G.: A report of RV-CuBES 2017. In: Reger, G., Havelund, K. (eds.) RV-CuBES 2017. An International Workshop on Competitions, Usability, Benchmarks, Evaluation, and Standardisation for Runtime Verification Tools. Kalpa Publications in Computing, vol. 3, pp. 1–9. EasyChair (2017). https://doi.org/10.29007/2496. https://easychair.org/publications/paper/MVXk
43. Reiter, R.: A theory of diagnosis from first principles. Artif. Intell. 32(1), 57–95 (1987). https://doi.org/10.1016/0004-3702(87)90062-2. http://www.sciencedirect.com/science/article/pii/0004370287900622
44. Groce, A., Visser, W.: What went wrong: explaining counterexamples. In: Ball, T., Rajamani, S.K. (eds.) SPIN 2003. LNCS, vol. 2648, pp. 121–136. Springer, Heidelberg (2003). https://doi.org/10.1007/3-540-44829-2_8
45. de Souza, H.A., Chaim, M.L., Kon, F.: Spectrum-based software fault localization: a survey of techniques, advances, and challenges. CoRR abs/1607.04347 (2016). http://arxiv.org/abs/1607.04347
46. Wotawa, F., Stumptner, M., Mayer, W.: Model-based debugging or how to diagnose programs automatically. In: Hendtlass, T., Ali, M. (eds.) IEA/AIE 2002. LNCS (LNAI), vol. 2358, pp. 746–757. Springer, Heidelberg (2002). https://doi.org/10.1007/3-540-48035-8_72. http://dl.acm.org/citation.cfm?id=646864.708248

Monitoring Cyber-Physical Systems: From Design to Integration

Maximilian Schwenger[✉]

CISPA Helmholtz Center for Information Security, Saarbrücken, Germany
maximilian.schwenger@cispa.saarland

Abstract. Cyber-physical systems are inherently safety-critical. The deployment of a runtime monitor significantly increases confidence in their safety. The effectiveness of the monitor can be maximized by considering it an integral component during its development. Thus, in this paper, I given an overview over recent work regarding a development process for runtime monitors alongside a cyber-physical system. This process includes the transformation of desirable safety properties into the formal specification language RTLola. A compiler then generates an executable artifact for monitoring the specification. This artifact can then be integrated into the system.

1 Introduction

Cyber-physical systems (CPS) directly interact with the physical world, rendering them inherently safety-critical. Integrating a runtime monitor into the CPS greatly increases confidence in its safety. The monitor assesses the health status of the system based on available data sources such as sensors. It detects a deterioration of the health and alerts the system such that it can e.g. initiate mitigation procedures. In this paper I will provide an overview regarding the development process of a runtime monitor for CPS based on recent work. For this, I will use the RTLola [13,14] monitoring framework.

The process ranges from designing specifications to integrating the executable monitor. It starts by identifying relevant properties and translating them into a formal specification language. The resulting specification is type-checked and validated to increase confidence in its correctness. Afterwards, it is compiled into an executable artifact, either based on software or hardware. Lastly, the artifact is integrated into the full system. This step takes the existing system architecture of the CPS into account and enables the monitor to support a post-mortem analysis. The full process is illustrated in Fig. 1.

This work was partially supported by the German Research Foundation (DFG) as part of the Collaborative Research Center "Foundations of Perspicuous Software Systems" (TRR 248, 389792660), and by the European Research Council (ERC) Grant OSARES (No. 683300).

J. Deshmukh and D. Ničković (Eds.): RV 2020, LNCS 12399, pp. 87–106, 2020.
https://doi.org/10.1007/978-3-030-60508-7_5

The first step of the process concerns the specification. It captures a detailed analysis of the system behavior, which entails computationally challenging arithmetic. Yet, since the monitor for the specification will be realized as an embedded component, its resource consumption must be statically bounded. Thus, the specification language has to provide sufficient expressiveness while allowing the monitor to retain a predictable and low resource footprint. In particular, an ideal specification language provides formal guarantees on the runtime behavior of its monitors such as worst case execution time or memory consumption. In general, however, expressiveness, formal guarantees, and predictably low resource consumption cannot be achieved at the same time. Desirable properties like "every request must be granted within a second" might come at the cost that the memory consumption of the monitor depends on the unpredictable input frequency of requests. Consequently, specification languages providing input-independent formal guarantees on the required memory must impose restrictions to prohibit such properties. These restriction can be direct, i.e., the syntax of the language renders the property inexpressible, or indirect, so the property can be expressed but falls into a language fragment unsuitable for monitoring. RTLola falls into the former category.

During the design phase of the CPS, the specifier defines properties spanning from validation of low-level input sensor readings to high-level mission-specific control decisions. The former are real-time critical, i.e., they demand a timely response from the monitor, whereas the latter include long-term checks and statistical analysis [6] where slight delays and mild inaccuracies are unsubstantial. Just like code is not a perfect reflection of what the programmer had in mind, the specification might deviate from the specifiers intention. To reduce the amount of undetected bugs, the specification needs to be validated. This increases confidence in it and—by proxy—in the monitor. The validation consists of two parts: type checks and validation based on log data. The former relies solely on the specification itself and checks for type errors or undefined behavior. The latter requires access to recorded or simulated traces of the system and interprets the specification over the given traces. The output of the monitor can then be compared against the expected result.

After successfully validating the specification, a compiler for the specification language generates an executable artifact. This artifact is either a hardware or a software solution, depending on the requirements of the system architecture. If, for example, the architecture does not allow for adding additional components, a software solution is preferable as it does not require dedicated hardware; the monitor can be part of the control computer. Hardware solutions, on the other hand, are more resource efficient and allow for parallelization with nearly-0 cost. In any case, the compiler can inject additional annotations for static code-level verification [15] or traceability [5] to further increase confidence in the correctness of the monitor.

Finally, deploying the monitor into the CPS harbors additional pitfalls. As an external safety component, the monitor should not influence the regular operation of the system unless upon detection of a safety violation. As a result, the system architecture needs to enable non-intrusive data flow from the system to

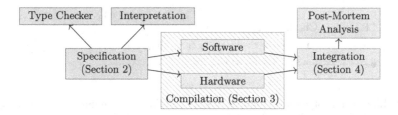

Fig. 1. Illustration of the paper structure. It is divided into three phases: specification, compilation, and integration.

the monitor and intrusive data flow from the monitor to the controller. The controller then has to react on an alarm appropriately. Such a reaction can e.g. be a switch from the regular controller to a formally verified controller with significantly reduced complexity responsible for a graceful shutdown of the system [16], as suggested in the Simplex Architecture [37].

After terminating a mission, the output of the monitor provides valuable data for the post-mortem analysis. Regular system logs might be insufficient as they do not contain the entire periphery data due to resource constraints. The monitor, however, filters and aggregates the data specifically to assess information regarding the system's status w.r.t. safety, thus providing valuable feedback.

2   Specifications: From Sensors to Missions

When designing specifications for CPS, the specifier has to keep in mind that not all properties are equal. They fall into a spectrum from low-level properties concerned with concrete sensor readings to high-level properties validating mission-specific criteria. Properties on the least end of the spectrum work on raw data points of single sensors. Most common are simple bounds checks (*the altitude may not be negative*) or frequency checks (*the barometer must provide between 9 and 11 readings per second*). Less low-level properties work on refined data points, e.g. to check whether several sensors contradict each other (*the altitude measured by the sonic altimeter must not deviate more than ϵ from the altitude based on the air pressure*). Such a sensor cross-validation requires refinement of raw values as they cannot be compared without further ado. While a barometer provides the air pressure, it needs further information such as pressure and temperature at sea level to accurately estimate the current altitude. Similarly, validating the position provided by the *global navigation satellite system* (GNSS) module against the position estimated by the *inertial measurement unit* (IMU) requires double integration of the measured acceleration. On the highest end of the spectrum reside mission-level properties. When checking such properties, the source of information is mostly discarded and the values are assumed to be correct. For example, consider an aircraft that traverses a set of dynamically received waypoints. Mission-level properties could demand that a waypoint is reached in time or that the traveled distance does deviate more than a factor from the actual distance between two points.

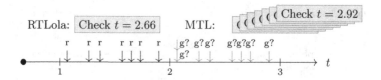

Fig. 2. Illustration of monitor obligations for checking if a request ("r") is granted ("g?") within a second. While the MTL interpretation is more precise, it requires statically unbounded memory. The RTLola under-approximation requires constant memory.

Properties are usually expressed in natural language as above and translated into a specification language. Consider the first property: *the altitude may not be negative.* Evidently, the properties harbors little challenge in terms of arithmetic. However, timeliness is critical. If the altimeter reports a negative altitude, clearly something is wrong and the system needs to be informed near-instantaneously. In RTLola, the property translates to the following specification:

```
input altitude: Float32
input orientation: Float32
trigger altitude < 0 "Altimeter reports negative altitude."
trigger orientation > 2 * π "Orientation exceeds 2π."
```

The first two lines declare input streams of name `altitude` and `orientation`, both with type `Float32`. The remaining lines contain trigger conditions with message to be sent to the system for the case a condition turns true. Whenever the monitor receives a new value from the altimeter or gyroscope, the respective condition is checked immediately. Note that RTLola allows for *asynchronous* input behavior, i.e., one input stream can produce a new value while the other does not. Thus, when the gyroscope produces a value, the respective trigger condition is checked regardless of the altimeter. This timing dependency from inputs to expressions is part of RTLola's type system.

The type system is two-dimensional: every stream and expression has a *value type* and a *pacing type*. Value types are common within programming languages, they indicate the shape and interpretation of data. The input streams, for example, are of value type `Float32`, so storing a single value requires 32 bits and the bits should be interpreted as a floating point number. The pacing type, however, states *when* expressions are evaluated and thus when streams produce new values. In case of the trigger expressions, the pacing types are *event-based*, i.e., they are coupled to the reception of new values from the altimeter or gyroscope.

The pacing type can also be *periodic*, effectively decoupling the evaluation of expressions from input streams in terms of timing. As an example, consider the second low-level property: *the barometer must provide between 9 and 11 readings per second.* An RTLola specification for this property is:

```
input pressure: Float32
output readings_per_sec @ 1Hz := pressure.aggregate(over: 1s, using:
    count)
trigger readings_per_sec < 9 "Barometer produces too few readings."
trigger readings_per_sec > 11 "Barometer produces too many readings."
```

Here, `readings_per_sec` is an output stream with a timing annotation @ 1 Hz prompting the monitor to only evaluate the expression of the stream once per second. Thus, the timing of the evaluation is decoupled from the reception of new input values.

The expression itself is a sliding window aggregation, i.e., whenever evaluated, the expression counts how many data points the barometer generated in the last second. If the count falls below 9 or exceeds 11, the monitor raises an alarm. While the logic behind a an efficient sliding window implementation is rather complex and requires a great deal of bookkeeping, RTLola provides a simple primitive for it. This alleviates the need for the specifier to manually take care of the implementation details.

Note that the specification does not precisely represent the property. Assume the system alternates between receiving 7 readings in the first half of a second and receiving 3 readings in the second half. Then, every other second, the system receives a total of 14 readings per second—unbeknownst to the monitor. In RTLola, it is impossible to specify the property correctly as it lacks the necessary expressiveness by design: sliding window expressions can only occur in streams with a timing annotation. This annotation renders the stream *isochronous*, i.e., the point in time when its expression will be evaluated are determined statically. The reason behind it is that the original properties lies in a category of properties that generally need a statically unbounded amount of memory to be monitored. To understand this, consider the property *Every request must be granted within one second*. A sound monitor for the property needs to check whether a request was granted exactly one second after receiving a request. However, there is no static bound on the amount of requests the monitor receives within this frame of time. Since it has to store their arrival times, the memory consumption might exceed any bound. The problem is illustrated in Fig. 2. There are specification logics such as *metric temporal logic* (MTL) [20], in which the property can be expressed. In such a case, the memory consumption of the monitor is linear in the number of events receives within the second. Since RTLola only provides constant memory monitors, it rejects specifications for such properties and instead enables constant-memory under-approximations. This design decision is a requirement to guarantee that the monitor cannot possible run out of memory during the execution.

RTLola provides primitives for more abstract constraints such as sensor cross-validations as well:

```
input velocity_1: Int64
input velocity_2: Int64
output deviation := abs(velocity_1 - velocity_2)
output lasting_dev := deviation > 5 ∧ deviation.offset(by: -1,
    default: 0) > 5 ∧ deviation.offset(by: -2, default: 0) > 5
trigger lasting_deviation "Lasting deviation in measured velocities."
```

The specification declares two input streams providing different readings for the velocity of the system, and two output streams `deviation` and `lasting_dev` that computes the absolut deviation of the readings and checks whether the deviation exceeds a threshold three consecutive times. The first conjunct of the stream expression accesses the current, i.e., the latest value of the deviation stream, whereas the offset(by: -n, default: v) function allows for accessing the nth-to-latest value of the stream for $n \in \mathbb{N}^1$. This value does not exist at the beginning of the monitor execution, so the specifier has to supply a default value v. Here, the specification refers to the abstract notion of "the last value" rather than considering the real-time behavior, assuming that low-level validation already took place.

Note that deviation accesses both velocity streams without supplying a default value. This indicates a *synchronous* access and prompts the monitor to only evaluate deviation when both input receive a new value. This is not necessarily the case since RTLola considers inputs to be asynchronous. The pacing type of deviation captures the information that the stream is only evaluated when the two inputs happen to arrive at the same time: it is event-based and the conjunction of both input streams. In contrast to that, a different definition of deviation could look like:

```
output deviation_disj @ velocity_1 ∨ velocity_2 :=
    abs(velocity_1.hold(or: 0) - velocity_2.hold(or: 0))
```

Here, the output stream has a disjunctive type, so when it is extended, at least one of the two inputs received a new value, not necessarily both. In such a case, RTLola forces the specifier to declare precisely how it should handle potentially old values. The specifier can, as in the example of deviation_disj, turn the synchronous accesses into sample and hold accesses. When evaluating the expression, the monitor will access the latest—yet potentially old—value of the input stream with a 0-order hold. If the specifier attempted to access either stream synchronously, RTLola would reject the specification because it contains an inner contradiction. These kinds of type checks greatly increase confidence in the correctness of the specification as they point out imprecise and potentially flawed parts.

Lastly, consider two mission-level properties for an aircraft flying a dynamic list of waypoints: the monitor should issue a warning if the aircraft deviated from the straight-line distance by at least ε, and it should issue an error if such a deviation occurred more than 10 times.

```
input wp: (Float64, Float64)
input pos: (Float64, Float64)
output start: (Float64, Float64) := (0, 0)
output exp_dist @ wp := wp - wp.offset(by: -1, default: start)
output dist_since_wp @ pos := pos - pos.offset(by: -1, default: start)
    + dist_since_wp.offset(by: -1, default: 0)
output distance_deviation @ wp :=
    abs(exp_dist.offset(by: -1, default: 0) - dist_since_wp.hold(or: 0))
trigger distance_deviation > ε "Warn: Path deviation detected."
output deviations := deviations.offset(by: -1, default: 0)
    + if distance_deviation > ε then 1 else 0
trigger deviations > 10 "Err: Too many path deviations!"
```

---

[1] As a result, RTLola does not allow for accessing future values.

The specification declares two clearly asynchronous input streams: the current waypoint wp and the current position pos. The start stream is a constant stream only containing the initial position of the aircraft. exp_dist contains the distance between the current and the last waypoint whereas dist_since_wp aggregates the distance the aircraft has traveled since reaching the last waypoint/starting the mission. The deviation in distance is then the absolut difference between these two distances. Note that this value is only valid when the aircraft just reached a new waypoint, hence the @ wp annotation. This prompts the monitor to only evaluate the stream when it receives a new waypoint. Lastly, the deviations stream counts the number of times the deviation exceeded its threshold.

The specification contains several pacing type annotations. This, however, is for illustration, as most of the time, RTLola can infer both types from the stream expression. Yet, the specifier always has the option to annotate types for clarity or if the timing of a stream should deviate from the standard behavior, e.g. for disjunctive event-based types.

Note that this was only a brief overview of RTLola. For more details on the theory, refer to [36], and for the implementation, refer to [13].

2.1 Specification Validation by Interpretation

RTLola's type system already rules out several sources for incorrect behavior of the monitor. Yet, a validation of the specification is crucial to increase confidence in the *correctness* of the specification. The validation requires access to records of previous runs of the system. These can be simulated, collected during test runs, or logs from sufficiently similar systems. Just like when testing software, developers annotate the trace data with points in time when they expect the monitor to raise an alarm. Then, they execute a monitor for the given specification on the trace and compare the result with their annotations. Deviations mainly root from either an error when designing the specification, or a discrepancy in the mental image of different people regarding the correct interpretation of a property.

A key point for the specification validation is that the process should incur as little cost as possible to enable rapid prototyping. Hence, interpreting the specification rather than compiling it is preferable—especially when the target platform is hardware-based. After all, realizing a specification on an FPGA usually takes upwards of 30 min [7]. While interpretation is considerably less performant than compiled solutions, the RTLola interpreter manages to process a single event in 1.5 µs. This enables a reasonably fast validation of specifications even against large traces.

2.2 Static Analysis for RTLola Specifications

After type checking the specification and validating its correctness based on test traces, RTLola provides static checks to further analyze it. For this, RTLola generates a dependency graph where each stream is a node and each stream access is an edge. This information suffices to perform a memory analysis and a running time analysis. The analysis identifies the resource consumption—both spatial and temporal—of each stream, granting fine-grained control to the specifier.

Memory. For the memory consumption of stream s, the analysis identifies the access of another stream to s with the greatest offset n_s^*. Evidently, the monitor only has to retain n_s^* values of s to successfully resolve all accesses. Moreover, note that all types in RTLola have a fixed size. Let T_s be the type of s with bit-size $|T_s|$. Then, the memory consumption of s induced by accesses through other streams amounts to $n_s^* \cdot |T_s|$.

Sliding window expressions within the stream expression of s incur additional memory overhead. Suppose $w_1, \ldots, w_k$ are the windows occurring in s where for $w_i = (\gamma_i, d_i)$, γ_i is the aggregation function and d_i is the length of the window. If $k > 0$, RTLola demands s to be periodic with frequency π_s. The memory consumption of s induced by sliding windows consists of the number of *panes* required. Here, a pane represents the time interval between two consecutive evaluations of the window. The pane consists of a single value which contains the aggregated information of all values that arrived in the respective time interval. This implementation of sliding windows is inspired by Li et al. [23] and only works for list homomorphisms [25]. A window thus has $d_i \cdot \pi_s$ panes, which has to be multiplied by the size of the value stored within a pane: T_{γ_i}. This value is statically determined and depends on the aggregation function: for summation, it is merely the sum of the values, for the average it is the intermediate average plus the number of values that occurred within the pane.

The overall memory consumption of s is therefore

$$\mu(s) = n_s^* |T_s| + \mathbb{1}_{k>0} \sum_{i=1}^{k} d_i \pi_i |T_{\gamma_i}|$$

Here, $\mathbb{1}_{\varphi}$ is the indicator function evaluating to 1 if φ is true and 0 otherwise.

Running Time. The running time cannot be fully determined based on the specification alone as it depends on the hardware of the CPS. For this reason, RTLola provides a preliminary analysis that can be concretized given the concrete target platform. The preliminary analysis computes a) the complexity of each evaluation cycle given a certain event or point in time, and b) the parallelizability of the specification.

For the former metric, note that the monitor starts evaluation cycles either when it receives an event, or at predetermined points in time (*deadlines*). An event always updates a set of input streams and a statically determined set of output streams. Recall the mission-level specification computing the deviation from the flight path including the `deviation_disj` stream. The specification declares two input streams, thus allowing for three possible non-empty events. An event covering either `velocity` stream but not the other only triggers an evaluation of `deviation_disj`. Only if the event covers both inputs, `deviation` and the trigger are evaluated as well.

Consider a specification containing periodic streams and suppose the monitor has a deadline at time t. It then evaluates all periodic streams due at t, i.e., all streams with frequency π where $\pi \cdot t$ is a natural number. Thus, the set of streams affected by an evaluation cycle is pre-determined.

The next step in the analysis is concerned with *evaluation layers* They are closely related to the parallelizability of the monitor as they indicate how many stream evaluations can take place at once. The analysis yields a partition of the set of streams where all streams within an element of the partition are *independent*, enabling a parallel evaluation. The (in-)dependence relation is based on the dependency graph. If a stream accesses another *synchronously*, i.e., without an offset, than the target stream needs to be evaluated before the accessing stream. This definition entails an *evaluation order* on output streams. The aforementioned partition is then the coarsest partition such that any two streams in the same set are incomparable with respect to the transitive closure of the evaluation order. Each element of the partition is an evaluation layer. By construction, streams within the same layer can be evaluated in an arbitrary order—in particular also in parallel. The order in which layers are evaluated, however, still needs to follow the evaluation order. In the example specification before, the partition would be {{wp, pos, start} < {exp_dist, dist_since_wp} < {distance_deviation} < {deviations, trigger_warn} < {trigger_err}}.

The evaluation layer analysis immediately provides information regarding the parallelizability of the monitor. The running time analysis takes the number of evaluations into account as well as how many streams are affected by an evaluation cycle, and how complex their expressions are. Intuitively, if an event or deadline affects streams in a multitude of layers, then the evaluation is slow as computations depend on each other and thus require a sequential order. Conversely, if an event only affects few streams, all within the first layer, the evaluations are independent and thus highly parallelizable. As a result, the running time of the monitor is low.

Note, however, that for software monitors the degree to which computations should run in parallel requires careful consideration, since spawning threads incurs a constant overhead. For hardware monitors, the overhead does not apply.

3   Compilation: Generating Monitors

While interpretation of specifications enables rapid prototyping, its logic is far more complex than a compiled monitor, at the same time resulting in subpar performance. This renders compilation preferable. Additionally, the compiler can inject additional information into the generated code. Such annotations can benefit the certification process of the CPS either by providing a notion of traceability, or by outright enabling the static verification of the monitor. The target platform of the compilation can either be hardware or software, both coming with advantages and drawbacks.

In this section, I will present and discuss a hardware compilation for RTLola specifications, and a software compilation for Lola, i.e., a subset of RTLola, with verification annotations.

3.1   RTLola on FPGA

Realizing an RTLola specification on hardware has several advantages. For one, the hardware monitor does not share resources with the controller of the system apart from power, eliminating potential negative interference. Moreover, special purpose hardware tends to be smaller, lighter, and require less energy than their general purpose counterparts. Secondly, hardware enables parallel computations at minimal cost. This synergizes well with RTLola, where output streams within the same evaluation layer can be evaluated in parallel.

The realization of RTLola on hardware [7] works in two steps: an RTLola specification is translated into VHDL code, out of which an FPGA (field-programmable gate array) implementation is synthesized. The synthesis provides additional static information regarding the required board size in terms of memory[2] and lookup-up tables. This allows for validating whether the available hardware suffices to host the monitor. Moreover, the synthesis indicates the idle and peak power consumption of the monitor, information that is invaluable when integrating the monitor into the system.

The aforementioned advantages are not only valid for FPGA but also for other hardware realization such as application-specific integrated circuits (ASIC) and complex programmable logic device (CPLD). While ASIC have significant advantages over FPGA when it comes to mass-producibility, power consumption and performance, FPGA are preferable during the development phase as they are orders of magnitude cheaper, have a lower entry barrier, and allow for rapid development. CPLD, on the other hand, are just too small to host realistic/nontrivial specifications.

Hardware Realization. Managing periodic and event-based streams under a common hardware clock poses the key challenging when realizing an RTLola monitor in hardware. Yet, this distinction only affects the part of the monitor logic deciding *when* to evaluate stream expressions; the evaluation itself is agnostic to it. For this reason, the monitor is split into two modules. The *high-level controller* (HLC) is responsible for scheduling evaluations, i.e., to decide when and which streams to evaluation. It passes the information down to the second module, the *low-level controller* (LLC), which is responsible for managing the evaluation. A FIFO queue between the controllers buffers information sent from the HLC to the LLC.

Recall the specification from Sect. 2 checking for strong deviations in readings of two velocimeters. As a running example for the hardware compilation, we extend the specification by the following declarations.

```
output avg_dev @10mHz := dev.aggregate(over: 10min, using: avg)
trigger avg_dev > 4 "High average deviation."
```

---

[2] The hardware realization might require temporary registers and working memory. This can slightly increase the computed memory consumption.

The specification checks whether two velocimeters disagree strongly over three consecutive measurements and whether the average disagreement is close to the disagreement-threshold. Note that all streams are event-based except for avg_dev and the second trigger.

Figure 3 illustrates the overall structure of the monitor. As can be seen, the HLC accepts input events from the monitored system. Such an event has a fixed size of $2 \cdot (32 + 1)$ bits, i.e., 32 due to the input types and an additional bit per stream to indicate whether the stream received an update. For periodic streams, the HLC has access to the system clock. Based on the current time and arrival of events, the HLC triggers evaluation cycles by sending relevant information to the queue while rising the *push* signal. Such a data package consists of $2 \cdot (32 + 1) + 64 + 5$ bits. The first component of the sum represents the potential input event. If the evaluation only serves to update periodic streams, these bits will all be 0. The following 64 bits contain the timestamp of the evaluation, crucial information for the computation of sliding window expressions. The last 5 bits each represent an output stream or trigger and indicate whether the respective entity is affected by the evaluation cycle. As a result, the LLC does not have to distinguish between event-based and periodic streams; it merely has to evaluate all streams the HLC marked as affected.

The communication between the queue and the LLC consists of three data lines: the *pop* bit is set by the LLC and triggers the queue to send another data packet down to it—provided the *empty* bit is 0. In this case, the queue puts the oldest evaluation information on the *dout* wires.

Internally, the LLC consists of two state machines. The first one handles the communication with the queue. While the first machines resides in the *eval* state, the second state machine manages the evaluation. To this end, it cycles through different states, each representing an evaluation layer. The first state ("1") copies the information about input stream updates into the respective memory region. In each consecutive state, the monitor enables the modules responsible for evaluating the respective stream expression by raising the *enable* bit. It then waits on the *done* bits. Upon receiving all of them, the monitor proceeds to the next state. During this process, the outputs of trigger expressions are not persisted locally, but directly piped down to the monitored system.

Resource Consumption. When compiling the specification into VHDL and realizing it on a ZYNQ-7 ZC702 Evaluation Board, using the Vivado Design Suite[3], the hardware synthesizer provides information regarding the overall resource consumption. In this case, the monitor requires 10,700 lookup tables and 1735 bits of memory. The energy consumption amounts to 144 μW when idle, and 1.699 W under peak pressure. Even though the specification is rather small, it gives a glimpse at how low the resource consumption actually is. Baumeister et al. [6] successfully synthesized larger specifications designed for autonomous aircraft on the same FPGA.

---

[3] https://www.xilinx.com/products/design-tools/vivado.html.

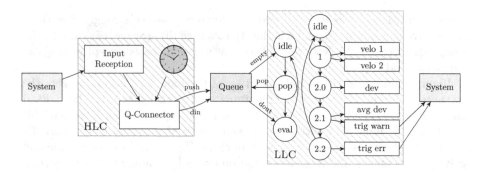

Fig. 3. Illustration of the hardware realization of an RTLola monitor. It is composed of two components connected by a queue. The HLC receives inputs from the system and manages the timing of periodic and event-based streams. The LLC controls the evaluation process with a state machine where each state represents an evaluation layer of the underlying specification. The LLC passes violations of safety properties on to the system.

3.2 Lola to Rust

While a compilation of RTLola specifications into software is a topic for future work, a compilation for Lola does exist, presented by Finkbeiner et al. [15]. Lola [10] is a synchronous and discrete-time subset of RTLola. As such, it does not have a notion of real-time, thus neither sliding windows nor periodic streams are an issue. Moreover, Lola assumes all input streams to receive new values at the same time, prompting all output streams to be extended as well. This renders sample and hold accesses obsolete. Lola does, however, allow for future lookups, i.e., a stream may refer to the *next* value of another stream.

The example specification for the software compilation is another mild variation of the velocimeter cross-validation from Sect. 2. The modification replaces the `lasting_dev` stream by the following:

```
output lasting_dev := dev > 5 ∧ dev.offset(by: +1, default: 0) > 5 ∧
    dev.offset(by: -1, default: 0) > 5
```

Here, `lasting_dev` access the last, current and *next* value of `deviation`.

The compilation presented in this section translates the Lola specification into Rust[4] code that enables a static verification. Rust as a target language comes with several advantages. First, as a system language with an LLVM[5] backend, it is compatible with a wide array of platforms. Secondly, a key paradigm of the language is to enforce static checks on the code and thus reduce dynamic failures. This goes hand in hand with the goal of verifying the functional correctness and absence of dynamic failures of the generated monitor. Lastly, Rust allows for fine-grained control low-level constructs such as memory management, enabling

---

[4] https://www.rust-lang.org/.

[5] https://llvm.org/.

the programmer—or in the case, the Lola compiler—to write highly performant code.

The compiler injects verification annotations into the code as well. This enables the static verifier Viper to prove functional correctness of the monitor in two steps. First, it relates the working memory of the monitor to the semantic model of Lola. The key challenge here is that the semantics of Lola argues about infinite data sequences while the monitor operates on a finite working memory. Next, the verification relates the verdict of the monitor, i.e., the boolean indicator of whether a trigger should go off is correct given the current state of the working memory. In combination we can conclude that the monitor only emits an alarm if the semantic model demands so.

Dealing with Fallible Accesses. While future offsets provide a natural way to specify temporal dependencies, the monitor has to compensate for them by delaying the evaluation of the accessing streams. Thus, the evaluation of `lasting_dev` needs to be delayed by one step since they access a future value of `dev`. This delay is propagated through the dependency graph: the trigger transitively accesses a future value, so its evaluation needs to be delayed, too.

With the delay operation in place, accesses via a future offset will always succeed up until the system terminates, and thus no longer produces new inputs. In this case, the monitor continues to evaluate delayed streams until they have the same length as the input streams. This phase is the *postfix* phase of the monitor execution. Here, future offsets fail because the accesses values do not exist and never will. Similarly, past offsets fail at the beginning of the monitor execution, the *prefix*.

In the very first iteration of the monitor, only the inputs and `dev` can be evaluated, the other output stream and the trigger are delayed. In the next iteration, the input is updated and all output streams and the trigger are evaluated. Evaluating `lasting_dev` accesses both values of `dev`. In addition to that, the past lookup refers to the -1st value of `altitude`, a value, that will never exist. Thus, the monitor statically substituted the access with the default value.

Clearly, the monitor goes through three phases: a prefix, in which past offsets fail unconditionally, a loop phase, in which both past and future offsets succeed unconditionally, and a postfix phase, in which future offsets fail unconditionally. In light of this, the compiler faces a trade-off: it can generate a general-purpose loop containing conditional statements resolving offsets dynamically, or it can take the three phases into account by generating code specific to them. The former option contains conditional statements not found in the original specification, resulting in far less performant code. The latter option, however, requires more code, resulting in a larger executable file. The compiler outlined in this section opts for the latter option.

```
                                    Prelude
struct Memory { ... }
impl Memory { ... }
[[ Evaluation Functions ]]
fn get_input() ->
       Option<(T_{s_1}, ..., T_{s_ℓ})> {
  [[ Communicate with system ]]
}
fn emit(output: &(T_{s_1}, ..., T_{s_n})) {
  [[ Communicate with system ]]
}
fn main() {
  let mut memory = Memory::new();
  let early_exit = prefix(&mem);
  if !early_exit {
    while let Some(input) = get_input() {
      mem.add_input(&input1);
      [[ Evaluation Logic ]]
    }                        Monitor Loop
  }
  postfix(&mem);
}
```

```
fn prefix(mem: &mut Memory) -> bool {
  if let Some(input) = get_input() {
    mem.add_input(&input);
    [[ Evaluation Logic ]]
  } else {
    return true // Jump to Postfix.
  }
  [[ Repeat η_φ^← times. ]]
  false   // Continue with Monitor Loop.
}
                        Execution Prefix
```

```
fn postfix(mem &Memory) {
  [[ Evaluation Logic ]]
  [[ Repeat η_φ^→ times. ]]
}
                        Execution Postfix
```

Listing 1.1: Structure of the generated Rust code. The prelude is highlighted in orange, the monitor loop in blue, the execution prefix in green, and the execution postfix in violet.

Listing 1.1 illustrates the abstract structure of the generated Rust code. The first portion of the code is the *prelude* containing declaration for data structures and I/O functions. Most notably, the `Memory` struct represents the monitor's working memory and is of a fixed size. For this, it utilizes the memory analysis from Sect. 2.2. Note also, that the `get_input` function returns an optional value: either it contains new input data or it indicates that the system terminated.

The `main` function is the entry point of the monitor. It allocates the working memory and transitions to the prefix. Here, the monitor code contains a static repetition of code checking for a new input, and evaluating all streams. In the evaluation, stream access are either translated into immediate access to memory or substituted by constant default values. The `prefix` function returns a boolean flag indicating whether the system terminated before the prefix was completed. This prompts the `main` function to jump to the postfix immediately. Otherwise, the main monitor loop begins following the same scheme of the prefix: retrieve new input values, commit them to memory, evaluate streams, repeat until the system terminates. Note that all stream accesses during the monitor loop translate to accesses to the working memory. Lastly, the `main` function triggers the computation of the postfix. The structure is similar to the prefix except that it does not check for new input values.

The evaluation logic for streams is a straight-forward translation of the Lola specification as conditional statements, constants, and arithmetic functions are syntactically and semantically almost identical in Lola and Rust. Only stream accesses requires special attention as they boil down to accesses to the `Memory` struct. Lastly, the compilation has to order the evaluation of streams to comply with the evaluation order from Sect. 2.2. Streams in the same evaluation can be ordered arbitrarily or parallelized. The latter leads to a significant runtime overhead and only pays off if computational complexity of the stream expressions is sufficiently high.

Verification. The compilation injects verification annotations in the Rust code to enable the Prusti [1] plugin of the Viper framework [28] to verify functional correctness of the monitor. The major challenge here is to verify that the finite memory available to the monitor suffices to accurately represent the infinite evaluation model of Lola. The compilation achieves this by introducing a dynamically growing list of values, the ghost memory. With this, the correctness proof proceeds in two steps. First, whenever the monitor receives or computes a new value, it commits it both to the ghost memory and the working memory. Here, the working memory acts as a ring buffer: as soon as its capacity is reached, the addition of a new value overwrites and thus evicts the oldest value. Therefore, the working memory is an excerpt of the ghost memory and thus the evaluation model. Ergo, the computation of new values is valid with respect to the evaluation model because memory accesses yield the same values as the evaluation model would. The newly computed, correct values, are then added into the memory, concluding the inductive proof of memory compliance.

Secondly, the verdict of a trigger in the theoretical model needs to be equivalent to the concrete monitor realization. This amounts to proving that the trigger condition was translated properly. Here, memory accesses are particularly interesting, because the theoretical computation uses entries of the ghost memory whereas the realization accesses the working memory only. The agreement of the ghost memory and the working memory for the respective excerpts conclude this proof.

Note that for the monitor the ghost memory is write-only, whereas the verification procedure "reads" it, i.e., it refers to its theoretical values. The evaluation logic of the monitor uses data from the system to compute output values. Different components of the verification than access these values either directly or over the ghost memory (GM). Clearly, the information flow is unidirectional: information flows from the monitor to the verification but not vice versa. As a result, upon successful verification, the ghost memory can safely be dissected from the realization.

Conclusion. Not only does the compilation from Lola to Rust produce performant runtime monitors, the injection of verification annotations answers the question *"Quis custodiet ipsos custodes?*[6]*"* rendering it an important step into the direction of verified runtime monitor. The applicability of Lola for CPS is limited to high-level properties where neither asynchrony, nor real-time play a significant role. Further research in this direction especially relating to RTLola can significantly increase the value and practical relevance of the compilation.

---

[6] *"Who will guard the guards themselves?"*.

4   Integration and Post-mortem

A key task when integrating a monitor into a CPS is finding a suitable spot in the system architecture. Improper placement can lead to ineffective monitoring or negative interference, jeopardizing the safety of the entire system.

4.1   Integration

The integration is considerably easier when the architecture is not yet fully determined. When adding the monitor retroactively, only minimal changes to the architecture are possible. Larger changes would render previous tests void since the additional component might physically change the system, e.g. in terms of weight distribution and power consumption, or logically offset the timing of other components. Consider, for example, a monitor that relies on dedicated messages from the controller as input data source. If the processor of the controller was already almost fully utilized, the additional communication leads to the controller missing deadlines. This can lead to safety hazards, as timing is critical for the safe operation of a CPS. Taking the placement of the monitor into account early on increases the degree of freedom, which helps avoid such problems.

The amount of interference the monitor imposes on the system also depends on the method of instrumentation. Non-intrusive instrumentation such as bus snooping grants the monitor access to data without affecting other modules. The effectiveness of this approach hinges on the amount of data available on the bus.

Consider, for example, the system architecture of the autonomous aircraft superARTIS of the German Aerospace Center (DLR) depicted in Fig. 4. When integrating a monitor for the optical navigation rail into the aircraft [6], the monitor was placed near the logging component. By design, the logger had access to all relevant data. This enabled monitoring of properties from the entire spectrum: The specification contained single-sensor validation, cross-validation, and geo-fence compliance checks. Note that in this particular case, the utilization of the logger was low. This allowed it to forward the information from the bus to the monitor. In a scenario where performance is critical, snooping is the preferable option.

4.2   Post-mortem Analysis

After termination of a flight, the post-mortem analysis allows for assessing the performance of the system and finding culprits for errors. The analysis relies on data recorded during the mission; a full record enables a perfect reconstruction of the execution from the perspective of the system. Resource restrictions, however, limit the amount of data, so full records are often not an option. Thus, data needs to be filtered and aggregated rigorously.

A main task of the monitor is exactly this: refining input data by filtering and aggregation to obtain an accurate assessment of the system state. Based on this assessment, the monitor determines whether a property is violated. While

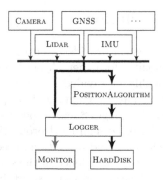

(a) An image of the superARTIS aircraft.

(b) A schematic of the superARTIS system architecture.

Fig. 4. Information on the superARTIS aircraft of the German Aerospace Center.

this binary verdict is the major output of the monitor, the intermediate results provide valuable insight into the evolution of the system over time. Hence, logging this data can improve the post-mortem analysis and alleviates the need to filter and aggregate data in another component as well.

5   Bibliographic Remarks

Early work on runtime monitoring was mainly based on temporal logics [12, 17,18,21,22,33]. Their notion of time was limited to discrete time, leading to the development of real-time logics like STL [24] and MTL [20]. Not only do algorithms for runtime monitoring exist for these logics [3,4,11,29], there is also work realizing it on an FPGA [19]. The R2U2 [27,35] tool in particular implements MTL monitors on FPGA while allowing for future-time specifications. Further, there are approaches for generating verified monitors for logics [2,34].

Apart from these temporal logics, there are other specification languages specifically for CPS such as differential dynamic logic [32]. The ModelPlex [26] framework translates such a specification into several verified components monitoring both the environment w.r.t. the assumed model and the controller decisions.

Other approaches—such as the one presented in this paper—completely forgo logics. Similar to the compiler from Lola to Rust, there is a verified compiler for synchronous Lustre [8] programs to C code. Moreover, the Copilot [30,31] toolchain is based on a functional, declarative, stream language with real-time capabilities. Copilot enables the verification of generated monitors using the CBMC model checker [9]. As opposed to the verification with Viper, their verification is limited to the absence of various arithmetic errors, lacking functional correctness.

In terms of integration, both the R2U2 [27] and the Copilot [31] tool were successfully integrated into an aircraft.

6   Conclusion

In this paper, I provided an overview of recent work on the development of a runtime monitor for cyber-physical systems from design to integration. The process can roughly be divided into three phases. In the specification phase, specifiers transform natural language descriptions of properties into a suitable formal specification language. Such properties range from low-level properties validating a single sensor to high-level properties overseen the quality of the entire mission. Type checking and validation based on log data from previous or simulated missions increase confidence in the specification. The compilation phase transforms the specification into an executable software or hardware artifact, potentially injecting annotations to enable static verification of the monitor. This process can help increase the effectiveness of the monitor, which directly translates into safer systems.

Acknowledgements. This paper is based on a tutorial at the 20th International Conference on Runtime Verification. The work summarized in this paper is based on several earlier publications [6,7,13–15] and I am grateful to all my co-authors. I especially would also like to thank Jan Baumeister and Bernd Finkbeiner for providing valuable feedback and comments.

References

1. Astrauskas, V., Müller, P., Poli, F., Summers, A.J.: Leveraging rust types for modular specification and verification. Proc. ACM Program. Lang. **3**(OOPSLA), 147:1–147:30 (2019). https://doi.org/10.1145/3360573
2. Basin, D., et al.: A formally verified, optimized monitor for metric first-order dynamic logic. In: Peltier, N., Sofronie-Stokkermans, V. (eds.) IJCAR 2020. LNCS (LNAI), vol. 12166, pp. 432–453. Springer, Cham (2020). https://doi.org/10.1007/978-3-030-51074-9_25
3. Basin, D.A., Klaedtke, F., Müller, S., Zalinescu, E.: Monitoring metric first-order temporal properties. J. ACM **62**(2), 15:1–15:45 (2015). https://doi.org/10.1145/2699444
4. Basin, D.A., Krstic, S., Traytel, D.: AERIAL: almost event-rate independent algorithms for monitoring metric regular properties. RV-CuBES **2017**, 29–36 (2017)
5. Baumeister: Tracing Correctness: a practical Approach to Traceable Runtime Monitoring. Master thesis, Saarland University (2020)
6. Baumeister, J., Finkbeiner, B., Schirmer, S., Schwenger, M., Torens, C.: RTLola cleared for take-off: monitoring autonomous aircraft. In: Lahiri, S.K., Wang, C. (eds.) CAV 2020. LNCS, vol. 12225, pp. 28–39. Springer, Cham (2020). https://doi.org/10.1007/978-3-030-53291-8_3
7. Baumeister, J., Finkbeiner, B., Schwenger, M., Torfah, H.: FPGA stream-monitoring of real-time properties. ACM Trans. Embedded Comput. Syst. **18**(5s), 88:1–88:24 (2019). https://doi.org/10.1145/3358220
8. Bourke, T., Brun, L., Dagand, P., Leroy, X., Pouzet, M., Rieg, L.: A formally verified compiler for lustre. In: Cohen, A., Vechev, M.T. (eds.) PLDI 2017, pp. 586–601. ACM (2017). https://doi.org/10.1145/3062341.3062358

9. Clarke, E., Kroening, D., Lerda, F.: A tool for checking ANSI-C programs. In: Jensen, K., Podelski, A. (eds.) TACAS 2004. LNCS, vol. 2988, pp. 168–176. Springer, Heidelberg (2004). https://doi.org/10.1007/978-3-540-24730-2_15

10. D'Angelo, B., et al.: Lola: runtime monitoring of synchronous systems. In: TIME 2005, pp. 166–174. IEEE Computer Society Press, June 2005

11. Deshmukh, J.V., Donzé, A., Ghosh, S., Jin, X., Juniwal, G., Seshia, S.A.: Robust online monitoring of signal temporal logic. Formal Methods Syst. Des. **51**(1), 5–30 (2017). https://doi.org/10.1007/s10703-017-0286-7

12. Drusinsky, D.: The temporal rover and the ATG rover. In: SPIN Model Checking and Software Verification, pp. 323–330 (2000). https://doi.org/10.1007/10722468_19

13. Faymonville, P., et al.: StreamLAB: stream-based monitoring of cyber-physical systems. In: Dillig, I., Tasiran, S. (eds.) CAV 2019. LNCS, vol. 11561, pp. 421–431. Springer, Cham (2019). https://doi.org/10.1007/978-3-030-25540-4_24

14. Faymonville, P., Finkbeiner, B., Schwenger, M., Torfah, H.: Real-time Stream-based Monitoring. CoRR abs/1711.03829 (2017). http://arxiv.org/abs/1711.03829

15. Finkbeiner, B., Oswald, S., Passing, N., Schwenger, M.: Verified rust monitors for lola specifications. In: RV 2020. LNCS. Springer (2020)

16. Finkbeiner, B., Schmidt, J., Schwenger, M.: Simplex architecture meets RTLola. In: MT@CPSWeek 2020 (2020). https://www.react.uni-saarland.de/publications/FSS20.pdf

17. Finkbeiner, B., Sipma, H.: Checking finite traces using alternating automata. Formal Methods Syst. Des. **24**(2), 101–127 (2004). https://doi.org/10.1023/B:FORM.0000017718.28096.48

18. Havelund, K., Rosu, G.: Synthesizing monitors for safety properties. TACAS **2002**, 342–356 (2002). https://doi.org/10.1007/3-540-46002-0_24

19. Jaksic, S., Bartocci, E., Grosu, R., Kloibhofer, R., Nguyen, T., Nickovic, D.: From signal temporal logic to FPGA monitors. MEMOCODE **2015**, 218–227 (2015). https://doi.org/10.1109/MEMCOD.2015.7340489

20. Koymans, R.: Specifying real-time properties with metric temporal logic. Real-Time Syst. **2**(4), 255–299 (1990). https://doi.org/10.1007/BF01995674

21. Kupferman, O., Vardi, M.Y.: Model checking of safety properties. Formal Methods Syst. Des. **19**(3), 291–314 (2001). https://doi.org/10.1023/A:1011254632723

22. Lee, I., Kannan, S., Kim, M., Sokolsky, O., Viswanathan, M.: Runtime assurance based on formal specifications. PDPTA **1999**, 279–287 (1999)

23. Li, J., Maier, D., Tufte, K., Papadimos, V., Tucker, P.A.: No pane, no gain: efficient evaluation of sliding-window aggregates over data streams. SIGMOD Rec. **34**(1), 39–44 (2005). https://doi.org/10.1145/1058150.1058158

24. Maler, O., Nickovic, D.: Monitoring temporal properties of continuous signals. In: FORMATS 2004 and FTRTFT 2004, pp. 152–166 (2004). https://doi.org/10.1007/978-3-540-30206-3_12

25. Meertens, L.: Algorithmics: towards programming as a mathematical activity (1986)

26. Mitsch, S., Platzer, A.: Modelplex: verified runtime validation of verified cyber-physical system models. Formal Methods Syst. Des. **49**(1–2), 33–74 (2016). https://doi.org/10.1007/s10703-016-0241-z

27. Moosbrugger, P., Rozier, K.Y., Schumann, J.: R2U2: monitoring and diagnosis of security threats for unmanned aerial systems. Formal Methods Syst. Des. **51**(1), 31–61 (2017). https://doi.org/10.1007/s10703-017-0275-x

28. Müller, P., Schwerhoff, M., Summers, A.J.: Viper: a verification infrastructure for permission-based reasoning. In: Jobstmann, B., Leino, K.R.M. (eds.) VMCAI 2016. LNCS, vol. 9583, pp. 41–62. Springer, Heidelberg (2016). https://doi.org/10.1007/978-3-662-49122-5_2

29. Nickovic, D., Maler, O.: AMT: A property-based monitoring tool for analog systems. FORMATS **2007**, 304–319 (2007). https://doi.org/10.1007/978-3-540-75454-1_22

30. Pike, L., Goodloe, A., Morisset, R., Niller, S.: Copilot: a hard real-time runtime monitor. In: Barringer, H., Falcone, Y., Finkbeiner, B., Havelund, K., Lee, I., Pace, G., Roşu, G., Sokolsky, O., Tillmann, N. (eds.) RV 2010. LNCS, vol. 6418, pp. 345–359. Springer, Heidelberg (2010). https://doi.org/10.1007/978-3-642-16612-9_26

31. Pike, L., Wegmann, N., Niller, S., Goodloe, A.: Copilot: monitoring embedded systems. ISSE **9**(4), 235–255 (2013). https://doi.org/10.1007/s11334-013-0223-x

32. Platzer, A.: Differential dynamic logic for hybrid systems. J. Autom. Reason. **41**(2), 143–189 (2008). https://doi.org/10.1007/s10817-008-9103-8

33. Pnueli, A.: The temporal logic of programs. In: FOCS 1977, pp. 46–57. IEEE Computer Society (1977). https://doi.org/10.1109/SFCS.1977.32

34. Schneider, J., Basin, D., Krstić, S., Traytel, D.: A formally verified monitor for metric first-order temporal logic. In: Finkbeiner, B., Mariani, L. (eds.) RV 2019. LNCS, vol. 11757, pp. 310–328. Springer, Cham (2019). https://doi.org/10.1007/978-3-030-32079-9_18

35. Schumann, J., Moosbrugger, P., Rozier, K.Y.: R2U2: monitoring and diagnosis of security threats for unmanned aerial systems. In: Bartocci, E., Majumdar, R. (eds.) RV 2015. LNCS, vol. 9333, pp. 233–249. Springer, Cham (2015). https://doi.org/10.1007/978-3-319-23820-3_15

36. Schwenger, M.: Let's not Trust Experience Blindly: Formal Monitoring of Humans and other CPS. Master thesis, Saarland University (2019)

37. Sha, L.: Using simplicity to control complexity. IEEE Softw. **18**(4), 20–28 (2001). https://doi.org/10.1109/MS.2001.936213

BDDs for Representing Data in Runtime Verification

Klaus Havelund[1]([✉]) and Doron Peled[2]

[1] Jet Propulsion Laboratory, California Institute of Technology, Pasadena, USA
klaus.havelund@jpl.nasa.gov
[2] Department of Computer Science, Bar Ilan University, Ramat Gan, Israel
doron.peled@gmail.com

Abstract. A BDD (Boolean Decision Diagram) is a data structure for the compact representation of a Boolean function. It is equipped with efficient algorithms for minimization and for applying Boolean operators. The use of BDDs for representing Boolean functions, combined with symbolic algorithms, facilitated a leap in the capability of model checking for the verification of systems with a huge number of states. Recently BDDs were considered as an efficient representation of data for Runtime Verification (RV). We review here the basic theory of BDDs and summarize their use in model checking and specifically in runtime verification.

1 Introduction

Achieving compact representation of Boolean functions has the immediate benefit of lowering the production costs and footprint of digital circuits. A later use of Boolean functions is analysis of software and hardware [9], where BDDs represent sets of states as Boolean functions. For these applications, there is a need not only to achieve a compact representation, but also to have efficient procedures for applying Boolean operators. In particular, the conjunction of Boolean functions that represent sets of states returns the intersection of these sets, and the disjunction returns their union.

More specifically, a *Boolean Decision Diagram* or BDD, is a rooted directed acyclic graph (DAG), with nonleaf nodes labeled by Boolean variables, and leafs labeled with 0 (*false*) or 1 (*true*). BDDs were already used for representing Boolean functions since the middle of the previous century [21]. However, it was only in the 80s that Bryant [6] presented their reduced ordered version (ROBDD), where the ordering between the Boolean variables are fixed along each path from the root to a leaf, and isomorphic parts are combined.

The ability to encode sets of states and relations between values and to apply Boolean operators on ROBDDs was exploited in *model checking* (see, [10]). It resulted

The research performed by the first author was carried out at Jet Propulsion Laboratory, California Institute of Technology, under a contract with the National Aeronautics and Space Administration. The research performed by the second author was partially funded by Israeli Science Foundation grant 1464/18: "Efficient Runtime Verification for Systems with Lots of Data and its Applications".

J. Deshmukh and D. Ničković (Eds.): RV 2020, LNCS 12399, pp. 107–128, 2020.
https://doi.org/10.1007/978-3-030-60508-7_6

in a huge increase in the size of systems that can be checked over previous techniques. Recently ROBDDs have been used to support *runtime verification* of execution traces containing large amounts of data, e.g., in monitoring of sequences with data-carrying events against first-order past-time LTL formulas [15]. In this paper we survey these applications of BDDs with emphasis on runtime verification.

The paper is organized as follows. Section 2 provides a brief introduction to BDDs. Section 3 outlines how to represent sets and relations with BDDs. Section 4 gives a brief introduction to their use in symbolic model checking. Section 5 presents the use of BDDs in runtime verification of first-order past-time LTL for representing the data quantified over in traces. Section 6 expands on this framework and illustrates how BDDs can be used to monitor timed events against first-order past-time LTL with time constraints.

2   Introduction to OBDDs

A Boolean function $f : \{0,1\}^k \mapsto \{0,1\}$ maps k-tuples of Boolean values 1 and 0 (for *true* and *false*, respectively) to Boolean values. Each k-tuple can be considered as an assignment $\Gamma : \mathcal{V} \mapsto \{0,1\}$ from variables in a fixed set $\mathcal{V}$ to a Boolean value. A Boolean function can be expressed using *literals*, which denote the Boolean variables, and Boolean operators: conjunction (*and*), disjunction (*or*) and negation (*not*). Conjunction is denoted here, in a standard way, using concatenation, disjunction is denoted with $+$ and negation is denoted by putting a line over the negated part; conjunction has priority over disjunction. A *minterm* is a conjunction of literals, e.g., $x_1\overline{x_3}x_4$ (standing for $x_1 \wedge \neg x_3 \wedge x_4$). Each Boolean function can be written in *disjunctive normal form* as a sum (disjunction) of minterms.

An OBDD $G = ((Q, v_0, E), \mathcal{V}, <, L)$ consists of the following components:

- (Q, v_0, E) is a rooted directed acyclic graph where
  - Q is finite set of *nodes*. Each non-leaf node has two distinguished *successor* nodes $l(v)$ and $h(v)$.
  - $v_0 \in Q$ is the *root* node.
  - $E \subseteq Q \times Q$ is a finite set of directed edges. Each non-leaf node has exactly two outgoing edges to its successors: the *low* edge $(v, l(v)) \in E$ and the *high* edge $(v, h(v)) \in E$.
- $\mathcal{V}$ is a finite set of *Boolean variables* (or *BDD variables* or simply *bits*).
- $<$ is a total order on $\mathcal{V}$, extended with two *maximal* values: 0 and 1.
- $L : Q \mapsto \mathcal{V} \cup \{0,1\}$ is a mapping that satisfies the following conditions:
  - The leafs are mapped to $\{0,1\}$ and the non-leaf nodes are mapped to $\mathcal{V}$.
  - If $(v, v') \in E$, then $L(v) < L(v')$, i.e., variables that label nodes on any path of the graph appear according to the order $<$, hence the name *Ordered BDD*.

An OBDD G represents a Boolean function (expression) over the variables $\mathcal{V}$. The interpretation of a BDD as a formula is based on the *Shannon expansion*

$$f = \overline{x}f[0/x] + xf[1/x] \tag{1}$$

where $f[0/x]$ ($f[1/x]$, respectively) denotes the function f when fixing x as 0 (1, respectively); thus, Eq. (1) separates the function f into two components, according to the truth value of the variable x. Each node $v \in Q$ in the OBDD represents the formula

$$f_v = \begin{cases} L(v), & \text{for a leaf } v \\ \overline{L(v)} f_{l(v)} + L(v) f_{h(v)}, & \text{for a non-leaf } v. \end{cases} \tag{2}$$

An OBDD G represents the formula f_{v_0} of the root node v_0. Another way to interpret an OBDD is that a path $F \subset E$ that starts at the root and ends at a leaf w corresponds to an assignment Γ, where for each nonleaf node $v \in Q$,

$$\Gamma(L(v)) = \begin{cases} 0, & \text{if } (v, l(v)) \in F \\ 1, & \text{if } (v, r(v)) \in F \end{cases} \tag{3}$$

and where each variable $x \in \mathcal{V}$ that does not label any node on the path $\Gamma(x)$ can be either 0 or 1. The Boolean function returns for the assignment Γ the truth value $L(w)$. We will, from now on, use the convention of calling OBDDs simply BDDs.

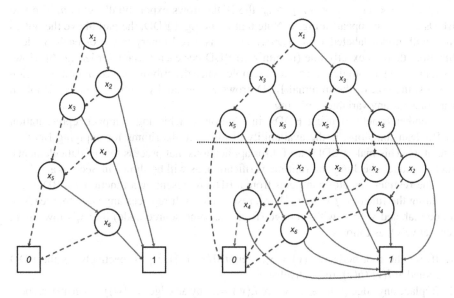

Fig. 1. The effect of variable order.

BDDs are typically depicted as in Fig. 1 (both left and right), where each nonleaf node is denoted with a circle, and the leafs are denoted with rectangles. Edges of the form $(v, l(v))$ are dashed, while edges of the form $(v, h(v))$ are full lines.

A benefit of using BDDs is the ability to *minimize* them, often producing a representation that is considerably smaller than other representations. The minimization allows combining isomorphic subgraphs, using the following rules, applied from the leafs upwards.

1. Combine all the leaf nodes that are labeled 1 and all the leaf nodes that are labeled 0. Redirect incoming edges to the resulting leafs.
2. When $l(f) = l(g)$ and $h(f) = h(g)$, combine the nodes f and g and redirect incoming edges to the single copy.
3. For a node f such that $l(f) = h(f)$, remove f and redirect its incoming edges to $l(f)$.

The term *minimal* BDD is sometimes used to emphasize that it is a *Reduced* Ordered Boolean Decision Diagram. The algorithm is linear in the size of the BDD[1].

As an example, consider the Boolean function f over the variables x_1, x_2 and x_3 that returns the parity (the sum modulo 2) of $x_1 + x_2 + x_3$. The full binary tree for this function, where $x_1 < x_2 < x_3$, appears in Fig. 2**A**. We obtain Fig. 2**B** by combining leafs with the same Boolean values, then Fig. 2**C** by combining the middle two x_3 nodes, and finally Fig. 2**D** by combining the exterior two x_3 nodes. No further minimization steps are available.

The order of variables in the BDD can greatly impact the size of the BDD. A classical example is the expression $x_1x_2 + x_3x_4 + \ldots x_{n-1}x_n$. Given the variable order $x_1 < x_2 < \ldots < x_{n-1} < x_n$, the BDD grows linearly with n. But for the order $x_1 < x_3 < \ldots x_{n-1} < x_2 < x_4 < \ldots < x_{n-2} < x_n$, the BDD grows exponentially with n. The two BDDs for $n = 6$ appear in Fig. 1. Note that in the right BDD, the part above the dotted line, with nodes labeled with $x_1, x_3, \ldots, x_{n-1}$, is a full binary tree. For each Boolean function, there is exactly one (minimized) BDD per each variable ordering [6]. However, in some pathological cases, for example, when describing bit-vector multiplication circuits, the size of the minimal BDD grows exponentially with the number Boolean variables for any variables ordering.

Another benefit of using BDDs, in addition to achieving compact representation of Boolean functions, is the availability of efficient algorithms for applying Boolean operators. This makes BDDs useful for applications that process sets of data elements, such as model checking and runtime verification, as will be shown in Sects. 4 and 5.

The **restrict** operator computes from a BDD representing a function f a BDD representing the function $f[0/x_i]$ ($f[1/x_i]$, respectively). It replaces any edge that leads to a node labeled with x_i with an edge (from the same source node) into x_i's low (high, respectively), as follows:

1. If, for the root node v, $L(v) = x_i$, then $f[0/x_i]$ ($f[1/x_i]$, respectively) is the BDD rooted at $l(v)$ ($h(v)$, respectively).
2. Replace any edge $(v, w) \in E$, where $L(w) = x_i$, by an edge $(v, l(w))$ ($(v, h(w))$, respectively), and remove w.
3. Minimize the BDD.

In Fig. 3, the left BDD represents some function f, and the right BDD is $f[1/x_2]$.

The operator **apply#** applies an arbitrary Boolean operator # (e.g., *and*, *or*) on BDDs. It is based on the fact that restriction distributes over function decomposition,

---

[1] To achieve linearity, for rule 2, bucket sort is applied to cluster together the nodes with the same variable and the same outgoing l edge. Then within each bucket, bucket sort is applied again according to the outgoing h edge.

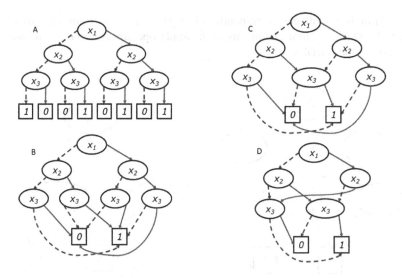

Fig. 2. A: original, B: reduce leafs, C: combine middle x_3's, D: combine other x_3's.

i.e.,

$$(f \# g)[a/x] = f[a/x] \# g[a/x]$$

for $a \in \{0, 1\}$ and $x \in \mathcal{V}$. Then, using Shannon's expansion, see Eq. (1), we have:

$$(f \# g) = \bar{x}(f \# g)[0/x] + x(f \# g)[1/x] = \bar{x}(f[0/x] \# g[0/x]) + x(f[1/x] \# g[1/x])$$

We calculate the BDD for $f \# g$, for BDDs f and g, using the following recursive procedure $apply\#(v_f, v_g)$, called initially with the roots of the two BDDs.

1. If v_f and v_g are leafs, then return a leaf v with $L(v) = L(v_f) \# L(v_g)$. Otherwise,
2. if $L(v_f) = L(v_g)$ (both parameters are labeled with the same variable), then return a node v with $l(v) = apply\#(l(v_f), l(v_g))$ and $h(v) = apply\#(h(v_f), h(v_g))$,
3. if $L(v_f) < L(v_g)$ (there is no node labeled with $L(v_f)$ in the current path of recursive calls in the BDD g) then return a node v with $l(v) = apply\#(l(v_f), v_g)$ and $h(v) = apply\#(r(v_f), v_g)$.
   The symmetric case is handled similarly.

A naive application of this procedure can repeatedly recalculate subgraphs starting from the same pair of BDD nodes. This is avoided by using a dynamic programming principle, where the results of the recursive calls are hashed according to the call parameters (v_f, v_g). This is demonstrated in Fig. 4, where some (arbitrary) Boolean operator # is applied to the two BDDs that appear at the left. The tree in the middle of Fig. 4 is obtained by using the recursive procedure without using dynamic programming. The DAG on the right is obtained using dynamic programming. Further reduction may be possible. Note that the leafs in the middle appear as pairs of nodes, whereas the corresponding leafs on the right appear as the Boolean # combinations between the leafs, e.g., R_5, S_4 in the middle part corresponds to $L(R_5) \# L(S_4)$ on the right. The size of the resulting BDD and the time complexity of the **apply** operator is limited to the product of the sizes of these BDDs.

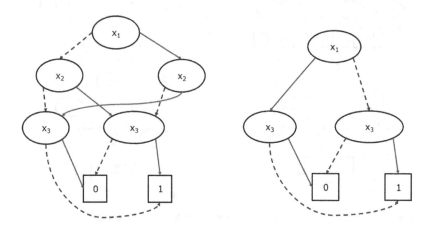

Fig. 3. A BDD f on the left, and $f[1/x_2]$ on the right.

The negation operator on BDDs is trivial; it requires reversing the labeling on the leafs, from 0 to 1 and from 1 to 0. Another useful operator is existential quantification over a Boolean variable, i.e., calculating $\exists x f$ for a BDD representing f. Since $\exists x f = f[0/x] \vee f[1/x]$, this operator can be implemented using **restrict** twice and then **apply** with $\# = \vee$ on the result.

Alternative Representations. *ZDDs*, for *Zero-suppressed Decision Diagrams*, were suggested by Minato [23]. ZDDs typically demonstrate better reduction than BDDs for Boolean functions in which the assignments that are satisfied are sparse. The reduction of ZDDs is slightly different than for BDDs. Reduction rules 1 and 2 remain the same. Reduction rule 3, which removes a node whose low and high edges point at the same node and redirects any incoming edge to its successor, is replaced with the following rule: a node v where its *high* successor is the constant 0, i.e., $L(h(v)) = 0$, is removed, and any incoming edge is redirected to $l(v)$.

Although ZDDs may produce a more compact representation than BDDs, the compaction that can be achieved is not exponential, but rather by a factor of the number of BDD variables $\mathcal{V}$.

Multi Terminal Binary Decision Diagrams (MTBDDs) [3] extend the BDD notation to mappings from Boolean variables to a domain $\mathcal{D}$ that can be different than the Boolean values. Then, the **apply** operator can be used with, e.g., arithmetic operators like addition and multiplication instead of the Boolean operators. This is useful, for example, for the symbolic verification of probabilistic systems [1].

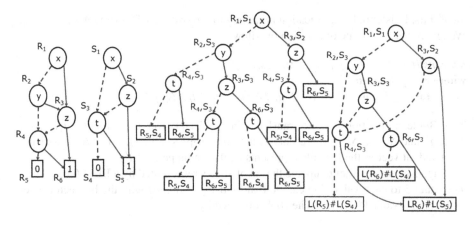

Fig. 4. *apply#* on BDDs (left) without (middle) and with (right) dynamic programming.

3 Representing Sets and Relations Using BDDs

A Boolean function, and consequently a BDD, can represent a set of integer values. Each integer value i is, in turn, represented as a bit vector (i.e., as a binary number) $x_m \ldots x_1$ where $i = x_1 \times 1 + x_2 \times 2 + \ldots x_m \times 2^m$. For example, the integer 6 can be represented as the bit vector $x_3 x_2 x_1 = 110$. To represent a *set* of integers, the BDD returns *true* for any bit vector that represents an element in the set. For example, to represent the set $\{4, 6\}$, we first convert 4 into the bit vector $x_3 x_2 x_1 = 100$ and 6 into $x_3 x_2 x_1 = 110$. The Boolean function over x_1, x_2, x_3 is then $\overline{x_1} x_3$, which returns *true* exactly for these two bit vector combinations. To keep common conventions, we write a list of Boolean variables with the least indexed variable at the left but bit vectors and binary numbers with the least significant digit at the right.

This representation can be extended to represent relations, or, equivalently, a set of tuples over integers. The Boolean variables are partitioned into n bit vectors $x_1 = x^1_{k_1}, \ldots, x^1_1, x_n = x^n_{k_n}, \ldots, x^n_1$, each one of them representing an integer value. These bit vectors are then concatenated.

3.1 BDDs over Integers

BDDs can represent a set of integers, where each value is kept as a bit vector, i.e., using its binary representation, using the BDD variables. This can be used, e.g., to represent integer values that an ALU processes or values of discrete timers. An advantage of this representation is that one can perform *arithmetic* operations and comparisons over sets of values, e.g., add a constant value Δ to each value in a set, or restrict a set to values that are bigger than a constant Δ, using BDD operations. We demonstrate how such operations are translated to BDDs.

The Boolean formula $addconst(t, t', \Delta)$ is satisfied by a triple of integer values t, t' and Δ, represented as the bit vectors $t_m \ldots t_1, t'_m \ldots t'_1$ and $\Delta_m \ldots \Delta_1$, respectively, such that $t' = t + \Delta$. The formula uses additional bits $r_1, \ldots, r_m$, where r_i is the *carry-over* from the ith bits. Existential quantification is applied to remove the BDD variables $r_1, \ldots, r_m$. We ignore here the issue of addition overflow.

$$addconst(t, t', \Delta) = \bigwedge_{1 \leq i \leq m} (t'_i \leftrightarrow (t_i \oplus \Delta_i \oplus r_i))$$
where $r_1 = false$ **and**
$\qquad$ **for** $1 \leq i < m$: $r_{i+1} = ((r_i \wedge (t_i \vee \Delta_i)) \vee (\neg r_i \wedge t_i \wedge \Delta_i))$

This Boolean function can be translated into a BDD over the variables $t_1, \ldots, t_m$, $t'_1, \ldots, t'_m$ and $\Delta_1, \ldots, \Delta_m$. It represents a relation on triples (t, t', Δ). When Δ is restricted to a fixed bit vector, the formula represents a relation on pairs (t, t').

Suppose that we want to update the set of values represented by a BDD B by adding a constant 3 to each value. We can do that by using *addconst* with the bit vector Δ set to the binary value $00 \ldots 011$. The BDD obtained by

$$\exists t_1 \ldots \exists t_m (B \wedge addconst(t, t', \Delta)) \tag{4}$$

is over the variables $t'_1, \ldots, t'_m$. It represents the values in B incremented by 3. Now we need to rename the variables $t'_1 \ldots t'_m$ back to $t_1, \ldots, t_m$. Renaming variables is a standard BDD operation, and we will denote this as $rename(C, t', t)$, where C is a BDD and t' and t are bit vectors. We obtain

$$rename(\exists t_1 \ldots \exists t_m (B \wedge addconst(t, t', \Delta)), t', t) \tag{5}$$

As another example, the formula $gtconst(t, \Delta)$ is satisfied by integers that are bigger than Δ (limited to the value $2^m - 1$, where the number of Boolean variables is m). Both t and Δ are integers represented as bit vectors, as before. Again, this is encoded as binary comparison, with Boolean variables $r_0, \ldots, r_m$ used to propagate the result of the comparison. As before, these variables are later removed using existential quantifiers

$$gtconst(t, \Delta) = r_m$$
where $r_0 = false$ **and**
$\qquad$ **for** $1 \leq i \leq m$: $r_i = ((t_i \wedge \neg \Delta_i) \vee ((t_i \leftrightarrow \Delta_i) \wedge r_{i-1}))$

The functions *addconst* and *gtconst* can be adapted for signed integers as well.

3.2   BDDs over Enumerations of Values

A disadvantage of the representation suggested in Sect. 3.1 is that the number of BDD variables required can be very large. Representing integers requires $\lceil \log p \rceil$ bits, where p is the largest possible value. The problem can intensify when the represented data is over strings with varying lengths.

To alleviate this problem, sets of values and relations can be represented as BDDs over *enumerations* of values. When a value associated with a variable in the specification appears for the first time in the computation (e.g., during runtime verification, see Sect. 5), a new *enumeration* is associated with it. Enumeration values can be assigned consecutively according to their binary value; however, a refined algorithm can reuse enumerations that were used for values that can no longer affect subsequent results, see [13]. A hash table is used to point from the value to its enumeration so that in subsequent appearances of this value the same enumeration will be used. The use of enumerations instead of the actual values allows a representation with a smaller number of bits. In addition, enumerations of values that are not far apart often share large bit patterns, which can also contribute to the BDD compactness.

BDDs can represent relations over mixed domains, where some of them are encoded using enumerations, and others as binary numbers.

4   Using BDDs for Model Checking

BDDs have gained a huge popularity in the automated verification of finite state systems referred to as *model checking*. Comprehensive analysis of systems requires reasoning about their states and execution sequences, and the main bottleneck is state space explosion. A BDD can represent a Boolean function that encodes a set of states. Then, it is possible to apply operators on BDDs to process sets of states, rather than handling the states one at a time.

Consider a finite-state system with state space St and initial states $I \subseteq St$. The property we want to check is that its execution must *never* arrive at states from $F \subseteq St$ (the *failure* states). Let $prec(s) \subseteq St$ be the set of states from which the system can move to $s \in St$ by performing one atomic transition, i.e., the *predecessor states* of s, and generalize it to $P(S) = \bigcup_{s \in S} prec(s)$. Checking that failure states cannot be reached from initial states is equivalent to checking that $I \cap P^*(F) \neq \emptyset$, where P^* denotes applying P repeatedly, 0 or more times. This can be described using the following pseudo-code:

$X1 := \emptyset; X2 := F;$
while $X1 \neq X2$ do
  $X1 := X2; X2 := X1 \cup P(X1);$
If $X1 \cap I \neq \emptyset$ then Return('failed');

Calculating $P(X1)$ and $X1 \cap I \neq \emptyset$ state by state is typically very expensive. This can severely limit the number of states that can processed. In *symbolic model checking* [9], all these operations are performed on BDDs, representing Boolean functions that encode sets of states. States are assignments a some fixed set of system (or program) variables, and a set of states corresponds to a relation over the domains of these variables. Section 3.1 demonstrated how arithmetic operators can be applied to sets of integer values. This would work for the simple case where states consist of the value of a single integer variables but can be extended to operate on relations over mixed domains.

Let $I, F, X1$ and $X2$ be represented as the BDDs $fI, fF, fX1$, and $fX2$, respectively. A less trivial step is encoding P: instead of a function P, one can use a relation between the current states, represented as bit vectors, using the Boolean variables $x = x_m \ldots x_1$, and the previous states, represented as bit vector using $x' = x'_m \ldots x'_1$. The BDD R represents this relation over the BDD variables of x and x'. $R \wedge fX1$ restricts this relation so that the current state values satisfy $fX1$. Then $\exists x_1 \ldots x_n(fX1 \wedge R)$ keeps only the state values of the predecessors to states satisfying $fX1$. The BDD operation *rename* is used to rename the variables of x' back to x. Finally, we apply disjunction to the obtained BDD and $fX1$ to obtain the union of the sets.

$fX1 := false; fX2 := fF;$
while $fX1 \neq fX2$ do
        $fX1 := fX2; fX2 := fX1 \lor rename(\exists x_1 \ldots x_n(fX1 \land R), x', x);$
If $(fX1 \land fI) \neq false$ then Return('failed');

5   Using BDDs for Runtime Verification

Runtime verification provides techniques for monitoring system executions against a formal specification. The monitored system is instrumented to report to the monitor on the occurrence of relevant events. The monitor observes the input events and keeps an internal *summary* of the prefix of the execution observed so far, which allows computing whether an evidence for a violation of the specification is already available.

Propositional Linear temporal logic (LTL) asserts about the evolution of an execution in time, using the future-time modalities $\Box$ (always), $\Diamond$ (sometimes), $\bigcirc$ (next-time) and $\mathcal{U}$ (until) [22]. It is possible to add to these modalities their corresponding past-time versions **H** (history), **P** (past), $\ominus$ (previous-time) and $\mathcal{S}$ (since), although adding them does not increase the expressive power [12].

RV often focuses on properties expressed in past-time Linear Temporal Logic (LTL), which includes the modalities **H**, **P**, $\ominus$ and $\mathcal{S}$, where it is implicitly assumed that the specification needs to hold for *all* the prefixes of the execution. This assumption is equivalent to prefixing each property with the $\Box$ operator. These properties correspond to temporal *safety properties* [2], where a failure can always be detected on a finite prefix as soon as it occurs [20].

First-order past-time LTL is obtained by adding predicates and quantification over data. An example of a first-order temporal specification is the following.

$$\forall f (close(f) \rightarrow \mathbf{P} open(f)) \tag{6}$$

It asserts that every file that is closed was opened before. Here, we need to keep in the summary a *set* of all the opened files so that we can compare them to the closing of files. In general, the summary in this case extends the one used for the propositional case by keeping for each subformula the set of assignments, essentially a relation between the free variables occurring in a formula and the values that make the formula true.

Traces. Assume a finite set of domains $D_1, \ldots, D_k$. Assume further that the domains are infinite, e.g., they can be the integers or strings[2]. Let P a set of *names* of unary predicates with typical instances p, q, r. Each predicate name p is associated with some domain $D_i = domain(p)$. A *ground predicate* is constructed from a predicate name and a constant of the same type. Thus, if the predicate name is p one can form ground predicates such as $p(\text{"gaga"})$ and $q(42)$. The restriction to unary predicates is not due to any principle limitation, but simplifies the presentation. An *event* is a finite set of ground predicates. For example, if $P = \{p, q, r\}$, then the set $\{p(\text{"gaga"}), q(42)\}$ is an event. A *trace* $\sigma = e_1 e_2 \ldots e_n$ is a finite sequence of events enumerated from 1. We denote the ith event e_i in σ by $\sigma[i]$.

---

[2] For dealing with finite domains see [15].

5.1 Syntax

Let V be a finite set of *variables*, with typical instances x, y, z. A predicate is constructed from a predicate name, and a variable or a constant (in which case it is a ground predicate) of the same type. Thus, if the predicate name p and the variable x are associated with the domain of strings, we have predicates like $p(\text{“gaga”})$ and $p(x)$. The syntax is as follows:

$$\varphi ::= true \mid p(a) \mid p(x) \mid \neg\varphi \mid (\varphi \wedge \varphi) \mid \ominus\varphi \mid (\varphi\, \mathcal{S}\, \varphi) \mid \exists x\, \varphi$$

The formula $p(a)$, where a is a constant in $domain(p)$, means that the ground predicate $p(a)$ occurs in the most recent event. The formula $p(x)$, for a variable $x \in V$, holds with a binding of x to the value a if a ground predicate $p(a)$ appears in the most recent event. The formula $\exists x\, \varphi$ has the obvious meaning that there exists some x such that φ (in which x can appear free) holds. In addition, We can derive the universal quantification as $\forall x\, \varphi = \neg\exists x\neg\varphi$ and other forms: $(\varphi \vee \psi) = \neg(\neg\varphi \wedge \neg\psi)$, $(\varphi \to \psi) = (\neg\varphi \vee \psi)$, $\mathbf{P}\, \varphi = (true\, \mathcal{S}\, \varphi)$, and $\mathbf{H}\, \varphi = \neg\mathbf{P}\, \neg\varphi$.

5.2 Semantics

Assignments of values to variables are at the core of this semantics. An *assignment* over a set of variables $W \subseteq V$ maps each variable $x \in W$ to a value from its associated domain $domain(x)$. For example $[x \to 5, y \to \text{“abc”}]$ maps x to 5 and y to "abc". By $\gamma[x \mapsto a]$ we mean the overriding of the assignment γ with the binding $[x \mapsto a]$. We denote by ε the empty assignment. Let $free(\varphi)$ be the set of free (i.e., unquantified) variables of a formula φ. Furthermore, let $\gamma|_{free(\varphi)}$ denote the restriction (projection) of an assignment γ to the free variables appearing in φ.

Predicate Semantics. We define a classic semantics for first-order past-time LTL. The assertion $(\gamma, \sigma, i) \models \varphi$ means that the trace $\sigma = e_1 e_2 \ldots e_n$ satisfies the formula φ for an assignment γ over $free(\varphi)$, where $1 \leq i \leq n$ (the relevant part of the execution is only the prefix $e_1 e_2 \ldots e_i$).

- $(\gamma, \sigma, i) \models true$.
- $(\gamma, \sigma, i) \models p(a)$ iff $p(a) \in \sigma[i]$.
- $(\gamma[x \mapsto a], \sigma, i) \models p(x)$ iff $p(a) \in \sigma[i]$.
- $(\gamma, \sigma, i) \models \neg\varphi$ iff not $(\gamma, \sigma, i) \models \varphi$.
- $(\gamma, \sigma, i) \models (\varphi \wedge \psi)$ iff $(\gamma, \sigma, i) \models \varphi$ and $(\gamma, \sigma, i) \models \psi$.
- $(\gamma, \sigma, i) \models \ominus\varphi$ iff $i > 1$ and $(\gamma, \sigma, i-1) \models \varphi$.
- $(\gamma, \sigma, i) \models (\varphi\, \mathcal{S}\, \psi)$ iff there exists $1 \leq j \leq i$ such that $(\gamma, \sigma, j) \models \psi$ and for all $j < k \leq i$ it holds that $(\gamma, \sigma, k) \models \varphi$.
- $(\gamma, \sigma, i) \models \exists x\, \varphi$ iff there exists $a \in domain(x)$ such that $(\gamma[x \mapsto a], \sigma, i) \models \varphi$.

For a finite trace σ, we write $\sigma \models \varphi$ to mean $\forall i(1 \leq i \leq length(\sigma) \to (\varepsilon, \sigma, i) \models \varphi)$.

Set Semantics. It helps the presentation of the BDD-based algorithm to first refine the semantics of the logic as a function that calculates the set of assignments satisfying a formula. Let $I[\varphi, \sigma, i]$ be the *interpretation function*, defined below, that returns a set of assignments such that $(\gamma, \sigma, i) \models \varphi$ iff $\gamma|_{free(\varphi)} \in I[\varphi, \sigma, i]$. The empty set of assignments $\emptyset$ behaves as the Boolean constant *false* and the singleton set $\{\varepsilon\}$ that contains the empty assignment behaves as the Boolean constant *true*. We define the union $\bigcup$ and intersection $\bigcap$ operators on sets of assignments, even if they are defined over non identical sets of variables. In this case, the assignments are extended to the union of the variables. Thus intersection between two sets of assignments A_1 and A_2 is defined like a database "join" operator; i.e., it consists of the assignments whose projection on the *common* variables agrees with an assignment in A_1 and with an assignment in A_2. Union is defined as the dual operator of intersection.

Furthermore, let A be a set of assignments over the set of variables W; we denote by $hide(A, x)$ (for "hiding" the variable x) the set of assignments obtained from A after removing from each assignment the mapping from x to a value. In particular, if A is a set of assignments over only the variable x, then $hide(A, x)$ is $\{\varepsilon\}$ when A is nonempty, and $\emptyset$ otherwise. $A_{free(\varphi)}$ is the set of all possible assignments of values to the variables that appear free in φ. We add a 0 position for each sequence σ (an "initial state"), where I returns the empty set for each formula. The assignment-set semantics is shown in the following. For all occurrences of i, it is assumed that $i \geq 1$.

- $I[\varphi, \sigma, 0] = \emptyset$.
- $I[true, \sigma, i] = \{\varepsilon\}$.
- $I[p(a), \sigma, i] = $ if $p(a) \in \sigma[i]$ then $\{\varepsilon\}$ else $\emptyset$.
- $I[p(x), \sigma, i] = \{[x \mapsto a] \mid p(a) \in \sigma[i]\}$.
- $I[\neg\varphi, \sigma, i] = A_{free(\varphi)} \setminus I[\varphi, \sigma, i]$.
- $I[(\varphi \wedge \psi), \sigma, i] = I[\varphi, \sigma, i] \bigcap I[\psi, \sigma, i]$.
- $I[\ominus\varphi, \sigma, i] = I[\varphi, \sigma, i-1]$.
- $I[(\varphi \mathrel{S} \psi), \sigma, i] = I[\psi, \sigma, i] \bigcup (I[\varphi, \sigma, i] \bigcap I[(\varphi S \psi), \sigma, i-1])$.
- $I[\exists x \, \varphi, \sigma, i] = hide(I[\varphi, \sigma, i], x)$.

5.3 Algorithm

A runtime verification algorithm for first-order LTL was presented in [4], based on applying database operations to relations. We present here an RV algorithm that is based on BDDs [15].

BDDs for Runtime Verification. We saw in Sect. 3 how a set of integers can be represented as a BDD: the BDD returning true for all bit-patterns corresponding to the binary encoding of the integers in the set. It was also explained how a value from an arbitrary value domain D, e.g. strings, can be represented as an integer while recording the mapping from the value to the integer in a hash map. E.g. the string "abc" can be represented as the number 6, which has the binary encoding 110. Consequently a set of values from the domain D can be represented as a BDD that is satisfied by the binary encodings of the corresponding integers.

First-order LTL formulas can contain multiple variables; a BDD can represent a set of assignments to variables as tuples of integers, each tuple position corresponding to a particular variable. This is the same as representing a relation over the domains of the variables. As shown in Sect. 3, such a tuple can be represented by concatenating the bit vectors of the individual tuple elements. For example, consider the assignment

$[x \rightarrow 5, y \rightarrow$ "abc"]. This can be thought of as the tuple $(5,$ "abc") if we associate the first tuple position with x and the second tuple position with y. If we map 5 and "abc" to integers, e.g. 1 and 2, the assignment can be thought of as being represented by the tuple $(1, 2)$. This tuple can then finally be represented as the concatenation of the binary representations 001 and 010 of these integers: 001010. This insight is the core idea in the BDD representation, first presented in [15], and implemented in the tool DEJAVU. Operations on BDDs, such as negation (corresponding to set complementation), conjunction (corresponding to set intersection), and disjunction (corresponding to set union) are very efficient. With k bits used for representing the enumerations for a variable, the BDD can represent 2^k values for each variable [8]. Furthermore, we often do not pay much in overhead for keeping surplus bits. Thus, we can start with an overestimated number of bits k such that it is unlikely to see more than 2^k different values for the domain they represent. We can also incrementally extend the BDD with additional bits when needed during runtime.

Example. Consider the formula $\exists x\, \mathbf{P}p(x)$ (there exists an x such that $p(x)$ occurred in the past). Consider furthermore the two-event trace $\langle\{p(\text{"ab"})\}, \{p(\text{"cd"})\}\rangle$. We will focus on the sub-formulas $p(x)$ and $\mathbf{P}p(x)$ and the BDDs that need to be calculated for them to keep a summary of the observed sequence of events during analysis of this trace. Figure 5 shows the generated BDDs. After the first event $p(\text{"ab"})$, when computing the BDD for $p(x)$, x is bound to "ab". We allocate an enumeration, an integer, in this case 0, and map "ab" to 0 in a hashmap. For the subformula $p(x)$ we create the BDD in Fig. 5a that is satisfied exactly by its binary value 000. For the subformula $\mathbf{P}p(x)$, we need a BDD that is satisfied by all the binary encodings of enumerations for values seen so far. Since we only observed the value "ab" as an argument to p, the same BDD in Fig. 5a is also used for $\mathbf{P}p(x)$. After the second event, the new value "cd" is mapped to the integer 1 (updating the hashmap), and the BDD in Fig. 5b that is satisfied by its binary value 001 is created for the subformula $p(x)$. For the subformula $\mathbf{P}p(x)$ we build the BDD in Fig. 5c that represents the set $\{\text{"ab"}, \text{"cd"}\}$, satisfied by the binary values 000 and 001. This BDD is obtained using the $\vee$-operation on the BDD in Fig. 5b constructed at the current step for $p(\text{"cd"})$ and the BDD in Fig. 5a, constructed in the previous step. Splitting the variable x into its bits: $x_3x_2x_1$, with x_1 the least significant bit, the figure shows the Boolean expressions over these bits corresponding to the BDDs.

Some Basic BDD Operations. We first introduce some basic functions used by the algorithm. Given some ground predicate $p(a)$ observed in the execution, matching with $p(x)$ in the monitored property, let **lookup**(x, a) be the enumeration of a in binary form. If this is the first occurrence of a, then it will be assigned a new enumeration. Otherwise, **lookup** returns the enumeration that a received before. We can use a counter[3], for each variable x, counting the number of different values appearing so far for x. When a new value appears, this counter is incremented, and the value is converted to the binary representation as discussed above. Enumerations that at any point in time have not yet been used represent the values not yet seen. In particular, we always leave one

---

[3] In [13] a form of *garbage collection* is applied, where enumerations for values that no longer affect the checked property are reclaimed for later reuse. This involves a more complicated enumeration mechanism.

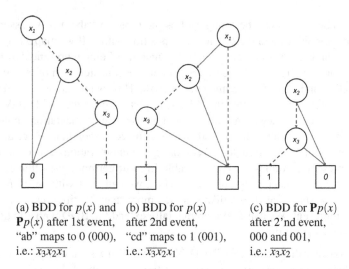

(a) BDD for $p(x)$ and $\mathbf{P}p(x)$ after 1st event, "ab" maps to 0 (000), i.e.: $\overline{x_3}\overline{x_2}\overline{x_1}$

(b) BDD for $p(x)$ after 2nd event, "cd" maps to 1 (001), i.e.: $\overline{x_3}\overline{x_2}x_1$

(c) BDD for $\mathbf{P}p(x)$ after 2'nd event, 000 and 001, i.e.: $\overline{x_3}\overline{x_2}$

Fig. 5. BDDs for the sub-formulas $p(x)$ and $\mathbf{P}p(x)$ for the trace $\langle \{p(\text{"ab"})\}, \{p(\text{"cd"})\} \rangle$, mapping "ab" to the integer 0 (binary 000), and mapping "cd" to the integer 1 (binary 001).

enumeration, $11\ldots11$ (all 1's), for this purpose. This enumeration is never allocated to represent observed data but represents all data not yet seen. This allows us to use a finite representation and quantify existentially and universally over *all* values in infinite domains. Where $11\ldots11$ represents the infinite set of values not yet seen. Even though at any point we may have not seen the entire set of values that will show up during the execution, we can safely (and efficiently) perform complementation: values that have not appeared yet in the execution are being accounted for and their enumerations are reserved already in the BDD before these values appear.

The function **build**(x,A) returns a BDD that represents the set of assignments where x is mapped to (the enumeration of) v for $v \in A$. For example, assume that we use three Boolean variables (bits) x_1, x_2 and x_3 for representing enumerations over x (with x_1 being the least significant bit), and assume that $A = \{a,b\}$, **lookup**$(x,a) = 011$ and **lookup**$(x,b) = 001$. Then **build**(x,A) is a BDD representation of the Boolean function $x_1 \wedge \neg x_3$.

Intersection and union of sets of assignments are translated simply to conjunction and disjunction of their BDD representation, respectively, and complementation becomes BDD negation. We will denote the Boolean BDD operators as **and**, **or** and **not**. To implement the existential (universal, respectively) operators, we use the BDD existential (universal, respectively) operators over the Boolean variables that represent (the enumerations of) the values of x. Thus, if B_φ is the BDD representing the assignments satisfying φ in the current state of the monitor, then **exists**$(\langle x_1, \ldots, x_k \rangle, B_\varphi)$ is the BDD that represents the assignments satisfying $\exists x\ \varphi$ in the current state. Finally, $\text{BDD}(\bot)$ and $\text{BDD}(\top)$ are the BDDs that return always 0 or 1, respectively.

The BDD Based Algorithm. The algorithm shown below extends the algorithm for the propositional case shown in [18]. It is based on the observation that the semantics of a formula in the current step can be cast in terms of the semantics of its subformulas in the current and the previous step. In particular, $\ominus\varphi$ holds in the current step if φ held in the previous step. The formula $(\varphi\,\mathcal{S}\,\psi)$ is equivalent to $(\psi\vee(\varphi\wedge\ominus(\varphi\mathcal{S}\psi)))$, which means that $(\varphi\,\mathcal{S}\,\psi)$ holds in the current step exactly if ψ holds now, or both φ holds now and $(\varphi\,\mathcal{S}\,\psi)$ held in the previous step. Thus, one only needs to look one step, or event, backwards in order to compute the new truth value of a formula. The algorithm operates on a summary of the sequence of events observed so far that consists of two vectors (arrays) of values indexed by subformulas: now calculated for the current event, and pre calculated for the previous event. While in the propositional case [18] these vectors contain Boolean values, here they contain BDDs.

1. Initially, for each subformula φ of the specification η, $\mathsf{now}(\varphi) := \mathrm{BDD}(\bot)$.
2. Observe a new event s (a set of ground predicates) as input.
3. Let $\mathsf{pre} := \mathsf{now}$.
4. Make the following updates for each subformula. If φ is a subformula of ψ then $\mathsf{now}(\varphi)$ is updated before $\mathsf{now}(\psi)$.
   - $\mathsf{now}(\textit{true}) := \mathrm{BDD}(\top)$.
   - $\mathsf{now}(p(a)) := $ if $p(a) \in s$ then $\mathrm{BDD}(\top)$ else $\mathrm{BDD}(\bot)$.
   - $\mathsf{now}(p(x)) := \mathbf{build}(x,A)$ where $A = \{a \mid p(a) \in s\}$.
   - $\mathsf{now}(\neg\varphi) := \mathbf{not}(\mathsf{now}(\varphi))$.
   - $\mathsf{now}((\varphi\wedge\psi)) := \mathbf{and}(\mathsf{now}(\varphi),\mathsf{now}(\psi))$.
   - $\mathsf{now}((\ominus\varphi)) := \mathsf{pre}(\varphi)$.
   - $\mathsf{now}((\varphi\,\mathcal{S}\,\psi)) := \mathbf{or}(\mathsf{now}(\psi),\mathbf{and}(\mathsf{now}(\varphi),\mathsf{pre}((\varphi\mathcal{S}\psi))))$.
   - $\mathsf{now}(\exists x\,\varphi) := \mathbf{exists}(\langle x_1,\ldots,x_k\rangle,\mathsf{now}(\varphi))$.
5. if $\mathsf{now}(\eta) = \mathrm{BDD}(\bot)$ then report "error".
6. Goto step 2.

Example. We shall illustrate the monitor generation using an example. Consider the following property stating that if a file f is closed, it must have been opened in the past with some access mode m (e.g. 'read' or 'write' mode):

$$\forall f\,(close(f) \longrightarrow \exists m\,\mathbf{P}\,open(f,m))\tag{7}$$

Figure 6 (left) shows the monitor evaluation function generated by DEJAVU for this property. It relies on the enumeration of the subformulas shown in the Abstract Syntax Tree (AST) in Fig. 6 (right). Two arrays are declared, indexed by subformula indexes: pre for the previous state and now for the current state, although here storing BDDs instead of Boolean values as in [18]. For each observed event, the function evaluate() computes the nowarray from highest to lowest index, and returns true (property is satisfied in this position of the trace) iff now(0) is not $\mathrm{BDD}(\bot)$. At composite subformula nodes, BDD operators are applied. For example for subformula 4, the new value is now(5).or(pre(4)), which is the interpretation of the formula $\mathbf{P}$ open(f, m) corresponding to the law: $\mathbf{P}\varphi = (\varphi\vee\ominus\mathbf{P}\varphi)$. As can be seen, for each new event, the evaluation of a formula results in the computation of a BDD for each subformula.

```
class Formula_p extends Formula {
  var pre: Array[BDD] = Array. fill (6)(False)
  var now: Array[BDD] = Array. fill (6)(False)
  var tmp: Array[BDD] = null
  val var_f :: var_m :: Nil =
    declareVariables("f", "m")

  override def evaluate(): Boolean = {
    now(5) = build("open")(V("f"),V("m"))
    now(4) = now(5).or(pre(4))
    now(3) = now(4).exist(var_m)
    now(2) = build("close")(V("f"))
    now(1) = now(2).not().or(now(3))
    now(0) = now(1).forAll(var_f)
    val result = !now(0).isZero
    tmp = now; now = pre; pre = tmp
    result
  }
}
```

Fig. 6. Monitor (left) and AST (right) for the property.

We shall evaluate the example formula on a trace. Assume that each variable f and m is represented by three BDD bits: $f_3 f_2 f_1$ and $m_3 m_2 m_1$ respectively, with f_1 and m_1 being the least significant bits. Consider the input trace, consisting of three events:

$$\langle \{open(input, read)\}, \{open(output, write)\}, \{close(out)\} \rangle \tag{8}$$

When the monitor evaluates subformula 5 on the first event $open$(input, read), it will create a bit string composed of a bit string for each parameter f and m. As previously explained, bit strings for each variable are allocated in increasing order: 000, 001, 010, ... For this first event the bit pattern $f_3 f_2 f_1$ is therefore mapped to 000 and the bit pattern $m_3 m_2 m_1$ is mapped to 000 as well. Hence, the assignment [f ↦ input, m ↦ read] is represented by the concatenation of the two bit strings $m_3 m_2 m_1 f_3 f_2 f_1 = 000000$, where the three rightmost bits represent the assignment of input to f and the three leftmost bits represent the assignment of read to m. Figure 7a shows the corresponding BDD B_1. In this BDD all the bits have to be zero in order to be accepted by the function represented by the BDD. We will not show how all the tree nodes evaluate, except observing that node 4 (all the seen values in the past) assumes the same BDD value as node 5, and conclude that since no $close(...)$ event has been observed, the top-level formula (node 0) holds at this position in the trace.

Upon the second $open$(output, write) event, new values (output, write) are observed as argument to the $open$ event. Hence a new bit string for each variable f and m is allocated, in both cases 001 (the next unused bit string for each variable). The new combined bit string for the assignments satisfying subformula 5 then becomes $m_3 m_2 m_1 f_3 f_2 f_1 = 001001$, forming a BDD representing the assignment [f ↦ output, m ↦ write], and appearing in Fig. 7b as B_2. The computation of the BDD for node 4 is

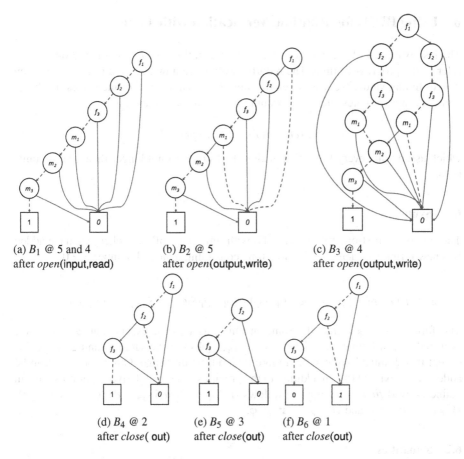

(a) B_1 @ 5 and 4
after *open*(input,read)

(b) B_2 @ 5
after *open*(output,write)

(c) B_3 @ 4
after *open*(output,write)

(d) B_4 @ 2
after *close*(out)

(e) B_5 @ 3
after *close*(out)

(f) B_6 @ 1
after *close*(out)

Fig. 7. Selected BDDs, named $B_1,\ldots,B_6$, computed after each event at various subformula nodes, indicated by B_i @ *node* (see Fig. 6), during processing of the trace $\langle\{open(\text{input,read})\},$ $\{open(\text{output,write})\}, \{close(\text{out})\}\rangle$.

computed by now(4) = now(5).or(pre(4)), which results in the BDD B_3, representing the set of the two assignments observed so far ($B_3 = $ **or**(B_1, B_2)).

Upon the third *close*(out) event, a new value out for f is observed, and allocated the bit pattern $f_3 f_2 f_1 = 010$, represented by the BDD B_4 for subformula 2. At this point node 4 still evaluates to the BDD B_3 (unchanged from the previous step), and the existential quantification over m in node 3 results in the BDD B_5, where the bits m_1, m_2 and m_3 for m have been removed, and the BDD compacted. Node 1 is computed as **or**(**not**(B_4), B_5), which results in the BDD B_6. This BDD represents all the possible bit patterns for f except for 010, which corresponds to the value out. This means, however, that the top-level formula in node 0 is not true (it is violated by bit pattern 010), and hence the formula is violated on the third event.

6 Using BDDs for Runtime Verification with Time

The last extension of the logic we shall consider in this paper is to allow properties to refer to the progress of time. The reported events are now assumed to appear with an integer timing value. We leave open the unit of measurement for time values (milliseconds, seconds, minutes, etc.). An example of such a specification is

$$\forall f \, (closed(f) \rightarrow \mathbf{P}_{\leq 20} \, open(f)) \qquad (9)$$

which asserts that every file f that is closed was opened not longer than 20 time units before.

6.1 Syntax

The syntax for first-order past-time LTL with time is as follows, where we have added two new formulas, each referring to a time constraint, a natural number $\delta \geq 0$:

$$\varphi ::= true \mid p(a) \mid p(x) \mid \neg\varphi \mid (\varphi \wedge \varphi) \mid \ominus\varphi \mid (\varphi S\varphi) \mid (\varphi S_{\leq\delta}\varphi) \mid (\varphi S_{>\delta}\varphi) \mid \exists x \, \varphi$$

The formula $(\varphi S_{\leq\delta}\psi)$ has the same meaning as $(\varphi S\psi)$, except that ψ must have occurred within δ time units. The formula $(\varphi S_{>\delta}\psi)$ has the same meaning as $(\varphi S\psi)$, except that ψ must have occurred more than δ time units ago. Other operators can be added, as shown in [14]. In addition to the previously defined derived operators we can define derived *timed* operators as follows: $\mathbf{P}_{\leq\delta}\varphi = (true S_{\leq\delta}\varphi)$, $\mathbf{P}_{>\delta}\varphi = (true S_{>\delta}\varphi)$, $\mathbf{H}_{\leq\delta}\varphi = \neg\mathbf{P}_{\leq\delta}\neg\varphi$, and $\mathbf{H}_{>\delta}\varphi = \neg\mathbf{P}_{>\delta}\neg\varphi$.

6.2 Semantics

A *timed event* is a pair (e,t) consisting of an event e and a time stamp t (a natural number). A *trace* $\sigma = (e_1,t_1)(e_2,t_2)\ldots(e_n,t_n)$ is a finite sequence of timed events, enumerated from 1. We denote the ith timed event (e_i,t_i) in σ by $\sigma[i]$. We let $\sigma_e[i]$ denote the event e_i and we let $\sigma_t[i]$ denote the time t_i.

We define the predicate semantics for the two new timed operators below. The semantic equations for the remaining formulas are as shown in Sect. 5.2, although defined on timed traces, and where $\sigma[i]$ should be read as $\sigma_e[i]$.

- $(\gamma,\sigma,i) \models (\varphi \, S_{\leq\delta} \, \psi)$ iff there exists $1 \leq j \leq i$ such that $\sigma_t[i] - \sigma_t[j] \leq \delta$ and $(\gamma,\sigma,j) \models \psi$, and for all $j < k \leq i$ it holds that $(\gamma,\sigma,k) \models \varphi$.
- $(\gamma,\sigma,i) \models (\varphi S_{>\delta}\psi)$ iff there exists $1 \leq j < i$ such that $\sigma_t[i] - \sigma_t[j] > \delta$ and $(\gamma,\sigma,j) \models \psi$, and for all $j < k \leq i$ it holds that $(\gamma,\sigma,k) \models \varphi$.

6.3 Algorithm

We describe now *changes* to the algorithm in Sect. 5.3 for handling the two new formulas with the timing constraints. Recall that for each subformula φ of a formula, the algorithm in Sect. 5.3 updates two array positions: $now(\varphi)$ and $pre(\varphi)$. These BDDs represent assignments to free variables that occur in the formula, represented as a concatenated bit vector of the binary enumerations of the values assigned to the BDD variables: $x_k^n \ldots x_1^n \ldots x_k^1 \ldots x_1^1$. To keep track of the time, each such bit vector is augmented with a bit vector $t_m \ldots t_1$ being the binary code of the time that has passed since that assignment was observed, obtaining $t_m, \ldots, t_1 x_k^n, \ldots, x_1^n \ldots x_k^1, \ldots, x_1^1.\ x_k^n, \ldots, x_1^n, \ldots, x_k^1, \ldots, x_1^1$ We add two new arrays, $\tau pre(\varphi)$ and $\tau now(\varphi)$, which for each subformula records the BDDs that include these time values. These BDDs are then used to compute $now(\varphi)$ and $pre(\varphi)$ by removing the time values (by existential quantification over the time values).

Example. We add a timing constraint to the formula (7), stating that when a file is closed it must have been opened within 3 time units in the past:

$$\forall f\,(close(f) \longrightarrow \exists m\,\mathbf{P}_{\leq 3}\,open(f,m)) \tag{10}$$

Let us apply this property to the following trace, which is the trace (8) augmented with the time values 1, 2, and 3 respectively. We keep the time constraint and time values small and consecutive to keep the BDD small for presentation purposes:

$$\langle(\{open(input,read)\},1),(\{open(output,write)\},2),(\{close(out)\},3)\rangle \tag{11}$$

The BDD for the subformula $\mathbf{P}_{\leq 3}\,open(f,m)$ at the third event $close(out)$, shown in Fig. 8, reflects that two (010 in binary) time units have passed since $open(input,read)$ occurred (follow leftmost path), and one time unit (001 in binary) has passed since $open(output,write)$ has occurred (follow rightmost path). The BDD is effectively an augmentation of the BDD in Fig. 7c, with the additional three BDD variables t_1, t_2, and t_3 for the timer values, with t_1 being the least significant bit.

The BDD-Based Algorithm with Time. When a new event occurs, for a subformula with a timing constraint δ, we need to update the timers in τnow that count the time that has passed since a tuple (assignment) of values satisfying the formula was observed. The difference between the clock value of the current event and the clock value of the previous one is Δ. In order to keep the representation of time small, $2\delta + 1$ is the biggest value of t that is stored. To see that this is sufficient, and necessary, consider the following. First, during computation, when we observe a Δ that is bigger than δ, we cut it down to $\delta + 1$ before we add to t. This is valid since we just need to know that it passed δ. Second, after we add Δ to t, we compare the new t against δ, and if now t goes beyond δ we can store just $\delta + 1$. Finally, since adding $\Delta = \delta + 1$ to a $t \leq \delta$ (since we only add Δ if $t \leq \delta$) gives max $2\delta + 1$, then this is the biggest number we need to store in a BDD. Consequently, the number of bits needed to store time for a formula with a time constraint δ is $log_2(2\delta + 1)$.

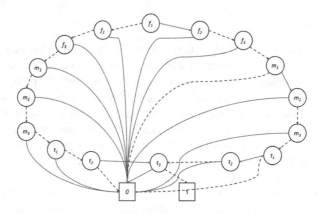

Fig. 8. The BDD for the formula $\mathbf{P}_{\leq 3}\, open(f,m)$ at the third event.

The algorithm for first-order past-time LTL with time is obtained by adding the statements below to step 4 of the algorithm shown in Sect. 5.3, and by adding the update $\tau pre := \tau now$ in step 2.

Algorithm for $(\varphi\, S_{\leq \delta}\, \psi)$**:** We will use $BDD0(x)$ to denote the BDD where all the x_i bits are a constant 0, representing the Boolean expression $\neg x_1 \wedge \ldots \wedge \neg x_k$. The statements updating τnow and now are as follows.

$\tau now(\varphi S_{\leq \delta}\psi) := (now(\psi) \wedge BDD0(t)) \vee (\neg now(\psi) \wedge now(\varphi) \wedge$
$\quad rename(\exists t_1 \ldots t_m\, (addconst(t,t',\Delta) \wedge \neg gtconst(t',\delta) \wedge \tau pre(\varphi S_{\leq \delta}\psi)), t', t))$;
$now(\varphi S_{\leq \delta}\psi) := \exists t_1 \ldots t_m\, \tau now(\varphi S_{\leq \delta}\psi)$;

That is, either ψ holds now and we reset the timer t to 0, or ψ does not hold now but φ does, and the previous t value is determined by $\tau pre(\varphi S_{\leq \delta}\psi))$, to which we add Δ, giving t', which must not be greater than δ. Then t is removed by quantifying over it, and t' renamed to t (t' becomes the new t). The BDD for $now(\varphi S_{\leq \delta}\psi)$ is obtained from $\tau now(\varphi S_{\leq \delta}\psi)$ by projecting out the timer value.

Algorithm for $(\varphi S_{> \delta}\psi)$**:** We will use $EQ(t,c)$ to denote that the bit sting t is equal to c. This is technically defined as $EQ(t,c) = \exists z_1 \ldots z_m\, (BDD0(z) \wedge addconst(z,t,c))$, stating that $z = 0$ added to c yields t. The updates to τnow and now are as follows.

$\tau now(\varphi S_{> \delta}\psi) :=$
$\quad (now(\psi) \wedge (\neg pre(\varphi S_{> \delta}\psi) \vee \neg now(\varphi)) \wedge BDD0(t)) \vee$
$\quad (now(\varphi) \wedge rename(previous, t', t))$
where $previous = \exists t_1 \ldots t_m\, (\tau pre(\varphi S_{> \delta}\psi) \wedge ((\neg gtconst(t,\delta) \wedge addconst(t,t',\Delta)) \vee$
$\quad (gtconst(t,\delta) \wedge EQ(t',\delta+1))))$;
$now(\varphi S_{> \delta}\psi) := \exists t_1 \ldots t_m\, (\tau now(\varphi S_{> \delta}\psi) \wedge gtconst(t,\delta))$;

That is, when ψ currently holds and either $\varphi S_{> \delta}\psi$ did not hold in the previous step or φ does not hold now, we reset the timer t to 0. Alternatively, when φ holds we compute t' using the **where**-clause as follows and then rename it to t: t takes its value from $\tau pre(\varphi S_{> \delta}\psi)$, which is calculated based on the previous step. This means that $(\varphi S_{> \delta}\psi)$

held in the previous step. If t was then not greater than δ, we add Δ to t to obtain t'. Otherwise (t was already greater than δ), we set t' to $\delta + 1$ to reduce the size of the time values we have to store.

References

1. de Alfaro, L., Kwiatkowska, M., Norman, G., Parker, D., Segala, R.: Symbolic model checking of probabilistic processes using MTBDDs and the Kronecker representation. In: Graf, S., Schwartzbach, M. (eds.) TACAS 2000. LNCS, vol. 1785, pp. 395–410. Springer, Heidelberg (2000). https://doi.org/10.1007/3-540-46419-0_27
2. Alpern, B., Schneider, F.B.: Recognizing safety and liveness. Distrib. Comput. **2**(3), 117–126 (1987)
3. Bahar, R.I., et al.: Algebraic decision diagrams and their applications. Formal Methods Syst. Des. **10**(2/3), 171–206 (1997)
4. Basin, D.A., Klaedtke, F., Müller, S., Zalinescu, E.: Monitoring metric first-order temporal properties. J. ACM **62**(2), 1–45 (2015)
5. Bensalem, S., Havelund, K.: Dynamic deadlock analysis of multi-threaded programs. In: Ur, S., Bin, E., Wolfsthal, Y. (eds.) HVC 2005. LNCS, vol. 3875, pp. 208–223. Springer, Heidelberg (2006). https://doi.org/10.1007/11678779_15
6. Bryant, R.E.: Graph-based algorithms for boolean function manipulation. IEEE Trans. Comput. **35**(8), 677–691 (1986)
7. Bryant, R.E.: Symbolic boolean manipulation with ordered binary-decision diagrams. ACM Comput. Surv. **24**(3), 293–318 (1992)
8. Bryant, R.E.: On the complexity of VLSI implementations and graph representations of boolean functions with application to integer multiplication. IEEE Trans. Comput. **40**(2), 205–213 (1991)
9. Burch, J.R., Clarke, E.M., McMillan, K.L., Dill, D.L., Hwang, L.J.: Symbolic model checking: 10^{20} states and beyond, pp. 428–439, LICS (1990)
10. Clarke, E.M., Grumberg, O., Peled, D.: Model Checking. MIT Press, Cambridge (2001)
11. Clarke, E.M., McMillan, K.L., Zhao, X.G., Fujita, M., Yang, J.C.-Y.: Spectral transforms for large boolean functions with applications to technology mapping. Formal Methods Syst. Des. **10**(2/3), 137–148 (1997)
12. Gabbay, D.M., Pnueli, A., Shelah, S., Stavi, J.: On the Temporal Basis of Fairness, POPL, pp. 163–173. ACM Press (1980)
13. Havelund, K., Peled, D.: BDDs on the run. In: Margaria, T., Steffen, B. (eds.) ISoLA 2018. LNCS, vol. 11247, pp. 58–69. Springer, Cham (2018). https://doi.org/10.1007/978-3-030-03427-6_8
14. Havelund, K., Peled, D.: First-order timed runtime verification using BDDs. In: ATVA. LNCS. Springer (to appear, 2020)
15. Havelund, K., Peled, D., Ulus, D.: First-order temporal logic monitoring with BDDs. In: FMCAD, pp. 116–123. IEEE (2017)
16. Havelund, K., Peled, D., Ulus, D.: First-order temporal logic monitoring with BDDs. Formal Methods Syst. Des. 1–21 (2019). https://doi.org/10.1007/s10703-018-00327-4
17. Havelund, K., Reger, G., Thoma, D., Zălinescu, E.: Monitoring events that carry data. In: Bartocci, E., Falcone, Y. (eds.) Lectures on Runtime Verification. LNCS, vol. 10457, pp. 61–102. Springer, Cham (2018). https://doi.org/10.1007/978-3-319-75632-5_3
18. Havelund, K., Roşu, G.: Synthesizing monitors for safety properties. In: Katoen, J.-P., Stevens, P. (eds.) TACAS 2002. LNCS, vol. 2280, pp. 342–356. Springer, Heidelberg (2002). https://doi.org/10.1007/3-540-46002-0_24

19. JavaBDD. http://javabdd.sourceforge.net
20. Kupferman, O., Vardi, M.Y.: Model checking of safety properties. Formal Methods Syst. Des. **19**(3), 291–314 (2001)
21. Lee, C.Y.: Representation of switching circuits by binary-decision programs. Bell Syst. Tech. J. **38**, 985–999 (1959)
22. Manna, Z., Pnueli, A.: Completing the temporal picture. Theor. Comput. Sci. **83**, 91–130 (1991)
23. Minato, S.: Zero-Suppressed BDDs for set manipulation in combinatorial problems. In: Design Automation Conference, pp. 272–277. ACM/IEEE (1993)

Runtime Verification for Autonomy

Runtime-Safety-Guided Policy Repair

Weichao Zhou[1(✉)], Ruihan Gao[2], BaekGyu Kim[3], Eunsuk Kang[4],
and Wenchao Li[1]

[1] Boston University, Boston, MA, USA
{zwc662,wenchao}@bu.edu
[2] Nanyang Technological University, Singapore, Singapore
GAOR0007@e.ntu.edu.sg
[3] Toyota Motor North America R&D, Mountain View, CA, USA
baekgyu.kim@toyota.com
[4] Carnegie Mellon University, Pittsburgh, PA, USA
eskang@cmu.edu

Abstract. We study the problem of policy repair for learning-based control policies in safety-critical settings. We consider an architecture where a high-performance learning-based control policy (e.g. one trained as a neural network) is paired with a model-based safety controller. The safety controller is endowed with the abilities to predict whether the trained policy will lead the system to an unsafe state, and take over control when necessary. While this architecture can provide added safety assurances, intermittent and frequent switching between the trained policy and the safety controller can result in undesirable behaviors and reduced performance. We propose to reduce or even eliminate control switching by 'repairing' the trained policy based on runtime data produced by the safety controller in a way that deviates minimally from the original policy. The key idea behind our approach is the formulation of a trajectory optimization problem that allows the joint reasoning of policy update and safety constraints. Experimental results demonstrate that our approach is effective even when the system model in the safety controller is unknown and only approximated.

1 Introduction

Data-driven methods such as imitation learning have been successful in learning control policies for complex control tasks [4]. A major shortcoming that impedes their widespread usage in the field is that the learnt policies typically do not come with any safety guarantee. It has been observed that when encountering states not seen in training, the learnt policy can produce unsafe behaviors [3,27].

A common approach to mitigate the safety problem at runtime is to pair the learning-based controller[1] (LC) with a high-assurance safety controller (SC)

---

[1] We use the terms 'controller' and 'control policy' (or simply 'policy') interchangeably in this paper. The latter is more common in the machine learning literature.

© Springer Nature Switzerland AG 2020
J. Deshmukh and D. Ničković (Eds.): RV 2020, LNCS 12399, pp. 131–150, 2020.
https://doi.org/10.1007/978-3-030-60508-7_7

that can take over control in safety-critical situations, such as the Simplex architecture first proposed in [32]. The safety controller is tasked with predicting an impending safety violation and taking over control when it deems necessary. Such controllers are often designed based on conservative models, has inferior performance compared to its learning-based counterpart, and may require significant computation resources if implemented online (e.g. model predictive control). Moreover, frequent and intermittent switching between the controllers can result in undesirable behaviors and further performance loss.

In this paper, we propose to *leverage the runtime interventions carried out by the safety controller to repair the learnt policy*. We do not assume access to the original training data of the LC but we assume that the policy is parameterized, differentiable and given as a white-box. This means that while fine-tuning the LC from scratch is not possible, it is still possible to improve the controller based on new data that is gathered during deployment. In particular, we introduce the concept of *policy repair* which uses the outputs of the safety controller to synthesize new training data to fine-tune the LC for improved safety. Furthermore, we formalize a notion of *minimal deviation* with respect to the original policy in order to mitigate the issue of performance degradation during policy repair. The main idea in *minimally deviating policy repair* is the formulation of a trajectory optimization problem that allows us to *simultaneously reason about policy optimization and safety constraints*. A key novelty of this approach is the synthesis of new safe 'demonstrations' that are the most likely to be produced by the original unsafe learnt policy. In short, we make the following contributions.

- We formalize the problems of *policy repair* and *minimally deviating policy repair* for improving the safety of learnt control policies.
- We develop a novel algorithm to solve the policy repair problem by iteratively synthesizing new training data from interventions by the safety controller to fine-tune the learnt policy.
- We demonstrate the effectiveness of our approach on case studies including a simulated driving scenario where the true dynamics of the system is unknown and is only approximated.

2   Related Work

Model-based control is a well-studied technique for controlling dynamical systems based on the modelling of the system dynamics. Algorithms such as iterative Linear Quadratic Regulator (iLQR) [33] have achieved good performance even in complex robotic control tasks. One important advantage of model-based control is its ability to cope with constraints on the dynamics, controls and states. Constrained Model Predictive Control [15] has been studied extensively and proven to be successful in solving collision avoidance problems [5,6] as well as meeting complex high-level specifications [10]. In this paper, we utilize model-based control techniques to verify the existence of safe control as well as synthesize new training data to guide the policy learning.

Imitation learning provides a way of transferring skills for a complex task from a (human) expert to a learning agent [20]. It has been shown that data-driven methods such as behavior cloning are effective in handling robotics and autonomous driving tasks [25,28] when an expert policy is accessible at training time. Model-based control techniques have already been introduced to imitation learning to guide the policy learning process [22]. Our work shares similarity with [22] in using a model predictive controller to generate training examples. What distinguishes our work from theirs is that in [22] the model predictive controller operates based on a given cost function whereas in our work we do not assume we know any cost function. An outstanding challenge in the imitation learning area is the lack of safety assurance during both training and final deployment. Efforts on addressing this challenge include [17,36], where multiple machine learning models cooperate to achieve performance and safety goals. However, the learned models can not provide guarantees on runtime safety by themselves. In fact,even when the dynamical model is given, existing imitation learning algorithms lack the means to incorporate explicit safety requirements. In this paper, we use imitation learning to formulate the problem of minimally deviating policy repair such that a repaired policy can match the performance of the original learnt policy while being safe.

Safe Learning research has experienced rapid growth in recent years. Many approaches consider safety requirement as constraints in the learning process. For example, [1,9] encodes safety as auxiliary costs under the framework of Constrained Markov Decision Processes (CMDPs). However, the constraints can only be enforced approximately. [9] developed a Lyapunov-based approach to learn safe control policies in CMDPs but is not applicable to parameterized policy and continuous control actions. Formal methods have also been applied to certain learning algorithms for establishing formal safety guarantees. In [37], safety is explicitly defined in probabilistic computational tree logic and a probabilistic model checker is used to check whether any intermediately learned policy meets the specification. If the specification is violated, then a counterexample in the form of a set of traces is used to guide the learning process. Providing assurance for runtime safety of learning-based controller has also garnered attention recently. [12] combines offline verification of system models with runtime validation of system executions. In [2], a so-called shield is synthesized to filter out unsafe outputs from a reinforcement learning (RL) agent. It also promotes safe actions by modifying the rewards. A similar idea can be seen in [23] where a so-called neural simplex architecture is proposed and an online training scheme is used to improve the safety of RL agents by rewarding safe actions. However, in the context of RL, choosing the right reward is in general a difficult task, since incorrect choices often lead to sub-optimal or even incorrect solutions. In [8], a model predictive approach is proposed to solve for minimum perturbation to bend the outputs of an RL policy towards asymptotic safety enforced by a predefined control barrier certificate. A similar idea also appears in [34] where robust model predictive control is used to minimally perturb the trajectories of a learning-based controller towards an iteratively expanding safe target set.

Our method differs from [8, 34] as we improve the runtime safety of the learning-based control while preserving its performance from an imitation learning perspective.

3   Preliminaries

In this paper we consider a discrete-time control system (X, U, f, d_0) where X is the set of states of the system and U is the set of control actions. The function $f : X \times U \to X$ is the dynamical model describing how the state evolves when an control action is applied, and $d_0 : X \to \mathbb{R}$ is the distribution of the initial states. By applying control actions sequentially, a trajectory, or a trace, $\tau = \{(x_t, u_t)|t = 0, 1, \ldots\}$ can be obtained where x_t, u_t are the state and control action at time t. In typical optimal control problems, a cost function $c : X \times U \to \mathbb{R}$ is explicitly defined to specify the cost of performing control action $u \in U$ in state $x \in X$. The cumulative cost along a trajectory τ can be calculated as $\sum_{(x_t, u_t) \in \tau} c(x_t, u_t)$. An optimal control strategy is thus one that minimizes the cumulative cost.

Model Predictive Control (MPC) leverages a predictive model of the system to find a sequence of optimal control actions in a receding horizon fashion. It solves the optimal sequence of control actions for T steps as in (1) but only applies the first control action and propagates one step forward to the next state. Then it solves for a new sequence of optimal control actions in the next state.

$$\arg \min_{x_{0:T}, u_{0:T}} \sum_{t=0}^{T} c(x_t, u_t) \tag{1}$$

$$s.t. \ x_{t+1} = f(x_t, u_t) \qquad t = 0, 1, 2, \ldots, T \tag{2}$$

When the dynamics f in constraint (2) is nonlinear, the iterative Linear Quadratic Regulator (iLQR) algorithm [14] applies a local linearization of f along an existing trajectory which is called the nominal trajectory. It computes a feedback control law via LQR [13], which induces a locally optimal perturbation upon the nominal trajectory to reduce the cumulative cost. Formally, given a nominal trajectory $\{(x_0, u_0), \ldots, (x_T, u_T)\}$, perturbations can be added to each state and control action in this trajectory, i.e. $x_t \to x_t + \delta x_t, u_t \to u_t + \delta u_t$. The relationship between $\delta x_t, \delta u_t$ and δx_{t+1} is locally determined by the dynamics as well as the state and control actions in the nominal trajectory as in (4) where $\nabla_x f(x_t, u_t), \nabla_u f(x_t, u_t)$ are the partial derivatives of $f(x_t, u_t)$ w.r.t x, u. Meanwhile, based on the nominal trajectory, $\sum_{t=0}^{T} c(x_t, u_t)$ in the objective (1) is substituted by $\sum_{t=0}^{T} c(\delta x_t + x_t, \delta u_t + u_t) - c(x_t, u_t)$ while the decision variables become $\delta x_{0:T}, \delta u_{0:T}$. When adopting an online trajectory optimization strategy [33], the optimal control law has a closed form solution $\delta u_t = k_t + K_t \delta x_t$ in which k_t, K_t are determined by the dynamics and the cumulative cost along the nominal trajectory.

$$x_{t+1} = f(x_t, u_t) \qquad x_{t+1} + \delta x_{t+1} = f(x_t + \delta x_t, u_t + \delta u_t) \tag{3}$$

$$\delta x_{t+1}^T \approx \delta x_t^T \nabla_x f(x_t, u_t) + \delta u_t^T \nabla_u f(x_t, u_t) \tag{4}$$

A **control policy** in general is a function $\pi : X \to U$ that specifies the behavior of a controller in each state. Given a deterministic policy π, its trajectory can be obtained by sequentially applying control actions according to the outputs of π. Specifically, for an LC such as a deep neural network, the policy is usually parameterized and can be written as π_θ where the parameter θ belongs to some parameter set Θ (e.g. weights of a neural network). We assume that $\pi_\theta(x)$ is differentiable both in x and θ.

Imitation learning assumes that an expert policy π_E (e.g. a human expert) can demonstrate on how to finish a desired task with high performance. The learning objective for an agent is to find a policy π that matches the performance of π_E in the same task. Traditional approaches such as behavioral cloning consider the 0–1 error $e(x_t, \pi_E; \pi) = \mathcal{I}\{\pi(x) \neq \pi_E(x)\}$ where $\mathcal{I}$ is an indicator function. In this setting, an optimally imitating policy minimizes $\mathbb{E}_{x \sim d_{\pi_E}}[e(x, \pi_E; \pi)]$ where d_{π_E} is state visitation distribution of π_E. From another perspective, the difference between π and π_E can be estimated based on their trajectory distributions. When the trajectory distribution $Prob(\tau|\pi_E)$ is known, one can empirically estimate and minimize the KL divergence $D_{KL}[\pi_E||\pi]$ by regarding $Prob(\tau|\pi)$ as the probability of π generating trajectory τ under an additional Gaussian noise, i.e. $u_t \sim \mathcal{N}(\pi(x_t), \Sigma), \forall (x_t, u_t) \in \tau$. On the other hand, one can estimate and minimize the KL divergence $D_{KL}[\pi||\pi_E]$ by treating $Prob(\tau|\pi)$ as being induced from a Dirac delta distribution $u_t \sim \delta(\pi(x_t)) \ \forall (x_t, u_t) \in \tau$. Both KL-divergences are related to negative log-likelihoods.

4 Runtime Safety Assurance

In this section we discuss the runtime safety issues of LCs and introduce our basic strategy for safe control. We consider a runtime safety requirement Φ for finite horizon T, such as 'if the current state is safe at step t, do not reach any unsafe state within the next T steps'. Temporal logic can be used to formally capture this type of safety requirements [16,24]. Given an LC with a deterministic policy π_θ, if π_θ satisfies Φ globally, that is, at each time step along all its trajectories, we denote it as $\pi_\theta \models \Phi$; otherwise $\pi_\theta \not\models \Phi$.

We assume that for any satisfiable Φ, there exists an SC, which we represent as π^{safe}, that checks at runtime whether Φ is satisfiable if the output $\hat{u} = \pi_\theta(x)$ of the LC is directly applied. That is, whether there exists a sequence of control actions in the next $T - 1$ steps such that Φ is not violated. If true, then the final output $\pi^{safe}(x, \pi_\theta(x)) = \hat{u}$. Otherwise it overrides the LC's output with $\pi^{safe}(x, \pi_\theta(x)) \neq \hat{u}$. We formally define the SC below.

Definition 1. *Given a safety requirement Φ, the corresponding SC is a mapping π^{safe} from $X \times U$ to U. In each state $x \in X$, $\pi^{safe}(x, \pi_\theta(x)) = \pi_\theta(x)$ iff Φ is satisfiable after applying the control action $\pi_\theta(x)$; otherwise, π^{safe} intervenes by providing a substitute $\pi^{safe}(x, \pi_\theta(x)) \neq \pi_\theta(x)$ to satisfy Φ.*

We use $\langle \pi_\theta, \pi^{safe} \rangle$ to represent the LC and SC pair. Obviously the trajectories generated by this pair satisfy Φ everywhere if π^{safe} exists. There are multiple options of implementing the SC such as having a backup human safety driver or using automated reasoning. Depending on the safety requirement and task environment, the difficulty of implementing safe control varies. In this paper, we assume that a dynamical model of f is given, possibly constructed conservatively, and adopt a scheme known as Model Predictive Safe Control as detailed below.

4.1   Model Predictive Safe Control

This scheme exploits the dynamical model to predict safety in the future. Depending on the safety requirement Φ considered, a function $\varphi : X \rightarrow \mathbb{R}$ can be defined to quantify how safe any state x is, i.e. if $\varphi(x) \leq 0$, then x is safe; otherwise x is unsafe. Without loss of generality, we let the current step be $t = 0$. Then the safety requirement can be translated into the constraints $\forall t \in \{1, 2, \ldots, T\}, \varphi(x_t) \leq 0$. After the LC provides a candidate control output $u_0 = \pi_\theta(x_0)$, the SC first verifies the satisfiability of (7) by using an MPC-like formulation as (5)–(8).

$$\min_{x_{0:T}, u_{0:T}} \quad 0 \tag{5}$$

$$s.t. \ \ x_{t+1} = f(x_t, u_t) \qquad t = 0, 1, 2, \ldots, T - 1 \tag{6}$$

$$\varphi(x_t) \leq 0 \qquad t = 1, 2, \ldots, T \tag{7}$$

$$u_0 = \pi_\theta(x_0) \tag{8}$$

The formula differs from MPC in that it solves a feasibility problem to check the existence of a sequence of control actions satisfying the constraints. It is easier to solve than optimal control since optimality is not required here. If this problem is feasible, that is, (6)–(8) can be satisfied at the same time. Then $\pi_\theta(x_0)$ is deemed safe and the final output is $\pi^{safe}(x_0, \pi_\theta(x_0)) = \pi_\theta(x_0)$. Otherwise, the SC solves another feasibility problem which is the same as (5)–(7) and has (8) removed because the unsafe candidate control action $\pi_\theta(x_0)$ is to be substituted. Note that it is possible that (7) is unsatisfiable, in which case there is no feasible solution. This means a safety violation is inevitable based on the given model, but the SC can predict such outcome T steps in advance and more drastic actions (e.g. physically changing the model) may be applied to prevent an accident from occurring. If a feasible solution to (5)–(7) can be obtained, we let $\pi^{safe}(x_0, \pi_\theta(x_0)) = u_0$ and use this solved u_0 to evolve the system to the next state.

There have been works on model predictive control of cyber-physical systems subject to formal specifications in signal temporal logic (STL) and its probabilistic variant [26,29]. Techniques have been proposed to synthesize safety constraints from formal specifications to accommodate optimal control of continuous systems and to reason about safety under uncertainty. In the semantics of STL, φ can be viewed as the negation of the robustness satisfaction value.

In this paper, at the beginning of each time step, before solving the feasibility problem (5)–(8), we forward simulate the policy π_θ for T steps. If the simulated trajectory satisfies the safety constraint (7) already, then there is no need to query the SC at all. Otherwise, we use the constrained iLQR approach from [7] to solve the feasibility problem. This approach treats the simulated trajectory as nominal trajectory and iteratively update the nominal trajectory. Also, this approach turns the safety constraint (7) into a penalty $\sum_{t=0}^{T} exp(M_t \psi(x_t))$ with sufficiently large $\{M_t\}_{t=0}^{T}$. And the penalty is added to the objective. By using this approach, even if the feasibility problem cannot be solved, at least a low-penalty solution can be provided.

Monitoring Overhead. Model Predictive Safe Control (MPSC) can provide assurance for a variety of runtime safety requirements. However, it can be more expensive to implement in practice compared to an LC due to the need to repeatedly solve a (nonlinear) optimization online as opposed to performing inference on a neural network [35]. Frequently using an SC to both verify safety and solve safe control at runtime can be computationally taxing for the entire control system. For instance, suppose the LC's inference time is t_{LC}, the time for solving (5)–(8) is $t_{SC}^{(1)}$ and the time for solving (5)–(7) is $t_{SC}^{(2)}$. Typically, t_{LC} is much smaller than $t_{SC}^{(1)}$ or $t_{SC}^{(2)}$. At each step, forward simulation of the LC for T steps takes at least $T * t_{LC}$ time. If (7) is violated in the forward simulation, the SC would need to be invoked and the total overhead will grow to $T * t_{LC} + t_{SC}^{(1)}$. If the problem based on the LC's candidate control output is infeasible and the SC is required to intervene with a substitute control value, then the SC will have to solve another MPC-like problem and the overhead will grow to $T * t_{LC} + t_{SC}^{(1)} + t_{SC}^{(2)}$. Thus, it would be more economical to have an inherently safe LC such that the SC is less triggered. Motivated by this, we propose to *repair* the LC so that it becomes safer and requires less intervention from the SC. In the next section, we formally introduce the policy repair problem and describe our solution in detail.

5   Policy Repair

We first give a formal definition of the policy repair problem below.

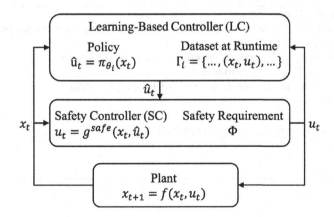

Fig. 1. Architecture of pairing LC's policy π_θ with an SC π^{safe}.

Definition 2. *Given a deterministic policy π_θ paired with an SC π^{safe} as defined in Definition 1, **policy repair** is the problem of finding a new policy π_{θ^*} such that $\theta^* = \underset{\theta \in \Theta}{\arg\min} \; \mathbb{E}_{x \in X}[\mathcal{I}\{\pi^{safe}(x, \pi_\theta(x)) = \pi_\theta(x)\}]$ where $\mathcal{I}\{\cdot\} \in \{0, 1\}$ is an indicator function.*

Definition 2 implies that a repaired policy generates safe controls most of the time and thus the SC rarely intervenes. The first idea is to treat controls generated by the SC as repairs at specific states, and then use this data to repair the whole policy. A solution based on this idea is described as follows.

5.1   Naive Policy Repair

During the execution of the LC and SC pair $\langle \pi_\theta, \pi^{safe} \rangle$, due to the presence of the SC, all the generated traces are safe. The basic idea of the naive policy repair approach is to let the unsafe LC learn from the interventions produced by the SC. Specifically, we iteratively execute the LC and SC pair to generate new safe traces. After each iteration, the state-action pairs in all the previously generated traces are used as training data to update the policy of the LC. We present the steps in Algorithm 1 and illustrate them with a high-level diagram in Fig. 1, where Γ_i is the set of traces of the $\langle \pi_{\theta_i}, \pi^{safe} \rangle$ pair at the ith iteration. We use supervised learning to fine-tune the policy parameter to minimize the expected error $\mathbb{E}_{(x,u) \sim \Gamma_i}[e(x, u; \pi_\theta)]$ as in line 9 of Algorithm 1. Note that at this stage, with a slight abuse of notation, we view Γ_i as a data set containing (x, u) pairs. In line 5–7, if the SC no longer intervenes, then we have a high confidence that the current policy is safe. According to the law of large numbers, this confidence increases with increasing number of sampled traces. The algorithm also terminates if a maximum iteration number is reached, in which case the SC may still intervene and the policy repair is only partially successful.

Algorithm 1. Naive_Policy_Repair

1: **Input** an initial policy π_{θ_0};
2: **Given** an SC π^{safe}; iteration parameter $N > 0$; policy parameter set Θ.
3: **for** iteration $i = 0$ to N **do**
4:      Run the $\langle \pi_{\theta_i}, \pi^{safe} \rangle$ pair to generate a set Γ_i of trajectories.
5:      **if** $\forall(x, u) \in \Gamma_i, u = \pi_{\theta_i}(x)$ **then**
6:          π^{safe} never intervenes $\Rightarrow \pi_{\theta_i} \models \Phi$ with high probability.
7:          **return** π_{θ_i}, Γ_i
8:      **end if**
9:      $\theta_{i+1} = \underset{\theta \in \Theta}{\arg\min} \; \mathbb{E}_{(x,u) \sim \cup_{j=0}^{i} \Gamma_j}[e(x, u; \pi_\theta)]$
10: **end for**
11: **return** $\pi_{\theta_N}, \emptyset$

5.2   Analysis of Performance Degradation Due to SC Intervention

In this section, we analyze the performance degradation due to the application of safe controls from the SC and use it to motivate the study of better policy repair strategies. We assume that the initial learnt policy π_{θ_0} is given as a white-box and its parameter θ_0 has already been optimized for the control task. Inspired from lemma 1 in [30], we analyze the performance degradation of naive policy repair in a fixed-horizon task with maximum step length H. Recall the definition of cost function c in Sect. 3. Without loss of generality, we simplify it into a function of state, that is, from $c(x, u)$ to $c(x)$ and normalize it to the range $[0, 1]$. We use $\eta(\pi) = \mathbb{E}_{\tau \sim \pi}[\sum_{t=0}^{H} c(x_t)]$ to denote the expected cumulative cost of following a policy π from initialization to step H. Define the value function $V_{\pi}(x_t) = \mathbb{E}_{x_t, u_t, x_{t+1} \ldots \sim \pi}[\sum_{l=t}^{H} c(x_l)]$ as the expected cost accumulated by following π after reaching state x_t at step t till step H. Define the state-action value function $Q_{\pi}(x_t, u_t) = \mathbb{E}_{x_t, x_{t+1}, u_{t+1} \ldots \sim \pi, u_t}[\sum_{l=t}^{H} c(x_l)]$ as the expected cost accumulated by executing u_t in state x_t, then following π henceforth til step H. We use an advantage function $A_{\pi}(x_t, u_t) = Q_{\pi}(x_t, u_t) - V_{\pi}(x_t)$ to evaluate the additional cost incurred by applying control action u_t in x_t instead of adhering to π. Based on the lemma 1 in [30] for infinite-horizon scenario, we have the Eq. (9) for any two policies $\pi, \hat{\pi}$ in finite-horizon scenario.

$$\mathbb{E}_{\tau \sim \hat{\pi}}[\sum_{t=0}^{H} A_{\pi}(x_t, u_t)] = \mathbb{E}_{\tau \sim \hat{\pi}}[\sum_{t=0}^{H} c(x_t) + V_{\pi}(x_{t+1}) - V_{\pi}(x_t)]$$

$$= \mathbb{E}_{\tau \sim \hat{\pi}}[-V_{\pi}(x_0) + \sum_{t=0}^{H} c(x_t)] = \mathbb{E}_{x_0 \sim d_0}[-V_{\pi}(x_0)] + \mathbb{E}_{\tau \sim \hat{\pi}}[\sum_{t=0}^{H} c(x_t)] = \eta(\hat{\pi}) - \eta(\pi) \quad (9)$$

Assuming that $\eta(\pi_{\theta_0})$ is the minimum for the desired task, i.e. π_{θ_0} is the optimal policy with respect to a cost function c, we bound the additional cost $\eta(\pi^{safe}) - \eta(\pi)$ incurred by possible interventions of π^{safe}.

Theorem 1. *Given a $\langle \pi_{\theta_0}, \pi_{safe} \rangle$ pair, let ϵ_1, ϵ_2 and ϵ_3 be the probability of $\langle \pi_{\theta_0}, \pi_{safe} \rangle$ generating a H-length trajectory where $\pi^{safe}(x, \pi_{\theta_0}(x)) \neq \pi_{\theta_0}(x)$ happens in at least one, two and three states respectively. Then, $\eta(\pi^{safe}) - \eta(\pi_{\theta_0}) \leq \epsilon_1 H + \epsilon_2 (H-1) + \frac{\epsilon_3 (H-1) H}{2}$.*

The theorem[2] shows the additional cost can grow quadratically in H when the probability of multiple interventions from the SC becomes higher. The implication of this is that even if the repaired policy π_{θ^*} replicates π^{safe} with zero error, the repaired policy can still suffer from significant performance degradation. Since the training error is non-zero in practice, $\pi_{\theta^*}(x) \neq \pi_{\theta_0}(x)$ may happen in more states where $\pi^{safe}(x, \pi_{\theta_0}(x)) \neq \pi_{\theta_0}(x)$. One major challenge in mitigating this performance loss is that the training information of π_{θ_0}, especially the cost function c, could be unknown. In the next section, we describe our approach of repairing a policy so that it also minimally deviates from the original one.

---

[2] Proof can be found in the extended version https://arxiv.org/abs/2008.07667.

5.3   Minimally Deviating Policy Repair via Trajectory Synthesis

We firstly formally define the minimally deviating policy repair problem.

Definition 3. *Given an initial policy π_{θ_0} and an SC π^{safe} as defined in Definition 1,* **minimally deviating policy repair** *is the problem of finding a policy π_{θ^*} where $\theta^* = \arg\min\limits_{\theta \in \Theta} \mathbb{E}_{x \sim d_{\pi_\theta}}[e(x, \pi_{\theta_0}; \pi_\theta)]$ subject to $\pi^{safe}(x, \pi_\theta(x)) = \pi_\theta(x), \forall x \in X$.*

Informally, the objective of this repair problem is to reduce the chance of $\pi_{\theta^*}(x) \neq \pi_{\theta_0}(x)$ while maintaining the safety of π_{θ^*}. Observe that the error term $e(\cdot)$ in Definition 3 resembles the one in an imitation learning setting. Then minimizing the expected error can be viewed as imitating π_{θ_0}. On the other hand, the equality constraint in Definition 3 can be understood as requiring π_{θ^*} to satisfy (7) at all steps in all its trajectories. Hence, the minimally deviating policy repair is essentially a problem of optimizing an imitation learning objective with safety constraints. The major challenge is that, the decision variable for the imitation learning objective is the policy parameter θ while for safety constraints (7) it is the state x.

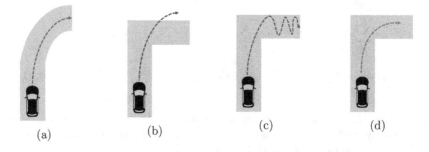

(a)   (b)   (c)   (d)

Fig. 2. (a) The grey area is the lane. The green dashed curve is the trajectory of the vehicle. (b) The red dashed curve is the trajectory of the initial policy. (c) The blue dashed curve is the trajectory of the policy and safety controller pair. (d) The magenta dashed curve is the trajectory produced by the repair policy that deviates minimally from the original one. (Color figure online)

We use a simple example below to illustrate our problem setting and desired solution. Consider a policy that was trained to steer a vehicle around a specific corner as shown in Fig. 2(a). When deployed in a slightly different environment as shown in Fig. 2(b), the policy fails to keep the vehicle inside the lane. Figure 2(c) illustrates that with the basic simplex setup as shown in Fig. 1, although the safety controller manages to keep the vehicle inside the lane, frequent switching between the two controllers can lead to undesirable behaviors such as an oscillating trajectory. Fig. 2(d) shows a more desirable trajectory produced by a new policy trained using minimally deviating policy repair. Our approach to the

problem stated in Definition 3 is to 'imitate' the original policy by first synthesizing and then learning from new trajectories that are similar to ones produced
by the original policy but instead do not violate the safety requirements. The
synthesis algorithm works by iteratively improving the trajectories produced by
a naively repaired policy such as the one in Fig. 2(c) until trajectories such as
the one in Fig. 2(d) are obtained. The improvement is achieved by solving a
trajectory optimization problem of which the objective is transformed from the
imitation learning objective in Definition 3. We mainly focus on showing such
transformation in the rest of this section.

As mentioned in Sect. 3, to solve an imitation learning problem, we can
minimize the KL-divergence which is related to maximal log-likelihood, i.e.
$\arg\min_{\theta \in \Theta} D_{KL}[\pi_\theta || \pi_{\theta_0}] = \arg\max_{\theta \in \Theta} \mathbb{E}_{\tau \sim \pi_\theta}[\log Prob(\tau | \pi_{\theta_0})]$. Note that $Prob(\tau | \pi_\theta)$
is induced from a Dirac Delta distribution $u \sim \delta(\pi(x))$ and $Prob(\tau | \pi_{\theta_0})$ is car-
ried out by adding to π_{θ_0} an isotropic Gaussian noise $\mathcal{N}(0, \Sigma)$ with diagonal
$\Sigma = \sigma^2 I$. When a finite set Γ of trajectories of π_θ is obtained, the log-likelihood
is equivalent to (10).

$$\mathbb{E}_{\tau \sim \pi_\theta}[\log Prob(\tau | \pi_{\theta_0})] \approx \frac{1}{|\Gamma|} \sum_{\tau \in \Gamma} \log Prob(\tau | \pi_{\theta_0})$$

$$\propto \sum_{\tau \in \Gamma} \log\{ \prod_{(x_t, u_t) \in \tau} exp[-\frac{(\pi_\theta(x_t) - \pi_{\theta_0}(x_t))^T \Sigma^{-1}(\pi(x_t, \theta) - \pi_{\theta_0}(x_t))}{2}]\}$$

$$\propto -\frac{1}{2} \sum_{\tau \in \Gamma} \sum_{(x_t, u_t) \in \tau} ||\pi_\theta(x_t) - \pi_{\theta_0}(x_t)||_2^2 \tag{10}$$

Suppose that at iteration $i \geq 1$, a safe policy π_{θ_i} is obtained and executed
to generate a set Γ_i of safe traces. Define $l_{x_t, \pi_{\theta_i}} = \frac{1}{2}||\pi_{\theta_0}(x_t) - \pi_{\theta_i}(x_t)||_2^2$ and
$J_{\Gamma_i}(\pi_{\theta_i}) = \sum_{\tau \in \Gamma_i} \sum_{(x_t, u_t) \in \tau} l_{x_t, \pi_{\theta_i}}$. To decrease J_{Γ_i}, a new policy parameter
$\theta_{i+1} = \theta_i + \delta\theta_i$ can be obtained by solving $\delta\theta_i = \arg\min_{\delta\theta} J_{\Gamma_i}(\pi_{\theta_i + \delta\theta}) - J_{\Gamma_i}(\pi_{\theta_i})$.
We further use the Gauss-Newton step [19] to expand this as shown in (11)
below.

$$\arg\min_{\delta\theta} \delta\theta^T \nabla_\theta J_{\Gamma_i}(\pi_{\theta_i}) + \frac{1}{2}\delta\theta^T \nabla_\theta J_{\Gamma_i}(\pi_{\theta_i}) \nabla_\theta J_{\Gamma_i}(\pi_{\theta_i})^T \delta\theta$$

$$= \arg\min_{\delta\theta} \sum_{\tau \in \Gamma_i} \sum_{(x_t, u_t) \in \tau} \delta\theta_i \nabla_\theta \pi_{\theta_i}(x_t) \nabla_{\pi_{\theta_i}} l_{x_t, \pi_{\theta_i}}$$

$$+ \frac{1}{2}\delta\theta_i^T \nabla_\theta \pi_{\theta_i}(x_t) \nabla_{\pi_{\theta_i}} l_{x_t, \pi_{\theta_i}} \nabla_{\pi_{\theta_i}} l_{x_t, \pi_{\theta_i}}^T \nabla_\theta \pi_{\theta_i}(x_t)^T \delta\theta_i \tag{11}$$

We note that the changes of the policy control output $u_t = \pi_{\theta_i}(x_t)$ at arbitrary
state x_t can be locally linearized as from (12) to (13).

$$u_t + \delta u_t = \pi_{\theta_i + \delta\theta_i}(x_t + \delta x_t) \qquad u_t = \pi_{\theta_i}(x_t) \tag{12}$$

$$\delta u_t^T - \delta x_t^T \nabla_x \pi_{\theta_i}(x_t) \approx \delta\theta_i^T \nabla_\theta \pi_{\theta_i}(x_t) \tag{13}$$

It implies that due to $\delta\theta_i$, each trajectory $\tau = \{(x_0, u_0), (x_1, u_1), \ldots\}$ of π_{θ_i} is approximately perturbed by $\delta\tau = \{(\delta x_0, \delta u_0), (\delta x_1, \delta u_1), \ldots\}$. Motivated by the fact that $\pi_{\theta_i + \delta\theta_i}$ is safe if all of the trajectories are still safe after such perturbations, we optimize w.r.t the trajectory perturbations $\delta\tau$'s instead of $\delta\theta_i$ by exploiting the relation between each $(\delta x_t, \delta u_t) \in \delta\tau$ and $\delta\theta_i$ as in (13). Interpolating the LHS of (13) in (11), we obtain a trajectory optimization problem (14) with linear and quadratic costs as shown in (15)–(19). Note that this trajectory optimization problem treats the trajectories from Γ_i as nominal trajectories and solves for optimal perturbations to update those nominal trajectories. Local linearization is used to derive the dynamics constraints as in (20) for each noiminal trajectory. By adding the safety constraints (21), the trajectories can remain safe after adding the solved perturbations. Here, we use the constrained iLQR approach from [7] to resolve this constrained trajectory optimization problem.

$$\underset{\{\delta x_{0:H}, \delta u_{0:H}\}}{\arg\min} \quad \frac{1}{4|\Gamma_i|} \sum_{\tau \in \Gamma_i} \sum_{(x_t, u_t) \in \tau} \begin{bmatrix} 1 \\ \delta x_t \\ \delta u_t \end{bmatrix}^T \begin{bmatrix} 0 & Q_x^T & Q_u^T \\ Q_x & Q_{xx} & Q_{xu} \\ Q_u & Q_{xu}^T & Q_{uu} \end{bmatrix} \begin{bmatrix} 1 \\ \delta x_t \\ \delta u_t \end{bmatrix} \tag{14}$$

$$where \quad Q_x = -2\nabla_x \pi_{\theta_i}(x_t) \nabla_{\pi_{\theta_i}} l_{x_t, \pi_{\theta_i}} \tag{15}$$

$$Q_u = 2\nabla_{\pi_{\theta_i}} l_{x_t, \pi_{\theta_i}} \tag{16}$$

$$Q_{xx} = \nabla_x \pi_{\theta_i}(x_t) \nabla_{\pi_{\theta_i}} l_{x_t, \pi_{\theta_i}} \nabla_{\pi_{\theta_i}} l_{x_t, \pi_{\theta_i}}^T \nabla_x \pi_{\theta_i}(x_t)^T \tag{17}$$

$$Q_{xu} = \nabla_x \pi_{\theta_i}(x_t) \nabla_{\pi_{\theta_i}} l_{x_t, \pi_{\theta_i}} \nabla_{\pi_{\theta_i}} l_{x_t, \pi_{\theta_i}}^T \tag{18}$$

$$Q_{uu} = \nabla_{\pi_{\theta_i}} l_{x_t, \pi_{\theta_i}} \nabla_{\pi_{\theta_i}} l_{x_t, \pi_{\theta_i}}^T \tag{19}$$

$$s.t. \quad \delta x_{t+1}^T = \delta x_t^T \nabla_x f(x_t, u_t) + \delta u_t^T \nabla_u f(x_t, u_t) \qquad t = 0, 1, \ldots, H-1 \tag{20}$$

$$\varphi(x_t + \delta x_t) \leq 0 \qquad t = 0, 1, 2, \ldots, H \tag{21}$$

One major benefit of this formulation is that *imitation learning objective and safety constraints can be reasoned at the same time via optimal control.* As the optimization is now separable, (14)–(20) provide a lower bound for (11). By solving the linear Eq. (13), $\delta\theta_i$ can be inferred from the solved perturbations $\{\delta x_{0:H}, \delta u_{0:H}\}$, and then be used to modify θ_i. Alternatively, $\pi_{\theta_i + \delta\theta_i}$ can be obtained by training π_{θ_i} with the trajectories induced from $\{x_{1:H} + \delta x_{1:H}, u_{1:H} + \delta u_{1:H}\}$.

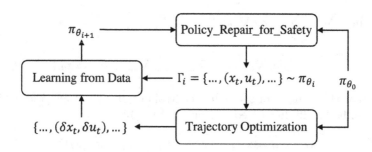

Fig. 3. Key steps in our minimally deviating policy repair algorithm. π_{θ_0} refers to the initial learnt policy.

The key steps of this iterative approach are shown in Fig. 3 and the details are in Algorithm 2. As indicated by line 2 and 6, Algorithm 1 is used to find safe policies and generate safe nominal trajectories. This is because safe nominal trajectories guarantee that the trajectory optimization problem (14)–(21) has feasible solutions, e.g. $\delta x = 0, \delta u = 0$. We terminate Algorithm 2 if Algorithm 1 fails to output a set of safe trajectories. In each iteration, we solve for the trajectory perturbations in line 4 and use them to update the policy as shown in line 5. The algorithm ends in line 7 if the trajectory optimization step no longer helps in decreasing the deviation.

Algorithm 2. Policy_Repair_for_Minimal_Deviation

1: **Given** an initial learnt policy π_{θ_0}; iteration parameters $\epsilon \in [0,1], N > 1$.
2: **Initialization** Obtain π_{θ_1}, Γ_1 from Naive_Policy_Repair(π_{θ_0}) via **Algorithm 1**;
   if Γ_1 is $\emptyset$, **then return** *fail*
3: **for** iteration $i = 1$ to $i = N$ **do**
4:     Solve the optimal $\{\delta x_{0:H}, \delta u_{0:H}\}$ from (14)–(21).
5:     Solve $\delta\theta_i$ via (13) and let $\theta_{i+1} = \theta_i + \delta\theta_i$.
       Alternatively, search for $\theta_{i+1} = \arg\min_{\theta \in \Theta} \mathbb{E}_{(x,u) \sim \Gamma_i}[e(x+\delta x, u+\delta u; \pi_\theta)]$ by training
       π_{θ_i} with $\{(x + \delta x, u + \delta u)|(x, u) \in \Gamma_i\}$.
6:     Obtain $\pi_{\theta_{i+1}}, \Gamma_{i+1}$ from Naive_Policy_Repair$(\pi_{\theta_{i+1}})$ via **Algorithm 1**;
       if Γ_{i+1} is $\emptyset$, **then return** π_{θ_i}
7:     **if** $|J_{\Gamma_{i+1}}(\pi_{\theta_{i+1}}) - J_{\Gamma_i}(\pi_{\theta_i})| \le \epsilon$, **then return** $\pi_{\theta_{i+1}}$
8: **end for**
9: **return** π_{θ_N}

Complexity Analysis. The main complexity of Algorithm 2 comes from solving the quadratic programming (QP) in (14)–(21). Since cost (14) is convex as indicated by (10), if the constraint (21) is also convex, then the QP can be solved in polynomial time [18]; otherwise, it is NP-hard [21]. The trajectory optimization in line 4 needs to be solved only once off-line at the beginning of each iteration based on the safe trajectories collected from the previous iteration. In our experiments, the trajectory optimization is solved in a receding horizon manner as an MPC. In this case, the QP will be solved repeatedly over time to determine an appropriate sequence of control outputs. The nominal trajectories are obtained at each step by forward simulating the policy for a number of steps. The total computation time will be the same as that of a standard MPC. Besides trajectory optimization, the time complexity of policy updates in line 5 is either the same as that of solving an approximated linear Eq. (13) or training a neural network in a standard supervised manner.

6 Experiments

We perform two case studies to evaluate the effectiveness of our proposed approach. The key metrics of evaluation are (1) safety of the repaired policy and (2) performance preservation with respect to the original policy. The experiments were performed on a computer with the following configurations: Intel Core i7-8700 CPU @ 3.2 GHz × 12 Processors, 15.4 GiB Memory, GeForce GTX 1050Ti, Ubuntu 16.04 LTS OS.

6.1 Mountaincar

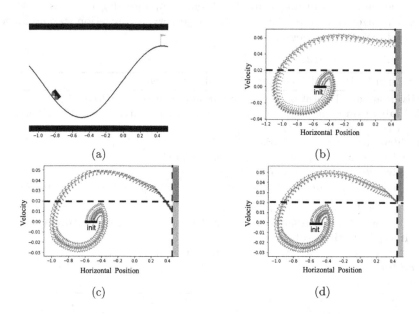

(a)

(b)

(c)

(d)

Fig. 4. (a) The mountaincar environment. (b) The red patterns represent a set of trajectories produced by executing the initial policy. The y-axis indicates the velocity and the x-axis indicates the horizontal position of the car. The car reaches the right mountain top in 83.8 steps on average with velocity higher than the safety threshold (0.02). (c) The interventions by the SC are indicated by the blue dots. A naively repaired policy takes the 89.3 steps on average to reach the mountaintop. (d) A minimally deviating repaired policy accomplishes the same task in 84.9 steps on average without violating the safety requirement. (Color figure online)

Our first case study is Mountaincar[3], as shown in Fig. 4(a). In this environment, the goal is to push an under-powered car from the bottom of a valley to the mountain top on the right with as few steps as possible. The state $\mathbf{x} = [p, v]$ includes the horizontal position $p \in [-1.2, 0.6]$ and the velocity $v \in [-0.07, 0.07]$ of the car. The control $u \in [-1.0, 1.0]$ is the force to be applied to the car. The car has a discrete-time dynamics that can be found in the source code the simulator. For the LC, we train a neural network policy via the Proximal Policy Optimization (PPO) algorithm [31]. The neural network takes the state variables as input and generates a distribution over the action space. An additional layer is

---
[3] https://gym.openai.com/envs/MountainCarContinuous-v0/.

added at the end of the network to calculate the expected action. In Fig. 4(b)–(d), the x and y axes indicate the horizontal position and the velocity respectively. The car starts from a state randomly positioned within $[-0.6, -0.4]$ as indicated by the black line above 'init'. The step length for the PPO-trained policy to reach the mountain top ($p \geq 0.45$) is 83.8 averaged over 1000 runs.

Now consider the safety requirement 'velocity v should not exceed 0.02 when reaching the mountain top at $p \geq 0.45$'. The goal states and unsafe states are indicated by the green and grey areas in Fig. 4(b). It can be observed that the PPO-trained policy does not satisfy this requirement as all the red trajectories in Fig. 4(b) end up at $p = 0.45$ with $v > 0.02$. Then an SC is implemented by following the Model Predictive Safe Control scheme introduced in Sect. 4.1. The function $\varphi(x)$ in (7) evaluates whether the state x is in the grey unsafe area. The LC and SC pair generates the red trajectories in Fig. 4(c). The blue dots indicate the intervention of the SC. While implementing Algorithm 1 and Algorithm 2, in each iteration we collect 20 trajectories in the trajectory set Γ_i. Algorithm 1 produces a naively repaired policy that can reach the green area with 89.3 steps on average. When using the minimally deviating policy repair algorithm (Algorithm 2), the resulting policy produces the red trajectories in Fig. 4(d). It shows that in all the runs the resulting policy satisfies the safety requirement and in addition the SC does not intervene. In terms of performance, the policy reaches the green area with only 84.9 steps on average, which is much closer to the performance of the original policy.

6.2   Traction-Loss Event in Simulated Urban Driving Environment

In this experiment, we show that our approach is effective even with an approximate dynamical model. The environment is in an open urban driving simulator, CARLA [11], with a single ego car on an empty road. The state variables include position, velocity and yaw angle of the car and the control variables include acceleration and steering angles. We use a simple bicycle model from [7] to approximate the unknown dynamical model of the car. The model simulates a discrete-time system where the control actions are supplied to the system at an interval of 0.03 s. For the LC, an initial neural network policy is trained with data collected from manually driving the car on different empty roads while maintaining a speed of 8 m/s and keeping the car to the middle of the lane. During testing, we put the vehicle in a roundabout as shown in Fig. 5(a) where the white curves are the lane boundary. The starting and finishing lines are fixed. The safety requirement can be described informally as 'once the vehicle crosses outside a lane boundary, the controller should drive the vehicle back to the original lane within 5 seconds'.

The initial, learnt policy drives the car well in the roundabout, as shown in Fig. 5(a). We then consider an unforeseen traction-loss event, as shown by the yellow rectangle in Fig. 5(a) where the friction is reduced to 0 (e.g. an icy surface). As a result, the vehicle skids out of the outer lane boundary. The initial policy alone does not satisfy the safety requirement, as it keeps driving the vehicle outside the lane boundary after the traction-loss event, as shown by the red trajectory in Fig. 5(a). An SC is implemented by following the Model

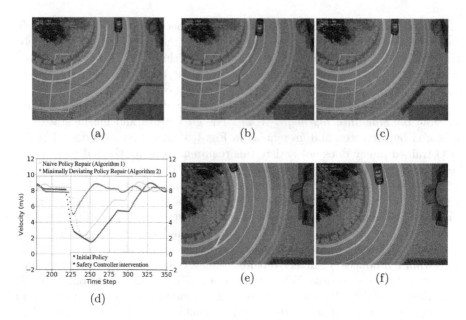

Fig. 5. The green trajectories represent normal trajectories of the car when there is no traction loss. The occurrence of the traction-loss event is indicated by the yellow rectangle. (a) Red trajectory: the initial policy fails to correct itself from skidding. (b) With interventions by the SC (the blue segment), the vehicle manages to return to the lane. (c) Magenta trajectory: policy repaired via Algorithm 2 corrects itself from skidding and does so better than using the SC. (d) The Y-axis represents velocity of the car and the X-axis represents time steps. The red curve indicates that the initial policy is in control and the blue segments represents the interventions from the SC. The cyan curve is generated by a policy repaired via Algorithm 1. The magenta curve is generated by a minimally deviating policy repaired via Algorithm 2. (e) Cyan trajectory: after the traction-loss area is removed, the naively repaired policy drives the vehicle towards the center of the roundabout, even going out the inner lane boundary for a short amount of time. (f) Magenta trajectory: after the traction-loss area is removed, by using Algorithm 2, the vehicle stays close to the middle of the lane. (Color figure online)

Predictive Safe Control scheme introduced in Sect. 4.1. The function $\varphi(x)$ in (7) checks whether the distance between the vehicle and the middle of the lane is larger than half of the lane width. In Fig. 5(b), the blue segment indicates the interventions of the SC. It shows that due to the coupling of the LC and SC, the vehicle satisfies the safety requirement as it moves back to the lane.

We next consider repairing the LC using Algorithm 1 and 2. We set ϵ to 0.001 in our experiments. For every intermediate policy in each iteration, 10 trajectories are collected in its trajectory set Γ. It takes 5 iterations for Algorithm 1 to synthesize a safe policy that does not require the SC to intervene. Starting with this safe policy, Algorithm 2 runs for 25 iterations before termination. The magenta trajectory in Fig. 5(c) is from the minimally deviating policy repaired via Algorithm 2. Obviously the policy is able to correct itself without any intervention from the SC. In Fig. 5(d), we compare the velocities of the vehicles controlled by different policies. It can be observed that the velocities of all policies drop drastically due to traction-loss at around step 220. The minimally deviating repaired policy performs the best in restoring the velocity back to 8 m/s. It is worth noting that velocity stability is important from the viewpoint of passenger comfort.

We summarize the results in Table 1. The performances of the algorithms are evaluated from multiple aspects. We evaluate how well the task is finished from 1) average speed (the closer to the target speed 8 m/s the better); 2) average distance of the vehicle to the middle of the lane (the smaller the better); 3) total time taken for the driving task in number of simulation steps (the fewer the better). We evaluate the smoothness of the trajectories based on the variances/standard deviations of speeds, distances, changes of speed and distance respectively in consecutive time steps. A smaller variance/standard deviation indicates a smoother navigation.

Table 1. Avg. Speed: average speed of the vehicle in each run. Lowest Speed: the lowest speed since the vehicle firstly reaches $8m/s$ in each run. Aveg. Distance: the average distance between the vehicle and the middle of the lane at each step. Tot. Steps: the total number of steps that the vehicle outputs control actions in one run. Var. Speed: the variance of the speed at each step in each run. Std Dev. Speed Change: the standard deviation of the speed changes between consecutive steps. Var. Distance: the variance of the distance between the vehicle and the middle of the lane at each step. Std Dev. Distance Change: the standard deviation of the distance (from vehicle to the middle of the lane) changes between consecutive steps. Initial policy is tested before and after the traction-loss area is placed. The initial policy and SC pair is tested after the traction-loss event occurs. 'Algorithm 1' and 'Algorithm 2' respectively refer to the policies repaired via those two algorithms.

	Avg. Speed (m/s)	Lowest Speed (m/s)	Avg. Distance (m)	Tot. Steps (0.03 s/step)
Initial Policy (No Traction-Loss Event)	8.0	7.1	0.27	396
Initial Policy	8.0	5.2	1.7	420
Initial Policy w/ SC	7.1	1.2	0.81	454
Algorithm 1	7.5	2.4	1.1	440
Algorithm 2	**7.9**	**5.2**	**0.63**	**413**

	Var. Speed	Std Dev. Speed Change	Var. Distance	Std Dev. Distance Change
Initial Policy (No Traction-Loss Event)	0.53	0.074	0.10	0.0096
Initial Policy	0.79	0.16	4.4	0.026
Initial Policy w/ SC	2.1	0.17	1.0	0.033
Algorithm 1	2.4	0.17	1.4	0.042
Algorithm 2	**0.73**	**0.15**	**1.0**	**0.033**

Before the traction-loss area is placed, the initial policy drives the vehicle at $8m/s$ on average and keeps the vehicle close to the middle of the lane. After the traction-loss event occurs, the initial policy still maintains the speed but the car slides out of the lane as indicated by the average distance. The initial policy and SC pair has the lowest average and lowest speed. As a result, the task time (represented by number of simulation steps) is also the longest. In terms of policy repair, both Algorithm 1 and 2 are successful in finding safe policies. The policy repaired via Algorithm 1 behaves similar to the initial policy and SC pair – the vehicle experiences significant speed changes and takes longer to finish the driving task. The minimally deviating policy repaired via Algorithm 2 behaves similarly to the initial policy in terms of maintaining the target speed, staying close to the middle of the lane while producing a smooth trajectory. In summary, the repaired policy using Algorithm 2 outperforms the initial policy with SC and the repaired policy using solely Algorithm 1 in almost all metrics. In terms of runtime overhead savings, the average neural network inference time on our machine configuration is 0.0003 s while the average time for SC to solve (3)–(8) is 0.39 s.

To further measure the impact of policy repair and evaluate the performance difference between a naive repair (using Algorithm 1) and a minimally deviating repair (using Algorithm 2), we remove the traction-loss area and execute both repaired policies in the original environment. It can be observed in Fig. 5(e) that the naively repaired policy cuts inside the lane, since it learns (possibly due to overfitting) to steer inward in the states where traction loss is supposed to occur. In contrast, the policy repaired using Algorithm 2 manages to keep the car in the lane, as it learns to imitate the original policy. This thus further validates our approach of finding a minimally deviating repair.

7 Conclusion

We consider a Simplex architecture where a learning-based controller is paired with a backup safety controller for ensuring runtime safety. We show that this setup, while provides added safety assurance, can produce undesired outputs or cause significant performance degradation. We propose to address this problem by fine-tuning the learning-based controller using interventions from the safety controller, and addressing the issue of performance degradation via imitation learning. Our experiments indicate that our proposed approach is effective in achieving both safety and performance even when the dynamical model used by the safety controller is not exact. In the future, we plan to consider other types of safety controllers and extend our techniques to end-to-end control settings.

Acknowledgements. We gratefully acknowledge the support from National Science Foundation (NSF) grants 1646497.

References

1. Achiam, J., Held, D., Tamar, A., Abbeel, P.: Constrained policy optimization. In: Proceedings of the 34th International Conference on Machine Learning, vol. 70, pp. 22–31. JMLR.org (2017)
2. Alshiekh, M., Bloem, R., Ehlers, R., Könighofer, B., Niekum, S., Topcu, U.: Safe reinforcement learning via shielding. In: Thirty-Second AAAI Conference on Artificial Intelligence (2018)
3. Amodei, D., Olah, C., Steinhardt, J., Christiano, P.F., Schulman, J., Mané, D.: Concrete problems in AI safety. CoRR, abs/1606.06565 (2016)
4. Argall, B.D., Chernova, S., Veloso, M., Browning, B.: A survey of robot learning from demonstration. Robot. Auton. Syst. 57(5), 469–483 (2009)
5. Bareiss, D., Van den Berg, J.: Reciprocal collision avoidance for robots with linear dynamics using LQR-Obstacles. In: 2013 IEEE International Conference on Robotics and Automation, pp. 3847–3853. IEEE (2013)
6. Borrelli, F., Keviczky, T., Balas, G.J.: Collision-free UAV formation flight using decentralized optimization and invariant sets. In: 2004 43rd IEEE Conference on Decision and Control (CDC) (IEEE Cat. No. 04CH37601), vol. 1, pp. 1099–1104. IEEE (2004)
7. Chen, J., Zhan, W., Tomizuka, M.: Constrained iterative LQR for on-road autonomous driving motion planning. In: 2017 IEEE 20th International Conference on Intelligent Transportation Systems (ITSC), pp. 1–7, October 2017
8. Cheng, R., Orosz, G., Murray, R.M., Burdick, J.W.: End-to-end safe reinforcement learning through barrier functions for safety-critical continuous control tasks. ArXiv, abs/1903.08792 (2019)
9. Chow, Y., Nachum, O., Duenez-Guzman, E., Ghavamzadeh, M.: A Lyapunov-based approach to safe reinforcement learning. In: Advances in Neural Information Processing Systems, pp. 8092–8101 (2018)
10. DeCastro, J.A., Kress-Gazit, H.: Guaranteeing reactive high-level behaviors for robots with complex dynamics. In: 2013 IEEE/RSJ International Conference on Intelligent Robots and Systems, pp. 49–756. IEEE (2013)
11. Dosovitskiy, A., Ros, G., Codevilla, F., Lopez, A., Koltun, V.: CARLA: an open urban driving simulator. In: Levine, S., Vanhoucke, V., Goldberg, K., (eds.), Proceedings of the 1st Annual Conference on Robot Learning, Proceedings of Machine Learning Research PMLR, vol. 78, pp. 1–16, 13–15 November 2017
12. Fulton, N., Platzer, A.: Safe reinforcement learning via formal methods: toward safe control through proof and learning. In: Thirty-Second AAAI Conference on Artificial Intelligence (2018)
13. Kwakernaak, H., Sivan, R.: Linear Optimal Control Systems, vol. 1. Wiley, New York (1972)
14. Li, W., Todorov, E.: Iterative linear quadratic regulator design for nonlinear biological movement systems. In: ICINCO (2004)
15. Maciejowski, J.: Predictive Control: With Constraints (2002)
16. Maler, O., Nickovic, D.: Monitoring temporal properties of continuous signals. In: Lakhnech, Y., Yovine, S. (eds.) FORMATS/FTRTFT -2004. LNCS, vol. 3253, pp. 152–166. Springer, Heidelberg (2004). https://doi.org/10.1007/978-3-540-30206-3_12
17. Menda, K., Driggs-Campbell, K., Kochenderfer, M.J..: EnsembleDAgger: a Bayesian approach to safe imitation learning. In: 2019 IEEE/RSJ International Conference on Intelligent Robots and Systems (IROS), pp. 5041–5048 (2019)

18. Nesterov, Y., Nemirovskii, A.: Interior-Point Polynomial Algorithms in Convex Programming. Society for Industrial and Applied Mathematics (1994)
19. Nocedal, J., Wright, S.: Numerical Optimization. Springer, Heidelberg (2006)
20. Osa, T., Pajarinen, J., Neumann, G., Bagnell, J.A., Abbeel, P., Peters, J.: An algorithmic perspective on imitation learning. Found. Trends® Robot. **7**(1–2), 1–179 (2018)
21. Pardalos, P.M., Vavasis, S.A.: Quadratic programming with one negative eigenvalue is NP-hard. J. Global Optim. **1**, 15–22 (1991)
22. Pereira, M., Fan, D.D., An, G.N., Theodorou, E.A.: MPC-inspired neural network policies for sequential decision making. CoRR, abs/1802.05803 (2018)
23. Phan, D., Paoletti, N., Grosu, R., Jansen, N., Smolka, S.A., Stoller, S.D.: Neural simplex architecture. ArXiv, abs/1908.00528 (2019)
24. Pnueli, A.: The temporal logic of programs. In: 18th Annual Symposium on Foundations of Computer Science (SFCS 1977), pp. 46–57. IEEE (1977)
25. Pomerleau, D.: ALVINN: an autonomous land vehicle in a neural network. In: NIPS (1988)
26. Raman, V., Donzé, A., Maasoumy, M., Murray, R.M., Sangiovanni-Vincentelli, A., Seshia, S.A.: Model predictive control with signal temporal logic specifications. In: 53rd IEEE Conference on Decision and Control, pp. 81–87. IEEE (2014)
27. Ross, S., Bagnell, D.: Efficient reductions for imitation learning. In: Proceedings of the Thirteenth International Conference on Artificial Intelligence and Statistics, pp. 661–668 (2010)
28. Ross, S., Gordon, G., Bagnell, D.: A reduction of imitation learning and structured prediction to no-regret online learning. In: Proceedings of the Fourteenth International Conference on Artificial Intelligence and Statistics, pp. 627–635 (2011)
29. Sadigh, D., Kapoor, A.: Safe control under uncertainty with probabilistic signal temporal logic. In: Proceedings of Robotics: Science and Systems XII, June 2016
30. Schulman, J., Levine, S., Abbeel, P., Jordan, M., Moritz, P.: Trust region policy optimization. In: International Conference on Machine Learning, pp. 1889–1897 (2015)
31. Schulman, J., Wolski, F., Dhariwal, P., Radford, A., Klimov, O.: Proximal policy optimization algorithms. CoRR, abs/1707.06347 (2017)
32. Seto, D., Krogh, B., Sha, L., Chutinan, A.: The simplex architecture for safe online control system upgrades. In: Proceedings of the 1998 American Control Conference. ACC (IEEE Cat. No. 98CH36207), vol. 6, pp. 504–3508, vol. 6 (1998)
33. Tassa, Y., Erez, T., Todorov, E.: Synthesis and stabilization of complex behaviors through online trajectory optimization. In: 2012 IEEE/RSJ International Conference on Intelligent Robots and Systems, pp. 4906–4913, October 2012
34. Wabersich, K.P., Zeilinger, M.N.: Linear model predictive safety certification for learning-based control. In: 2018 IEEE Conference on Decision and Control (CDC), pp. 7130–7135 (2018)
35. Wu, C.-J., et al.: Machine learning at Facebook: understanding inference at the edge. In: 2019 IEEE International Symposium on High Performance Computer Architecture (HPCA), pp. 331–344. IEEE (2019)
36. Zhang, J., Cho, K.: Query-efficient imitation learning for end-to-end simulated driving. In: AAAI (2017)
37. Zhou, W., Li, W.: Safety-aware apprenticeship learning. In: Chockler, H., Weissenbacher, G. (eds.) CAV 2018. LNCS, vol. 10981, pp. 662–680. Springer, Cham (2018). https://doi.org/10.1007/978-3-319-96145-3_38

PATRIoT: Policy Assisted Resilient Programmable IoT System

Moosa Yahyazadeh[1]([✉]), Syed Rafiul Hussain[2], Endadul Hoque[3], and Omar Chowdhury[1]

[1] The University of Iowa, Iowa City, IA 52242, USA
{moosa-yahyazadeh,omar-chowdhury}@uiowa.edu
[2] The Pennsylvania State University, University Park, PA 16802, USA
hussain1@psu.edu
[3] Syracuse University, Syracuse, NY 13244, USA
enhoque@syr.edu

Abstract. This paper presents PATRIoT, which efficiently monitors the behavior of a programmable IoT system at runtime and suppresses contemplated actions that violate a given declarative policy. Policies in PATRIoT are specified in effectively propositional, past metric temporal logic and capture the system's expected temporal invariants whose violation can break its desired security, privacy, and safety guarantees. PATRIoT has been instantiated for not only an industrial IoT system (EVA ICS) but also for two home representative automation platforms: one proprietary (SmartThings) and another open-source (OpenHAB). Our empirical evaluation shows that, while imposing only a moderate runtime overhead, PATRIoT can effectively detect policy violations.

Keywords: Runtime monitoring · IoT systems · Policy enforcement

1 Introduction

Programmable IoT systems, that have seen deployments in regular households as well as advanced manufacturing plants, enable one to carry out *specialized automation functions* by instructing a group of (COTS) actuators to perform different tasks based on sensor values, events, and business logic. For supporting diverse automation tasks, these systems allow one to develop and deploy *automation apps/units* whose complexity can range from simple if-then-else rules to complex machine learning based programs. As a simple example, an IoT app in a metal melting plant can command a lifter-robot (*i.e.*, actuator) to load scrap metal on a conveyor belt only when the weight sensor reads more than 100 lbs.

These automation apps that *(i)* can be possibly obtained from unvetted sources, *(ii)* can be malicious, *(iii)* may have logical bugs, or *(iv)* may interact in unanticipated ways with other apps, can render the system to unexpected states. Such unexpected state transitions can halt a production line, create safety-hazards, or violate security and privacy guarantees of such systems. For

© Springer Nature Switzerland AG 2020
J. Deshmukh and D. Ničković (Eds.): RV 2020, LNCS 12399, pp. 151–171, 2020.
https://doi.org/10.1007/978-3-030-60508-7_8

instance, an IoT app in a melting plant can instruct the lifter-robot to load scrap metal on an already loaded conveyor belt, severely damaging it and creating a safety hazard. *This paper focuses on developing a runtime policy enforcement approach for ensuring that a system under monitoring does not reach such unexpected states.*

A majority of the existing work relies on static analysis of apps to identify such undesired behavior [17,20,24,30,37,39] but suffers from one of the following limitations: *(i)* false positives due to conservative analysis; *(ii)* false negatives due to single app analysis; or *(iii)* scalability issues due to state-space explosion. Existing runtime enforcement based approaches [18,28,41], on the contrary, have one of the following limitations: *(i)* requires constructing the whole state-space of the global IoT system statically which is infeasible for large systems; *(ii)* cannot enforce rich temporal policies; *(iii)* policy specification is based on the transitions on the global state-space which is extremely inconvenient.

In this paper, we present PATRIoT which monitors the contemplated actions of programmable IoT apps at runtime and denies them only when they violate a declarative policy. The policy language of PATRIoT can refer to any past events/actions/system states, impose explicit-time constraints between any past events/states, and contain predicates over quantitative aspects of the system execution (*e.g.*, number of times an event has occurred in the last 10 s). Technically, this language can be automatically translated to a first-order, past-time metric temporal logic (MTL) with some aggregation functions (e.g., count, mean). The first-order logic portion of it, modulo aggregation functions, is restricted to a fragment of the Bernays–Schönfinkel class (or, effectively proposition logic or EPR). This conscious choice allows us not only to express a rich set of policies but also to enforce our policies efficiently by drawing inspirations from existing runtime monitoring algorithms [12–15,35,36]. Unlike first-order MTL, for enforcing our policies, it is sufficient to store only truth values of sub-formulas with auxiliary structures of the immediate previous state instead of any past variable substitutions.

To show PATRIoT's generality, we instantiated it for 3 representative IoT systems, namely, EVA ICS [4] in the context of Industrial IoT systems, and also Samsung SmartThings [7] and OpenHAB [5], in the context of home automation. For instantiating PATRIoT, we resort to inline reference monitoring in which we automatically instrument each app by guarding high-level APIs for performing actions with a call to the policy decision function. We develop automatic instrumentation approach for each of the platforms. In addition, as automation apps can run concurrently, one has to also use appropriate synchronization mechanisms (e.g., mutex) to avoid any inconsistencies during state update of the reference monitor. We needed to design such a synchronization mechanism for SmartThings (e.g., mutex) as its programming interface did not provide any.

In an empirical evaluation with two case studies, one based on metal melting plant and another based on home automation, we observed that PATRIoT was able to mitigate all the undesired state transitions while incurring an average of 137 ms of runtime overhead. We have also designed PatRIoT as a standalone library which other platforms can use to perform policy checking.

To summarize, the paper has the following technical contributions:

- We propose PatRIoT, which monitors the execution of an IoT system at runtime and prevents it from entering an undesired state by denying actions that violate a policy.
- We instantiate PatRIoT for three representative programmable IoT platforms, namely, EVA ICS [4], SmartThings [7], and OpenHAB [5]. Our evaluation with these instantiations show that they are not only effective in identifying non-compliant actions but also efficient in terms of runtime overhead.

2   Scope and Motivation

Most of the IoT ecosystems, despite being complex, share a similar architecture. Figure 1 shows a general IoT system consisting of a wide range of devices (*e.g.*, robot arm, surveillance cameras, smart lights) and a programmable IoT platform, which serves as a centralized backend of the system. The backend typically exposes some programming interfaces for IoT apps (or a system control panel) to automate the system (or directly control the devices, respectively).

The backend is a (logically) centralized server, dedicated for storage and computation, is responsible to synchronize the physical world with the cyber world. It can be physically co-located or placed in a remote cloud. Nevertheless, it provides a human machine interface to enable remote control and monitoring. Nowadays, most IoT platforms expose programming interfaces for programmers to develop flexible and customized IoT apps. The app execution engine coordinates the execution of all IoT apps in which the automated operations of the IoT system occur as they directly guide (and possibly, alter) the physical processes.

All actions taking place in an IoT system form its behavior. The actions in IoT apps are based on the automation tasks in that system. Given an IoT app's business logic, commanding an action might not only depend on the devices' events for which the IoT app (issuing the action) is registered but also hinge on the current context in the system. The current context for an action is formed by the snapshot of the system state right before taking the action. As the complexity of an IoT system (including its automation tasks) scales and grows, the dependency between actions and the system state becomes more tangled. Hence, to capture the expected behavior, this complexity of the dependency between action and the system state needs to be taken into account.

Policy. The expected behavior of an IoT system can be captured via a set of expressions, called *policies*. All policies must be invariably maintained by the system at runtime while the IoT apps are active and operating. A policy is maintained if it is satisfied by an impending action of any IoT app given the current execution trace. Thus, if an action respects every policy, then the system is considered to comply with the policies and allows the action to be executed. In case of a violation, an action must be denied to prevent potential repercussions.

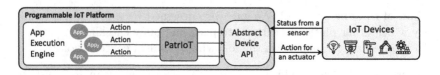

Fig. 1. A programmable IoT platform with PATRIoT installed. Without PATRIoT, every `Action` would be directly forwarded to the device API.

Threats. Any unwanted behavior, caused by single IoT app or *unintended interplays* among multiple IoT apps, can impose security, privacy, or safety threats to the IoT system. The security threats exist if an unwanted action impairs an IoT system by changing its state such that it cannot perform its intended functions (*i.e.*, targeting system integrity) or gives an unauthorized access to the protected data (*i.e.*, violating data confidentiality). Depending on the criticality level of the IoT apps, such unwanted actions can also threaten the safety of the system (*e.g.*, failing to turn on the fire sprinkler of the factory floor when there is a fire). Not to mention that allowing some of those action can also violate the privacy (*e.g.*, posting a tweet by a medicine-reminder app unbeknown to the user). An IoT system can face such threat due to a number of vulnerabilities including cross-app interference, race conditions due to concurrent executions of apps, a lack of fine-grained access control mechanisms in the underlying platforms, and semantic bugs in apps. As an example, let us let us consider cross-app interference vulnerabilities specialized for programmable IoT systems.

Since IoT app's action can change a device state and/or a physical processes (*i.e.*, the environment), it can generate additional trigger(s) which in turn can execute another IoT app. Such interplay among IoT apps can be either *explicit* or *implicit* [20]. In an explicit interplay, the outcome of an action directly triggers other IoT app. For instance, running *"if the weight sensor detects some weights then turn on the conveyor belt"* explicitly triggers *"if the conveyor belt is rolling then turn on the object detector"*. Contrarily, in an implicit interplay, the outcome of an action changes some attributes of the physical environment which can consequently trigger other IoT app. For example, *"if water temperature is greater than 200°F then open the outgoing valve of the cooler to drain hot water"* implicitly triggers *"if water level is low then open the incoming valve to refill the cooler with cold water"*.

Attacker Model. In this paper, we assume an attacker is capable of launching the unwanted behavior by *(i)* developing the malicious IoT apps exploiting the above vulnerabilities or *(ii)* simply misusing the existing faulty IoT apps, where the latter does not necessarily need to involve the attacker, yet is unwittingly introduced by a developer. For smart home based systems, a malicious app can creep in to the system through *unvetted* marketplaces from which users often obtain IoT apps. Contrarily, IoT systems like IIoT may not have open marketplaces, but they are prone to—(i) insiders who can carry and install malicious apps, and (ii) untrusted third-party developers. Any undesired situation resulted from compromised IoT devices, by exploiting vulnerabilities in firmware or communication protocols, and even the IoT backend itself is beyond our scope.

Motivating Example. Consider a smart building where access restrictions are imposed on the entry of several rooms. An IoT integrated reader installed near the entry unlocks the door when a presented credential (*e.g.*, smart card) is authenticated. This one-way security entrance operation is one of the most popular and simplest access control solutions for smart buildings in which once someone is authorized entering a room, then they can easily exit the room because the door is unlocked from inside. In this situation, an unwanted behavior could occur when an unauthorized person sneaks into the room through a window or ventilation pipe and then they can freely open the door and enter into the building. A security measure preventing this undesirable situation is to check the following temporal policy before unlocking the door from inside:

> **Allow** unlatching the door lock
> **only if** the **number** of granted door access requests is
> greater than the **number** of times door unlatched.

That is, unlatching the door from inside is allowed whenever someone entered into the room before.

3 Overview of PATRIOT

In this section, we present an abstract programmable IoT system model, our problem definition, and PATRIoT's architecture.

3.1 Abstract Model

A programmable IoT system $\mathcal{I}$ is viewed as a labeled transition system defined by the tuple $\langle \mathcal{S}, \mathcal{A}, \mathcal{P}, \mathcal{V}, \mathcal{T} \rangle$, where $\mathcal{S}$ is a non-empty, finite set of states, $\mathcal{A}$ is a finite set of high-level activities in the IoT system, $\mathcal{P}$ refers to a finite set of all possible IoT apps supported by the underlying platform, $\mathcal{V}$ refers to a finite but arbitrary set of *typed* variables, and $\mathcal{T}$ is the transition relation $\mathcal{T} \subseteq \mathcal{S} \times \mathcal{A} \times \mathcal{S}$ regulates how $\mathcal{I}$ changes its states while reacting to the activities. A state is total map that assigns each variable $v \in \mathcal{V}$ a value from an appropriate domain.

We consider $\mathcal{T}$ to be a *deterministic* and *left-total* relation (*i.e.*, no dead states). For all states $s_b, s_e \in \mathcal{S}$ and activity $a \in \mathcal{A}$, if $\langle s_b, a, s_e \rangle \in \mathcal{T}$ (alternatively, $s_b \xrightarrow{a} s_e$), then it suggests that when the system is in state s_b and an activity a is performed, then $\mathcal{I}$ will move to the state s_e. Given a state $s_b \in \mathcal{S}$ such that $s_b = [v_{\text{valve1}} \mapsto \text{close}, \ldots]$ and an activity $a = \langle \textit{caused\_by} \mapsto \text{app}_1, \textit{target\_device} \mapsto \text{valve1}, \textit{activity\_value} \mapsto \text{open} \rangle$ by an app (called $\text{app}_1 \in \mathcal{P}$), then $\mathcal{I}$ will transition to a state s_e, where $s_e = [v_{\text{valve1}} \mapsto \text{open}, \ldots]$.

3.2   Problem Definition

Given a programmable IoT system $\mathcal{I}$, let σ be a finite execution trace of it. A trace σ is a finite sequence of states $\sigma = \langle s_0, s_1, s_2, \ldots, s_{n-1} \rangle$. We use $|\sigma|$ to denote the length of the trace σ. For each trace σ, we require that there exists an activity $a \in \mathcal{A}$ such that $s_i \xrightarrow{a} s_{i+1} \in \mathcal{T}$ where $0 \leq i < |\sigma| - 1$. Given $\mathcal{I}$ and a policy Ψ, in this paper, we want to ensure that each *action* activity performed by an app $\in \mathcal{P}$ is compliant with Ψ, formalized as below. Given a programmable IoT system $\mathcal{I}$, a policy Ψ, a valid trace $\sigma = \langle s_0, s_1, \ldots, s_{n-1} \rangle$ of $\mathcal{I}$, and an action activity a_c, the *policy compliance problem* is to decide whether $\sigma' = \langle s_0, s_1, \ldots, s_{n-1}, s_n \rangle$ is compliant with Ψ where $s_{n-1} \xrightarrow{a_c} s_n \in \mathcal{T}$.

3.3   Architecture of PATRIOT

PATRIoT's reference monitor has the following three main components: *Policy Enforcement Point* (PEP), *Policy Decision Point* (PDP), and *Policy Information Point* (PIP). The PEP intercepts each action contemplated by apps installed in a programmable IoT system. It then consults the PDP to decide whether the action is compliant with the given policies. If the action is compliant, it is allowed to be carried out; otherwise, the action is denied. The PDP implements the *policy decision function* which takes as input an action, and returns ALLOW or DENY. It essentially solves the *policy compliance problem*. The PIP stores all the relevant information regarding the policy (*e.g.*, policy statements) and system information (*e.g.*, device status) that are necessary for policy decision.

4   Design of PatrIoT

In this section, we present the syntax and semantics of PATRIoT's policy language as well as PATRIoT's solution to policy compliance problem.

4.1   Policy Language Syntax

Note that, in what follows, we discuss the abstract syntax of our language. A policy consists of one or more *policy blocks*. Each policy block starts with a **Policy** keyword followed by an identifier. The body of each block can have one or more *policy statements* of the following form. Policy blocks are introduced to allow modularity; grouping similar policy statements under a named block.

```
allow/deny <target_clause>
    [only if <condition_clause>]
    [except <condition_clause>]
```

In a policy statement, we can use either **allow** or **deny** keyword to identify allow or deny statements, respectively. The *allow* (or, *deny*) statements capture the conditions under which certain actions are permitted (or, discarded, respectively). The <target_clause> is an expression that captures information about the actions for which the policy statement is applicable. It has the form of a non-temporal condition (i.e., Ψ) shown below. We allow a special wild-card keyword, **everything**, in place of <target_clause>, to denote all possible actions. The optional **only if** portion contains a <condition_clause> that expresses a logical condition under which the action, identified by the <target_clause>, will be allowed (or, denied). The optional **except** portion contains a <condition_clause> that captures the exceptional cases under which the restriction expressed by the <condition_clause> in **only if** portion can be disregarded.

$$\text{(Term)}\, t ::= v \mid c \mid f(\Phi)$$
$$\text{(Non-temporal Condition)}\Psi ::= \textbf{true} \mid \textbf{false} \mid \mathsf{P}(t_1, t_2) \mid \textbf{not}\,\Psi_1 \mid \Psi_1\textbf{or}\,\Psi_2 \mid \Psi_1\textbf{and}\,\Psi_2$$
$$\text{(Temporal Condition)}\Phi ::= \Psi \mid \mathsf{Since}_{[\ell,r]}(\Phi_1, \Phi_2) \mid \mathsf{Lastly}_{[\ell,r]}(\Phi_1) \mid \mathsf{Once}_{[\ell,r]}(\Phi_1) \mid$$
$$\textbf{not}\,\Phi_1 \mid \Phi_1\textbf{or}\,\Phi_2 \mid \Phi_1\textbf{and}\,\Phi_2$$
$$(\langle\text{condition\_clause}\rangle) ::= \Phi|\Psi$$

A condition clause can be either be a temporal condition or a non-temporal condition. A non-temporal formula (i.e., Ψ) can be **true**, **false**, a predicate or their logical combinations. We use **and**, **or**, and **not** to denote the logical conjunction, disjunction, and negation, respectively. We only consider binary *predicates* P where one of its arguments is a constant. A *term* is either a variable v, a constant c, or an aggregation function f. Currently, we have the following standard predicates: $>, \geq, =, \neq, \leq, <$. Examples of predicates could be Temperature ≥ 78 and Humidity < 30. We currently allow the Count aggregation function.

The condition clause can use three standard *past* temporal operators $\mathsf{Since}_{[\ell,r]}(\cdot, \cdot)$, $\mathsf{Lastly}_{[\ell,r]}(\cdot)$, and $\mathsf{Once}_{[\ell,r]}(\cdot)$. To enable condition clause to refer to explicit time differences between different state values, each of the temporal operators can optionally take an additional time interval $[\ell, r]$, where ℓ and r denote the lowerbound and upperbound such that $\ell, r \in \mathbb{R}^+ \cup \{0, \infty\}$ and $\ell \leq r$. If ℓ is 0, it points to the current state. r can be ∞ to allow temporal operators to refer to arbitrarily in the past. Using ℓ and r, we can adjust a time window on which a temporal operator can be applied.

Examples. Having understood the basics of policy language syntax, we can formally specify the policy given in motivating example 2 as follows:

```
POLICY Motivating_Example_1:
  ALLOW action_command = unlatch and action_device = door
  ONLY IF COUNT(ONCE(state(door_reader) = access_granted)) >
          COUNT(ONCE(state(door) = unlatched))
```

4.2   Policy Language Semantics

We provide the semantics of policy language by converting any given policy to a quantifier-free, first-order metric temporal logic (QF-MTL) formula.

A policy Ψ consists of a sequence of policy statements $\langle ps_1, ps_2, \ldots, ps_n \rangle$. Given that each policy statement ps_i can be converted into a QF-MTL formula

φ_i, the QF-MTL equivalent of Ψ denoted with φ can be logically viewed as combining φ_i with logical conjunctions (*i.e.*, $\varphi \equiv \bigwedge_{i=1}^{n} \varphi_i$). Conceptually, this is similar to using the "DENY overrides ALLOW" conflict resolution mechanism to combine compliance verdicts of the different policy statements. In this mechanism, an action is thus allowed only if all the policy statements have the ALLOW verdict (i.e., evaluates to true) for that action. Note that, if an action falsifies the <target_clause> component of each rule, then it is trivially allowed. It is also possible to easily extend the language to support other conflict resolution mechanisms (e.g., "ALLOW overrides DENY", "first applicable policy statement").

Our discussion of formal semantics will thus be complete as long as we describe how to convert each policy statement ps_i to its equivalent QF-MTL formula. In our presentation, $\varphi_{\text{applicable\_action}}$, $\varphi_{\text{condition}}$, and $\varphi_{\text{exception}}$ are meta-variables representing corresponding QF-MTL formulas capturing the applicable action, condition, and exception of a statement, respectively. We interpret the allow statement as the following QF-MTL formula: $\varphi_{\text{applicable\_action}} \Rightarrow \varphi_{\text{condition}} \wedge \neg \varphi_{\text{exception}}$. In the similar vein, we interpret the deny statement as the following QF-MTL formula: $\varphi_{\text{applicable\_action}} \Rightarrow \neg \varphi_{\text{condition}} \vee \varphi_{\text{exception}}$.

In case either the optional condition or exception block is missing, we consider them to be logical TRUE (*i.e.*, $\varphi_{\text{condition}} = \text{TRUE}$) or FALSE (*i.e.*, $\varphi_{\text{exception}} = \text{FALSE}$), respectively. When the condition block contains **everything**, we consider $\varphi_{\text{applicable\_action}} = \text{TRUE}$. Otherwise, obtaining $\varphi_{\text{applicable\_action}}$, $\varphi_{\text{condition}}$, and $\varphi_{\text{exception}}$ from policy syntax are straightforward. Each syntactic element are replaced by its logical equivalent (*e.g.*, **not** with $\neg$, **or** with $\vee$, and **and** with $\wedge$). Similarly, the temporal operators will be replaced by their usual equivalent. For a given temporal formula Φ, a trace σ, and a position i in it (i.e., $0 \leq i < |\Phi|$), we write $\sigma, i \models \Phi$ if and only if Φ evaluates to true in the ith position of σ [6].

4.3   Policy Decision Function

PATRIoT's policy decision function (Δ) takes as input an attempted action a_c, the current execution trace $\sigma = \langle s_0, s_1, \ldots, s_{n-1} \rangle$, and a policy Ψ (whose QF-MTL equivalent is φ), then decides whether a_c is compliant with Ψ. In case a_c is compliant (i.e., φ evaluates to true), Δ returns ALLOW; it returns DENY, otherwise. PATRIoT's decision function checks whether $\sigma', n \models^? \varphi$ where $\sigma' = \langle s_0, s_1, \ldots, s_{n-1}, s_n \rangle$ and $s_{n-1} \xrightarrow{a_c} s_n \in \mathcal{T}$. For checking $\sigma', n \models^? \varphi$, we rely on standard runtime monitoring algorithms from the literature [11,13–15,22,35,36].

5   Implementation

To demonstrate the generality of PATRIoT, we have instantiated it for both industrial IoT (EVA ICS [4]) and smart-home systems (SmartThings [7] and OpenHAB [5]). Although these systems share similar design principles with respect to other IoT platforms, each presents unique challenges for PATRIoT instantiation. Since EVA ICS, SmartThings, and OpenHAB do not provide native APIs support for policy enforcement, we hooked PATRIoT in these

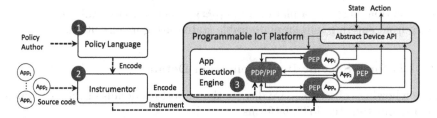

Fig. 2. The flowchart of automation tool to deploy PATRIoT with the necessary components inside the target programmable IoT platform.

platforms automation unit execution engine (shown in Fig. 2) such that all PATRIoT's necessary components are realized by code snippets (automatically generated by an accompanying toolchain, which we call as the *instrumentor*). That is, the auto-generated code can be deployed inside the IoT platform alongside the apps logics. This makes PATRIoT self-contained since it does not require any custom service from the target platforms and can enforce policy compliance by the platform's app execution engine.

As shown in Fig. 2, PATRIoT's instrumentor takes the policies and IoT apps as inputs and automatically generates instrumented-, ready-to-be-deployed-apps as outputs. The instrumentor is written as a Python script and internally uses its own parser (generated by ANTLR [1]) to parse policy language syntax (step ❶). Once parsed, its semantics will be encoded as a part of Policy Decision Point (PDP) in the platform's supporting language (step ❷). The PDP code is also accompanied by all the necessary codes retrieving information about the system/devices states. The instrumentor also parses the apps source code to find the actions of interest (*i.e.*, the function calls sending command). These actions are then guarded with an `if` block, predicated on a function call to PDP by passing the request context as its arguments. With that in place, PATRIoT can enforce the policies given the decision result from PDP at runtime. That is, the requested action is either allowed to be taken or simply needs to be dropped.

Note that, there are two main aspects need to be considered in the design of PDP. First, it should be deployed at a place reachable by every guarded action in the apps inside the execution engine, whilst preserving a global view of the entire system state. Second, each function call to PDP for each guarded action needs be synchronized. This is due to the fact that multiple action commands from different apps can be called roughly at the same time, which might cause some state change while the current thread running inside PDP has already read its old value. Therefore, once the decision has been made in PDP, it will be no longer valid since its premise might have changed. This is a well-known concurrency issue called Time-of-check Time-of-use (TOCTOU) race condition [3] which can be addressed by some synchronization mechanism. Note that, allowing only sequential actions is not restrictive, as eventually they will be serialized in the network modem; however, it may affect the performance of the system. Once the instrumentation is finished, the generated code can be run inside the automation execution engine of a platform (step ❸), which automatically prevents the system from entering into an undesirable state during its execution.

5.1 Platform-Specific Implementation Details

In the following subsections, we discuss the important details of the instrumentation in our targeted IoT platforms.

EVA ICS. EVA ICS is an IoT platform for the automated system development in both industrial and home environment [4]. The automation units in EVA ICS is called *macros* which mainly supports Python as its scripting language.

PEP. EVA ICS provides uniform APIs (e.g., `action()`, `action_toggle()`) for performing actions in a macro. Calling these functions with appropriate arguments result in a global state change. For instance, `action('zone1/lifter_-robot', status=1)` will activate `lifter_robot` residing in `zone1`. Our instrumentor uses its own custom parser to spot these actions in macros' source code. Once identified, its arguments (*e.g.*, `'zone1/lifter_robot'` and 1) are extracted to be then passed to PDP as part of the request context. The identified action is then guarded with an `if` block, whose condition is a function call to PDP to which the pre-extracted information such as the target device and command name are passed as its arguments. EVA ICS also provides native support for locking mechanism via `lock()` and `unlock()` functions, which can be used to address synchronization issue discussed earlier.

PDP/PIP. EVA ICS runs macros whose source codes reside in a specific folder in the system. If any piece of code needs to be shared among them, it has to be stored in `common.py` and also located in the same folder with the apps. Given that it can be readily accessed by the other macros and any code inside of it can see the entire system states, `common.py` file is our target to store the policy decision function encoding the semantics of policy language policies. There are other platform-supported features used to capture the request context inside the PDP function (*e.g.*, `_00` variable for obtaining current macro's full identifier and `_source` variable to access the item generated the event).

SmartThings. SmartThings is a cloud-based smart-home platform with a proprietary back-end that can provide automations among SmartThings-powered IoT devices. The automation units in SmartThings are called *SmartApps* which support a restricted subset of the groovy language [7].

PEP. SmartThings uses a variety of methods for performing an action. For example, it uses `on()` method of an object with `capability.switch` to turn it on (*e.g.*, `light1.on()`). Given a pre-compiled action list, the instrumentor parses the source code of SmartApps to find those actions and then guarding them with PEP-related statements. Since SmartApps are groovy-based programs, we use groovy meta-programming feature [2] which allows traversing the Abstract

Syntax Tree (AST) of a SmartApp. To this end, we use a groovy script that uses `ASTTransformation` class to write a custom `ASTNode` visitor to spot each method call in the pre-compiled action list and then replacing it with a ternary operator such that in the condition portion it checks whether the function call to PDP is evaluated to be true. In the true branch, it performs the guarded action while in the false branch it logs that the action is denied. The `ASTNode` visitor also extracts the necessary request context and passes them to PDP as arguments. After visitor's pass, our groovy script translates the AST back to the source code and spits it out as the instrumented SmartApp.

PDP/PIP. Recall that, PDP needs to have a global view of the entire system. In SmartThings, this can be achieved through the Parent-Child SmartApps relationship structure in which the PDP is defined as a function inside a parent SmartApp, so-called policy manager, while the previously instrumented SmartApps are considered as its children. This setup not only features all SmartApps to call the same PDP function but also enables the PDP to access the state of all devices used by the SmartApps. Unfortunately, SmartThings does not provide any built-in synchronization primitives. To address concurrency issues, we have built PATRIoT lock management server which is **(i) RESTful**: SmartApps requests for a lock by a simple HTTP post (*e.g.*, http://<domain : port>/locks/PatriotLock). The server notifies them whether lock is acquired or not by a HTTP response code (*e.g.*, 201: The lock is acquired; 408: lock is not acquired). SmartApps release the lock by a HTTP delete; **(ii) Queue-based**: It simply uses FIFO approach to give the lock to the oldest request. The further requests have to wait for the one who acquired the lock to release it and then the older request can acquire it (if the request has not gotten timed-out); **(iii) Starving-free**: The created lock has a lifetime in seconds which server starts counting down from each request which successfully acquires the lock. So, if the client does not release the lock before the lock lifetime, server simply releases the lock; and **(iv) Secure**: It uses HTTPS for each request and release. Each request/release is authenticated (using a pre-shared key) and replay protected; therefore, a malicious entity cannot make illegal lock request/release.

OpenHAB. OpenHAB is an open-source smart-home platform that can be deployed locally. The automation units in OpenHAB are called *rules* and are written in a domain specific language (DSL).

PEP. OpenHAB has a well-structured category of actions that can be used inside a rule to perform an action. Our instrumentor uses that to select the actions of interest. For instance, `sendCommand()` and `postUpdate()` are methods for sending a command to an item and updating an item's status, respectively. Since rules in OpenHAB are written in a DSL, we developed a custom parser to instrument a rule's source code. The synchronization issue in OpenHAB is handled using mutex lock provided by the platform.

Table 1. Item list used for EVA ICS chemical plant testbed

compound_valve01	liquid_level_indicator01 (lli01)
compound_valve02	presence_sensor01 (ps01)
conveyor_belt	presence_sensor02 (ps02)
drain_valve	quality_control_sensor01 (qc01)
lifter_robot	temperature_sensor01 (ts01)
lifting_arm	weight_sensor01(ws01)
mixing_robot	weight_sensor02 (ws02)
stopper	processed_sensor
water_valve	

Table 2. Automation units used in EVA ICS testbed

ID	AU Description
AU_1	ws01 sensed $\longrightarrow$ activate lifter_robot
AU_2	ws02 sensed $\longrightarrow$ activate stopper
AU_3	ps01 sensed $\longrightarrow$ activate mixing_robot
AU_4	mixing_robot activated $\longrightarrow$ if lli01 off: activate lifting_arm; open compound_valve01; open compound_valve02;
AU_5	ts01 on $\longrightarrow$ open water_valve
AU_6	qc01 passed $\longrightarrow$ if ts01 off: open drain_valve; deactivate mixing_robot;
AU_7	mixing_robot deactivated $\longrightarrow$ deactivate stopper
AU_8	ps02 sensed $\longrightarrow$ set processed;

PDP/PIP. In OpenHAB, rules written in the same file can share global variables and utilize the common functions. Given that, the instrumentor merge all rules into the single rule file and encode PDP as a common function.

6 Evaluation

In this section, we evaluate our instantiations of PATRIoT. The main goal of our evaluation is to demonstrate PATRIoT effectiveness in maintaining the user expectations and its efficiency in terms of runtime overhead on a host platform.

6.1 Effectiveness

To showcase the effectiveness of PATRIoT in each platform, we built a testbed containing several IoT devices and constructed different scenarios in which some undesired action(s) can occur.

EVA ICS

Testbed. The testbed is similar to a realistic production line of a chemical plant aiming to combine metal blocks with two other compounds in a furnace. Table 1

and Table 2 show the item list and simplified apps used for this testbed, respectively. To setup the testbed for EVA ICS, we deployed EVA ICS-3.2.4 [4] on a machine powered by an Intel Core i7-6700 3.40 GHz CPU and with 32 GB RAM.

The testbed production line is designed to receive a metal block at a time and deliver it to the furnace in order to be combined with two other compounds and then drain the mixture into another production line (not covered here) and start the whole process again for a new batch. In this periodic operation, each element in the system takes a fixed amount of time to perform its task and deliver its output to the next element. The design of the system guarantees that the overall time needed for each iteration is significantly longer than the total time needed by each element in isolation. Each iteration starts when a pallet carrying a metal block has been placed on a weight sensor $ws01$, which activates AU_1. The robot then lifts the pallet and places it on the conveyor belt. The conveyor belt's weight sensor $ws02$ notifies the stopper in the middle-end of the line about the incoming pallet via AU_2. Once arrived, the stopper engages the pallet and detaches it from conveyor belt. The presence sensor $ps01$ then detects package arrival and AU_3 activates the mixing robot. According to AU_4, the mixing robot then checks whether the liquid level indicator $11i01$ inside the furnace is off and then activates the lifting arm to take the metal block off the pallet and puts it inside the furnace. It then opens the compound valves 1 and 2, respectively. As the result of some chemical process, the temperature of the mixture goes up until the temperature sensor $ts01$ trips. In that case AU_5 opens the water valve to cool down the mixture. Once cooled, it reaches to the point making the quality control sensor $qc01$ to indicate "passed" signal. Then, AU_6 gets executed and monitors $ts01$ to double check whether it is safe to open the drain valve and reset the mixing robot. Deactivating the mixing robot then releases the stopper (AU_7) which puts the pallet back on the conveyor belt letting it to go towards the end of the line where presence sensor $ps02$ resides. Once $ps02$ tripped, it signals the batch process has completed (AU_8) and pallet will be removed automatically from the conveyor belt.

Although this production line works fine for most situations, there are some undesired cases that can cause fatal physical damages such as *conveyor belt blockage*, *liquid overflow*, and *ruining the batch*.

Scenario #1 - Conveyor Belt Blockage. There are several reasons that can cause multiple pallets to be on conveyor belt at the same time making the conveyor belt to break because of its weight tolerance limitation or crashing a few pallets into each other. Having multiple pallets at the same time can happen if the previous pallet got stuck on an obstacle next to conveyor belt or malfunctioning stopper. Therefore, after passing the iteration time limit, our simulation has shown that multiple pallets can be placed on the conveyor belt causing the blockage. This undesirable situation has been prevented by PATRIOT using the policy in the Listing 1.1 which says *"deny activating the lifter robot only if since the last time it was activated, no batch has been processed"*.

Listing 1.1. policy language Policy P1 to address conveyor belt blockage

```
POLICY P1:
  DENY action_command = on and action_device = g1/lifter_robot
  ONLY IF LASTLY(SINCE(state(unit:g1/lifter_robot) = on, value(g1/processed) = 0))
```

Scenario #2 - Liquid Overflow. The production line is also susceptible to furnace overflow causing severe physical damages. According to our simulation, this undesirable situation can occur if, for example, the drain valve is faulty such that it cannot completely drain the previous batch and some significant amount of mixture liquid has remained in the furnace, which is still below the lli01 threshold. Therefore, once the next batch comes in (including the metal block, compounds 1 and 2, and the water) it will cause liquid overflow. PATRIoT prevents such undesirable situation via the following policies which simply checks the liquid level before taking any actions causing adding a substance to the furnace. This scenario with policies (P2-P5) in place could still create a conveyor belt blockage which will be prevented by the policy P1.

Listing 1.2. policy language Policies to address liquid overflow

```
POLICY P2:
  DENY action_command = on and action_device = g1/lifting_arm
  ONLY IF value(sensor:g1/lli01) = on

POLICY P3:
  DENY action_command = on and action_device = g1/compound_valve01
  ONLY IF value(sensor:g1/lli01) = on

POLICY P4:
  DENY action_command = on and action_device = g1/compound_valve02
  ONLY IF value(sensor:g1/lli01) = on

POLICY P5:
  DENY action_command = on and action_device = g1/water_valve
  ONLY IF value(sensor:g1/lli01) = on
```

Scenario #3 - Ruining the Batch. This scenario is based on the requirement which warrants that water will be added to the mixture only after compounds 1 and 2 have been poured. If the metal block is placed in the furnace containing water, that batch will be considered as ruined. This situation can happen in our testbed when for some reason (*e.g.*, ts01) water valve opens before mixing robot is activated in an iteration. PATRIoT uses the following policy to avoid this situation. The policy *"allows activating the mixing robot only if since the last time it was activated, water valve has not been opened"*.

Listing 1.3. policy language Policy P1 to address conveyor belt blockage

```
POLICY P6:
  ALLOW action_command = on and action_device = g1/mixing_robot
  ONLY IF LASTLY(SINCE(state(unit:g1/mixing_robot) = off, state(unit:g1/water_valve) =
      off))
```

SmartThings and OpenHAB

Testbeds. To perform our evaluation on the smart-home platforms we built two testbeds for SmartThings and OpenHAB in which we leveraged 48 IoT devices for our setup [6].

In order to setup the testbed for OpenHAB, we deployed OpenHAB 2.4 [5] on a Raspberry Pi 3 Model B+ and created our virtual devices inside the platform. Virtual devices in OpenHAB can be controlled and monitored via a web-based interfaced provided by the platform. For SmartThings, we used SmartThings web-based IDE to create these virtual devices. In order to control and monitor the status of these devices, SmartThings provides a companion mobile app, so-called SmartThings, which we used for this experiment.

IoT Apps. For our experiment, we used 122 SmartApps for SmartThings and 20 rules for OpenHAB which we collected from SmartThings official repository [8], IoTBench [16], and the developer community forums. All rules have been manually investigated to establish the ground-truth and understand their semantics and intentions. Unlike static analysis approaches, PATRIoT provides runtime protection; therefore, to evaluate its effectiveness, all these rules need to be executed in different scenarios and through the pre-established ground-truth one should validate whether PATRIoT can maintain user-specified policies.

Policies. In our experiment, we used 33 policies which are listed in Table 3. These policies are specified after studying the literature and acquiring the necessary knowledge by manually investigating the rules. Although the English description of these policies are provided for exposition, the policy language representation of these policies can be found in [6]. Table 3 also shows the main goal of each policy. For instance, **P1** restricts sending SMS by the rules to only those that the user expects to do so. In that case, all other apps trying to send SMS, whether maliciously or not, will be blocked by the policy. This policy aims to protect the user against any privacy violation. Policy **P27** also protects the expensive appliances (*e.g.*, water pump) from any damage that might be caused by repeatedly turning them on and off which can be as a result of a loop of actions because of a semantic bug or a malicious intent. In order to evaluate the effectiveness of PATRIoT we created three sample scenarios to illustrate that the specified policies are maintained by the system at runtime.

- *Privacy.* In this scenario, the main focus is on Policies **P1** and **P2**. Given these policies, PATRIoT only allowed user's authorized apps to send SMS while denying the action for other apps. For instance, a malicious app pretending to strobe the alarm when CO2 is detected while maliciously sending an advertisement before strobing the alarm. However, PATRIoT is able to successfully block that advertisement by sms at runtime.
- *Overprivilege.* This scenario mainly focuses on Policies such as **P3** and **P14** and PATRIoT only allowed the authorized apps to unlock the door and open the garage. Those malicious apps such as the one that monitors the battery level of the lock but sneakily detects that nobody is at home and then unlocks the door, are successfully blocked.
- *Interplay.* The focus of this scenarios is on Policies that can protect users from some hidden- unwanted actions such as **P5**. Based on fire-sprinkler app and dry-the-wetspot app, actions might interfere and as a result water valve

gets closed while there is still fire to contain. Given the policy PATRIoT successfully blocked unwanted closing of water valve.

6.2 Efficiency

In order to measure the runtime overhead of PATRIoT incurred on EVA ICS, SmartThings, and OpenHAB, we calculate the computation time of executing each automation unit *with* and *without* PATRIoT in place and then compare them to each other. Figure 3 illustrates the runtime overhead incurred by PATRIoT in different platforms, which is on average 8.96%, 9.44%, and 11.52% for EVA ICS, OpenHAB, and SmartThings, respectively. This runtime overhead depends on: *(i)* the number of actions happening at the same time; *(ii)* the complexity of the policies related to an impending action; and *(iii)* synchronization mechanism support for a platform. To have a fair evaluation, we carefully established our testbeds to closely reflect real-world IoT setups. For the application we had, although this overhead is acceptable, this could be an interesting future work to discover tighter overhead threshold for different applications. Figure 4 also shows the portion of the PATRIoT overhead incurred by locking mechanism. Among these platforms, SmartThings has the most locking overhead since it uses our external https-based lock manager. The locking overhead can be reduced, if we have native synchronization support form SmartThings.

7   Related Work

Prior efforts in IoT security are broadly focused on devices [10,23,27,31,33,38], communication and authentication protocols [25,34,42,43]. There are significant efforts focusing on unexpected behavior on programmable IoT systems [9,17–21,24,26,28–30,32,37,40,44], which is also the focus of this paper. Broadly speaking, there are two main approaches to address this issue: static and runtime monitoring approaches. The static approaches [17,20,24,30,37] are mostly pre-deployment techniques used for either: *(i)* further investigation like taint analysis to find out how private data is consumed by the apps (*i.e.*, whether or not there is any unwanted operation performed on the data); *(ii)* verifying that it satisfies a set of properties described as its correct behavior; or *(iii)* rectification aiming to fix mistakes in writing the trigger-action rules in it. Runtime monitoring based approaches, on the other hand, aim to provide post-deployment solutions to prevent unsafe/undesired operations at runtime [18,28,41]. These prior efforts, however, either require human intervention or cannot support rich temporal policies. Extensive work has been done in developing efficient runtime monitors using different types of logic [12–15,22,35,36]. Prior works on IoT security, however, have not leveraged these rich policy languages and do not take advantage of the developments in the runtime verification community. Apart from these works, there have been efforts repairing or synthesizing rules based on given properties [44] to make sure IoT apps behave as expected.

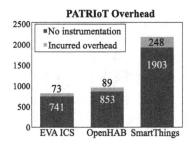

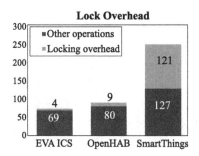

Fig. 3. Runtime overhead (in milliseconds) incurred by PATRIoT because of the instrumentation.

Fig. 4. Runtime overhead (in milliseconds) incurred by PATRIoT's synchronization mechanism.

8 Discussion

PatrIoT Policy Expressiveness. In contrast to existing IoT policy languages [18,28,41], PATRIoT policies have a formal semantics, are more expressive, and can specify existing IoT policies in the literature. With respect to MFOTL, however, PATRIoT policies neither support quantification nor arbitrary function symbols. Although such restrictions consciously limit the expressive power of the language to applicable to general policies, they are not only necessary for efficient monitoring but also sufficient to express existing IoT policies.

Authoring PatrIOT Policies. For PATRIoT's effectiveness, it is crucial for the users to be able to write the correct and consistent policies. To be practically deployable, one would require to consider the usability of the language as well as tool support for identifying inconsistent policies. To limit the scope of this paper, we focus on the technical foundations of PATRIoT and considering deployment issues are subjects of future work.

Extending PatrIoT Applicability. Current instantiation of PATRIoT assumes a centralized IoT architecture. However, one can envision extending PATRIoT for decentralized IoT architectures. For this extension, however, one would require the decomposition of global policies into local policies that are to be enforced on the IoT devices themselves. Additionally, the device-centric policy enforcement mechanisms would need to communicate to ensure the consistency of the global system and policy states. This is a subject of future work.

Performance Overhead of PatrIoT. We observed that PATRIoT on-average incurs <100 ms of runtime overhead in systems whose app programming interface have native support for synchronization mechanism (e.g., mutex). For Samsung SmartThings, PATRIoT on-average induces an overhead of 248 ms of which 48% is due to its web-based locking mechanism. Such overheads are tolerable in a non-safety-critical system such as a home automation system. For real-time systems,

Table 3. List of policies used in the evaluation

ID	Policy description	Main goal
P1	Allow sending SMS only if it is requested by flood-alert or energy-alerts or humidity-alert or mail-arrived or medicine-reminder or presence-change-text or ready-for-rain or laundry-monitor apps	Privacy
P2	Deny all http request	Privacy, security
P3	Allow unlocking the front door only if it is requested by enhanced-auto-lock-door app	Security
P4	Allow water valve to be closed only if the fire-sprinkler was not on in the last 5 h	Safety
P5	Allow water valve to be closed only if water leak sensor sensed wet within 1 min	Safety
P6	Allow any light to be turned on only if the system is not on vacation mode	Safety, Energy saving
P7	Deny surveillance camera to get turned off except user is at home	Security
P8	Allow light to be switched on only if user is at home	Safety, energy saving
P9	Allow hallway light to get turned on only if the hallway motion sensor has tripped within 20 s	Energy saving
P10	Allow siren to go off only if lastly smoke/co2 detector detects smoke/co2 with 1 min, or flood sensor sensed wet within 1 min, or motion is sensed within 1 min while user is not at home	Convenience
P11	Deny turning on the coffee machine only if the user is not at home	Safety
P12	Deny turning off the refrigerator or TV only if it is requested by energy-saver app	Convenience
P13	Allow light to be turned off only if lastly it was on within 30 s	Damage protection
P14	Deny opening the garage door except it is requested by garage-door-opener app	Security
P15	Deny unlock the front door only if user is not at home or the system is in sleep mode except smoke detector detects smoke within the last 60 s	Security, safety
P16	Allow AC to be switched on only if the heater is off	Convenience, energy saving
P17	Allow heater to be switched on only if the AC is off	Convenience, energy saving
P18	Allow living room window to be opened only if both heater and AC are off	Energy saving
P19	Allow living room Window to be opened only if lastly motion detector tripped within 60 s	Energy saving
P20	Allow living room window to be closed only if lastly it was open within 30 s	Damage protection
P21	Allow opening the interior door only if the exterior door is closed and lastly pod is empty	Security
P22	Deny irrigation to go off only if since moisture sensor sensed wet, it has been dry within 2 days	Energy saving
P23	Allow setting the mode to away only if my presence is not present	Security, safety
P24	Allow setting the mode to home only if my presence is present	Security, safety
P25	Allow turning off coffee machine only if lastly it was on within 30 s	Damage protection
P26	Allow turning off TV only if lastly it was on within 30 s	Damage protection
P27	Allow turning off water pump only if lastly it was on within 120 s	Damage protection
P28	Allow turning off water pump only if the basement moisture sensor senses dry	Safety
P29	Allow turning off thermostat only if lastly it was on within 120 s	Damage protection
P30	Allow changing light level only if user is at home	Security, energy saving
P31	Deny turning on TV only if it is after midnight	Energy saving
P32	Allow window to be opened only if the system is not on vacation mode	Safety, energy saving
P33	Allow window to be opened only if user is at home	Safety, energy saving

however, this overhead needs to be decreased. One possible solution to this high overhead is to realize PATRIOT by incorporating it in the back-end.

Limitation. Currently, PATRIOT can only regulate actions contemplated by IoT apps. Actions triggered by third-party service (e.g., IFTTT) or user interaction with the companion mobile app cannot be regulated by PATRIOT. To mitigate this limitation, one would require installing PATRIOT in the backend. Installing PATRIOT in the backend may require app instrumentation for collecting context information. Extending PATRIOT with such support is future work.

9 Conclusion

We presented PATRIOT, a runtime monitor that dynamically ensures that actions performed by IoT apps installed in an IoT system do not violate desired policies crucial for assuring the security, privacy, and safety of the users and system. To express policies, PATRIOT provides a platform-independent policy language policy language that can effectively capture system invariants as well as different temporal behaviors including explicit timing restrictions and counting operator. For compliance checking, PATRIOT uses an existing, efficient dynamic programming algorithm which encodes the relevant information in the system's execution history into summary structures that can be quickly looked up during policy checking. Finally, we evaluated PATRIOT's generality, efficacy, and efficiency by instantiating it for three popular open-source IoT platforms We tested 33 policies against 122 SmartThings, 10 policies against 20 OpenHAB, and 6 policies against 8 EVA ICS automation units. The performance overhead induced by PATRIOT is as low as 248 ms for SmartThings, 89 ms for OpenHAB, and 73 ms for EVA ICS, demonstrating the efficiency of our proposed framework.

Acknowledgments. We are grateful to the anonymous reviewers for their insightful comments and suggestions. This work was supported by DARPA CASE program award N66001-18-C-4006. Any opinions, findings, conclusions, or recommendations expressed herein are those of the authors, and do not necessarily reflect those of the US Government or DARPA.

References

1. Antlr. https://www.antlr.org. Accessed 16 Feb 2019
2. Apache Groovy - runtime and compile-time metaprogramming. http://groovy-lang.org/metaprogramming.html. Accessed 13 Sep 2019
3. CWE-367 - time-of-check time-of-use (toctou) race condition. https://cwe.mitre.org/data/definitions/367.html. Accessed 13 Sep 2019
4. EVA ICS. https://www.eva-ics.com. Accessed 13 Sep 2019
5. OpenHAB - a vendor and technology agnostic open source automation software for your home. https://www.openhab.org. Accessed 16 Feb 2019
6. PatrIoT. https://github.com/yahyazadeh/patriot.git. Accessed 16 Aug 2020
7. Smartthings. https://www.smartthings.com/. Accessed 16 Feb 2019

8. SmartThings Public GitHub Repo. https://github.com/SmartThingsCommunity/SmartThingsPublic. Accessed 17 Feb 2019

9. Alrawi, O., Lever, C., Antonakakis, M., Monrose, F.: Sok: security evaluation of home-based IoT deployments. In: S&P. IEEE (2019)

10. Antonakakis, M., et al.: Understanding the mirai botnet. In: USENIX Security Symposium, pp. 1092–1110 (2017)

11. Basin, D., Klaedtke, F., Marinovic, S., Zălinescu, E.: Monitoring of temporal first-order properties with aggregations. Formal Methods Syst. Design **46**(3), 262–285 (2015). https://doi.org/10.1007/s10703-015-0222-7

12. Basin, D., Klaedtke, F., Müller, S.: Policy monitoring in first-order temporal logic. In: Touili, T., Cook, B., Jackson, P. (eds.) CAV 2010. LNCS, vol. 6174, pp. 1–18. Springer, Heidelberg (2010). https://doi.org/10.1007/978-3-642-14295-6_1

13. Basin, D., Klaedtke, F., Müller, S., Zălinescu, E.: Monitoring metric first-order temporal properties. JACM **62**(2), 1–45 (2015)

14. Bauer, A., Leucker, M., Schallhart, C.: Runtime verification for LTL and TLTL. TOSEM **20**(4), 1–64 (2011)

15. Calzavara, S., Focardi, R., Maffei, M., Schneidewind, C., Squarcina, M., Tempesta, M.: {WPSE}: fortifying web protocols via browser-side security monitoring. In: USENIX Security Symposium, pp. 1493–1510 (2018)

16. Celik, Z.B., et al.: Sensitive information tracking in commodity IoT. In: USENIX Security Symposium, pp. 1687–1704 (2018)

17. Celik, Z.B., McDaniel, P., Tan, G.: Soteria: automated IoT safety and security analysis. In: ATC, pp. 147–158. USENIX (2018)

18. Celik, Z.B., Tan, G., McDaniel, P.: IoTGuard: dynamic enforcement of security and safety policy in commodity IoT. In: NDSS (2019)

19. Chen, J., et al.: Iotfuzzer: Discovering memory corruptions in IoT through app-based fuzzing. In: NDSS (2018)

20. Chi, H., Zeng, Q., Du, X., Yu, J.: Cross-app interference threats in smart homes: Categorization, detection and handling. CoRR abs/1808.02125 (2018)

21. Ding, W., Hu, H.: On the safety of IoT device physical interaction control. In: CCS, pp. 832–846. ACM (2018)

22. Du, X., Liu, Y., Tiu, A.: Trace-length independent runtime monitoring of quantitative policies in LTL. In: Bjørner, N., de Boer, F. (eds.) FM 2015. LNCS, vol. 9109, pp. 231–247. Springer, Cham (2015). https://doi.org/10.1007/978-3-319-19249-9_15

23. Edwards, S., Profetis, I.: Hajime: analysis of a decentralized internet worm for IoT devices. Rapidity Netw. **16** (2016)

24. Fernandes, E., Jung, J., Prakash, A.: Security analysis of emerging smart home applications. In: S&P, pp. 636–654. IEEE, May 2016

25. Gong, N.Z., et al.: Piano: proximity-based user authentication on voice-powered Internet-of-Things devices. In: ICDCS, pp. 2212–2219. IEEE (2017)

26. He, W., et al.: Rethinking access control and authentication for the home Internet of Things (IoT). In: USENIX Security, pp. 255–272 (2018)

27. Ho, G., Leung, D., Mishra, P., Hosseini, A., Song, D., Wagner, D.: Smart locks: lessons for securing commodity Internet of Things devices. In: ASIACCS, pp. 461–472. ACM (2016)

28. Jia, Y.J., et al.: ContexIoT: towards providing contextual integrity to appified IoT platforms. In: NDSS (2017)

29. Lee, S., et al.: Fact: functionality-centric access control system for IoT programming frameworks. In: SACMAT, pp. 43–54. ACM (2017)

30. Nguyen, D.T., Song, C., Qian, Z., Krishnamurthy, S.V., Colbert, E.J., McDaniel, P.: IoTSan: fortifying the safety of IoT systems. In: CoNEXT, pp. 191–203. ACM (2018)
31. Notra, S., Siddiqi, M., Gharakheili, H.H., Sivaraman, V., Boreli, R.: An experimental study of security and privacy risks with emerging household appliances. In: CNS, pp. 79–84. IEEE (2014)
32. Rahmati, A., Fernandes, E., Eykholt, K., Prakash, A.: Tyche: a risk-based permission model for smart homes. In: SecDev, pp. 29–36. IEEE (2018)
33. Ronen, E., Shamir, A.: Extended functionality attacks on IoT devices: the case of smart lights. In: EuroS&P, pp. 3–12. IEEE (2016)
34. Ronen, E., Shamir, A., Weingarten, A.O., O'Flynn, C.: IoT goes nuclear: creating a zigbee chain reaction. In: S&P (2017)
35. Rosu, G., Havelund, K.: Synthesizing dynamic programming algorithms from linear temporal logic formulae (2001)
36. Soewito, B., Vespa, L., Mahajan, A., Weng, N., Wang, H.: Self-addressable memory-based FSM: a scalable intrusion detection engine. IEEE Netw. **23**(1), 14–21 (2009)
37. Tian, Y., et al.: Smartauth: User-centered authorization for the Internet of Things. In: USENIX Security (2017)
38. Ur, B., Jung, J., Schechter, S.: The current state of access control for smart devices in homes. In: HUPS (2013)
39. Wang, Q., Datta, P., Yang, W., Liu, S., Bates, A., Gunter, C.A.: Charting the attack surface of trigger-action IoT platforms. In: CCS (2019)
40. Wang, Q., Hassan, W.U., Bates, A., Gunter, C.: Fear and logging in the Internet of Things. In: ISOC NDSS (2018)
41. Yahyazadeh, M., Podder, P., Hoque, E., Chowdhury, O.: Expat: expectation-based policy analysis and enforcement for appified smart-home platforms. In: SACMAT, pp. 61–72. ACM (2019)
42. Yu, T., Sekar, V., Seshan, S., Agarwal, Y., Xu, C.: Handling a trillion (unfixable) flaws on a billion devices: rethinking network security for the Internet-of-Things. In: HotNets (2015)
43. Zhang, J., Wang, Z., Yang, Z., Zhang, Q.: Proximity based IoT device authentication. In: INFOCOM, pp. 1–9. IEEE (2017)
44. Zhang, L., He, W., Martinez, J., Brackenbury, N., Lu, S., Ur, B.: AutoTap: synthesizing and repairing trigger-action programs using LTL properties. In: ICSE (2019)

Runtime Verification of Autonomous Driving Systems in CARLA

Eleni Zapridou[1] , Ezio Bartocci[2] , and Panagiotis Katsaros[1(✉)]

[1] Aristotle University of Thessaloniki, 54124 Thessaloniki, Greece
{zapridou,katsaros}@csd.auth.gr
[2] Vienna University of Technology (TU Wien), Vienna, Austria
ezio.bartocci@tuwien.ac.at

Abstract. Urban driving simulators, such as CARLA, provide 3-D environments and useful tools to easily simulate sensorimotor control systems in scenarios with complex multi-agent dynamics. This enables the design exploration at the early system development stages, reducing high infrastructure costs and high risks. However, due to the high-dimensional input and state spaces of closed-loop autonomous driving systems, their testing and verification is very challenging and it has not yet taken advantage of the recent developments in theory and tools for runtime verification. We show here how to integrate the recently introduced `rtamt` library, for runtime verification of STL (Signal Temporal Logic) specifications, with the CARLA simulator. Finally, we also present the obtained results from monitoring quantitatively interesting requirements for an experimental Adaptive Cruise Control system tested in CARLA.

Keywords: Autonomous driving · Simulation · Signal Temporal Logic · Runtime verification

1 Introduction

Controllers design for autonomous driving systems is based, to a large extent, on high-fidelity simulators, such as CARLA [7], for their validation in urban driving scenarios with traffic intersections, pedestrians, street signs, street lights etc. CARLA is a versatile simulator that supports multiple approaches of autonomous driving, including a system decomposition into perception, planning and control, as well as the training of autonomous systems with machine learning (ML) components. CARLA is continuously developed towards a richer set of environment models, driving scenarios and ML use cases, but little is done for providing adequate means of model evaluation. CARLA and similar simulators, in their basic configuration, can export simulation traces to be further post-processed. However, this is not enough to effectively validate simulated systems.

Recent advances in runtime verification render it a promising perspective, for a multitude of reasons. First, closed-loop reachability analysis of control systems

© Springer Nature Switzerland AG 2020
J. Deshmukh and D. Ničković (Eds.): RV 2020, LNCS 12399, pp. 172–183, 2020.
https://doi.org/10.1007/978-3-030-60508-7_9

is characterized by theoretical limitations [1], which render them inapplicable to real-scale industrial problems [9]. Second, runtime verification of simulation traces allows validating systems in realistic urban driving scenarios with complex dynamics between the traffic agents and the environment. Third, the runtime verification of STL (Signal Temporal Logic) properties [11] enables systematic design space exploration (e.g. through property falsification and parameter synthesis) [4]. These analysis capabilities also open prospects for testing and verifying the robustness of autonomous driving systems with ML components.

We present here the first step towards this perspective, i.e. the runtime verification of STL properties for autonomous driving systems in CARLA. Specifically, we have extended CARLA by integrating the rtamt library [12], for online runtime verification of STL properties. rtamt supports the qualitative and quantitative (property robustness) verification of STL specifications. This new tool combination allowed (i) the design space exploration of an Adaptive Cruise Control (ACC) system, with respect to various PID (proportional-integral-derivative) control parameters and (ii) the quantitative verification of performance requirements that are necessary for an ACC system [14]. Our experimentation with the CARLA model took place on a set of diversified scenarios, which guarantee that the ACC system is effectively validated under realistic urban driving conditions.

Section 2 presents the CARLA simulator, its configuration and integration with the rtamt library. Section 3 discusses the experimental results from our ACC system. In Sect. 4, we review the related work and in the last section we summarize the achievements and the future research prospects.

2   Online Runtime Verification of STL Properties in CARLA

CARLA is a driving simulation environment [7] built on top of the Unreal Engine 4 game engine. It features a variety of digital assets for urban driving scenarios, including a sensor suite, various actors placed/moving on the map and the capability to control them, as well as the simulated environmental conditions.

A simulation is composed of: (i) the CARLA Simulator that computes the physics and renders the scene and all actor properties, (ii) client scripts written using a Python API, to spawn actors, attach sensors to them and, then, retrieve the sensor data, process them and compute the parameters needed by the controller (throttle, brake and steering). Computed values are then sent back to CARLA Simulator, thus forming an ever-running client-server interaction loop.

A client script consists of two parts:

- In the first part, connection with the CARLA Simulator is established, sensors are attached to the controlled vehicles and the actors of the simulated scenario are spawned or destroyed.
- The second part (Fig. 1a) contains the control algorithm and the client-server interaction loop. The client retrieves the simulated world (get_world()) and the sensor signals, and then responds (via the carla.VehicleControl object) with the vehicle control signals that are subsequently applied to the Vehicle object (method apply_control()).

The simulated world, maintained by the server, has its own clock and time. The time-step can be fixed or variable depending on the user preferences. CARLA runs, by default, in asynchronous mode: the server runs the simulation, without waiting for the client, which receives sensor data via a callback function that is called whenever there is new sensor data. In synchronous mode, the client imposes total control over the simulation and its information: the server waits for a client tick (`world.tick()`), before updating to the next simulation step.

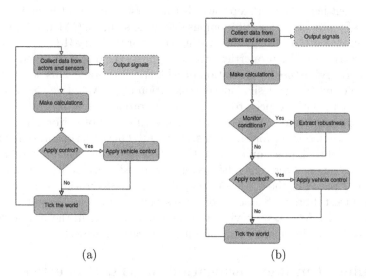

(a)   (b)

Fig. 1. CARLA (a) main simulation loop, and (b) online monitoring

The time-step duration affects the computation of physics. As time progresses and more variables are involved, the simulation may become imprecise. Therefore, physics must be computed within time-steps not greater than 0.1 sec. An important consideration is the reproducibility of simulation scenarios. This is achieved using functions of the Python API that enable and stop a simulation recorder. Then, the obtained file can be playback.

To inspect the actor behavior (e.g. location, velocity, acceleration), there are client functions to access values at the latest tick. If the simulation runs in synchronous mode (Fig. 1a), data is stored in signals and it is reliable. For online monitoring (Fig. 1b), we use the synchronous mode with fixed time-step, ensuring that the simulation time and physics will be in synchrony and the sensed signals are reliable. There are, however, challenges regarding the properties that can be monitored, since online monitoring is restricted to a single pass through the simulation trace. To assess the performance of closed-loop autonomous systems, we need to be able to determine the satisfaction/violation of a property specification based on a robustness degree function, i.e. a means to indicate how far is the monitored trace from satisfying or violating a specification. This allows to interpret the performance of the system design under various parameters, scenario events (e.g. street signs) and environment perturbations, as opposed to the binary pass/fail answer of qualitative verification, which is not very informative.

We rely on the rtamt library [12] that generates online robustness monitors from bounded-future STL specifications [4,11] that can express temporal properties for continuous signals. Monitoring takes place through evaluating the (equivalent) past STL specification, according to its quantitative semantics, interpreted in discrete or dense time [6]. For a signal given as a sequence of (time, value) pairs, rtamt computes at different instants how far is the signal from satisfying or violating the property. When using discrete-time monitors, sensing of inputs and output generation are done at a periodic rate, whereas dense-time monitors compute the min and max of a numeric sequence over a sliding window.

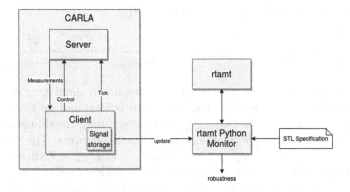

Fig. 2. STL runtime verification of CARLA simulations with the rtamt library

Figure 2 shows how an rtamt monitor is integrated with a CARLA simulation in synchronous mode and fixed time-step. The (time, value(s)) pairs with data, for every car with the autonomous system enabled, are stored by the client at each step. This requires monitoring events, like that the host (ego) vehicle is behind another car. If these conditions hold true, the monitor's update function computes the robustness measures from the signals. This is a non-intrusive solution, since all computations take place, while the simulated time is frozen.

3   Experimental Results for an ACC System

3.1   An Experimental ACC System

ACC systems extend the functionality of conventional cruise control systems by the capability to adjust the host vehicle's velocity and assuring a safety distance to the preceding vehicle through controlling its throttle and/or brake. A key part of ACC is the range sensor, which is used to measure the distance from the preceding vehicle. We use the CARLA obstacle detector that detects obstacles, including vehicles, located within a specified distance from the host vehicle, towards its traveling direction. The ACC system of the host vehicle is enabled, when the preceding vehicle is too close (distance below a fixed threshold r) or if it is moving slowly. In this case, the ACC controls the throttle and the brake, in order to keep the distance higher or equal to the safety distance, which is dynamically calculated, as in Definition 1. In the absence of a preceding vehicle, the velocity of the host vehicle is controlled by the CARLA server.

Definition 1. [13] *A longitudinal distance between a car c_h that drives behind another car c_p, where both cars are driving at the same direction, is safe w.r.t. a response time ρ, if for any braking of at most $a_{brake_{max}}$, performed by c_p, if c_h will accelerate by at most $a_{accel_{max}}$ during the response time, and from there on will brake by at least $a_{brake_{min}}$ until a full stop, then it won't collide with c_p.*

Let v_h, v_p be the longitudinal velocities of the cars. Then, the safe longitudinal distance between c_h and c_p is ($[x]_+ := max\{x, 0\}$):

$$SD = \left[v_h \cdot \rho + \frac{1}{2} a_{accel_{max}} \cdot \rho^2 + \frac{(v_h + \rho \cdot a_{accel_{max}})^2}{2 \cdot a_{brake_{min}}} - \frac{v_p^2}{2 \cdot a_{brake_{max}}} \right]_+$$

In our case, ρ is equal to the time elapsed between two simulation steps, since we the simulation runs in synchronous mode this is fixed and set to 0.05 s.

For $a_{accel_{max}}$, $a_{brake_{min}}$ and $a_{brake_{max}}$ we parameterized the simulation model using values from vehicle specifications by car manufacturers. The values used are: $a_{accel_{max}} = 5.4\,\mathrm{m/sec^2}$, $a_{brake_{min}} = 2.9\,\mathrm{m/sec^2}$, $a_{brake_{max}} = 9.8\,\mathrm{m/sec^2}$.

The ultimate aim of ACC is to allow the host vehicle traveling with a velocity v_h at most equal to v_p, lower than the road speed limit (imposed by CARLA), while minimizing the distance d from the preceding vehicle, without violating SD. The available time, before the two vehicles get closer than SD is:

$$time_{safe} = \frac{d - SD}{v_h - v_p}$$

Thus, the target velocity v_{tar} and target acceleration a_{tar} for the host vehicle to have in next simulation sample (time-step) are:

$$a_{tar} = \frac{min\{v_p, speed_{limit}\} - v_h}{time_{safe}}$$

$$v_{tar} = v_h + \rho \cdot a_{tar}$$

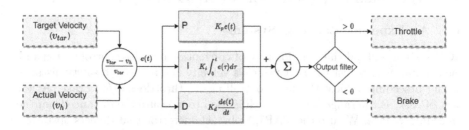

Fig. 3. PID controller for the ACC system

The ACC function is driven by the PID controller of Fig. 3, which computes the needed throttle and brake based on v_{tar} and the actual velocity (v_h). The PID controller continuously calculates an error value $e(t)$, as the difference between the desired set point (in our case v_{tar}) and a measured process variable (v_h), and applies a correction based on three terms, namely the proportional, the integral, and the derivative (denoted respectively by P, I and D). In practice, the PID controller applies a responsive correction to the controlled function.

3.2   Design Space Exploration w.r.t. PID Parameters

When designing a PID controller, it is important to understand how to improve the system's performance. As a rule of thumb, by increasing the proportional gain (K_P) we achieve a proportional increase of the control signal for the same level of $e(t)$. In this way, the system reacts more quickly, but it tends to exceed its target more (overshoot). The parameter of derivative control (K_D) affects the capability of damping, which is important to decrease overshoot. The value of integral parameter (K_I) affects the capability to limit the steady error, but the system may become more sluggish and oscillatory, if it is not properly tuned.

Our runtime verification approach can help to adjust the gains K_P, K_I, and K_D with the aim to eventually achieve a satisfactory overall response. We present here the experimental results obtained for two different sets of parameter values:

$$K_{P_A} = 1,\ K_{I_A} = 1,\ K_{D_A} = 0.0005$$
$$K_{P_B} = 2,\ K_{I_B} = 0.01,\ K_{D_B} = 0.4$$

Since the primary aim of the ACC system is to keep the safe distance from the preceding vehicle, we evaluate the requirement,

$$R := d - SD > 0$$

in order to find the parameter set that seems to be more appropriate. For the runtime verification of R and for all other experiments that are reported henceforward, we employed the rtamt library to generate discrete-time monitors that were integrated with the CARLA simulation of our ACC system.

Figure 4 shows the robustness of R, when monitoring similar driving scenarios with the two mentioned sets of parameters (A and B). These scenarios refer to the route of two cars moving one behind the other in the CARLA urban environment with junctions, stop signs and traffic lights. While following the same route, the scenarios differ slightly with respect to the duration of the red traffic lights.

In Fig. 4a, no robustness value is shown in specific simulation steps, when the preceding vehicle was too far and the ACC of the host vehicle was disabled. For parameters $K_{P_A}, K_{I_A}, K_{D_A}$, R is strongly violated, when the cars stop at the second traffic light, and it is violated, for more than 300 steps, while waiting for the green traffic light. For $K_{P_B}, K_{I_B}, K_{D_B}$ (Fig. 4b), R is slightly violated at the same instant, but the system adjusts quickly and the host vehicle stops at the traffic light maintaining the safety distance. By simulating more similar scenarios, we found that R is violated for $K_{P_A}, K_{I_A}, K_{D_A}$ at the second traffic light

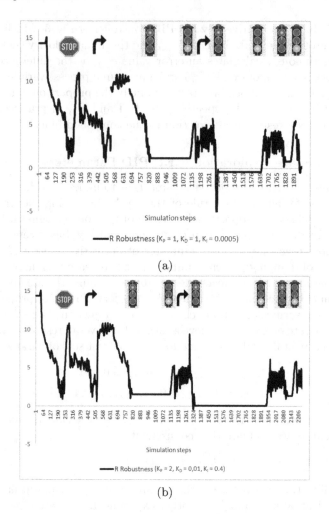

Fig. 4. Robustness of R for (a) $K_{P_A}, K_{I_A}, K_{D_A}$ and (b) $K_{P_B}, K_{I_B}, K_{D_B}$

and every next time the vehicles stop for a long period. The problem vanishes for $K_{P_B}, K_{I_B}, K_{D_B}$ that was chosen for the experiments reported hereafter.

A more detailed view of the same scenario, extended by additional steps, is shown in Fig. 5. These graphs show the distance between the two vehicles and how it compares with the safety distance (Fig. 5a), and their velocities (Fig. 5b). We observe that in a stop signal, the host car stops when the preceding has already left and similarly in a traffic light, the vehicles stop and start moving with a time difference. In Fig. 5a, we see that d gets closer to SD, as the PID controller adjusts by using more historic data.

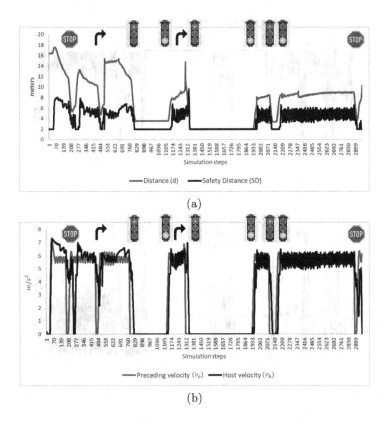

(a)

(b)

Fig. 5. Distance (a) between host and preceding vehicle and (b) their velocities

3.3 Requirements for an ACC System

According to [14], any ACC system has to fulfill the following performance requirements, in order to be used in public roads:

R_1. Relative difference $v_p - v_h$ should not be too high, except when the preceding vehicle is out of range or the host vehicle has decelerated, due to a stop signal or a red traffic light, while the preceding vehicle is moving ahead.

R_2. Acceleration of the host vehicle (a_h) must be greater than or equal to G, except if the preceding vehicle's acceleration (a_p) is less than this limit,

$$G := -0.25 \cdot \frac{T_{hw} + 1}{m}$$

with m the vehicle's mass and T_{hw} a constant time headway, i.e. the distance between the two vehicles in time expressing the degree to which the safety distance varies proportionally to the vehicles velocity (spacing policy).

The STL property for the first mentioned requirement is:

$$R_1 := v_p - v_h < c \lor d > r \lor stopped_h$$

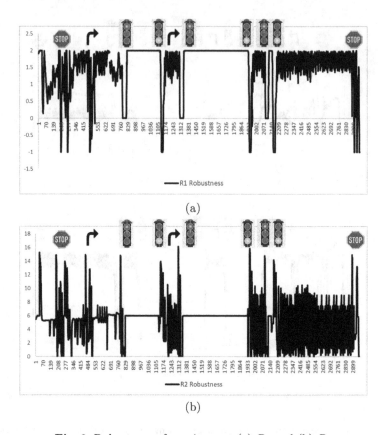

Fig. 6. Robustness of requirement (a) R_1 and (b) R_2

where c is a threshold for the relative difference between velocities, r is the distance threshold under which the ACC system is enabled and $stopped_h$ is **true**, when the host vehicle decelerates, due to a stop signal or a red traffic light. We set the threshold for the difference between the velocities $c = 1.5\,\text{m/s}$.

The STL property for the R_2 requirement is ($\boxminus$ is the *historically* operator):

$$R_2 := a_h \geq G \vee \boxminus_{[0:t]} a_p < G$$

where $[0 : t]$ is the time interval for the host vehicle to adjust its acceleration back to normal, after an extreme deceleration of the preceding vehicle.

Figure 6a shows the robustness of R_1 for the scenario of Sect. 3.2. We observe violations after stop signals and green traffic lights. In stop signals, when the host vehicle stops, the preceding has already moved ahead, causing an excessive difference in velocities. When a traffic light turns to green, the host vehicle needs more steps to start accelerating and the velocities difference is also increased. These performance perturbations, due to usual driving incidents, do not invalidate our system. R_1 is satisfied and robustness raises as time proceeds, showing that the ACC adjusts to acceleration changes of the preceding vehicle.

Figure 6b shows the robustness of R_2 for the same scenario. In this experiment, we have set $T_{hw} = 1.5$ s, $t = 3$ and $m = 1200$ kg (mass of "Seat Leon" that is the host vehicle in our experiments). The ACC fulfills the requirement, although the robustness in some steps is low (host vehicle's acceleration is close to G). By increasing/decreasing T_{hw} we could find the lowest time headway that still fulfills R_2 or a higher time headway, for which the robustness is increased.

4 Related Work

In contrast with other systems, automotive control systems exhibit complex behaviors that are difficult to anticipate at design time. Their performance requirements typically arise out of test driving scenarios.

The VERIFAI toolkit [8] analyzes simulation traces (also from CARLA) of systems with ML components. It has a wider scope from our work, aiming to address the absence of specifications for perception components, the analysis of ML components and environment modeling (e.g. distribution assumptions made by ML components). It works through offline monitoring system-level properties in Metric Temporal Logic (MTL) [2]. Monitors can output falsifying traces and a feedback to direct sampling to find falsifying scenarios. Such an analysis may be also possible in our case, since rtamt can be easily used for offline monitoring.

Through simulation-based analysis, we can also identify behaviours that can be then captured as requirements. In [10], a set of automotive behavior classes is identified that control engineers typically want to avoid (ringing, excessive overshoot, slow response time, steady state error etc.) and a library of signal templates for STL is proposed, such that it will be easier to specify STL requirements that exclude them. These requirements are easier to be checked over simulation traces produced by a Simulink model of the system under design, whereas for our ACC requirements (adopted from [14]) in Sect. 3.3, we advocate their validation over realistic driving scenarios generated by CARLA.

Worth to mention are the S-TaLiRo [3] and Breach [5] tools, for sensitivity analysis and falsification testing over Simulink traces. Sensitivity analysis of model robustness to STL requirements is based on uniformly varying model parameters, whereas falsification looks for an input signal that violates a requirement. Another interesting prospect is the requirements-driven testing [15].

5 Conclusion and Future Research Prospects

We presented an approach for integrating CARLA simulations with runtime monitors generated by the rtamt library[1]. Our proposal enables the validation of autonomous driving control by online monitoring STL specifications over realistic driving scenarios. We believe that this is a means for design space exploration and has the potential to uncover undesired behaviours or check important

---

[1] The CARLA client scripts for our ACC system with the integrated rtamt monitors can be accessed online at http://depend.csd.auth.gr/software/carla.

performance requirements. We showed the results from applying our approach, in order to find appropriate parameters for the PID control of an experimental ACC system and for checking it against important performance requirements.

Our work is a first step towards additional contributions that will allow testing and verification of autonomous driving systems with ML components. CARLA already supports the simulation of such systems, but we need to further develop our approach towards automating property falsification, parameter synthesis, sensitivity analysis and systematic scenario testing.

References

1. Henzinger, T.A., Kopke, P.W., Puri, A., Varaiya, P.: What's decidable about hybrid automata? J. Comput. Syst. Sci. **57**(1), 94–124 (1998)
2. Alur, R., Henzinger, T.A.: Logics and models of real time: a survey. In: de Bakker, J.W., Huizing, C., de Roever, W.P., Rozenberg, G. (eds.) REX 1991. LNCS, vol. 600, pp. 74–106. Springer, Heidelberg (1992). https://doi.org/10.1007/BFb0031988
3. Annpureddy, Y., Liu, C., Fainekos, G., Sankaranarayanan, S.: S-TaLiRo: a tool for temporal logic falsification for hybrid systems. In: Abdulla, P.A., Leino, K.R.M. (eds.) TACAS 2011. LNCS, vol. 6605, pp. 254–257. Springer, Heidelberg (2011). https://doi.org/10.1007/978-3-642-19835-9_21
4. Bartocci, E., Deshmukh, J., Donzé, A., Fainekos, G., Maler, O., Ničković, D., Sankaranarayanan, S.: Specification-based monitoring of cyber-physical systems: a survey on theory, tools and applications. In: Bartocci, E., Falcone, Y. (eds.) Lectures on Runtime Verification. LNCS, vol. 10457, pp. 135–175. Springer, Cham (2018). https://doi.org/10.1007/978-3-319-75632-5_5
5. Donzé, A.: Breach, a toolbox for verification and parameter synthesis of hybrid systems. In: Touili, T., Cook, B., Jackson, P. (eds.) CAV 2010. LNCS, vol. 6174, pp. 167–170. Springer, Heidelberg (2010). https://doi.org/10.1007/978-3-642-14295-6_17
6. Donzé, A., Maler, O.: Robust satisfaction of temporal logic over real-valued signals. In: Chatterjee, K., Henzinger, T.A. (eds.) FORMATS 2010. LNCS, vol. 6246, pp. 92–106. Springer, Heidelberg (2010). https://doi.org/10.1007/978-3-642-15297-9_9
7. Dosovitskiy, A., Ros, G., Codevilla, F., Lopez, A., Koltun, V.: CARLA: an open urban driving simulator. In: Proceedings of the 1st Annual Conference on Robot Learning, pp. 1–16 (2017)
8. Dreossi, T., et al.: VerifAI: a toolkit for the formal design and analysis of artificial intelligence-based systems. In: Dillig, I., Tasiran, S. (eds.) CAV 2019. LNCS, vol. 11561, pp. 432–442. Springer, Cham (2019). https://doi.org/10.1007/978-3-030-25540-4_25
9. Jin, X., Deshmukh, J.V., Kapinski, J., Ueda, K., Butts, K.: Powertrain control verification benchmark. In: Proceeding of 17th International Conference on Hybrid Systems: Computation and Control, pp. 253–262. HSCC '14, Association for Computing Machinery, New York, NY, USA (2014)
10. Kapinski, J., et al.: St-lib: a library for specifying and classifying model behaviors. In: SAE Technical Paper. SAE International (2016)
11. Maler, O., Nickovic, D.: Monitoring temporal properties of continuous signals. In: Lakhnech, Y., Yovine, S. (eds.) FORMATS/FTRTFT -2004. LNCS, vol. 3253, pp. 152–166. Springer, Heidelberg (2004). https://doi.org/10.1007/978-3-540-30206-3_12

12. Nickovic, D., Yamaguchi, T.: RTAMT: online robustness monitors from STL. CoRR abs/2005.11827 (2020). https://arxiv.org/abs/2005.11827
13. Shalev-Shwartz, S., Shammah, S., Shashua, A.: On a formal model of safe and scalable self-driving cars. CoRR abs/1708.06374 (2017). http://arxiv.org/abs/1708.06374
14. Takahama, T., Akasaka, D.: Model predictive control approach to design practical adaptive cruise control for traffic jam. Int. J. Autom. Eng. **9**, 99–104 (2018)
15. Tuncali, C.E., Fainekos, G., Prokhorov, D., Ito, H., Kapinski, J.: Requirements-driven test generation for autonomous vehicles with machine learning components. IEEE Trans. Intell. Veh. **5**(2), 265–280 (2020)

SOTER on ROS: A Run-Time Assurance Framework on the Robot Operating System

Sumukh Shivakumar[1], Hazem Torfah[1(✉)], Ankush Desai[2], and Sanjit A. Seshia[1]

[1] University of California, Berkeley, USA
{sumukhshiv,torfah,sseshia}@berkeley.edu
[2] Amazon, Cupertino, CA, USA
ankushpd@amazon.com

Abstract. We present an implementation of SOTER, a run-time assurance framework for building safe distributed mobile robotic (DMR) systems, on top of the Robot Operating System (ROS). The safety of DMR systems cannot always be guaranteed at design time, especially when complex, off-the-shelf components are used that cannot be verified easily. SOTER addresses this by providing a language-based approach for run-time assurance for DMR systems. SOTER implements the reactive robotic software using the language P, a domain-specific language designed for implementing asynchronous event-driven systems, along with an integrated run-time assurance system that allows programmers to use unfortified components but still provide safety guarantees. We describe an implementation of SOTER for ROS and demonstrate its efficacy using a multi-robot surveillance case study, with multiple run-time assurance modules. Through rigorous simulation, we show that SOTER enabled systems ensure safety, even when using unknown and untrusted components.

Keywords: Distributed mobile robotics · Autonomous systems · Runtime assurance

1 Introduction

The design of runtime monitoring components has become an integral part of the development process of distributed mobile robotic (DMR) systems. Runtime monitoring is essential for maintaining situational awareness, assessing the health of a robot, and most importantly for detecting any irregularities at runtime and consequently deploying the necessary countermeasures when such irregularities occur. The growing complexity of DMR systems, along with the utilization of uncertified off-the-shelf components and complex machine-learning models that are difficult to verify at design time, has made runtime assurance a crucial component for building robust DMR systems [15].

© Springer Nature Switzerland AG 2020
J. Deshmukh and D. Ničković (Eds.): RV 2020, LNCS 12399, pp. 184–194, 2020.
https://doi.org/10.1007/978-3-030-60508-7_10

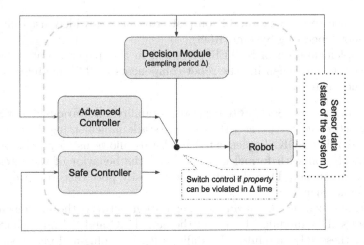

Fig. 1. RTA module in SOTER.

In this paper, we present an implementation of SOTER [2], a runtime assurance framework for building safe distributed mobile robotics, on top of the Robot Operating System (ROS)[1]. In SOTER, components of a DMR system are defined as runtime assurance (RTA) modules implementing a Simplex architecture [16]. An RTA module based on Simplex (see Fig. 1) consists of two controllers, an *advanced controller* (AC) and a *safe controller* (SC), and a *decision module* that implements a switching logic between the AC and SC. The AC is used for operating the system under nominal circumstances. This is usually an optimized controller based on advanced heuristics or complex learning-enabled components such as machine-learning-based perception modules. This makes it hard to provide any guarantees on the behavior of the AC, especially, when it is an off-the-shelf component that cannot be verified at design time. To, nevertheless, guarantee the safety of a system using such controllers, the system can always default to a certified back-up controller, the SC, that takes over operating the system when anomalies in the behavior of the AC are detected. For example, the SC could be based only on reliable sensors that navigate a robot to a safe state. The detection of faulty behavior is guaranteed by the decision module, which is a certified monitor that observes the state of the robot. The decision module decides whether it is necessary to switch from the AC to the SC to keep the robot in a safe state and when to switch back to the AC to utilize the high performance of the AC to optimally achieve the objectives of the robot. In DMR systems, components within the robot as well as any systems connected to the robot are communicating asynchronously. In SOTER, the various robot components are implemented as asynchronously communicating RTA modules. This is realized by implementing the modules in the language P [3], a verifiable programming language designed for writing asynchronous event-driven code, which can be

---

[1] https://www.ros.org.

compiled down to code executable on platforms such as widely used platforms as the Robot Operating System (ROS).

The implementation of SOTER presented in this paper maintains a similar approach to implementing the robot components as RTA modules with the following new extensions:

- A refactorization of SOTER to support portability onto various Robot SDK's. The refactorization separates the software stack implementing the robot from the used robot SDK. Implemented in P, this allows us to provide a robot implementation with formal guarantees on the behavior of the interacting robot components. This also allows us to easily port this framework on to other robot SDK's.
- The refactorization also includes a separation between the implementation of robot's RTA modules' logic and the actual AC and SC implementations used in these RTA modules. This allows us, in a plug-and-play fashion, to easily link the calls of the AC's and SC's in the RTA modules to external implementations of the controllers.
- A concrete integration of the SOTER framework onto widely used robot SDK ROS. We provide an implementation of a software interface that implements the communication with the ROS SDK. Integration onto other robot SDK's can be done in a similar way.

The implementation of the framework, details and videos on the examples presented in Sect. 3, and a guideline for using the framework can be found on the following website https://github.com/Drona-Org/SOTERonROS. This includes instructions on how to execute the examples presented in the paper.

2   Architecture of SOTER on ROS

In this section, we outline the architecture of the new implementation of the SOTER framework. The framework borrows from the Drona framework [4] and is similarly comprised of three layers. The *application* layer, the robot *software stack*, and the *robot SDK*. The application layer implements an application related task planner that is responsible for computing application related tasks and distributing them amongst the robots for execution. The *software stack* of each robot consists of an interface to establish the communication with task planner, a motion planner, and a plan executor, in addition to a set of decision modules. In contrast to the Drona framework, the motion planner and the plan executor are implemented as RTA modules that are linked to one of the decision modules and to implementations of their safe and advanced controllers.

The implementation of the monitors used by the decision modules, and also the implementation of the safe and advanced controllers for both the motion planner and the plan executor are provided as C++ modules in a separate library. The library also plays the role of the interface which abstracts away many of the underlying details needed for the robot SDK, and make them accessible to the modules in the software stack as well as to the task planner.

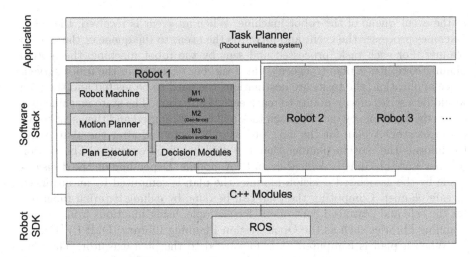

Fig. 2. SOTER framework architecture.

In the following, we give some details on the implementation of each of the three layers and the integration into robot SDK's such as ROS. We use a robot surveillance application to elaborate on some of the implementation details.

Task Planner. A task planner is implemented specifically for a certain application. For example, a task planner for a surveillance application computes certain way-points on the map that should be visited by the robots. A task planner in our framework is implemented as a state machine in the language P [3]. This allows asynchronous communication between the task planner and P state machines defining the robots. A state machine in P has its own event queue on which it receives events published by other machines that communicate with this machine. The task planner can send events defining tasks to the queues of the robot machines for execution. In its initial state, the task planner state machine, spawns a number of robots to execute application related tasks. After initializing the robots, the task planner computes the tasks to be executed and publishes the tasks to the event queues of the different robots.

Robot Software Stack. The software stack consists of three predefined P state machines, the robot machine, the motion planner, and the plan executor, in addition to other application-dependent P state machine defining the decision modules used by the motion planner and the plan executor. When the task planner spawns a robot, a new software stack is setup with a new robot machine, motion planner, plan executor and all the decision modules, In the following, we provide some details on the state machines defining the robot machine, motion planner, and plan executor. All implementations can be found on the frameworks webpage under the software stack directory.

The robot machine serves as the interface between the task planner and the motion planner of a robot. The tasks assigned by the task planner are queued in the event queue of the robot machine. When an event is received, the robot machines processes the event and forwards the event to the queue of the motion planner. For each task, processed and sent by the robot machine, the motion planner computes a plan to execute this task. For example, in the robot surveillance application, the tasks are destinations the need to be visited and the plan would be a series of way-points to reach each destination. The state machine processes the tasks one by one. For each task a plan is computed and then sent to the plan executor. A plan for the next task is only computed after the plan executor informs the motion planner that the plan has been executed. The motion planner state machine is defined as an RTA module. Depending on the decisions made by the associated decision module, the plan is computed by an advanced or safe planner. Computing the plan can be done by calling external functions for the safe and advanced controllers, for example, using functions from motion planning libraries such as the Open Motion Planning Library (OMPL) [17].

When a plan is computed, it is forwarded to the plan executor. The plan executor is a state machine that implements another RTA module. For each step of the plan, the plan executor consults a decision module on what type of controller to use. For example, in the surveillance application, if a step is leading to a collision with another robot, the plan executor will use a safe controller to guide the robot around the other robot. If the battery level is low, the safe controller might decide to first go to the charging station before going to the next point given by the plan. When the plan is executed, the plan executor informs the motion planner and waits for the next plan to be sent by the motion planner.

ROS Integration. The software stack is built on top of a software interface given as a library of C++ modules. The library contains all foreign functions that implement the monitors for the decision modules and the safe and advanced controller for the RTA modules. We chose C++ for writing the external function because P programs can be compiled in to C++ programs, which in turn can compiled to ROS executables. To build the ROS executables, we used the Catkin build system (http://wiki.ros.org/catkin/conceptual_overview). Catkin build system (popularly used for ROS projects) contains a source space where programmers include their source code. We have modified it so that this source space can support P files. This is done using the P compiler and Cmake to compile the P programs into executables that can be run on ROS.

3   Case Studies

We present two case studies with multiple runtime assurance modules. We use the case studies to show how to use SOTER on ROS framework to build safe robotics that provide safety guarantees while maintaining performance, and to demonstrate the re-usability of the framework on a variety of robotics applications. In SOTER, application task planners, the Cpp module layer, and their RTA modules, need to be implemented independently for each application. The software stack in SOTER on ROS is largely reusable for many applications. The implementation and videos of these case studies can be found on https://github. com/Drona-Org/SOTERonROS.

```
machine DroneSurveillanceTaskPlanner {          state StartSurveillance {

    var drones: seq[machine];                       entry {
    var numRobots: int;                                 var destinations: seq[locations];
                                                        var i: int;
    start state Init {                                  i = 0;
                                                        while (i < numRobots) {
        entry {                                             destinations = SurveillanceDesinations();
            numRobots = workspaceSetupDrone();              send drones[i], DestinationsEvent,
            drones =                                            destinations;
                createRobotMachine(numRobots);          }
            raise Done;                                 raise Done;
        }                                           }

        on Done goto StartSurvillanceState;         on Done goto EndSurveillance;
    }                                           }

                                                ...
}                                           }
```

Fig. 3. Application level code for Drone Surveillance Protocol. This is a simplified version of the task planner. For the full P state machine we refer the reader to the surveillance application directory on the frameworks webpage.

3.1 Drone Surveillance Protocol

The Drone Surveillance Protocol case study demonstrates how to develop a SOTER on ROS application. In this case study, there is a single drone exploring a 5 × 5 grid with 4 walls on the boundaries of the workspace. The goal of the drone is to explore the workspace (visit a series of locations), while ensuring the drone does not collide with the walls. To implement the case study, the programmer must first implement the application level goals in the task planner, which is implemented as a P state machine. The task planner, as depicted in Fig. 3, consists of two states, the initialization state (Init) and the surveillance state (StartSurveillance). The former is used to initialize the relevant workspace information and the robots within the application. The surveillance state is used to send destination information to the different robots, which in the case of the machine in Fig. 3 is done in the order of the robot's id's. Here, DestinationsEvent is the event queued into the robot machine, and destinations is the corresponding payload of the event.

The P state machine implementing the robot machine in the drone's software stack is responsible for setting up communication with the drone's own motion planner, and initializing with ROS, which is done using a foreign function RobotROSSetup() that the programmer implements to connect the P machine with its ROS node. The robot machine forwards the destination point from the task planner to the motion planner, which then computes a series of way points to reach that destination. In our case studies, we use the Open Motion Planning Library's motion planner [17], and make it accessible in P using a foreign function. Finally, these sequence of way points are sent to the drone's plan executor, that physically executes this plan on the drone. It does so, using a series of foreign functions from the C++ modules that implement the drone's controllers, which is provided by the programmer.

In our case study, the motion planner has no knowledge of the obstacles present in the workspace. As a result, the drone occasionally visits points that are very close to the walls. In order to ensure the drone does not collide with the walls, we construct a collision avoidance runtime assurance module. The RTA module defining the plan executor guides the robot to visit a series of locations across the workspace. The decision module monitors the location of the drone, and specifically checks to see if the next way point is located in a problematic location on the workspace. The decision module also has a parameter Δ, that has the ability to look ahead to the next Δ way points of the drone's current motion plan and confirm none are in dangerous locations in the workspace. If the decision module finds that the one of the next Δ way points bring the drone too close to one of the walls, it transfers control to the safe controller. The safe controller brings the drone back to safety in the middle of the workspace. The decision module is able to perform this look ahead and return an answer in a non-substantial amount of time (near instantaneous).

This decision module is implemented in the decision module P state machine, where the programmer implements their decision logic to determine if the robot is in a safe/unsafe state. The plan executor communicates with this decision module machine to determined whether to execute the AC or the SC.

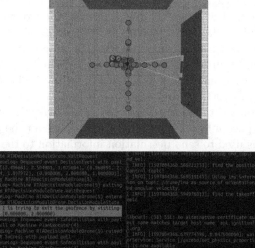

Fig. 4. Drone Surveillance Protocol. (Color figure online)

Figure 4 contains a snapshot of the simulation and the terminal used to run our application. We execute our application by first launching our gazebo simulator in one window (right) and executing the ROS executable (left). The ROS executable also displays application related information such as the controller that is being used and the reason why the decision module decided to switch to one of the controllers. We also demonstrate the effect of the Δ parameter of the decision module in our case study. Increasing values of Δ cause the decision module to look ahead further into the drone's motion plan, and in turn makes its behavior more conservative in how close the drone can fly near the walls. Figure 4, compares the drone's path with $\Delta = 1$ in red and $\Delta = 2$ in blue.

3.2 Robot Delivery

In the Robot Delivery case study, we demonstrate the ability to have multiple robots running asynchronously using decision modules over multiple monitors. There are two robots (TurtleBot3) that explore a grid with static obstacles. The goal of the robots is to randomly visit points on the grid indefinitely, while avoiding the static obstacles. The task planner sends each robot randomized empty destinations on the grids. Each robot has its own copy of the motion planner and plan executor. The robot machine forwards destination information to the motion planner, which in this case is the third party Open Motion Planning Library's motion planner [17]. The motion planner computes way points to reach this destination while avoiding the static obstacles of the workspace. The motion planner also forwards the plan to the plan executor to execute. This process occurs concurrently on both robots so multiple robots can simultaneously navigate the workspace.

In this case study, we define a decision module with 3 different runtime monitors: (1) Battery Safety, (2) Geo Fencing, and (3) Collision Avoidance.

The first monitor is battery safety, where we prioritize safely bringing the robot to its charging station. Here our advanced controller is a node that computes control information given the current motion plan and drives the robot to the next way point in the plan. The safe controller is a certified planner that safely brings the robot to its corresponding charging station from its current position. The decision module observes battery percentage at each way point to ensure whether there is sufficient battery for executing the next Δ way points.

The geo-fencing monitor checks whether the robot moves outside of our 5×5 grid. The RTA using this monitor can then ensure that the robot does not navigate to this region. Here our advanced controller is a node that computes control information given the current motion plan and drives the robot to the next way point in the plan. The safe controller prevents further execution of the plan and skips to the next destination, ensuring the robot remains in the safe region. The decision module observes the next Δ at each step, and determines whether the current robot would eventually explore an unsafe region.

The third safety guarantee is collision avoidance. In the event that the two robots are simultaneously trying to visit the same destination, we ensure that a collision does not occur. The advanced controller executes the current motion plan way point by way point. The safe controller has one of the robots wait until the other finishes reaching the destination, and then proceeds. The decision module observes the next Δ way points of both robot, given their current location and motion plan, and determines whether a collision is imminent.

In this case study, the decision module machine has 3 different aspects of the robot it must monitor simultaneously. Each RTA module also has its own AC and SC and each of the RTA modules must be composed to provide the desired security guarantees. Hence, the decision module must have an implicit prioritization of the 3 monitors, to decide which safe controller the Plan executor must run in the event multiple monitors report unsafe. In our case study, we prioritized the RTA modules in the following order: collision avoidance, geo-fencing, and battery safety. The decision module is able to perform this monitoring task and return an answer non-substantial time.

4   Related Work

There is a rich body of work on the design of runtime assurance components for safety-critical systems [1,5–11,13]. Some of these works present language-based approaches that instrument an implementation of a system to assure that certain executions are enforced to satisfy certain requirements, other approaches combine design time techniques with runtime verification techniques to assure that environment assumptions made at design time also hold at runtime [1]. For black-box robotic systems, or robotic systems that include off-the-shelf machine-learning-based components that are hard to verify at design time, Simplex-based approaches like SOTER are more suitable. Frameworks based on the Simplex (or Simplex-like) architecture include those presented in [9,11–13]. These frameworks are however designed for single component systems, or wrap the entire system using a single Simplex module, making the design of monitoring components for a distributed setting extremely difficult and complicated. In comparison, with SOTER, we provide a framework for the design of Simplex-based RTA modules for distributed robotic systems that builds on a formally verified robotic software stack and is compatible with a variety of robot SDK's. We also note that decision modules in SOTER allow for a principled and safe way to switch back from the safe controller to the advanced controller to keep performance penalties to a minimum [2]; subsequently, an alternative approach for realizing the reverse switching mechanism was presented by Phan et al. [12].

5   Outlook

With SOTER we presented a framework for building safe distributed robotics with integrated runtime assurance modules. SOTER separates the implementation of the robot logic from the underlying robot SDK making it compatible with many robotic platforms. For now combining multiple monitoring decisions of the decision modules is still a manual step. For the future, we plan on providing a systematic way to coordinate the different decisions. We also plan to integrate the framework with a broader class of robotics platforms, planning tools, simulators, and techniques such as introspective environment modeling [14].

Acknowledgments. This work is supported in part by NSF grant CNS-1545126, the DARPA Assured Autonomy program, Berkeley Deep Drive, and by the iCyPhy center.

References

1. Desai, A., Dreossi, T., Seshia, S.A.: Combining model checking and runtime verification for safe robotics. In: Lahiri, S., Reger, G. (eds.) RV 2017. LNCS, vol. 10548, pp. 172–189. Springer, Cham (2017). https://doi.org/10.1007/978-3-319-67531-2_11

2. Desai, A., Ghosh, S., Seshia, S.A., Shankar, N., Tiwari, A.: SOTER: a runtime assurance framework for programming safe robotics systems. In: 49th Annual IEEE/IFIP International Conference on Dependable Systems and Networks, DSN 2019, Portland, OR, USA, June 24–27, 2019, pp. 138–150. IEEE (2019). https://doi.org/10.1109/DSN.2019.00027

3. Desai, A., Gupta, V., Jackson, E.K., Qadeer, S., Rajamani, S.K., Zufferey, D.: P: safe asynchronous event-driven programming. In: Boehm, H., Flanagan, C. (eds.) ACM SIGPLAN Conference on Programming Language Design and Implementation, PLDI '13, Seattle, WA, USA, June 16–19, 2013, pp. 321–332. ACM (2013). https://doi.org/10.1145/2491956.2462184

4. Desai, A., Saha, I., Yang, J., Qadeer, S., Seshia, S.A.: DRONA: a framework for safe distributed mobile robotics. In: Martínez, S., Tovar, E., Gill, C., Sinopoli, B. (eds.) Proceedings of the 8th International Conference on Cyber-Physical Systems, ICCPS 2017, Pittsburgh, Pennsylvania, USA, April 18–20, 2017, pp. 239–248. ACM (2017). https://doi.org/10.1145/3055004.3055022

5. Hofmann, A.G., Williams, B.C.: Robust execution of temporally flexible plans for bipedal walking devices. In: Long, D., Smith, S.F., Borrajo, D., McCluskey, L. (eds.) Proceedings of the Sixteenth International Conference on Automated Planning and Scheduling, ICAPS 2006, Cumbria, UK, June 6–10, 2006, pp. 386–389. AAAI (2006). http://www.aaai.org/Library/ICAPS/2006/icaps06-047.php

6. Huang, J., et al.: ROSRV: runtime verification for robots. In: Bonakdarpour, B., Smolka, S.A. (eds.) RV 2014. LNCS, vol. 8734, pp. 247–254. Springer, Cham (2014). https://doi.org/10.1007/978-3-319-11164-3_20

7. Kim, M., Viswanathan, M., Kannan, S., Lee, I., Sokolsky, O.: Java-mac: a run-time assurance approach for java programs. Formal Methods Syst. Des. **24**(2), 129–155 (2004). https://doi.org/10.1023/B:FORM.0000017719.43755.7c

8. Masson, L., Guiochet, J., Waeselynck, H., Cabrera, K., Cassel, S., Törngren, M.: Tuning permissiveness of active safety monitors for autonomous systems. In: Dutle, A., Muñoz, C., Narkawicz, A. (eds.) NFM 2018. LNCS, vol. 10811, pp. 333–348. Springer, Cham (2018). https://doi.org/10.1007/978-3-319-77935-5_23

9. Mitsch, S., Platzer, A.: ModelPlex: verified runtime validation of verified cyber-physical system models. In: Bonakdarpour, B., Smolka, S.A. (eds.) RV 2014. LNCS, vol. 8734, pp. 199–214. Springer, Cham (2014). https://doi.org/10.1007/978-3-319-11164-3_17

10. Pettersson, O.: Execution monitoring in robotics: a survey. Robot. Auton. Syst. **53**(2), 73–88 (2005). https://doi.org/10.1016/j.robot.2005.09.004

11. Phan, D., et al.: A component-based simplex architecture for high-assurance cyber-physical systems. In: 17th International Conference on Application of Concurrency to System Design, ACSD 2017, Zaragoza, Spain, June 25–30, 2017, pp. 49–58. IEEE Computer Society (2017). https://doi.org/10.1109/ACSD.2017.23

12. Phan, D.T., Grosu, R., Jansen, N., Paoletti, N., Smolka, S.A., Stoller, S.D.: Neural simplex architecture. In: Lee, R., Jha, S., Mavridou, A. (eds.) NFM 2020. LNCS, vol. 12229, pp. 97–114. Springer, Cham (2020). https://doi.org/10.1007/978-3-030-55754-6_6

13. Schierman, J.D., et al.: Runtime assurance framework development for highly adaptive flight control systems (2015)

14. Seshia, S.A.: Introspective environment modeling. In: 19th International Conference on Runtime Verification (RV), pp. 15–26 (2019)

15. Seshia, S.A., Sadigh, D., Sastry, S.S.: Towards verified artificial intelligence. ArXiv e-prints, July 2016

16. Sha, L.: Using simplicity to control complexity. IEEE Softw. **18**(4), 20–28 (2001). https://doi.org/10.1109/MS.2001.936213

17. Sucan, I.A., Moll, M., Kavraki, L.E.: The open motion planning library. IEEE Robot. Autom. Mag. **19**(4), 72–82 (2012). https://doi.org/10.1109/MRA.2012.2205651

Runtime Verification for Software

Scalable Online Monitoring of Distributed Systems

David Basin[ID], Matthieu Gras, Srđan Krstić$^{(\boxtimes)}$[ID], and Joshua Schneider$^{(\boxtimes)}$[ID]

Institute of Information Security, Department of Computer Science, ETH Zürich,
Zurich, Switzerland
{srdan.krstic,joshua.schneider}@inf.ethz.ch

Abstract. Distributed systems are challenging for runtime verification. Centralized specifications provide a global view of the system, but their semantics requires totally-ordered observations, which are often unavailable in a distributed setting. Scalability is also problematic, especially for online first-order monitors, which must be parallelized in practice to handle high volume, high velocity data streams. We argue that scalable online monitors must ingest events from multiple sources in parallel, and we propose a general model for input to such monitors. Our model only assumes a low-resolution global clock and allows for out-of-order events, which makes it suitable for distributed systems. Based on this model, we extend our existing monitoring framework, which slices a single event stream into independently monitorable substreams. Our new framework now slices multiple event streams in parallel. We prove our extension correct and empirically show that the maximum monitoring latency significantly improves when slicing is a bottleneck.

1 Introduction

Runtime verification (or monitoring) is a technique that verifies systems while they run in their operational environment. It is realized using *monitors*, which are programs that systematically validate a specification by searching for counterexamples in sequences of observations recorded during system execution. *Online monitors* incrementally process the observations, which arrive as an unbounded stream while the system is running [4].

The specification language used significantly influences the monitors' efficiency. Monitors for propositional languages are very efficient and can process millions of observations per second [5,36,37]. However, these monitors are limited as they distinguish only a fixed, finite set of observations. The observations are often parameterized by values from (possibly) infinite domains, such as IP addresses and user names. Propositional monitors cannot look for patterns that take such parameters into account. In contrast, *first-order monitors* [10,15,30,31,38,39,42] do not suffer from this limitation, but they must be parallelized to reach the performance of propositional monitors [6,29,38–41].

In practice, even small IT systems are often built from many interacting subsystems, which are distributed across multiple machines. When monitored,

© Springer Nature Switzerland AG 2020
J. Deshmukh and D. Ničković (Eds.): RV 2020, LNCS 12399, pp. 197–220, 2020.
https://doi.org/10.1007/978-3-030-60508-7_11

each subsystem provides information about its behavior as a separate observation sequence. Some approaches adopt specification languages that refer to multiple observation sequences explicitly [21,33], or whose semantics is defined on partially-ordered observations [35,43]. However, it is challenging to express global system properties using such decentralized specification languages [25] as they couple the system's behavior with its distributed architecture. Moreover, the specifications must be adapted whenever the system's runtime architecture changes, e.g., when the system is scaled up or down.

We instead focus on *centralized specification languages* [25] that provide a global view of the distributed system. These languages abstract from the system architecture and are thus resilient to its changes. However, centralized specifications often assume totally-ordered observations and without additional information, the multiple observation sequences obtained from distributed systems induce only a partial order. Checking centralized specifications then becomes intractable, since exponentially many compatible total orders must be checked [8]. One therefore needs alternative solutions.

Some approaches opt for a *global clock* to tag every observation across every subsystem with the time when it was made. A global clock abstracts over a collection of local clocks used by each subsystem and synchronized using a clock synchronization protocol like NTP [34]. A clock's resolution is the number of its increments in a time period. The global clock establishes the true total order of observations if the local clocks have sufficient resolutions and are accurate [20] up to a small-enough error. In practice, it is difficult to achieve both conditions for distributed systems that provide observations at high rates [17]. Moreover, even when the observations are totally ordered, they may be received by a monitor in a different order. This can occur if the observations are transmitted over unreliable channels where messages can be delayed, dropped, or reordered [11].

Finally, existing monitors for centralized specifications typically verify a single observation sequence. This *single-source* design limits the monitors' throughput and thus their applicability to the online monitoring of large distributed systems. In previous work, scalable monitors with more than one source have so far been restricted to propositional [14,18] or decentralized specifications [23,33] (Sect. 2).

In this paper we develop a *multi-source* monitoring framework for centralized first-order specifications that takes multiple observation sequences as parallel inputs. It extends our scalable monitoring framework [40,41], which parallelizes the online monitoring of specifications expressed in Metric First-Order Temporal Logic (MFOTL) [10]. The main idea behind the existing framework is to slice the input stream into multiple substreams (Sect. 3). Each substream is monitored independently and in parallel by a first-order (sub)monitor, treated as a black box. When instantiated by a concrete submonitor, the framework becomes an online monitor. However, the existing framework supports only a single source, which hampers scalability. It also cannot handle partially-ordered observations, which arise in distributed systems. We address both limitations in this work.

Our new multi-source framework can be used to monitor distributed systems. The framework's topology is independent of the system's topology, and the framework itself can be distributed. The notion of sources abstracts from the nature of the observation's origin. For example, each source could correspond to an independent component of the monitored system, but it may also be the result of aggregating other streams.

We require that all sources have access to a *low-resolution* global clock. Such a clock must have sufficient resolution to decide whether the given specification is satisfied, but it need not necessarily induce a total order on the observations. We argue that global clocks cannot be avoided when monitoring metric specifications as they refer to differences in real time. We account for the fact that observations may have the same creation time (according to the low-resolution clock) and in such cases restrict the specification language to a fragment that guarantees unambiguous verdicts [8]. Our multi-source framework additionally copes with out-of-order observations. This is important even if the sources use reliable channels, as the framework interleaves observations from different sources and its internal components exchange information concurrently.

We generalize the concept of a *temporal structure (TS)*, which models totally-ordered observations, to a *partitioned temporal structure (PTS)*, which represents partially-ordered observations that may be received out-of-order from multiple sources (Sect. 4.1). We introduce and explain the assumptions on the observation order in a PTS, which are sufficient to uniquely determine whether the specification is satisfied. To monitor a PTS, we add multiple input sources and a reordering step (Sect. 4.2) to our existing monitoring framework. We prove that this extended framework remains sound and complete: the submonitors collectively find exactly those patterns that exist in the input PTS. We extended the implementation (Sect. 5) and empirically evaluated it, showing that it significantly improves monitoring performance (Sect. 6).

In summary, our main contributions are: 1) the definition of the partitioned temporal structure as an input model for multi-source monitors; 2) the extension of our monitoring framework to support multiple sources; 3) its correctness proof, which has been formally verified in the Isabelle proof assistant; and 4) an empirical evaluation showing a significant performance improvement over the single-source framework. Overall, our work lays the foundations for the efficient, scalable, online monitoring of distributed systems using expressive centralized specifications languages like MFOTL.

2   Related Work

Centralized Monitors. Parametric trace slicing [38,39] performs data slicing on a single input stream to improve monitoring expressivity, rather than its scalability. The stream-based language Lola 2.0 [26] extends parametric trace slicing with dynamic control over the active parameter instances. Lola 2.0 supports multiple input streams, but they must be modeled explicitly in the specification and, moreover, their monitoring is centralized.

Basin et al. [8] monitor distributed systems using a single-source, centralized monitor. They preprocess and merge locally collected traces prior to monitoring. Preprocessing assumes that observations with equal time-stamps happen simultaneously and restricts the specification to a fragment where the order of such observations does not influence the monitor's output. Our approach generalizes this idea, whereby it becomes a special case.

Monitors that handle missing and out-of-order observations [11,13] are resilient to network failures, which commonly occur in large distributed systems. These centralized monitors, which support MTL and its variant with freeze quantifiers, are orthogonal to our approach and can be instantiated within our monitoring framework.

Decentralized Monitors. Our work builds on top of existing work on parallel black-box monitoring. Basin et al. [6] introduce the concept of slicing temporal structures. They provide composable operators that slice both data and time and support parallel offline monitoring using MapReduce. In prior work [40,41], we generalized their data slicer and implemented it using the Apache Flink stream processing framework [19].

According to the distributed monitoring survey's terminology [27], the organization of our monitoring framework can be seen as orchestrated or choreographed. In the survey, the notion of a global clock implies the true total observation order, while we assume a low-resolution global clock. Our monitoring framework supports a more expressive specification language than the state-of-the-art alternatives reported on in the survey, which are mostly limited to LTL and the detection of global state predicates.

Bauer and Falcone [14] exploit the locality of the observations in monitored subsystems to organize the monitors hierarchically based on the structure of an LTL formula. In contrast, our parallel monitors each monitor the same (global) formula. By decomposing the specification, Bauer and Falcone reduce the communication overhead, but the monitors still must synchronize on every time-point in the trace. Similarly, El-Hokayem and Falcone [23,24] propose a framework for decentralised monitoring of LTL and (automata-based) regular specifications. However, they focus only on propositional specifications, which limits the expressiveness of their framework.

Leucker et al. [33] describe a concurrent online monitor for multiple non-synchronized input streams. Unlike our work, the authors assume the existence of a global clock that establishes a total order. It is difficult to compare their specification language TeSSLa with ours. TeSSLa refers to multiple input streams directly, while our specification language specifies (global) properties of distributed systems. It is generally easier to write a centralized specification when observations can originate from multiple streams. In TeSSLA, one must either encode all possible interactions between the streams, or merge the streams first, which offsets any gains from the concurrent evaluation.

Stream Processing. A common mechanism for dealing with out-of-order observations in database and stream processing systems [3] is watermarks [2], which are special markers inserted in the data streams to provide a lower bound on the progress of time. Alternatively, a slack parameter [1] can be specified, which denotes the maximum number of positions that any observation can be delayed at a stream operator. It is used to allocate an appropriately sized buffer for each input of the stream operator to perform reordering. Observations delayed more than the slack value are discarded. Punctuations [45] are more general than watermarks in that they indicate the end of some subset of the stream. The semantics of punctuations can vary, e.g., there will be no more observations having certain attribute values in the stream. Heartbeats [44] resemble watermarks and can be seen as special punctuations about temporal attribute values.

3 Preliminaries

We recap the syntax and semantics of Metric First-Order Temporal Logic [10] and summarize our scalable monitoring framework [40], which slices a single temporal structure.

Metric First-Order Temporal Logic (MFOTL). We fix a set of names $\mathbb{E}$ and for simplicity assume a single infinite domain $\mathbb{D}$ of values. The names $r \in \mathbb{E}$ have associated arities $\iota(r) \in \mathbb{N}$. An *event* $r(d_1, \ldots, d_{\iota(r)})$ is an element of $\mathbb{E} \times \mathbb{D}^*$. We further fix an infinite set $\mathbb{V}$ of variables, such that $\mathbb{V}$, $\mathbb{D}$, and $\mathbb{E}$ are pairwise disjoint. Let $\mathbb{I}$ be the set of nonempty intervals $[a, b) := \{x \in \mathbb{N} \mid a \leq x < b\}$, where $a \in \mathbb{N}$, $b \in \mathbb{N} \cup \{\infty\}$, and $a < b$. Formulas φ are defined inductively, where t_i, r, x, and I range over $\mathbb{V} \cup \mathbb{D}$, $\mathbb{E}$, $\mathbb{V}$, and $\mathbb{I}$, respectively:

$$\varphi ::= r(t_1, \ldots, t_{\iota(r)}) \mid t_1 \approx t_2 \mid \neg\varphi \mid \varphi \vee \varphi \mid \exists x.\varphi \mid \bullet_I \varphi \mid \bigcirc_I \varphi \mid \varphi \, \mathsf{S}_I \, \varphi \mid \varphi \, \mathsf{U}_I \, \varphi.$$

Formulas of the form $r(t_1, \ldots, t_{\iota(r)})$ are called *event formulas*. The temporal operators $\bullet_I$ (previous), $\bigcirc_I$ (next), S_I (since), and U_I (until) may be nested freely. We derive other operators: truth $\top := \exists x. \, x \approx x$, inequality $t_1 \not\approx t_2 := \neg(t_1 \approx t_2)$, conjunction $\varphi \wedge \psi := \neg(\neg\varphi \vee \neg\psi)$, implication $\varphi \rightarrow \psi := \neg\varphi \vee \psi$, eventually $\Diamond_I \varphi := \top \, \mathsf{U}_I \, \varphi$, always $\square_I \varphi := \neg\Diamond_I \neg\varphi$, and once $\blacklozenge_I \varphi := \top \, \mathsf{S}_I \, \varphi$. The set $\mathbb{V}_\varphi$ denotes the set of free variables of φ. A formula has *bounded future* iff all subformulas of the form $\bigcirc_{[a,b)} \alpha$ and $\alpha \, \mathsf{U}_{[a,b)} \, \beta$ (including derived operators) satisfy $b < \infty$.

MFOTL formulas are interpreted over *temporal structures (TS)*, which model totally-ordered observation sequences (or streams). A temporal structure ρ is an infinite sequence $(\tau_i, D_i)_{i \in \mathbb{N}}$, where $\tau_i \in \mathbb{N}$ is a discrete time-stamp, and the *database* $D_i \in \mathbb{DB} = \mathcal{P}(\mathbb{E} \times \mathbb{D}^*)$ is a finite set of events that happen concurrently in the monitored system. Databases at different time-points $i \neq j$ may have the same time-stamp $\tau_i = \tau_j$. The sequence of time-stamps must be *monotone* ($\forall i. \, \tau_i \leq \tau_{i+1}$) and *progressing* ($\forall \tau. \, \exists i. \, \tau < \tau_i$).

The relation $v, i \models_\rho \varphi$ defines the satisfaction of the formula φ for a valuation v at an index i with respect to the temporal structure $\rho = (\tau_i, D_i)_{i \in \mathbb{N}}$; see Fig. 1. Whenever ρ is fixed and clear from the context, we omit the subscript on $\models$. The valuation v is a mapping $\mathbb{V}_\varphi \rightarrow \mathbb{D}$, assigning domain elements to the free

$$v, i \models r(t_1, \ldots, t_n) \text{ if } r(v(t_1), \ldots v(t_n)) \in D_i \quad | \quad v, i \models \exists x. \varphi \text{ if } v[x \mapsto d], i \models \varphi \text{ for some } d \in \mathbb{D}$$
$$v, i \models t_1 \approx t_2 \qquad \text{if } v(t_1) = v(t_2) \qquad\qquad | \quad v, i \models \bullet_I \varphi \text{ if } i > 0, \tau_i - \tau_{i-1} \in I, \text{ and } v, i-1 \models \varphi$$
$$v, i \models \neg\varphi \qquad\qquad \text{if } v, i \not\models \varphi \qquad\qquad\quad | \quad v, i \models \bigcirc_I \varphi \text{ if } \tau_{i+1} - \tau_i \in I \text{ and } v, i+1 \models \varphi$$
$$v, i \models \varphi \vee \psi \qquad\quad \text{if } v, i \models \varphi \text{ or } v, i \models \psi$$
$$v, i \models \varphi \, \mathsf{S}_I \, \psi \qquad \text{if } v, j \models \psi \text{ for some } j \leq i, \tau_i - \tau_j \in I, \text{ and } v, k \models \varphi \text{ for all } k \text{ with } j < k \leq i$$
$$v, i \models \varphi \, \mathsf{U}_I \, \psi \qquad \text{if } v, j \models \psi \text{ for some } j \geq i, \tau_j - \tau_i \in I, \text{ and } v, k \models \varphi \text{ for all } k \text{ with } i \leq k < j$$

Fig. 1. Semantics of MFOTL

variables of φ. Overloading notation, v is also the extension of v to the domain $\mathbb{V}_\varphi \cup \mathbb{D}$, setting $v(t) = t$ whenever $t \in \mathbb{D}$. We write $v[x \mapsto d]$ for the function equal to v, except that the argument x is mapped to d.

Monitors. An *online monitor* for a formula φ receives time-stamped databases that are a finite prefix π of some TS ρ (denoted by $\pi \prec \rho$). The monitor incrementally computes a verdict, which is a set of valuations and time-points that satisfy φ given π. (Typically, one is interested in the violations of a specification $\square \, \psi$, which can be obtained by monitoring $\neg\psi$ instead.) A monitor is *sound* if the verdict for π contains (v, i) only if $v, i \models_\rho \varphi$ for all $\rho \succ \pi$. It is *complete* if whenever $\pi \prec \rho$ is such that $v, i \models_{\rho'} \varphi$ for all $\rho' \succ \pi$, then there is another prefix $\pi' \prec \rho$ for which the verdict contains (v, i). In our formal treatment, we consider the monitor's output in the limit as the input prefix grows to infinity. Thus, a monitor implements an abstract *monitor function* $\mathcal{M}_\varphi : (\mathbb{N} \times \mathbb{DB})^\omega \to \mathcal{P}((\mathbb{V}_\varphi \to \mathbb{D}) \times \mathbb{N})$ that maps a TS ρ to the union of all verdicts obtained from all possible prefixes of ρ. We shall assume that the monitor implementing $\mathcal{M}_\varphi$ is sound and complete. If φ has bounded future, it follows that $\mathcal{M}_\varphi(\rho) = \{(v, i) \mid v, i \models_\rho \varphi\}$.

Slicing Framework. In prior work, we parallelized online first-order monitoring by slicing [40,41] the temporal structure into N temporal structures that can be independently monitored. Figure 2 shows the dataflow graph constructed by our monitoring framework to monitor a given formula φ. The framework utilizes N parallel submonitors, which are independent instances of the monitor function $\mathcal{M}_\varphi$. Let $[n]$ denote the set $\{1, \ldots, n\}$. The slicer $\mathcal{S}_g$ is parameterized by a *slicing strategy* $g : [N] \to \mathcal{P}(\mathbb{V}_\varphi \to \mathbb{D})$ satisfying $\bigcup_{k \in [N]} g(k) = (\mathbb{V}_\varphi \to \mathbb{D})$. The slicing strategy specifies the set of valuations $g(k)$ for which the submonitor k is responsible. Next, we describe which events the submonitor k receives to evaluate φ correctly on all $v \in g(k)$. Given an event e, let $sfmatches(\varphi, e)$ be the set of all valuations v for which there is an event subformula ψ in φ with $v(\psi) = e$. (Here v is extended to event subformulas, such that $v(r(t_1, \ldots, t_{\iota(r)})) = r(v(t_1), \ldots, v(t_{\iota(r)}))$, and we assume that φ's bound variables are disjoint from its free variables.) For a database D and a set of valuations R, we write $D \downarrow R$ for the restricted database $\{e \in D \mid sfmatches(\varphi, e) \cap R \neq \varnothing\}$. The same notation restricts the TS $\rho = (\tau_i, D_i)_{i \in \mathbb{N}}$ pointwise, i.e., $\rho \downarrow R = (\tau_i, D_i \downarrow R)_{i \in \mathbb{N}}$. Then, it is sufficient if the submonitor k receives the slice $\mathcal{S}_{g,k}(\rho) = \rho \downarrow g(k)$. The slicer $\mathcal{S}_g$ thus outputs N streams $\mathcal{S}_{g,1}(\rho), \ldots, \mathcal{S}_{g,N}(\rho)$.

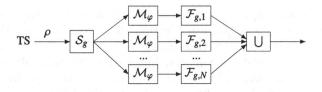

Fig. 2. Dataflow in the single-source monitoring framework

The output of the monitor function $\mathcal{M}_\varphi$ on ρ can be reconstructed from the parallel submonitors' output on the N slices. Formally, $\mathcal{M}_\varphi(\rho) = \bigcup_{k \in [N]}(\mathcal{F}_{g,k}(\mathcal{M}_\varphi(\mathcal{S}_{g,k}(\rho))))$, where $\mathcal{F}_{g,k}(X) = X \cap (g(k) \times \mathbb{N})$. Note that Fig. 2 illustrates the right-hand side of the equation defining $\mathcal{M}_\varphi(\rho)$. In [40], we proved this equation assuming a stronger completeness property of the online monitor. However, it can also be shown for the abstract function $\mathcal{M}_\varphi$, which operates on a TS. The intersection with $g(k) \times \mathbb{N}$ is needed to avoid spurious verdicts for some formulas, such as those involving equality.

Example 1. Consider an access control policy for a service operating on medical records, where *whenever a user requests to process a record, the service does so only if the user was authorized to access that record.* The policy is formalized in MFOTL as $\square\, \Phi_1$ with $\Phi_1 \equiv \forall u.\ \mathsf{proc}(u, r) \rightarrow \blacklozenge\mathsf{auth}(u, r)$. The formula $\mathsf{proc}(u, r)$ denotes that u requested to process r and $\mathsf{auth}(u, r)$ denotes that u is authorized to access r. For the sake of this example, we leave r as the only free variable and assume numeric identifiers for u and r.

We monitor $\varphi \equiv \neg\Phi_1$ as shown in Fig. 2, using the slicing strategy $g(k) = \{v \mid v(r) \bmod 3 = k - 1\}$ with $N = 3$ slices. Recall that the set $g(k)$ contains valuations, which are mappings from the free variables $\{r\}$ to $\mathbb{D}$. The TS ρ models a service execution with the first database $D = \{\mathsf{auth}(1, 1), \mathsf{auth}(1, 2), \mathsf{auth}(1, 3), \mathsf{proc}(1, 3), \mathsf{proc}(1, 4)\}$. The submonitor 1 receives $D \downarrow g(1) = \{\mathsf{auth}(1, 1), \mathsf{proc}(1, 4)\}$ as its first database and reports the verdict $\{(\{r \mapsto 4\}, 0)\}$ as a violation of Φ_1, which is the only violation evident from D. Submonitors 2 and 3 receive databases $\{\mathsf{auth}(1, 2)\}$ and $\{\mathsf{auth}(1, 3), \mathsf{proc}(1, 3)\}$ and output empty verdicts after processing them, respectively.

Example 2. Now consider a centralized system running many instances of the service from the previous example. Each service handles user requests either by directly processing a record, or by recursively triggering requests to other (local) services. So, now *a service is allowed to process a record only if this was initially requested by a user authorized to access the record.* Notice that data processing can now happen after a chain of requests involving multiple services. Therefore, we assume that the services attach a unique session number s to all requests caused directly or indirectly by a user's request.

The MFOTL formula $\square\, \Phi_2$ with $\Phi_2 \equiv (\blacklozenge\mathsf{req}(u, s)) \wedge \mathsf{proc}(s, r) \rightarrow \blacklozenge\mathsf{auth}(u, r)$ formalizes the new specification, now with free variables $\{u, s, r\}$. The new event formulas are $\mathsf{req}(u, s)$ (user u sends a request, starting a session s), and $\mathsf{proc}(s, r)$ (record r is processed within the session s). Let $N = 8$ and $g(k) = \{v \mid 4 \cdot (v(u) \bmod 2) + 2 \cdot (v(s) \bmod 2) + v(r) \bmod 2 = k - 1\}$ be a slicing strategy. Note that according to g, submonitor 1 receives only valuations where each variable has an even value. When we monitor ρ with the first database $D = \{\mathsf{req}(2, 2), \mathsf{auth}(2, 1), \mathsf{proc}(2, 2)\}$, each event in D is sent to two submonitors. For instance, $\mathsf{req}(2, 2)$ is sent both to submonitors 1 and 2, whereas $\mathsf{proc}(2, 2)$ is sent to submonitors 1 and 5. Such a slicing scheme ensures that submonitor 1 receives sufficient information to output the verdict $\{(\{u \mapsto 2, s \mapsto 2, r \mapsto 2\}, 0)\}$.

4   Monitoring Distributed Systems

We consider the online monitoring of a distributed system. A first problem that we must solve is the lack of a total order on the observations of the individual subsystems (machines, processes, threads, etc.). As explained in the introduction, such a total order is required by the semantics of centralized specifications, but it does not exist unless the subsystems' execution is perfectly synchronized. This cannot be assumed in general as one usually desires some parallelism in distributed systems.

A second problem is that distributed systems are often developed to achieve scalability, and online monitors used with such systems should be scalable as well. A monitor that physically combines observations from different sources into a single stream cannot satisfy this requirement: if the workload increases and additional events are generated, the processes working with the single stream will eventually be overloaded. Scalable online monitors must therefore ingest observations in parallel.

We solve the above problems by viewing online monitoring as an instance of distributed stream processing. Observations enter the monitor in multiple parallel streams, called *sources*. We give a general model of sources that captures a variety of distributed monitoring scenarios, while still allowing the efficient monitoring of metric specifications (Sect. 4.1). The model logically decouples the monitor from the monitored system, which ensures that the system's topology can be chosen independently. We then extend the slicing framework to utilize multiple sources (Sect. 4.2). The resulting multi-source framework does not require a total order on the observations, and it scales better than the single-source version, even if the monitored system is not truly distributed.

4.1   Input Model

We model the monitor's input as a *Partitioned Temporal Structure (PTS)*, which we define formally later in this section. We believe that this model is useful beyond our implementation using slicing. The model is based on several assumptions about the problem at hand. Below, we explain these assumptions, show how they are reflected in the PTS, and give examples of possible applications.

Assumption 1. We assume that the monitored specification has the form $\Phi = \Box \neg \varphi$, where φ has bounded future. We also assume that the specification is centralized, i.e., its event formulas are interpreted over all events from the entire system.

The restriction on the formula's structure is common for first-order monitors. It guarantees that every violation can be detected in finite time [10]. The assumption that the specification is centralized rules out various monitoring approaches. We already argued that centralized monitors are ill-suited for scalable distributed systems. Moreover, note that centralized specifications cannot be easily split into smaller parts that are handled by local monitors, as illustrated by the following example.

Example 3. Consider now the services from Example 2 deployed on a microservice architecture that is running on a cluster of machines. Each service generates its own TS. As requests span arbitrarily many machines, the specification cannot be checked locally.

We therefore treat the monitored system and the monitor as independent entities. They are connected by M sources, which are parallel observation streams. The sources may correspond the monitored system's components, e.g., the services in Example 3. This is not required by the model, which we will show in a later example.

The next assumption imposes an important restriction: it must be possible to arrive at a definite monitoring verdict even if the observations are only partially ordered. Otherwise, we would need to construct all possible interleavings of the concurrent observations, which is generally infeasible. We avoid relying on system-specific information, such as vector clocks, to reduce the number of interleavings [35] as this would diminish the generality of our approach.

Assumption 2. There exists a TS $\rho^\star$ that describes the actual sequence of events as they occur in real time. The time-stamps in $\rho^\star$ are obtained from the real time truncated to the precision used in the specification. (We do not assume that $\rho^\star$ can be observed directly.) The sources must have access to a global clock that provides time-stamps from $\rho^\star$ as well as sufficient information about the event order to decide whether $\rho^\star$ satisfies Φ.

Note that the system satisfies the specification Φ iff $\rho^\star$ satisfies Φ. We model the information provided by the global clock using *indices*, which are natural numbers attached to every observation. If the index of observation o_1 is less than the index of observation o_2, then o_1 must have happened before o_2. At one extreme, the index is simply the position of the observation in $\rho^\star$, i.e., a global sequence number. Then every specification has a definite verdict. A distributed system providing such sequence numbers would need a global clock with very high resolution, which is often unrealistic. However, centralized applications, which have access to sequence numbers, can be more efficiently monitored with a multi-source monitor than with a single-source monitor.

Example 4. Kernel event tracing creates streams with high event rates [22]. We may improve the monitor's throughput by distributing the events over multiple streams (see Sect. 6). For a single processor, its hardware counters provide global sequence numbers.

At the other extreme, the indices could simply be the time-stamps. We say that a clock providing such indices is *low resolution*, as its resolution may not be high enough to establish the true total order. Yet not all specifications can be monitored if the indices have lower resolution than global sequence numbers. We follow the *collapse* approach by Basin et al. [8], where events with the same time-stamp are collapsed into a single instantaneous observation. We generalize the collapse from time-stamps to indices, which unifies the presentation. We then rephrase the requirement on the global clock from Assumption 2 in terms of the collapse: monitoring the collapsed sequence must result in essentially the same output as monitoring $\rho^\star$. To make this precise, we add the indices to $\rho^\star$ itself, which results in the indexed temporal structure $\hat{\rho}^\star$.

Definition 1. *An* indexed temporal structure (ITS) *is a TS over extended tuples* (α_i, τ_i, D_i), *where* $\alpha_i \in \mathbb{N}$ *are indices. The indices must increase monotonically* $(\forall i.\ \alpha_i \leq \alpha_{i+1})$, *and they must refine time-stamps* $(\forall i.\ \forall j.\ \alpha_i \leq \alpha_j \implies \tau_i \leq \tau_j)$.

Definition 2. *The generalized collapse* $\mathcal{C}(\hat{\rho}) = (\tau_i^c, D_i^c)_i$ *of an ITS* $\hat{\rho}$ *is characterized by the unique monotone and surjective function* $f : \mathbb{N} \to \mathbb{N}$ *that maps (only) positions with the same index to a common value* $(\forall i.\ \forall j.\ \alpha_i = \alpha_j \iff f(i) = f(j))$. *Then* $\forall i.\ \tau_{f(i)}^c = \tau_i$ *and* $\forall j.\ D_j^c = \bigcup\{D_i \mid f(i) = j\}$.

Since $\hat{\rho}^\star$ is the idealized totally-ordered sequence, its indices must increase monotonically. Indices must also refine time-stamps so that the generalized collapse is a TS. This requirement, which may seem quite strong, is necessary because the semantics of a metric specification language (like MFOTL) is defined with respect to a TS. Note, however, that the resolution of time-stamps is not fixed (Assumption 2). The resolution of time-stamps and thus indices can be quite low as long as it is possible to formalize the specification faithfully.

Definition 3. *We call* $\hat{\rho}$ adequate *for the formula* φ *iff* $v, i \models_{\mathcal{C}(\hat{\rho})} \varphi \iff (\exists j.\ f(j) = i \wedge v, j \models_\rho \varphi)$ *for all* v *and* i, *where* ρ *is obtained from* $\hat{\rho}$ *by omitting the indices.*

Monitoring a formula φ on the generalized collapse of an adequate ITS finds the same satisfying valuations as monitoring the ITS itself (modulo the remapping of time-points).

Lemma 1. *Suppose that* $\hat{\rho}$ *is adequate for the formula* φ. *Then* $\mathcal{M}_\varphi(\mathcal{C}(\hat{\rho})) = \{(v, f(j)) \mid (v, j) \in \mathcal{M}_\varphi(\rho)\}$, *where* f *is as in Definition 2.*

If the indices of an ITS are global sequence numbers (e.g., $\forall i.\ \alpha_i = i$), the ITS is adequate for all φ. To gain intuition for other ITS, we focus again on the case where indices are time-stamps (*time-ITS*, $\forall i.\ \alpha_i = \tau_i$). Basin et al. [8] define the notion of *collapse-sufficient* formulas, which are essentially those formulas that can be monitored correctly on a time-based collapse. They provide an efficiently decidable fragment of formulas with this property. (More precisely, a time-ITS $\hat{\rho}$ is adequate for φ iff φ satisfies the properties ($\models\exists$) and ($\not\models\forall$) given in [8], which implies that $\Phi = \square\ \neg\varphi$ is collapse-sufficient.) Often, a formula can be made collapse-sufficient by replacing subformulas $\blacklozenge_{[0,t]}\alpha$ (note the interval's zero bound) with $\blacklozenge_{[0,t]}\lozenge_{[0,0]}\alpha$, and dually for $\lozenge_{[0,t]}$. More complicated replacements are however needed for S and U.

Example 5. To obtain a collapse-sufficient formula from the specification in Example 2, we restrict the authorizations to happen at least one second before their use. Furthermore, we ignore the order of requests and process events (using the $\lozenge_{[0,0]}$ operator) as long as they have the same time-stamp. The specification is formalized as $\square\ \Phi_3$ with $\Phi_3 \equiv (\blacklozenge\lozenge_{[0,0]}\mathsf{req}(u,s)) \wedge \mathsf{use}(s,d) \to \blacklozenge_{[1,60]}\mathsf{auth}(u,d)$.

It is common practice in distributed systems to process, aggregate, and store logging information in a dedicated service. The observations fed to the monitor are then taken from this service. In Example 3, the microservices could first send their events to a distributed message broker such as Kafka [32]. As a result, events from different services may be interleaved before they reach the monitor. We therefore allow that individual sources provide observations in a different order than their temporal order. This generalization adds almost no complexity to the monitor's design (Sect. 4.2): we must anyway reorder the observations, even for correctly ordered streams, to synchronize them across sources. Handling out-of-order observations thus comes almost for free.

Assumption 3. Sources may provide observations in any order. However, the delay of each observation must be bounded.

The latter condition ensures that the monitor does not get stuck. We enforce it by adding watermarks, which are lower bounds on future indices, to the sources. Then, the observations' delay is bounded if the watermarks always eventually increase. In our implementation, watermarks are interspersed between regular observations. We simplify the formal definitions below by assuming that every database has an associated watermark, which is the one most recently seen. Note that an input model with watermarks is strictly more permissive than one without. If we know that the observations will be in the correct order, we can simply set each watermark equal to the next index.

We are now ready to give a formal definition of our input model. We recall the main idea: The monitor's input is a PTS, which partitions some ITS $\hat{\rho}^\star$ into multiple sources. If $\hat{\rho}^\star$ is adequate for the formula φ, it suffices to monitor the generalized collapse $\mathcal{C}(\hat{\rho}^\star)$ via the PTS to achieve the goal of monitoring $\rho^\star$.

Definition 4. *A partitioned temporal structure (PTS) is a finite list $\rho_1,\ldots,\rho_M$ of $M \geq 1$ sources. A source ρ_k is an infinite sequence of tuples $(\alpha_{k,i}, \beta_{k,i}, \tau_{k,i}, D_{k,i})_{i\in\mathbb{N}}$, where $\alpha_{k,i} \in \mathbb{N}$ is an index, $\beta_{k,i} \in \mathbb{N}$ is a watermark, and $\tau_{k,i}$ and $D_{k,i}$*

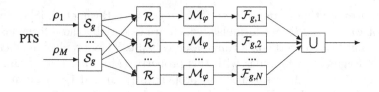

Fig. 3. Dataflow in the multi-source monitoring framework

are as in temporal structures. For all $k \in [M]$, ρ_k must satisfy (P1) monotone watermarks ($\forall i.\ \beta_{k,i} \leq \beta_{k,i+1}$); (P2) progressing watermarks ($\forall \beta.\ \exists i.\ \beta \leq \beta_{k,i}$); (P3) watermarks bound future indices ($\forall i.\ \forall j.\ i < j \implies \beta_{k,i} \leq \alpha_{k,j}$); and (P4) progressing time-stamps ($\forall \tau.\ \exists i.\ \tau \leq \tau_{k,i}$).

A PTS $\rho_1, \ldots, \rho_n$ partitions an ITS $(\alpha_j, \tau_j, D_j)_{j \in \mathbb{N}}$ iff it is (Q1) sound ($\forall k.\ \forall i.\ \exists j.\ \alpha_{k,i} = \alpha_j \wedge \tau_{k,i} = \tau_j \wedge D_{k,i} \subseteq D_j$); and (Q2) complete wrt. indices ($\forall j.\ \exists k.\ \exists i.\ \alpha_{k,i} = \alpha_j \wedge \tau_{k,i} = \tau_j$) and events ($\forall j.\ \forall e \in D_j.\ \exists k.\ \exists i.\ \alpha_{k,i} = \alpha_j \wedge \tau_{k,i} = \tau_j \wedge e \in D_{k,i}$).

Conditions P1–P3 have already been explained, while condition P4 is inherited from temporal structures. Conditions Q1–Q2 encode that the PTS contains the same information as the ITS. Specifically, the sources must have access to a low-resolution global clock providing the time-stamps in $\hat{\rho}^\star$. Its resolution is defined by the specification. For instance, we could use NTP-synchronized time in seconds in Example 5, where the specification requires recent authorization on the order of seconds.

We need both completeness wrt. indices and events (Q2) because the latter is trivially true for empty databases, but we must ensure that the corresponding index (and time-stamp) occurs in the PTS. Note that for every ITS, there is at least one PTS that partitions it into $M \geq 1$ sources: let $(\alpha_{k,i}, \beta_{k,i}, \tau_{k,i}, D_{k,i}) = (\alpha_j, \alpha_j, \tau_j, D_j)$ with $j = i \cdot M + k - 1$.

4.2 Slicing Framework with Multiple Sources

Figure 3 shows the slicing framework's dataflow after extending it to multiple sources. Arrows represent streams of elements, and rectangles are stream transducers with possibly multiple inputs and outputs. The input consists of the M sources of a PTS. We apply the slicer $\mathcal{S}_g$ independently to each source, using the given slicing strategy g. The input of $\mathcal{S}_g$ thus carries additional indices and watermarks. Since slicing only affects the databases, we can easily lift it to source streams. Let the stream $\rho_{k,k'}$ be the output of the kth slicer on its k'th outgoing edge, where $k' \in [N]$. The k'th instance of $\mathcal{R}$ (described below) receives an interleaving of the streams $\rho_{1,k'}, \ldots, \rho_{M,k'}$. Stream processor implementations usually do not guarantee a particular order for such an interleaving. This also applies to our implementation (Sect. 5). Therefore, we assume that the interleaving is nondeterministic, with the only guarantee being one of fairness, namely that every input stream is visited infinitely often. We further assume that the elements in the streams $\rho_{k,k'}$ are tagged with their origin k.

The crucial new component is the *reordering algorithm* $\mathcal{R}$, which fulfills two purposes. First, it collapses databases according to their indices. This has an effect only if indices are time-stamps, i.e., the underlying ITS is time-indexed. Second, $\mathcal{R}$ ensures that the input to the monitor function $\mathcal{M}_\varphi$ is sorted correctly. Even if observations arrive in the correct order at PTS sources, reordering is necessary due to the shuffling between $\mathcal{S}_g$ and $\mathcal{R}$.

The pseudocode for $\mathcal{R}$ is given in Algorithm 1. It uses two global variables, *marks* and *buffer*, both finite associative maps. The expression keys(m) denotes the set of keys in the associative map m. If $x \in$ keys(m), then $m[x]$ is the unique value that m associates with x. The map *marks* stores the largest watermark seen so far for each input stream. (Recall that the input to $\mathcal{R}$ is an interleaving of one slice from each input stream.) The map *buffer* maps indices to pairs of time-stamps and databases. Intuitively, *buffer* keeps all indices that may occur in the future as the watermarks have not advanced past them.

The procedure INITIALIZE(M) is called once when the monitor starts, where M is the number of sources. The watermarks are initially zero, which is a lower bound for all indices. The procedure PROCESS(x) is called for every stream element x received by $\mathcal{R}$. The first element of the tuple $x = (k, \alpha, \beta, \tau, D)$ identifies the source from which it originates, while the remaining elements are from the sliced PTS. Line 4 restores the invariant for *marks*. In lines 5–9, D's contents are added to the buffer. If the index α is already mapped by *buffer*, we take the union with the previously stored database to implement the collapse. Otherwise, τ and D are inserted into *buffer*. The value θ computed in line 10 is the minimum of all the latest watermarks across all inputs. By condition P3 of PTS (Definition 4), we know that all future indices that $\mathcal{R}$ will receive must be at least θ. Therefore, it is safe (only) to output everything in *buffer* with a smaller index. This happens in lines 11–13. Note that we iterate over the indices in ascending order, which ensures that the output is sorted correctly. The sequence of $\mathcal{R}$'s output elements (which are pairs of time-stamps and databases) forms the stream that is sent to the monitor $\mathcal{M}_\varphi$ in Fig. 3.

The following theorem establishes the correctness of the multi-source framework. It is formalized [7] and verified along with Lemma 1 in the Isabelle/HOL proof assistant.

Theorem 1. *Let $\rho_1, \ldots, \rho_M$ be a PTS that partitions $\hat{\rho}^\star$. For all slicing strategies g, the result of the dataflow in Fig. 3 (with inputs $\rho_1, \ldots, \rho_M$) is equal to $\mathcal{M}_\varphi(\mathcal{C}(\hat{\rho}^\star))$.*

Note that this theorem holds for all possible partitions of $\hat{\rho}^\star$ and all possible interleavings that can result from the shuffling step. However, it is only a statement about the infinite sequence of verdicts. Each verdict may be delayed by an arbitrary (but finite) amount of time, depending on the watermarks in the input and the shuffling implementation. Theorem 1 does not assume that $\hat{\rho}^\star$ is adequate for φ because it refers directly to the generalized collapse $\mathcal{C}(\hat{\rho}^\star)$. If we additionally know that $\hat{\rho}^\star$ is adequate, we get the same verdicts as if we were monitoring $\rho^\star$ directly, modulo the mapping of time-points (Lemma 1).

Algorithm 1. Reordering algorithm $\mathcal{R}$

1: **procedure** INITIALIZE(M)
2:     $marks \leftarrow \{k \mapsto 0 \mid k \in [M]\}, \quad buffer \leftarrow \{\}$
3: **procedure** PROCESS(($k, \alpha, \beta, \tau, D$))
4:     $marks[k] \leftarrow \beta$
5:     **if** $\alpha \in \text{keys}(buffer)$ **then**
6:         $(\tau', D') := buffer[\alpha]$
7:         $buffer[\alpha] \leftarrow (\tau', D \cup D')$
8:     **else**
9:         $buffer[\alpha] \leftarrow (\tau, D)$
10:     $\theta := \min\{marks[k] \mid k \in \text{keys}(marks)\}$
11:     **for** $i \in \text{keys}(buffer)$ in ascending order, while $i < \theta$ **do**
12:         **output** $buffer[i]$
13:         delete i from $buffer$

Example 6. We use the multi-source monitoring framework to monitor $\varphi \equiv \neg \Phi_3$ (Example 5) on $M = 2$ distributed services (Example 3), using $N = 8$ submonitors and the splitting strategy g (Example 2). The dataflow is shown in Fig. 3. The input PTS consists of two sources ρ_1 and ρ_2 with prefixes $(0, 0, 0, \{\text{req}(2, 2)\})$, $(3, 0, 3, \{\text{proc}(1, 1)\})$, $(1, 0, 1, \{\text{req}(2, 1)\})$, $(4, 4, 4, \{\})$ and $(0, 0, 0, \{\text{proc}(2, 2), \text{auth}(2, 1)\})$, $(4, 4, 4, \{\})$, respectively. Note that the indices are equal to the time-stamps. As in Example 2, submonitor 1 receives events $\text{req}(2, 2)$ and $\text{proc}(2, 2)$ and produces the same verdict. However, the reordering algorithm sends these events only after receiving watermark 4 from both sources. All of the remaining events are sent to submonitor 3. The reordering algorithm ensures that they are received in the order defined by their indices. Hence, $\text{auth}(2, 1)$ is received first, followed by $\text{req}(2, 1)$, and then by $\text{proc}(1, 1)$. Due to the reordering, submonitor 3 correctly produces an empty verdict for the given prefixes.

We conclude with a remark about the time and space complexity of Algorithm 1. Both are unbounded in the worst case because of the problem with unbounded watermark delays mentioned above. However, we obtain a more meaningful result under reasonable additional assumptions. For example, assume that each database in the input has size at most d, that every index occurs at most c times, and that the number of stream elements between an index α and the time that θ (line 10) becomes greater than α is at most z. The parameter c is upper bounded by the *time-point rate* (Sect. 6) multiplied by M. The parameter z depends on the *watermark frequency* and the *maximum (event) delay* (Sect. 6), and also on the additional delay introduced by the shuffle step between slicing and reordering.

There are at most z different keys in *buffer* at any given time, each mapping to a database of size at most $c \cdot d$. The space complexity is thus $O(M + c \cdot d \cdot z)$ in the uniform RAM model, where M is the number of sources. By using a self-balancing search tree for *buffer* and hash tables for the databases contained therein, one invocation of PROCESS has an amortized average time complexity of $O(M + d + \log z)$, again in the uniform model. The summand M can be reduced to $\log M$ by using a binary heap to maintain θ instead of recomputing it in every invocation.

5   Implementation

We implemented a multi-source online monitoring framework based on the ideas outlined in Sect. 4. It extends our previous single-source framework [40,41] and is available online [7]. The implementation instantiates the submonitors with MonPoly [12], which supports a monitorable fragment of MFOTL [10] where, in particular, formulas must have bounded future. We modified about 4k lines of code (3.2k added and 0.8k deleted). In Sect. 4, we omitted many details, e.g., how events are delivered to and exchanged within the framework, which effect the efficiency and usability of the framework. We explain some implementation choices here and further details can be found in [28,40].

Our multi-source framework is built on top of Apache Flink [19], which provides an API and a runtime for fault tolerant distributed stream processing. Fault tolerance is important for distributed online monitors since increasing the number of machines on which a monitor runs also increases the risk of failures, which would otherwise disrupt the monitor's operation. The implementation's dataflow corresponds roughly to the dataflow in Fig. 3, except that the streams' elements are individual events instead of databases. The events are interleaved with other control elements that carry additional metadata. We use Flink's API to define the logical dataflow graph, whose vertices are operators that transform potentially unbounded data streams. At runtime, operators can have multiple instances as defined by their degree of parallelism. Each operator instance works on a partition, i.e., a substream. Stream elements are repartitioned according to some strategy if the degree of parallelism changes from one operator to the next. In Fig. 3, the parallelism changes from M to N at the shuffling step. Each slicer outputs is a single stream of elements labeled with their destination submonitor. Based on these labels, a stream partitioner ensures that the elements reach their intended destination.

We use two types of source operators (TCP and Kafka) with different trade-offs. In Flink, sources are operators without incoming edges in the dataflow graph. Their degree of parallelism, which must be chosen before execution starts, determines the number M of input streams. The TCP source reads simple text streams from multiple sockets by connecting to a list of address and port pairs. It is fast and thus useful for benchmarking the other components, but it is not fault tolerant. The Kafka [32] source operator implements a distributed persistent message queue and provides fault tolerance. However, we exclude it from the evaluation as it incurred a significant overhead in our preliminary experiments.

The slicer, submonitors, filtering, and verdict union are nearly unmodified (see [40]). However, there are now multiple instances of the slicing operator. The reordering function $\mathcal{R}$ is a straightforward implementation of Algorithm 1.

$$\varphi_s \equiv P(x,y) \wedge \left((\blacklozenge_{[1,3s]} Q(x,z)) \wedge \blacklozenge_{[1,3s]} R(x,w) \right)$$

$$\varphi_i \equiv insert(u,db1,p,d) \wedge d \not\approx null \wedge \neg \lozenge_{[0,30h]} (\exists u'. insert(u',db2,p,d) \vee delete(u',db1,p,d))$$

$$\varphi_d \equiv \Big((delete(u,db1,p,d) \wedge d \not\approx null \wedge \neg \blacklozenge_{[0,30h]} \exists u'. \exists p'. insert(u',db1,p',d)) \vee$$

$$(delete(u,db1,p,d) \wedge d \not\approx null \wedge (\exists u'. \exists p'. (\blacklozenge_{[0,30h]} insert(u',db1,p',d)) \vee$$

$$(\lozenge_{[0,30h]} insert(u',db2,p',d)))) \Big) \wedge \neg \lozenge_{[0,30h]} \exists u'. \exists p'. delete(u',db2,p',d)$$

Fig. 4. MFOTL formulas used in the evaluation

In our implementation, the *buffer* is simply a hash table, and we access it by probing for increasing indices. A more efficient approach can be used if this becomes a bottleneck. Our implementation currently supports time-points and time-stamps as indices (see Sect. 4.1). With out-of-order input, only time-stamps are supported, but it should be easy to generalize the framework to time-points. We rely on *order elements*, which are a type of control elements, instead of associating watermarks with every database. For in-order inputs, the order elements are separators between databases, which are inserted by the input parser. In this case, we can synthesize the watermark from the database's time-point or time-stamp. If the input is out-of-order, watermarks must be provided as annotations in the input data. The input parser extracts the watermarks and embeds them in newly created order elements.

6   Evaluation

To assess the scalability of our extended framework we organized our evaluation (available online [7]) in terms of the following research questions (RQs).

RQ1: How do the input parameters affect the multi-source framework's scalability?

RQ2: What is the impact of imbalanced input sources on performance?

RQ3: Can multiple sources be used to improve monitoring performance?

RQ4: How much overhead does event reordering incur?

RQ1 and RQ2 assess the impact of input parameters (specifically, the event rate and time-point rate, defined below, as well as the number of inputs and submonitors) on our framework's performance. When events arrive out of order, we additionally control their maximum delay and the watermark frequency. We assess RQ1 by monitoring multiple traces with the same event rate, while for RQ2 we relax this restriction. RQ3 aims to evaluate the overall performance gain of introducing multiple inputs. We aim to validate our hypothesis that the slicer is no longer the performance bottleneck. We also assess the overhead introduced by the newly added reorder function (RQ4).

We run our experiments on both synthetic and real traces. The former are monitored with the collapse-sufficient formula φ_s (Fig. 4), which is the common *star* database query [16] augmented with temporal operators. It contains only

Table 1. Summary of the parameters used in the experiments

Experiment groups	$Synthetic_1$	$Synthetic_2$	$Synthetic_3$	$Nokia_1$	$Nokia_2$
Formulas	φ_s	φ_s	φ_s	φ_i, φ_d	$\neg\top$
Source distribution	all uniform except in $Synthetic_3$, which also has $\left(\frac{2}{3},\frac{1}{9},\frac{1}{9},\frac{1}{9}\right)$, $\left(\frac{1}{3},\frac{1}{3},\frac{1}{6},\frac{1}{6}\right)$				
Event order	total, partial	partial	partial	partial	partial
Ingestion order	in-order	out-of-order	in-order	in-order	in-order
No. of input sources	1, 2, 4	1, 2, 4	4	1, 2, 4	1, 2, 4
No. of submonitors	16	16	16	1, 4, 16	16
Acceleration	1	1	1	3k, 5k, 7k	3k, 5k, 7k
Trace time span	60s	60s	60s	a one day fragment from the Nokia trace with 9.5 million events	
Event rate ($1/s$)	500k, 700k, 900k	900k	500k, 700k, 900k		
Time-point rate ($1/s$)	1, 2k, 4k	1	1		
Maximum delay (s)	n/a	1, 2, 4	n/a		
Watermark period (s)	n/a	1, 2, 4	n/a		
Use reorder function	✓	✓	✓	✓	✓, ✗
Repetitions	10	5	1	1	5

past temporal operators because these can be monitored more efficiently, which puts a higher load on the framework's input and slicers. We use a trace generator [40] to create random traces with configurable time span, event names, rate, and time-point rate. The trace's *time span* is the difference between the highest and the lowest time-stamp in the trace. Given a trace and a time-stamp, the *event rate* is the number of events with that time-stamp, while the *time-point rate* is the number of databases with that time-stamp. The generator synthesizes traces with the same event and time-point rates at all time-stamps, choosing randomly between the event names P, Q, and R. We configured the generator to produce mostly R events (99.8%). The events' parameters are sampled from the natural numbers less than 10^9. There is some correlation between the parameters of events with different names (see [40]), which is not relevant for our experiments because of the prevalence of R events. In general, it is highly unlikely that the generated traces satisfy φ_s.

The generator is extended to determine the order in which the events are supplied to the monitor by explicitly generating the *emission time* for each event. The emission times are relative to the monitoring start time. For traces received in-order, the events' emission times correspond to their time-stamps decreased by the value of the first time-stamp in the trace. Otherwise, each event's emission time is additionally delayed by a value sampled from a truncated normal distribution $\mathcal{N}(0, \sigma^2)$ over the interval $(0, \delta_{max})$. In our experiments we fix $\sigma = 2$ and vary the *maximum delay* δ_{max} of events. The generator also adds a watermark after fixed time-stamp increments called *watermark periods*.

Besides the synthetic traces, we also use a real system execution trace from Nokia's Data Collection Campaign [8]. The trace captures how Nokia's system handled the campaign's data. Namely, it collected phone data of 180 participants and propagated it through three databases: db1, db2, and db3. The data was uploaded directly to db1, while the system periodically copied the data to db2, where data was anonymized and copied to db3. The participants could query and delete their own data stored in db1. The system must propagate the deletions to all databases, which is formalized by formulas φ_i and φ_d (Fig. 4). Since the trace spans a year, to evaluate our tool in a reasonable amount of time, we pick a one day fragment (starting at time-stamp 1282921200) containing roughly 9.5 million events with a high average event rate of about 110 events per second.

To perform online monitoring, we use a replayer tool [40] that emits the trace in real time based on its time-stamps or (the generated) explicit emission times. The tool can be configured to accelerate the emission of the trace proportionally to its event rate, which allows for a meaningful performance evaluation since the trace characteristics are retained. For our multi-source monitor we use one replayer instance per input source. We evaluate only the implementation that uses TCP sockets. The k input sources are obtained by assigning each event to one of the sources based on a discrete probability distribution called *source distribution*, e.g., the source distribution $\left(\frac{1}{4}, \frac{1}{4}, \frac{1}{4}, \frac{1}{4}\right)$ is the uniform distribution for $k = 4$. We use other source distributions to investigate RQ2. Both the Nokia and the synthetic traces have explicit time-points, which are used as the partitions' indices. To simulate partially-ordered events, we replace the indices with the appropriate time-stamps.

Table 1 summarizes the parameters used in all our experiments. There are five experiment groups: three using the synthetic traces and two using the Nokia traces. We perform a separate monitoring run for each combination of parameters within one group.

We used a server with two sockets, each containing twelve Intel Xeon 2.20GHz CPU cores with hyperthreading. This effectively supports up to 48 independent parallel computations. We measure the worst-case latency achieved during our experiments.

In general, monitor latency is the difference between the time a monitor consumes an event and the time it finishes processing the event. Thus, at regular intervals, the replayer injects a *latency marker*, which is a special event tagged with its creation time and a sequence number local to its source. Each such marker is then propagated by our framework, preserving its order relative to other events from the same input source. It is treated as part of the preceding event, effectively measuring its processing time. The slicers duplicate and forward latency markers to all parallel submonitors, such that each submonitor receives every latency marker from each source. Finally, for every sequence number, the last operator in the framework aggregates all latency markers (coming both from the different input sources and the different parallel submonitors) and calculates the worst-case latency. For a single monitoring run, we report the maximum of the worst-case latency aggregated over the entire run. To avoid spurious latency spikes, some experiments are repeated (see Table 1) and the mean value is reported with error bars showing two standard errors.

The results of our experiments are shown in Figs. 5, 6, 7 and 8. The experiments $Synthetic_1$ and $Synthetic_2$ (Fig. 5) answer RQ1. Increasing the number of

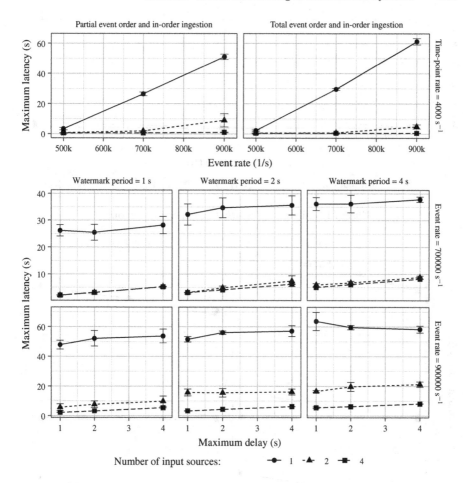

Fig. 5. Results of the *Synthetic*₁ (first row) and *Synthetic*₂ (second and third row) experiment groups

input sources decreases the worst-case latency, which is particularly evident with high event rates. For instance, when monitoring traces with event rate 900k, we improve the maximum latency by 10 s if we double the number of input sources. The relationship between the maximum event rate at a fixed latency and the number of sources appears to be slightly sublinear. We conjecture that this is due to duplicate events that the slicers necessarily emit for some formulas [40]. Therefore, having more slicers increases the framework's total load.

As expected, *Synthetic*₂ shows that the watermark period and the maximum delay establish a lower bound on the maximum latency. These parameters determine the minimum amount of time the reorder function must buffer out-of-order events, which our latency measurements capture. We note that the time-point rate has not influenced the monitoring performance in our experiments; we there-

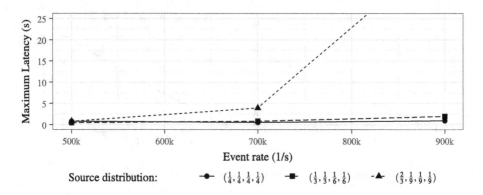

Fig. 6. Results of the $Synthetic_3$ experiment group

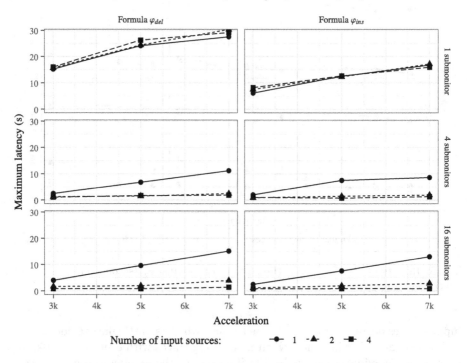

Fig. 7. Results of the $Nokia_1$ experiment group

fore omitted the plots that show different time-point rates and fix the time-point rate to 4000 in $Synthetic_1$.

RQ2 is answered by experiment $Synthetic_3$ (Fig. 6) where we fix the number of input sources to 4 and change the source distribution. The maximum latency is only affected for high event rates and highly skewed source distributions (i.e., when most of the events belong to one source). Otherwise, our framework shows robust performance.

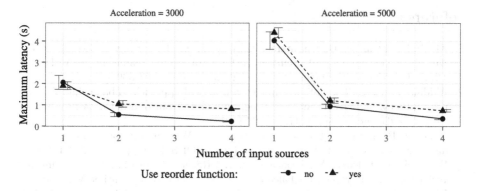

Fig. 8. Results of the $Nokia_2$ experiment group

The results of $Nokia_1$ (Fig. 7) answer RQ3 and validate our hypothesis that increasing the number of sources can improve monitoring performance in realistic monitoring use cases. Increasing the number of sources is ineffective only when parallel submonitors are themselves the performance bottleneck (e.g., when using only one submonitor).

In $Nokia_2$ we monitor the Nokia trace without using the reorder function (RQ4). To retain soundness, we monitor the formula $\neg\top$. The experiment shows that the reorder function introduces negligible overhead: less than 1 s of maximum latency.

7   Conclusion

We have developed the first scalable online monitor for centralized, first-order specifications that can efficiently monitor executions of distributed systems. Specifically, we have defined a partitioned temporal structure (PTS) that models an execution of a distributed system, i.e., a sequence of partially-ordered observations received out-of-order. We have extended our monitoring framework to support multiple sources and proved its correctness. Moreover, we empirically show a significant performance improvement over the framework's single-source variant. For example, in our experiments with real data, we could more than double the event rate, from an average of about 330k to 770k events per second by using two sources instead of one, while achieving the same maximum latency. As future work, we plan to combine our framework with monitors that inherently support out-of-order observations [13] or imprecise time-stamps [9], and make our (now parallel) slicing adaptive [41] with respect to changes in the trace characteristics.

Acknowledgment. Dmitriy Traytel and the anonymous reviewers helped us improve this paper. This research is funded by the US Air Force grant "Monitoring at Any Cost" (FA9550-17-1-0306) and by the SNSF grant "Big Data Monitoring" (167162). The authors are listed alphabetically.

References

1. Abadi, D.J., Carney, D., Çetintemel, U., Cherniack, M., Convey, C., Lee, S., et al.: Aurora: a new model and architecture for data stream management. VLDB J. **12**(2), 120–139 (2003). https://doi.org/10.1007/s00778-003-0095-z
2. Akidau, T., et al.: The dataflow model: a practical approach to balancing correctness, latency, and cost in massive-scale, unbounded, out-of-order data processing. Proc. VLDB Endow. **8**(12), 1792–1803 (2015)
3. Babcock, B., Babu, S., Datar, M., Motwani, R., Widom, J.: Models and issues in data stream systems. In: Popa, L., et al. (eds.) PODS 2002, pp. 1–16. ACM (2002)
4. Bartocci, E., Falcone, Y., Francalanza, A., Reger, G.: Introduction to runtime verification. In: Bartocci, E., Falcone, Y. (eds.) Lectures on Runtime Verification. LNCS, vol. 10457, pp. 1–33. Springer, Cham (2018). https://doi.org/10.1007/978-3-319-75632-5_1
5. Basin, D., Bhatt, B.N., Krstić, S., Traytel, D.: Almost event-rate independent monitoring. FMSD **54**(3), 449–478 (2019). https://doi.org/10.1007/s10703-018-00328-3
6. Basin, D., Caronni, G., Ereth, S., Harvan, M., Klaedtke, F., Mantel, H.: Scalable offline monitoring of temporal specifications. FMSD **49**(1–2), 75–108 (2016). https://doi.org/10.1007/s10703-016-0242-y
7. Basin, D., Gras, M., Krstić, S., Schneider, J.: Implementation, experimental evaluation, and Isabelle/HOL formalization associated with this paper (2020). https://github.com/krledmno1/krledmno1.github.io/releases/download/v1.0/multi-source.tar.gz
8. Basin, D., Harvan, M., Klaedtke, F., Zălinescu, E.: Monitoring data usage in distributed systems. IEEE Trans. Softw. Eng. **39**(10), 1403–1426 (2013)
9. Basin, D., Klaedtke, F., Marinovic, S., Zălinescu, E.: On real-time monitoring with imprecise timestamps. In: Bonakdarpour, B., Smolka, S.A. (eds.) RV 2014. LNCS, vol. 8734, pp. 193–198. Springer, Cham (2014). https://doi.org/10.1007/978-3-319-11164-3_16
10. Basin, D., Klaedtke, F., Müller, S., Zălinescu, E.: Monitoring metric first-order temporal properties. J. ACM **62**(2), 15:1–15:45 (2015)
11. Basin, D., Klaedtke, F., Zălinescu, E.: Failure-aware runtime verification of distributed systems. In: Harsha, P., Ramalingam, G. (eds.) FSTTCS 2015. LIPIcs, vol. 45, pp. 590–603. Schloss Dagstuhl - Leibniz-Zentrum für Informatik (2015)
12. Basin, D., Klaedtke, F., Zălinescu, E.: The MonPoly monitoring tool. In: Reger, G., Havelund, K. (eds.) RV-CuBES 2017. Kalpa Publications in Comp., vol. 3, pp. 19–28. EasyChair (2017)
13. Basin, D., Klaedtke, F., Zălinescu, E.: Runtime verification over out-of-order streams. ACM Trans. Comput. Log. **21**(1), 5:1–5:43 (2020)
14. Bauer, A., Falcone, Y.: Decentralised LTL monitoring. FMSD **48**(1–2), 46–93 (2016). https://doi.org/10.1007/978-3-642-32759-9_10
15. Bauer, A., Küster, J.-C., Vegliach, G.: From propositional to first-order monitoring. In: Legay, A., Bensalem, S. (eds.) RV 2013. LNCS, vol. 8174, pp. 59–75. Springer, Heidelberg (2013). https://doi.org/10.1007/978-3-642-40787-1_4
16. Beame, P., Koutris, P., Suciu, D.: Communication steps for parallel query processing. J. ACM **64**(6), 40:1–40:58 (2017)
17. Becker, D., Rabenseifner, R., Wolf, F., Linford, J.C.: Scalable timestamp synchronization for event traces of message-passing applications. Parallel Comput. **35**(12), 595–607 (2009)

18. Bersani, M.M., Bianculli, D., Ghezzi, C., Krstić, S., San Pietro, P.: Efficient large-scale trace checking using MapReduce. In: Dillon, L., et al. (eds.) ICSE 2016, pp. 888–898. ACM (2016)
19. Carbone, P., Katsifodimos, A., Ewen, S., Markl, V., Haridi, S., Tzoumas, K.: Apache Flink™: stream and batch processing in a single engine. IEEE Data Eng. Bull. **38**(4), 28–38 (2015)
20. Coulouris, G., Dollimore, J., Kindberg, T.: Distributed Systems - Concepts and designs, 3rd edn. International Computer Science Series, Addison-Wesley-Longman (2002)
21. D'Angelo, B., Sankaranarayanan, S., Sánchez, C., Robinson, W., Finkbeiner, B., et al.: LOLA: runtime monitoring of synchronous systems. In: TIME 2005, pp. 166–174. IEEE (2005)
22. Desnoyers, M., Dagenais, M.R.: The LTTng tracer: a low impact performance and behavior monitor for GNU/Linux. In: OLS 2006, pp. 209–224 (2006)
23. El-Hokayem, A., Falcone, Y.: THEMIS: a tool for decentralized monitoring algorithms. In: Bultan, T., Sen, K. (eds.) ISSTA 2017, pp. 372–375. ACM (2017)
24. El-Hokayem, A., Falcone, Y.: On the monitoring of decentralized specifications: semantics, properties, analysis, and simulation. ACM Trans. Softw. Eng. Methodol. **29**(1), 1:1–1:57 (2020)
25. Falcone, Y., Krstić, S., Reger, G., Traytel, D.: A taxonomy for classifying runtime verification tools. Int. J. Softw. Tools Technol. Transf. (2020, to appear)
26. Faymonville, P., Finkbeiner, B., Schirmer, S., Torfah, H.: A stream-based specification language for network monitoring. In: Falcone, Y., Sánchez, C. (eds.) RV 2016. LNCS, vol. 10012, pp. 152–168. Springer, Cham (2016). https://doi.org/10.1007/978-3-319-46982-9_10
27. Francalanza, A., Pérez, J.A., Sánchez, C.: Runtime verification for decentralised and distributed systems. In: Bartocci, E., Falcone, Y. (eds.) Lectures on Runtime Verification. LNCS, vol. 10457, pp. 176–210. Springer, Cham (2018). https://doi.org/10.1007/978-3-319-75632-5_6
28. Gras, M.: Scalable multi-source online monitoring. Bachelor's thesis, ETH Zürich (2020)
29. Hallé, S., Khoury, R., Gaboury, S.: Event stream processing with multiple threads. In: Lahiri, S., Reger, G. (eds.) RV 2017. LNCS, vol. 10548, pp. 359–369. Springer, Cham (2017). https://doi.org/10.1007/978-3-319-67531-2_22
30. Havelund, K., Peled, D., Ulus, D.: First order temporal logic monitoring with BDDs. In: Stewart, D., Weissenbacher, G. (eds.) FMCAD 2017, pp. 116–123. IEEE (2017)
31. Havelund, K., Reger, G., Thoma, D., Zălinescu, E.: Monitoring events that carry data. In: Bartocci, E., Falcone, Y. (eds.) Lectures on Runtime Verification. LNCS, vol. 10457, pp. 61–102. Springer, Cham (2018). https://doi.org/10.1007/978-3-319-75632-5_3
32. Kreps, J., Narkhede, N., Rao, J., et al.: Kafka: a distributed messaging system for log processing. In: NetDB 2011, vol. 11, pp. 1–7 (2011)
33. Leucker, M., Sánchez, C., Scheffel, T., Schmitz, M., Schramm, A.: Runtime verification of real-time event streams under non-synchronized arrival. Softw. Qual. J. **28**(2), 745–787 (2020). https://doi.org/10.1007/s11219-019-09493-y
34. Mills, D.L.: Internet time synchronization: the network time protocol. RFC **1129**, 1 (1989)
35. Mostafa, M., Bonakdarpour, B.: Decentralized runtime verification of LTL specifications in distributed systems. In: IPDPS 2015, pp. 494–503. IEEE (2015)

36. Raszyk, M., Basin, D., Krstić, S., Traytel, D.: Multi-head monitoring of metric temporal logic. In: Chen, Y.-F., Cheng, C.-H., Esparza, J. (eds.) ATVA 2019. LNCS, vol. 11781, pp. 151–170. Springer, Cham (2019). https://doi.org/10.1007/978-3-030-31784-3_9

37. Raszyk, M., Basin, D., Traytel, D.: Multi-head monitoring of metric dynamic logic. In: Hung, D.V., Sokolsky, O. (eds.) ATVA 2020. LNCS, vol. 12302. Springer (2020, to appear)

38. Reger, G., Rydeheard, D.: From First-order Temporal Logic to Parametric Trace Slicing. In: Bartocci, E., Majumdar, R. (eds.) RV 2015. LNCS, vol. 9333, pp. 216–232. Springer, Cham (2015). https://doi.org/10.1007/978-3-319-23820-3_14

39. Rosu, G., Chen, F.: Semantics and algorithms for parametric monitoring. Log. Methods Comput. Sci. **8**(1), 1–47 (2012)

40. Schneider, J., Basin, D., Brix, F., Krstić, S., Traytel, D.: Scalable online first-order monitoring. In: Colombo, C., Leucker, M. (eds.) RV 2018. LNCS, vol. 11237, pp. 353–371. Springer, Cham (2018). https://doi.org/10.1007/978-3-030-03769-7_20

41. Schneider, J., Basin, D., Brix, F., Krstić, S., Traytel, D.: Adaptive online first-order monitoring. In: Chen, Y.-F., Cheng, C.-H., Esparza, J. (eds.) ATVA 2019. LNCS, vol. 11781, pp. 133–150. Springer, Cham (2019). https://doi.org/10.1007/978-3-030-31784-3_8

42. Schneider, J., Basin, D., Krstić, S., Traytel, D.: A formally verified monitor for metric first-order temporal logic. In: Finkbeiner, B., Mariani, L. (eds.) RV 2019. LNCS, vol. 11757, pp. 310–328. Springer, Cham (2019). https://doi.org/10.1007/978-3-030-32079-9_18

43. Sen, K., Vardhan, A., Agha, G., Rosu, G.: Efficient decentralized monitoring of safety in distributed systems. In: Finkelstein, A., et al. (eds.) ICSE 2004, pp. 418–427. IEEE (2004)

44. Srivastava, U., Widom, J.: Flexible time management in data stream systems. In: Beeri, C., Deutsch, A. (eds.) PODS 2004, pp. 263–274. ACM (2004)

45. Tucker, P.A., Maier, D.: Exploiting punctuation semantics in data streams. In: Agrawal, R., Dittrich, K.R. (eds.) ICDE 2002, p. 279. IEEE (2002)

Actor-Based Runtime Verification
with MESA

Nastaran Shafiei[1]([⊠]), Klaus Havelund[2], and Peter Mehlitz[1]

[1] NASA Ames Research Center/KBR, Inc., Moffett Field,
Mountain View, CA 94035, USA
{nastaran.shafiei,peter.c.mehlitz}@nasa.gov

[2] Jet Propulsion Laboratory, California Institute of Technology,
Pasadena, CA 91109, USA
klaus.havelund@jpl.nasa.gov

Abstract. This work presents a runtime verification approach implemented in the tool MESA (MEssage-based System Analysis) which allows for using concurrent monitors to check for properties specified in data parameterized temporal logic and state machines. The tool is implemented as an internal Scala DSL. We employ the actor programming model to implement MESA where monitors are captured by concurrent actors that communicate via messaging. The paper presents a case study in which MESA is used to effectively monitor a large number of flights from live US airspace data streams. We also perform an empirical study by conducting experiments using monitoring systems with different numbers of concurrent monitors and different layers of indexing on the data contained in events. The paper describes the experiments, evaluates the results, and discusses challenges faced during the study. The evaluation shows the value of combining concurrency with indexing to handle data rich events.

1 Introduction

Distributed computing is becoming increasingly important as almost all modern systems in use are distributed. Distributed systems usually refer to systems with components that communicate via message passing. These systems are known to be very hard to reason about due to certain characteristics, e.g. their concurrent nature, non-determinism, and communication delays [16,27]. There has been a wide variety of work focusing on verifying distributed systems including dynamic verification techniques such as runtime verification [14,29] which checks if a run of a System Under Observation (SUO) satisfies properties of interest. Properties are typically captured as formal specifications expressed in forms of linear temporal logic formulas, finite state machines, regular expressions, etc. Some of the

---

K. Havelund—The research performed by this author was carried out at Jet Propulsion Laboratory, California Institute of Technology, under a contract with the National Aeronautics and Space Administration.

J. Deshmukh and D. Ničković (Eds.): RV 2020, LNCS 12399, pp. 221–240, 2020.
https://doi.org/10.1007/978-3-030-60508-7_12

proposed runtime verification techniques related to distributed computing themselves employ a distributed system for monitoring for a variety of reasons such as improving efficiency [5,8,9,11,17,18]. Exploiting parallelism, one can use additional hardware resources for running monitors to reduce their online overhead [9]. Moreover, using concurrent monitors instead of one monolithic monitor, one can achieve higher utilization of available cores [17].

In this paper, we propose a runtime verification approach for analyzing distributed systems which itself is distributed. Our approach is generic and is not tied to a particular SUO. It is motivated by a use case which aims to analyze flight behaviors in the *National Airspace System* (NAS). NAS refers to the U.S. airspace and all of its associated components including airports, airlines, air navigation facilities, services, rules, regulations, procedures, and workforce. NAS is a highly distributed and large system with over 19000 airports including public, private, and military airports, and up to 5000 flights in the U.S. airspace at the peak traffic time. NAS actively evolves under the NextGen (Next Generation Air Transportation System) project, led by the Federal Aviation Administration (FAA), which aims to modernize NAS by introducing new concepts, and technologies. Considering the size and complexity of NAS, efficiency is vital to our approach. Our ultimate goal is to generate a monitoring system that handles high volume of live data feeds, and can be used as a ground control station to analyze air traffic data in NAS.

Our approach is based on employing concurrent monitors, and adopts *the actor programming model*, a model for building concurrent systems. The actor model was proposed in 1973 as a way to deal with concurrency in high performance systems [23]. Concurrent programming is notoriously difficult due to concurrency errors such as race conditions and deadlocks. These errors occur due to lack of data encapsulation to avoid accessing objects' internal state from outside. Thus, mechanisms are required to protect objects' state such as blocking synchronization constructs which can impact scalability and performance. The actor programming model offers an alternative which eliminates these pitfalls. Primary building blocks in the actor programming model are *actors*, which are concurrent objects that do not share state and only communicate by means of asynchronous messages that do not block the sender. Actors are fully independent and autonomous and only become runnable when they receive a message in their buffer called *mailbox*. The model also guarantees that each runnable actor only executes in one thread at a time, a property which allows to view an actor's code as a sequential program.

We create a framework, MESA, using the Akka toolkit [1,38], which provides an implementation of the actor model in Scala. The actor model is adopted by numerous frameworks and libraries. However, what makes Akka special is how it facilitates the implementation of actor-based systems that refrain users from dealing with the complexity of key mechanisms such as scheduling actors and communication. We also use the Runtime for Airspace Concept Evaluation (RACE) [30,31] framework, another system built on top Akka and extending it with additional features. RACE is a framework to generate airspace simulations, and provides actors to import, translate, filter, archive, replay, and visualize data from NAS, that can be directly employed in MESA when checking for properties in the NAS domain.

MESA supports specification of properties in data parameterized temporal logic and state machines. The support for formal specification is provided by integrating the trace analysis tools TraceContract [6,22] and Daut (Data automata) [20,21], implemented as domain specific languages (DSLs) [2]. TraceContract, which was also used for command sequence verification in NASA's LADEE (Lunar Atmosphere And Dust Environment Explorer) mission [7], supports a notation that combines data-parameterized state machines, referred to as data automata, with temporal logic. Daut is a modification of TraceContract which, amongst other things, allows for more efficient monitoring. In contrast to general-purpose languages, *external* DSLs offer high levels of abstractions but usually limited expressiveness. TraceContract and Daut are, in contrast, *internal* DSLs since they are embedded in an existing language, Scala, rather than providing their own syntax and runtime support. Thus, their specification languages offer all features of Scala which adds adaptability and richness.

As a basic optimization technique, MESA supports indexing, a restricted form of slicing [32,36]. Indexing slices the trace up into sub-traces according to selected data in the trace, and feeds each resulting sub-trace to its own sub-monitor. As an additional optimization technique, MESA allows concurrency at three levels. First, MESA runs in parallel with the monitored system(s). Second, multiple properties are translated to multiple monitors, one for each property. Third, and most importantly for this presentation, each property is checked by multiple concurrent monitors by slicing the trace up into sub-traces using indexing, and feeding each sub-trace to its own concurrent sub-monitor. One can configure MESA to specify how to check a property in a distributed manner. We present a case study demonstrating the impact of using concurrent monitors together with indexing. In this case study it is flight identifiers that are used as slicing criteria. We evaluate how different concurrency strategies impact the performance. The results are positive, demonstrating that concurrency used to handle slices of a trace can be beneficial. This is not a completely obvious result considering the cost of scheduling threads for small tasks. The main contribution of the paper is providing an extensive empirical assessment of asynchronous concurrent monitors implemented as actors. The paper also presents a new runtime verification tool, MESA, and its application on a real case study.

2   Related Work

Amongst the most relevant work is that of Basin et al. [8]. In this work the authors use data parallelism to scale rst-order temporal logic monitoring by slicing the trace into multiple sub-traces, and feeding these sub-traces to different parallel executing monitors. The approach creates as many slices as there are monitors. The individual monitors are considered black boxes, which can host any monitoring system fitting the expected monitor interface. Another attempt in a similar direction is that of Hallé et al. [18], which also submits trace slices to parallel monitors, a development of the author's previous work on using MapReduce for the same problem [5]. Reger in his MSc dissertation [35] experimented with similar ideas, creating parallel monitors to monitor subsets of value ranges. However, in that early work the results were not promising, possibly due to the less mature state of support for parallelism in Java and hardware at the time. Berkovich et al. [9] also address the splitting of the trace according to data into parallel executing monitors. However, differently from the other approaches, the monitors run on GPUs instead of on CPUs as the system being monitored does. Their monitoring approach incurs minimal intrusion, as the execution of monitoring tasks takes place in different computing hardware than the execution of the system under observation. Francalanza and Seychell [17] explore structural parallelism, where parallel monitors are spawned based on the structure of the formula. E.g. a formula $p \wedge q$ will cause two parallel monitors, one for each conjunct, co-operating to produce the combined result. El-Hokayem and Falcone [13] review different approaches to monitoring multi-threaded Java programs, which differs in perspective from the monitoring system itself to be parallel. Francalanza et al. [16] survey runtime verification research on how to monitor systems with distributed characteristics, solutions that use a distributed platform for performing the monitoring task, and foundations for decomposing monitors and expressing specifications amenable for distributed systems.

The work by Burlò et al. [10] targets open distributed systems and relies on session types for verification of communication protocols. It applies a hybrid verification technique where the components available pre-deployments are checked statically, and the ones that become available at runtime are verified dynamically. Their approach is based on describing communication protocols via session types with assertions, from the lchannels Scala library, which are used to synthesize monitors automatically. The work by Neykova and Yoshida [33] applies runtime verification to ensure a *sound* recovery of distributed Erlang processes after a failure occurs. Their approach is based on session types that enforce protocol conformance. In [28], Lavery et al. present an actor-based monitoring framework in Scala, that similar to our approach is built using the Akka toolkit. The monitoring system does not, as our approach, provide a temporal logic API for specifying properties, which is argued to be an advantage. Daut as well as TraceContract allow defining monitors using any Scala code as well. A monitor *master* actor can submit monitoring tasks to *worker* actors in an automated round robin fashion manner. This, however, requires that the worker monitors do not rely on an internal state representing a summary of past events. The work by Attard and Francalanza [3] targets asynchronous distributed systems. Their approach allows for generating partitioned traces at the instrumentation level where each partitioned trace provides a localized view for a subset of the system under observation. The work focuses on global properties that can be cleanly decomposed into a set of local properties which can be verified against local components. It is suggested that one could use the partitioned traces to infer alternative merged execution traces of the system. The implementation of the approach targets actor-based Erlang systems, and includes concurrent localized monitors captured by Erlang actors.

3   An Overview of MESA

MESA is a framework for building actor-based monitoring systems. An overview of a system that can be built using MESA is shown in Fig. 1. A MESA system is solely composed of actors that implement a pipeline of four processing steps. The vertical lines between actors represent publish-subscribe communication channels resembling pipelines where outputs from one step are used as inputs for the following step. The first step is *data acquisition* which extracts data from the SUO. The second step is *data processing* which parses raw data extracted by the previous step and generates a trace composed of events that are relevant to the properties of interest. Next step is *monitoring* which checks the trace obtained from the previous step against the given properties. Finally, the last step is *reporting* which presents the verification results. What MESA offers are the building blocks to create actors for each step of the runtime verification. Often one needs to create application specific actors to extend MESA towards a particular domain. Besides the NAS domain, MESA is extended towards the UxAS project which is developed at Air Force Research Laboratory and provides autonomous capabilities for unmanned systems [34].

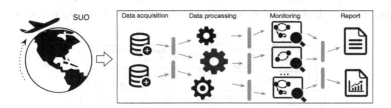

Fig. 1. Overview of a MESA actor-based monitoring system.

Akka actors can use a point-to-point or publish-subscribe model to communicate with one another. In point-to-point messaging, the sender sends a message directly to the receiver, whereas, in publish-subscribe messaging, the receivers subscribe to the channel, and messages published on that channel are forwarded to them by the channel. Messages sent to each actor are placed on its mailbox. Only actors with a non-empty mailbox become runnable. Actors extend the `Actor` base trait and implement a method `receiveLive` of type `PartialFunction[Any, Unit]` which captures their core behavior. It includes a list of `case` statements, that by applying Scala pattern matching over parameterized events, determine the messages that can be handled by the actor and the way they are processed. To create a MESA monitoring system (Fig. 1) one needs to specify the actors and the way they are connected with communication channels in a HOCON configuration file used as an input to MESA.

Figure 2 shows the MESA framework infrastructure and the existing systems incorporated into MESA. These systems are all open source Scala projects. MESA is also written in Scala and in the process of becoming open source. Akka provides the actor model implementation. RACE, built on top of Akka, is mainly used for connectivity to external systems. MESA employs a non-intrusive approach since for safety-critical systems such as NAS, sources are either not available or are not allowed to be modified for security and reliability reasons. RACE provides dedicated actors, referred to as importers, that can subscribe to commonly-used messaging system constructs, such as JMS server and Kafka. Using an importer actor from RACE in the data acquisition step, we extract data from the SUO, in a nonintrusive manner.

TraceContract and Daut are trace analysis DSLs where given a program trace and a formalized property, they determine whether the property holds for the trace. `Monitor` is a main class in these DSLs which encapsulates property specification capabilities and implements a key method, `verify`, that for each incoming event updates the state of the monitor accordingly. Instances of `Monitor` are referred to as monitors from here on. Similar to actors `receiveLive` method, `Monitor.verify` includes a series of `case` statements that determine the events that can be handled by the monitor and the behavior triggered for each event. The properties described in this paper are specified using Daut since it also provides an indexing capability within monitors to improve their performance. It allows for defining a function from events to keys where keys are used as entries in a hash map to obtain those states which are relevant to the event. Using indexing, a Daut monitor only iterates over an indexed subset of states.

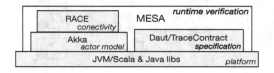

Fig. 2. The MESA framework infrastructure.

Properties in MESA are defined as subclasses of `Monitor`. The actors in the monitoring step (Fig. 1), referred to as *monitor actors*, hold an instance of the `Monitor` classes and feed them with incoming event messages. MESA provides components referred to as *dispatchers* which are configurable and can be used in the monitoring step to determine how the check for a property is distributed among different monitor actors. Dispatchers, implemented as actors, can generate monitor actors on-the-fly and distribute the incoming trace between the monitor actors, relying on identifiers extracted by data parametrized events.

4   Monitoring Live Flights in the U.S. Airspace

This section presents the case study where MESA is applied to check a property known as RNAV STAR adherence, referred to as P_{RSA} in this paper. A STAR is a standard arrival procedure designed by the FAA to transition flights from the en-route phase to the approach phase where descent starts. Every STAR specifies a set of flight routes that merge together, and each route is specified by a sequence of *waypoints*, accompanied by vertical and speed profiles specifying altitude and airspeed restrictions. A waypoint is a geographical position with latitude and longitude coordinates. A STAR is a form of communication between the flight crew and air traffic controllers. When the air traffic controller gives a clearance to the pilot to take a certain STAR route, they communicate the route, altitude, and airspeed. A STAR route, assigned to a flight, is encoded in the flight plan presented to the pilot as a sequence of waypoints. STARs are specfically designed for flights operated under Instrument Flight Rules under which the aircraft is navigated by reference to the instruments in the aircraft cockpit rather than using visual references. STAR routes can only be used by aircrafts equipped with a specific navigation system called RNAV.

One of the ongoing focus points of the FAA is to increase the utilization of STAR procedures. From 2009 to 2016, as part of the NextGen project, 264 more STAR procedures were implemented on an expedited timeline [41] which led to safety concerns raised by airlines and air traffic controllers including numerous unintentional pilot deviations [12,24]. A possible risk associated with deviating from a procedure is a loss of separation which can result in a midair collision. The work presented in [40] studies RNAV STAR adherence trends based on a data mining methodology, and shows deviation patterns at major airports [4].

The case study applies runtime verification to check if flights are compliant with the designated STAR routes in real-time. A navigation specification for flights assigned to a STAR requires a lateral navigation accuracy of 1 NM[1] for at least 95% of the flight time [25]. Our approach focuses on lateral adherence where incorporating a check for vertical and speed profiles becomes trivial. We informally define the RNAV STAR lateral adherence property as follows, adopted by others [40].

P_{RSA} : *a flight shall cross inside a 1.0 NM radius around each waypoint in the assigned RNAV STAR route, in order.*

4.1   Formalizing Property P_{RSA}

For a sake of brevity, we say a flight *visits* a waypoint if the flight crosses inside a 1.0 NM radius around the waypoint. We say an event occurs when the aircraft under scrutiny visits a waypoint that belongs to its designated STAR route. For example, in Fig. 3, where circles represent 1.0 NM radius around the waypoints, the sequence of events for this aircraft is MLBEC MLBEC JONNE.

We define a state machine capturing Property P_{RSA}. Let L be a set including the labels of all waypoints in the STAR route. Let *first* and *last* be predicates on L that denote the initial and final waypoints, respectively. Let *next* be a partial function, $L \hookrightarrow L$, where given a non-final waypoint in L it returns the subsequent

---

[1] NM, nautical mile is a unit of measurement equal to 1,852 m.

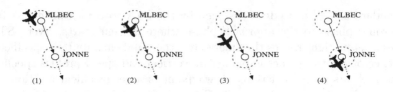

Fig. 3. The sequence of events for the aircraft is MLBEC MLBEC JONNE.

waypoint in the route. For example, $next(\text{MLBEC})$ returns JONNE (Fig. 3). The finite state machine for Property P_{RSA} is the tuple $(Q, \Sigma, q_0, F, \delta)$ where

- $Q = L \cup \{init, err, drop\}$
- $\Sigma = \{e_t | t \in L \cup \{FC, SC\}\}$
- $q_0 = init$
- $F = \{err, drop\} \cup \{q \in L \mid last(q)\}$
- $\delta : Q \times \Sigma \to Q$

Q is the set of all states, and $init$ is the initial state. Σ is the set of all possible events. The event e_t where $t \in L$ indicates that the aircraft visits the waypoint t. The event e_{FC} indicates that the flight is completed, and e_{SC} indicates that the flight is assigned to a new STAR route. Note that FC stands for flight completed and SC stands for STAR changed. F is the set of final states where $last$ represents the set of accept states indicating that the flight adhered to the assigned STAR route. The state err represents an error state indicating the violation of the property. The state $drop$ represents a state at which the verification is dismissed due to assignment of a new STAR route. The transition function δ is defined as below.

$$\delta(q, e_t) = \begin{cases} t & if(q = init \ \& \ first(t)) \\ & \quad \text{or } (q \in \{x \in L \mid \neg last(x)\} \ \& \ t \in \{q, next(q)\}) \\ err & if(q = init \ \& \ t \neq SC \& \neg first(t)) \\ & \quad \text{or } (q \in \{x \in L \mid \neg last(x)\} \ \& \ t \notin \{q, next(q), SC\}) \\ drop & if(q \neq err \ \& \ t = SC) \end{cases}$$

At $init$, if the flight visits the first waypoint of the assigned route, the state machine advances to the state representing the first waypoint. Alternatively, if at waypoint q, the flight can only visit q or the next waypoint in the route, $next(q)$. Otherwise, if at $init$, and it visits any waypoint other than the first waypoint of the route, the state machine advances to err. Likewise, if the flight visits any waypoint not on the route, the state advances to err. Finally, at any state other than err, if the flight gets assigned to a new route ($t = SC$), the state machine advances to $drop$.

4.2 P_{RSA} Monitor Implementation

All the events and types encapsulated by them are implemented as Scala `case` classes due to their concise syntax and built-in pattern matching support that

```
1   class P_RSA(config: Config) extends daut.Monitor(config) {
2     always {
3       case e@Visit(info@Info(_, track: Track), wp: Waypoint) if (isValid(e)) =>
4         if(wp == first) nextState(wp, track.cs) else error(msg)
5       case e@Completed(ti) if (isValid(e)) => error(msg)
6     }
7
8     def nextState(wp: Waypoint, cs: String): state = {
9       val next = star.next(wp)
10      watch {
11        case Visit(Info(State('cs', _,_,_), _),'wp') => nextState(wp, cs)
12        case Visit(Info(State('cs', _,_,_), track: Track),'next') =>
13          if(next == last) accept(last, track) else nextState(next, cs)
14        case Visit(Info(State('cs', _,_,_), _),_),_),_) => error(msg)
15        case Completed(Track('cs',_,_)) => error(msg)
16        case StarChanged(Track('cs',_,_)) => drop(cs)
17      }
18    }
19    def accept(wp: Waypoint, track: Track): state = {report(msg);ok}
20    def error(msg: String): state = {report(msg);err}
21    def drop(cs: String): state = {dropMonitor(cs);ok} ...
22  }
```

Fig. 4. Implementation of Property P_{RSA}.

facilitates the implementation of data-parametrized state machines. The class Visit represents an event where the flight visits the given waypoint, Waypoint. Completed indicates that the flight is completed. StarChanged indicates that the given flight is assigned to a new STAR route.

```
case class Visit(info: Info, wp: Waypoint)
case class Completed(track: Track)
case class StarChanged(track: Track)
```

We implement P_{RSA} as a Daut monitor (Fig. 4). A Daut monitor maintains the set of all *active* states representing the current states of the state machines. For each incoming event, new target states of transitions may be created and the set of active states updated. A state is presented by an object of type state, and the set of transitions out of the state is presented by an instance of Transitions, which is a partial function of type PartialFunction[E, Set[state]] where E is a monitor type parameter.

The functions always and watch act as states. They accept as argument a partial function of type Transitions and return a state object. The case statements, representing transitions at states, are matched against incoming events. The verification starts from the state always, and watch represents a state at which the flight visits a waypoint. For case statements in always, isValid is used as a pattern guard to narrow down the set of events triggered on the state to the ones relevant to the STAR routes assigned to the monitor. Moreover, since

always is always an active state, **isValid** ensures that only one event per flight is triggered on **always**. The first **case** in **always** matches against the event **Visit** where a flight visits a waypoint. Then, it checks if the waypoint, **wp**, visited by the flight is the first waypoint of the route. If so, the method **nextState** is invoked which advances the state to **watch**. Otherwise, the method **error** advances the state to **err**. The second **case** matches against **Completed**, indicating that the flight is completed without visiting any waypoints, and invokes **error**.

The **watch** state waits to receive an event that triggers one of its transitions and then leaves the state. The input parameters of **nextState**, **wp** and **cs**, represent the waypoint being visited by the flight and the flight call sign. To ensure that only events associated with this flight can match against **case** statements, all the patterns match the call sign for the incoming event, **cs**, against the value of the flight call sign. This is done by using back-quotes for associated parameter in the typed patterns, **cs**. The first **case** in **watch** matches against the event where the flight visits the current waypoint, and calls **nextState(wp, cs)** to remain in the current state. The variable **next** is set to the next waypoint in the STAR route. The second **case** matches against the event where the flight visits the waypoint **next**. It checks if **next** is the last waypoint, and if so, it calls **accept** which returns the object **ok**, representing the accepting state. If **next** is not the last waypoint, it calls **nextState(next, cs)** to advance to the state corresponding to **next**. Next **case** matches against **Completed** which calls **error** to advance to the **err** state. Finally, last **case** matches against **StarChanged** which calls **drop** to discard the analysis for the flight.

4.3   A MESA Monitoring System for P_{RSA}

Figure 5 illustrates the MESA monitoring system used to verify Property P_{RSA}. The data acquisition step extracts the data relevant to the property which includes flight information, position, navigation specification, flight plan, etc. To get this data, we connect to an FAA system, SWIM (System Wide Information Management) [19]. SWIM implements a set of information technology principles in NAS which consolidates data from many different sources, e.g. flight data, weather data, surveillance data, airport operational status. Its purpose is to provide relevant NAS data, in standard XML formats, to its authorized users such as airlines, and airports. SWIM has a service-oriented architecture which adopts the *Java Message Service (JMS)* interface [37] as a messaging API to deliver data to JMS clients subscribed to its bus. We use the RACE actor **SFDPS-importer** which is a JMS client configured to obtain en-route real-time fight data from a SWIM service, SFDPS (SWIM Flight Data Publication Service) [15]. **SFDPS-importer** publishes the data to the channel **sfdps**.

The data processing step parses the SFDPS data obtained from the previous stage and generates a trace, composed of event objects, relevant to the property. This done via a pipeline of actors that parse the SFDPS messages in XML (**sfdps2track** and **sfdps2state**), filter irrelevant data (**filter**), and finally generate **Visit**, **Completed**, and **StarChanged** events, which are known to the monitor P_RSA (**event-gen**) and published to the channel **trace**.

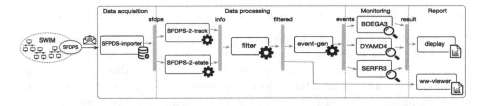

Fig. 5. A MESA instance for verifying Property P_{RSA} for STARs at SFO.

Fig. 6. Flight deviation from assigned RNAV STARs detected at SFO.

The monitoring step includes monitor actors that encapsulate an instance of the monitor P_RSA (Fig. 4). They subscribe to the channel `trace`, and feed their underlying P_RSA object with incoming events. Each monitor actor in Fig. 5 is associated to a STAR procedure at SFO which checks for the flights assigned to that STAR, and published the verification result on the channel `result`. Using the dispatcher feature of MESA, one can distribute the monitoring differently, for example using one monitor actor per flight. Finally, the last step displays the results. The actor `display` simply prints data published on `result` on the console. We also use a RACE actor, `ww-viewer`, that uses NASA WorldWind system to provide interactive geospatial visualization of flight trajectories.

Using the MESA system shown in Fig. 5, we discovered violations of P_{RSA}. Figure 6 includes snapshots from our visualization illustrating two cases where P_{RSA} was violated. It shows that the flight United 1738 missed the waypoint LOZIT, and the flight Jazz Air 743 missed the initial waypoint BGGLO.

5 Experiments

This section presents our experiments evaluating the impact of using concurrent monitors and indexing. More details on the experiments can be found in [39]. The experiments uses a property which checks if the sequence of SFDPS messages with the same call sign received from SWIM is ordered by the time tag attached to the messages. This property is motivated by observations where the SFDPS messages did not send in the right order by SWIM. We use the state of flights as events captured by `State` instances, and specify the property p as a data-parameterized finite state machine using Daut as follows, where t1 and t2 represent the event time.

```
always {case State(cs,_,_,t1)=>watch {case State('cs',_,_,t2)=>t2.isAfter(t1)}}
```

This property is simple and it leads to a small *service time*, the time used to process the message within the monitor object. To mitigate issues associated with microbenchmarking, we use a feature of Daut that allows for defining sub-monitors within a monitor object. We implement a Daut monitor P_SEQ which maintains a list of monitor instances, all capturing the same *p*, as its sub-monitors.

We evaluate the impact of concurrency in the context of indexing. Indexing can be applied both at the monitor level or the dispatcher level. Indexing at the monitor level is supplied by Daut. We activate this feature by implementing an indexing function in the Daut monitor that uses the call signs carried by events to retrieve the set of relevant states for analysis instead of iterating over all the current states. At the dispatcher level, indexing is applied by keeping the monitor instances or references to monitor actors in a hash map, using the call signs carried by events as entries to the hash map.

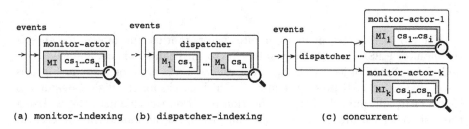

(a) monitor-indexing   (b) dispatcher-indexing   (c) concurrent

Fig. 7. Actor-based monitoring systems used in the experiment.

5.1 Monitoring Systems

The experiments use four different MESA systems which are only different in their monitoring step. They all use the same actors to extract the recorded SFDPS data, generate a trace composed of State objects, and publish the trace to a channel, events, accessed in the monitoring step. The monitoring step for each system is illustrated in Fig. 7. Let n be the total number of different call signs in the input sequence. The outermost white boxes represent actors, and gray boxes represent monitor instances held by the actor. Let M refer to P_SEQ monitor instances with no indexing capability, and MI refer to P_SEQ instances with indexing. The white box inside each monitor instance includes call signs monitored by this instance. Next, we explain the monitoring step for the monitoring systems, the features of which are summarized in Table Fig. 8.

– monitor-indexing - the monitoring step includes one actor with a single MI monitor which checks for all the events in the input sequence published to events. In a way, the monitoring step of this configuration is equivalent to directly using the Daut tool to process the trace sequentially.

- `dispatcher-indexing` - the monitoring step includes a dispatcher actor which creates monitor instances of type M, and feeds them with incoming events. The dispatcher actor generates one monitor instance per call sign, and applies indexing by storing the monitor instances in a hash map. The dispatcher obtains event objects from the channel `events`, and starting with an empty hash map, for each new call sign, it adds a new monitor instance to the hash map. For an event object with the call sign cs_i, the dispatcher invokes the `verify` method of the monitor instance M_i.

- `concurrent` - the trace analysis is performed concurrently by employing multiple monitor actors, generated on-the-fly. One can configure the dispatcher to set a limit on the number of monitor actors. If no limit is set, one monitor actor is generated for each call sign and the indexing within the monitor is deactivated. By setting a limit, one monitor actor could be assigned to more than one call sign. The latter is referred to as `bounded-concurrent`. Indexing is also applied at the dispatcher level, using a hash map that stores monitor actor references with call signs as entries to the map. For each event object, the dispatcher forwards the event object to the associated monitor actor via point-to-point communication. Then the monitor actor invokes the `verify` method on its underlying monitor instance.

	monitor indx	dispatcher indx	concurrency
monitor-indexing	✓	✗	✗
dispatcher-indexing	✗	✓	✗
concurrent	✗	✓	✓
bounded-concurrent	✓	✓	✓

Fig. 8. The main features of the monitoring systems presented in Fig. 7.

5.2 System Setup

All experiments are performed on an Ubuntu 18.04.3 LTS machine, 31.1 GB of RAM, using a Intel®Xeon®W-2155 CPU (10 cores with hyperthreading, 3.30 GHz base frequency). We use an input trace, T, including 200,000 messages obtained from an archive of recorded SFDPS data in all experiments. T includes data from 3215 different flights, that is, n in Fig. 7 is 3215. The number of sub-monitors in P_SEQ is set to 2000. The Java heap size is set to 12 GB. Our experiment uses a default setting of the Akka scheduler which associates all actors to a single thread pool with 60 threads, and uses the default value 5 for actors *throughput*, the maximum number of messages processed by the actor before the assigned thread is returned to the pool.

5.3   Evaluation

Using a bash script, each MESA monitoring system is run 10 consecutive times on the trace T, and the average of the runs is used for evaluation. Figure 7 compares the run times for the monitoring systems presented in Fig. 9. The legend bcon stands for bounded-concurrent followed by the number of monitor actors. Considering the 3215 different call signs in T, monitor-indexing includes one monitor actor including one monitor object that tracks all 3215 flights. The dispatcher-indexing system creates one actor with a hash map of size 3215 storing the monitor objects where each object monitors events from one flight. The concurrent monitoring system creates 3215 monitor actors where each actor monitors events from one flight. The bounded-concurrent system creates 250 monitor actors where each actor monitors events from 12 or 13 flights.

The results show that the systems with concurrent monitors perform considerably better than the systems with a single monitor actor. The system monitor-indexing performs worse than dispatcher-indexing. Considering the similarity between their indexing mechanisms, the difference mostly amounts to the implementation. The CPU utilization profiles for the system are obtained by the VisualVM profiler which represent the percentage of total computing resources in use during the run (Fig. 10). The CPU utilization for monitor-indexing is mostly under 30% and for dispatcher-indexing is mostly between 40% and 50%. For concurrent and bounded-concurrent, the CPU utilization is mostly above 90% which shows the impact of using concurrent monitor actors. The VisualVM heap data profiles reveal that all the system exhibit a similar heap usage which mostly remains under 10G.

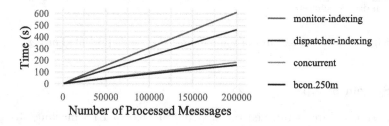

Fig. 9. Comparing the run times of different MESA actor systems.

Figure 9 shows that limiting the concurrent monitors to 250 results in a better performance than using one monitor actor per flight in concurrent. To evaluate how the number of monitor actors impact the performance, bounded-concurrent is run with different numbers of monitor actors, 125, 250, 500, 1000, 2000, and 3215. We increase the number of monitor actors up to 3215 since this is the number of total flights in the trace T. The results are compared in Table Fig. 11. The system performs best with 250 monitor actors, and from there as the number of monitor actors increases the run time increases. Increasing the number of monitor actors decreases the load on each monitor actor, however, it increases the

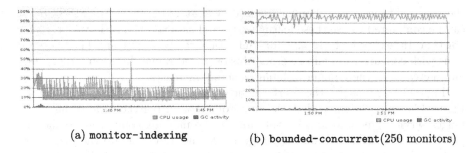

(a) monitor-indexing   (b) bounded-concurrent(250 monitors)

Fig. 10. The CPU utilization profiles obtained by VisualVM.

overhead from their scheduling and maintenance. Note that the optimal number of monitor actors depends on the application and the value of input parameters. Tweaking inputs parameters could lead to a different optimal number of monitor actors. Our results also show that depending on the number of flights tracked by each monitor actor, Daut indexing could lead to overhead, e.g. it leads to 11% overhead when using 3215 monitor actors, and improves the performance by 45% when using 125 monitor actors.

#monitors	125m	250m	500m	1000m	2000m	3215m
time (s)	169	161	167	169	183	208

Fig. 11. Comparing the run times of different MESA actor systems.

5.4 Actor Parameter Evaluation

We also evaluate performance parameters for individual dispatcher and monitor actors in each monitoring system, including the average service time, and the average wait time for messages in the mailbox. The relevant points for measuring these parameters are when a message is enqueued into and dequeued from the mailbox, and when the actor starts processing and finishes processing a message. We provide mechanisms for actors to wrap the relevant data into container objects and publish them to a channel accessed by an actor, stat-collector, which collects this information and reports when the system terminates.

To measure service time, the default actor behavior, recieveLive, is replaced by an implementation that for each message, invokes recieveLive, records the time before and after the invocation, and publishes a data container with the recorded times to the channel accessed by stat-collector. To obtain information from actor mailboxes, we implement a new mailbox that extends the default Akka mailbox implementation with a mechanism that records the message entry time to and the exit time from the mailbox, and publishes a data container with the recorded times to the channel accessed by `stat-collector`. Any MESA actor can be configured to use these features, referred as ASF. The ASF overheads for `monitor-indexing` and `dispatcher-indexing` are about 20% and 11%. For systems with concurrent monitor actors, this overhead ranges between 20% to 28% and increases as the number of monitor actors increases.

Figure 12 compares the performance parameters for individual actors. Figure 12a and 12b show that the monitor actor in `monitor-indexing` has a longer service time and longer wait time in the mailbox comparing to the dispatcher in `dispatcher-indexing`. Figure 12c and 12d compare the dispatcher performance metrics for `bounded-concurrent` with different numbers of monitor actors. Figure 12e and 12f present the monitor actors performance metrics for the same systems. The average service time for the dispatcher and monitor actors increases as the number of actors increases. Increasing the monitor actors increases the load on the dispatcher since it needs to generate more monitor actors. Decreasing the number of monitor actors increases the load on individual monitor actors since each actor monitors more flights. On the other hand, applying indexing within the monitor actors improves their performance, however for monitors that track small number of flights, indexing can lead to overhead leading to longer service times.

The message wait time in the dispatcher mailbox increases as the number of actors increases (Fig. 12d). In general, with a constant thread pool size, increasing actors in the system can increase the wait for actors to get scheduled, leading to longer wait for messages in mailboxes. However, in the case of monitor actors the mailbox wait is longer with smaller number of actors (Fig. 12f). This is due to higher arrival rate of messages in these systems since each monitor actor is assigned to higher number of flights.

6 Discussion

Applying MESA on NAS demonstrates that our approach can be used to effectively detect violations of temporal properties in a distributed SUO. We show the impact of using concurrent monitors for verification. Our evaluation includes a setting that resembles using an existing trace analysis tool, Daut, directly. Comparing this setting to the concurrent monitoring setting reveals that employing concurrent actors can considerably improve the performance. MESA is highly extensible, and provides flexibility in terms of incorporating new DSLs. It can be viewed as a tool that provides concurrent monitoring platform for existing trace analysis DSLs.

To maximize the performance, one needs to limit the number of concurrent monitor actors. Due to a variety of overhead sources, the optimal number of actors is application specific and cannot be determined a priori. The following factors need to be taken into consideration when configuring values of the related parameters. Limiting the number of monitor actors on a multi-core machine can lead to a low CPU utilization. One can elevate the CPU utilization by increasing concurrency. However, there is overhead associated with actors. Assigning actors

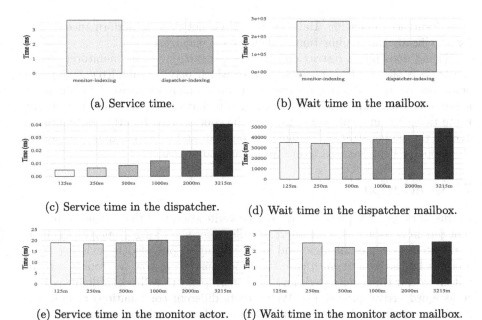

(a) Service time.

(b) Wait time in the mailbox.

(c) Service time in the dispatcher.

(d) Wait time in the dispatcher mailbox.

(e) Service time in the monitor actor.

(f) Wait time in the monitor actor mailbox.

Fig. 12. Comparing the monitors performance metrics for MESA systems.

to threads from the thread pool and context switching between them impose overhead. MESA is a highly configurable platform that can facilitate finding the optimal number of monitor actors to maximize the performance. One can easily tune relevant parameters in the configuration file to evaluate the monitoring systems.

As shown in Fig. 2, our framework runs on top of JVM and relies on the Akka framework. There are mechanisms, such as garbage collection at the JVM level and actor scheduling at the Akka level, that cannot be controlled from a MESA system. Therefore, MESA is not suitable for verifying hard real-time systems where there are time constraints on the system response. One of the challenges that we faced in this work is microbenchmarking on JVM which is a well-known problem. Certain characteristics of JVM such as code optimization can impact accuracy of the results, specially when it comes to smaller time measures such as service time and wait time for messages in the actor mailboxes. However, there are tools such as JMH that provide accurate benchmarking [26].

Several of the mentioned works [3,8,9,18], support the observation that concurrency in one form or other, using asynchronous message passing, can improve performance of runtime verification systems. The works most relevant to our combination of slicing and concurrency are [8,18]. Basin et al. [8] provide performance results for the use of slicing together with concurrency, but do not compare these with runs without concurrency. However, the logs analyzed contain billions of events, supporting the observation that exactly this use of concurrency is performance enhancing. Hallé et al. [18] do not provide performance results for specifically the combination of slicing and concurrency.

Slicing does put a restriction on what properties can be monitored. Since the trace is sliced into subtraces, each of which may be submitted to its own actor, one cannot express properties that relate difference slices. An example of a property that cannot be stated in e.g. this particular case study is that the route taken by an airplane depends on the routes taken by other airplanes. In MESA the slicing strategy is manually defined, and attention must be paid to the property being verified to ensure a sound approach.

7   Conclusion

In this work we have presented a runtime verification tool that employs concurrent monitors as actors. Our approach allows for specifying properties in data-parameterized temporal logic and state machines, provided by existing trace analysis DSLs. We present a case study demonstrating how the tool is used to obtain live air traffic data feeds and verify a property that checks if flights adhere to assigned arrival procedures. We evaluate different combinations of indexing and concurrency, and observe that there are clear benefits to monitor a single property with multiple concurrent actors processing different slices of the input trace. This is not an obvious result since there is a cost to scheduling of small tasks.

References

1. Akka (2020). http://doc.akka.io/docs/akka/current/scala.html
2. Artho, C., Havelund, K., Kumar, R., Yamagata, Y.: Domain-specific languages with scala. In: Butler, M., Conchon, S., Zaïdi, F. (eds.) ICFEM 2015. LNCS, vol. 9407, pp. 1–16. Springer, Cham (2015). https://doi.org/10.1007/978-3-319-25423-4_1
3. Attard, D.P., Francalanza, A.: Trace partitioning and local monitoring for asynchronous components. In: Cimatti, A., Sirjani, M. (eds.) SEFM 2017. LNCS, vol. 10469, pp. 219–235. Springer, Cham (2017). https://doi.org/10.1007/978-3-319-66197-1_14
4. Avrekh, I., Matthews, B.L., Stewart, M.: RNAV adherence data integration system using aviation and environmental sources. Technical report, NASA Ames Research Center, June 2018
5. Barre, B., Klein, M., Soucy-Boivin, M., Ollivier, P.-A., Hallé, S.: MapReduce for parallel trace validation of LTL properties. In: Qadeer, S., Tasiran, S. (eds.) RV 2012. LNCS, vol. 7687, pp. 184–198. Springer, Heidelberg (2013). https://doi.org/10.1007/978-3-642-35632-2_20
6. Barringer, H., Havelund, K.: TRACECONTRACT: a scala DSL for trace analysis. In: Butler, M., Schulte, W. (eds.) FM 2011. LNCS, vol. 6664, pp. 57–72. Springer, Heidelberg (2011). https://doi.org/10.1007/978-3-642-21437-0_7
7. Barringer, H., Havelund, K., Kurklu, E., Morris, R.: Checking flight rules with tracecontract: application of a scala DSL for trace analysis. Technical report, Jet Propulsion Laboratory, National Aeronautics and Space Administration, Pasadena, CA, USA (2011). http://hdl.handle.net/2014/42194

8. Basin, D., Caronni, G., Ereth, S., Harvan, M., Klaedtke, F., Mantel, H.: Scalable offline monitoring of temporal specification. Formal Methods Syst. Des. **49**, 75–108 (2016). https://doi.org/10.1007/s10703-016-0242-y
9. Berkovich, S., Bonakdarpour, B., Fischmeister, S.: Runtime verification with minimal intrusion through parallelism. Formal Methods Syst. Des. **46**(3), 317–348 (2015). https://doi.org/10.1007/s10703-015-0226-3
10. Bartolo Burlò, C., Francalanza, A., Scalas, A.: Towards a hybrid verification methodology for communication protocols (short paper). In: Gotsman, A., Sokolova, A. (eds.) FORTE 2020. LNCS, vol. 12136, pp. 227–235. Springer, Cham (2020). https://doi.org/10.1007/978-3-030-50086-3_13
11. Colombo, C., Francalanza, A., Mizzi, R., Pace, G.J.: polyLARVA: runtime verification with configurable resource-aware monitoring boundaries. In: Eleftherakis, G., Hinchey, M., Holcombe, M. (eds.) SEFM 2012. LNCS, vol. 7504, pp. 218–232. Springer, Heidelberg (2012). https://doi.org/10.1007/978-3-642-33826-7_15
12. Department of Transportation, Federal Aviation Administration: Implementation of Descend Via into Boston Terminal area from Boston ARTCC (2015)
13. El-Hokayem, A., Falcone, Y.: Can we monitor all multithreaded programs? In: Colombo, C., Leucker, M. (eds.) RV 2018. LNCS, vol. 11237, pp. 64–89. Springer, Cham (2018). https://doi.org/10.1007/978-3-030-03769-7_6
14. Falcone, Y., Havelund, K., Reger, G.: A tutorial on runtime verification. In: Broy, M., Peled, D., Kalus, G. (eds.) Engineering Dependable Software Systems, NATO Science for Peace and Security Series - D: Information and Communication Security, vol. 34, pp. 141–175. IOS Press, January 2013. https://doi.org/10.3233/978-1-61499-207-3-141
15. SWIM Flight Data Publication Service (2020). https://www.faa.gov/air_traffic/technology/swim/sfdps/
16. Francalanza, A., Pérez, J.A., Sánchez, C.: Runtime verification for decentralised and distributed systems. In: Bartocci, E., Falcone, Y. (eds.) Lectures on Runtime Verification. LNCS, vol. 10457, pp. 176–210. Springer, Cham (2018). https://doi.org/10.1007/978-3-319-75632-5_6
17. Francalanza, A., Seychell, A.: Synthesising correct concurrent runtime monitors. Formal Methods Syst. Des. **46**(3), 226–261 (2014). https://doi.org/10.1007/s10703-014-0217-9
18. Hallé, S., Khoury, R., Gaboury, S.: Event stream processing with multiple threads. In: Lahiri, S., Reger, G. (eds.) RV 2017. LNCS, vol. 10548, pp. 359–369. Springer, Cham (2017). https://doi.org/10.1007/978-3-319-67531-2_22
19. Harris Corporation: FAA Telecommunications Infrastructure NEMS User Guide (2013)
20. Havelund, K.: Data automata in scala. In: Symposium on Theoretical Aspects of Software Engineering Conference, pp. 1–9. Changsha, China (2014). https://doi.org/10.1109/TASE.2014.37
21. Havelund, K.: Daut (2020). https://github.com/havelund/daut
22. Havelund, K.: TraceContract (2020). https://github.com/havelund/tracecontract
23. Hewitt, C., Bishop, P., Steiger, R.: A universal modular ACTOR formalism for artificial intelligence. In: Proceedings of the 3rd International Joint Conference on Artificial Intelligence, pp. 235–245. Morgan Kaufmann Publishers Inc., San Francisco (1973)
24. International Air Line Pilots Associations: FAA Suspends OPD Arrivals for Atlanta International Airport (2016)
25. International Civil Aviation Organization (ICAO): Performance-based Navigation (PBN) Manual, 3 edn., May 2008

26. JMH - Java Microbenchmark Harness (2020). https://openjdk.java.net/projects/code-tools/jmh/
27. Joyce, J., Lomow, G., Slind, K., Unger, B.: Monitoring distributed systems. ACM Trans. Comput. Syst. **5**(2), 121–150 (1987). https://doi.org/10.1145/13677.22723
28. Lavery, P., Watanabe, T.: An actor-based runtime monitoring system for web and desktop applications. In: Hochin, T., Hirata, H., Nomiya, H. (eds.) International Conference on Software Engineering, Artificial Intelligence, Networking and Parallel/Distributed Computing, pp. 385–390. IEEE Computer Society (2017)
29. Leucker, M., Schallhart, C.: A brief account of runtime verification. J. Logic Algebraic Program. **78**(5), 293–303 (2009). https://doi.org/10.1016/j.jlap.2008.08.004
30. Mehlitz, P.: RACE (2020) http://nasarace.github.io/race/
31. Mehlitz, P., Shafiei, N., Tkachuk, O., Davies, M.: RACE: building airspace simulations faster and better with actors. In: Digital Avionics Systems Conference (DASC), pp. 1–9, September 2016. https://doi.org/10.1109/DASC.2016.7777991
32. Meredith, P.O., Jin, D., Griffith, D., Chen, F., Roşu, G.: An overview of the MOP runtime verification framework. Int. J. Softw. Tech. Technol. Transf. **14**, 249–289 (2011). https://doi.org/10.1007/s10009-011-0198-6
33. Neykova, R., Yoshida, N.: Let it recover: multiparty protocol-induced recovery. In: Wu, P., Hack, S. (eds.) International Conference on Compiler Construction, pp. 98–108. ACM (2017). https://doi.org/10.1145/3033019.3033031
34. Rasmussen, S., Kingston, D., Humphrey, L.: A brief introduction to unmanned systems autonomy services (UxAS). In: 2018 International Conference on Unmanned Aircraft Systems (ICUAS), pp. 257–268 (2018). https://doi.org/10.1109/ICUAS.2018.8453287
35. Reger, G.: Rule-Based Runtime Verification in a Multicore System Setting. Master's thesis, University of Manchester (2010)
36. Reger, G., Cruz, H.C., Rydeheard, D.: MARQ: monitoring at runtime with QEA. In: Baier, C., Tinelli, C. (eds.) TACAS 2015. LNCS, vol. 9035, pp. 596–610. Springer, Heidelberg (2015). https://doi.org/10.1007/978-3-662-46681-0_55
37. Richards, M., Monson-Haefel, R., Chappell, D.A.: Java Message Service, 2nd edn. O'Reilly Media Inc., Newton (2009)
38. Roestenburg, R., Bakker, R., Williams, R.: Akka in Action, 1st edn. Manning Publications Co., Greenwich (2015)
39. Shafiei, N., Havelund, K., Mehlitz, P.: Empirical study of actor-based runtime verification. Technical report, NASA Ames Research Center, June 2020
40. Stewart, M., Matthews, B.: Objective assessment method for RNAV STAR adherence. In: DASC: Digital Avionics Systems Conference (2017)
41. U.S. Department of Transportation. Federal Aviation Administration: Performance Based Navigation PBN NAS Navigation Strategy (2016)

Placement of Runtime Checks
to Counteract Fault Injections

Benedikt Maderbacher$^{(\boxtimes)}$ ⒾD, Anja F. Karl ⒾD, and Roderick Bloem ⒾD

Graz University of Technology, Graz, Austria
{benedikt.maderbacher,anja.karl,roderick.bloem}@iaik.tugraz.at

Abstract. Bitflips form an increasingly serious problem for the correctness and security of software and hardware, whether they occur inadvertently as soft errors or on purpose as fault injections. Error Detection Codes add redundancy and make it possible to check for faults during runtime, making systems more resilient to bitflips. Codes require data integrity to be checked regularly. Such checks need to be used sparingly, because they cause runtime overhead.

In this paper, we show how to use static verification to minimize the number of runtime checks in encoded programs. We focus on loops, because this is where it is important to avoid unnecessary checks. We introduce three types of abstractions to decide correctness: depending on (i) whether we keep track of errors precisely or of their Hamming weights, (ii) how we check whether faults can still be detected, and (iii) whether we keep track of the data or not. We show that checks in loops induce simple and natural loop invariants that we can use to speed up the verification process.

The abstractions let us trade verification time against the number of required runtime checks, allowing us to find efficient sets of integrity checks for critical program fragments in reasonable time. Preliminary experimental data shows that we can reduce the number of runtime checks by up to a factor of ten.

1 Introduction

Fault injection attacks and soft errors [BBKN12] are a significant and growing concern in software security. By flipping bits, an attacker can reveal cryptographic secrets, change branching decisions, circumvent privilege evaluations, produce system failures, or manipulate the outcome of calculations. For instance, Boneh et al. [BDL97] showed how to break several implementations of cryptographic algorithms by injecting register faults. To prevent such attacks, they propose to protect the data integrity with error detection measures. Such countermeasures have been studied in detail for cryptographic algorithms [LRT12,SFES18,MAN+18], but not as much for secure software in general, where fault attacks may also be problematic [YSW18]. Similarly, radiation can lead to random bit flips known as *soft errors* or *single event upsets*. Such errors

© Springer Nature Switzerland AG 2020
J. Deshmukh and D. Ničković (Eds.): RV 2020, LNCS 12399, pp. 241–258, 2020.
https://doi.org/10.1007/978-3-030-60508-7_13

were initially only problematic for hardware used in space, but with decreasing feature sizes, they have also become relevant for consumer electronics [MER05].

We address error detection with Error Detecting Codes (EDCs) [Ham50, Dia55]. The fundamental principle of EDCs is an injective mapping of data words to code words in an encoded domain. The mapping cannot be surjective, indeed, if a code word is valid (the image of a data word), then flipping a few bits should not yield another valid code word. Thus, limited faults can be detected using runtime checks.

We are interested in error detecting codes that are homomorphic over certain operations. For example, arithmetic codes preserve (some) arithmetic operations, and binary linear codes preserve bitwise logical operations. Thus, we can execute certain programs in an encoded domain, without the need to decode and reencode in-between operations.

We define the distance between code words as their Hamming distance (we will be more precise below). For a given code, the minimal distance between two valid code words is called the *distance of the code*, denoted by d_{min}. The maximal number of bitflips that a code can detect is thus $d_{min} - 1$. In a program, bitflips may propagate and grow. For instance, if a variable a contains one bitflip, 3 * a may contain two.

We need to ensure that errors are not *masked*, which happens if combining two invalid code words results in a valid code word. We prevent masking by inserting *runtime checks* in the program that halt the program if the variable passed to the check is not a valid code word. Because checks cost runtime, we want to insert as few checks as possible.

In this paper, we show how to use static reasoning to minimize the number of runtime checks in encoded programs, building on the formal verification techniques presented in [KSBM19]. We pay special attention to the verification of checks inside loops, as their impact on correctness and on verification complexity is especially high. In order to help minimize the placement of checks, we make two contributions.

As a first contribution, we introduce a refined abstraction scheme. Where [KSBM19] only tracks the weight of the errors, we introduce a four-tiered abstraction scheme in which an error is tracked either by weight or by precise value; checks are performed either by checking the weight of error or by checking that a fault is not a valid code word itself, and finally the actual values of the variables are either abstracted away or kept precisely.

The second contribution is based on the observation that checks that are placed in loops induce simple loop invariants. We thus propose invariants that along with generated checks are used to reduce the verification of the runtime checks in the program to straight-line code.

We show experimentally that our approach allows us to significantly minimize the number of necessary runtime checks, by up to a factor of ten. The different levels of abstraction allow us to trade off the number of runtime checks in the program (we can prove programs with fewer checks correct if we have a finer abstraction) against the scalability of the approach (which is better if we abstract more strongly). The resulting approach allows us to insert efficient sets of checks into programs with reasonable computational effort.

2   Preliminaries

2.1   Fundamentals of Error Detecting Codes

Before introducing specific arithmetic codes, let us introduce some theory that is common across these types of codes. The fundamental operating principle of EDCs is the extension of every value with additional, redundant information. The key component of each EDC is the *encode* function. This function defines how a data word w of the decoded domain $\mathcal{W}$, $w \in \mathcal{W}$, is mapped to a code word c in the encoded domain $\mathcal{C}$:

$$\texttt{encode} : \mathcal{W} \mapsto \mathcal{C}.$$

Typically, both domains are an interval of non-negative integers. The function encode should be injective but not surjective, so that we can decode code words and detect (some) corruptions of code words. We call code word c *valid*, if it is part of the image of encode, i.e., $\exists w \in \mathcal{W} : c = \texttt{encode}(w)$, and *invalid* otherwise.

For the error detecting codes that are of interest here, we can define a distance function $d : \mathcal{C} \times \mathcal{C} \rightharpoonup \mathbb{N}$ on the encoded domain. (Distance functions fulfill the usual properties of non-negativity, identity, symmetry, and the triangle inequality.) We use these distances to measure faults (as distances to the intended value) and we will see below that they allow us to track these faults through certain types of operations.

The error detection capabilities of an error detecting code are limited by the minimum distance d_{min} between any two valid code words [Ham50]. We define d_{min} as the minimum distance between any two valid code words, i.e., $d_{min} = \min_{c_v, c_v'} d(c_v, c_v')$. We also define a weight function weight : $\mathcal{C} \mapsto \mathbb{N}$ as the distance between a code word and the identity encode(0), i.e., weight(c) = $d(c, \texttt{encode}(0))$. Finally, we define a partial function decode : $\mathcal{C} \rightharpoonup \mathcal{W}$, as the inverse of the encode function, and a function isvalid : $\mathcal{C} \mapsto \mathbb{B}$, which maps valid code words to true and invalid code words to false. The result of decode is only defined for valid code words.

Most EDCs are homomorphic over a set of supported operations $\circ$, i.e.,

$$\texttt{encode}(w_1 \circ w_2) = \texttt{encode}(w_1) \circ \texttt{encode}(w_2),$$

which allows us to encode a whole program and execute the calculation directly in the encoded domain.

2.2   Arithmetic Codes

Our work targets programs protected by codes that are homomorphic over arithmetic operations.

Arithmetic Codes are homomorphic over operations like addition. The distance and weight functions are defined as the (base-2) *arithmetic distance* and *weight*, resp. [Mas64]:

$$\text{weight}_{\text{arit}}(c) = \min\left\{n \mid c = \sum_{i=0}^{n} a_i \cdot 2^{k_i} \text{ for some } a_i \in \{-1,1\} \text{ and } k_i \geq 0\right\}$$

and

$$d_{\text{arit}}(c_1, c_2) = \text{weight}_{\text{arit}}(|c_2 - c_1|).$$

For instance, $d_{\text{arit}}(9,2) = \text{weight}_{\text{arit}}(7) = 2$, because $7 = 8 - 1$. The distance between a value c and a value c' that differ only in one bit is one.

For any linear operation $\circ$, we have the propagation laws $d_{\text{arit}}(c_1 \circ c_2, c_1' \circ c_2') \leq d_{\text{arit}}(c_1, c_1') + d_{\text{arit}}(c_2, c_2')$ and $d_{\text{arit}}(c \circ c, c' \circ c') \leq d_{\text{arit}}(c, c')$.

Example 1. Separate multiresidue codes. Separate multiresidue codes [Rao70, RG71] are arithmetic codes. Every code word is a $(k+1)$-tuple and operations are performed separately on each element [Gar66, Pet58]. Every code is defined by k constants, $m_1, \ldots, m_k$ and we encode a data word as

$$\texttt{encode}(w) = (w, |w|_{m_1}, \ldots, |w|_{m_k}),$$

where each check digit $|w|_{m_i}$ equals $w \bmod m_i$. Every operation on the check digits is performed modulo its check base, so that

$$|w_1 \circ w_2|_{m_i} = ||w_1|_{m_i} \circ |w_2|_{m_i}|_{m_i},$$

making separate multiresidue codes are homomorphic over these operations. The constant d_{min} depends on the choice of the check bases $m_1, \ldots m_k$ [MS09].

Example 2. AN-codes. For AN-codes, we fix a constant A and we define $\texttt{encode}(w) = A \cdot w$. A code word is valid if its residue after division by A is zero. Note that multiplication by A distributes over addition and subtraction. The d_{min} of the code does not follow by easy inspection of A, but we often choose A to be a prime. (Note that a power of two would be a particularly poor choice with $d_{min} = 1$.)

2.3   Error Propagation

When considering computations, we consider both the *correct* value c^0 of a variable c, which occurs in an execution in which no faults are introduced, and its possible *faulty* counterpart c^*, which occurs in the corresponding execution where faults have been introduced. The *error weight* e_c is defined as the distance $d(c^*, c^0)$ between the correct and actual code values. Recall that if $e_c \geq d_{min}$, then c^* may equal the encoding of a different data word, and it may no longer be possible to detect a fault. On the other hand, if we can guarantee that $e_c < d_{min}$ for all variables c, then faults will remain detectable.

We will assume that faults are introduced as one or more individual bitflips. If a single bitflip is introduced in an otherwise correct variable c^*, we have that $d(c^0, c^*) = 1$ and a bitflip introduced in an existing variable increases the error weight by at most one. By the propagation laws stated above, for any operation $\circ$, we have that $e_{c \circ c'} \leq e_c + e_{c'}$. Thus, faults may spread across an execution and "grow up": a variable may eventually have an error weight that is larger than the total number of bitflips introduced into the program. For example: $e_{(c \circ c') \circ c} \leq 2 * e_c + e_{c'}$ which can be larger than the sum of the injected errors $e_c + e_{c'}$.

Table 1 summarizes the propagation rules, where we use arithmetic error weights.

Table 1. Error propagation rules for arithmetic codes. The symbol $\pm$ stands for addition or subtraction.

$$e_{v \pm v'} \leq e_v + e_{v'}$$
$$e_{v \pm v} \leq e_v$$
$$e_{-v} = e_v$$

2.4   Fault Model

Our approach is relatively independent of the precise fault model chosen, as long as it can be modeled by a program transformation.

We illustrate our approach using a simple fault model in which faults consist of bit flips on memory variables. We model faults to be transient in the sense that the occurrence of a failure at a given program location does not mean the failure will occur again when the program location is visited again. We do, however, assume that errors persist in the sense that when the value of a variable has changed, it does not automatically change back again. This models faults in memory rather that faults on, say, the data path of a processor.

To model faults, we assume a minimal programming language with assignments, arithmetic operations, jumps, conditionals, and a runtime check statement. When called on a code word c, check(c) halts the program when c is not a valid code word and continues otherwise. Note that this check will not detect code words that contain such a large error that they equal a different code word.

We model faults by a simple program transformation in which a program P is transformed to an *annotated program* P_f. In P_f, we add a new statement flip(v) before every use of a variable v. This statement may nondeterministically flip one bit of the value of v. We will also typically have an *error assumption* φ_ε that limits the number of bit flips that can be inserted into a run of the program. An example would be a specification that says that the total number of inserted bit flips is smaller than d_{min}. We refer to [KSBM19] for a formalization of this approach.

We assume that the control flow of the program is protected using other means [SWM18, WUSM18].

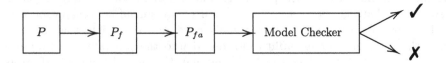

Fig. 1. Overview of the verification algorithm.

3   Error Tracking

In this section and the next, we describe how we verify the correctness of the checks in a program. We will thus define a code transformation from a program with loops into a set of loop-free programs with assumptions and assertions such that the correctness of the original program under the fault model is guaranteed if all of the loop-free code fragments are correct. This is done by tracking the values of the arithmetic errors in addition to the values of the variables. This section introduces increasingly precise abstractions for error variables, to make the error tracking feasible. In the next section, we will describe how to generate the invariants necessary to handle loops.

Figure 1 contains a schematic of our verification approach. Starting with an encoded program P in the first step the fault model is made explicit resulting in a program P_f. In the next step we apply one of the error abstractions described in this section, abstract the control flow and add assertions. This program P_{fa} is then given to a model checker, which gives a verdict whether the program is secure.

The idea of the abstraction is to track the errors in the variables separately from their (intended, uncorrupted) values. In order to do this, we need the following property.

Definition 1. *An error-correcting code is error-homomorphic for a set F of operations, if for any $f \in F$ there is an f' such that*

$$f(a + \varepsilon_a) = f(a) + f'(\varepsilon_a) \text{ and}$$
$$f(a + \varepsilon_a, b + \varepsilon_b) = f(a, b) + f'(\varepsilon_a, \varepsilon_b),$$

where $+$ denotes addition, as we are dealing with arithmetic codes.

AN-codes and multiresidual codes are error-homomorphic for addition and multiplication with constants. Multiresidual codes are error-homomorphic for multiplication as well, but AN-codes are not.

In effect, these constraints state that we can track the values of the variables separately from the errors. This is important for verification, because it means we can distinguish between three situations: (1) a value may be *correct*, that is, the error is zero. We denote this by $\text{corr}(\varepsilon)$; (2) the error may be *detectable* in a given code, denoted by $\text{detect}(\varepsilon)$; (3) the error may be *masked*, meaning that it is not zero but cannot be detected using the given code, denoted by $\text{masked}(\varepsilon)$. The third case is the one we want to avoid.

Example 3. For an AN code with constant A, $\text{corr}(\varepsilon)$ is defined as $\varepsilon = 0$, $\text{detect}(\varepsilon) = (\varepsilon \mod A \neq 0)$ and $\text{masked}(\varepsilon) = (\varepsilon > 0 \wedge \varepsilon \mod A = 0)$

We will construct a program P_{fa} from P_f. For every variable v in P_f, P_{fa} will have two variables, v and ε_v. We distinguish our abstractions along three dimensions:

1. The first question is how to keep track of errors that are introduced. We can track the actual arithmetic error, or we can abstract it away by keeping track of the weight of the error only.
2. We can vary how we check whether the induced errors can be handled by the given code: we can either check whether the concrete error can be detected by the given code, or we can abstract this to a check whether the weight of the fault is greater than d_{min}.
3. Finally, we can keep the actual values of the variables or we can fully abstract these away.

The abstractions are modeled as follows. In the following, we will assume static single assignment form and we will introduce assumptions on relations between variables when we cannot use assignments.

1. If we keep track of errors by their actual values, then for every v, ε_v is a bitvector that models the error and the statement flip(v) is replaced by a statement $\text{flip}^a(\varepsilon_\text{v})$ that nondeterministically flips one of the bits in ε_v. We replace an assignment u := f(v,w) in P_f by the two statements u := f(v,w); $\varepsilon_\text{u} := f'(\varepsilon_\text{v}, \varepsilon_\text{w})$, using error homomorphism.
   If we keep only the weights of the errors, then ε_v is a positive number, and $\text{flip}^a(\varepsilon_\text{v})$ nondeterministically adds one to ε_v. In these cases we replace an assignment u := f(v,w) by the statements u := f(v,w); $\text{assume}(\varepsilon_\text{u} \leq f'(\varepsilon_\text{v},\varepsilon_\text{w}))$. The value of ε_u can be anything satisfying the assumption. Note that for arithmetic codes and additions, for instance, the weight of the error of the sum of two variables can be smaller than the sum of the weights of the errors.
2. A check whether the weight of a given error is greater than d_{min} is easily implemented, whether or not we keep track of the concrete value of the error or only of its weight. If we keep track of the concrete value of an error, we can check make sure that the error value can be detected. For multiresidual codes with constants $m_1, \ldots, m_k$, this is the case if ε_v is not a common multiple of $m_1, \ldots, m_k$; for AN-codes it is the case if it is not a multiple of A.
3. Finally, if we abstract away the values of the concrete variable of the program, we simply remove all assignments to the variables and replace conditionals with nondeterministic choices.

Based on these three dimensions, we define four levels of abstraction, as sketched in Table 2.

The abstract program is extended by adding assumptions and assertions. Whenever a variable gets assigned it may not contain error masking. The error must be either zero or detectable by the code.

- For only checking the weight of the variables the assertion for a variable v is `assert`(weight(ε_v) < d_{min}).
- If we check the actual code words the assertion instead is `assert`(corr(ε_v) $\vee$ detect(ε_v)).

After a check on variable we added an assumption that the error on this variable is zero, as the program would abort otherwise. We can slightly reduce the number of assertions by only checking the variables when they are checked or used in some form of output.

Table 2. Abstraction levels

Level	Errors	Checks	Values
3	Weight	Weight	Abstract
2	Precise	Weight	Abstract
1	Precise	Code Word	Abstract
0	Precise	Code Word	Precise

Theorem 1. *If no assertion in the abstract program P_{fa} is violated then either the program P_f with faults conforming to the fault model φ_ε raises an error or the output of P and P_f is equal.*

We overapproximate the control flow and the propagation of errors. Thus if no assertion is violated we can guarantee that no fault can lead to error masking and no manipulated values are in the program output. The other direction, however, is not true. There are programs that are rejected by our approach, that are secure against the fault model.

Example 4. The different behaviors of these abstraction levels can be demonstrated with a simple example. Let the following program, P, be protected by an AN code with $A = 7$, for which we have $d_{min} = 2$:

```
m := m + a;
check(m); check(a);
```

For the sake of a simpler presentation we only consider one error injection location on the variable a at the beginning of the program, so that our annotated program P_f becomes

```
flip(a);
m := m + a;
check(m); check(a);
```

Let us assume that at most one bit is flipped. Using Abstraction Level 3 we obtain an abstract program P_{fa}. Combining that with the specification that puts the error at zero at the beginning at the program and requires safe errors at the end, we get the following.

$$\text{assume}(\varepsilon_a = 0 \wedge \varepsilon_m = 0);$$
$$\varepsilon_a' := \text{flip}^a(\varepsilon_a); \qquad // \ \varepsilon_a' = 1, \ \varepsilon_m = 0$$
$$\text{assume}(\varepsilon_m' \leq \varepsilon_m + \varepsilon_a'); \qquad // \ \varepsilon_a' = 1, \ \varepsilon_m' = 1$$
$$\text{assert}(\varepsilon_m' < d_{min} \wedge \varepsilon_a' < d_{min});$$

The variables a and m are replaced by their respective error weights and the comments on the right side of the code show one possible execution in which a bitflip is introduced in a and the bitflip propagates to m. The final checks are replaced by checks whether both errors are not masked, i.e., smaller than d_{min}. It it easy to verify (by hand or mechanically) that the assertion always holds.

To make things a little more interesting, let us extend the program by repeating the first statement:

```
m := m + a;
m := m + a;
check(m); check(a);
```

This program can no longer be verified using Abstraction Level 3, because a single bitflip in a at the beginning can result in $\varepsilon_m = 2$ at the end, which is equal to d_{min}. However, we can use Abstraction Level 2 to show that all errors will be detected:

$$\text{assume}(\varepsilon_a = 0 \wedge \varepsilon_m = 0);$$
$$\varepsilon_a' := \text{flip}^a(\varepsilon_a); \qquad // \ \varepsilon_a' = 2, \ \varepsilon_m = 0$$
$$\varepsilon_m' := \varepsilon_m + \varepsilon_a'; \qquad // \ \varepsilon_a' = 2, \ \varepsilon_m' = 2$$
$$\varepsilon_m'' := \varepsilon_m' + \varepsilon_a'; \qquad // \ \varepsilon_a' = 2, \ \varepsilon_m'' = 4$$
$$\text{assert}(\text{weight}(\varepsilon_m'') < d_{min} \wedge \text{weight}(\varepsilon_a') < d_{min});$$

The variables ε_a and ε_b now keep track of the precise faults. The comments show possible values for one execution with a bitflip on the second bit, which in the third line leads to a value with the third bit flipped. In general, injecting one bit flip in a variable and adding it to itself always results in a value with only one flipped bit, and such errors can be detected by a code with $d_{min} = 2$.

Extending our example once more, we get

```
m := m + a;
m := m + a;
m := m + a;
check(m); check(a);
```

An attempt to verify this program using Abstraction Level 2 fails, because the error weight of m can reach d_{min} at the end. However, we can use Abstraction

Level 1 to show that the check on m is still sufficient to find all faults in this program.

```
assume(εₐ = 0 ∧ εₘ = 0);
ε'ₐ := flipᵃ(εₐ);                    // ε'ₐ = 2, εₘ = 0
ε'ₘ := εₘ + ε'ₐ;                     // ε'ₐ = 2, ε'ₘ = 2
ε''ₘ := ε'ₘ + ε'ₐ;                   // ε'ₐ = 2, ε''ₘ = 4
ε'''ₘ := ε''ₘ + ε'ₐ;                 // ε'ₐ = 2, ε'''ₘ = 6
assert((ε'''ₘ = 0 ∨ ε'''ₘ mod A ≠ 0) ∧ (ε'ₐ = 0 ∨ ε'ₐ mod A ≠ 0));
```

Instead of checking only the weight of the error variables we check if the error variable is zero or a valid code word in the AN code. This is done by testing if the value is divisible by A. The comments again show one possible execution of the program. It is also easy to see that this is correct in general. The value of m at the end is m+3∗a; any error introduced at the beginning is also multiplied by 3. Error masking cannot occur, since 3 is not a factor of $A = 7$.

Abstraction Level 0 keeps the precise values of all variables. Essentially, this amounts to not using any abstraction. We will not go into details for this abstraction level, but of course, it is easy to come up with an example in which the concrete values of the variables are needed to show the program is secure.

4   Invariants

The abstract program defined in the last section can be passed to a model checker as is. However, such programs may be difficult for off-the-shelf model checkers to handle, especially in the presence of loops. It may, however, be easy to generate loop invariants for the classes of faults that we use, thus reducing the verification of an annotated program to the verification of a set of loop-free code segments in order to reduce the number of runtime checks.

Let us assume our annotated program P_f contains a loop body L that uses a set of variables $V = \{v_1, \ldots, v_n\}$ with the associated error variables $\varepsilon_V = \{\varepsilon_1, \ldots, \varepsilon_n\}$ and let $E \subseteq \mathbb{N}^n$ be the set of possible values for ε_V. Without loss of generality, let us assume that at the end of each loop iteration, we check variables $\{v_1, \ldots, v_k\}$ for a detectable error.

We will assume that we have an error specified by φ_ε on the level of the loop that limits the bit flips to l, i.e., l is the total number of bit flips that can be inserted during the execution of the loop. We denote the resulting value of variable v_i (error ε_i) of executing L with variable values $a = (a_1, \ldots, a_n)$ and error values $e = (e_1, \ldots, e_n)$ and the total number of bitflips introduced in this iteration b by $a'_i(a, e, b)$ ($e'_i(a, e, b)$, resp.).

Definition 2. *For a loop L, a set $E^* \subseteq E \times \mathbb{N}$ is an* error invariant *if the following two conditions hold.*

1. *For any $(e_1, \ldots, e_n, b) \in E^*$, we have $\bigwedge_{i \leq k} \mathrm{corr}(e_i)$ and $\bigwedge_{i > k} \neg\,\mathrm{masked}(e_i)$ and $b \leq l$.*

2. *For any $(e, b) \in E^*$, any valuation a of V, and any number of new bitflips*
   $b' \leq l - b$, one of two things holds
   (a) $\bigvee_{i \leq k} \text{detect}(e'_i(a, e, b'))$ or
   (b) $(e'_1(a, e, b'), \ldots, e'_n(a, e, b'), b + b') \in E^*$.

Thus, if we start the loop body with the errors in the checked variables equal to zero and no masked errors, we know that at the end of the loop the program either terminates because it finds an error, or there are no masked errors. In addition to the errors on the variables the invariant also tracks the number of introduced bitflips and limits them to conform to the program wide fault model.

We will consider a loop to be correct if it has an error invariant, noting that if required, we can check for detectable error on variables $v_{k+1}, \ldots, v_n$ after the loop has finished.

Theorem 2. *Assume E^* is an error invariant for a loop with body L. If L is executed with error values and introduced bitfilps in E^* and at the end either an error is raised or the values are in E^* then executing the loop* while(*): { L } *with values in E^* either results in raising an error or after the loop all values are in E^*.*

The general definition of invariants is independent of the abstraction level, but the invariants differ in the actual value of E^*. The main challenge is to find a good E^*. Many programs can be verified by using a few simple invariants.

- If all variables are checked at every loop iteration, we use $\{(0, \ldots, 0, b) \mid b \in [0, l]\}$ as a (candidate) error invariant.
- For Abstraction Level 3 we can use the invariant that all unchecked error variables are below d_{min}. The same can be done for Abstraction Level 2, but in this case we require that the Hamming weight of all variables be below d_{min}.
- For Abstraction Level 1 we can define E^* as the set of detectable errors, according to the used code.
- Another stricter version for Abstraction Level 1 is to restrict the values to only what can be introduced with a single error injection and no accumulation.

These invariants assume a fault model that limits the amount of fault injections for one program execution. The invariants can be adapted to support other fault models. For instance only the number of bitflips per loop iteration could be bounded, without an upper limit for the whole execution.

Example 5. We use a variant of the example from the previous section to demonstrate our invariants. A simple multiplication algorithm can be build from repeated addition. The following code multiples a and b and stores the result in m.

```
m  := 0;
while(i<b):
    i := i + 1;
    m := m + a;
    check(m); check(a);
```

The variables i and b are assumed to be checked by the control flow protection. We can therefore obtain the following program with abstracted control flow.

```
m := 0;
while(*):
    m := m + a;
    check(m); check(a);
```

Here both variables m and a are checked at the end of the loop body. Using Abstraction Level 2, we keep track of the errors and check their weights, resulting in the following program. In this case we can use the invariant that both ε_a and ε_m are zero, which gives the following program P_{fa} using Definition 2.

```
assume(εₐ = 0 ∧ εₘ = 0);
ε'ₐ := flipᵃ(εₐ);
ε'ₘ := εₘ + εₐ;
assert(0 < weight(ε'ₘ) < dₘᵢₙ ∨ 0 < weight(ε'ₐ) < dₘᵢₙ ∨ ε'ₘ = 0 ∧ ε'ₐ = 0);
```

We assume that both errors are zero at the start and we check that we can find potential errors in the variables after executing the loop body.

Suppose we want to only check one of the variables. Using Abstraction Level 1 and checking only m, we can define an invariant $\mathrm{inv}(\varepsilon_a)$ that does not allow masked values. We obtain the program:

```
assume(εₘ = 0 ∧ inv(εₐ));
ε'ₐ := flipᵃ(εₐ);
ε'ₘ := εₘ + ε'ₐ;
assert(detect(ε'ₘ) ∨ ε'ₘ = 0 ∧ inv(εₐ))
```

The last line in the listing can be realized by checking $\varepsilon'_m \neq 0 \wedge \varepsilon'_m \bmod A \neq 0 \vee \varepsilon'_m = 0 \wedge \mathrm{inv}(\varepsilon'_a)$. For the invariant on ε_a we could use $\varepsilon_a = 0$. This invariant holds, because any bitflip that is introduced in the second line will be found by the check on m.

5   Experimental Results

In order to evaluate how the overhead of runtime checks can be minimized using our method, we ran our technique on two examples, The CORDIC algorithm for numerical trigonometry [Vol59] and a Fibonacci number generator [Bon02]. These algorithms contain a loop in which almost all of the work is done, so that small performance improvements can have a large impact on the overall performance of the programs. To further reduce the number of required runtime check we also consider variants of these programs where the loop has been unrolled n times. In these cases, checks are only inserted every n iterations. We also use these two algorithms to compare the static verification results and performance of our approaches.

In our experiments, we used CPAchecker version 1.9 [BK11] running on a laptop with an Intel i5-6200U CPU under Ubuntu 18.04 with 12 GB of RAM.

Listing 1. CORDIC program and abstraction

```
// concrete program
for (k in 0 to n):
  if (theta >=0 ):
    t_cosin := cosin - (sin>>k);
    t_sin := sin + (cosin>>k);
    theta := theta - table[k];
  else:
    t_cosin := cosin + (sin>>k);
    t_sin := sin - (cosin>>k);
    theta := theta + table[k];
  cosin := t_cosin;
  sin := t_sin;


// abstraction
while(*):
  if (*):
    (cosin, sin) := (cosin - (sin>>k)), (sin + (cosin>>k));
  else:
    (cosin, sin) := (cosin + (sin>>k)), (sin - (cosin>>k));
```

To verify invariants, we use the following settings in CPAchecker: MATHSAT5 solver, disabled outputs and disabled Java assertions. For comparison, we also verify the abstract programs when leaving the loops intact and not introducing invariants. Here we use the same settings with CPAchecker's k-induction configuration.[1]

5.1   CORDIC

The CORDIC algorithm is used to calculate sine and cosine on devices without hardware support. It only requires addition, subtraction and right shifts. The results of the algorithm become more precise the more iterations are performed. Listing 1 shows an implementation for fixpoint arithmetic in two versions, first the original program and second the program with abstract control flow. The variable `table` refers to a precomputed array of constants that has been omitted from this listing. The abstract version of the program no longer contains the variables n and `theta` as they are already included in the control flow protection. The variable k is also checked as part of the control flow and we can assume that it does not contain errors. This makes the shifts conform to the error homomorphism property.

Our error assumption is that at most one arithmetic error is injected during the execution of the program. Our baseline comparison is to check each variable after each loop iteration. Using our abstractions we can show that it is sufficient to only check the variables every three loop iterations without reducing the fault resilience of the program, which reduces the runtime overhead by factor three.

---

[1] Our scripts are available at https://extgit.iaik.tugraz.at/scos/rv20-fault-injection-checks.

Table 3 shows the experimental results for the CORDIC algorithm. It shows the abstraction level, the number of iterations of the loop that are performed before the variables are checked for errors, whether the technique can prove the approach correct or not and how much time it needs. The latter two categories are presented both for the techniques using invariants and for a plain run of CPAchecker. The program is protected by an AN-code where A is the prime number 7919, which results in $d_{min} = 4$. Using Abstraction Level 3 (only tracking the weight of the error) we can prove that performing checks every second iteration is sufficient. However, this abstraction level is not precise enough to verify that we can perform three iterations of the loop before checking the variables. All these checks are completed in under four seconds.

Listing 2. Fibonacci program

```
(a, b) := (1, 1);
while(*):
    (a, b) := (a+b, a);
    check(a); check(b);
```

A more precise abstraction allows us to prove programs with fewer checks, at the cost of a longer verification time. We note that Abstraction Level 2 is unsuitable for this specific program. Testing the Hamming weight instead of the arithmetic weight performs worse than using Abstraction Level 3. However, calculating the arithmetic weight during model checking is too expensive.

With Abstraction Level 1 we are able to establish that checks every three loop iterations are sufficient. This takes around 45 min, significantly longer than using the simpler abstraction. The runtime overhead of the checks, however, is reduced by a further 33%. Although the runtime differences between a plain run of CPAchecker and a run using invariants are not large, the most efficient configuration (two checks for every three iterations) can only be proved using invariants.

Table 3. CORDIC verification results

		Invariants		Loops	
Abstr. Lvl	Iterations	Success	Time [s]	Success	Time [s]
3	1	✓	2.71	✓	3.43
	2	✓	3.19	✓	4.78
	3	✗	3.77	✗	6.82
2	1	✗	4.37	✗	4.47
1	1	✓	9.25	✓	15.26
	2	✓	224.00	✓	200.33
	3	✓	2649.86	?	>3600
	4	?	>3600	?	>3600

5.2 Fibonacci

As a second case study we analyze a Fibonacci number generator. The program consists of a loop and two variables a and b. We compare our techniques based on the static verification time and the number of required runtime checks. To do this, we vary both the number of iterations before checks are performed and the variables that are checked. The program is protected by an AN code with $A = 13$ and $d_{min} = 2$. The error assumption is that at most one arithmetic error is injected during the execution of the program. Our baseline comparison is a check on variables a and b after every iteration of the loop, giving us two checks per iteration. The code of the Fibonacci program with abstracted control flow is shown in Listing 2.

Table 4. Fibonacci experimental results

	Configuration			Invariants		Loops	
Abstr Lvl	Checked Vars	Iter	Checks/Iter	Success	Time [s]	Success	Time [s]
3	a, b	1	2	✓	2.78	✓	3.03
	a, b	2	1	✗	2.81	✗	3.54
	a	1	1	✓	2.45	✓	3.81
	a	2	0.5	✗	2.75	✗	3.51
2	a, b	1	2	✓	3.45	✓	4.48
	a, b	2	1	✓	6.65	✓	10.16
	a, b	3	0.67	✗	5.54	✗	9.34
	a	1	1	✓	3.60	✓	6.33
	a	2	0.5	✓	7.80	✓	17.61
	a	3	0.33	✗	7.01	✗	9.41
1	a, b	1	2	✓	4.32	✓	8.76
	a, b	2	1	✓	6.57	✓	16.00
	a, b	3	0.67	✓	15.99	✓	46.62
	a, b	4	0.5	✓	43.92	✓	56.80
	a, b	5	0.4	✓	34.08	✓	190.94
	a, b	6	0.33	✗	38.85	✗	82.52
	a	1	1	✓	4.72	✓	15.26
	a	2	0.5	✓	11.36	✓	88.84
	a	3	0.33	✓	21.14	?	>600
	a	4	0.25	✓	132.25	?	>600
	a	5	0.2	✓	121.51	?	>600
	a	6	0.17	✗	14.06	✗	85.99

Table 4 shows the results of the Abstraction Levels 3 to 1. As before, we used both the approach with invariants and a vanilla run of CPAchecker. When checking only one variable we use the error invariant that the unchecked variable has a error weight less than d_{min} for both Abstraction Levels 2 and 3. The number of checks per iteration is our final measure of runtime overhead.

We can observe that lower levels of abstraction allow us to verify programs with fewer runtime checks. When using Abstraction Level 3 we need at least one check per loop iteration on average. The verification time is around two to four seconds and using invariants performs slightly better than loops.

Moving to Abstraction Level 2 allows us to reduce the number of runtime checks per iteration to 0.5 checks when checking only one variable. The verification time increases, but is still relatively low.

Abstraction Level 1 provides the greatest benefits in terms of reducing the runtime overhead of the program. It allows us to reduce the required checks to only one check in every 5 iterations, an improvement of a factor of 10 over the original. These cases could not be verified using plain CPA within ten minutes.

For this algorithm, the final reduction in runtime overhead for checks is a factor of 10.

Table 5. Fibonacci encoding parameter selection

A	Checks/Iter	Checked Vars	Max Iter	Time [s]
7	0.33	a, b	6	61.03
	0.2	a	5	93.39
	0.25	b	4	36.43
10	0.67	a, b	3	17.05
	0.33	a	3	12.36
	0.33	b	3	22.53
11	0.25	a, b	8	68.07
	0.2	a	5	74.20
	0.25	b	4	39.45
13	0.4	a, b	5	33.02
	0.2	a	5	127.20
	0.25	b	4	27.34
17	0.29	a, b	7	189.06
	0.2	a	5	472.71
	0.25	b	4	29.55

Finding an Optimal Value for A. As a second experiment on the Fibonacci program, we used invariants and Abstraction Level 1 to search for a good encoding parameter A and the optimal placement of runtime checks. We tried five different values for A: 7, 10, 11, 13, and 17 that all have the same d_{min} of 2. Three patterns for placing checks are explored: checking both the variables a and b, only checking a and only checking b. In all cases we maximize the number of loop iterations by increasing the iterations until the verification fails for the first time.

The results of this experiment are presented in Table 5. The maximum number of loop iterations between checks varies greatly based on the used encoding parameter. For $A = 10$ the program can only perform three iterations before it needs to check the variables, whereas for $A = 11$ we can do eight iterations if both variables are checked. The smallest runtime overhead can be achieved by using one of the prime numbers and performing a check on the variable a every five loop iterations. This results in only 0.2 checks per iteration, a significant improvement over the 2 checks per iteration from the naive check placement. As multiple coding parameters can achieve the same low runtime overhead we can look at the memory overhead as a tiebreaker. A smaller encoding parameter also results in a smaller memory overhead in the protected program. Thus, the most runtime efficient protection for this program is to use $A = 7$ and place a check on a every fifth iteration.

6 Conclusions

We have presented a method to analyze the necessity of runtime checks in programs using error correcting codes to achieve resilience against fault injections. Our method uses a combination of novel abstractions and simple recipes for loop invariants to achieve scalable verification times. We have shown that for simple examples we can reduce the overhead of runtime checks by factor of up to 10.

In future work, we will look at the use of different error detection codes, and we will consider combinations of secure hardware and software design to shield against fault injections.

Acknowledgements. We would like to thank Stefan Mangard and Robert Schilling for contributing their expertise on error correcting codes. We gratefully acknowledge the support of Graz University of Technology through the LEAD Project "Dependable Internet of Things in Adverse Environments".

References

[BBKN12] Barenghi, A., Breveglieri, L., Koren, I., Naccache, D.: Fault injection attacks on cryptographic devices: theory, practice, and countermeasures. Proc. IEEE **100**(11), 3056–3076 (2012)

[BDL97] Boneh, D., DeMillo, R.A., Lipton, R.J.: On the importance of checking cryptographic protocols for faults. In: Fumy, W. (ed.) EUROCRYPT 1997. LNCS, vol. 1233, pp. 37–51. Springer, Heidelberg (1997). https://doi.org/10.1007/3-540-69053-0_4

[BK11] Beyer, D., Keremoglu, M.E.: CPACHECKER: a tool for configurable software verification. In: Gopalakrishnan, G., Qadeer, S. (eds.) CAV 2011. LNCS, vol. 6806, pp. 184–190. Springer, Heidelberg (2011). https://doi.org/10.1007/978-3-642-22110-1_16

[Bon02] Leonardo Bonacci. Liber Abaci. 1202

[Dia55]   Diamond, J.M.: Checking codes for digital computers. Proc. IRE **43**(4), 483–490 (1955)

[Gar66]   Garner, H.L.: Error codes for arithmetic operations. IEEE Trans. Electron. Comput. **15**(5), 763–770 (1966)

[Ham50]   Hamming, R.W.: Error detecting and error correcting codes. Bell Syst. Tech. J. **29**(2), 147–160 (1950)

[KSBM19] Karl, A.F., Schilling, R., Bloem, R., Mangard, S.: Small faults grow up - verification of error masking robustness in arithmetically encoded programs. In: Enea, C., Piskac, R. (eds.) VMCAI 2019. LNCS, vol. 11388, pp. 183–204. Springer, Cham (2019). https://doi.org/10.1007/978-3-030-11245-5_9

[LRT12]   Lomné, V., Roche, T., Thillard, A.: On the need of randomness in fault attack countermeasures - application to AES. In: Bertoni, G., Gierlichs, B. (eds.) 2012 Workshop on Fault Diagnosis and Tolerance in Cryptography, Leuven, Belgium, 9 September 2012, pp. 85–94. IEEE Computer Society (2012)

[MAN+18] De Meyer, L., Arribas, V., Nikova, S., Nikov, V., Rijmen, V.: M&M: Masks and macs against physical attacks. Cryptology ePrint Archive, Report 2018/1195 (2018). https://eprint.iacr.org/2018/1195

[Mas64]   Massey, J.L.: Survey of residue coding for arithmetic errors. Int. Comput. Center Bull. **3**(4), 3–17 (1964)

[MER05]   Mukherjee, S.S., Emer, J., Reinhardt, S.K.: The soft error problem: an architectural perspective. In: 11th International Symposium on High-Performance Computer Architecture, pp. 243–247 (2005)

[MS09]   Medwed, M., Schmidt, J.-M.: Coding schemes for arithmetic and logic operations - how robust are they? In: Youm, H.Y., Yung, M. (eds.) WISA 2009. LNCS, vol. 5932, pp. 51–65. Springer, Heidelberg (2009). https://doi.org/10.1007/978-3-642-10838-9_5

[Pet58]   Peterson, W.W.: On checking an adder. IBM J. Res. Dev. **2**(2), 166–168 (1958)

[Rao70]   Rao, T.R.N.: Biresidue error-correcting codes for computer arithmetic. IEEE Trans. Comput. **19**(5), 398–402 (1970)

[RG71]   Rao, T.R.N., Garcia, O.N.: Cyclic and multiresidue codes for arithmetic operations. IEEE Trans. Inf. Theory **17**(1), 85–91 (1971)

[SFES18] Seker, O., Fernandez-Rubio, A., Eisenbarth, T., Steinwandt, R.: Extending glitch-free multiparty protocols to resist fault injection attacks. IACR Trans. Cryptogr. Hardw. Embed. Syst. **2018**(3), 394–430 (2018)

[SWM18]   Schilling, R., Werner, M., Mangard, S.: Securing conditional branches in the presence of fault attacks. In: 2018 Design, Automation & Test in Europe Conference & Exhibition, pp. 1586–1591. IEEE (2018)

[Vol59]   Volder, J.: The cordic computing technique. In: Papers presented at the the 3–5 March 1959, Western Joint Computer Conference, pp. 257–261 (1959)

[WUSM18] Werner, M., Unterluggauer, T., Schaffenrath, D., Mangard, S.: Sponge-based control-flow protection for IoT devices. In: 2018 IEEE European Symposium on Security and Privacy, pp. 214–226 (2018)

[YSW18]   Yuce, B., Schaumont, P., Witteman, M.: Fault attacks on secure embedded software: threats, design, and evaluation. J. Hardware Syst. Secur. **2**(2), 111–130 (2018)

Empirical Abstraction

Vivian M. Ho[1], Chris Alvin[2], Supratik Mukhopadhyay[1(✉)], Brian Peterson[1],
and Jimmie D. Lawson[3]

[1] Department of Computer Sciences, Louisiana State University, Baton Rouge, USA
whe1@lsu.edu, Supratik@csc.lsu.edu
[2] Department of Computer Sciences, Furman University, Greenville, USA
ctalvin@gmail.com
[3] Department of Mathematics, Louisiana State University, Baton Rouge, USA
lawson@math.lsu.edu

Abstract. Given a program analysis problem that consists of a program
and a property of interest, we use an empirical approach to automatically
construct a sequence of abstractions that approach an ideal abstraction
suitable for solving that problem. This process begins with an infinite
concrete domain that maps to a finite abstract cluster domain defined by
statistical procedures. Given a set of properties expressed as formulas in
a restricted and bounded variant of CTL, we can test the success of the
abstraction with respect to a predefined performance measure. In addition, we can perform iterative abstraction-refinement of the clustering
by tuning hyperparameters that determine the accuracy of the cluster
representations (abstract states) and determine the number of clusters.

1 Introduction

Abstract interpretation [7] provides a practical and effective method to verify
properties of both finite and infinite state systems (programs). Classical abstraction frameworks, such as predicate abstraction [13], require the user to input
predicates that enable the creation of a "good" abstraction of the program. This
step necessitates that the user has a thorough understanding of the whole program. However, the author of a program and the person verifying it may be
different; as such, the latter may not be well-versed in the intricacies of the
program. In classical abstraction-based program analysis [7], the behavior of a
program analysis tool is not quantitatively characterized through true positive
rate (TPR) [11], false positive rate (FPR) [11], and the number of abstract states.
There are no "hyperparameters" to tune to obtain "better abstractions" eventually approaching an optimal "operating point" for a given program analysis
problem.

In this paper, we present both a theoretical framework for empirical abstraction and a practical tool for program analysis, using a clustering technique based
on a distance metric that results in an abstract cluster domain. Our technique
applies an empirical, query-guided refinement process, which refines the abstract

© Springer Nature Switzerland AG 2020
J. Deshmukh and D. Ničković (Eds.): RV 2020, LNCS 12399, pp. 259–278, 2020.
https://doi.org/10.1007/978-3-030-60508-7_14

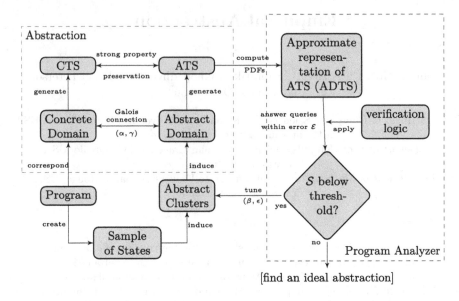

[find an ideal abstraction]

Fig. 1. A flow chart of empirical abstraction process (where CTS means concrete transition system).

model by tuning hyperparameters that in turn results in modification of the abstract cluster domain.

Our empirical abstraction process is composed of the following steps. A flow chart of our empirical abstraction procedure is shown in Fig. 1.

1. The program analysis problem in our case consists of a program P (along with program points of interest) and a query φ_k specified in the verification logic, a restricted variant of CTL that specifies properties over computation trees of bounded depth.

Example 1. Consider a C program in Fig. 2. The program point of interest in this case is "main_A" (highlighted brown in Fig. 2). We want to determine if the verification logic formula $\varphi_k = \mathbf{E}_k \mathbf{X}(\mathbf{E}_{k-1}\mathbf{X}(x > y)), k = 2$, holds true for all states at the program point "main_A". A state, in this case, is represented by the pair (x, y) where $x, y \in [0, 200)$. The property $\varphi_k, (k = 2)$, holds true on a state if, starting from it, it is possible to reach a state in exactly two steps where $x > y$ holds true.

2. The user instruments the program P to sample states occurring at the instrumented program points during the execution of the program. For example, we instrument and execute the program in Fig. 2 to obtain a sample of states occurring at the location "main_A". Other points in the program can be instrumented (not shown in Fig. 2) to generate a sample of states.

3. Given a set of sampled program states, we show the existence of an abstract domain of clusters of states in which states having similar behavior up to a

```
1   int x, y;
2   x = rand() % 200;
3   y = rand() % 200;
4   writeState(locals ,2 ,
5       "main_A");
6   while (true) {
7       x++;
8       y++;
9       if (x >= 200) break;
10      if (y >= 200) break;
11  }
```

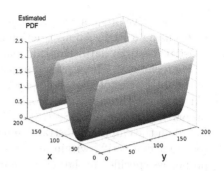

Fig. 2. A simple C program; high-lighted code indicates a program point of interest.

Fig. 3. An estimated PDF for a cluster

certain number of transition steps belong to the "same" cluster. In Example 1, the states $(110, 192)$ and $(5, 42)$ behave similarly for 9-steps starting from program point "main_A". We then establish a Galois connection [7] linking the concrete domain of program states and the abstract domain of clusters.

4. We then provide a procedure for drawing from each cluster a sample of program states (call it a cluster sample) that satisfy a criterion depending on two hyperparameters β and ϵ that modulate the characteristics of the clusters.

5. For each cluster, using the sample of program states drawn above, we estimate a probability density function (PDF) representing the distribution of states corresponding to that cluster. Each cluster can now be implicitly approximated by a PDF. The estimated PDF of a cluster obtained corresponding to the set of states sampled at the program point "main_A" in Fig. 2 is shown in Fig. 3. The clusters form the basis of an abstract transition system (ATS), and the PDFs form the basis of an abstract density transition system (ADTS), approximating the semantics of the program.

6. As mentioned above, queries are specified in the verification logic, a restricted and bounded variant of CTL. The ADTS allows us to answer queries about the program with an error probability $\mathcal{E}$ that depends on the hyperparameters β and ϵ.

7. We define a quantitative performance measure $\mathcal{S}$ for the program analyzer, in terms of TPR, FPR, and the size of ADTS. In case $\mathcal{S}$ falls below a threshold δ, we can refine the abstraction by tuning the hyperparameters β and ϵ towards achieving an optimal operating point for the given program analysis problem.

Our framework is flexible, since users do not need to understand the logic or intricacies of the entire program. Users need only provide program points of interest and specifications to be verified.

Contributions. This paper makes the following contributions:

- It introduces a new paradigm of automated program analysis based on empirical abstraction (Sects. 2 and 4). The key ideas are to treat a concrete program as a generative process and symbolically approximate a possibly infinite set of states using a PDF. An abstraction of the concrete program is automatically constructed from data sampled from the instrumented program using a clustering technique. The abstractions can be created without full understanding of the intricacies of the whole program under analysis.

- It introduces the verification logic, a bounded variant of CTL, for specifying properties of programs (Sect. 3).
- Based on the empirical abstraction framework, we provide a program analysis tool that can verify, within an error probability, if a given program satisfies properties specified in the verification logic. We experimentally show the effectiveness of the tool on a test suite of programs from GNU coreutils, diffutils, and grep (Sect. 5).
- It quantitatively characterizes the behavior of a program analyzer in terms of its true and false positive rates as well as the number of abstract states (Sect. 5).
- The framework allows one to acquire different abstractions by tuning the hyperparameters β and ϵ. This helps quantitative evaluation of the performance of the tool at different abstraction levels. Based on a performance measure, one can determine an "optimal operating point" that serves as an "ideal" abstraction suitable to solve a program analysis problem (Sect. 5).

The proofs of all propositions and theorems, and details of experiments in this paper are provided in [15].

2   Theory

2.1   Program States and Distances

A program $P = (\Sigma, \mathcal{L}, \mathcal{T}, L)$ comprises a set Σ of all program states, a set $\mathcal{L}$ of statement locations, a set $\mathcal{T}$ of transitions where each transition $t \in \mathcal{T}$ is a relation $t \subseteq \Sigma \times \Sigma$, and a proposition labeling function L, mapping each state to a collection of atomic propositions true in that state [7]. A *program state* is a mapping from program variables $\boldsymbol{X}$ to values in the corresponding program domain $\mathcal{D}$. We will denote a program state $\boldsymbol{x} \in \Sigma$ (consisting of ℓ variables) as $\boldsymbol{x} = (x_1, \ldots, x_\ell)$, where $x_j \in \mathbb{R}$ for $1 \leq j \leq \ell$. For states $\boldsymbol{p}, \boldsymbol{q} \in \Sigma$ and a transition $t \in \mathcal{T}$, we say $\boldsymbol{p} \xrightarrow{t} \boldsymbol{q}$ if $(\boldsymbol{p}, \boldsymbol{q}) \in t$.

We now define *bounded bisimilarity* between program states and a distance metric over the program state space, that respects the bisimilarity relation. Let $\overline{\mathbb{N}} = \mathbb{N} \cup \{0, \infty\}$. Let $k \in \overline{\mathbb{N}}$. The idea of $\boldsymbol{p}$ being k-step bisimilar to $\boldsymbol{q}$ is that $\boldsymbol{p}$ can imitate the behaviour of $\boldsymbol{q}$ for up to k steps, and vice versa, and "divergence" takes place in $(k+1)$th step, as shown in Fig. 4 (for simplicity, we consider only one successor of a state for each transition). We say $\boldsymbol{p}$ and $\boldsymbol{q}$ are 0-step bisimilar if $L(\boldsymbol{p}) = L(\boldsymbol{q})$ and they are not 1-step bisimilar. If two program states are k-step bisimilar, they are not s-step bisimilar for any $s \in \overline{\mathbb{N}}$ with $s > k$.

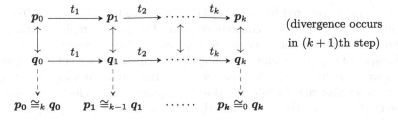

(divergence occurs
in $(k+1)$th step)

Fig. 4. A sequence of program executions

Definition 1 (k-step bisimilarity). *The k-step bisimilarity on Σ is defined to be the largest symmetric relation $\cong_k \subseteq \Sigma \times \Sigma$ such that for any two states $\boldsymbol{p}, \boldsymbol{q} \in \Sigma$, $\boldsymbol{p} \cong_k \boldsymbol{q}$ implies that $L(\boldsymbol{p}) = L(\boldsymbol{q})$, and $k \in \overline{\mathbb{N}}$ is the largest number for which the following hold: (1) for any sequence of transitions of length k, $\boldsymbol{p}_0 \xrightarrow{t_1} \boldsymbol{p}_1 \xrightarrow{t_2} \cdots \xrightarrow{t_k} \boldsymbol{p}_k$ with $\boldsymbol{p}_0 := \boldsymbol{p}$, there exists a sequence of transitions of length k, $\boldsymbol{q}_0 \xrightarrow{t_1} \boldsymbol{q}_1 \xrightarrow{t_2} \cdots \xrightarrow{t_k} \boldsymbol{q}_k$ with $\boldsymbol{q}_0 := \boldsymbol{q}$, such that $\boldsymbol{p}_j \cong_{k-j} \boldsymbol{q}_j$ for each $1 \le j \le k$; and (2) the same as (1) with the roles of $\boldsymbol{p}_j$ and $\boldsymbol{q}_j$ interchanged.*

Given a bounded bisimilarity relation between program states, we would like to construct a clustering which assigns bisimilar (at least k-step bisimilar for some k) pairs of states into the same cluster. Therefore, a good metric needs to respect the k-step bisimilarity relationships between program states, i.e., assign small distances between bounded bisimilar pairs of states.

Definition 2 (Distances between program states). *Let $\boldsymbol{p}, \boldsymbol{q} \in \Sigma$. The distance between program states is a function $d : \Sigma \times \Sigma \to [0,1]$ defined by $d(\boldsymbol{p}, \boldsymbol{q}) = 2^{-k}$, where $k \in \overline{\mathbb{N}}$ is the number such that $\boldsymbol{p}$ and $\boldsymbol{q}$ are k-step bisimilar.*

It is possible that $\boldsymbol{p}$ and $\boldsymbol{q}$ are ∞-bisimilar and thus $d(\boldsymbol{p}, \boldsymbol{q})$ is zero even for $\boldsymbol{p} \ne \boldsymbol{q}$. So the function d defines a pseudometric on the program state space Σ.

2.2   The Concrete and Abstract Domains of a Program

We equip both the set of program states and its power set with partial orders, and use them to define the concrete and abstract domains required for abstract interpretation.

Definition 3 (Concrete domain). *Let P be a program with corresponding space Σ of program states. The concrete domain for P, $\mathcal{C} = (\Sigma, \le)$, is the set Σ of program states equipped with a partial order $\le$ where for two states $\boldsymbol{x} = (x_1, \ldots, x_\ell)$ and $\boldsymbol{y} = (y_1, \ldots, y_\ell)$, $\boldsymbol{x} \le \boldsymbol{y}$ if $x_j \le y_j$ for all $1 \le j \le \ell$.*

We assume the concrete domain is a subset of $\mathbb{R}^\ell$ that forms a *complete lattice*[1] with a supremum $\top_\mathcal{C}$ and an infimum $\bot_\mathcal{C}$. In Example 1, the mentioned

---

[1] The set of extended reals ($\mathbb{R}^\ell \cup \{\top, \bot\}$ where for all $x \in \mathbb{R}^\ell$, $\bot < x < \top$) with the usual ordering is a complete lattice. This case also works for our framework.

two elements are ordered by $(5, 42) < (110, 192)$. We have $\Sigma = ([0, 200) \cap \mathbb{Z}) \times ([0, 200) \cap \mathbb{Z}) \subseteq \mathbb{R}^2$, and this concrete domain $(\Sigma, \leq)$ is a complete lattice.

Our proposed empirical technique depends on the concept of a cluster, a well-known concept in machine learning. Our technique does not learn clusters from a set of points in the traditional sense. Instead we iteratively construct clusters in an abstract domain based on *root* points. Each cluster consists of a downset[2] of the root. We shall define the abstract domain for a program P as a set of clusters.

Definition 4 (Abstract cluster rooted at a point). *Let $p \in \mathcal{C}$. The abstract cluster rooted at p is the downset $B_p = \downarrow p := \{q \in \mathcal{C} \mid q \leq p\}$.*

The root of a cluster uniquely determines the cluster. When the context is clear, we will refer to a cluster without specifying its root. Next, we establish a hierarchy among all clusters in a domain, and define the abstract domain as the set of all clusters rooted at points in the concrete domain.

Lemma 1. *For root points $p, q \in \mathcal{C}$ we have $q \leq p$ if and only if $B_q \subseteq B_p$.*

Definition 5 (Abstract domain). *For a program P with concrete domain $\mathcal{C} = (\Sigma, \leq)$, let $\mathcal{P} = \{B_p \mid p \in \mathcal{C}\} \subseteq 2^\Sigma$ where for $p \in \Sigma$, B_p is the cluster rooted at p. The abstract domain $\mathcal{A} = (\mathcal{P}, \subseteq)$ is defined to be the set $\mathcal{P}$ of clusters, partially ordered by inclusion $\subseteq$.*

Lemma 2. *The abstract domain $\mathcal{A}$ defines a complete lattice.*

2.3 Mappings and the Abstract Transition System

We begin by defining the abstraction mapping to take a state in the concrete domain and map it to the cluster corresponding to the closest root above it. We assume a finite set of n root points $\{r_1, \ldots, r_n\}$ with $r_i \in \Sigma$. We assume that $d(r_i, r_j) \geq \epsilon$ for $i \neq j$, where ϵ is a hyperparameter. In Sect. 4, we will show how these root points can be sampled from Σ satisfying this constraint.

Definition 6 (Abstraction Mapping). *Let P be a program with corresponding space Σ of program states. Let $\mathcal{C}$ be the concrete domain for P, and $\mathcal{A}$ the abstract domain with $C_1, \ldots, C_n$ the n clusters of $\mathcal{A}$, each with unique respective root $r_1, \ldots, r_n$.*

The abstraction mapping $\alpha : \mathcal{C} \to \mathcal{A}$ is defined by $\alpha(p) = C_i$, $p \in \mathcal{C}$, where C_i (for some $1 \leq i \leq n$) is determined such that (1) $p \leq r_i$ and (2) if $p \leq r_j$ then $d(p, r_i) \leq d(p, r_j)$ for all $j \neq i$ with ties broken arbitrarily.

Definition 6 maps a state p in the concrete domain to the cluster in abstract domain $\mathcal{A}$ whose root is greater than or equal to p and is closer to p than any other root. In particular, $\alpha(p)$ identifies the element in $\mathcal{A}$ that most precisely represents the state p.

---

[2] Let $(X, \leq)$ be a poset and $A \subseteq X$. Then A is a *downset* of X if $x \in X$, $x \leq y$, $y \in A$ implies $x \in A$.

Since a cluster is defined by a root point, we have a natural definition of a concretization mapping from a cluster in the abstract domain to a state in the concrete domain; specifically, a cluster is mapped to its root in the concrete domain.

Definition 7 (Concretization Mapping). *Let $B_p \in \mathcal{A}$ be a cluster rooted at a state $p \in \mathcal{C}$. The concretization mapping $\gamma : \mathcal{A} \to \mathcal{C}$ is defined by $\gamma(B_p) = p$.*

The following result ensures that (α, γ) is a Galois connection [22].

Proposition 1. *The maps α and γ in Definitions 6 and 7 satisfy a Galois connection: $p \leq \gamma(\alpha(p))$ and $\alpha(\gamma(A)) \subseteq A$ for any $p \in \mathcal{C}$ and $A \in \mathcal{A}$.*

Definition 8 (Abstract Transitions). *For each transition $t \subseteq \Sigma \times \Sigma$, we create an abstract transition $t^\# \subseteq \mathcal{P} \times \mathcal{P}$ such that $t^\# = \alpha \circ t \circ \gamma$.*

In abstraction-based verification, we would like to construct an abstraction that *strongly preserves* properties, i.e., a property holds on the abstract domain if and only if it holds on the concrete domain. In this case, the abstract transition $t^\#$ is a *sound and complete* approximation for the concrete transition t (see Theorem 2).

Definition 9 (Concrete and Abstract Transition System). *A (concrete) transition system (CTS) is a pair $(\mathcal{C}, \mathcal{T})$, with $\mathcal{C}$ being the concrete domain, and $\mathcal{T}$ being the collection of transitions $t \subseteq \Sigma \times \Sigma$. Similarly, the abstract transition system is defined as $(\mathcal{A}, \mathcal{T}^\#)$, with $\mathcal{A}$ being the abstract domain, and $\mathcal{T}^\#$ being the set of abstract transitions on $\mathcal{P} \times \mathcal{P}$.*

3 Verification Logic

We define a logic CTL_k, a bounded fragment of the standard computation tree logic [10] that expresses properties that hold true over sequences of transitions of length k with $k \in \overline{\mathbb{N}}$:

$$\varphi_k ::= ap \mid \neg\varphi_k \mid \varphi_k^1 \vee \varphi_k^2 \mid \mathbf{E}_k \mathbf{X}(\varphi_{k-1}) \mid \mathbf{E}_k \mathbf{G}(ap) \mid \mathbf{E}_k(ap_1 \ \mathbf{U} \ ap_2) \quad (3.1)$$

where ap is an atomic proposition. Setting $k = \infty$, we get full CTL from CTL_k. Restriction to a finite k allows respecting k-bisimilarity (as shown below) which in turn is tied to the distance pseudometric d that will be used for clustering. We naturally express bounded temporal properties of a program by the CTL_k logic. We show the correspondence between the behavioral equivalence defined by k-bisimilarity between states and the logical equivalence induced by CTL_k logic.

Theorem 1. *Let $p, q \in \Sigma$ and $k \in \overline{\mathbb{N}}$. Then the following are equivalent: (1) $p \cong_k q$; and (2) For all CTL_k formulas φ_k, $p \models \varphi_k$ if and only if $q \models \varphi_k$.*

The following theorem relates the concrete transition system and the abstract transition system with respect to verification of CTL_k properties.

Theorem 2. *For a concrete transition system $(\mathcal{C}, \mathcal{T})$ where $\mathcal{C} = (\Sigma, \leq)$, $\boldsymbol{p} \in \Sigma$, a corresponding abstract transition system $(\mathcal{A}, \mathcal{T}^{\#})$ where $\mathcal{A} = (\mathcal{P}, \subseteq)$, and a CTL_k formula φ_k, if $d(\boldsymbol{p}, \gamma(\alpha(\boldsymbol{p}))) \leq 2^{-k}$ then $(\mathcal{C}, \mathcal{T}), \boldsymbol{p} \models \varphi_k$ if and only if $(\mathcal{A}, \mathcal{T}^{\#}), \alpha(\boldsymbol{p}) \models \varphi_k$.*

Based on Theorem 2, to verify $(\mathcal{C}, \mathcal{T}), \boldsymbol{p} \models \varphi_k$, where $\mathcal{C} = (\Sigma, \leq)$, $\boldsymbol{p} \in \Sigma$, one needs to use the abstraction map α to determine the abstract cluster $\alpha(\boldsymbol{p})$ corresponding to $\boldsymbol{p}$, and if $d(\boldsymbol{p}, \gamma(\alpha(\boldsymbol{p}))) \leq 2^{-k}$ then we verify $(\mathcal{A}, \mathcal{T}^{\#}), \alpha(\boldsymbol{p}) \models \varphi_k$ on the abstract transition system. However, computing $\alpha(\boldsymbol{p})$ requires comparing among $d(\boldsymbol{p}, \boldsymbol{r})$ for each root $\boldsymbol{r} \geq \boldsymbol{p}$; this may be computationally expensive.

We will use an approach where each cluster C_i will be approximately represented by a *probability density function* (PDF) that determines the probability that C_i is the abstract cluster corresponding to a set of states $U \subseteq \Sigma$. To verify $(\mathcal{C}, \mathcal{T}), \boldsymbol{p} \models \varphi_k$, one needs to check if $(\mathcal{C}, \mathcal{T}), U \models \varphi_k$ where $U \subseteq \Sigma$ is a neighborhood of $\boldsymbol{p}$ and $(\mathcal{C}, \mathcal{T}), U \models \varphi_k$ if and only if for all $\boldsymbol{u} \in U$, $(\mathcal{C}, \mathcal{T}), \boldsymbol{u} \models \varphi_k$.

For a state $\boldsymbol{p} \in \Sigma$, if $\alpha(\boldsymbol{p}) = C_i$, then the root $\boldsymbol{r}_i$ is closest to $\boldsymbol{p}$ among all root points $\boldsymbol{r} \geq \boldsymbol{p}$. The probability density function approximately representing C_i will provide a measure of the closeness of a set U of states to the root $\boldsymbol{r}_i$ of C_i. An abstract cluster C_i will correspond to a set of states $U \subseteq \Sigma$ if the probability of its closeness to the root $\boldsymbol{r}_i$ is greater than that of its closeness to all other roots $\boldsymbol{r}$ (ties broken arbitrarily). Let $\mathcal{F}$ be the set of all PDFs f_C corresponding to $C \in \mathcal{A}$.

Probability density functions can be estimated using a kernel density estimation procedure [28]. We use Gaussian kernels to estimate the desired PDFs in the implementation (see Sect. 5).

4   Algorithms for Program Analysis

Sampling for Cluster Roots. We assume a program P with the corresponding state space Σ. To induce the clusters in the abstract domain, we first sample program states as root points of clusters. Specifically, we construct a *net* N from the program state space Σ such that if $\boldsymbol{p}$ and $\boldsymbol{q}$ are in N, then $d(\boldsymbol{p}, \boldsymbol{q}) \geq \epsilon$ where ϵ is a hyperparameter. The size of N, $n = |N|$, is finite (we will estimate n in Sect. 4.2). Each state in N will be the root of a cluster. Each state in the net must be at least a distance of ϵ away from all other states in the net so that root points are "spread out" enough, and the resulting clusters rooted at these root points can cover the concrete domain (see Lemma 4).

Lemma 3. *Let $E_n[X]$ be the expectation of the number X of trials needed to get n root points. There exists a constant χ, where $0 \leq \chi \leq \frac{1}{\epsilon}$, such that $E_n[X] = n \cdot (1 - \chi\epsilon)^{n(1-n)/2}$.*

4.1   Inducing the Abstract Domain

Assuming a finite net of the concrete state space, $N \subseteq \Sigma$, we construct a (sampling) abstract domain. For each $\boldsymbol{r} \in N$, we construct a cluster rooted at $\boldsymbol{r}$. Recall that the concrete domain $\mathcal{C}$ has the supremum element $\top_{\mathcal{C}}$.

Lemma 4 (Finite Coverage of Concrete Domain). *For a program P with the program state space Σ, a finite sample $N \subseteq \Sigma$ will induce a set of clusters $\mathcal{C}_N = B_{\top_c} \cup \left(\bigcup_{r \in N} B_r \right)$ that is a finite cover of the concrete domain $\mathcal{C}$.*

It is natural to define a (sampling) abstract domain to be $\mathcal{A} := \mathcal{C}_N$.

Sampling for Clusters. To approximate a probability density function that can be used to estimate for each abstract cluster C_i with root r_i, the likelihood that for a state p, $\alpha(p) = C_i$, we need to draw a finite sample for each cluster that is an approximate representation of states p such that $\alpha(p) = C_i$ (we call this sample the cluster sample for C_i). Observe that if $p \leq r_i$ and $d(p, r_i) < \epsilon/2$ then $\alpha(p) = C_i$ (by triangle inequality). For a state $p \leq r_i$ such that $\epsilon/2 \leq d(p, r_i) \leq 1$, it is possible that $\alpha(p) = C_i$ with likelihood increasing with closeness to r_i.

We form n cluster samples (for the n clusters) from the program state space Σ such that (1) each cluster sample contains m program states (m can be pre-specified; we assume $m \geq 30$ for statistical significance); and (2) if r is the root point of a cluster and x is any state in the cluster sample, then

$$d(r, x) \leq \beta, \quad \text{and} \quad x \leq r \tag{4.1}$$

where β is a hyperparameter determining the accuracy of the sample.

Algorithm *BuildCluster*(Σ, r, β) (cf. Algorithm 2 in [15]) is based on the condition (4.1), that acquires a cluster sample of program states. Choosing an appropriate value for β depends on the coarseness of the desired abstraction.

4.2 Estimate the Number of Clusters

We introduce Algorithm 1 to determine the number n of clusters constructed from observed data, using a stopping criterion. We fix a level of significance $\nu \in (0, 1]$ to indicate the fraction of unclustered program states. The basic idea is to make the probability of unclustered program states (i.e., states for which equation (4.1) does not hold true for any of these n clusters) less than or equal to the level of significance ν. The following proposition gives an upper bound for the expected number n of clusters.

Proposition 2. *An upper bound for the expected number n of clusters is given by $E[n] = \log \nu - \log \varpi$, $\varpi := 2 - (c + \chi_1 \beta) - c\chi_1 \beta$, where $\chi_1 \in [0, \frac{1}{\beta}]$, and c is the probability of a state being less than or equal to a root point.*

Proposition 3 (Correctness of Algorithm 1). *The following hold true for Algorithm 1: (1) It determines the number n of clusters (this is also the number of root points) and generates n cluster samples; (2) Each state in a cluster sample is within β-distance from the root point of the cluster; and (3) Any two root points of clusters are at least ϵ-distance away from each other.*

Proposition 4 (Upper Bound on the Expected Runtime of Algorithm 1). *Without loss of generality, we assume that each cluster sample has the same size. The expected run time of Algorithm 1 is upper bounded by*

Algorithm 1. Determine the Number of Clusters

1: **procedure** $NOC(\Sigma, \beta, \epsilon, \nu)$
2:    $i \leftarrow 1, N \leftarrow \emptyset$
3:    $\boldsymbol{p}_i \leftarrow choose(\Sigma), N \leftarrow N \cup \{\boldsymbol{p}_i\}$
4:    $S_i \leftarrow BuildCluster(\Sigma, \boldsymbol{p}_i, \beta)$ ▷ S_i: cluster samples
5:    **while** $\varpi^i > \nu$ **do**
6:        $i \leftarrow i + 1$
7:        **repeat**
8:            $\boldsymbol{p}_i \leftarrow choose(\Sigma \setminus (S_1 \cup \cdots \cup S_{i-1}))$
9:            $\min \leftarrow d(\boldsymbol{p}_i, \boldsymbol{p}_1)$
10:           **for all** $j = 2 : (i - 1)$ **do**
11:               **if** $d(\boldsymbol{p}_i, \boldsymbol{p}_j) < \min$ **then** $\min \leftarrow d(\boldsymbol{p}_i, \boldsymbol{p}_j)$
12:           **until** $\min \geq \epsilon$
13:           $N \leftarrow N \cup \{\boldsymbol{p}_i\}$
14:           $S_i \leftarrow BuildCluster(\Sigma, \boldsymbol{p}_i, \beta)$
        return $\langle i, N \rangle$

$$\frac{\Gamma}{(1 - \chi\epsilon)^{\Gamma(\Gamma-1)/2}} + \frac{m\Gamma}{c\chi_1\beta}, \ \Gamma := \log\left(\frac{\nu}{\varpi}\right)$$

where c, χ_1 and ϖ are the same as in Proposition 2, and χ is the same as in Lemma 3.

4.3   Abstract Density Map and Abstract Density Transition System

For each cluster C_i corresponding to root $\boldsymbol{r}_i \in N$, we estimate a PDF f_{C_i} from its cluster sample. This f_{C_i} provides an approximate representation of C_i. We define an abstract density map η mapping $U \subseteq \Sigma$ to the PDF f_{C_i} for $C_i \in \mathcal{A}$ if $\int_U f_{C_i}(\boldsymbol{x})d\boldsymbol{x} \geq \int_U f_{C_j}(\boldsymbol{x})d\boldsymbol{x}$ for all j (ties broken arbitrarily). For instance, in Example 1, the abstract density map assigns to the (neighborhood of the) state $\boldsymbol{p} = (12, 139)$ at program point "main_A" in Fig. 2 the PDF shown in Fig. 3. Based on the abstract density map, we define an abstract density transition system (ADTS) as follows.

Definition 10 (ADTS). *For each abstract transition* $t^\# \in \mathcal{T}^\#$, *we define an abstract density transition* $\theta^\# \subseteq \mathcal{F} \times \mathcal{F}$ *such that* $(f_{C_i}, f_{C_j}) \in \theta^\#$ *if and only if* $(C_i, C_j) \in t^\#$. *Let* $\Theta^\#$ *be the set of all abstract density transitions. The abstract density transition system (ADTS) is defined to be the pair* $(\mathcal{F}, \Theta^\#)$.

To verify $(\mathcal{C}, \mathcal{T}), U \models \varphi_k$, we verify if $(\mathcal{F}, \Theta^\#), \eta(U) \models \varphi_k$. The ADTS $(\mathcal{F}, \Theta^\#)$ and $(\mathcal{C}, \mathcal{T})$ are related by the following theorem.

Theorem 3. *For a program* P *with the state space* Σ *and* $U \subseteq \Sigma$, *and a* CTL_k *formula* φ_k, *if* $\eta(U) = f_C \in \mathcal{F}$ *and* $f_C \models \varphi_k$ *in the density transition system, then in the concrete program* $P, U \models \varphi_k$ *with an error probability* $\mathcal{E}$ *upper bounded by* $1 - (c'\epsilon)/2^{k+1}$, *where* $c' \in [0, \frac{2^{k+1}}{\epsilon}]$ *is a constant.*

4.4   Abstraction and Refinement

For a program together with a set of properties that it is supposed to satisfy, our approach generates an abstraction on which we verify properties. The associated abstract density transition system allows us to answer queries about the program within an error probability $\mathcal{E}$.

Performance Evaluation. We can compare the verification results obtained based on the ADTS with ground truth, and can classify them into the following types: true positives (TP), false positives (FP), true negatives (TN), and false negatives (FN) [11]. The estimated probability of error for the program analyzer at an abstraction level is computed by $\mathcal{E} = \frac{FP+FN}{TP+FT+TN+FN}$ [11].

We present a way to offer a viable performance measure for the empirical abstraction framework. The performance measure is defined by a weighted sum of true positive rate (TPR) [11] and false positive rate (FPR) [11], and the number n of clusters:

$$\mathcal{S} := w_1 \log_2(TPR + 1) - w_2 \log_2(FPR + 1) - w_3 \log_2(n) \qquad (4.2)$$

where $TPR = \frac{TP}{TP+FN}$ [11], $FPR = \frac{FP}{FP+TN}$ [11], and w_i's ($i = 1, 2, 3$) are weighting factors in $[0, 1]$ that determine the relative strength of TPR, FPR, and the number n of clusters, respectively. We can change these parameters to control the relative importance of each term. A high value of w_1 and a low value of w_2 will reward an abstraction that achieves a high TPR at the cost of a high FPR. On the other hand, a high value of w_1 and a high value of w_2 will reward an abstraction that has a low FPR even at the cost of a reduced TPR. A high value of w_3 will penalize those abstractions with a large number of abstract states (for computational inefficiency). A good choice can be to assign high values to w_1, w_2, and w_3. The choices of these three factors are independent.

An abstraction enables ideal performances when it has high TPR, low FPR, and relatively small number n of clusters (for computational efficiency). We observe the relation between these three terms and the hyperparameter β, and create an evaluation curve by plotting the weighted sum $\mathcal{S}$ against the (modified) hyperparameter $\log_2 \beta$. This curve illustrates the variation in performance of the program analyzer created based on the empirical abstraction framework as its discrimination hyperparameter is varied.

Refinement. We compute $\mathcal{S}$ for an abstraction generated by our method using (4.2). If the value of $\mathcal{S}$ is below a threshold δ, we vary β and the least distance ϵ between cluster root points to generate distinct levels of abstractions, on which we can again answer queries. Based on the computation of the quantitative measure $\mathcal{S}$, we may iteratively repeat this process until $\mathcal{S}$ reaches a stable and optimal value: an ideal abstraction for the given program analysis problem then occurs. The iterative process of varying the hyperparameters while searching for an optimal operating point can be automated. More details on how the hyperparameters β and ϵ are varied can be found in Sect. 5.

Cross Validation. To understand whether the performance provided by the empirical abstraction framework will generalize to other program analysis problems for the same program, we perform Monte Carlo cross validation (MCCV). We randomly partition the set of concrete states sampled from a program point of interest (instrumented) into two sets, the first of which is used to compute abstractions (called the *abstraction set*) while the second is used to validate their performance (we call the latter the *validation set*). For the validation set, we obtain the ground truth by evaluating the property of interest on concrete states in it. We vary the hyperparameters β and ϵ and iteratively compute a sequence of abstractions (ADTS) from the abstraction set. The validation set is used to compute the performance provided by these abstractions and an optimal operating point is determined. This procedure is repeated κ times, randomly partitioning the set of concrete states sampled from a program point of interest into an abstraction set and a validation set and the average performance measure for the optimal operating points determined in these iterations is computed; κ is user-defined.

Revisiting Example 1. For the property $\varphi_k, k = 2$ in Example 1, we observe that when $\beta \approx 2^{-44}$ and $\epsilon \approx 2^{-43}$, the corresponding abstraction obtained the performance measure $\mathcal{S} = 0.6613$ and the error probability $\mathcal{E} = 0.146$, that gives an optimal operating point of our empirical abstraction approach for the given program analysis problem.

5   Experimental Evaluation

Our experiments were executed on a desktop running Ubuntu Linux 4.4.0-53. For details of the program instrumentation framework, we refer the reader to Appendix in [15]. We present the verification results obtained by using the empirical abstraction framework on a test suite of C programs mostly selected from the open-source GNU coreutils, diffutils, and grep: base64, cat, cmp, comm, cp, csplit, dd, diff, du, fmt, fold, grep, truncate, and wc.

Benchmark Selection. Programs were selected for instrumentation if they fulfilled several criteria. Programs that utilized generic text file input were selected, as we can vary the input easily by simply providing a variety of input files, generated from dictionary data. We picked programs that were intended to take command line input and run to completion with no user input during execution. Therefore, we are able to run each instrumented program many times with little difficulty.

Generate Sample Data. We chose to instrument programs manually in this paper. But users may use available automated instrumentation tools to instrument programs, for example, one based on CIL [6] or LLVM [18].

   To instrument a program, one needs to save the states of variables, and the sequence of statements executed for one execution of the program. Then one would develop a set of input arguments to run the program, and properties that vary over those input arguments.

Within an instrumented program, we record two types of information. The first is the states of certain variables, global and local, in a set of meaningful code locations[3] of the program, for a variety of inputs. The first data set enables comparing the actual variable values at particular locations. The second is the sequential set of statements that were actually executed in a run. The second data set, which we will call the traces, allows us to compare any two sequences of executions across any of our runs and determine bisimilarity (we call the resulting values *bisimilarity data*).

For our experiments we require data on variable values throughout the execution of a program. To gather this data we have instrumented the above mentioned programs in the test suite.

Clustering Data. We next cluster the trace data based on the hyperparameter β, which determines the quality of the abstraction, according to the clustering algorithm (Algorithm 1). Kernel density estimation (with Gaussian kernel, bandwidth $= 0.15$) is used to estimate PDFs to approximately represent the abstract clusters. Suppose we are going to verify a property φ_k for a fixed $k \in \overline{\mathbb{N}}$. We set $\beta = 1/2^{\overline{k}}$ and $\epsilon \geq 2\beta$ (to guarantee clusters do not mutually overlap), and tune these hyperparameters (by varying $\overline{k}$ and ϵ) until the quality of the abstraction is satisfactory. While tuning, we would like to achieve a trade-off between the quality of the abstraction and the number of clusters which affect computational efficiency.

Verify Properties. Properties of interest are specified as CTL_k formulas. Atomic propositions are boolean formulas on the values of variables from the instrumented program. At each location in a program's execution at which we record the variable values, we can also calculate the truth value of the atomic propositions based on those variable values.

Obtain an optimal operating point. Recall that we cluster the trace data (with hyperparameters $\beta = 2^{-\overline{k}}$ and $\epsilon \geq 2\beta$), and then use the resulting ADTS to verify a given property φ_k. This abstraction may be too rough to verify φ_k, for example, there may be an unacceptable number of false positives. We then perform abstraction refinement by tuning the hyperparameters β and ϵ to generate a new abstraction. We may repeat the process until the abstraction can verify the properties accurately or within an acceptable error probability. At that point, the abstraction obtained is an ideal one with respect to a given program analysis problem.

To generate an ideal abstraction, we would like to determine optimal values for the hyperparameters β and ϵ that determine the quality of the abstraction. This amounts to tuning the values of $\overline{k}$ and $\epsilon \geq 2 \cdot 2^{-\overline{k}}$ until the performance measure $\mathcal{S}$ cannot be significantly improved. This is the point where the values of the hyperparameters β and ϵ reach an optimal value (and thus provide an optimal operating point of the program analyzer).

---

[3] A meaningful code location refers to a statement that has a side-effect.

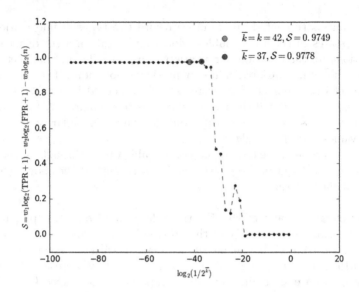

Fig. 5. Performance evaluation on *cat*: $w_1 = w_2 = 1$, $w_3 = 0.005$ (Color figure online)

Table 1. Statistical results for program *cat* at location main_EH

$\overline{k}$	n	φ_k ($k = 42$)			$\mathcal{S}$	Execution time (in sec)
		TPR	FPR	$\mathcal{E}$		
1	1	0.2	0.2	0.2938	−0.005	0.3477
19	3	0	0	0.1597	−0.01	0.3572
25	4	0.2	0.0968	0.2046	0.118	0.3645
29	6	0.4667	0.0606	0.138	0.454	0.3751
31	9	0.5	0.0629	0.1287	0.48	0.3962
33	14	1.0	0.0257	0.0217	0.944	0.4327
37	22	1.0	0	0	0.978	0.5018
39	27	1.0	0	0	0.976	0.5516
42	32	1.0	0	0	0.975	0.6225
49	39	1.0	0	0	0.973	0.6837
59	39	1.0	0	0	0.973	0.6861
69	39	1.0	0	0	0.973	0.6890
79	39	1.0	0	0	0.973	0.7041
89	39	1.0	0	0	0.973	0.7223

Example. The following is one of our experimental results taken for the program `cat.c`. The sample data was drawn at a chosen location main_EH in the instrumented `cat.c` program. Suppose we want to verify a property

Table 2. Statistical results for observed benchmark programs

Program	Point of interest	n	Verify property					Optimal $\overline{k}$	Optimal $\mathcal{S}$
			φ_k	k	TPR	FPR	$\mathcal{E}$		
base64	main_AO	3	(5.2)	12	1.0	0	0	8	0.9920
cat	main_AS	22	(5.3)	19	1.0	0	0	36	0.9778
cmp	main_J	5	(5.4)	18	0.81	0.03	0.1	50	0.8029
comm	main_AE	14	(5.5)	50	0.90	0.16	0.1158	43	0.6937
cp	main_BD	10	(5.6)	4	1.0	0.06	0.0519	3	0.9001
csplit	main_Q	4	(5.7)	88	0.8	0	0.0449	89	0.8379
dd	main_ABG	16	(5.8)	7	1.0	0.06	0.0273	28	0.8899
diff	main_DL	11	(5.9)	53	0.79	0.21	0.2135	101	0.5492
du	main_S	45	(5.10)	2	0.98	0.12	0.0676	44	0.7906
fmt	main_R	9	(5.11)	4	1.0	0	0	4	0.9841
fold	main_AB	11	(5.12)	13	0.91	0.04	0.0629	41	0.8676
grep	main_CO	5	(5.13)	63	1.0	0	0	63	0.9883
truncate	main_BF	4	(5.14)	3	1.0	0	0	3	0.99
wc	main_EU	4	(5.15)	19	0.66	0	0.0496	20	0.7217

$$\varphi_k = \mathbf{E}_k \mathbf{F}(\text{show\_ends} = T), \ k = 42 \tag{5.1}$$

where show_ends is a boolean variable in the program cat.c. The property φ_k ($k = 42$) holds true on a state if a path of length 42 starting from that state exists such that show_ends=true at some state in that path.

Figure 5 provides quantitative evaluations for the performance of the program analyzer on a set of program states (called the validation set; each state corresponding to a neighborhood around itself) for different abstractions used to verify the property (5.1), along with an optimal operating point. For each abstraction, we compute a performance measure $\mathcal{S}$ after applying Monte Carlo Cross Validation (MCCV) on the sample data. Figure 5 describes a plot of $\mathcal{S}$ values for the different abstractions with respect to β on a log scale. Table 1 describes statistics about the performance of the program analyzer for different abstractions. The column $\mathcal{E}$ (both in Tables 1 and 2) shows the estimated probability of error for the program analyzer at a particular abstraction level. We notice two important things:

(1) an optimal $\overline{k}$ value (we set $\epsilon = 2(2^{-\overline{k}})$ for this experiment) for which the value of the performance measure $\mathcal{S}$ reaches its maximum (highlighted by blue bullet) and
(2) the value of the performance measure $\mathcal{S}$ for the case $\overline{k} = 42$ (highlighted by red bullet).

It can be seen from Fig. 5 and the statistical result in Table 1, that the performance of the abstraction ($\mathcal{S} = 0.9778$) is optimal when $\overline{k} = 37$ (with true positive rate of 1 and false positive rate of 0; see Fig. 5 for the values of the

Table 3. Properties chosen for verification on observed programs

Program	base64
Property	$\mathbf{E}_k\mathbf{F}(\text{ignore\_garbage} = T \land \text{decode} = T)$ (5.2)

Program	cat
Property	$\mathbf{E}_k\mathbf{F}(\text{show\_ends} = T)$ (5.3)

Program	cmp
Property	$\mathbf{E}_k\mathbf{X}^k(\text{opt\_print\_bytes} = T)$ (5.4)

Program	comm
Property	$\mathbf{E}_k\mathbf{X}^k((\text{both} = T) \lor (\text{only\_file\_2} = F))$ (5.5)

Program	cp
Property	$\mathbf{E}_k\mathbf{X}^k((\text{no\_target\_directory} = T) \lor (\text{copy\_contents} = T))$ (5.6)

Program	csplit
Property	$\mathbf{A}_k\mathbf{G}((\text{remove\_files} = T) \lor (\text{elide\_empty\_files} = T))$ (5.7)

Program	dd
Property	$\mathbf{E}_k\mathbf{X}^k((\text{w\_partial} = F) \land (\text{w\_full} = F))$ (5.8)

Program	diff
Property	$\mathbf{E}_k\mathbf{F}(\text{new\_file} = T)$ (5.9)

Program	du
Property	$\mathbf{A}_k\mathbf{G}((\text{hash\_all} = F) \land (\text{human\_output\_opts} = F))$ (5.10)

Program	fmt
Property	$\mathbf{E}_k\mathbf{X}^k((\text{crown} = T) \land (\text{tagged} = T))$ (5.11)

Program	fold
Property	$\mathbf{E}_k\mathbf{X}^k(\text{break\_spaces} = T)$ (5.12)

Program	grep
Property	$\mathbf{E}_k\mathbf{F}((\text{out\_invert} = T) \land (\text{suppress\_errors} = F))$ (5.13)

Program	truncate
Property	$\mathbf{E}_k\mathbf{F}((\text{got\_size} = T) \land (\text{errors} = F))$ (5.14)

Program	wc
Property	$\mathbf{A}_k\mathbf{G}((\text{print\_chars} = F) \land (\text{print\_lines} = F))$ (5.15)

parameters w_1, w_2, and w_3). For $\overline{k} = 42$ (this is the k-value corresponding to the one in equation (5.1)), the value of $\mathcal{S}$ reduces slightly to 0.9749, and reduces to 0.973 for $\overline{k} > 42$ and stabilizes to that value while the execution time keeps increasing. The value $\overline{k} = 37$ provides the optimal operating point (highlighted by blue bullet) among all observed abstractions.

We also demonstrate empirically that even when we increased $\overline{k}$ to 90 or further, both the ratio of TPR and FPR, and the number of generated clusters did not have a significant improvement anymore. The performance of the constructed abstraction stabilized after the hyperparameter β passed a critical point (in this example, the critical point occurred at $\overline{k} = 37$).

Last, we present in Table 2 the statistical results of the empirical abstraction approach applied to the chosen benchmark programs. The values for the column φ_k in Table 2 refer to properties of interest for that verification effort listed in Table 3. Each row in Table 2 provides results obtained for the abstraction corresponding to the optimal operating point for the analysis problem for a benchmark program.

6 Related Work

Sharma et al. [26] theoretically quantified the precision of an abstraction using Vapnik-Chervonenkis dimension [4]. They used trade-offs between bias and variance to understand how the performance of a program analyzer varies across different abstractions. In contrast, our empirical abstraction framework quantifies the performance of a program analyzer using a particular abstraction in terms of TPR, FPR, and the number of abstract states. It uses this quantification to determine an optimal operating point for a given program analysis problem. There has been some research on generating [12, 23–25], pre-conditions and invariants from source code using an empirical approach. There has been some research on generating [12, 23], pre-conditions and invariants from source code using an empirical approach.

In [21], the authors presented the Yogi program analyzer that combines static analysis and testing to for verifying C programs.

Yogi [21] uses Synergy [14], defines an algorithm that combines a procedure for finding bugs with a procedure for proof search.

Zhang et al. [30] used a counter-example guided query-driven analysis that performs iterative refinement to identify the cheapest abstraction (minimal set of parameters) or prove that no such abstraction can prove the query. In contrast, our technique is empirical that refines abstractions by tuning hyperparameters.

Liang et al. [17] use machine learning techniques to determine the coarsest possible abstraction needed to answer a set of points-to analysis queries. In contrast, our framework uses an empirical approach to obtain an optimal operating point (abstraction) for a given program analysis problem.

Chen et al. [5] provided a PAC learning-based framework for creating a model abstracting a program. In contrast, our framework uses an empirical approach to obtain an ideal abstraction suitable for solving a program analysis problem.

In [3], the authors provide an automatic technique that infers a static analyzer, from a dataset containing programs, approximating their behavior. In contrast, our approach uses states sampled from an instrumented program to approximate its semantics. In [2], the authors presented a generative model for programs. We approximate the semantics of a program using an empirical approach. In [16], the authors present a framework for learning disjunctive predicates to distinguish between positive and negative examples drawn from a concrete domain.

Probabilistic abstract interpretation [8, 19, 27] assumes that the distribution of a program is known, while our approach uses a nonparametric density estimation technique to approximately represent abstract states.

In [9], the authors used the Skorokhod metric for conformance checking for dynamical systems. The pseudo-metric d in this paper is designed to respect bounded bisimilarity between states.

7   Conclusions

This paper presents an empirical abstraction framework and experimental evidence demonstrating its practicality for program analysis.

Given a program and a property, the aim is to find a "good" abstraction that derive an accurate yet efficient program analysis to verify the property. We compute abstractions from concrete states of program executions without the full knowledge of the program. An abstract cluster is given by a set of program states such that any two states in the same cluster have certain step bisimilarity to each other. The coarseness of an abstraction can be controlled by parameterizing how concrete states are clustered into abstract states. Abstract states (possibly infinite sets of states) are approximated by probability density functions. At a given level of abstraction, the property can be verified by the resulting abstract densities. The performance of the abstraction is quantified by a measure in terms of true and false positives and a regularization for computation efficiency. We perform iterative query-guided refinements of the clustering in order to maximize that measure and eventually generate an ideal abstraction with minimal manual intervention.

While the framework relies on sampling program states for constructing abstractions, there is no underlying assumption regarding any particular distribution on the program state space from which the states are sampled. Moreover, we apply a cross validation technique on sampling data of program states, to assure the performance provided by the empirical abstraction framework can generalize to other program analysis problems for the same program.

Future work includes application of the framework for analysis of timed systems [20] and object/service oriented systems [1, 29].

References

1. Alvin, C., Peterson, B., Mukhopadhyay, S.: *StaticGen*: static generation of UML sequence diagrams. In: Huisman, M., Rubin, J. (eds.) FASE 2017. LNCS, vol. 10202, pp. 173–190. Springer, Heidelberg (2017). https://doi.org/10.1007/978-3-662-54494-5_10
2. Bielik, P., Raychev, V., Vechev, M.T.: PHOG: probabilistic model for code. In: Proceedings of the 33nd International Conference on Machine Learning, ICML 2016, New York City, NY, USA, 19–24 June 2016, pp. 2933–2942 (2016)
3. Bielik, P., Raychev, V., Vechev, M.: Learning a static analyzer from data. In: Majumdar, R., Kunčak, V. (eds.) CAV 2017. LNCS, vol. 10426, pp. 233–253. Springer, Cham (2017). https://doi.org/10.1007/978-3-319-63387-9_12
4. Blumer, A., Ehrenfeucht, A., Haussler, D., Warmuth, M.K.: Learnability and the Vapnik-Chervonenkis dimension. J. ACM **36**(4), 929–965 (1989)
5. Chen, Y., et al.: PAC learning-based verification and model synthesis. In: Proceedings of the 38th International Conference on Software Engineering, ICSE 2016, Austin, TX, USA, 14–22 May 2016, pp. 714–724 (2016)
6. CIL: C intermediate language. https://people.eecs.berkeley.edu/~necula/cil/
7. Cousot, P., Cousot, R.: Abstract interpretation: a unified lattice model for static analysis of programs by construction or approximation of fixpoints. In: Conference Record of the Fourth Annual ACM SIGPLAN-SIGACT Symposium on Principles of Programming Languages, pp. 238–252. ACM Press, New York (1977)
8. Cousot, P., Monerau, M.: Probabilistic abstract interpretation. In: Seidl, H. (ed.) ESOP 2012. LNCS, vol. 7211, pp. 169–193. Springer, Heidelberg (2012). https://doi.org/10.1007/978-3-642-28869-2_9
9. Deshmukh, J.V., Majumdar, R., Prabhu, V.S.: Quantifying conformance using the Skorokhod metric. Formal Methods Syst. Des. **50**(2–3), 168–206 (2017)
10. Emerson, E.A., Clarke, E.M.: Using branching time temporal logic to synthesize synchronization skeletons. Sci. Comput. Program. **2**(3), 241–266 (1982)
11. Flach, P.: Machine Learning: The Art and Science of Algorithms That Make Senseof Data. Cambridge University Press, New York (2012)
12. Gehr, T., Dimitrov, D., Vechev, M.: Learning commutativity specifications. In: Kroening, D., Păsăreanu, C.S. (eds.) CAV 2015. LNCS, vol. 9206, pp. 307–323. Springer, Cham (2015). https://doi.org/10.1007/978-3-319-21690-4_18
13. Graf, S., Saïdi, H.: Construction of abstract state graphs with PVS. In: Grumberg, O. (ed.) CAV 1997. LNCS, vol. 1254, pp. 72–83. Springer, Heidelberg (1997). https://doi.org/10.1007/3-540-63166-6_10
14. Gulavani, B.S., Henzinger, T.A., Kannan, Y., Nori, A.V., Rajamani, S.K.: SYNERGY: a new algorithm for property checking. In: Proceedings of the 14th ACM SIGSOFT International Symposium on Foundations of Software Engineering, FSE 2006, Portland, Oregon, USA, 5–11 November 2006, pp. 117–127 (2006)
15. Ho, V.M., Alvin, C., Mukhopadhyay, S., Peterson, B., Lawson, J.: Empirical abstraction. Technical report (2020). https://rb.gy/ggllbr
16. Jobstmann, B., Leino, K.R.M. (eds.): VMCAI 2016. LNCS, vol. 9583. Springer, Heidelberg (2016). https://doi.org/10.1007/978-3-662-49122-5
17. Liang, P., Tripp, O., Naik, M.: Learning minimal abstractions. In: POPL, pp. 31–42 (2011)
18. LLVM: The LLVM project. https://llvm.org/
19. Monniaux, D.: Abstract interpretation of programs as Markov decision processes. In: Cousot, R. (ed.) SAS 2003. LNCS, vol. 2694, pp. 237–254. Springer, Heidelberg (2003). https://doi.org/10.1007/3-540-44898-5_13

20. Mukhopadhyay, S., Podelski, A.: Beyond region graphs: symbolic forward analysis of timed automata. In: Rangan, C.P., Raman, V., Ramanujam, R. (eds.) FSTTCS 1999. LNCS, vol. 1738, pp. 232–244. Springer, Heidelberg (1999). https://doi.org/10.1007/3-540-46691-6_18

21. Nori, A.V., Rajamani, S.K., Tetali, S.D., Thakur, A.V.: The YOGI project: software property checking via static analysis and testing. In: Kowalewski, S., Philippou, A. (eds.) TACAS 2009. LNCS, vol. 5505, pp. 178–181. Springer, Heidelberg (2009). https://doi.org/10.1007/978-3-642-00768-2_17

22. Ore, O.: Galois connexions. Trans. Am. Math. Soc. **55**, 493–513 (1944)

23. Padhi, S., Sharma, R., Millstein, T.D.: Data-driven precondition inference with learned features. In: Proceedings of the 37th ACM SIGPLAN Conference on Programming Language Design and Implementation, PLDI 2016, Santa Barbara, CA, USA, 13–17 June 2016, pp. 42–56 (2016)

24. Sankaranarayanan, S., Chaudhuri, S., Ivancic, F., Gupta, A.: Dynamic inference of likely data preconditions over predicates by tree learning. In: Proceedings of the ACM/SIGSOFT International Symposium on Software Testing and Analysis, ISSTA 2008, Seattle, WA, USA, 20–24 July 2008, pp. 295–306 (2008)

25. Sharma, R.: Data-driven verification. Ph.D. thesis, Stanford (2016)

26. Sharma, R., Nori, A.V., Aiken, A.: Bias-variance tradeoffs in program analysis. In: POPL, pp. 127–138 (2014)

27. Smith, M.J.A.: Probabilistic abstract interpretation of imperative programs using truncated normal distributions. Electr. Notes Theor. Comput. Sci. **220**(3), 43–59 (2008)

28. Wasserman, L.: All of Nonparametric Statistics (Springer Texts in Statistics). Springer, New York (2006). https://doi.org/10.1007/0-387-30623-4

29. Yau, S.S., et al.: Automated situation-aware service composition in service-oriented computing. Int. J. Web Serv. Res. (IJWSR) **4**(4), 59–82 (2007)

30. Zhang, X., Naik, M., Yang, H.: Finding optimum abstractions in parametric dataflow analysis. In: PLDI, pp. 365–376 (2013)

Test4Enforcers: Test Case Generation for Software Enforcers

Michell Guzman, Oliviero Riganelli$^{(\boxtimes)}$ ⓘ, Daniela Micucci ⓘ,
and Leonardo Mariani ⓘ

University of Milano-Bicocca, 20126 Milan, Italy
{michell.guzman,oliviero.riganelli,
daniela.micucci,leonardo.mariani}@unimib.it

Abstract. Software enforcers can be used to modify the runtime behavior of software applications to guarantee that relevant correctness policies are satisfied. Indeed, the implementation of software enforcers can be tricky, due to the heterogeneity of the situations that they must be able to handle. Assessing their ability to steer the behavior of the target system without introducing any side effect is an important challenge to fully trust the resulting system. To address this challenge, this paper presents Test4Enforcers, the first approach to derive thorough test suites that can validate the impact of enforcers on a target system. The paper also shows how to implement the Test4Enforcers approach in the DroidBot test generator to validate enforcers for Android apps.

Keywords: Runtime enforcement · Testing enforcers · Test case generation · Android apps

1 Introduction

To prevent undesired behaviors that may result in software failures and crashes, runtime enforcement techniques have been used to modify the runtime behavior of software systems, forcing the systems to satisfy a set of correctness policies [16, 27]. So far, runtime enforcement has been already applied to multiple domains, including security [21], resource management [35,36], and mobile computing [12, 43].

The enforcement logic is often defined with an input/output [29] or an edit automaton [25] that is used to guide the implementation of the actual software enforcer. Although sometimes part of the code of the enforcer can be obtained automatically, the implementation of the final component that can be injected in the actual system normally requires the manual intervention of the developers, to make it fit well with the complexity of the runtime context. In particular, manual intervention is necessary to handle those aspects that are abstracted (i.e., not represented) in the enforcement model, such as handling the values of the parameters that are not represented in the model but must be used in function calls, adding the code to extract data from the runtime events produced by the

© Springer Nature Switzerland AG 2020
J. Deshmukh and D. Ničković (Eds.): RV 2020, LNCS 12399, pp. 279–297, 2020.
https://doi.org/10.1007/978-3-030-60508-7_15

monitored system, adding the code necessary to obtain security permissions, and more in general handling any other aspect or optimization not fully represented in the model.

As a consequence, the correctness of the resulting enforcer is threaten by three possible sources of problems:

- *Model inaccuracies*: This is the case of a wrong enforcement model that consequently leads to the implementation of a wrong software enforcer. Wrong models are the results of a bad design activity. When all the elements of the system can be accurately modelled (e.g., the environment, the monitored system, and the enforcer), this problem can be mitigated using verification techniques [37];
- *Inconsistent implementations*: This is the case of a software implementation that is not perfectly compliant with the model. This may happen when developers unintentionally introduce bugs while implementing an enforcer starting from its enforcement model. In some cases, code generation techniques can be used to obtain part of the code automatically and mitigate this problem [12];
- *Faulty additional code*: This is the case of a fault in the code that must be added to the software enforcer, which is distinct from the code that directly derives from the enforcement model, to obtain a fully operational enforcer that can be deployed in the target environment. The amount of additional code that is needed can be significant, depending on the complexity of the involved elements (e.g., the environment, the monitoring technology, and the monitored application). No simple strategy to mitigate the problem of verifying the correctness of this code is normally available.

To guarantee the correctness of a software enforcer before it is deployed in the target system, in addition to validating the enforcement model, it is necessary to extensively test the enforcer against all these possible threats. Compared to a regular testing scenario, testing software enforcers requires approaches that are able to target the specific events relevant to the enforcer and assess their impact on the runtime behavior of the system. In particular, *test case generation should check that a software enforcer both modifies executions according to the expected strategy and leaves executions unaltered when the observed computation does not require any intervention.*

In this paper we present Test4Enforcers, the first test case generation approach designed to address the challenge of testing the correctness of software enforcers. Note that enforcers typically act on the internal events of a software system, while test case generation works on its interface, and thus the testing strategy must discover *how to activate the proper sequences of internal events from the application interface.* Test4Enforcers originally combines the knowledge of the enforcement strategy with GUI exploration techniques, to discover how to generate the right sequences of interactions that validate the interactions between the target software system and the enforcer. The resulting test cases are executed on both the application with and without the enforcer in place to detect undesired behavioral differences (e.g., side effects) and unexpected similarities (e.g., lack of effect of the enforcer) to the tester. We also concretely show

how to implement Test4Enforcers for Android apps by extending the DroidBot test case generation technique [24].

The paper is organized as follows. Section 2 provides background information about policy enforcement. Section 3 presents the Test4Enforcers test case generation strategy. Section 4 reports our experience with Test4Enforcers applied to an Android app. Section 5 discusses related work. Finally, Sect. 6 provides concluding remarks.

2   Policy Enforcement

In this section we introduce the notion of runtime policy and policy enforcement.

2.1   Runtime Policy

A runtime policy is a predicate over a set of executions. More formally, let Σ be a finite set of observable program actions a. An *execution* σ is a finite or infinite non-empty sequence of actions $a_1; a_2; \ldots; a_n$. Σ^* is the set of all finite sequences, Σ^ω is the set of infinite sequences, and $\Sigma^\infty = \Sigma^* \cup \Sigma^\omega$ is the set of all sequences. Given a set of executions $\chi \subseteq \Sigma^\infty$, a *policy* is a predicate P on χ. A policy P is satisfied by a set of executions χ if and only if $P(\chi)$ evaluates to *true*.

Policies may concern different aspects of the runtime behavior of a software, such as resource usages, security, and privacy. For example, a policy about resource usage for the Android framework requires that anytime an app stops using the Camera, the app explicitly releases the Camera to make it available to the other applications [1]. More precisely, *"if an activity[1] is using the camera and the activity receives an invocation to the callback method* onPause()*[2], the activity must release the camera"*. We use this policy throughout the paper to describe our approach.

2.2   Policy Enforcement Models

A policy enforcement model is a model that specifies how an execution can be altered to make it comply with a given policy. Policy enforcers can be represented with both edit and input/output automata. In Fig. 1 we show the model of an enforcer specified as an input/output automaton that addresses the before-mentioned policy about the Camera. The inputs are requests intercepted at runtime (these events are labeled with the *req* subscript) by the software enforcer and the outputs are the events emitted by the enforcer in response to the intercepted requests (these events are labeled with the *api* subscript). When the label

---

[1] *Activities are fundamental components of Android apps and they represent the entry point for a user's interaction with the app* https://developer.android.com/guide/components/activities.

[2] onPause() is a callback method that is invoked by the Android framework when an activity is paused.

of the output is the same than the label of the input (regardless of the subscript), the enforcer is just forwarding the requests without altering the execution. If the output is different from the input, the enforcer is manipulating the execution suppressing and/or adding requests.

When the current state is state s_0, the Camera has not been acquired yet and the `activity.onPause()` callback can be executed without restrictions. If the camera is acquired by executing `camera.open()` (transition from s_0 to s_1), the camera must be released before the activity is paused (as done in the transition with the input `activity.release()` from s_1 to s_0). If the activity is paused before the camera is released, the enforcer modifies the execution emitting the sequence `camera.release() activity.onPause()`, which guarantees that the policy is satisfied despite the app is not respecting it.

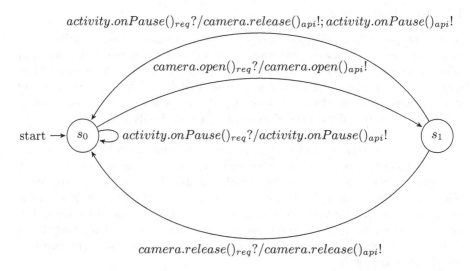

Fig. 1. Enforcer for systematically releasing the camera when the activity is paused.

This enforcement strategy must be translated into a suitable software component to achieve runtime enforcement. With reference to the main classes of errors introduced in the paper, the following types of bugs may affects its implementation:

- *Model Inaccuracies:* Although the designer may believe the enforcement model is correct, the strategy might end up being incorrect. For instance, the enforcer in Fig. 1 releases the camera when an activity is paused but does not acquire the camera back when the execution of the activity is resumed. This is a source of problems when the activity does not automatically re-acquire the camera once resumed. The strategy is thus inaccurate and should be extended to also include this stage. For simplicity in this paper we use the enforcer in Fig. 1 without complicating the model with the part necessary to acquire again a forcefully released camera.

- *Inconsistent Implementations:* The model must be translated into working code. Concerning the behavior specified in the model, the corresponding code can be easily produced automatically, thus preventing inconsistencies (unless the generator is faulty). If the code is implemented manually, still the conformance of the code with the model has to be verified.
- *Faulty Additional Code:* In order to achieve code that can be deployed, a non-trivial amount of scaffolding code must be implemented, as well as many details should be worked out at the code level. For instance, the software enforcer derived from the model in Fig. 1 must be integrated with the monitoring solution used to capture events. This may already require a significant amount of code to be implemented. Moreover, although not shown in the model, an implementation of the enforcer that also acquires back the camera has to track both all the parameters used to initialize the camera and all the changes performed to these parameters to later recreate a correctly configured camera. These details are typically worked out by the engineers at the code level and are not present in the model.

Test4Enforcers automatically generates tests that target the above listed issues.

3   Test4Enforcers

Test4Enforcers generates test cases in 4 steps, as illustrated in Fig. 2. The first step, namely *Generation of Test Sequences with HSI*, generates the test sequences that must be covered to thoroughly test the behavior of the enforcer based on the behavior specified in the enforcement model. To obtain concrete test cases that cover these sequences, Test4Enforcers explores (second and third steps) the application under test to determine what user interface (UI) interactions generate the events that belong to the alphabet of the enforcement model. In particular, the second step, namely *Monitor Generation*, uses the events in the alphabet of the enforcer to obtain a monitor that observes when these events are executed. The third step, namely *GUI Ripping Augmented with Runtime Monitoring*, runs a GUI Ripping process [31] that systematically explores the UI of the application under test while logging the events relevant to the enforcer with the generated monitor. The output is the Test4Enforcers model, which is a finite state model that represents the GUI states that have been exercised, the UI interactions that cause transitions between these states, and the events relevant to the monitor that have been produced during transitions. Note that although we present the steps in this order, the second and third steps can be executed in parallel with the first step. Finally, the fourth step, namely *Generation of the Concrete Test Cases*, looks for the sequences of UI interactions that exactly cover the test sequences identified in the first step and deemed as relevant to verify the behavior of the enforcer. These UI interactions, enriched with program oracles, are the test cases that can be executed to validate the activity of the enforcer. In the following, we describe each step in details.

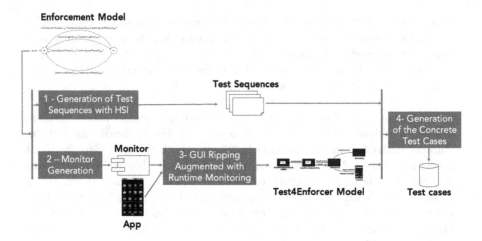

Fig. 2. Test case generation with Test4Enforcers.

3.1   Generation of Test Sequences

In this step, Test4Enforcers generates the sequences of operations that must be covered with testing based on the behavior specified in the enforcement model. A notable method to generate these sequences from finite state models is the *W-method* [4,23,39].

The *W-method* has been designed to unveil possible errors in the implementation, such as, erroneous next-states, extra/missing states, etc. The main idea of the method is that starting from a state-based representation of a system, it is possible to generate sequences of inputs to reach every state in the model, cover all the transitions from every state, and identify all destination states to ensure that their counter-parts in the implementation are correct.

One limitation of the W-method is that it requires the model of the system to be *completely specified*, that is, in every state of the model there must be a transition for every possible input. This is however not the case for enforcers, since the inputs are generated by other components and frameworks, and not all the combinations of inputs can be feasibly generated (e.g., `onPause()` and `onResume()` are callbacks produced when an activity is paused and resumed, respectively, as a consequence it is impossible to produce a sequence of two `onPause()` events without an intermediate `onResume()` event). In order to tackle this limitation, we use the *Harmonized State Identifiers* (HSI) method, which is a variante of the W-method that does not require the model of the system to be completely specified [2,28]. HSI exploits a few key concepts that are introduced below.

We first define an *Input/Output Automaton* A as a tuple $\langle S, s_0, sig, T \rangle$, where S is a finite set of states; $s_0 \in S$ is the initial state; sig is the set of actions of A partitioned into input actions in, internal actions int, and output actions out; $T \subseteq S \times \{in \cup int\} \times out^* \times S$ is a set of transitions (the symbol * denotes a sequence of actions). Note that differently from classic Input/Output Automaton, here we consider models that are not input-enabled, that is, every input cannot be received from every state, as mentioned due to the requirements of the environment where the enforcer is executed. Moreover, the automaton can produce zero or more outputs, denoted with out^*, in response to a single input as a consequence of the activity of the enforcer.

A sequence $in_1, \ldots, in_k$ with $in_j \in in, \forall j = 1 \ldots k$ is an input sequence for state $s \in S$, if there exist states $s_1, \ldots, s_{k+1}$ such that $s = s_1$ and $\langle s_i, in_i, o, s_{i+1} \rangle \in T, \forall i = 1 \ldots k$ (note o is not bounded to any value). $\Omega(s)$ is used to denote all input sequences defined for state s. Similarly, given a state s and an input sequence $\gamma = \langle in_1, \ldots, in_k \rangle \in \Omega(s)$, the function $\lambda(s, \gamma)$ denotes the output sequence $o_1, \ldots, o_m$ emitted by the automaton when accepting γ.

To generate an effective test suite, it is important to be able to distinguish the covered states. We say that two states $s_i, s_j \in S$ are *distinguishable* if there exists a *separating sequence* $\gamma \in \Omega(s_i) \cap \Omega(s_j)$, such that $\lambda(s_i, \gamma) \neq \lambda(s_j, \gamma)$, otherwise they are not distinguishable.

To generate a thorough test suite, HSI exploits the notions of *transition cover* and *separating families*. We say that the set P is a *transition cover* of A if for each transition x from state s there exists the sequence $\alpha x \in P$ such that $\alpha \in \Omega(s_0)$ and s is the state reached by accepting α. By definition, P also includes ϵ.

For instance, a transition cover P for the enforcer in Fig. 1 is given by the following set

$P = \{$

$\quad \epsilon,$

$\quad activity.onPause()_{req},$

$\quad camera.open()_{req},$

$\quad camera.open()_{req}\ activity.onPause()_{req},$

$\quad camera.open()_{req}\ camera.release()_{req}$

$\}.$

The sequences in the transition cover, each one defined to cover a different transition, are extended with actions aimed at determining if the right state has been finally reached once the sequence is executed. To this end, HSI computes the *separating families*, which are sets of input sequences, one set for each state, that can be executed to distinguish a state from the other states of the system. In particular, a separating family is a set of input sequences $H_i \subseteq \Omega(s_i)$ for $s_i \in S$ satisfying the following condition: For any two distinguishable states s_i, s_j there exist sequences $\beta \in H_i, \gamma \in H_j$, such that α is a common prefix of β and γ and $\lambda(s_i, \alpha) \neq \lambda(s_j, \alpha)$.

Computing the separating families for the automaton in Fig. 1 is straightforward since the two states have a single input in common that produces different outputs, allowing to distinguish the states. Thus $H_0 = H_1 = \{activity.onPause()_{req}\}$.

The HSI method can take into consideration the case the actual states of the implementation differ from the number of states in the model. However, we expect the software enforcer to have exactly the same number of states reported in the model. In such a case, the resulting test sequences are obtained by concatenating the transition coverage set P with the separating families H_i. Note that the concatenation considers the state reached at the end of each sequence in P, namely s_i, to concatenate such a sequence with the sequences in the corresponding separating family, namely H_i.

In our example, this process generates the following sequences to be covered with test cases:

$activity.onPause()_{req}$,
$activity.onPause()_{req}\ activity.onPause()_{req}$,
$camera.open()_{req}\ activity.onPause()_{req}$,
$camera.open()_{req}\ activity.onPause()_{req}\ activity.onPause()_{req}$,
$camera.open()_{req}\ camera.release()_{req}\ activity.onPause()_{req}$

HSI also includes a step to remove duplicates and prefixes from the generated set. Test4Enforcers only removes duplicates. In fact, removing a sequence that is a prefix of another sequence may drop a feasible test sequence in favour of an infeasible one (e.g., the longer sequence might be impossible to generate due to constraints in the environment, while it might be still possible to test the shorter sequence). In our example, since the list includes no duplicates, it is also the set of sequences that Test4Enforcer aims to cover to assess the correctness of the enforcer in Fig. 1.

3.2   Monitor Generation

This step is quite simple. It consists of the generation of a monitor that can trace the execution of the events that appear in the enforcement model. Since we focus on enforcers that intercept and produce method calls, the captured events are either API calls (e.g., the invocation of `open()` and `release()` on the Camera) or callbacks (e.g., the invocation of `onPause()` on the activity). In this phase, the user of Test4Enforcer can also specialize the general enforcement strategy to the target application, if needed. For instance, the user can specify the name of the target activity that must be monitored replacing the placeholder name `activity` that occurs in the model with the name of an actual activity in the application (e.g., `MainActivity`). Multiple copies of the same enforcer can be generated, if multiple activities must be monitored.

In our implementation, we consider Xposed [42] as instrumentation library for Android apps. The monitoring module is implemented once and simply configured every time with the set of methods in the alphabet of the enforcer.

3.3   GUI Ripping Augmented with Monitoring

GUI Ripping is an exploration strategy that can be used to explore the GUI of an application under test with the purpose of building a state-based representation of its behavior [31]. In particular, GUI ripping generates the state-based model of the application under test by systematically executing every possible action on every state encountered during the exploration, until a given time or action budget expires. Our implementation of Test4Enforcers targets Android apps and uses DroidBot [24] configured to execute actions in a breadth-first manner to build the state-based model.

The model represents each state of the app according to its set of visible views and their properties. More rigorously, a state of the app under test is a set of views $s = \{v_i | i = 1 \ldots n\} \in S_{app}$, and each view is a set of properties $v_i = \{p_{i1}, \ldots, p_{ik}\}$. For instance, an `EditText` is an Android view that allows the users to enter some text in the app. The `EditText` has a number of properties, such as `clickable`, which indicates if the view reacts to click events, and `text`, which represents the text present in the view.

Operations that change the set of visible views (e.g., because an activity is closed and another one is opened) or the properties of the views (e.g., because some text is entered in an input field) change the state of the app. DroidBot uses the following set of actions A_{app} during GUI ripping: *touch* and *long touch*, which execute a tap and a long tap on a clickable view, respectively; *setText*, which enters a pre-defined text inside an editable view; *keyEvent*, which presses a navigation button; and *scroll*, which scrolls the current window.

The actual state-based representation of the execution space of an app produced by GUI Ripping consists of the visited states and the executed actions. Test4Enforcers extends the model generated by GUI ripping by adding the information generated by the monitor, that is, the list of the relevant internal events (i.e., the events in the alphabet of the enforcer) executed during each transition. The state-based model thus shows both the UI interactions that can be executed on the app, their effect on the state of the app, and the internal events that are activated when they are executed.

More formally, the model resulting from the GUI ripping phase is a tuple (S_{app}, s_0, T_{app}), where S_{app} is the set of visited states, $s_0 \in S_{app}$ is the initial state, $T_{app} \subseteq S_{app} \times A_{app} \times in^* \times S_{app}$ is a set of transitions $\langle s_1, a_{app}, \langle in_1, \ldots, in_k \rangle, s_2 \rangle$, where s_1 and s_2 are the source and target states of the transition, respectively, a_{app} is the UI interaction that causes the transition, and $\langle in_1, \ldots, in_k \rangle$ is a possibly empty sequence of internal events observed during the transition (note these events are exactly the input actions of the enforcer). The resulting model includes everything needed to obtain the concrete test cases (i.e., the sequences of UI operations that must be performed on the app) that cover the test sequences derived with HSI (i.e., the sequences of input operations of the enforcer that must be generated). Figure 3 shows an excerpt of the model obtained by running the ripping phase on the `fooCam` app while considering the alphabet of the enforcer shown in Fig. 1. The `fooCam` app is briefly introduced in Sect. 4. For simplicity, we represent the states with the screenshots of the app. The labels above transitions represent UI interactions, while the labels below transitions, when present, represent internal events collected by the monitor. For instance, when the *KeyEvent(Back)* UI interaction is executed and the app moves from the state *MainActivity* to the state *Launcher*, the sequence of internal events *camera.release() activity.onPause()* is observed.

Note that Test4Enforcers assumes that the software under test has a deterministic behavior, that is, an action performed on a given state always produces the same computation. For Android apps this is often true, and even if this constraint is sometime violated, the test case generation algorithm presented in the next section can compensate this issue by trying multiple sequences of operations, until emitting the correct sequence of events. However, if the behavior of the tested software is highly non-deterministic, it might be difficult for Test4Enforcer to obtain the right set of test cases.

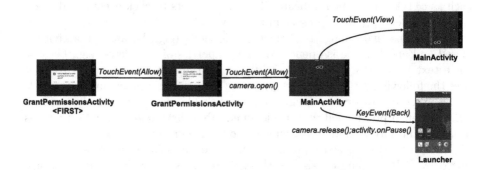

Fig. 3. Excerpt of a model derived with GUI ripping.

3.4 Generation of Concrete Test Cases

Generating concrete (i.e., executable) test cases consists of finding the sequences of GUI interactions that cause the execution of the desired sequences of internal events, as identified by the HSI method. To this end, Test4Enforcers exploits both the state-based model of the application under test and the sequences generated with the HSI method. Algorithm 1 shows the generation process, which takes an app, its GUI model, and a set of sequences to be covered as input, and returns a test suite that contains executable test cases that cover the identified sequences of events. When the algorithm returns the test cases, the mapping between the test case and the covered sequence is maintained.

Algorithm 1 starts by initializing the test suite to the empty set (line 1), then for each sequence in the set of sequences to be covered, the algorithm searches for a test that covers the sequence (for loop starting at line 2), and, if successful, it both adds an oracle to the test and adds the test to the test suite (lines 8 and 9 respectively). To identify the concrete test case that can cover a sequence, the algorithm searches for one or more paths in the model that generate the desired sequence of events (line 3). For instance, if the sequence to be covered is *camera.open() camera.release() activity.onPause()* and the GUI model is the one in Fig. 3, the algorithm can derive the sequence *TouchEvent(v1) TouchEvent(v2) KeyEvent(BACK)* as the concrete test to execute. In fact, the execution of the identified UI events is expected to produce the desired computation (based on the labels on the transitions). Since an arbitrarily large number of paths covering the desired sequence can be often determined, and not necessarily any path will deterministically produce the desired set of events internal to the app, the algorithm identifies the N (e.g., N = 10) shortest paths of the model that cover the sequence (stored in variable *testCases* in the algorithm). Each path of UI events is tested by actually running the application to make sure that both its execution is feasible and it indeed generates the intended sequence of events (for loop at line 5). Our implementation of Test4Enforcers uses again DroidBot to reproduce a sequence of UI events.

Algorithm 1: Algorithm for generating concrete test cases

Input: App app, RippingModel appModel, TestSequences testSequences
Output: Set of <TestCase, TestSequences> testSuite

1   $testSuite \leftarrow \emptyset$
2   **foreach** $ts \in testSequences$ **do**
3      $testCases \leftarrow$ generateEventSequences(ts, $appModel$)
4      $isCovered \leftarrow$ FALSE
5   **foreach** $tc \in testCases \wedge \neg isCovered$ **do**
6         $isCovered \leftarrow$ runTestCase(tc, ts, app)
7   **if** $isCovered$ **then**
8   tc $\leftarrow$ *addOracle*(tc, ts)
9   testSuite.add(tc, ts)

10 **return** testSuite

If the right test is found, the algorithm embeds a *differential oracle* in the test case, before adding it to the test suite. A differential oracle is an oracle that determines the correctness of a test execution by comparing two executions of the same tests on two different programs. In our case, the compared programs are the app *with* and *without* the enforcer deployed. Test4Enforcers can inject two different differential oracles, depending on the characteristics of the sequence of events $in_1, \ldots, in_k$ covered by the test $tc = a_1, \ldots, a_n$ where the oracle must be embedded: the transparent-enforcement oracle and the actual-enforcement oracle.

Transparent-Enforcement Oracle. If the sequence is not the result of any change performed by the enforcer, that is, it covers a path of the enforcement model where the inputs and the outputs are always the same, the test is annotated as a test that must *produce the same result if executed on both the application with and without the enforcer.* More rigorously, if the output $o_1, \ldots, o_m$ is produced by the enforcement model for the inputs $in_1, \ldots, in_k$, this oracle applies when $k = m$ and $in_i = o_i, \forall i = 1 \ldots k$. The resulting oracle checks the correctness of the execution by first capturing the intermediate states traversed during test execution, as done during the construction of the GUI model, and comparing them when collected from the app with and without the enforcer deployed. More rigorously, if the states cs_i and cs'_i are the states reached after executing the action a_i on the app without and with the enforcer, respectively, the oracle checks if $cs_i = cs'_i, \forall i = 1 \ldots n$. If the check fails, the enforcer *is not non-intrusive*, although it was supposed to be, and a failure is reported. For instance, the input sequence *camera.open() camera.release() activity.onPause()* is not altered by the enforcer in Fig. 1 and thus the transparent-enforcement oracle is used to determine the correctness of the test that covers this sequence, that is, no behavioral difference must be observed when this sequence is executed in both the app without and the app with the enforcer.

Actual-Enforcement Oracle. If the tested sequence corresponds to a path that requires the intervention of the enforcer, the test is annotated as producing an execution that may produce a different outcome when executed on the app with and without the enforcer in place. In such a case, given a sequence of events $in_1, \ldots, in_k$, $\exists v, s.t.$ $in_i = o_i \forall i < v$ and $in_v \neq o_v$. The resulting oracle checks the equality of the states visited by the test case executed on the app with and without the enforcer until the event in_v is produced, and checks for the possible presence of a difference in the following states. More rigorously, if a_v is the GUI action that generates event in_v, the actual-enforcement oracle first checks $cs_i = cs'_i, \forall i < v$. If the check fails, the enforcer is unexpectedly intrusive and a failure is reported. For the remaining portion of the execution, it is not possible to know a priori if the activity of the enforcer must result in an effect visible on the GUI. The actual-enforcement oracle thus looks for such a difference, and if the difference is not found, it only issues a warning, suggesting that the enforcer may have failed its activity. Formally, the oracle checks if $\exists p, s.t., cs_p \neq cs'_p$ with $p \geq v$, if it is not the case the warning is issued. For instance, the input sequence *camera.open() activity.onPause()* causes the intervention of the enforcer shown in Fig. 1, which outputs an extra event *camera.release()*. The test corresponding to that sequence is thus labeled as *producing the same result until the activity.onPause() event, and a potentially different result afterwards*, and the actual-enforcement oracle is embedded in the test.

4   Case Study

As initial validation of the approach, we applied Test4Enforcers to the software enforcer that we implemented from the camera release policy shown in Fig. 1 and validated its behavior when injected in the `fooCam` app, which is a HDR camera app that can take multiple shots with different exposure settings. The app is available on the Google Play Store[3]. We selected this app because it is rather simple, although realistic, it is open source, and we can thus control its execution by manually cross-checking the impact of the enforcer and the behavior of the test cases generated by Test4Enforcers.

To consider both the scenario in which the app violates and does not violate the policy, we produced a faulty version of the app by removing the invocation to the `release()` operation that the app performs when paused. In the rest of this

---

[3] https://play.google.com/store/apps/details?id=net.phunehehe.foocam2&hl=EN.

section, we refer to the correct and faulty apps as $fooCam_c$ and $fooCam_f$, respectively. Moreover, we indicate the apps augmented with the software enforcer for the Camera policy as $fooCam_{c+enf}$ and $fooCam_{f+enf}$, respectively.

As reported in Sect. 3.1, Test4Enforcers identified the following 5 test sequences that should be covered to test the enforcer:

$activity.onPause()_{req}$,
$activity.onPause()_{req}$ $activity.onPause()_{req}$,
$camera.open()_{req}$ $activity.onPause()_{req}$,
$camera.open()_{req}$ $activity.onPause()_{req}$ $activity.onPause()_{req}$,
$camera.open()_{req}$ $camera.release()_{req}$ $activity.onPause()_{req}$

Note that, not all these sequences are necessarily feasible. In fact, depending on the specific implementation of the app, some sequences might be impossible to execute.

To obtain the concrete test cases, we performed steps 2 and 3 of the technique, that is, we configured the Xposed module [42] that we designed for Test4Enforcers to trace the execution of the events in the alphabet of the enforcer and we ran DroidBot on both $fooCam_c$ and $fooCam_f$ obtaining two Test4Enforcers models. We configured DroidBot to produce 750 UI events, which correspond to about 30 min of computation. We report information about the size of the resulting models in Table 1.

Table 1. Size of Test4Enforcers models.

App	Test4Enforcers model	
	#States	#Transitions
$fooCam_c$	54	295
$fooCam_f$	63	276

The exploration covered a number of states considered the relative simplicity of the app. The difference in the number of states and transitions is due to the randomness of some choices taken during the exploration activity by the tool. Interestingly, the model can now be used to derive the concrete test cases.

The behavior of the app immediately reveals that some sequences cannot be covered in this case. For instance, since fooCam opens the Camera when the MainActicity is started, it is infeasible to execute the MainActivity.onPause() callback without first executing the Camera.open() API call. As a consequence, all the test sequences starting with an invocation to MainActivity.onPause() without a preceding invocation to Camera.open() are infeasible in both $fooCam_c$ and $fooCam_f$. We would like to remark two aspects: (i) this is true for this app, but it is not necessarily true for another app that may open the camera at a different point of the execution, for instance when a button is pressed and not when an activity is started, thus obtaining more feasible test sequences; (ii) the analysis of the model allows Test4Enforcers to not waste time trying to cover sequences that cannot be covered, focusing on the feasible combination of events.

Table 2. Tests automatically generated by Test4Enforcers.

App	Test sequences	Coverage
$fooCam_c$	$activity.onPause()_{req}$	infeasible: $camera.open()_{req}$ must be the first event
	$activity.onPause()_{req}$ $activity.onPause()_{req}$	infeasible: see the above reason
	$camera.open()_{req}$ $activity.onPause()_{req}$	infeasible: $camera.release()_{req}$ is invoked from $activity.onPause()_{req}$, thus it is impossible to have $activity.onPause()_{req}$ without $camera.release()_{req}$
	$camera.open()_{req}$ $activity.onPause()_{req}$$activity.onPause()_{req}$	infeasible: see the above reason
	$camera.open()_{req}$ $camera.release()_{req}$ $activity.onPause()_{req}$	feasible: it is a legal sequence of operations monitored by the enforcer that does not require its intervention. The corresponding test is thus associated with the *transparent-enforcement oracle*
$fooCam_f$	$activity.onPause()_{req}$	infeasible: $camera.open()_{req}$ must be the first event
	$activity.onPause()_{req}$ $activity.onPause()_{req}$	infeasible: see the above reason
	$camera.open()_{req}$ $activity.onPause()_{req}$	feasible: it is the sequence that violates the policy and requires the intervention of the enforcer. The corresponding test is thus associated with the *actual-enforcement oracle*
	$camera.open()_{req}$ $activity.onPause()_{req}$ $activity.onPause()_{req}$	infeasible: once the activity is paused, it must be resumed to be paused again; resuming the activity causes the execution of $camera.open()_{req}$ in fooCam, thus the sequence is infeasible
	$camera.open()_{req}$ $camera.release()_{req}$ $activity.onPause()_{req}$	feasible: it is a legal sequence of operations monitored by the enforcer that does not require its intervention. In the faulty app this sequence can be obtained by interacting with view elements that cause the release of the camera, even if the camere is not automatically released on $activity.onPause()_{req}$. The corresponding test is thus associated with the *transparent-enforcement oracle*

Table 2 summarizes the results about the feasibility of covering the test sequences in both apps. Column *App* indicates the app that is tested. Column *Test Sequences* indicates the specific sequences of internal events that must be covered. Column *Coverage* reports the outcome obtained using Test4Enforcers in terms of the capability to cover the corresponding sequence. Interestingly, different sequences are feasible in the faulty and correct apps.

Test4Enforcers derived test cases that cover all the feasible test sequences. The execution of the tests on the apps with and without the enforcer confirmed the correctness of the enforcer for the $fooCam$ app. In particular, the test case derived from the $fooCam_c$ confirmed that both $fooCam_c$ and $fooCam_{c+enf}$ behave the same. In fact, the app is correct and the enforcer simply monitored the execution never altering it. The execution of the two test cases derived from $fooCam_f$ on both $fooCam_f$ and $fooCam_{f+enf}$ revealed no differences in the behavior of the app. This raised a warning for the test that was expected to activate the intervention of the enforcer. However, the manual inspection of the execution confirmed that a different behavior was observed, since an extra release operation that makes the execution to satisfy the policy is produced when the enforcer is in place. In this specific case, to turn the impact of the enforcer into a visible behavior the test should open a different app that uses the camera, which is outside the capability of DroidBot.

We can conclude that Test4Enforcers interestingly generated different test cases based on the implementation of the app under test to validate the effect of the enforcers while covering the most relevant feasible test sequences.

5   Related Work

The contribution described in this paper spans three related research areas: runtime enforcement, model-based testing, and verification of runtime enforcement.

Runtime enforcement solutions can be used to prevent a software system from behaving incorrectly with respect to a set of known policies. In particular, runtime enforcement strategies modify executions assuring that policies are satisfied despite the potentially incorrect behavior of the monitored software [14,22]. Enforcement strategies can be specified using a variety of models, including models specifically designed to represent runtime enforcement, such as All or Nothing Automata [3], Late Automata [3], Mandatory Results Automata [9], and Edit Automata [26]. Runtime enforcement solutions have been applied in multiple application domains, including mobile applications [6,12,33,35] operating systems [40], web-based applications [30], and cloud systems [5]. An overview of techniques to prevent failures by enforcing the correct behaviour at runtime has been recently published by Falcone et al. [15]. Among these many domains, in this paper we focus on the Android environment, which has been already considered in the work by Falcone et al. [12], who studied how to enforce privacy policies by detecting and disabling suspicious method calls, and more recently by Riganelli et al. [34–36], who studied how to augment classic Android libraries with proactive mechanisms able to automatically suppress and insert API calls to enforce resource usage policies.

While runtime enforcement strategies focus on the definition of models and strategies to specify and implement the enforcers, Test4Enforcers is complemental to this effort, since it derives the test cases that should be executed on applications with and without the enforcers to verify the correctness of the implemented enforcer.

Model-based testing (MBT) refers to the automatic generation of a suite of test cases from models extracted from requirements [7,8]. The purpose of the generated test suite is to determine whether an implementation is correct with respect to its specification. MBT approaches are often organized around three main steps [41]: building the model, choosing the test selection criteria and building the test case specifications, and generating tests. MBT has been extensively used in the software safety domain, where conformance of the implementation with respect to the model is critical, as shown in the survey by Gurbuz et al. [19]. Test4Enforcers is also a MBT approach, in fact it uses a model, it defines a coverage criterion, and it generates the corresponding test cases.

A variety of models have been used to guide test case generation, including finite state machines, UML diagrams (statechart, class, activity, and others), and Z specifications [8]. Indeed, finite-state models are among the most used ones [20]. Interestingly, there are various methods to derive test cases from finite-state machines. For instance, the W [4], Wp [17], UIO [38], DS [18], HSI [32], and the H [11] are well-know test derivation methods [10]. Test4Enforcers exploits HSI due to the characteristics of the models used to represent the behavior of the enforcers. Furthermore, Test4Enforcers defines a strategy to produce the target sequences of events while interacting with the UI of an application.

Verification of runtime enforcement concerns with checking that the software enforcer is indeed delivering the intended behavior. In fact, although the enforcer is meant to correct the behavior of a monitored software, the enforcer itself might still be wrong and its activity might compromise the correctness of the system rather than improving it. A recent work in this direction is the one by Riganelli et al. [37] that provides a way to verify if the activity of multiple enforcers may interfere. The proposed analysis is however entirely based on the models and the many problems that might be introduced by the actual software enforcers cannot be revealed with that approach. Test4Enforcers provides a complemental capability, that is, it can test if the implementation of the enforcer behaves as expected once injected in the target system.

6   Conclusions

Runtime enforcement is a useful technique that can be used to guarantee that certain correctness policies are satisfied while a running software application. However, specifying enforcement strategies and implementing the corresponding software enforcers might be challenging. In particular, translating an enforcement model into a software enforcer might be difficult because of the significant adaptation and instrumentation effort required to close the gap between the abstraction of the models and the actual implementation, which must take under consideration the requirements of the target execution environment. Indeed, enforcers may easily introduce side effects in the attempt of modifying executions. These are well-known shortcomings of software enforcement solutions [3, 37].

To address these problems, this paper describes Test4Enforcers, a test case generation technique that can automatically derive a test suite that can be used to validate the correctness of the software enforcers derived from enforcement models. The resulting test cases are executed on the same application with and without the enforcer in place. The observed behavioral differences are used to reveal faults and issue warnings.

Although the approach is not specific to the Android environment, in this paper we focus on the case of software enforcement for Android apps. This domain is particularly relevant because the apps that are downloaded and installed by end-users have been often developed by unknown, and potentially untrusted, parties. Enriching the environment with enforcers can improve multiple aspects, including security and reliability. Studying how to apply Test4Enforcers to other domains is indeed part of our future work.

In addition, Test4Enforcers is designed to reveal misbehaviors that relate to the ordering of events, as represented in the enforcement model. There are of course classes of misbehaviours that go beyond the ones considered in this paper. For instance, timed properties can be used as policies and enforcers that take time information into account can be designed [13]. Extending the test case generation capabilities of Test4Enforcers to other class of properties is also part of our future work.

References

1. Android Docs: Camera API (2020). https://developer.android.com/guide/topics/media/camera
2. Belli, F., Beyazıt, M., Endo, A.T., Mathur, A., Simao, A.: Fault domain-based testing in imperfect situations: a heuristic approach and case studies. Softw. Qual. J. **23**(3), 423–452 (2014). https://doi.org/10.1007/s11219-014-9242-6
3. Bielova, N., Massacci, F.: Do you really mean what you actually enforced? Int. J. Inf. Secur. **10**, 239–254 (2011)
4. Chow, T.S.: Testing software design modeled by finite-state machines. IEEE Trans. Softw. Eng. **3**, 178–187 (1978)
5. Dai, Y., Xiang, Y., Zhang, G.: Self-healing and hybrid diagnosis in cloud computing. In: Jaatun, M.G., Zhao, G., Rong, C. (eds.) CloudCom 2009. LNCS, vol. 5931, pp. 45–56. Springer, Heidelberg (2009). https://doi.org/10.1007/978-3-642-10665-1_5
6. Daian, P., et al.: RV-Android: efficient parametric android runtime verification, a brief tutorial. In: Bartocci, E., Majumdar, R. (eds.) RV 2015. LNCS, vol. 9333, pp. 342–357. Springer, Cham (2015). https://doi.org/10.1007/978-3-319-23820-3_24
7. Dalal, S.R., et al.: Model-based testing in practice. In: Proceedings of the International Conference on Software Engineering (ICSE) (1999)
8. Dias Neto, A.C., Subramanyan, R., Vieira, M., Travassos, G.H.: A survey on model-based testing approaches: a systematic review. In: Proceedings of the ACM International Workshop on Empirical Assessment of Software Engineering Languages and Technologies (WEASELTech) (2007)

9. Dolzhenko, E., Ligatti, J., Reddy, S.: Modeling runtime enforcement with mandatory results automata. Int. J. Inf. Secur. **14**(1), 47–60 (2014). https://doi.org/10.1007/s10207-014-0239-8

10. Dorofeeva, R., El-Fakih, K., Maag, S., Cavalli, A.R., Yevtushenko, N.: FSM-based conformance testing methods: a survey annotated with experimental evaluation. Inf. Softw. Technol. **52**(12), 1286–1297 (2010)

11. Dorofeeva, R., El-Fakih, K., Yevtushenko, N.: An improved conformance testing method. In: Wang, F. (ed.) FORTE 2005. LNCS, vol. 3731, pp. 204–218. Springer, Heidelberg (2005). https://doi.org/10.1007/11562436_16

12. Falcone, Y., Currea, S., Jaber, M.: Runtime verification and enforcement for android applications with RV-Droid. In: Qadeer, S., Tasiran, S. (eds.) RV 2012. LNCS, vol. 7687, pp. 88–95. Springer, Heidelberg (2013). https://doi.org/10.1007/978-3-642-35632-2_11

13. Falcone, Y., Pinisetty, S.: On the runtime enforcement of timed properties. In: Finkbeiner, B., Mariani, L. (eds.) RV 2019. LNCS, vol. 11757, pp. 48–69. Springer, Cham (2019). https://doi.org/10.1007/978-3-030-32079-9_4

14. Falcone, Y.: You should better enforce than verify. In: Barringer, H., et al. (eds.) RV 2010. LNCS, vol. 6418, pp. 89–105. Springer, Heidelberg (2010). https://doi.org/10.1007/978-3-642-16612-9_9

15. Falcone, Y., Mariani, L., Rollet, A., Saha, S.: Runtime failure prevention and reaction. In: Bartocci, E., Falcone, Y. (eds.) Lectures on Runtime Verification. LNCS, vol. 10457, pp. 103–134. Springer, Cham (2018). https://doi.org/10.1007/978-3-319-75632-5_4

16. Falcone, Y., Mounier, L., Fernandez, J.C., Richier, J.L.: Runtime enforcement monitors: composition, synthesis, and enforcement abilities. Formal Methods Syst. Des. **38**(3), 223–262 (2011)

17. Fujiwara, S., von Bochmann, G., Khendek, F., Amalou, M., Ghedamsi, A.: Test selection based on finite state models. IEEE Trans. Softw. Eng. **17**(6), 591–603 (1991)

18. Gonenc, G.: A method for the design of fault detection experiments. IEEE Trans. Comput. **C–19**(6), 551–558 (1970)

19. Gurbuz, H.G., Tekinerdogan, B.: Model-based testing for software safety: a systematic mapping study. Softw. Qual. J. **26**(4), 1327–1372 (2017). https://doi.org/10.1007/s11219-017-9386-2

20. Hierons, R.M., Turker, U.C.: Parallel algorithms for generating harmonised state identifiers and characterising sets. IEEE Trans. Comput. **65**(11), 3370–3383 (2016)

21. Khoury, R., Tawbi, N.: Corrective enforcement: a new paradigm of security policy enforcement by monitors. ACM Trans. Inf. Syst. Secur. **15**(2), 1–27 (2012)

22. Khoury, R., Tawbi, N.: Which security policies are enforceable by runtime monitors? A survey. Comput. Sci. Rev. **6**(1), 27–45 (2012)

23. Lee, D., Yannakakis, M.: Principles and methods of testing finite state machines-a survey. Proc. IEEE **84**(8), 1090–1123 (1996)

24. Li, Y., Ziyue, Y., Yao, G., Xiangqun, C.: DroidBot: a lightweight UI-guided test input generator for android. In: Proceedings of the International Conference on Software Engineering Companion (ICSE) (2017)

25. Ligatti, J., Bauer, L., Walker, D.: Run-time enforcement of nonsafety policies. ACM Trans. Inf. Syst. Secur. **12**(3), 1–41 (2009)

26. Ligatti, J., Bauer, L., Walker, D.: Edit automata: enforcement mechanisms for run-time security policies. Int. J. Inf. Secur. **4**, 2–16 (2005)

27. Ligatti, J., Reddy, S.: A theory of runtime enforcement, with results. In: Gritzalis, D., Preneel, B., Theoharidou, M. (eds.) ESORICS 2010. LNCS, vol. 6345, pp. 87–100. Springer, Heidelberg (2010). https://doi.org/10.1007/978-3-642-15497-3_6

28. Luo, G., Petrenko, A., Bochmann, G.V.: Selecting test sequences for partially-specified nondeterministic finite state machines. In: Mizuno, T., Higashino, T., Shiratori, N. (eds.) Protocol Test Systems. ITIFIP, pp. 95–110. Springer, Boston, MA (1995). https://doi.org/10.1007/978-0-387-34883-4_6

29. Lynch, N.A.: An introduction to input/output automata. PN (1988)

30. Magalhães, J.A.P., Silva, L.M.: Shōwa: a self-healing framework for web-based applications. ACM Trans. Autonom. Adapt. Syst. **10**(1), 4:1–4:28 (2015)

31. Memon, A.M., Banerjee, I., Nguyen, B.N., Robbins, B.: The first decade of GUI ripping: extensions, applications, and broader impacts. In: Proceedings of the Working Conference on Reverse Engineering (WCRE) (2013)

32. Petrenko, A., Yevtushenko, N., v. Bochmann, G.: Testing deterministic implementations from nondeterministic FSM specifications. In: Baumgarten, B., Burkhardt, H.-J., Giessler, A. (eds.) Testing of Communicating Systems. ITIFIP, pp. 125–140. Springer, Boston, MA (1996). https://doi.org/10.1007/978-0-387-35062-2_10

33. Riganelli, O., Micucci, D., Mariani, L.: Healing data loss problems in android apps. In: Proceedings of the International Workshop on Software Faults (IWSF), Co-Located with the International Symposium on Software Reliability Engineering (ISSRE) (2016)

34. Riganelli, O., Micucci, D., Mariani, L.: Increasing the reusability of enforcers with lifecycle events. In: Margaria, T., Steffen, B. (eds.) ISoLA 2018. LNCS, vol. 11247, pp. 51–57. Springer, Cham (2018). https://doi.org/10.1007/978-3-030-03427-6_7

35. Riganelli, O., Micucci, D., Mariani, L.: Policy enforcement with proactive libraries. In: Proceedings of the IEEE/ACM International Symposium on Software Engineering for Adaptive and Self-Managing Systems (SEAMS) (2017)

36. Riganelli, O., Micucci, D., Mariani, L.: Controlling interactions with libraries in android apps through runtime enforcement. ACM Trans. Autonom. Adapt. Syst. **14**(2), 8:1–8:29 (2019)

37. Riganelli, O., Micucci, D., Mariani, L., Falcone, Y.: Verifying policy enforcers. In: Lahiri, S., Reger, G. (eds.) RV 2017. LNCS, vol. 10548, pp. 241–258. Springer, Cham (2017). https://doi.org/10.1007/978-3-319-67531-2_15

38. Sabnani, K., Dahbura, A.: A protocol test generation procedure. Comput. Netw. ISDN Syst. **15**(4), 285–297 (1988)

39. Sidhu, D.P., Leung, T.K.: Formal methods for protocol testing: a detailed study. IEEE Trans. Softw. Eng. **15**(4), 413–426 (1989)

40. Sidiroglou, S., Laadan, O., Perez, C., Viennot, N., Nieh, J., Keromytis, A.D.: ASSURE: automatic software self-healing using rescue points. In: Proceedings of the International Conference on Architectural Support for Programming Languages and Operating Systems (ASPLOS) (2009)

41. Utting, M., Pretschner, A., Legeard, B.: A taxonomy of model-based testing approaches. Softw. Testing Verification Reliabil. **22**(5), 297–312 (2012)

42. XDA: Xposed (2020). http://repo.xposed.info/

43. Xu, R., Saïdi, H., Anderson, R.: Aurasium: practical policy enforcement for android applications. In: Proceedings of the USENIX Conference on Security Symposium (Security) (2012)

SharpDetect: Dynamic Analysis Framework for C#/.NET Programs

Andrej Čižmárik and Pavel Parízek[✉]

Department of Distributed and Dependable Systems, Faculty of Mathematics
and Physics, Charles University, Prague, Czech Republic
cizmarik.andrej@gmail.com, parizek@d3s.mff.cuni.cz

Abstract. Dynamic analysis is a popular approach to detecting possible runtime errors in software and for monitoring program behavior, which is based on precise inspection of a single execution trace. It has already proved to be useful especially in the case of multithreaded programs and concurrency errors, such as race conditions. Nevertheless, usage of dynamic analysis requires good tool support, e.g. for program code instrumentation and recording important events. While there exist several dynamic analysis frameworks for Java and C/C++ programs, including RoadRunner, DiSL and Valgrind, we were not aware of any framework targeting the C# language and the .NET platform. Therefore, we present SharpDetect, a new framework for dynamic analysis of .NET programs — that is, however, focused mainly on programs compiled from the source code written in C#. We describe the overall architecture of SharpDetect, the main analysis procedure, selected interesting technical details, its basic usage via command-line, configuration options, and the interface for custom analysis plugins. In addition, we discuss performance overhead of SharpDetect based on experiments with small benchmarks, and demonstrate its practical usefulness through a case study that involves application on NetMQ, a C# implementation of the ZeroMQ messaging middleware, where SharpDetect found one real concurrency error.

1 Introduction

Dynamic analysis is a popular approach to detecting possible runtime errors in software and for monitoring program behavior, which is applied within the scope of testing and debugging phases of software development. A typical dynamic analysis tool, such as Valgrind [5], records certain events and runtime values of program variables during execution of a subject program, and based on this information it can very precisely analyze behavior of the given program on the particular observed execution trace (and on few other closely-related traces). For example, dynamic bug detectors usually look for suspicious event sequences in the observed trace. Usage of dynamic analysis has already showed as beneficial especially in the case of multithreaded programs and search for concurrency

© Springer Nature Switzerland AG 2020
J. Deshmukh and D. Ničković (Eds.): RV 2020, LNCS 12399, pp. 298–309, 2020.
https://doi.org/10.1007/978-3-030-60508-7_16

errors, such as race conditions and deadlocks (cf. [2] and [6]), where the reported errors and fragments of the execution trace can be further inspected offline.

The main benefits of dynamic analysis include a very high precision and therefore also minimal number of reported false warnings, all of that because the actual concrete program execution is observed. On the other hand, usage of dynamic analysis requires good tool support, which is needed for tasks such as program code instrumentation and processing of recorded important events. Tools should also have practical overhead with respect to performance and memory consumption.

While robust dynamic analysis frameworks have been created for Java and C/C++ programs, including RoadRunner [3], DiSL [4], Valgrind [5] and Thread-Sanitizer [7], we were not aware of any framework targeting programs written in C# and running on the .NET platform. For that reason, we have developed SharpDetect, a framework for dynamic analysis of .NET programs, that we present in this paper.

SharpDetect takes executable .NET assemblies as input, performs offline instrumentation of the CIL (*Common Intermediate Language*) binary intermediate code with API calls that record information about program behavior, and runs the actual dynamic analysis of the instrumented subject program according to user configuration. Although the .NET platform supports many different programming languages, when developing and testing SharpDetect we focused mainly on programs compiled from the source code written in C#. Still, most programs written in other popular .NET languages, such as VB.NET and F#, should be also handled without any problems because SharpDetect manipulates the intermediate CIL binary code, but we have not tested it on any VB.NET and F# programs. In particular, the F# compiler may generate CIL code fragments different from those produced by C# compilers. We also want to emphasize that SharpDetect targets the modern cross-platform and open-source implementation of the .NET platform, which is called .NET Core. It runs on all major operating systems that are supported by .NET Core, that means recent distributions of Windows, Linux and Mac OS X. The output of SharpDetect includes a log of recorded events and a report of possibly discovered errors. Note, however, that SharpDetect is primarily a framework responsible for the dynamic analysis infrastructure. Specific custom analyses, including bug detectors, are actually performed by plugins that are built on top of the core framework. In order to demonstrate that the core framework (and its plugin API) is mature and can be used in practice, we have implemented two well-known algorithms for detecting concurrency errors, Eraser [6] and FastTrack [2], as plugins for SharpDetect. We have used the Eraser plugin in a case study that involves the NetMQ messaging middleware. Nevertheless, despite our focus on analyses related to concurrency, SharpDetect is a general framework that supports many different kinds of dynamic analyses.

Contribution and Outline. The main contributions presented in this paper include:

- SharpDetect, a new general and highly extensible framework that enables dynamic analysis of .NET programs;
- evaluation of runtime performance overhead incurred by usage of SharpDetect based on experiments with several benchmark programs written in C#;
- realistic case study that involves NetMQ, a C# implementation of the ZeroMQ messaging middleware, and demonstrates practical usefulness of SharpDetect for the purpose of detecting real concurrency errors.

The source code of a stable release of SharpDetect, together with example programs, is available at https://gitlab.com/acizmarik/sharpdetect-1.0.

Due to limited space, we provide only selected information about SharpDetect in this paper. Additional details can be found in the master thesis of the first author [1].

Structure. The rest of this paper is organized as follows. We describe the overall architecture and main workflow of SharpDetect in Sect. 2. Then we provide a brief user guide (Sect. 3), discuss the case study involving NetMQ (Sect. 4) and results of performance evaluation (Sect. 5), and finish with an outline of current work in progress and plans for the future.

2   Architecture and Main Workflow

SharpDetect consists of two parts, compile-time modules and runtime modules, that also correspond to main phases of its workflow, namely offline instrumentation and run of the dynamic analysis. The compile-time modules, Console and Injector, are responsible mainly for the offline CIL instrumentation. The runtime modules, Core and Plugins, perform the actual dynamic analysis during execution of the subject program. In addition, the module Common implements basic functionality, including the definitions of analysis events and necessary data structures, that is used by all other modules. Figure 1 shows a high-level overview of the architecture and workflow of SharpDetect. Both compile-time modules are displayed in the left frame with the label "Instrumentation", while runtime modules are displayed in the right frame with the label "Output Program". A very important aspect of the architecture of SharpDetect is that dynamic analysis runs in the same process as the subject program, in such a way that both our tool and the subject program share their memory address spaces. Now we provide details about individual modules and phases of the whole process.

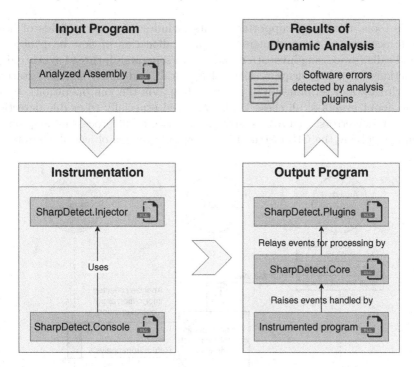

Fig. 1. High-level architecture and workflow of SharpDetect

The Console module is a .NET Core frontend of SharpDetect that has the form of a console application. It parses all configuration files and the command-line (Sect. 3), reads the input C# project and creates a self-contained package that includes the .NET program to be analyzed, drives the offline instrumentation process, and finally executes the actual dynamic analysis using the instrumented assemblies.

The Injector module uses dnlib [8] for manipulation with CIL bytecode. Its main purpose is to instrument the subject program with new code (classes, methods, and fields) that records the relevant events and other information about program state through calls of the SharpDetect API, when the dynamic analysis is executing. Note that SharpDetect instruments also .NET System libraries, especially the Base Class Library (BCL). This is needed, for example, to observe usage of collections in the subject program.

During the first phase, SharpDetect also completely removes native code from all the processed assemblies to enforce that CLR (Common Language Runtime), the virtual machine of .NET Core, actually loads the instrumented CIL bytecode instead of native images produced by the C# compiler based on the original CIL bytecode.

The Core module is the main component of SharpDetect that is used at run-time. It is responsible mainly for registering event handlers and dispatching of recorded analysis events to plugins. Like in the case of some other dynamic analysis tools, the list of supported events includes: accesses to fields of heap objects, accesses to array elements, dynamic allocation of new heap objects, method calls (processing invocation and return separately), thread synchronization actions (e.g., lock acquire, lock release, wait and notify signals), start of a new thread, and termination of a thread (e.g., via the join operation). Information about events of all these kinds is needed especially to enable detection of concurrency errors. Figure 2 illustrates the main event processing loop on an example involving the CIL instruction newobj for dynamic object allocation.

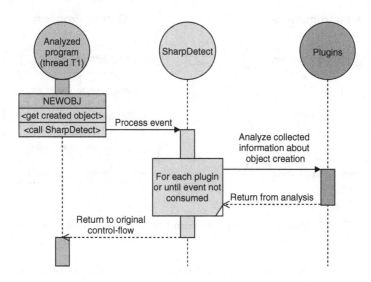

Fig. 2. Main event-processing loop illustrated on the CIL instruction newobj

The last part is the plugin API, an interface through which the core notifies plugins about observed events. Developers of custom plugins have to be aware of the fact that, due to SharpDetect running in the same process as the subject program, analysis of each individual event is carried out by the same thread that raised it. For each recorded event, the dynamic analysis engine takes control of the corresponding thread in the subject program for the duration of event's processing by all plugins. We provide more details about the plugin API from the user's perspective in Sect. 3.

A closely related aspect, which is not specific just to SharpDetect, is that when the analyzed program uses multiple threads, event handlers may be invoked concurrently and, therefore, events may be received in a wrong order by the analysis plugins. Consider the following example. Thread T_1 releases a lock L at some point during the program execution. But right before SharpDetect core notifies plugins about the corresponding event, a thread preemption happens and thread T_2 now runs instead of T_1. Immediately after the preemption, T_2 takes the lock L and SharpDetect notifies all plugins about this event. Plugins then receive information about T_2 acquiring L before the notification from T_1

about the release of L. We plan to address this challenge in future, using an approach that we discuss in Sect. 6.

One important limitation of the current version of SharpDetect is that it can track only information about user-defined threads. Specifically, it does not track analysis events related to threads retrieved from thread pools, because almost no information about such threads is available from the managed C# code.

3   User Guide

SharpDetect currently provides only a simple command-line interface. Figure 3 shows all three commands that must be executed in order to analyze a given C# program. The symbol rid in the first command stands for a runtime identifier, which needs to be specified in order to create a fully self-contained package. A complete list of supported runtime identifiers is provided in the official documentation for .NET Core [12].

```
// [optional] build the C# project and prepare it for
    instrumentation by generating a self-contained package
dotnet SharpDetect.Console.dll build <path_to_csproj> \
        --rid <platform_rid> --output <output_folder>

// instrument target assemblies based on the configuration
dotnet SharpDetect.Console.dll instrument <path_to_config>

// run the dynamic analysis
dotnet SharpDetect.Console.dll run \
        <path_to_instrumented_assembly> \
        --config <plugins_registration>
```

Fig. 3. Example usage of SharpDetect through its command-line interface

Configuration. Before the subject program can be analyzed, the user has to prepare the configuration of SharpDetect. In a local configuration file, specific to a given program, the user can (1) disable some categories of analysis events and (2) further restrict the set of reported events by defining patterns for names of methods and object fields that should be tracked. Figure 4 shows an example configuration, written in the JSON syntax, that:

- enables analysis events related to field accesses, method calls, and object allocation;
- completely disables all events related to arrays;
- restricts the set of reported field access events for the assembly MyAssembly1.dll just to the class C1 in the namespace nsA;
- and finally restricts the set of reported method call events for the assembly just to the class C1 in the namespace nsA and the method Mth3 in the class C2 from the namespace nsB.

The main purpose of all these configuration options is to allow users to specify events relevant for a particular run of dynamic analysis, so that the overall number of reported events is significantly reduced and the output can be therefore more easily inspected.

```
{
    "TargetAssembly" : "MyAssembly1.dll",
    "FieldPatterns" : [ "nsA.C1" ],
    "MethodPatterns" : [ "nsA.C1", "nsB.C2::Mth3" ],

    "FieldInjectors" : true,
    "MethodInjectors" : true,
    "ObjectCreateInjector" : true,
    "ArrayInjectors" : false
}
```

Fig. 4. Example content of a local configuration for a specific dynamic analysis.

Users also need to decide upfront whether they want to enable JIT optimizations. The difference can be observed, for example, in the case of programs that use multiple threads or the Task Parallel Library (TPL) with one simple lambda function as a task body. If the JIT optimizations are enabled, then each execution of the lambda function might be performed by the same thread, regardless of the usage of TPL. On the other hand, when the JIT optimizations are disabled, each execution of the lambda function is performed by a different thread.

Plugins. We have already indicated that a very important feature of SharpDetect is the possibility to use custom analysis plugins. Developers of such plugins need to implement the abstract class BasePlugin that belongs to the Core module. In Fig. 5, we show those methods of the abstract class that correspond to the most commonly used analysis events. Signatures of the remaining methods follow the same design pattern. The full source code of the BasePlugin class is available in the project repository and it is also documented on the project web site.

The command that executes actual dynamic analysis (Fig. 3) takes as one parameter the list of plugin names in the format plugin1 | plugin2 | ... | pluginN. SharpDetect then looks for available plugins in the directory specified by the environment variable SHARPDETECT_PLUGINS. During the analysis run, every observed event is dispatched by SharpDetect to the first plugin in the chain. A plugin that received an event may consume the event or forward it to the next plugin. Note that the default implementation of all event handler methods on the abstract class BasePlugin forwards the information about events to the next plugin in the chain, if such plugin exists.

Additional technical details regarding the development of custom plugins are illustrated by two example plugins that we released together with SharpDetect,

```
public abstract string PluginName { get; }
void AnalysisStart(MethodDescriptor entryMethod);
void AnalysisEnd(MethodDescriptor entryMethod);
void FieldRead(int threadId, object obj, FieldDescriptor fd);
void FieldWritten(int threadId, object obj, FieldDescriptor fd,
    object newValue);
void LockAcquireAttempted(int threadId, MethodDescriptor mth,
    object lockObj, (int, object)[] parameters);
void LockAcquireReturned(int threadId, MethodDescriptor mth,
    object lockObj, bool result, (int, object)[] parameters);
void LockReleased(int threadId, MethodDescriptor mth, object
    lockObj);
void MethodCalled(int threadId, (int, object)[] parameters,
    MethodDescriptor mth);
void MethodReturned(int threadId, object retValue, bool valid,
    (int, object)[] parameters, MethodDescriptor mth);
void ObjectCreated(int threadId, object obj);
void UserThreadStarted(int threadId, Thread thread);
void UserThreadJoined(int threadId, Thread thread);
```

Fig. 5. Selected methods defined by the abstract class BasePlugin

i.e. our implementations of the algorithms Eraser and FastTrack that can be found in the module SharpDetect.Plugins.

4   Case Study

We have applied SharpDetect to the NetMQ library [9], which is a C# implementation of the ZeroMQ high-performance asynchronous messaging middleware, in order to see how well it can help with debugging of concurrency issues in realistic programs. To be more specific, the first author used SharpDetect when searching for the root cause of a particular timing issue in NetMQ that occurred very rarely.

The source code of a test program that uses NetMQ, together with the configuration of SharpDetect, is in the directory src/SharpDetect/SharpDetect.Examples/CaseStudy of the repository at https://gitlab.com/acizmarik/sharpdetect-1.0. It is a standard .NET Core console application that runs two threads (server and client). Here we describe just a fragment of the SharpDetect's output and a fragment of the NetMQ source code that contains the root cause of this particular concurrency issue.

Figure 6 shows output produced by the run of dynamic analysis with the Eraser plugin, which can detect possible data races. The last two entries in Fig. 6 represent the warning reported by Eraser, which points to possible data races on the static fields s_lastTsc and s_lastTime defined by the class NetMQ.Core.Utils.Clock. In the corresponding revision of NetMQ [10], both static fields are read and written only by the method NowMS whose source code is displayed in Fig. 7.

```
// Field s_lastTime was written by thread with ID=3
21:12:57 [INF] [3] Field: System.Int64 NetMQ.Core.Utils.Clock::
    s_lastTime was written with value 27266154.

// Field s_lastTsc was read by thread with ID=4
21:12:57 [INF] [4] Field: System.Int64 NetMQ.Core.Utils.Clock::
    s_lastTsc was read from.

// Field s_lastTime was read by thread with ID=3
21:12:57 [INF] [3] Field: System.Int64 NetMQ.Core.Utils.Clock::
    s_lastTime was read from.

// Field s_lastTsc was written by thread with ID=4
21:12:57 [INF] [4] Field: System.Int64 NetMQ.Core.Utils.Clock::
    s_lastTsc was written with value 54333378824957.

21:12:57 [ERR] [Eraser] detected data-race on a static field
    System.Int64 NetMQ.Core.Utils.Clock::s_lastTsc
21:12:57 [ERR] [Eraser] detected data-race on a static field
    System.Int64 NetMQ.Core.Utils.Clock::s_lastTime
```

Fig. 6. Output produced by SharpDetect with the Eraser plugin for the program that uses NetMQ

Log entries at the level INF, which are presented in Fig. 6, indicate that the method NowMS is actually executed by multiple threads without any synchronization of the critical section.

5 Performance Evaluation

In this section we report and discuss the overhead of dynamic analysis with SharpDetect, and the impact on analyzed programs, in terms of the running time and memory consumption. For that purpose, we performed experiments with two small benchmark programs on the following hardware and software configuration: Intel Core i7-8550U CPU with the clock speed 1.80 GHz and 4 cores, 16 GB of memory, 64-bit version of Windows 10, and .NET Core 2.1.

The first benchmark program uses Task Parallel Library (TPL) to process a big array in an unsafe way, such that individual threads are not synchronized and therefore a data race may happen at each access to array elements. The second benchmark program is a simple implementation of the producer-consumer pattern, where (i) both the producer and consumer are implemented as separate Task objects that share a common queue and (ii) access to the queue is guarded by a lock. Source code of both programs is available in the SharpDetect repository in the directories src/SharpDetect/SharpDetect.Examples/(Evaluation1,Evaluation2). Even though these programs are quite small, their execution generates a lot of analysis events, which makes them useful for the purpose of measuring the overhead of analysis with SharpDetect.

```
public static long NowMs() {
    long tsc = Rdtsc();
    if (tsc == 0) return NowUs() / 1000;

    /* Beginning of critical section */
    if (tsc - s_lastTsc <= Config.ClockPrecision / 2
            && tsc >= s_lastTsc) {
        return s_lastTime;
    }

    s_lastTsc = tsc;
    s_lastTime = NowUs() / 1000;
    return s_lastTime;
    /* End of critical section */
}
```

Fig. 7. Source code of the method NowMS that contains root cause of the concurrency issue.

Each measurement was repeated 50 times. In tables with results, we present average values together with the corresponding standard deviations. The baseline values of running time and memory consumption, respectively, were recorded using the subject programs before instrumentation.

Table 1 contains results for the first benchmark and several configurations of SharpDetect. Data in the table show that usage of SharpDetect, together with the Eraser plugin, is responsible for a slow-down by the factor of 4 with respect to the baseline. Memory overhead is caused by tracking analysis information for each array element.

Table 1. The running time and memory consumption of the first benchmark program

Configuration		Results	
Instrumented	Plugins	Time (s)	Memory (KiB)
No (baseline)	–	0.19 ± 0.01	333
Yes	EmptyPlugin	0.44 ± 0.01	541 ± 5
Yes	FastTrack	0.56 ± 0.01	4223 ± 37
Yes	Eraser	0.79 ± 0.03	7216 ± 6

Table 2 contains results for the second benchmark. In this case, we observed slow-down at most by the factor of 3.7. Memory consumption apparently increased by the factor of 16, but, in fact, there is a constant memory overhead of about 4000 KiB, regardless of the configuration. The main cause is that SharpDetect needs to track a lot of information during the program execution, such as method call arguments and return values, even when plugins do not use much of the data.

Table 2. The running time and memory consumption of the second benchmark program

Configuration		Results	
Instrumented	Plugins	Time (s)	Memory (KiB)
No (baseline)	–	0.145 ± 0.003	261.1
Yes	EmptyPlugin	0.51 ± 0.01	4265.7 ± 0.5
Yes	Eraser	0.53 ± 0.02	4267.5 ± 0.5
Yes	FastTrack	0.54 ± 0.02	4268.3 ± 0.7

Overall, results of our experiments indicate that SharpDetect has a relatively small overhead that enables usage of the tool in practice. Note that baseline measurements of the memory consumption did not deviate at all for both programs, because non-instrumented variants of the programs allocate very few objects on the heap.

6   Future Work

We plan to continue our work on SharpDetect in various directions, implementing new features and improving its performance.

One way to reduce the effects of dynamic analysis with SharpDetect on the behavior and performance of subject programs is to use the .NET Profiling API [11], which enables online instrumentation at the level of CIL bytecode during execution of a subject program. In addition, usage of the .NET Profiling API allows clients to observe specific events raised by the .NET execution engine, CoreCLR, even without code instrumentation. We are currently working on the implementation of a new version, SharpDetect 2.0, that will (1) utilize the .NET Profiling API, (2) execute dynamic analysis using the out-of-process approach where the analysis runs in a different process than the subject program, and (3) contain many additional improvements. The process of the subject program will contain just the minimal necessary amount of injected code to record events and forward them to the analysis process (which involves all the plugins, too).

Another goal is to address the issues related to possible concurrent invocation of event handlers that we described at the end of Sect. 2. We plan to implement a solution that will impose more strict ordering of analysis events from multiple threads, based on some form of vector clock, such that SharpDetect could delay dispatching of an event until all observed preceding events are processed.

Acknowledgments. This work was partially supported by the Czech Science Foundation project 18-17403S and partially supported by the Charles University institutional funding project SVV 260588.

References

1. Cizmarik, A.: Dynamic Analysis Framework for C#/.NET Programs. Master thesis, Charles University, Prague, (2020) https://is.cuni.cz/webapps/zzp/detail/209472/45410198
2. Flanagan, C., Freund, S.N.: FastTrack: efficient and precise dynamic race detection. In Proceedings of PLDI 2009, pp. 121–133. ACM (2009) https://doi.org/10.1145/1542476.1542490
3. Flanagan, C., Freund, S.N.: The RoadRunner dynamic analysis framework for concurrent programs. In Proceedings of PASTE 2010, pp. 1–8. ACM (2010) https://doi.org/10.1145/1806672.1806674
4. Marek, L., et al.: Java bytecode instrumentation made easy: the DiSL framework for dynamic program analysis. In: Jhala, R., Igarashi, A. (eds.) APLAS 2012. LNCS, vol. 7705, pp. 256–263. Springer, Heidelberg (2012). https://doi.org/10.1007/978-3-642-35182-2_18
5. Nethercote, N., Seward, J.: Valgrind: a framework for heavyweight dynamic binary instrumentation. In Proceedings of PLDI 2007, pp. 89–100. ACM (2007) https://doi.org/10.1145/1250734.1250746
6. Savage, S., Burrows, M., Nelson, G., Sobalvarro, P., Anderson, T.: Eraser: a dynamic data race detector for multithreaded programs. ACM Trans. Comput. Syst. (TOCS) 15(4), 391–411 (1997). https://doi.org/10.1145/265924.265927
7. Serebryany, K., Iskhodzhanov, T.: ThreadSanitizer: data race detection in practice. In Proceedings of WBIA 2009, pp. 62–71. ACM (2009) https://doi.org/10.1145/1791194.1791203
8. Dnlib, https://github.com/0xd4d/dnlib. Accessed Jun 2020
9. The NetMQ library, https://netmq.readthedocs.io/en/latest/. Accessed Jun 2020
10. NetMQ Custom Clock Implementation, https://github.com/zeromq/netmq/blob/e4dfcf9e8190f85bf4fab9fc657e2c7da820c7f4/src/NetMQ/Core/Utils/Clock.cs#L88. Accessed Jun 2020
11. .NET Profiling API Reference, https://docs.microsoft.com/en-us/dotnet/framework/unmanaged-api/profiling/. Accessed Jun 2020
12. A complete list of supported Runtime Identifiers (RID), https://docs.microsoft.com/en-us/dotnet/core/rid-catalog. Accessed Jun 2020

Efficient Runtime Assertion Checking for Properties over Mathematical Numbers

Nikolai Kosmatov[1,2]($\boxtimes$) (ID), Fonenantsoa Maurica[1,3], and Julien Signoles[1]

[1] CEA, LIST, Software Safety and Security Laboratory, Palaiseau, France
nikolaikosmatov@gmail.com, julien.signoles@cea.fr
[2] Thales Research & Technology, Palaiseau, France
[3] Billee, Neuilly-sur-Seine, France
fonenantsoa.maurica@billee.fr

Abstract. Runtime assertion checking is the discipline of detecting at runtime violations of program properties written as formal code annotations. These properties often include numerical properties, which may rely on either (bounded) machine representations or (unbounded) mathematical numbers. The verification of the former is easier to implement and more efficient at runtime, while the latter are more expressive and often more adequate for writing specifications. This short paper explains how the runtime assertion checker E-ACSL reconciles both approaches by presenting a type system that allows the tool to generate efficient machine-number based code when it is safe to do so, while generating arbitrary-precision code when it is necessary. This type system and the code generator not only handle integers but also rational arithmetics. As far as we know, it is the first runtime verification tool that supports the verification of properties over rational numbers.

Keywords: Typing · Runtime assertion checking · Numerical properties · Rational numbers · Optimized code generation

1 Introduction

Runtime assertion checking is the discipline of detecting at runtime violations of program properties written as formal code annotations [1,2]. This way, it allows the developer to better support testing, to make debugging easier by reducing the distance between the execution of a bug and the manifestation of its effects, to serve as executable comments about preconditions and postconditions[1], and can act as an intermediate step before applying formal proof. Its main drawback is the slowdown of the program execution. It may also lead to additional runtime failures when used incorrectly by a developer.

---

[1] https://blog.regehr.org/archives/1091.

© Springer Nature Switzerland AG 2020
J. Deshmukh and D. Ničković (Eds.): RV 2020, LNCS 12399, pp. 310–322, 2020.
https://doi.org/10.1007/978-3-030-60508-7_17

Formal code annotations usually express properties about program variables or/and program inputs and outputs. Most of them are mathematical properties or, at least, involve some mathematical operations. The semantics of these properties may involve either bounded machine representations (e.g., machine integers and floating-point numbers), or unbounded mathematical numbers (e.g., mathematical integers in $\mathbb{Z}$ and real numbers in $\mathbb{R}$). The former one allows for efficient runtime checking and remains close to the semantics of the underlying programming language, so easy to grasp for a developer. However, it is less expressive than the latter and, most often, it does not correspond to the informal specifications that writers or readers have in mind because they usually think in terms of usual mathematics [3]. It can lead to incorrect specifications [4]. Yet the latter is harder to implement and leads to less efficient code [5].

The oldest formal specification languages such as Eiffel [6] and Spec# [7] rely on a bounded semantics. JML [8] historically used this semantics but now accepts three different modes (bounded integers with modulo when overflowing, bounded integers that raises exceptions when overflowing, and unbounded integers). Spark2014 [9] also offers both bounded and unbounded integer modes. ACSL [10] and Why3 [11] rely on an unbounded semantics. Kosmatov et al. [12] provide a more complete comparison of Spark2014, ACSL and Why3.

This paper presents a type system that allows to rely on the unbounded mathematical semantics when writing formal specifications, while soundly using bounded machine integers most of the time when executing the code. This way, it reconciles both approaches by combining the expressiveness of the mathematical semantics and the efficiency of machine integers. It supports not only integers, but also rational numbers in $\mathbb{Q}$, thus making it possible to conveniently express and verify at runtime many useful numerical accuracy properties. This technique is implemented in E-ACSL [13], the runtime assertion checker of Frama-C [14]. This type system has also been adapted to Spark2014 by Adacore (but only for integers). As far as we know, E-ACSL is the only tool that supports runtime assertion checking of properties over rational numbers. The paper also provides initial experiments that demonstrate the gain of efficiency of E-ACSL because of its type system. To sum up, **the contributions of this paper** are threefold:

- a type system that allows a runtime assertion checker to soundly rely on machine code for evaluating mathematical integers and rational numbers;
- an implementation of this type system in E-ACSL that allows the tool to efficiently check at runtime properties over both integer and rational numbers;
- an initial evaluation of this type system to measure the gain of efficiency.

The outline of the paper is as follows. Section 2 gives a general overview and a motivating example. Section 3 introduces a small formal specification language on which the type system is designed in Sect. 4. Section 5 provides some insights about our evaluation and experiments before concluding in Sect. 6.

```
1  short Mo,Tu,We,Th,Fr,Sa,Su; // daily prices in cents
2  int main{
3  ... // read recorded prices over a week
4  // compute the average price as a floating-point number
5  float avg=(Mo+Tu+We+Th+Fr+Sa+Su)/7.0;
6  // check the error is at most 0.0001
7  /*@ assert (Mo+Tu+We+Th+Fr+Sa+Su)/7.0-0.0001 ≤ avg ≤
8       (Mo+Tu+We+Th+Fr+Sa+Su)/7.0+0.0001; */
9  }
```

Fig. 1. Toy example computing an average, and an ACSL assertion on its precision.

2   Overview and Motivating Example

To illustrate a property with mathematical numbers, consider a simple example of Fig. 1, broadly inspired by well-known numerical accuracy issues (in critical software[2] or in computations of stock prices[3]). It computes, given daily prices of a merchandise (say, in cents), its average price (as a floating-point value) over a week. The considered property states that, for a given $\varepsilon > 0$, the computed average avg has a maximal (absolute) error ε with respect to the exact (ideal) average A_{id}: $A_{id} - \varepsilon \leq avg \leq A_{id} + \varepsilon$. For $\varepsilon = 0.0001$, this property can fail: e.g., $17293/7 \approx 2470.428571$ while the division result in a float is 2470.428467.

The ACSL semantics guarantees that all computations in annotations remain mathematically precise. It allows us to specify the numerical accuracy property of the result in the simplest form, as in the assertion. Indeed, unlike ACSL, in C code, a sum of integers can overflow, and a division in floating-point numbers can be rounded. In our example, the developer avoids the risk of an integer overflow by taking the prices in short, automatically promoted to int to compute the sum (line 5), but the rounding cannot be avoided.

The expression (Mo + ... + Su)/7.0 in the assertion (lines 7–8) can have a different value than in the code (line 5) because it assumes mathematical numbers and operators in $\mathbb{Z}$ or $\mathbb{R}$. To verify the assertion at runtime, it cannot be translated into C by the same expression in machine numbers. In our example, the property translated in such a way would be always true, while the assertion can in fact fail. Precise computations in mathematical integer and rational numbers can rely e.g. on the GMP library[4] for C programs, but its usage has a cost.

The purpose of our work is twofold. First, we present a pre-analysis step that allows to identify computations for which machine numbers (of a suitable type) can be used without loss of precision. In our example, the sums on lines 7–8 can be safely computed in an int variable without GMP calls. Second, we add a support for rational numbers that makes it possible to easily specify and verify at runtime properties over rational numbers, including some accuracy properties.

---

[2] See e.g. http://www-users.math.umn.edu/~arnold/disasters/patriot.html.

[3] See e.g. https://en.wikipedia.org/wiki/Vancouver_Stock_Exchange.

[4] https://gmplib.org/.

$$
\begin{array}{ll}
a ::= \texttt{/*@ assert } p\texttt{; */} & \text{assertion} \\
p ::= p \; rel \; p & rel \in \{\wedge, \vee, \Rightarrow\} \\
\quad | \; \neg p & \text{negation} \\
\quad | \; t \; cmp \; t & cmp \in \{\equiv, <, >, \leq, \geq\} \\
\quad | \; \texttt{let } x = t; \; p & \text{local binding} \\
\quad | \; \blacklozenge \; \tau \; x; \; t \leq x < t, \; p & \blacklozenge \in \{\forall, \exists\} \\
\tau ::= \gamma \; | \; \mathbb{Z} \; | \; \mathbb{Q} & \gamma \in \textsf{C types}
\end{array}
\qquad
\begin{array}{ll}
t ::= x & \text{logic binder} \\
\quad | \; lv & \text{left-values} \\
\quad | \; zcst & zcst \in \mathbb{Z} \\
\quad | \; qcst & qcst \in \mathbb{Q} \\
\quad | \; t \; op \; t & op \in \{+, -, \times, /\} \\
\quad | \; (\tau)t & \text{cast}
\end{array}
$$

Fig. 2. Formal syntax of the specification language.

3   Formal Specification Language

Our work is based on the E-ACSL specification language [15], derived from the ACSL specification language [10]. The differences between both languages [5] are of no importance for our work. This section introduces a small common sublanguage sufficient for presenting our type system. It is rich enough to express the assertion at lines 7–8 of Fig. 1. Its formal syntax is shown in Fig. 2.

Logic statements are assertions enclosed in special comments /*@ ...*/ that may be written before any C instruction. Assertions are typed predicates which include logical relations, comparison operators over terms, local bindings à la ML and bounded first-order quantifiers over integers. Terms are logic binders, C left-values (variables, pointer dereferences, array and struct accesses, etc.), mathematical constants (either integers or rationals; e.g., the constant 7.0 on lines 7–8 in Fig. 1 is seen as a rational number because of the decimal notation)[5], numerical operators, and (explicit) casts. Terms are typed. Types are the standard C types extended with mathematical integers and rationals. The typing rules are left implicit here, but are straightforward. A numerical operation is an integer one if both arguments are integers; otherwise it is an operation over rational numbers (and the integer argument, if any, is automatically promoted to the corresponding rational number).

It is worth noting that all constants and numerical operators are over mathematical numbers (either integers in $\mathbb{Z}$, or rationals in $\mathbb{Q}$ depending on the context). C integers and floating-point values (that come from C left values) are implicitly coerced to their mathematical counterparts. For the sake of simplicity, we assume no NaN, -0.0 nor $\pm\infty$ values, as well as no runtime errors when evaluating C left-values. In practice, the necessary code for checking the absence of runtime errors is generated by an independent mechanism [5,16].

4   Type System

Preamble. The illustrative examples of this section assume a toy architecture that supports a set of C types limited to $\{\texttt{char}, \texttt{int}, \texttt{float}\}$ in which the values of type char are included in the interval $[-32; 31]$, while those of type int are included in $[-128; 127]$. The possible floating-point values are left unspecified.

---

[5] E-ACSL also supports floating-point constants such as $0.1f$ but they are excluded here for the sake of simplicity.

```
1  { /* declaring temporary variables */
2    mpz_t __e_acsl_x, __e_acsl, __e_acsl_add, __e_acsl_2;
3    int __e_acsl_le;
4    /* computing x+1 */
5    __gmpz_init_set_si(__e_acsl_x, x);
6    __gmpz_init_set_si(__e_acsl, 1);
7    __gmpz_init(__e_acsl_add);
8    __gmpz_add(__e_acsl_add, __e_acsl_x, __e_acsl);
9    /* comparing x+1 and 127 */
10   __gmpz_init_set_si(__e_acsl_2, 127);
11   __e_acsl_le = __gmpz_cmp(__e_acsl_add, __e_acsl_2);
12   e_acsl_assert(__e_acsl_le <= 0);
13   /* freeing the allocated GMP numbers */
14   __gmpz_clear(__e_acsl_x);
15   __gmpz_clear(__e_acsl);
16   __gmpz_clear(__e_acsl_add);
17   __gmpz_clear(__e_acsl_2); }
```

Fig. 3. GMP code generated by E-ACSL for /*@ assert $x + 1 \leq 127;$ */ on a toy architecture. The comments have been manually inserted for readability.

Illustrative Examples. Consider the assertion /*@ assert $x + 1 \leq 127;$ */ with x of type int. When $x = 127$, it is invalid. Yet, using machine-integer code for evaluating it would be unsound since $x + 1$ would overflow. To circumvent this issue, a code generator should rely on a dedicated mathematical library such as GMP in C. For instance, the E-ACSL runtime assertion checker [13] of Frama-C [14] would generate the (slightly simplified) code of Fig. 3.

While sound, the generated arbitrary-precision code is not as efficient as machine-number based code, while not being always necessary. Consider for instance the assertion /*@ assert $c + 1 \equiv 0;$ */ with c of type char: it would be more efficient and fully sound to use machine-number based code for evaluating the assertion since $c + 1$ cannot overflow if computed over type int (the values of c vary from -32 to 31, thus the values of $c + 1$ are included in $[-128; 127]$).

Based on (over-approximated) intervals of possible values of integer-valued expressions, our type system decides whether the code generator can soundly rely on machine-number based code. On our small examples, it infers that the type of $x + 1$ should be $\mathbb{Z}$ because its possible values vary from -128 to 128, so does not fit in any existing type of our toy architecture, while the type of $c + 1$ can be int because its possible values vary from -32 to 32. The domains of values are computed thanks to a simple interval analysis. In most cases, using a machine-number based code instead of arbitrary-precision code is possible.

Our type system also supports rational arithmetics. Yet, our type system allows to optimize only comparisons between floating-point variables (e.g., $f \leq g$) but no rational operations. Indeed, an interval-based reasoning does not allow optimizing rational arithmetics (e.g., $f + 1$.) by floating-point operations without being unsound (as any non-singular interval of rationals contains an infinite number of values non-representable as floating-point numbers). It explains why the rational extension of our type system does not rely on interval arithmetics: it directly infers either a floating-point type for variables and comparisons between them, or type $\mathbb{Q}$ for any other rational number or operator.

Language Type System. We assume the existence of a type system at the level of the formal specification language: $\Sigma(t)$ denotes the type of a term t and the primitive isinteger(t) (resp., isfloat(t)) is true if and only if $\Sigma(t)$ is a subtype of $\mathbb{Z}$ (resp., a floating-point type). The relation $\preccurlyeq_\tau$ is the subtyping relation (expressing that all values of one type are also values of the other). On our illustrative examples, $\Sigma(x) = \text{int}$ and $\Sigma(c) = \text{char}$ because x (resp. c) is an int (resp. a char), while $\Sigma(x+1) = \Sigma(c+1) = \mathbb{Z}$ since any logical integer operation relies on an unbounded semantics. Furthermore, char $\preccurlyeq_\tau$ int $\preccurlyeq_\tau \mathbb{Z}$.

Integer Intervals. We consider (unbounded) integer intervals with partial order $\preccurlyeq_I$. Let $\emptyset$ be the empty interval, $\mathbb{T}(I)$ be the smallest C integral type containing interval I (e.g., int if $I = [18; 42]$ since $I \not\subseteq [-32; 31]$), or $\mathbb{Z}$ otherwise, and $\mathbb{I}(t)$ be an interval that contains all the possible values of the term t. On our illustrative examples, $\mathbb{I}(x + 1) = [-128; 128]$ and $\mathbb{I}(c + 1) = [-32; 32]$, thus $\mathbb{T}(x + 1) = \mathbb{Z}$ and $\mathbb{T}(c + 1) = \text{int}$. In practice, E-ACSL relies on a simple syntactic type-based inference system to compute $\mathbb{I}(t)$ [17].

Kinds. Kinds extend integer intervals to floating-point and rational numbers. They are required since integer arithmetics and rational arithmetics should remain separated: as already explained, integer type inference relies on interval arithmetics, while it is not the case for rationals. Kinds define a lattice structure. They are the core information used by our type system. More formally, let $(\mathbb{K}, \preccurlyeq)$ be the lattice of kinds defined as follows:

$$\mathbb{K} ::= \mathcal{Z}\ I \quad \text{an integer interval } I \qquad \mathcal{Z}\ I_1 \preccurlyeq \mathcal{Z}\ I_2 \iff I_1 \preccurlyeq_I I_2$$
$$\mid\ \mathcal{F}\ \gamma \quad \text{a floating-point type } \gamma \qquad \mathcal{F}\ \gamma_1 \preccurlyeq \mathcal{F}\ \gamma_2 \iff \gamma_1 \preccurlyeq_\tau \gamma_2$$
$$\mid\ \mathcal{Q} \quad \text{the set of rationals } \mathbb{Q} \qquad \mathcal{Z}\ I \preccurlyeq \mathcal{F}\ \gamma \iff \mathbb{T}(I) \preccurlyeq_\tau \gamma$$
$$K \preccurlyeq \mathcal{Q} \quad \text{(for all } K \in \mathbb{K}\text{)}.$$

The kind $\mathcal{Z}\ \emptyset$ (resp., $\mathcal{Q}$) is the minimum (resp., maximum) element of the lattice. Let $\sqcup$ (resp., $\sqcap$) denote the union (resp., intersection) over kinds induced by their lattice structure. The kind of a term t, denoted $\kappa(t)$, and the type of a kind k, denoted $\theta(k)$, are defined as follows:

$$\kappa(t) = \mathcal{Z}\ \mathbb{I}(t) \quad \text{if isinteger}(t) \qquad\qquad \theta(\mathcal{Z}\ I) = \mathbb{T}(I)$$
$$\kappa(t) = \mathcal{F}\ \Sigma(t) \quad \text{if isfloat}(t) \qquad\qquad \theta(\mathcal{F}\ \tau) = \tau$$
$$\kappa(t) = \mathcal{Q} \quad \text{if } \neg\, \text{isfloat}(t) \qquad\qquad \theta(\mathcal{Q}) = \mathbb{Q}.$$

While we will use an integer interval I for soundly representing a range of machine-integer values as soon as $\mathbb{T}(I)$ is not $\mathbb{Z}$, it would be unsound to use a non-singular rational interval R to do the same for a range of floating-point values since R contains (an infinite number of) rationals that are not representable as floating-point values. The operator κ naturally extends from terms to types. The

$$\frac{}{\varGamma \vdash cst : \theta(\kappa(cst) \sqcup \kappa(\text{int}))} \text{[Cst]} \qquad \frac{}{\varGamma \vdash lv : \varSigma(lv)} \text{[Lv]} \qquad \frac{}{\varGamma \vdash x : \varGamma(x)} \text{[Bind]}$$

$$\frac{\varGamma \vdash t : \tau_t \quad \tau' = \theta(\kappa((\tau)t))}{\varGamma \vdash (\tau)t : \tau'} \text{[Cast]} \qquad \frac{\tau = \theta(\kappa(t_1) \sqcup \kappa(t_2) \sqcup \kappa(t_1 \text{ op } t_2)) \quad \varGamma \vdash t_1 : \tau \quad \varGamma \vdash t_2 : \tau}{\varGamma \vdash t_1 \text{ op } t_2 : \tau \hookleftarrow \tau} \text{[Op]}$$

$$\frac{\varGamma \vdash t : \tau' \quad \tau' \preccurlyeq_\tau \tau}{\varGamma \vdash t : \tau} \text{[Sub]} \qquad \frac{\varGamma \vdash t : \tau' \hookleftarrow \tau' \quad \tau \prec_\tau \tau' \quad \theta(\kappa(t)) \preccurlyeq_\tau \tau}{\varGamma \vdash t : \tau \hookleftarrow \tau'} \text{[↓]}$$

$$\frac{\varGamma \vdash_p p_1 : \text{int} \quad \vdash_p p_2 : \text{int}}{\varGamma \vdash_p p_1 \text{ rel } p_2 : \text{int}} \text{[Rel]} \qquad \frac{\varGamma \vdash_p p : \text{int}}{\varGamma \vdash_p \neg p : \text{int}} \text{[Neg]}$$

$$\frac{\tau = \theta(\kappa(t_1) \sqcup \kappa(t_2)) \quad \varGamma \vdash t_1 : \tau \quad \varGamma \vdash t_2 : \tau}{\varGamma \vdash_p t_1 \text{ cmp } t_2 : \text{int} \hookleftarrow \tau} \text{[Cmp]} \qquad \frac{\varGamma \vdash t : \tau \quad \varGamma, x : \tau \vdash_p p : \text{int}}{\varGamma \vdash_p \text{ let } x = t; \ p : \text{int}} \text{[Let]}$$

$$\frac{\tau' = \theta(\kappa(t_1) \sqcup \kappa(t_2)) \quad \varGamma \vdash t_1 : \tau' \quad \varGamma \vdash t_2 : \tau' \quad \varGamma, \ x : \theta(\kappa(\tau) \sqcap \kappa(\tau')) \vdash_p p : \text{int}}{\varGamma \vdash_p \blacklozenge \tau \ x; \ t_1 \leq x < t_2, \ p \ : \text{int}} \text{[Quantif]}$$

Fig. 4. Type system inferring the types of terms and predicates for the generated code.

operator θ converts a kind to a type. For integers, it means converting intervals to types, while, for rationals, it means choosing between a floating-point types and rationals. On our illustrative examples, one gets:

$$\theta(\kappa(x + 1)) = \theta(\mathcal{Z} \ [-128; 128]) = \mathbb{Z}$$
$$\theta(\kappa(c + 1)) = \theta(\mathcal{Z} \ [-32; 32]) \quad = \text{int}$$
$$\theta(\kappa(f + 1.)) = \theta(\mathcal{Q}) \qquad\qquad = \mathbb{Q}.$$

Type System. Figure 4 presents the type system. An earlier version limited to integers has already been published in French [17]. A type judgment, written $\varGamma \vdash t : \tau_1 \hookleftarrow \tau_2$ for terms (resp., $\varGamma \vdash_p p : \tau_1 \hookleftarrow \tau_2$ for predicates), means "in the typing environment $\varGamma$, the C expression generated for t (resp., p) may soundly have type τ_1, but, in the case of an operator (resp., a comparison), it must be computed over type τ_2". The type τ_2 is omitted when irrelevant (e.g. for constants). Actually, it may only differ from τ_1 for comparisons and decreasing arithmetic operators (the division "/" in our formal specification language). Predicates return an int. For instance, assuming two variables x and y of type char and int respectively, the term $x/(y + 1)$ requires GMP code because $y + 1$ does not fit into any C type of our toy architecture. However, its result fits into an int, so it may soundly be compared to 42 with the usual C equality. Therefore, its type is int $\hookleftarrow \mathbb{Z}$. Figure 5 details the derivation tree of $x/(y + 1) \equiv 42$ and $f - 0.1 \leq g$ (with both f and g of type float).

A constant is evaluated within the smallest possible type with respect to its value (rule [Cst]), but this type is actually never more precise than int (e.g., never char). This optimization avoids superfluous casts in the generated code, because of the C99 promotion rule [18, §6.3.1.1] that states (among others) that any expression more precise than int is automatically promoted to int when used in arithmetic operands. A left-value keeps its C type ([Lv]), while a logic binder takes it from the typing context ([Bind]). A cast $(\tau)t$ uses the interval inference system to downcast the resulting type of t to a possibly more precise type τ' (e.g. char for both $(\text{int})4$ and $(\text{char})42$, cf. rule [Cast]). As usual with explicit

$$
\cfrac{
  \cfrac{
    \cfrac{\dfrac{\vdash x : \mathsf{char}}{\vdash x : \mathbb{Z}}
      \quad
      \cfrac{\dfrac{\vdash y : \mathsf{int}}{\vdash y : \mathbb{Z}}\,[\textsc{Sub}] \quad \dfrac{\vdash 1 : \mathsf{int}}{\vdash 1 : \mathbb{Z}}}{\vdash y+1 : \mathbb{Z} \hookleftarrow \mathbb{Z}}\,[\textsc{Op}]
    }{\vdash x/(y+1) : \mathbb{Z} \hookleftarrow \mathbb{Z}}\,[\textsc{Op}]
    \qquad \mathsf{int} \prec_\tau \mathbb{Z} \qquad \theta(\kappa(x/(y+1))) \preccurlyeq_\tau \mathsf{int}
  }{\vdash x/(y+1) : \mathsf{int} \hookleftarrow \mathbb{Z}}\,[\downarrow]
  \qquad \vdash 42 : \mathsf{int}
}{\vdash_p x/(y+1) \equiv 42 : \mathsf{int}}\,[\textsc{Cmp}]
$$

$$
\cfrac{
  \cfrac{\dfrac{\vdash f : \mathsf{float}}{\vdash f : \mathbb{Q}}\,[\textsc{Sub}] \quad \vdash 0.1 : \mathbb{Q}}{\vdash f - 0.1 : \mathbb{Q} \hookleftarrow \mathbb{Q}}\,[\textsc{Op}]
  \qquad
  \dfrac{\vdash g : \mathsf{float}}{\vdash g : \mathbb{Q}}\,[\textsc{Sub}]
}{\vdash_p f - 0.1 \le g : \mathsf{int} \hookleftarrow \mathbb{Q}}\,[\textsc{Cmp}]
$$

$$
\cfrac{
  \dfrac{0 : \mathsf{int}}{\vdash 0 : \mathsf{char}}\,[\downarrow]
  \quad
  \dfrac{4 : \mathsf{int}}{4 : \mathsf{char}}\,[\downarrow]
  \quad
  \cfrac{
    \cfrac{x : \mathsf{char} \vdash 2 : \mathsf{int} \quad \dfrac{x : \mathsf{char} \vdash x : \mathsf{char}}{x : \mathsf{char} \vdash x : \mathsf{int}}\,[\textsc{Sub}]}{x : \mathsf{char} \vdash 2 \times x : \mathsf{int}}\,[\textsc{Op}] \quad x : \mathsf{char} \vdash 6 : \mathsf{int}
  }{x : \mathsf{char} \vdash_p 2 \times x \le 6 : \mathsf{int} \hookleftarrow \mathsf{int}}\,[\textsc{Cmp}]
}{\vdash_p \forall\ \mathsf{int}\ x;\ 0 \le x < 4,\ 2 \times x \le 6 : \mathsf{int}}\,[\textsc{Quantif}]
$$

Fig. 5. Derivation trees for predicates $x/(y+1) \equiv 42$ (top), $f - 0.1 \le g$ (middle) and $\forall\ \mathsf{int}\ x;\ 0 \le x < 4, 2 \times x \le 6$ (bottom). The unlabeled rules are axioms or [Sub].

coercions, it is up to the user to enforce safety. E-ACSL is also able to verify this safety property but that is outside the scope of this paper. The typing rule [Op] for an operator computes the kind of its operands and its result, merges them to get the most precise interval containing all of their possible values, and converts the result into the corresponding C type. The last two rules for terms are coercion rules. Rule [Sub] is a standard subsumption rule [19] (e.g., stating that any term of type char may have type int as well), while rule [↓] soundly downcasts a term to a smaller type than its own type if its inferred kind fits in. For instance, the term x/(y+1) of Fig. 5 has type $\mathbb{Z} \hookleftarrow \mathbb{Z}$ after applying rule [Op], but since any possible result of the division fits into an int (i.e., $\theta(\kappa(x/(y+1))) \preccurlyeq_\tau \mathsf{int}$), it may soundly be coerced to this type. Yet its operands are still computed over $\mathbb{Z}$. Typing rules [Rel] and [Neg] for relations are straightforward. Rule [Cmd] for comparisons is similar to rule [Op], but the result is necessarily an int (actually either 0 or 1). A let-binding extends the typing context when evaluating the predicate ([Let]). A quantifier does the same ([Quantif]). In this latter case, the type associated to x is the smallest possible type with respect to its declared type and the one of its bounds. For instance, the inferred type of x is char for both $\forall\ \mathsf{char}\ x;\ -3 \le x < 4,\ 2 \times x \le 6$ and $\forall\ \mathsf{int}\ x;\ 0 \le x < 4,\ 2 \times x \le 6$ because x fits in $[0; 4]$ in each case. Figure 5 shows the derivation for the latter formula. As for casts, it is up to the user to enforce safety of the type declaration, but this property may be verified independently.

Code Generation. Generating code from the information computed by the type system is quite straightforward. Yet we may notice that the inference system is *not* an algorithm since several rules can be applied for a given term because of the coercion rules. A good implementation strategy consists in applying these coercions rules only when no other rules apply. This way, a cast must be introduced in the generated code if and only if a coercion rule is applied. Thus, this strategy introduces a minimal number of casts in the generated code. For instance, the code generated for the assertion /*@ assert $x/(y+1) \equiv 42 \wedge f - 0.1 \le g$; */ with the first operand of $\equiv$ of type int $\hookleftarrow \mathbb{Z}$, and f and g of type double would be as follows (the comments are manually added for readibility).

```
1  /* compute x/(y+1) with GMP integers */
2  mpz_t _x, _y, _cst_1, _add, _div; int _div2, _and;
3  mpz_init_set_si(_x, x); mpz_init_set_si(_y, y); mpz_init_set_si(_cst_1, 1);
4  mpz_init(_add); mpz_add(_add, _y, _cst_1);
5  mpz_init(_div); mpz_tdiv_q(_div, _x, _add);
6  /* soundly downcast the result of the division from GMP to int;
7     it corresponds to the application of rule [↓] in Fig 5. */
8  _div2 = mpz_get_si(_div);
9  if (_div2 == 42) {
10    /* compute f-0.1 ≤ g with GMP rationals */
11    mpq_t _f, _cst, _g, _sub; int _le;
12    mpq_init(_cst); mpq_set_str(_cst,"01/10",10);
13    mpq_init(_f); mpq_set_d(_f, f);
14    mpq_init(_sub); mpq_sub(_sub, _f, _cst);
15    mpq_init(_g); mpq_set_d(_g, g);
16    /* getting the result of the predicate as an int */
17    _le = mpq_cmp(_sub, _g);
18    _and = _le ≤ 0;
19    /* de-allocate the allocated GMP variables for rationals */
20    mpq_clear(_cst); mpq_clear(_f); mpq_clear(_sub); mpq_clear(_g);
21  } else
22    _and = 0;
23  /* runtime check the conjunction */
24  assert(_and);
25  /* de-allocate the allocated GMP variables for integers */
26  mpz_clear(_x); mpz_clear(_y); mpz_clear(_cst_1); mpz_clear(_add);
27  mpz_clear(_div);
```

It is worth noting that, at line 9, the code uses the C equality "==" to compare the result of the division to 42 thanks to our type system. The rational operations (lines 10–20) cannot be optimized because of the rational subtraction that cannot be soundly computed in any floating-point type, as we explained above. If the comparison were $f \le g$, then the generated code would use a floating-point comparison. The effect of the type system is even clearer for the assertion /*@ assert $c + 1 \equiv 0$; */ in which the term $c + 1$ has type int: the generated code is as simple as the C assertion assert(c+1 == 0);

5   Experiments

We evaluate the benefits of the optimized code generation on several simple examples (cf. Fig. 6). The first one is a simple computational program similar to Fig. 1. It computes, given daily prices of a merchandise, its average price (as a floating-point value) over a year. The considered property states that the returned average has a maximal error ε with respect to the exact average. The other four examples are simple C programs with ACSL annotations involving integer numbers: three programs manipulating an array (binary search, search for a maximal element, search for repetitions), and a program dealing with a matrix (checking if a matrix is symmetric).

Since these examples are rather simple and their execution is very fast, we perform N runs (for various values of parameter N) of the computational part

		$N = 100$	$N = 1,000$	$N = 10,000$	$N = 100,000$	$N = 1,000,000$
average	All-GMP	0.008s	0.070s	0.719s	7.167s	73.817s
	Optimized	0.001s	0.006s	0.053s	0.567s	5.428s
	Speedup	88%	91%	93%	92%	93%
binary_search	All-GMP	0.041s	0.413s	4.625s	—	—
	Optimized	0.001s	0.005s	0.045s	0.474s	4.797s
	Speedup	98%	99%	99%		
max_seq	All-GMP	0.155s	1.620s	15.413s	—	—
	Optimized	0.003s	0.028s	0.278s	2.815s	29.793s
	Speedup	98%	98%	98%		
pair	All-GMP	0.142s	1.524s	15.813s	—	—
	Optimized	0.003s	0.026s	0.273s	2.603s	26.437s
	Speedup	98%	98%	98%		
symmetry	All-GMP	0.073s	0.758s	—	—	—
	Optimized	0.003s	0.021s	0.211s	2.106s	22.293s
	Speedup	96%	97%			

Fig. 6. Execution time of the intrumented examples with and without optimization, where "—" indicates that the execution exceeded the heap allocation limit of 128 MB and thus the speedup cannot be computed.

of each example, including annotations to be evaluated. This is done for two reasons. First, a unique execution is always instantaneous and thus the speedup computed for it is meaningless. Second, performing several iterations of the computational part simulates more complex examples where the evaluation of annotations represents a more significant part of the whole execution.

Figure 6 shows the execution time of the non-optimized (all-GMP) and optimized versions for different values of parameter N. It shows that the optimized code brings a speedup between 88% and 99% by replacing GMP code by machine-number based code. Moreover, some of the executions of the non-optimized version ran out-of-memory because of numerous heap allocations performed by the GMP code. Thanks to our optimization, this problem did not happen on the optimized version, where no GMP calls were required. Finally, the results of both versions were identical, giving confidence in the soundness of the optimization. Regarding the **average** example, it was executed with $\varepsilon = 0.001$. Our experiments also demonstrate that if the result type is **float**, the specified precision property is true for $\varepsilon = 0.001$, but fails for $\varepsilon = 0.0001$. If the computation result type is **double**, a much greater precision is achieved.

In general, the benefit of the proposed optimization for other programs can depend on the considered annotations and the amount of computation necessary to evaluate them with respect to the rest of the code. An evaluation of this optimization on real-life programs is left as future work, even if this optimization was already turned-on when benchmarking [20] or experimenting [21] E-ACSL.

These experiments also suggest that runtime assertion checking with the E-ACSL tool can be a very useful and easily performed step to empirically identify numerical properties (in particular, with respect to the exact result in mathematical numbers specified in ACSL) of a given code before attempting to perform their formal proof.

6   Conclusion and Future Work

We presented a type system parameterized by an interval analysis in order to rely on machine-number based code as often as possible when checking at runtime properties over integer and rational numbers. It is implemented in the E-ACSL tool and has been adapted (for integers only) by Adacore to Spark2014. To the best of our knowledge, E-ACSL is the only runtime verification tool that is able to verify numerical properties over rational numbers. Our initial experiments confirm the soundness and the efficiency of our approach. More generally, it has already been used on large use cases a number of times without detecting soundness issues. Yet, evaluating the precise efficiency gain on larger use cases, as well as proving the soundness of the type system, are left as future work. Future work also includes more efficient generated code when dealing with $\mathbb{Q}$, and a richer support when dealing with numbers in $\mathbb{R}$.

Code Generation. When dealing with rationals, arbitrary-precision code can be further reduced by using floating-point arithmetics when appropriate. Indeed, floating-point computations are exact under precisely defined circumstances. First, any multiplication and division by an integer power of two is exact: it simply corresponds to a change of the exponent in the binary representation of the floating-point number. Then, the Hauser theorem states that any floating-point addition is exact if both operands are small enough, while the Sterbenz lemma states that any floating-point subtraction is exact if the second operand is small enough [22, Theorem 3 and Lemma 2]. Several other floating-point number properties can be used in a similar way.

Expressiveness. The Richardson theorem states that equality over rational expressions extended with the sine function is undecidable [23]. Hence formal specifications that use the sin function, and any other trigonometric function by extension, cannot always be translated into *terminating* code. More generally, exact runtime assertion checking of properties over real numbers is not possible in finite time. To circumvent this issue, we could rely on sound approximations and partial verdicts (i.e., the tool would sometimes answer "I don't know").

Acknowledgment. The authors thank Thales Research & Technology for support of this work, the Frama-C team for providing the tool, as well as the anonymous reviewers for their helpful comments.

References

1. Clarke, L.A., Rosenblum, D.S.: A historical perspective on runtime assertion checking in software development. SIGSOFT Softw. Eng. Notes **31**(3), 25–37 (2006)
2. Kosmatov, N., Signoles, J.: A lesson on runtime assertion checking with frama-C. In: Legay, A., Bensalem, S. (eds.) RV 2013. LNCS, vol. 8174, pp. 386–399. Springer, Heidelberg (2013). https://doi.org/10.1007/978-3-642-40787-1_29

3. Chalin, P.: JML support for primitive arbitrary precision numeric types: definition and semantics. J. Object Technol. **3**(6), 57–79 (2004)
4. Chalin, P.: Improving JML: for a safer and more effective language. In: Araki, K., Gnesi, S., Mandrioli, D. (eds.) FME 2003. LNCS, vol. 2805, pp. 440–461. Springer, Heidelberg (2003). https://doi.org/10.1007/978-3-540-45236-2_25
5. Delahaye, M., Kosmatov, N., Signoles, J.: Common specification language for static and dynamic analysis of C programs. In: Symposium on Applied Computing (SAC), March 2013
6. Meyer, B.: Eiffel: The Language. Prentice-Hall, Upper Saddle River (1992)
7. Barnett, M., Leino, K.R.M., Schulte, W.: The spec# programming system: an overview. In: Barthe, G., Burdy, L., Huisman, M., Lanet, J.-L., Muntean, T. (eds.) CASSIS 2004. LNCS, vol. 3362, pp. 49–69. Springer, Heidelberg (2005). https://doi.org/10.1007/978-3-540-30569-9_3
8. Leavens, G.T., Baker, A.L., Ruby, C.: JML: a notation for detailed design. In: Kilov, H., Rumpe, B., Simmonds, I. (eds.) Behavioral Specifications of Businesses and Systems. SECS, vol. 523, pp. 175–188. Springer, Boston (1999). https://doi.org/10.1007/978-1-4615-5229-1_12
9. Dross, C., Filliâtre, J.-C., Moy, Y.: Correct code containing containers. In: Gogolla, M., Wolff, B. (eds.) TAP 2011. LNCS, vol. 6706, pp. 102–118. Springer, Heidelberg (2011). https://doi.org/10.1007/978-3-642-21768-5_9
10. Baudin, P., Filliâtre, J.C., Marché, C., Monate, B., Moy, Y., Prevosto, V.: ACSL: ANSI/ISO C specification language. http://frama-c.com/acsl.html
11. Filliâtre, J.-C., Paskevich, A.: Why3—where programs meet provers. In: Felleisen, M., Gardner, P. (eds.) ESOP 2013. LNCS, vol. 7792, pp. 125–128. Springer, Heidelberg (2013). https://doi.org/10.1007/978-3-642-37036-6_8
12. Kosmatov, N., Marché, C., Moy, Y., Signoles, J.: Static versus dynamic verification in Why3, Frama-C and SPARK 2014. In: Margaria, T., Steffen, B. (eds.) ISoLA 2016. LNCS, vol. 9952, pp. 461–478. Springer, Cham (2016). https://doi.org/10.1007/978-3-319-47166-2_32
13. Signoles, J., Kosmatov, N., Vorobyov, K.: E-ACSL, a runtime verification tool for safety and security of C programs. Tool paper. In: International Workshop on Competitions, Usability, Benchmarks, Evaluation, and Standardisation for Runtime Verification Tools (RV-CuBES), September 2017
14. Kirchner, F., Kosmatov, N., Prevosto, V., Signoles, J., Yakobowski, B.: Frama-C: a software analysis perspective. Formal Aspects Comput. **27**, 573–609 (2015)
15. Signoles, J.: E-ACSL: executable ANSI/ISO C specification language. http://frama-c.com/download/e-acsl/e-acsl.pdf
16. Signoles, J.: From static analysis to runtime verification with Frama-C and E-ACSL, Habilitation thesis, July 2018
17. Jakobsson, A., Kosmatov, N., Signoles, J.: Rester statique pour devenir plus rapide, plus précis et plus mince. In: Journées Francophones des Langages Applicatifs (JFLA), January 2015. (In French)
18. ISO: ISO C Standard 1999. Technical report (1999)
19. Pierce, B.: Types and Programming Languages. MIT Press, Cambridge (2002)
20. Vorobyov, K., Signoles, J., Kosmatov, N.: Shadow state encoding for efficient monitoring of block-level properties. In: International Symposium on Memory Management (ISMM), June 2017
21. Pariente, D., Signoles, J.: Static analysis and runtime assertion checking: contribution to security counter-measures. In: Symposium sur la Sécurité des Technologies de l'Information et des Communications (SSTIC), June 2017

22. Muller, J., et al.: Handbook of Floating-Point Arithmetic. Birkhäuser, Boston (2010)
23. Richardson, D., Fitch, J.P.: The identity problem for elementary functions and constants. In: International Symposium on Symbolic and Algebraic Computation (ISSAC), July 1994

BISM: Bytecode-Level Instrumentation for Software Monitoring

Chukri Soueidi, Ali Kassem, and Yliès Falcone[(✉)]

Univ. Grenoble Alpes, Inria, CNRS, Grenoble INP, LIG, 38000 Grenoble, France
{chukri.a.soueidi,ali.kassem,ylies.falcone}@inria.fr

Abstract. BISM (Bytecode-level Instrumentation for Software Monitoring) is a lightweight Java bytecode instrumentation tool which features an expressive high-level control-flow-aware instrumentation language. The language follows the aspect-oriented programming paradigm by adopting the joinpoint model, advice inlining, and separate instrumentation mechanisms. BISM provides joinpoints ranging from bytecode instruction to method execution, access to comprehensive context information, and instrumentation methods. BISM runs in two modes: build-time and load-time. We demonstrate BISM effectiveness using two experiments: a security scenario and a general runtime verification case. The results show that BISM instrumentation incurs low runtime and memory overheads.

Keywords: Instrumentation · Runtime verification · Monitoring · Java bytecode · Aspect-oriented programming · Control flow · Static and dynamic contexts

1 Introduction

Instrumentation is essential to the software monitoring workflow [2,9]. Instrumentation allows extracting information from a running software to abstract the execution into a trace that is fed to a monitor. Depending on the information needed by the monitor, the granularity level of the extracted information may range from coarse (e.g., a function call) to fine (e.g., an assignment to a local variable, a jump in the control flow).

Aspect-oriented programming (AOP) [13] is a popular and convenient paradigm where instrumentation is a cross-cutting concern. For Java programs, runtime verification tools [1,7] have for long relied on AspectJ [12], which is one of the reference AOP implementations for Java. AspectJ provides a high-level pointcut/advice model for convenient instrumentation. However, AspectJ does not offer enough flexibility to perform some instrumentation tasks that require to reach low-level code regions, such as bytecode instructions, local variables of a method, and basic blocks in the control-flow graph (CFG).

Yet, there are several low-level Java bytecode manipulation frameworks such as ASM [5] and BCEL [18]. However, instrumenting programs with such frameworks is tedious and requires expertise on the bytecode. Other Java bytecode

© Springer Nature Switzerland AG 2020
J. Deshmukh and D. Ničković (Eds.): RV 2020, LNCS 12399, pp. 323–335, 2020.
https://doi.org/10.1007/978-3-030-60508-7_18

instrumentation frameworks, from which DiSL [15] is the most remarkable, enable flexible low-level instrumentation and, at the same time, provide a high-level language. However, DiSL does not allow inserting bytecode instructions directly but provides custom transformers where a developer needs to revert to low-level bytecode manipulation frameworks. This makes various scenarios tedious to implement in DiSL and often at the price of a considerable bytecode overhead.

Contributions. In this paper, we introduce BISM (Bytecode-Level Instrumentation for Software Monitoring), a lightweight Java bytecode instrumentation tool that features an expressive high-level instrumentation language. The language inspires from the AOP paradigm by adopting the joinpoint model, advice inlining, and separate instrumentation mechanisms. In particular, BISM provides a separate Java class to specify instrumentation code, and offers a variety of *joinpoints* ranging from bytecode instruction to basic block and method execution. BISM also provides access to a set of comprehensive joinpoint-related *static* and *dynamic contexts* to retrieve some relevant information, and a set of *instrumentation methods* to be called at joinpoints to insert code, invoke methods, and print information. BISM is control-flow aware. That is, it generates CFGs for all methods and offers this information at joinpoints and context objects. Moreover, BISM provides a variety of control-flow properties, such as capturing conditional jump branches and retrieving successor and the predecessor basic blocks. Such features provide support to future tools using a control-flow analysis, for instance, in the security domain, to detect control-flow attacks, such as test inversions and arbitrary jumps.

We demonstrate BISM effectiveness using two complementary experiments. The first experiment shows how BISM can be used to instrument a program to detect test inversion attacks. For this purpose, we use BISM to instrument AES (Advanced Encryption Standard). The second experiment demonstrates a general runtime verification case where we use BISM to instrument seven applications from the DaCapo benchmark [4] to verify the classical **HasNext**, **UnsafeIterator** and **SafeSyncMap** properties. We compare the performance of BISM, DiSL, and AspectJ in build-time and load-time instrumentation, using three metrics: size, memory footprint, and execution time. In build-time instrumentation, the results show that the instrumented code produced by BISM is smaller, incurs less overhead, and its execution incurs less memory footprint. In load-time instrumentation, the load-time weaving and the execution of the instrumented code are faster with BISM.

Paper Organization. Section 2 overviews the design goals and the features of BISM. Section 3 introduces the language featured by BISM. Section 4 presents the implementation of BISM. Section 5 reports on the case studies and a comparison between BISM, DiSL, and AspectJ. Section 6 discusses related work. Section 7 draws conclusions.

2   BISM Design and Features

BISM is implemented on top of ASM [5], with the following goals and features.
Instrumentation Mechanism. BISM language follows the AOP paradigm.
It provides a mechanism to write separate instrumentation classes. An instrumentation class specifies the instrumentation code to be inserted in the target program at chosen joinpoints. BISM offers joinpoints that range from bytecode instruction to basic block and method execution. It also offers several instrumentation methods and, additionally, accepts instrumentation code written in the ASM syntax. The instrumentation code is eventually compiled by BISM into bytecode instructions and inlined in the target program.

Access to Program Context. BISM offers access to complete static information about instructions, basic blocks, methods, and classes. It also offers dynamic context objects that provide access to values that will only be available at runtime such as values of local variables, stack values, method arguments, and results. Moreover, BISM allows accessing instance and static fields of these objects. Furthermore, new local variables can be created within the scope of a method to (for instance) pass values between joinpoints.

Control Flow Context. BISM generates the CFGs of target methods out-of-the-box and offers this information within joinpoints and context objects. In addition to basic block entry and exit joinpoints, BISM provides specific control-flow related joinpoints such as `OnTrueBranchEnter` and `OnFalseBranchEnter`, which capture conditional jump branches. Moreover, it provides a variety of control-flow properties within the static context objects. For example, it is possible to traverse the CFG of a method to retrieve the successors and the predecessors of basic blocks. Furthermore, BISM provides an optional feature to display the CFGs of methods before and after instrumentation.

Compatibility with ASM. BISM uses ASM extensively and relays all its generated class representations within the static context objects. Furthermore, it allows for inserting raw bytecode instructions by using the ASM data types. In this case, it is the responsibility of the user to write instrumentation code free from compilation and runtime errors. If the user unintentionally inserts faulty instructions, the code might break. The ability to insert ASM instructions provides highly expressive instrumentation capabilities, especially when it comes to inlining the monitor code into the target program.

Bytecode Coverage. BISM can run in two modes: *build-time* (as a standalone application) with static instrumentation, and *load-time* with an agent (utilizing `java.lang .instrument`) that intercepts all classes loaded by the JVM and instruments before the linking phase. In build-time, BISM is capable of instrumenting all the compiled classes and methods[1]. In load-time, BISM is capable

---

[1] Excluding the native and abstract methods, as they do not have bytecode representation.

of instrumenting additional classes, including classes from the Java class library that are flagged as modifiable. The modifiable flag keeps certain core classes outside the scope of BISM. Note, modifying such classes is rather needed in dynamic program analysis (e.g., profiling, debugging).

3 BISM Language

We demonstrate the language in BISM, which allows developers to write *transformers* (*i.e.,*instrumentation classes). The language provides joinpoints which capture exact execution points, static and dynamic contexts which retrieve relevant information at joinpoints, and instrumentation methods used to instrument a target program.

Joinpoints. Joinpoints identify specific bytecode locations in the target program. BISM offers joinpoints that capture bytecode instruction executions: `BeforeInstruction` and `AfterInstruction`, conditional jump branches: `OnTrueBranchEnter` and `OnFalseBranchEnter`, executions of basic blocks: `OnBasicBlockEnter` and `OnBasicBlockExit`, method executions: `OnMethodEnter` and `OnMethodExit`, and method calls: `BeforeMethodCall` and `AfterMethodCall`.

```
public class BasicBlockTransformer extends Transformer {
  @Override
  public void onBasicBlockEnter(BasicBlock bb){
    String id = bb.method.className+"."+bb.method.name+"."+bb.id;
    print("Entered block:" + id); }
  @Override
  public void onBasicBlockExit(BasicBlock bb){
    String id = bb.method.className+"."+bb.method.name+"."+bb.id;
    print("Exited block:" + id); }
}
```

Listing 1.1: A transformer for intercepting basic block executions.

Static Context. Static context objects provide relevant static information at joinpoints. These objects can be used to retrieve information about a bytecode instruction, a method call, a basic block, a method, and a class. BISM performs static analysis on target programs and provides additional control-flow-related static information such as basic block successors and predecessors. Listing 1.1 shows a transformer using joinpoints `onBasicBlockEnter` and `onBasicBlockExit` to intercept all basic block executions. The static context `BasicBlock bb` is used to get the block id, the method name, and the class name. Here, the instrumentation method `print` inserts a print invocation in the target program before and after every basic block execution.

```
public class IteratorTransformer extends Transformer {
@Override
public void afterMethodCall(MethodCall mc,
  MethodCallDynamicContext dc){
  if (mc.methodName.equals("iterator") &&
    mc.methodOwner.endsWith("List")) {
  DynamicValue callingClass = dc.getThis(mc); // Access to
  DynamicValue list = dc.getMethodReceiver(mc); // dynamic
  DynamicValue iterator = dc.getMethodResult(mc); // data
  StaticInvocation sti = // Instrumenting to invoke a monitor
    new StaticInvocation("IteratorMonitor","iteratorCreation");
  sti.addParameter(callingClass);
  sti.addParameter(list);
  sti.addParameter(iterator);
  invoke(sti); }
}}
```

Listing 1.2: A transformer that intercepts the creation of an iterator from a List.

Dynamic Context. Dynamic Context objects provide access to dynamic values that are possibly only known during execution. BISM gathers this information from local variables and operand stack, then weaves the necessary code to extract this information. In some cases (e.g., when accessing stack values), BISM might instrument additional local variables to store them for later use. We list the methods available in dynamic contexts: getThis, getLocalVariable, getStackValue, getInstanceField and getStaticField, and the values related to these methods: getMethodReceiver, getMethodArgs, and getMethodResult. BISM also allows inserting and updating new local variables within the scope of a method. Listing 1.2 presents a transformer using afterMethodCall joinpoint to capture the return of an Iterator created from a List object, and retrieving dynamic data from the dynamic context object MethodCallDynamicContext dc. The example also shows how to limit the scope using an if-statement to a specific method. Note that BISM also provides a general notion of *scope* that can be specified as an argument to match packages, classes, and methods by names (using possibly wildcards).

Instrumentation Methods. A developer instruments the target program using specified instrumentation methods. BISM provides print methods with multiple options to invoke a print command. It also provides (i) invoke methods for static method invocation and (ii) insert methods for bytecode instruction insertion. These methods are compiled by BISM into bytecode instructions and inlined at the exact joinpoint locations. Listing 1.1 shows the use of print to print the constructed id of a basic block. Listing 1.2 shows how a method invocation is instrumented after a method call.

4   BISM Implementation

BISM is implemented in Java with about 4,000 LOC and 40 classes distributed in
separate modules [16]. It uses ASM for bytecode parsing, analysis, and weaving.
Figure 1 shows BISM internal workflow.

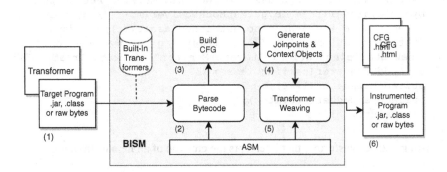

Fig. 1. Instrumentation process in BISM.

(1) User Input. In build-time mode, BISM takes a target program bytecode
(*.class* or *.jar*) to be instrumented, and a transformer which specifies the instrumentation logic. In load-time mode, BISM only takes a transformer used to
instrument every class being loaded by the JVM. BISM provides several built-in
transformers that can be directly used. Moreover, users can specify a scope to
filter target packages, classes, or methods. %, and can enable storing CFGs into
html files.

(2) Parse Bytecode. BISM uses ASM to parse the bytecode and to generate
a tree object which contains all the class details, such as fields, methods, and
instructions.

(3) Build CFG. BISM constructs the CFGs for all methods in the target class.
If the specified transformer utilizes control-flow joinpoints (i.e., `onTrueBranch`
and `onFalseBranch`), BISM eliminates all *critical edges* from the CFGs to avoid
instrumentation errors. This is done by inserting empty basic blocks in the middle of critical edges. Note, BISM keeps copies of the original CFGs. Users can
optionally enable the *visualizer* to store CFGs in HTML files on the disk.

(4) Generate Joinpoints and Context Objects. BISM iterates over the target class to generate all joinpoints utilizing the created CFGs. At each joinpoint,
the relevant static and dynamic context objects are created.

(5) Transformer Weaving. BISM evaluates the used dynamic contexts based
on the joinpoint static information and weaves the bytecode needed to extract
concrete values from executions. It then weaves instrumentation methods by
compiling them into bytecode instructions that are woven into the target program at the specified joinpoint.

(6) Output. The instrumented bytecode is then output back as a *.class* file in
build-time mode, or passed as raw bytes to the JVM in load-time mode. In case

of instrumentation errors, e.g., due to adding manual ASM instructions, BISM emits a weaving error. If the visualizer is enabled, instrumented CFGs are stored in HTML files on the disk.

5   Evaluation

We compare BISM with DiSL and AspectJ using two complementary experiments. To guarantee fairness, we switched off adding exception handlers around instrumented code in DiSL. In what follows, we illustrate how we carried out our experiments and the obtained results[2].

5.1   Inline Monitor to Detect Test Inversions

We instrument an external AES (Advanced Encryption Standard) implementation in build-time mode to detect test inversions. The instrumentation deploys inline monitors that duplicate all conditional jumps in their successor blocks to report test inversions. We implement the instrumentation as follows:

- In BISM, we use built-in features to duplicate conditional jumps utilizing insert instrumentation method to add raw bytecode instructions. In particular, we use the beforeInstruction joinpoint to capture all conditional jumps. We extract the opcode from the static context object Instruction and we use the instrumentation method insert to duplicate the needed stack values. We then use the control-flow joinpoints OnTrueBranchEnter and onFalseBranchEnter to capture the blocks executing after the jump. Finally, at the beginning of these blocks, we utilize insert to duplicate conditional jumps.
- In DiSL, we implement a custom InstructionStaticContext object to retrieve information from conditional jump instructions such as the index of a jump target and instruction opcode. Note, we use multiple BytecodeMarker snippets to capture all conditional jumps. To retrieve stack values, we use the dynamic context object. Finally, on successor blocks, we map opcodes to Java syntax to re-evaluate conditional jumps using switch statements.

We use AES to encrypt and then decrypt input files of different sizes, line by line. The bytecode size of the original AES class is 9 KB. After instrumentation, it is 10 KB (+11.11%) for BISM, and 128 KB (+1,322%) for DiSL. The significant overhead in DiSL is due to the inability to inline the monitor in bytecode and having to instrument it in Java. We note that it is not straightforward in DiSL to extract control-flow information in Markers, whereas BISM provides this out-of-the-box. Figure 2 reports runtime and memory footprint with respect to file size (KB)[3]. For each input file, we performed 100 measurements and reported

---

[2] More details about the experiments are at https://gitlab.inria.fr/monitoring/bism-experiments.

[3] Note, AspectJ is not suited for inline monitoring, and that is why it is not included.

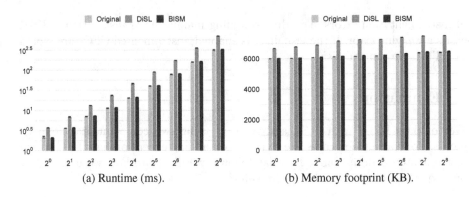

(a) Runtime (ms).   (b) Memory footprint (KB).

Fig. 2. Runtime and memory footprint by AES on files of different sizes.

the mean and the standard deviation. The latter is very low. We use Java JDK 8u181 with 4 GB maximum heap size on a standard PC (Intel Core i7 2.2 GHz, 16 GB RAM) running macOS Catalina v10.15.5 64-bit. The results show that BISM incurs less overhead than DiSL for all file sizes. Table 1 reports the number of events (corresponding to conditional jumps).

Table 1. Number of events according to the file input to AES (in millions).

Input File (KB)	2^0	2^1	2^2	2^3	2^4	2^5	2^6	2^7	2^8
Events (M)	0.92	1.82	3.65	7.34	14.94	29.53	58.50	117.24	233.10

5.2 DaCapo Benchmarks

Experimental Setup. We compare BISM, DiSL, and AspectJ in a general runtime verification scenario[4]. We instrument the benchmarks in the DaCapo suite [4] (dacapo-9.12-bach), to monitor the classical **HasNext**, **UnSafeIterator**, and **SafeSyncMap** properties[5]. We only target the packages specific to each benchmark and do not limit our scope to `java.util` types; instead, we match freely by type and method name. We implement an external monitor library with stub methods that only count the number of received events.

We implement the instrumentation as follows:

– In BISM, we use the static context provided at method call joinpoints to filter methods by their names and owners. To access the method calls' receivers and results, we utilize the methods available in dynamic contexts.

---

[4] We use the latest DiSL version from https://gitlab.ow2.org/disl/disl and AspectJ Weaver 1.9.4.

[5] **HasNext** property specifies that a program should always call `hasNext()` before calling `next()` on an iterator. **UnSafeIterator** property specifies that a collection should not be updated when an iterator associated with it is being used. **SafeSyncMap** property specifies that a map should not be updated when an iterator associated with it is being used.

- In DiSL, we implement custom Markers to capture the needed method calls and use argument processors and dynamic context objects to access dynamic values.
- In AspectJ, we use the call pointcut, type pattern matching and joinpoint static information to capture method calls and write custom advices that invoke the monitor.

We use Java JDK 8u251 with 2 GB maximum heap size on an Intel Core i9-9980HK (2.4 GHz. 8 GB RAM) running Ubuntu 20.04 LTS 64-bit. All our measurements correspond to the mean of 100 runs on each benchmark, calculating the standard deviation. We run our experiment in two modes: load-time and build-time. The first mode is to compare the performance of the tools in load-time instrumentation and the second mode to examine the performance of the generated instrumentation bytecode.

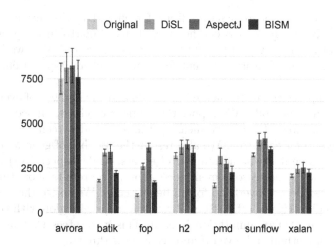

Fig. 3. Load-time instrumentation runtime (ms).

Load-time Evaluation. Figure 3 reports the execution time in ms for the benchmarks. We do not measure the used memory since DiSL performs instrumentation on a separate JVM process. BISM shows better performance over DiSL and AspectJ in all benchmarks. DiSL shows better performance than AspectJ except for the pmd benchmark. For the pmd benchmark, this is mainly due to the fewer events emitted by AspectJ (see Table 2). We notice that AspectJ captures fewer events in benchmarks batik, fop, pmd, and sunflow. This is due to its inability to instrument synthetic bridge methods generated by the compiler after type erasure in generic types.

Build-time Evaluation. We replace the original classes in the benchmarks with statically instrumented classes from each tool. Figure 4 reports the execution time and memory footprint of the benchmarks. For memory, we measure

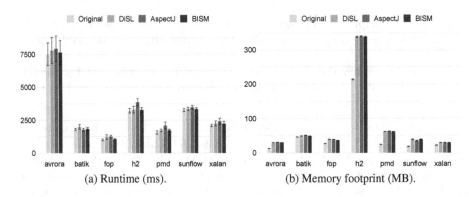

Fig. 4. Build-time execution.

the used heap and non-heap memory after a forced garbage collection at the end of each run[6]. BISM shows less overhead in all benchmarks in execution time, except for batik where AspectJ emits fewer events. BISM also shows less overhead in used-memory footprint, except for sunflow, where AspectJ emits much fewer events.

Table 2 compares the instrumented bytecode and the number of events emitted after running the code. We report the number of classes in scope (Scope) and the instrumented (Instr.), we measure the overhead percentage (Ovh.) on the bytecode size for each tool. We also report the number of generated events. BISM and DiSL emit the same number of events, while Aspect (AJ) produces fewer events due to the reasons mentioned above. The results show that BISM incurs less bytecode size overhead for all benchmarks. We notice that even with exception-handlers turned off, DiSL still wraps a targeted region with try-finally blocks when the @After annotation is used. This guarantees that an event is emitted after a method call, even if an exception is thrown.

Table 2. Generated bytecode size and events emitted.

	Scope	Instr.	Ref	BISM		DiSL		AspectJ		Events (M)	
			KB	KB	Ovh.%	KB	Ovh.%	KB	Ovh.%	#	AJ
avrora	1,550	35	257	264	2.72	270	5.06	345	34.24	2.5	2.5
batik	2,689	136	1,544	1,572	1.81	1,588	2.85	1,692	9.59	0.5	0.4
fop	1,336	172	1,784	1,808	1.35	1,876	5.16	2,267	27.07	1.6	1.5
h2	472	61	694	704	1.44	720	3.75	956	37.75	28	28
pmd	721	90	756	774	2.38	794	5.03	980	29.63	6.6	6.3
sunflow	221	8	69	71	2.90	74	7.25	85	23.19	3.9	2.6
xalan	661	9	100	101	1.00	103	3.00	116	16.00	1	1

---

[6] The DaCapo callback mechanism captures the end of each run.

6   Related Work and Discussion

Low-level code instrumentation is widely used for monitoring software and implementing dynamic analysis tools. To this end, several tools and frameworks, in different programming languages, have been proposed and adopted. We focus our comparison on Java-related instrumentation tools. Yet, there are several tools to instrument programs in different programing languages. For instance, to instrument C/C++ programs AspectC/C++ [6,17] (high-level) and LLVM [14] (low-level) are widely used.

ASM [5] is a bytecode manipulation framework utilized by several tools, including BISM. ASM offers two APIs that can be used interchangeably to parse, load, and modify classes. However, to use ASM, a developer has to deal with the low-level details of bytecode instructions and the JVM. BISM offers extended ASM compatibility and provides abstraction with its aspect-oriented paradigm.

DiSL is a bytecode-level instrumentation framework designed for dynamic program analysis [15]. DiSL adopts an aspect-oriented paradigm. It provides an extensible joinpoint model and access to static and dynamic context information. Even though BISM provides a fixed set of joinpoints and static context objects, it performs static analysis on target programs to offer out-of-the-box additional and needed control-flow joinpoints with full static information. As for dynamic context objects, both BISM and DiSL provide equal access. However, DiSL provides typed dynamic objects. Also, both are capable of inserting synthetic local variables (restricted to primitive types in BISM). Both BISM and DiSL require basic knowledge about bytecode semantics from their users. In DiSL, writing custom markers and context objects also requires additional ASM syntax knowledge. However, DiSL does not allow the insertion of arbitrary bytecode instructions but provides a mechanism to write custom transformers in ASM that runs before instrumentation. Whereas, BISM allows to directly insert bytecode instructions, as seen in Sect. 5.1. Such a mechanism is essential in many runtime verification scenarios. All in all, DiSL provides more features (mostly targeted for writing dynamic analysis tools) and enables dynamic dispatch amongst multiple instrumentations and analysis without interference [3], while BISM is more lightweight as shown by our evaluation.

AspectJ [12] is the standard aspect-oriented programming [13] framework highly adopted for instrumenting Java applications. It provides a high-level language used in several domains like monitoring, debugging, and logging. AspectJ cannot capture bytecode instructions and basic blocks directly, forcing developers to insert additional code (like method calls) to the source program. With BISM, developers can target single bytecode instructions and basic block levels, and also have access to local variables and stack values. Furthermore, AspectJ introduces a significant instrumentation overhead, as seen in Sect. 5.2, and provides less control on where instrumentation snippets get inlined. In BISM, the instrumentation methods are weaved with minimal bytecode instructions and are always inlined next to the targeted regions.

7   Conclusions

BISM is an effective tool for low-level and control-flow aware instrumentation, complementary to DiSL, which is better suited for dynamic analysis (e.g., profiling). Our first evaluation (Sect. 5.1) let us observe a significant advantage of BISM over DiSL due to BISM's ability to insert bytecode instructions directly, hence optimizing the instrumentation. Our second evaluation (Sect. 5.2) confirms that BISM is a lightweight tool that can be used generally and efficiently in runtime verification. We notice a similar bytecode performance between BISM and DiSL after static instrumentation since, in both tools, the instrumentation (monitor invocation) is always inlined. On the other hand, AspectJ instruments calls to advice methods that, in turn, invoke the monitors. In load-time instrumentation, the gap between BISM and DiSL is smaller in benchmarks with a large number of classes in scope and a small number of instrumented classes. This stems from the fact that BISM performs a full analysis of the classes in scope to generate its static context. While DiSL generates static context only after marking the needed regions, which is more efficient.

Overall, we believe that BISM can be used as an alternative to AspectJ for lightweight and expressive runtime verification and even runtime enforcement (cf. [8,10,11]) thanks to its ability to insert bytecode instructions.

References

1. Bartocci, E., et al.: First international competition on runtime verification: rules, benchmarks, tools, and final results of CRV 2014. Int. J. Softw. Tools Technol. Transf. **21**(1), 31–70 (2019)
2. Bartocci, E., Falcone, Y., Francalanza, A., Reger, G.: Introduction to runtime verification. In: Bartocci, E., Falcone, Y. (eds.) Lectures on Runtime Verification. LNCS, vol. 10457, pp. 1–33. Springer, Cham (2018). https://doi.org/10.1007/978-3-319-75632-5_1
3. Binder, W., Moret, P., Tanter, É., Ansaloni, D.: Polymorphic bytecode instrumentation. Softw. Pract. Exp. **46**(10), 1351–1380 (2016)
4. Blackburn, S.M., et al.: The DaCapo benchmarks: Java benchmarking development and analysis. In: Tarr, P.L., Cook, W.R. (eds.) Proceedings of the 21th Annual ACM SIGPLAN Conference on Object-Oriented Programming, Systems, Languages, and Applications, OOPSLA 2006, October 22–26, 2006, Portland, Oregon, USA, pp. 169–190. ACM (2006)
5. Bruneton, E., Lenglet, R., Coupaye, T.: ASM: a code manipulation tool to implement adaptable systems. In: Adaptable and extensible component systems, (2002) https://asm.ow2.io
6. Coady, Y., Kiczales, G., Feeley, M.J., Smolyn, G.: Using AspectC to improve the modularity of path-specific customization in operating system code. In: Tjoa, A.M., Gruhn, V. (eds.) Proceedings of the 8th European Software Engineering Conference held jointly with 9th ACM SIGSOFT International Symposium on Foundations of Software Engineering 2001, Vienna, Austria, September 10–14, 2001, pp. 88–98. ACM (2001) https://doi.org/10.1145/503209.503223

7. Falcone, Y., Krstić, S., Reger, G., Traytel, D.: A taxonomy for classifying runtime verification tools. In: Colombo, C., Leucker, M. (eds.) RV 2018. LNCS, vol. 11237, pp. 241–262. Springer, Cham (2018). https://doi.org/10.1007/978-3-030-03769-7_14

8. Falcone, Y.: You should better enforce than verify. In: Barringer, H., Falcone, Y., Finkbeiner, B., Havelund, K., Lee, I., Pace, G., Roşu, G., Sokolsky, O., Tillmann, N. (eds.) RV 2010. LNCS, vol. 6418, pp. 89–105. Springer, Heidelberg (2010). https://doi.org/10.1007/978-3-642-16612-9_9

9. Falcone, Y., Havelund, K., Reger, G.: A tutorial on runtime verification. In: Broy, M., Peled,D.A., Kalus, G. (eds.) Engineering Dependable Software Systems, NATO Science for Peaceand Security Series, D: Information and Communication Security, vol. 34, pp. 141–175. IOSPress (2013). https://doi.org/10.3233/978-1-61499-207-3-141

10. Falcone, Y., Mariani, L., Rollet, A., Saha, S.: Runtime failure prevention and reaction. In: Bartocci, E., Falcone, Y. (eds.) Lectures on Runtime Verification. LNCS, vol. 10457, pp. 103–134. Springer, Cham (2018). https://doi.org/10.1007/978-3-319-75632-5_4

11. Falcone, Y., Pinisetty, S.: On the runtime enforcement of timed properties. In: Finkbeiner, B., Mariani, L. (eds.) RV 2019. LNCS, vol. 11757, pp. 48–69. Springer, Cham (2019). https://doi.org/10.1007/978-3-030-32079-9_4

12. Kiczales, G., Hilsdale, E., Hugunin, J., Kersten, M., Palm, J., Griswold, W.G.: Getting started with AspectJ. Commun. ACM 44(10), 59–65 (2001)

13. Kiczales, G., et al.: Aspect-oriented programming. In: Akşit, M., Matsuoka, S. (eds.) ECOOP 1997. LNCS, vol. 1241, pp. 220–242. Springer, Heidelberg (1997). https://doi.org/10.1007/BFb0053381

14. Lattner, C., Adve, V.S.: LLVM: a compilation framework for lifelong program analysis & transformation. In: 2nd IEEE / ACM International Symposium on Code Generation and Optimization (CGO 2004), 20–24 March 2004, San Jose, CA, USA, pp. 75–88. IEEE (2004) https://doi.org/10.1109/CGO.2004.1281665

15. Marek, L., Villazón, A., Zheng, Y., Ansaloni, D., Binder, W., Qi, Z.: DiSL: a domain-specific language for bytecode instrumentation. In: Hirschfeld, R., Tanter, É., Sullivan, K.J., Gabriel, R.P. (eds.) Proceedings of the 11th International Conference on Aspect-oriented Software Development, AOSD, Potsdam, Germany, pp. 239–250. ACM (2012)

16. Soueidi, C., Kassem, A., Falcone, Y.: BISM: Bytecode-level Instrumentation for Software Monitoring, (2020) https://gitlab.inria.fr/monitoring/bism-tool

17. Spinczyk, O., Lohmann, D., Urban, M.: AspectC++: an AOP extension for C++. Softw. Developer's J. 5, 68–76 (2005)

18. The Apache Software Foundation: Apache commons. https://commons.apache.org. Accessed 18 Jun 2020

Runtime Verification with Temporal Logic Specifications

Property-Directed Verified Monitoring
of Signal Temporal Logic

Thomas Wright$^{(\boxtimes)}$ (ID) and Ian Stark (ID)

School of Informatics, University of Edinburgh, Edinburgh, UK
thomas.wright@ed.ac.uk

Abstract. Signal Temporal Logic monitoring over numerical simulation
traces has emerged as an effective approach to approximate verification
of continuous and hybrid systems. In this paper we explore an exact
verification procedure for STL properties based on monitoring verified
traces in the form of Taylor model flowpipes as produced by the *Flow**
verified integrator. We explore how tight integration with Flow*'s symbolic flowpipe representation can lead to more precise and more efficient
monitoring. We then show how the performance of monitoring can be
increased substantially by introducing masks, a property-directed refinement of our method which restricts flowpipe monitoring to the time
regions relevant to the overall truth of a complex proposition. Finally,
we apply our implementation of these methods to verifying properties of
a challenging continuous system, evaluating the impact of each aspect of
our procedure on monitoring performance.

1 Introduction

Signal Temporal Logic (STL) [35] is an established and effective framework for
describing and monitoring temporal properties of real-valued signals in continuous time, enabling verification of both continuous and hybrid systems. Much
work on STL has focused on monitoring signals derived from numerical simulation traces. This is a powerful technique, but the approximate nature of such
traces can lead to erroneous signal values at some timepoints whilst the signals do not account for uncertainties in the underlying model. Recently Ishii,
Yonezaki and Goldsztejn [27] have explored combining signal-based monitoring
techniques with interval analysis to perform exact verification of STL properties
over traces produced via verified integration.

In this paper we propose a new verified STL monitoring algorithm based on
preconditioned Taylor model flowpipes [34] generated with the *Flow** verified
integrator [13]. Our algorithm starts from such a Flow* flowpipe, which tracks
our uncertain knowledge of the system state at each point in time (whether due
to numerical errors or uncertain model parameters), and produces a *three-valued
signal* reflecting our resulting uncertain knowledge in the truth value of a STL
property over time. One of Flow*'s key features is its sophisticated symbolic
flowpipe representation, which allows it to handle a wide range of non-linear

© Springer Nature Switzerland AG 2020
J. Deshmukh and D. Ničković (Eds.): RV 2020, LNCS 12399, pp. 339–358, 2020.
https://doi.org/10.1007/978-3-030-60508-7_19

continuous and hybrid systems [15], but poses challenges to effectively monitoring properties over these flowpipes, since over-approximating the value of the flowpipe at a given timepoint can be expensive and requires a careful tradeoff between accuracy and efficiency. We tackle these challenges by tightly integrating our monitoring strategy for atomic propositions with Flow*'s flowpipe representation, in contrast to most previous verified monitoring approaches which treat the flowpipe as a closed box by evaluating it as an interval function. This allows us to vary our evaluation strategy on demand at each timepoint, as required to verify a given atomic proposition. We are thus able to maximize precision for complex atomic propositions by utilizing Taylor model arithmetic to avoid the *dependency problem* [9], or fall back to simpler interval evaluation strategies when this suffices to determine the value of the signal at the current timepoint.

We further refine our method by introducing *masks*, a special type of signal representing the region of time for which each proposition of a STL formula is required by the overall monitoring process. We present methods for computing masks in a top-down manner, complementing the normal bottom-up signal monitoring process. We also see how to efficiently monitor each atomic proposition under a given mask. This allows us to handle the monitoring of each atomic proposition as a single-pass offline verification problem with a mask providing a condensed view of the regions of interest; we are hence able to utilize Taylor model methods to refine the signal in the most crucial time regions whilst avoiding unnecessary work elsewhere. Altogether, this gives a property-directed algorithm for efficient and precise STL monitoring over Flow* flowpipes.

The structure of this paper is as follows. In Sect. 1.1 we review related work. Section 2 covers necessary background information regarding interval arithmetic, Taylor Models, Flow*, and STL, and establishes our notation. In Sect. 3 we introduce our verified monitoring algorithm by defining three-valued signals and our method of monitoring atomic propositions over Flow* flowpipes. In Sect. 4 we present masks and show how they may be used to perform property-directed monitoring. In Sect. 5 we evaluate the benefits of each part of our method for monitoring STL properties in a complex continuous system. Finally, in Sect. 6 we present our conclusions and discusses future directions.

1.1   Related Work

The most closely related work is the verified STL monitoring algorithm of Ishii et al. [25–27]. We build upon their approach of monitoring atomic propositions using interval root finding to derive verified signals; however, whilst their method treats the result of verified integration as a generic interval function, we work directly with the symbolic Taylor model flowpipes produced by Flow*. Our formulation of verified signals is also quite different, representing signals using three-valued logic rather than inner and outer interval approximations. Other works have looked at three-valued extensions of STL [5,32], but have not applied this in the context of exact, interval-based, formal verification of continuous systems. Three-valued logic has also been applied to model checking Linear Temporal Logic (LTL) properties over discrete systems with partially known state spaces [11]. Fisman and Kugler [23] also investigated a more general semantics for LTL and STL over a number of different forms of incomplete traces.

A variety of different approaches have been explored for formal verification of temporal logics over hybrid and continuous systems. Early methods include [2] which initially focused on linear systems and the temporal logic TCTL. Piazza et al. [40] developed methods for temporal logic verification of semi-algebraic hybrid systems based on quantifier elimination. Bresolin [10] developed a method for encoding LTL properties of hybrid systems as hybrid automata reachability problems, extending the common automata theoretic approach [42] to temporal logic verification, allowing existing reachability tools to be applied to LTL model checking. Cimatti et al. [16] presented another approach to reducing LTL verification on hybrid systems to reachability analysis. The dynamic temporal logic dTL^2 [28] takes a rather different approach, including both hybrid systems and nested temporal modalities as part of the logic whilst providing a proof calculus.

A number of recent works have focused specifically on exact STL verification using ideas from reachability analysis. Roehm et al. [41] provided an approach to STL verification for hybrid automata based on checking (discrete) time sampled versions of STL formulae against reachsets produced by reachability analysis tools such as CORA [1]. Bae and Lee [4] introduced an approach to STL verification which translates properties into constraint problems which can be verified exactly using a SMT solver such as Z3 for linear systems [17] or the ε-complete decision procedure dReal for non-linear systems [24,30]. Their work is the closest to providing an automated property-directed model checking procedure for STL. The constraint solving tools on which this work relies are very different from verified integration tools such as Flow*, and currently which approach performs better depends heavily on the system at hand [15,31]. These exact verification-based methods also compete with approximate methods such as [3,5,19,22] which attempt to verify properties by sampling trajectories and may use quantitative measures of satisfaction [20,21] to give some assurance of robustness.

Our method has some similarities with online monitoring in that in both cases we have partial knowledge of the underlying signal, and wish to avoid unnecessary monitoring for atomic propositions. Deshmukh et al. [18] introduced an interval quantitative semantics for STL in order to perform online monitoring over partial traces. In their method partiality of traces is used to record the fact that part of the trace has not yet been received whereas in our method it reflects uncertainty in the underlying system. Both [18] and the earlier incremental marking procedure [36,38] attempt to avoid reevaluation of atomic propositions at timepoints unnecessary for the operators in which they occur similarly to masks, however, we statically calculate a mask for the timepoints of interest for a proposition, whilst online monitoring algorithms track (contiguous) time horizons for propositions each time they are revisited. Masks also play a quite different role to these optimizations, since masks are computed in a top-down manner to allow specific parts of the verified monitoring process to be avoided on a non-contiguous region throughout the time domain, whilst the role of these optimizations in online monitoring is to reduce memory usage by allowing time points outside of a proposition's time horizon to be forgotten or to allow early termination of simulations.

2 Background

In this section we review some background material including interval arithmetic and Taylor models, which will be central to our monitoring process.

2.1 Interval Arithmetic

We will work with interval arithmetic [37] over closed intervals and denote the lower and upper endpoint of interval $I = [l_I, u_I] \triangleq \{x \in \mathbb{R} \mid l_I \leq x \leq u_I\}$ by $l_I, u_I \in \mathbb{R} \cup \{-\infty, \infty\}$ respectively. Arithmetic operations can be computed using interval endpoints so that

$$I + J \triangleq \{x + y \mid x \in I, y \in J\} = [l_I + l_J, u_I + u_J]$$

and IJ and $I - J$ are computed similarly. We can also define set operations on intervals so $I \cap J = [\max\{l_I, l_J\}, \min\{u_I, u_J\}]$, and whilst the set-theoretic union $I \cup J$ is not necessarily an interval, we may over-approximate and use $I \cup J \triangleq [\min\{l_I, l_J\}, \max\{u_I, u_J\}]$ in its place.

Given a real-valued function $f : I \to \mathbb{R}$ over interval domain I, an interval valued function F is an *interval extension of f* if $f(x) \in F(X)$ for every point x and interval X such that $x \in X$. Assuming f is differentiable and we have an interval extension F' of its derivative f', we may apply the *Extended Interval Newton method*, a generalisation of the Newton root finding method, which uses interval evaluation of F to produce guaranteed interval enclosures of all roots of f [27,37, Chapter 8.1]; we denote the set of such intervals as $\mathrm{roots}(F, F', I)$.

2.2 Taylor Model Arithmetic

When used in verified numerical computation, interval arithmetic often leads to imprecise or inconclusive results due to the so called *dependency problem* in which the functional dependencies within an expression are ignored by an interval over-approximation, causing the approximation errors to be compounded throughout the computation. This motivates the use of symbolic methods such as Taylor models [9,33], which give a higher-order symbolic over-approximation of a function based on a Taylor series expansion and an interval remainder bound.

Definition 1. *Given a function $\mathbf{f} : \mathbf{D} \to \mathbb{R}^n$ with domain $\mathbf{D} \subseteq \mathbb{R}^m$, a kth-order Taylor model for $\mathbf{f}$ is a pair $(\mathbf{p}, \mathbf{I})$ of an n-dimensional vector $\mathbf{p}$ of kth-order m-variable polynomials and an n-dimensional box $\mathbf{I}$ such that $f(\mathbf{x}) \in \mathbf{p}(\mathbf{x}) + \mathbf{I}$ for all $\mathbf{x} \in \mathbf{D}$.*

The precision of the approximation increases as the order of the Taylor model increases and the size of the remainder decreases. Given two Taylor models $(\mathbf{p}, \mathbf{I})$ and $(\mathbf{q}, \mathbf{J})$ enclosing functions $\mathbf{f}$ and $\mathbf{g}$ respectively, we can carry out various operations symbolically. Addition and subtraction can be carried out componentwise, whilst other common operations including multiplication, division, and differentiation can be carried out with a suitable expansion of the remainder intervals [9]. Finally, we may define *symbolic composition* $(\mathbf{q}, \mathbf{J}) \square (\mathbf{p}, \mathbf{I})$, which symbolically substitutes $(\mathbf{p}, \mathbf{I})$ into $(\mathbf{q}, \mathbf{J})$ and is guaranteed to enclose the composition $\mathbf{g} \circ \mathbf{f}$ of the underlying functions [8].

2.3   Flow* Verified Integration

Consider a continuous system described by an n-dimensional collection of ODEs

$$\frac{d\mathbf{x}}{dt} = \mathbf{f}(\mathbf{x}, t) \tag{1}$$

with initial conditions $\mathbf{x}(0)$ in some starting set $S \subseteq \mathbb{R}^n$ and with $\mathbf{f}$ being, for example, Lipschitz continuous. Such a system has a unique solution $\mathbf{x_s}$ for any given initial condition $\mathbf{s} \in S$ [29]. The aim of *verified integration* is to find an interval function $\mathbf{F} : [0, T] \to \mathbb{R}^n$ enclosing every solution $\mathbf{x_s}$ for $\mathbf{s} \in S$ over a bounded time window $[0, T]$. Flow* [13] uses verified integration based on Taylor models [9] to compute such an enclosure covering the whole set S, soundly accounting for the uncertainty in the initial point $\mathbf{s}$ as well as floating point rounding errors. Flow* represents the solution as a *flowpipe* consisting of a sequence of *preconditioned Taylor models* [34], that is, over each interval time step $[t_k, t_{k+1}] \subseteq [0, T]$, the solution is enclosed in a composition of two Taylor models

$$\left(\mathbf{p}^{(k)}, \mathbf{I}^{(k)} \right) \triangleq \left(\mathbf{p}_{\text{post}}^{(k)}, \mathbf{I}_{\text{post}}^{(k)} \right) \square \left(\mathbf{p}_{\text{pre}}^{(k)}, \mathbf{I}_{\text{pre}}^{(k)} \right).$$

Whilst this representation is extremely powerful, allowing Flow* to handle nonlinear systems with complex continuous dynamics, it can be expensive to work with the generated flowpipes: each pair of preconditioned Taylor models must be composed symbolically (and then be placed into Horner form [12,39]) in order to carry out accurate interval evaluation. This step is a prerequisite for applying most forms of analysis to the flowpipe including reach-avoidance checking, plotting [13], and the verified monitoring algorithm [26].

2.4   Signal Temporal Logic

Signal Temporal Logic [35] specifies properties of continuous trajectories in dynamical systems such as Eq. (1). Propositions are defined according to the grammar,

$$\varphi, \psi ::= \rho \mid \varphi \wedge \psi \mid \varphi \vee \psi \mid \neg\varphi \mid \varphi \, \mathcal{U}_I \, \psi,$$

where I is an interval and atomic propositions consist of inequalities $\rho \triangleq p > 0$ defined by polynomials p over the system's variables.

The semantics for the connectives are defined by specifying when a system trajectory $\mathbf{x}$ satisfies a property φ at time t, written $(\mathbf{x}, t) \models \varphi$. Then the semantics for atomic propositions is given by $(\mathbf{x}, t) \models p > 0$ iff $p(\mathbf{x}(t)) > 0$ and the normal boolean connectives are extended to each time point so that, for example, $(\mathbf{x}, t) \models \varphi \wedge \psi$ iff $(\mathbf{x}, t) \models \varphi$ and $(\mathbf{x}, t) \models \psi$. The fundamental temporal modality *until* is defined by $(\mathbf{x}, t) \models \varphi \, \mathcal{U}_I \, \psi$ iff there exists $t' \in t + I$, such that $(\mathbf{x}, t') \models \psi$ and for all $t'' \in [t, t']$, $(\mathbf{x}, t'') \models \varphi$. We can also define the derived temporal modalities $\mathcal{F}_I(\varphi) \equiv \mathbf{T} \, \mathcal{U}_I \, \varphi$ *(eventually)* and $\mathcal{G}_I(\varphi) \equiv \neg \, \mathcal{F}_I(\neg \varphi)$ *(globally)*.

The problem of *verified monitoring* of a STL property φ at a time point $t \in [0, T]$ is to determine whether or not $(\mathbf{x}, t) \models \varphi$ for every possible trajectory $\mathbf{x}$ of a given system.

3   Three-Valued Monitoring over Flow* Flowpipes

In this section we present our basic verified monitoring algorithm for Signal Temporal Logic. In Sect. 3.1 we introduce three-valued signals and specify rules to combine these to derive signals for complex propositions. We then develop an efficient algorithm for monitoring signals of atomic propositions based over Flow* flowpipes in Sects. 3.2 and 3.3.

We have omitted some of the longer proofs which may be found in the extended technical report version of this paper [44].

3.1   Three-Valued Signals

Our verified monitoring algorithm is based on *three-valued signals*:

Definition 2. *A* three-valued signal *is a function* $s : [0, \infty) \to \{\mathbf{T}, \mathbf{U}, \mathbf{F}\}$.

These extend the boolean signals $s : [0, \infty) \to \{\mathbf{T}, \mathbf{F}\}$ used in numerical STL monitoring algorithms to track the validity of the answer at each time point $t \in [0, \infty)$, to allow a third answer, *Unknown* ($\mathbf{U}$), if we can neither verify nor refute the proposition. We interpret these logic values under the rules of Kleenian three-valued logic so $\mathbf{F} \vee \mathbf{U} \equiv \mathbf{U} \equiv \mathbf{T} \wedge \mathbf{U}$. A three-valued signal is consistent with the (boolean) truth values of a proposition φ if it soundly under-approximates the time-regions on which φ is True and False:

Definition 3. *Given a proposition φ and a three-valued signal s, we say s is a signal for φ (over the trajectories of a given system) if at every time t,*

$$s(t) = \mathbf{T} \quad \Longrightarrow \quad (\mathbf{x}, t) \models \varphi \quad \text{for every trajectory } \mathbf{x}$$
$$s(t) = \mathbf{F} \quad \Longrightarrow \quad (\mathbf{x}, t) \not\models \varphi \quad \text{for every trajectory } \mathbf{x}.$$

This definition allows a single proposition φ to be approximated by many different signals to differing degrees of precision. Indeed, the signal which is unknown everywhere is a valid (but uninformative) signal for every proposition.

For concrete computation we work with those three-valued signals s that can be represented by a finite set of nonempty disjoint intervals $I_j = [a_j, b_j]$ and logical values $s_j \in \{\mathbf{T}, \mathbf{F}\}$, with j ranging over some index set Γ. These values determine signal s on those intervals, with $\mathbf{U}$ assumed elsewhere, and we write $s = (I_j, s_j)_j$. For convenience we also admit some improper representations including empty intervals, values $s_j = \mathbf{U}$, and intervals with overlapping endpoints (but consistent logical values); these may all be rewritten as proper representations.

Given propositions φ and ψ with $s = (I_j, s_j)_j$ a signal for φ and $w = (I_j, w_j)_j$ a signal for ψ, we have the following constructions:

$\neg\varphi$ has a signal given by $\neg s = (I_j, \neg s_j)_j$
$\varphi \wedge \psi$ has a signal given by $s \wedge w = (I_j, s_j \wedge w_j)_j$
$\mathcal{F}_{[a,b]}\, \varphi$ has a signal given by $\mathcal{F}_{[a,b]}\, s = (K_j \cap [0,\infty), s_j)_j$ where

$$K_j = \begin{cases} I_j - [a, b] & \text{if } s_j = \mathbf{T} \\ (I_j - a) \cap (I_j - b) & \text{if } s_j = \mathbf{F} \end{cases}$$

In the above we have assumed, without loss of generality, that s and w are represented using a common set of intervals I_j; this is always possible by taking a common refinement of the representations of s and w respectively.

Whilst the pointwise semantics of the until operator could be extended directly to three-valued logic, it is somewhat trickier to define a closed representation, as required for interval-based verified monitoring. In the case of boolean signals, the until signal $s\, \mathcal{U}_J\, w$ is usually computed by subdividing s into *disjoint unitary signals* s_j (that is, signals which are indicator functions $s_j(t) = \mathcal{X}_{I_j}(t) = (\mathbf{T}$ if $t \in I_j$ otherwise $\mathbf{F})$ of pairwise disjoint intervals) [35]. For three-valued signals we will follow a similar approach, however we need an appropriate three-valued generalisation of unitary signals. To this end we define a *connected signal*.

Definition 4. *We say a three-valued signal s is* connected *if for every interval $[a, b]$ we have that,*

$$s(a) \wedge s(b) \leq s(t) \qquad \text{for all } t \in [a, b].$$

under the ordering $\mathbf{F} \lesssim \mathbf{U} \lesssim \mathbf{T}$.

Proposition 1. *A three-valued signal s is* connected *iff there exist intervals $J \subseteq I$ such that s is equal to the* three-valued indicator signal,

$$\mathcal{X}_{J,I}(t) \triangleq \begin{cases} \mathbf{T} & \text{if } t \in J \\ \mathbf{U} & \text{if } t \in I \setminus J \\ \mathbf{F} & \text{if } t \notin I \end{cases}$$

Proof. Given in [44].

We note that it is straightforward to compute a signal for $\varphi \, \mathcal{U}_K \, \psi$ on connected signals.

Proposition 2. *If s and w are respectively signals for φ and ψ, and s is connected then*

$$s \, \mathcal{U}_K \, w \triangleq s \wedge \mathcal{F}_K(s \wedge w)$$

is a signal for $\varphi \, \mathcal{U}_K \, \psi$.

Proof. Suppose $(s \, \mathcal{U}_K \, w)(t) = \mathbf{T}$. Then $s(t) = \mathbf{T}$ and for some $t' \in t + K$, $s(t') = \mathbf{T}$ and $w(t') = \mathbf{T}$. But then since s is connected, $s(t') = \mathbf{T}$ for all $t'' \in [t, t']$, showing that $(\mathbf{x}, t) \models \varphi \, \mathcal{U}_K \, \psi$.

Suppose $(s \, \mathcal{U}_K \, w)(t) = \mathbf{F}$. Then either $s(t) = \mathbf{F}$ in which case $(\mathbf{x}, t) \not\models \varphi \, \mathcal{U}_K \, \psi$, or for all $t' \in t + K$, $s(t) = \mathbf{F}$ or $w(t) = \mathbf{F}$, in which case again $(\mathbf{x}, t) \not\models \varphi \, \mathcal{U}_K \, \psi$.

We next decompose a three-valued signal into connected signals.

Proposition 3. *Given a three-valued signal s and disjoint intervals I_j such that $s^{-1}(\{\mathbf{T}, \mathbf{U}\}) = \biguplus_j I_j$, we have a decomposition $s = \bigvee_j \bigvee_k s_{j,k}$ of s into the connected components:*

- $s_{j,0} = \chi_{\varnothing, I_j}$ *whenever* $I_j \cap s^{-1}(\{\mathbf{T}\}) = \varnothing$;
- $s_{j,k} = \chi_{J_{j,k}, I_j}$ *given intervals $J_{j,k}$ such that $I_j \cap s^{-1}(\{\mathbf{T}\}) = \biguplus_k J_{j,k}$.*

Proof. Given in [44].

Example 1. Given the three-valued signal

$$s = (([0,1], \mathbf{F}), ([2,3], \mathbf{T}), ([4,5], \mathbf{T}), ([6,7], \mathbf{F}), ([7.5,8], \mathbf{T}), ([8.5,9], \mathbf{F}))$$

we have the decomposition (Fig. 1)

$$s = (s_{1,1} \vee s_{1,2}) \vee s_{2,1} \vee s_{3,0} = (\chi_{[2,3], (1,6)} \vee \chi_{[4,5], (1,6)}) \vee \chi_{[7.5,8], (7,8.5)} \vee \chi_{\varnothing, (9,\infty)}.$$

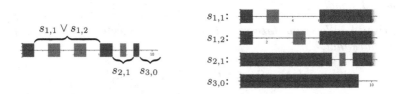

Fig. 1. The decomposition of s into components $s \equiv (s_{1,1} \vee s_{1,2}) \vee s_{2,1} \vee s_{3,0}$.

We now use this decomposition to construct a signal for $\varphi \, \mathcal{U}_K \, \psi$:

Proposition 4. *If φ has a three-valued signal $s = \bigvee_j \bigvee_k s_{j,k}$ with connected components $s_{j,k}$ and ψ has a signal w, then $\varphi \, \mathcal{U}_K \, \psi$ has a signal given by,*

$$s \, \mathcal{U}_K \, w \triangleq \bigvee_j \bigvee_k s_{j,k} \wedge \mathcal{F}_K(s_{j,k} \wedge w). \tag{2}$$

Proof. Given in [44].

3.2 Signals for Atomic Propositions

We now turn our attention to generating a signal for an atomic proposition $\rho \triangleq p > 0$ with defining polynomial p, based on a Flow* flowpipe.

We do this in a single pass algorithm which iterates over each time segment of the flowpipe and encloses all roots of p for the current timestep. For each timestep $[t_k, t_{k+1}]$, Flow* provides two Taylor models, $\left(\mathbf{q}_{\text{post}}^{(k)}, \mathbf{I}_{\text{post}}^{(k)}\right)$ and $\left(\mathbf{q}_{\text{pre}}^{(k)}, \mathbf{I}_{\text{pre}}^{(k)}\right)$ whose composition encloses all trajectories of the system over the time step. The value of p over system trajectories is hence enclosed by the Taylor model $G_p^{(k)}(\mathbf{s}, t)$ defined by the composition

$$G_p^{(k)} \triangleq p \,\square\, \left(\mathbf{q}_{\text{post}}^{(k)}, \mathbf{I}_{\text{post}}^{(k)}\right) \,\square\, \left(\mathbf{q}_{\text{pre}}^{(k)}, \mathbf{I}_{\text{pre}}^{(k)}\right) \tag{3}$$

where $t \in [t_k, t_{k+1}]$ and $\mathbf{s}$ ranges over the n-dimensional box $[-1,1]^n$ [12,34]. Therefore, we have an interval extension of p over the time interval $[t_k, t_{k+1}]$ given by the interval function $H_p^{(k)}(t) \triangleq G_p^{(k)}([-1,1]^n, t)$ which may be evaluated using interval arithmetic.

We may then determine a signal for ρ.

Proposition 5. *Given atomic proposition $\rho = p(\mathbf{x}) > 0$, the three-valued signal $s \triangleq (I_j, s_j)_j$ is a signal for ρ where I_j are the interval components of*

$$[0, T] \setminus \bigcup \left\{ x_0 \;\middle|\; x_0 \in \text{roots}\left(H_p^{(k)}, \frac{d}{dt} H_p^{(k)}, [t_k, t_{k+1}] \right) \text{ for some } k \right\},$$

and s_j is $\mathbf{T}$ iff $H_p^{(k)}(t') > 0$ for some k and $t' \in I_j \cap [t_k, t_{k+1}]$.

The unknown regions are given by amalgamating the roots of $H_p^{(k)}$ over each time step. These roots are found by applying Interval Newton method [7,27,37] to $H_p^{(k)}$ (using its derivative $\frac{d}{dt} H_p^{(k)}$ which may be derived by Taylor model differentiation [9]), and are guaranteed to soundly enclose the roots of p. Then ρ must have a consistent boolean value in between these roots, which we may sample by performing interval evaluation of $H_p^{(k)}$ (see Fig. 2).

3.3 Efficient Monitoring of Composed Taylor Models

The method described in Sect. 3.2 relies on being able to efficiently compute the interval function $H_p^{(k)}$ defined as a symbolic composition of Taylor models (Eq. 3). This is potentially very expensive since the composition involves symbolic operations on high-order polynomials and a Flowpipe may consist of thousands of time steps, each requiring a separate composition.

However, since we only need to deduce the signal for the atomic proposition, rather than the exact function value at each point, it will often be sufficient to inexpensively over-approximate the range of Eq. 3 over the current time step via interval arithmetic, which we do by replacing some of the Taylor model compositions (denoted $\square$) with functional compositions (denoted $\circ$). Hence, we use the following adaptive algorithm:

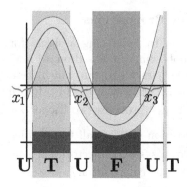

Fig. 2. Transition from root finding to three-valued signals.

– Perform the interval evaluation stepwise using interval arithmetic to check if

$$0 \in \text{range} \left[p \circ \left(\mathbf{q}_{\text{post}}^{(k)}, \mathbf{I}_{\text{post}}^{(k)} \right) \circ \left(\mathbf{q}_{\text{pre}}^{(k)}, \mathbf{I}_{\text{pre}}^{(k)} \right) \right]$$

– If so, perform one stage of symbolic composition and check if

$$0 \in \text{range} \left[p \circ \left(\mathbf{q}_{\text{post}}^{(k)}, \mathbf{I}_{\text{post}}^{(k)} \right) \square \left(\mathbf{q}_{\text{pre}}^{(k)}, \mathbf{I}_{\text{pre}}^{(k)} \right) \right]$$

– If the result is still ambiguous, perform full symbolic composition of $G_p^{(k)}$ for the current time step and apply root finding.

Hence, we are able to generate a precise signal for an atomic proposition over the whole time domain, whilst only performing symbolic Taylor model composition and root finding on demand where necessary to disambiguate the result of the signal (i.e. near the roots of the atomic proposition). We may additionally skip the composition of the preconditioned Taylor model on dimensions which do not correspond to any variable of p.

This method may, however, still spend effort trying to determine the truth value of the signal of an atomic proposition in regions of time which are not crucial to the truth of the overall signal; this issue is addressed in the next section with the introduction of *masks*.

4   Masks

In this section we introduce *masks* which allow us to direct the monitoring process to certain time-regions on the flowpipe. We then see how the mask required for each proposition may be constructed in a top-down manner, taking into account the context of an atomic proposition in the overall STL monitoring process (Sects. 4.2 and 4.3). Once we have an appropriate mask, in Sect. 4.4 we see how to reduce the cost of monitoring an atomic proposition by avoiding work associated within time points outside of the mask.

4.1   Basic Notions

Firstly we introduce *masks* as follows:

Definition 5. *A* mask *is a finite sequence* $m = (I_j)_j$ *of disjoint intervals* I_j. *We refer to these intervals as the* regions of interest *under the mask* m.

We can interpret a mask m as a boolean signal $m : [0, \infty) \to \{\mathbf{T}, \mathbf{F}\}$ such that $m(x) = \mathbf{T}$ iff $x \in \bigcup_j I_j$.

Such a mask represents the region of time for which we wish to monitor a given proposition. Since for soundness of monitoring we only need to over-approximate these regions of interest, in a practical implementation we may restrict ourselves to masks whose components are all closed intervals $I_j \triangleq [a_j, b_j]$ (using e.g. floating point endpoints) and consistently round outwards. We will however sometimes use other types of interval endpoints in what follows in order to state crisp results.

We can apply a mask to an existing signal, erasing any truth values that lie outside the mask.

Definition 6. *Given a signal s and a mask m, the* masked signal *of s by m is the signal $s|_m$ defined as*

$$s|_m(t) \triangleq \begin{cases} s(t) & \textit{if } m(t) = \mathbf{T} \\ \mathbf{U} & \textit{otherwise.} \end{cases}$$

Examples of Masking. Before laying out rules for using and computing masks, we will illustrate their use in two different examples, demonstrating the importance of the temporal and logical context of a proposition within a STL formula.

Example 2. Suppose we want to monitor the property $\varphi \triangleq \mathcal{F}_{[5,6]}\, \psi$ for 2 s (that is, over the time-domain $I \triangleq [0, 2]$). This would naively require computing a signal for ψ over 8 s, despite the fact that φ only looks at the behaviour of ψ between 5 and 6 s in the future—that is, within the absolute time-domain

$$I + [5, 6] = [0, 2] + [5, 6] = [5, 8].$$

This means that in checking φ it is sufficient to compute a signal for ψ under the mask $m \triangleq ([5, 8])$, allowing us to ignore more than half of the time-domain.

Example 3. Suppose we want to monitor the property $\varphi \triangleq \psi \vee \sigma$ for 5 s (that is, over the time-domain $I \triangleq [0, 5]$). This would normally require computing signals for ψ and σ over the whole time domain I. However, if we have already computed a signal for ψ such as

$$s \triangleq (([0, 1], \mathbf{F}), ([2, 4], \mathbf{T}))$$

then it is evident that computing a signal for φ only depends on the truth value of σ on the intervals $[0, 2)$ and $(4, 5]$. It thus suffices to compute a signal for σ under the mask $m \triangleq ([0, 2), (4, 5])$. This demonstrates how masks can enable a form of *temporal short-circuiting*.

Whilst in both of the above examples the required masks are quite simple, in general they quickly become much more complex depending on what signals we have already computed for other parts of the property (as in Example 3) and the position of the current proposition in a larger property. Later in this section we will see how the reasoning in these two examples can be generalised and combined to build up masks for arbitrary properties in a compositional manner.

Operations on Masks. We next need to define the operations with which masks can be build. Firstly, masks inherit all of the normal logical operations on boolean signals [35]. In particular, given masks $m_I = (I_k)_k$ and $m_J = (J_l)_l$ we have that $m_I \wedge m_J = (I_k \cap J_l)_{l,k}$, and we write the negation of a mask m as $\neg m$.

We will also need the temporal operators $\mathcal{P}_J \, m$ *(past)* and $\mathcal{H}_J \, m$ *(historically)* defined on masks by,

Definition 7. *Given a mask* $m_I = (I_k)_k$ *and an interval* $J = [a, b]$, *the* past mask *is defined by,*

$$\mathcal{P}_J \, m_I \triangleq (I_k + J)_k$$

whilst the historically mask *is defined by,*

$$\mathcal{H}_J \, m_I \triangleq \neg \mathcal{P}_J \, (\neg m) = ((I_k + a) \cap (I_k + b))_k \, .$$

4.2   Monitoring Contexts

Before we specify how the masks for the monitoring algorithm should be computed, we must first formalise what is required of a mask for it to be used at a given stage of the monitoring algorithm. This motivates us to define *contexts* which capture our existing knowledge at each recursive step of the monitoring algorithm, by recording the position of an argument ψ within the STL operator currently being monitored and the signals s we have already computed for any other arguments.

Definition 8. *A* monitoring context *is defined similarly to a STL formula except with subformulae replaced by concrete signals* s *and, in exactly one place, a hole* $[\cdot]$. *That is, a monitoring context is defined according to the grammar*

$$\mathcal{C}([\cdot]) ::= [\cdot] \mid s \vee \mathcal{C}([\cdot]) \mid s \wedge \mathcal{C}([\cdot]) \mid \neg \mathcal{C}([\cdot])$$
$$\mid \mathcal{F}_I(\mathcal{C}([\cdot])) \mid \mathcal{G}_I(\mathcal{C}([\cdot])) \mid s \, \mathcal{U}_I \, \mathcal{C}([\cdot]).$$

A monitoring context $\mathcal{C}([\cdot])$ *is a* monitoring context of the subformula ψ *of a STL formula* φ, *if* $\mathcal{C}([\cdot])$ *has the same structure as* φ *except that, in the place of each atomic proposition* ρ *of* φ, $\mathcal{C}([\cdot])$ *has a signal* s_ρ *that is a signal for* ρ, *and the hole* $[\cdot]$ *in place of* ψ.

Given a signal s, we can evaluate a monitoring context $\mathcal{C}([\cdot])$ to give a signal $\mathcal{C}(s)$ by substituting s in the place of the hole $[\cdot]$ and following the usual rules for combining signals. This means that a monitoring context captures how the signal for the overall formula depends on the signal for the proposition which remains to be monitored.

We are now able to define when a mask is sufficient for monitoring in a context.

Definition 9. *A mask m is* sufficient *for a monitoring context* $C([\cdot])$ *under mask* n, *if for any signal s we have that*

$$C(s)|_n = C(s|_m)|_n.$$

That is, a mask is sufficient if signals masked by it are *just as good* as unmasked signals for monitoring the overall formula.

We also wish to know when a mask is as small as possible for monitoring in a given context.

Definition 10. *A mask m is the* optimal *mask in context* $C([\cdot])$ *under mask n if it is the smallest sufficient mask in context* $C([\cdot])$ *under mask n with respect to the pointwise logical ordering* $\leq$.

It follows directly that the mask defined above is unique (for a given context and overall mask), allowing us to talk about *the mask* for a given context.

4.3 Monitoring Under a Mask: Complex Propositions

We are now ready to detail how our masked monitoring algorithm deals with complex propositions, by introducing suitable masks for each temporal and logical context.

Negation. Suppose we want to monitor a negation $\neg\varphi$ under mask m, then this is equivalent to monitoring φ under mask m and then negating the resulting signal. That is, m is sufficient and optimal in the context $C([\cdot]) = \neg[\cdot]$ under m.

Eventually ($\mathcal{F}_{[a,b]}\varphi$) and Globally ($\mathcal{G}_{[a,b]}\varphi$). Suppose we want to monitor the property $\mathcal{F}_{[a,b]}\,\varphi$ or $\mathcal{G}_{[a,b]}\,\varphi$, under mask $m = (I_j)_j$. In this case we should monitor φ under the past mask

$$\mathcal{P}_{[a,b]}\,m = (I_j + [a,b])_j.$$

because the truth of φ at time t could determine the truth of either $\mathcal{F}_{[a,b]}\,\varphi$ or $\mathcal{G}_{[a,b]}\,\varphi$ at any point between a and b seconds ago (in the former case by witnessing its truth, and in the latter case, by witnessing its falsehood)—this generalises the reasoning given in Example 2.

Proposition 6. *Given a context*

$$C([\cdot]) = \mathcal{F}_{[a,b]}[\cdot] \qquad or \qquad C([\cdot]) = \mathcal{G}_{[a,b]}[\cdot]$$

under the overall mask m, in each case the mask $\mathcal{P}_{[a,b]}\,m$ *is sufficient and optimal for* $C([\cdot])$.

Proof. Here we just prove sufficiency for $\mathcal{C}([\cdot]) = \mathcal{F}_{[a,b]}[\cdot]$ the results for $\mathcal{C}([\cdot]) = \mathcal{G}_{[a,b]}[\cdot]$ follow since $\mathcal{G}_{[a,b]} \varphi \equiv \neg \mathcal{F}_{[a,b]} \neg \varphi$. For sufficiency we need to show that

$$\mathcal{C}\big(s|_{\mathcal{P}_{[a,b]} m}\big)(t) = \mathcal{F}_{[a,b]}\big(s|_{\mathcal{P}_{[a,b]} m}\big)(t) = \mathcal{F}_{[a,b]}(s)(t) = \mathcal{C}(s)(t)$$

for any three-valued signal s and time point t such that $m(t) = \mathbf{T}$. We do this by showing that $\mathcal{P}_{[a,b]} m(t') = \mathbf{T}$ and hence $s|_{\mathcal{P}_{[a,b]} m}(t') = s(t')$ at each of the future time points $t' \in t + [a, b]$ to which both of the above $\mathcal{F}_{[a,b]}$ operators refer. This holds by contrapositive since if we had some $t' \in t + [a, b]$ for which $\mathcal{P}_{[a,b]} = \mathbf{F}$, then we would have $m(t'') = \mathbf{F}$ for all $t'' \in t' - [a, b]$ and, in particular, $m(t) = \mathbf{F}$.

Disjunctions and Conjunctions. Suppose we want to monitor a disjunction $\varphi \vee \psi$ under mask m. We should first monitor φ under the mask m to give the signal s. Then, generalising Example 3, we can use the signal s to generate a mask $m_s^\vee$, the *or-mask of s*.

Definition 11. *Given a three-valued signal $s = (I_j, s_j)_j$, the or-mask of s is the mask $m_s^\vee$ defined by $m_s^\vee(t) = \mathbf{T}$ iff $s(t) \in \{\mathbf{F}, \mathbf{U}\}$ so*

$$m_s^\vee = \bigwedge_{s_j = \mathbf{T}} m_j$$

where $m_j \triangleq \left(C_j^{(\ell)}, C_j^{(u)}\right)$ is the mask consisting of the two interval complements $C_j^{(\ell)}, C_j^{(u)}$ of I_j in $[0, \infty)$.

If this mask turns out to be empty (i.e. if $s(t) = \mathbf{F} = m_s^\vee(t)$ for all $x \in m$), then we can stop and conclude s is a signal for $\varphi \vee \psi$ under m. Otherwise, we monitor ψ under the mask $m_s^\vee$ giving a signal w, and hence the signal $s \vee w$ for $\varphi \vee \psi$ under m.

We see that the mask $m_s^\vee$ is optimal and sufficient for the context $\mathcal{C}([\cdot]) = s \vee [\cdot]$. We treat conjunctions similarly, and can see that the *and-mask $m_s^\wedge$* defined by $m_s^\wedge(t) = \bigwedge_{s_j = \mathbf{F}} m_j$ is an optimal and sufficient mask for conjunctions $\mathcal{C}([\cdot]) = s \wedge [\cdot]$.

Until ($\varphi \, \mathcal{U}_{[a,b]} \, \psi$). Finally, suppose we wish to monitor the signal for the property $\varphi \, \mathcal{U}_{[a,b]} \, \psi$ under the mask m. As in Sect. 3, we will compute the signal for $\varphi \, \mathcal{U}_{[a,b]} \, \psi$ based on signals for φ and ψ using Eq. (2), however we now need to monitor φ and ψ under appropriate masks. We start by monitoring φ under the mask $m \vee \mathcal{P}_{[a,b]} m$ (taking into account the two places in which it appears in Eq. (2)). Then we could find a suitable mask for ψ by applying the above rules for $\vee$, $\wedge$, and $\mathcal{F}_{[a,b]}$ to Eq. (2). However, it turns out that this mask may be computed directly using the historically operator, giving us the following result.

Proposition 7. *The mask*

$$m_s^{\mathcal{U}_a} \triangleq \mathcal{H}_{[0,a]}(m_s^\wedge)$$

is optimal and sufficient for monitoring context $\mathcal{C}([\cdot]) = s \, \mathcal{U}_{[a,b]} \, [\cdot]$.

Proof. Given in [44, Appendix A].

4.4   Monitoring Under a Mask: Atomic Propositions

Once we have determined a mask $m = (I_j)_j$ for a given atomic proposition ρ given its context in the monitoring process, we then aim to directly monitor a signal s for φ *under the mask* m. This means that we only care about the value of $s(t)$ at time points t for which $m(t)$ is true, and so can increase the efficiency of monitoring by avoiding work associated with time points outside of the mask. Whilst there is no way to save Flow* from having to generate the flowpipes for these time points (since they may be required for determining the future evolution of the system), we can avoid the effort associated with every subsequent step of the monitoring process.

We do this by modifying how we carry out monitoring of ρ (via $H_\rho^{(k)}$) on each flowpipe segment (Sect. 3.3) over its associated time domain $T_k = [t_k, t_{k+1}]$ as follows:

- if $m \wedge (T_k) = \varnothing$ then we set $s(t) = \mathbf{U}$ for all $t \in T_k$ and avoid monitoring over this segment;
- otherwise, we restrict the time domain to the interval $T_k' = \bigcup_j T_k \cap I_j$ and apply the normal monitoring process.

This immediately saves us from performing root finding on regions outside of the mask. Additionally, since we have already seen how the symbolic composition of the two halves of the flowpipe and between the flowpipe and the atomic propositions may be performed on demand, these expensive operations may also be avoided outside of the mask. Thus masks allow us to direct the monitoring of each atomic proposition based on its context within a wider STL formula.

5   Demonstration and Performance Analysis

We have implemented the monitoring techniques discussed in this paper as a Python library with Cython [6] code implementing interval and Taylor model operations by interfacing with Flow*'s internal C++ libraries; our implementation is available as part of the source repository[1]. In this section we will use this implementation to demonstrate the application of our method to verifying STL properties of a known challenging continuous system, the 9-dimensional genetic oscillator [14,43] involving non-linear (polynomial) ODEs over the variables $x_1, \ldots, x_9$ and an uncertain box of interval initial conditions $x_i \in [a_i, b_i]$ (given in full along with other details of our benchmarking approach in [44, Appendix B]). The evolution of the variables x_4 and x_6 over $5\,\mathrm{s}$ is shown in Fig. 3 which includes numerical traces from a sample of many different fixed initial conditions alongside a coarse interval over-approximation of a Flow* flowpipe covering the whole box of uncertain initial conditions. We can describe the temporal behaviour of this system much more precisely with STL properties such as $\varphi \triangleq \mathcal{G}_{[0,1]}\big(P \vee \mathcal{G}_{[3,3.5]}(Q)\big)$ in which we have polynomial atomic propositions

---

[1]   https://github.com/twright/Logic-of-Behaviour-in-Uncertain-Contexts.

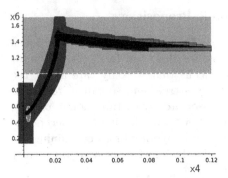

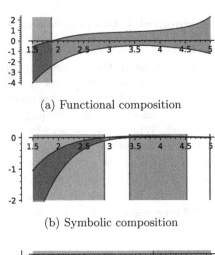

(a) Functional composition

(b) Symbolic composition

(c) Mask for Q in context

Fig. 3. An interval over-approximation of the Flow* flowpipe at each time step is illustrated in blue , numerical trajectories for different initial conditions in black , initial conditions in red , and the regions involved in properties P and Q are in orange and green respectively. (Color figure online)

Fig. 4. Monitoring Q.

$P \triangleq x_6 - 1 > 0$ and $Q \triangleq 0.032 - 125^2(x_4 - 0.003)^2 - 3(x_6 - 0.5)^2 > 0$. The property φ states that at any point within the first second, the system will either remain within the half-space P or, at any point between 3 and 3.5 s in the future will be within the elliptical region Q.

In Fig. 5 we break down the time taken to monitor φ for 0.5 s using a number of variants of our monitoring algorithm in order to evaluate the impact of each of its elements on monitoring cost and precision. First we consider the closed box monitoring approach where we first run Flow* to perform verified integration and flowpipe composition, before using interval analysis and functional composition to monitor φ over the entire flowpipe. Whilst the monitoring cost for the propositions P and Q is very small in comparison to the time it took Flow* to perform verified integration, the flowpipe composition stage is more expensive and takes almost as long as the verified integration itself. Next we monitor φ in the same way, but perform the flowpipe composition on demand as described in Sect. 3.3. We see that if we just monitor the simple atomic proposition P we save most of the cost of flowpipe composition, although once we also monitor Q we need to pay the full cost. These two methods also do not yield sufficient precision to verify φ, both producing a useless signal which is unknown everywhere. This imprecision can be seen in Fig. 4a which shows the result of monitoring the complex polynomial atomic proposition Q over the flowpipe using functional composition and the corresponding signal.

In order to produce a useful signal for φ we need to run our full monitoring algorithm, permitting symbolic composition at each stage. Whilst the monitoring cost for the simple proposition P is similar to before, the cost for the complex proposition Q is significantly higher. This, however, now gives a much more precise signal for Q as shown in Fig. 4b. This means we now get the overall signal $s = (([0, 0.0237], \mathbf{T}))$ for φ, allowing us to verify that φ is true at time 0 and that $P \vee \mathcal{G}_{[3,3.5]}(Q)$ holds for at least the first 1.0237 s. Finally, we reran our monitoring algorithm but monitored each atomic proposition under appropriate masks. For example, Q is monitored under the mask shown in Fig. 4c. This produced the same overall signal as the full unmasked monitoring algorithm but reduced the monitoring time for Q by 65%.

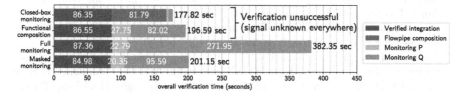

Fig. 5. Combined Flow* verified integration and STL monitoring times in seconds, showing the cost of each stage for a number of variants of our monitoring algorithm.

6   Conclusion and Future Work

In this paper we explored a symbolic algorithm for monitoring STL properties over Taylor model flowpipes via three-valued signals and introduced masking to direct the monitoring process to time regions critical to the property at hand. We saw that, whilst direct integration with the symbolic structure of flowpipes can add some overhead for complex propositions, it significantly increases the precision of the results generated and is sometimes necessary to produce definitive results at all. We have also seen that masking can have an important impact on reducing this cost, by avoiding the need to carry out symbolic operations for regions of time not necessary for the overall result of the monitoring algorithm.

Our current method relies on interval arithmetic to evaluate flowpipes over the whole set of uncertain initial conditions, whereas Flow*'s flowpipes in fact track the functional dependency of each system variable on the initial condition [9]. In future we intend to use this additional information to extend our algorithm to produce spatio-temporal signals exploring refinements of the initial conditions and introduce spatio-temporal masks to enable *spatio-temporal short-circuiting*.

Acknowledgements. We would like to thank Paul Jackson for many useful discussions of Taylor models and Flow*, Chris Banks for providing feedback on our approach, Kristjan Liiva for useful discussions of Flow*'s code and for his patches to Flow* for native floating point arithmetic, and Jos Gibbons and Juliet Cooke for providing feedback on drafts of this report. Thanks also go to our anonymous reviewers for helpful feedback, and for pointing out the connections of our work to [18].

This work was supported by the Engineering and Physical Sciences Research Council (grant EP/L01503X/1), EPSRC Centre for Doctoral Training in Pervasive Parallelism at the University of Edinburgh, School of Informatics.

References

1. Althoff, M.: An Introduction to CORA 2015. In: Proceedings of the Workshop on Applied Verification for Continuous and Hybrid Systems (2015)
2. Alur, R., Henzinger, T.A., Ho, P.-H.: Automatic symbolic verification of embedded systems. IEEE Trans. Softw. Eng. **22**(3), 181–201 (1996)
3. Annpureddy, Y., Liu, C., Fainekos, G., Sankaranarayanan, S.: S-TaLiRo: a tool for temporal logic falsification for hybrid systems. In: Abdulla, P.A., Leino, K.R.M. (eds.) TACAS 2011. LNCS, vol. 6605, pp. 254–257. Springer, Heidelberg (2011). https://doi.org/10.1007/978-3-642-19835-9_21
4. Bae, K., Lee, J.: Bounded model checking of signal temporal logic properties using syntactic separation. Proc. ACM Program. Lang. **3**(POPL), 51 (2019)
5. Banks, C.J., and Stark, I.: A more sensitive context. arXiv:1702.03288 (2017)
6. Behnel, S., Bradshaw, R., Citro, C., Dalcin, L., Seljebotn, D., Smith, K.: Cython: the best of both worlds. Comput. Sci. Eng. **13**(2), 31–39 (2011)
7. Berz, M., Hoefkens, J.: Verified high-order inversion of functional depedencies and interval newton methods. Reliable Comput. **7**(5), 379–398 (2001)
8. Berz, M., Hoffstätter, G.: Computation and application of Taylor polynomials with interval remainder bounds. Reliable Comput. **4**(1), 83–97 (1998)
9. Berz, M., Makino, K.: Verified integration of ODEs and flows using differential algebraic methods on high-order Taylor models. Reliable Comput. **4**(4), 361–369 (1998)
10. Bresolin, D.: HyLTL: a temporal logic for model checking hybrid systems. Electron. Proc. Theoret. Comput. Sci. **124**, 73–84 (2013)
11. Bruns, G., Godefroid, P.: Model checking partial state spaces with 3-valued temporal logics. In: Halbwachs, N., Peled, D. (eds.) CAV 1999. LNCS, vol. 1633, pp. 274–287. Springer, Heidelberg (1999). https://doi.org/10.1007/3-540-48683-6_25
12. Chen, X.: Reachability analysis of non-linear hybrid systems using taylor models. Ph.D thesis, Fachgruppe Informatik, RWTH Aachen University (2015)
13. Chen, X., Ábrahám, E., Sankaranarayanan, S.: Flow*: an analyzer for non-linear hybrid systems. In: Sharygina, N., Veith, H. (eds.) CAV 2013. LNCS, vol. 8044, pp. 258–263. Springer, Heidelberg (2013). https://doi.org/10.1007/978-3-642-39799-8_18
14. Chen, X., Sankaranarayanan, S.: Decomposed reachability analysis for nonlinear systems. In: 2016 IEEE Real-Time Systems Symposium (RTSS), pp. 13–24 (2016)
15. Chen, X., Schupp, S., Makhlouf, I.B., Ábrahám, E., Frehse, G., Kowalewski, S.: A benchmark suite for hybrid systems reachability analysis. In: Havelund, K., Holzmann, G., Joshi, R. (eds.) NFM 2015. LNCS, vol. 9058, pp. 408–414. Springer, Cham (2015). https://doi.org/10.1007/978-3-319-17524-9_29

16. Cimatti, A., Griggio, A., Mover, S., Tonetta, S.: Verifying LTL properties of hybrid systems with K-LIVENESS. In: Biere, A., Bloem, R. (eds.) CAV 2014. LNCS, vol. 8559, pp. 424–440. Springer, Cham (2014). https://doi.org/10.1007/978-3-319-08867-9_28

17. de Moura, L., Bjørner, N.: Z3: an efficient SMT solver. In: Ramakrishnan, C.R., Rehof, J. (eds.) TACAS 2008. LNCS, vol. 4963, pp. 337–340. Springer, Heidelberg (2008). https://doi.org/10.1007/978-3-540-78800-3_24

18. Deshmukh, J.V., Donzé, A., Ghosh, S., Jin, X., Juniwal, G., Seshia, S.A.: Robust online monitoring of signal temporal logic. Formal Methods Syst. Des. **51**(1), 5–30 (2017). https://doi.org/10.1007/s10703-017-0286-7

19. Donzé, A.: Breach, a toolbox for verification and parameter synthesis of hybrid systems. In: Touili, T., Cook, B., Jackson, P. (eds.) CAV 2010. LNCS, vol. 6174, pp. 167–170. Springer, Heidelberg (2010). https://doi.org/10.1007/978-3-642-14295-6_17

20. Donzé, A., Maler, O.: Robust satisfaction of temporal logic over real-valued signals. In: Chatterjee, K., Henzinger, T.A. (eds.) FORMATS 2010. LNCS, vol. 6246, pp. 92–106. Springer, Heidelberg (2010). https://doi.org/10.1007/978-3-642-15297-9_9

21. Fages, F., Rizk, A.: On temporal logic constraint solving for analyzing numerical data time series. Theoret. Comput. Sci. **408**(1), 55–65 (2008)

22. Fainekos, G.E., Pappas, G.J.: Robust sampling for MITL specifications. In: Raskin, J.-F., Thiagarajan, P.S. (eds.) FORMATS 2007. LNCS, vol. 4763, pp. 147–162. Springer, Heidelberg (2007). https://doi.org/10.1007/978-3-540-75454-1_12

23. Fisman, D., Kugler, H.: Temporal reasoning on incomplete paths. In: Margaria, T., Steffen, B. (eds.) ISoLA 2018. LNCS, vol. 11245, pp. 28–52. Springer, Cham (2018). https://doi.org/10.1007/978-3-030-03421-4_3

24. Gao, S., Kong, S., Clarke, E.M.: dReal: an SMT solver for nonlinear theories over the reals. In: Bonacina, M.P. (ed.) CADE 2013. LNCS (LNAI), vol. 7898, pp. 208–214. Springer, Heidelberg (2013). https://doi.org/10.1007/978-3-642-38574-2_14

25. Ishii, D., Goldsztejn, A.: HySIA: tool for simulating and monitoring hybrid automata based on interval analysis. In: Lahiri, S., Reger, G. (eds.) RV 2017. LNCS, vol. 10548, pp. 370–379. Springer, Cham (2017). https://doi.org/10.1007/978-3-319-67531-2_23

26. Ishii, D., Yonezaki, N., Goldsztejn, A.: Monitoring bounded LTL properties using interval analysis. Electron. Notes Theoret. Comput. Sci. **317**, 85–100 (2015)

27. Ishii, D., Yonezaki, N., Goldsztejn, A.: Monitoring temporal properties using interval analysis. IEICE Trans. Fundam. Electron. Commun. Comput. Sci. **99**(2), 442–453 (2016)

28. Jeannin, J.-B., Platzer, A.: dTL^2: differential temporal dynamic logic with nested temporalities for hybrid systems. In: Demri, S., Kapur, D., Weidenbach, C. (eds.) IJCAR 2014. LNCS (LNAI), vol. 8562, pp. 292–306. Springer, Cham (2014). https://doi.org/10.1007/978-3-319-08587-6_22

29. Kolmogorov, A.N., Fomin, S.V.: Introductory Real Analysis. Courier Corporation, Chelmsford (1975)

30. Kong, S., Gao, S., Chen, W., Clarke, E.: dReach: δ-reachability analysis for hybrid systems. In: Baier, C., Tinelli, C. (eds.) TACAS 2015. LNCS, vol. 9035, pp. 200–205. Springer, Heidelberg (2015). https://doi.org/10.1007/978-3-662-46681-0_15

31. Liu, J., Zhan, N., Zhao, H., Zou, L.: Abstraction of elementary hybrid systems by variable transformation. In: Bjørner, N., de Boer, F. (eds.) FM 2015. LNCS, vol. 9109, pp. 360–377. Springer, Cham (2015). https://doi.org/10.1007/978-3-319-19249-9_23

32. Luisa Vissat, L., Hillston, J., Loreti, M., Nenzi, L.: Automatic verification of reliability requirements of spatio-temporal analysis using three-valued spatio-temporal logic. In: Proceedings of the 11th EAI International Conference on Performance Evaluation Methodologies and Tools, pp. 225–226. ACM (2017)

33. Makino, K., Berz, M.: Efficient control of the dependency problem based on taylor model methods. Reliable Comput. **5**(1), 3–12 (1999)

34. Makino, K., Berz, M.: Suppression of the wrapping effect by Taylor model-based verified integrators: Long-term stabilization by preconditioning. Int. J. Diff. Equ. Appl. **10**(4), 385–403 (2011)

35. Maler, O., Nickovic, D.: Monitoring temporal properties of continuous signals. In: Lakhnech, Y., Yovine, S. (eds.) FORMATS/FTRTFT -2004. LNCS, vol. 3253, pp. 152–166. Springer, Heidelberg (2004). https://doi.org/10.1007/978-3-540-30206-3_12

36. Maler, O., Nickovic, D., Pnueli, A.: Checking temporal properties of discrete, timed and continuous behaviors. In: Avron, A., Dershowitz, N., Rabinovich, A. (eds.) Pillars of Computer Science. LNCS, vol. 4800, pp. 475–505. Springer, Heidelberg (2008). https://doi.org/10.1007/978-3-540-78127-1_26

37. Moore, R.E., Kearfott, R.B., Cloud, M.J.: Introduction to Interval Analysis. Siam, Philadelphia (2009)

38. Nickovic, D., Maler, O.: AMT: a property-based monitoring tool for analog systems. In: Raskin, J.-F., Thiagarajan, P.S. (eds.) FORMATS 2007. LNCS, vol. 4763, pp. 304–319. Springer, Heidelberg (2007). https://doi.org/10.1007/978-3-540-75454-1_22

39. Peña, J.M., Sauer, T.: On the multivariate horner scheme. SIAM J. Numer. Anal. **37**(4), 1186–1197 (2000)

40. Piazza, C., Antoniotti, M., Mysore, V., Policriti, A., Winkler, F., Mishra, B.: Algorithmic algebraic model checking I: challenges from systems biology. In: Etessami, K., Rajamani, S.K. (eds.) CAV 2005. LNCS, vol. 3576, pp. 5–19. Springer, Heidelberg (2005). https://doi.org/10.1007/11513988_3

41. Roehm, H., Oehlerking, J., Heinz, T., Althoff, M.: STL model checking of continuous and hybrid systems. In: Artho, C., Legay, A., Peled, D. (eds.) ATVA 2016. LNCS, vol. 9938, pp. 412–427. Springer, Cham (2016). https://doi.org/10.1007/978-3-319-46520-3_26

42. Vardi, M.Y., Wolper, P.: An automata-theoretic approach to automatic program verification. In: Proceedings of the First Symposium on Logic in Computer Science, pp. 322–331 (1986)

43. Vilar, J.M.G., Kueh, H.Y., Barkai, N., Leibler, S.: Mechanisms of noise resistance in genetic oscillators. Proc. Nat. Acad. Sci. **99**(9), 5988–5992 (2002)

44. Wright, T., Stark, I.: Technical report: property-directed verified monitoring of signal temporal logic. arXiv:2008.06589 (2020)

Logical Signal Processing: A Fourier Analysis of Temporal Logic

Niraj Basnet and Houssam Abbas[✉]

Oregon State University, Corvallis, OR 97330, USA
{basnetn,abbasho}@oregonstate.edu

Abstract. What is the frequency content of temporal logic formulas? That is, when we monitor a signal against a formula, which frequency bands of the signal are relevant to the logic and should be preserved, and which can be safely discarded? This question is relevant whenever signals are filtered or compressed before being monitored, which is almost always the case for analog signals. To answer this question, we focus on monitors that measure the robustness of a signal relative to a specification in Signal Temporal Logic. We prove that robustness monitors can be modeled using Volterra series. We then study the Fourier transforms of these Volterra representations, and provide a method to derive the Fourier transforms of entire formulas. We also make explicit the measurement process in temporal logic and re-define it on the basis of distributions to make it compatible with measurements in signal processing. Experiments illustrate these results. Beyond compression, this work enables the integration of temporal logic monitoring into common signal processing tool chains as just another signal processing operation, and enables a common formalism to study both logical and non-logical operations in the frequency domain, which we refer to as Logical Signal Processing.

Keywords: Robustness monitoring · Temporal logic · Volterra series · Fourier transform

1 Introduction: The Place of Runtime Verification in the Signal Processing Chain

Runtime monitors in Cyber-Physical Systems (CPS) process analog signals: that is, continuous-time, continuous-valued signals generated by the physics of the system, rather than digital signals generated by computations on values stored in memory. These analog signals are never pristine: to begin with, they are measured, and so incur some measurement distortion; they are noisy, and therefore are usually filtered to reduce noise; and if they get transmitted, they are compressed and de-compressed, which introduces further distortions. All of these operations are very common in signal processing toolchains - indeed, the act of measurement is inevitable. And all of these operations affect, a priori, the verdict of the runtime monitor. Yet we have little theory to *systematically* account for

© Springer Nature Switzerland AG 2020
J. Deshmukh and D. Ničković (Eds.): RV 2020, LNCS 12399, pp. 359–382, 2020.
https://doi.org/10.1007/978-3-030-60508-7_20

these effects. For instance, Fourier analysis is a standard powerful tool in signal processing, which is used to synthesize optimal filters meeting certain output requirements. If we want to synthesize a filter subject to monitorability requirements, how would we go about it? Conversely, how can we synthesize a monitor that accounts for the modifications introduced by a filter earlier in the processing chain? Today we have no way of answering these questions systematically, because we lack an account of the frequency content of temporal logic. That is, we lack a Fourier representation of the operation of a temporal logic monitor. Lacking such a uniform formalism, we remain in the awkward position of having to study the impact of frequency-domain operations in the time domain, using ad hoc assumptions like the availability of Lipschitz constants, and combining them somehow with the time-domain representation of monitors.

This paper presents a way of analyzing the frequency content of temporal logic, or equivalently, of analyzing temporal logic monitors in the Fourier domain. Because monitors are nonlinear operators, we resort to Volterra series, which generalize the convolution representation of time-invariant linear operators to time-invariant nonlinear operators, and have generalized Fourier representations. To apply the machinery of Volterra series, we work exclusively with robustness monitors, which output analog robustness signals.

As soon as we start thinking in the Fourier domain, we also realize that the basic measurement model in temporal logic is broken from a physical, and therefore, cyber-physical, perspective: in almost all temporal logics, it is assumed that one can make an *instantaneous* measurement. I.e., that it is possible to measure $x(t)$ exactly at t, and this is used to determine the truth value of an atomic proposition, e.g. '$x(t) \geq 0$'. However, it is well-known that instantaneous measurements of analog signals are impossible! Any measurement device has a finite resolution, so at best we can measure some aggregate of infinitely many signal values. For instance, in a camera the value recorded by a pixel equals the *average* illumination incident on that pixel, not the illumination in a specific point in space. This matters to us because an instantaneous measurement requires infinite bandwidth, thus rendering the entire frequency analysis trivial or useless. Instantaneous measurements also produce mathematical complications when working with sup norms and Lebesgue integrals which ignore sets of measure zero. We therefore re-define atomic propositions (and the measurement model) on the basis of the theory of distributions, and demonstrate that the resulting robust semantics are still sound and still yield robustness tubes that can be used in falsification.

Figure 1 shows an example of the results made possible by the methods of this paper, which we refer to as *Logical Signal processing*. The figure shows the first four Generalized Frequency Response Functions (GFRFs) of the formula $\boxminus_{[1,1.2]}\, p$, read 'Historically p'. Here, p is a given atomic proposition and $\boxminus$ is the Historically operation, the past equivalent of Always/Globally. The way to interpret Fig. 1 is, roughly, as follows: let X be the Fourier transform of the input monitored signal, and Y be the Fourier of the output robustness signal computed by the monitor. Then $H_1(\omega)$ weighs the contribution of $X(\omega)$ to $Y(\omega)$, $H_2(\omega_1, \omega_2)$

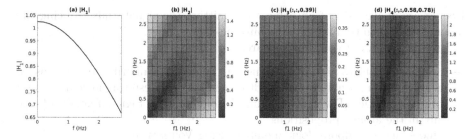

Fig. 1. Frequency response of the temporal logic formula Historically p. $H_1(\omega)$ captures the linear, or first-order, transfer function, while $H_2(\omega_1, \omega_2)$, $H_3(\omega_1, \omega_2, \omega_3)$, etc., are higher-order generalized frequency responses that capture the non-linear effects. By studying these response functions we can determine which frequencies of the monitored signal affect the monitor output. (Color in digital copy).

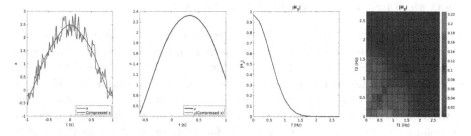

Fig. 2. Monitoring-safe compression enabled by Logical Signal Processing. (Left) Signal x (red) is compressed by eliminating frequencies above the formula's cut-off frequency (1.5 Hz). Resulting signal is in blue. (Second panel) Robustness of original and compressed signals relative to a formula ϕ. Despite the marked difference between the monitored signals, the robustness signals are almost identical, validating the fact that the compression was monitoring-safe. Right two panes show the order-1 and -2 frequency responses of the formula. (Color in digital copy). (Color figure online)

weighs the contribution of the product $X(\omega_1)X(\omega_2)$, $H_3(\omega_1, \omega_2, \omega_3)$ weighs the contribution of $X(\omega_1)X(\omega_2)X(\omega_3)$, etc. (Product terms appear because the monitor is a non-linear operator, as will be explained later). Using these GFRFs H_n, we can, for example, calculate frequencies ω s.t. $X(\omega)$ contributes very little to the output $Y(\omega)$, that is, frequencies of the signal that are irrelevant to the monitor. This is shown in Fig. 2: using the methods of this paper, we obtained the frequency responses of formula $\Diamond_{[0.2,0.4]} p$, read 'Once p'. From the responses we determined (roughly) that the H_n's are negligible above $\omega = 3\pi$ rad/s. Therefore, setting $X(\omega)$ to 0 above the cut-off should change the monitoring output very little. This analysis is confirmed by the experiment: Fig. 2 shows that there's a marked difference between original and compressed signals, and a priori there is no reason to assume that their robustnesses would be similar. And yet, the calculated robustness signals are almost indistinguishable, confirming that compression was done in a monitoring-safe manner. Thus, a codec can suppress all frequencies above the cut-off before transmitting the signal, thus reducing the amount of transmitted bits in a monitoring-safe manner.

In this paper, our contributions are:

- a definition of atomic propositions on the basis of distributions to ensure measurements have finite bandwidth, such that the resulting logic has sound robust semantics. The new logic differs from standard Signal Temporal Logic only in the atomic propositions.
- a modeling of temporal logic monitors using Volterra series
- the first frequency analysis of temporal logic formulas and their robustness monitors.

The proposed analysis using Volterra series can be used as a signal processing tool for frequency domain analysis of temporal logic monitors but it is not supposed to replace the monitors themselves. It can be used for example to design filters which respect the monitorability requirements.

Related Work. There are few works dealing with the dual aspects of time and frequency in temporal logic. In [8] the authors introduce a variant of Signal Temporal Logic (STL), called Time-Frequency Logic (TFL), to explicitly specify properties of the frequency spectrum of the signal - e.g. one formula might read "$|X(\omega, t)| > 5$ over the next three time units" (where $X(\omega, t)$ is obtained by a windowed Fourier transform and ω is given). What we do in this paper is orthogonal to [8]: given a standard STL formula, we want to analyze which frequencies of signal x contribute to the monitoring verdict. We do not require the formula to tell us that explicitly, as in TFL. In fact, our techniques are applicable to TFL itself: a TFL formula like the one above has a 'hidden' frequency aspect, namely the temporal restriction "in the next three time units". Our methods allow an automatic extraction of that.

The works [14] and [11] provide a general algebraic framework for the semantics of temporal logic based on semi-rings, opening the way to producing new semantics automatically by concretizing the semi-ring operations. In the special case of Metric Temporal logic, [14] shows a formal similarity between convolution and the classical semantics of some logical operations. However, no frequency analysis is made (and indeed that is not the objective of [14]).

In [16], the logic SCL is introduced which replaces the usual temporal operators (like Eventually) with a cross-correlation between the signal and a kernel, which resembles our use of it for atomic propositions (we preserve all temporal operators). The objective of [16] is to measure the fraction of time a property is satisfied, and no frequency analysis is made. We also mention [9] which derives continuous-time verdicts from discrete-time reasoning. The modified measurement in this paper should allow us to connect that work to the sampling process and therefore optimize it for monitoring (but we do not carry out that connection here).

Finally, the works [1,2] consider the impact of representation basis and out-of-order reconstruction on monitoring verdicts, thus also contributing to the study of how signal processing affects runtime verification. The work [2] implicitly replaces instantaneous measurements in the temporal operators with a scrambled, or locally orderless, measurement, but maintains instantaneous measurements in atoms. No frequency analysis is made.

2 Preliminaries: Signal Temporal Logic and Volterra Series

Terminology. Let $\mathbb{R} = (-\infty, \infty), \mathbb{R}_+ = [0, \infty), \overline{\mathbb{R}} = \mathbb{R} \cup \{\pm\infty\}, \mathbb{N} = \{0, 1, 2, \ldots\}$. We write $\mathbb{C}$ for the set of complex numbers and $i = \sqrt{-1}$. Given an interval $I \subset \mathbb{R}$ and $t \in \mathbb{R}$, $t - I := \{t' \mid \exists s \in I.t' = t - s\}$. E.g. $t - [a, b] = [t - b, t - a]$.

For a vector $x \in \mathbb{R}^d$, $|x|$ is its 2-norm and if $x \in \mathbb{C}$, $|x|$ is its modulus (i.e. $|a + ib| = \sqrt{a^2 + b^2}$). For a function f, $\|f\|$ is its essential supremum, defined as $\|f\| := \inf\{a \mid |f(t)| \le a$ on all sets of non-zero measure in the domain of $f\}$.

Given two sets A and B, A^B is the set of all functions from B to A. The space of bounded continuous functions $f : \mathbb{R}^n \to \mathbb{R}^m$ is denoted by $\mathcal{C}(\mathbb{R}^n, \mathbb{R}^m)$. An n-dimensional function is one whose domain is $\mathbb{R}^n$. The Fourier transform of function h will be written $\mathcal{F}\{h\}$. We adopt the convention of using capitalized letters for the transform, e.g. $\mathcal{F}\{h\} = H, \mathcal{F}\{g\} = G$, etc. The magnitude $|H|$ of a Fourier transform will be called the *spectrum*.

Dirac's delta distribution is δ. It is common to abuse notation and treat δ as a function; in that case recall that for any continuous function f and $\tau \in \mathbb{R}$, $\int f(t)\delta(t - \tau)dt = f(\tau)$, $\delta(0) = \infty$ and $\delta(t) = 0 \ \forall t \ne 0$.

In this paper, we reserve the word *operator* to mean a function $\mathcal{N}$ that maps signals to signals, e.g. $\mathcal{N} : \mathcal{C}(\mathbb{R}, \mathbb{R}) \to \mathcal{C}(\mathbb{R}, \mathbb{R})$. The composition of operators $\mathcal{N}$ and $\mathcal{M}$ is $\mathcal{N} \circ \mathcal{M}$. A *logical operation*, on the other hand, refers to an operation of a temporal logic, like negation, disjunction, Since and Once. Logical True is $\top$, False is $\bot$.

2.1 Signal Temporal Logic (STL)

Signal Temporal Logic (STL) [7,13] is a logic that allows the succinct and unambiguous specification of a wide variety of desired system behaviors over time, such as "The vehicle reaches its destination within 10 time units while always avoiding obstacles" and "While the vehicle is in Zone 1, it must obey that zone's velocity constraints".

We use a variant of STL which uses past temporal operators instead of future ones. For simplicity in this paper we work with scalar-valued signals. Formally, let $\mathcal{X} \subseteq \mathbb{R}$ be the state-space and let $E \subseteq \mathbb{R}_+$ be an open interval (which could be all of $\mathbb{R}_+$). A *signal* x is a continuous bounded function. Let $\{\mu_1, \ldots, \mu_L\}$ be a set of real-valued functions of the state: $\mu_k : \mathcal{X} \to \mathbb{R}$. Let $AP = \{p_1, \ldots, p_L\}$ be a set of atomic propositions.

Definition 1 (Past Bounded STL). *The syntax of the logic STL_{bdd}^{past} is given by*

$$\phi := \top \mid p \mid \neg\phi \mid \phi_1 \vee \phi_2 \mid \diamondsuit_I \phi \mid \boxminus_I \phi \mid \phi_1 \mathcal{S}_I \phi_2$$

where $p \in AP$ and $I \subset \mathbb{R}$ is a compact interval. The semantics are given relative to signals as follows.

$$(x, t) \models \top \quad \textit{iff} \quad \top$$
$$\forall p_k \in AP, (x, t) \models p_k \quad \textit{iff} \quad \mu_k(x(t)) \geq 0$$
$$(x, t) \models \neg\phi \quad \textit{iff} \quad (x, t) \not\models \phi$$
$$(x, t) \models \phi_1 \vee \phi_2 \quad \textit{iff} \quad (x, t) \models \phi_1 \ \textit{or} \ (x, t) \models \phi_2$$
$$(x, t) \models \Diamond_I \phi \quad \textit{iff} \quad \exists t' \in t - I \ . \ (x, t') \models \phi$$
$$(x, t) \models \boxminus_I \phi \quad \textit{iff} \quad \forall t' \in t - I \ (x, t') \models \phi$$
$$(x, t) \models \phi_1 \mathcal{S}_I \phi_2 \quad \textit{iff} \quad \exists t' \in t - I \ . \ (x, t') \models \phi_2 \ \textit{and} \ \forall t'' \in (t', t], \ (x, t'') \models \phi_1$$

It is possible to define the Once ($\Diamond$) and Historically ($\boxminus$) operations in terms of Since $\mathcal{S}$, but we make them base operations because we will work extensively with them.

The requirement of bounded intervals and past time is needed to enable the Volterra approximation of temporal logic operations, as will be made explicit in Sect. 4.

2.2   Robust Semantics

The robust semantics of an STL_{bdd}^{past} formula give a quantitative measure of how well a formula is satisfied by a signal x. Usually, robustness is thought of as a functional that maps a signal x and time instant t to a real value $\rho_\phi(x, t)$ which is the robustness of x relative to ϕ at t. In this paper, instead, we will think of it as an *operator* mapping signals x to robustness signals $\rho_\phi(x)$. This forms the starting point of our Volterra approximation and frequency domain modeling.

Definition 2 (Robustness [7,9]). *Let ϕ be a STL_{bdd}^{past} formula. The robustness ρ_ϕ of ϕ is an operator which maps signals $x : E \to \mathcal{X}$ to signals $\rho_\phi(x) : \mathbb{R} \to \overline{\mathbb{R}}$, and is defined as follows: for any $t \in \mathbb{R}$,*

$$\rho_\top(x)(t) = +\infty$$
$$\rho_{p_k}(x)(t) = \mu_k(x(t)) \ \forall p_k \in AP$$
$$\rho_{\neg\phi}(x)(t) = -\rho_\phi(x)(t)$$
$$\rho_{\phi_1 \vee \phi_2}(x)(t) = \max\{\rho_{\phi_1}(x)(t), \rho_{\phi_2}(x)(t)\}$$
$$\rho_{\Diamond_I \phi}(x)(t) = \max_{t' \in t - I} \rho_\phi(x)(t')$$
$$\rho_{\boxminus_I \phi}(x)(t) = \min_{t' \in t - I} \rho_\phi(x)(t')$$
$$\rho_{\phi_1 \mathcal{S}_I \phi_2}(x)(t) = \max_{t' \in (t - I)} \left\{ \min\{\rho_{\phi_2}(x)(t'), \min_{t'' \in (t', t]} \rho_{\phi_1}(x)(t'')\} \right\}$$

The following soundness property allows us to use robustness to monitor signals.

Theorem 1 (Soundness [9]**).** *For any signal x and STL_{bdd}^{past} formula ϕ, if $\rho_\phi(x)(t) < 0$ then x violates ϕ at time t, and if $\rho_\phi(x)(t) > 0$ then x satisfies ϕ at t. Moreover, for every signal y s.t. $\|x - y\| < \rho_\phi(x)(t)$, $(y, t) \models \phi$ if $(x, t) \models \phi$ and $(y, t) \not\models \phi$ if $(x, t) \not\models \phi$.*

2.3   Fourier Analysis

We give a brief overview of the Fourier transform and LTI systems; readers familiar with this material can skip this section without loss of continuity. Fourier analysis allows us to decompose a signal into its constituent frequencies, e.g. by decomposing it into a weighted sum of sinusoids or complex exponentials. We can then also compute how much energy is placed in a given frequency band.

The Fourier transform $X : \mathbb{R} \to \mathbb{C}$ of an input signal x is defined as:

$$X(\omega) = \int_{-\infty}^{\infty} x(t)e^{-i\omega t}dt \tag{1}$$

The real variable ω is the angular frequency measured in rad/sec and relates to the usual frequency f in Hz as $\omega = 2\pi f$. The magnitude $|X|$ is called the amplitude spectrum of x; the energy in frequency band $[\omega_1, \omega_2]$ is $\int_{\omega_1}^{\omega_2} |X(\omega)|^2 d\omega$. The Fourier transform is invertible and x can be obtained using the inverse Fourier transform:

$$x(t) = \frac{1}{2\pi} \int_{-\infty}^{\infty} X(\omega)e^{i\omega t}d\omega \tag{2}$$

Thus we can see that x at t is a weighted sum of complex exponentials, in which $e^{i\omega t}$ is weighted by $X(\omega)$. For a quick implementation on computers, the discrete version of Fourier transform is evaluated using the Fast Fourier Transform (FFT) algorithm.

The Fourier transform is a powerful tool for studying linear time-invariant (LTI) systems. An LTI system is characterized by its *impulse response* $h : \mathbb{R} \to \mathbb{R}$. For an input signal x, the system's output signal y is given by the convolution (represented by operator $*$) of x with the impulse response as follows

$$y(t) = (x * h)(t) = \int_{-\infty}^{\infty} h(\tau)x(t - \tau)d\tau \tag{3}$$

The Fourier Transform reduces this convolution to simply the product of the Fourier transforms:

$$y(t) = (x * h)(t) \leftrightarrow Y(\omega) = X(\omega)H(\omega) \tag{4}$$

Thus if we choose an LTI system such that $H(\omega) = 0$ above some frequency ω_c, we would get $y(t)$ without high frequency noise. Hence, the Fourier domain can be done for designing filters that pass or block specific frequency components of the input signal.

But Eq. (4) holds only for LTI systems, because complex exponentials are the eigenfunctions for linear, time invariant systems. Since robustness operators used in monitoring temporal logic monitors are nonlinear, they require separate treatment. A nonlinear extension is necessary which is provided by Volterra series.

2.4   Volterra Series Approximation of Non-Linear Operators

A *finite Volterra series operator* $\mathcal{N}$ is one of the form

$$(\mathcal{N}x)(t) := h_0 + \sum_{n=1}^{N} \int \cdots \int h_n(\tau_1, \ldots, \tau_n) \cdot x(t - \tau_1) \ldots x(t - \tau_n) d\tau_1 \ldots d\tau_n \quad (5)$$

where x is the input signal. A Volterra series generalizes the convolution description of linear time-invariant (LTI) systems to time-invariant (TI) but nonlinear systems. We will drop the parentheses to simply write $\mathcal{N}u$ for the output signal of $\mathcal{N}$. The n-dimensional functions $h_n : \mathbb{R}^n \to \mathbb{R}, n \geq 1$, are known as *Volterra kernels*, and their Fourier transforms $H_n : \mathbb{C}^n \to \mathbb{C}$ are know as Generalized Frequency Response Functions (GFRFs):

$$H_n(\boldsymbol{\Omega}) := \int_{\tau \in \mathbb{R}^n} \exp(-i\boldsymbol{\Omega}^T \boldsymbol{\tau}) h_n(\boldsymbol{\tau}) d\boldsymbol{\tau}$$

We will use Volterra series to approximate the robustness nonlinear operator because there exists a well-developed theory for studying their output spectra using the GFRFs. For instance, the Fourier of the output signal $y = \mathcal{N}x$ is $Y(\omega) = \sum_n Y_n(\omega)$ where [12]

$$Y_n(\omega) = \frac{1}{\sqrt{n}(2\pi)^{n-1}} \int_{\omega_1 + \ldots + \omega_n = \omega} H_n(\omega_1, \ldots, \omega_n) X(\omega_1) \ldots X(\omega_n) d\omega_1 \ldots d\omega_n \quad (6)$$

Equation 6 gives one way to determine which frequencies of signal x affect the output robustness signal. If a frequency ω^* is s.t. for almost all $\omega_1, \omega_2, \omega_3, \ldots$, all the following spectra are below some user-set threshold

$$H_1(\omega^*), H_2(\omega^*, \omega_2), H_2(\omega_1, \omega^*), H_3(\omega^*, \omega_2, \omega_3), H_3(\omega_1, \omega^*, \omega_3), H_3(\omega_1, \omega_2, \omega^*), \text{ etc.} \quad (7)$$

then $X(\omega^*)$ contributes very little to the formation of the monitoring output, and can be safely discarded.

Volterra series can approximate time-invariant (TI) operators with fading memory. Intuitively, an operator has fading memory if two input signals that are close in the near past, but not necessarily the distant past, yield present outputs that are close.

Definition 3 (Fading memory). *Operator $\mathcal{N}$ has fading memory on a subset K of $\mathcal{C}(\mathbb{R}, \mathbb{R})$ if there is an increasing function $w : (-\infty, 0] \to (0, 1]$, $\lim_{t \to -\infty} w(t) = 0$ s.t. for each $u \in K$ and $\epsilon > 0$ there is a constant $\delta > 0$ s.t.*

$$\forall v \in K, \ \sup_{t \leq 0} |u(t) - v(t)| w(t) < \delta \to |\mathcal{N}u(0) - \mathcal{N}v(0)| < \epsilon$$

Such a w is called a weight function *for $\mathcal{N}$.*

Theorem 2 (Volterra approximation [5]**).** *Let* $K_{M_1,M_2} := \{u \in \mathcal{C}(\mathbb{R},\mathbb{R}) \mid \|u\| \leq M_1, \|u(\cdot - \tau) - u\| \leq M_2\tau \ \forall \tau \geq 0\}$ *for some constants* M_1, M_2, *and let* $\epsilon > 0$. *Let* $\mathcal{R}$ *be any TI operator with fading memory on* K_{M_1,M_2}. *Then there is a finite Volterra series operator* $\mathcal{N}$ *such that for all* $u \in K_{M_1,M_2}$, $\|\mathcal{R}u - \mathcal{N}u\| < \epsilon$

In practice, how one obtains the Volterra approximation of a given non-linear operator depends on the operator. The probing method [12] can be used for systems given by ODEs or auto-regressive equations. However, it is not applicable in our case because it requires feeding complex exponentials to the operator, whereas our robustness operators can only be applied to real-valued signals. If the operator's behavior is given by a set of input-output pairs of signals, one can first fit a function to the data, then obtain the Volterra representation of that function - see [5,12].

2.5   Measurement Devices and the Spaces $\mathcal{D}(E)$ and $\mathcal{D}'_1$

A measurement device is modeled in classical Physics using the theory of distributions. Giving even a cursory overview of this theory is beyond the scope of this paper. We will provide the necessary mathematical definitions and refer the reader to [10] for a more comprehensive CS and Engineering-oriented introduction to this topic.

Let $\mathcal{D}(E)$ be the space of infinitely differentiable functions with compact support in E. A *measurement kernel* in this paper is a non-zero function $f : \mathbb{R} \to \mathbb{R}$ with L_1 norm at most 1, i.e., $\|f\|_1 := \int |f(t)|dt \leq 1$. Let $\mathcal{D}'_1$ be the space of all such functions. Note that $f \in \mathcal{D}'_1$ iff $-f \in \mathcal{D}'_1$ and that the shifted kernel $f(\cdot - t)$ is in $\mathcal{D}(E)$ for every t whenever $f \in \mathcal{D}(E)$. The measurement signal y is then obtained by taking the following inner product:

$$y(t) = \langle f(\cdot - t), x \rangle := \int_{-\infty}^{\infty} f(\tau - t)x(\tau)d\tau \quad \forall t \tag{8}$$

One can think of the measurement device as taking an f-weighted average of the values of x centered on t. Informally, the width of f dictates the resolution of the measurement: the narrower f, the higher the resolution. Different measurement devices use different filters $f \in \mathcal{D}'_1$. Note that Dirac's δ is not in $\mathcal{D}'_1$, but can be approximated arbitrarily well with narrow integrable functions.

3   Bounded-Bandwidth STL

The semantics of an atomic proposition, given in Definition 1, requires the ability to measure the instantaneous value $x(t)$. However, it is *physically impossible to do an instantaneous measurement* [10]: in (8), $y(t) = x(t)$ iff $f = \delta$, Dirac's delta. But δ is not realizable because it has infinite energy: $\int \delta^2(t)dt = \delta(0) = \infty$. In this paper, we must pay closer attention to how measurements are actually made in the physical world for two reasons:

- we are interested in analyzing runtime monitors when they are a part of a signal processing chain. If something is not physically possible, e.g., because it requires infinite energy, it makes little sense to model how other components in the chain will process its output.
- We are interested in analyzing the input-output relation of a temporal logic monitor in the frequency domain (its transfer function, as it were). Even if we kept using instantaneous measurements in the theory for convenience sake, we'd end up with the trivial result that all robustness monitors have infinite essential bandwidth [17] since $\mathcal{F}\{\delta\}(\omega) = 1$ $\forall \omega$. I.e., *all* frequency bands are relevant - clearly a useless analysis.

This motivates our introduction of a new logic, Bounded-Bandwidth STL (BB-STL, pronounced 'baby Steel'), that does away with punctual measurements while preserving the logical relations and the soundness of robust semantics.

BB-STL formulas are interpreted over signals in $\mathcal{D}(E)$, defined in Sect. 2.5. Let AP be a set of atomic propositions s.t. there exists a bijection between $\mathcal{D}'_1$ and AP. We write p_f for the atom corresponding to filter f.

Definition 4 (Bounded-Bandwidth STL). *The syntax of BB-STL is identical to that of* STL_{bdd}^{past}:

$$\phi := \top \mid p_f \mid \neg\phi \mid \phi_1 \wedge \phi_2 \mid \diamondsuit_I \phi \mid \boxminus_I \phi \mid \phi_1 \mathcal{S}_I \phi_2$$

where $p_f \in AP$ *and* $I \subset \mathbb{R}$ *is a compact interval. Its boolean semantics are identical to those of* STL_{bdd}^{past} *except for the atomic proposition case given here:*

$$(x, t) \models p_f \text{ iff } \langle f(\cdot - t), x \rangle \geq 0$$

Its robust semantics are identical to those of STL_{bdd}^{past} *except for the base case below.*

$$\rho_{p_f}(x)(t) = \langle f(\cdot - t), x \rangle$$

The robustness of any signal relative to any atomic proposition is finite: letting S_x be the compact support of signal x, it holds that $\langle f, x \rangle \leq \int_{S_x} |f| dt \cdot \int_{S_x} |x| dt$, which is finite since f is absolutely integrable and x is continuous and therefore bounded on any compact set. Thus $\rho_\phi(x) \leq \rho_\top(x)$ for any ϕ, as required for an intuitive interpretation of robustness.

The following theorem establishes that BB-STL can be monitored via its robust semantics.

Theorem 3 (Soundness of robust semantics). *For every signal* $x \in \mathcal{D}(E)$ *and BB-STL formula* ϕ, *if* $\rho_\phi(x)(t) < 0$ *then* x *violates* ϕ *at time* t, *and if* $\rho_\phi(x)(t) > 0$ *then* x *satisfies* ϕ *at* t. *Moreover, for every signal* y *s.t.* $d(x, y) < \rho_\phi(x)(t)$, $(y, t) \models \phi$ *if* $(x, t) \models \phi$ *and* $(y, t) \not\models \phi$ *if* $(x, t) \not\models \phi$.

Before proving the theorem, we make several remarks about the definition of BB-STL and the various restrictions we placed on the signal and kernel spaces. The measurement process $x \rightarrow \langle x, f(\cdot - t) \rangle$ can be written as a convolution

$(x * f^-)(t)$, where $f^-(t) = f(-t)$. So $\mathcal{F}\{f^-\}$ is the transfer function of the measurement process. By selecting an appropriate set of filters, we get rid of the problem of infinite bandwidth measurements. In particular, we make sure that δ is not in $\mathcal{D}'_1$.

STL and STL$^{\text{past}}_{\text{bdd}}$ use arbitrary functions μ_k in their atoms, which allows arbitrary processing of the signal. E.g. if some x is $1 - D$, and we want to express the requirement $x^2 - e^x \geq 0 \wedge x \geq 1$, we can do that by using $\mu_1(x) = x^2 - e^x$ and $\mu_2(x) = x - 1$. BB-STL does not have that expressiveness, but we are nevertheless able to compute arbitrary linear functionals of x and compare them. E.g. the requirement $\langle x, f \rangle \geq 2\langle x, g \rangle$ is captured as $\langle x, f - 2g \rangle \geq 0$. So the difference between STL and BB-STL, at the level of atomic propositions, is in the ability to generate auxiliary signals in a non-linear vs linear fashion.

The Volterra approximation of an operator requires the latter to be causal and have fading memory (causality is implied by the conditions of Theorem 2 [5]). Causality requires working with past time operations, and fading memory requires working with bounded temporal operators. This is why we derived BB-STL from STL$^{\text{past}}_{\text{bdd}}$ rather than STL.

To prove Theorem 3, we will first need to define a distance function $d :$ $\mathcal{D}(E) \times \mathcal{D}(E) \to \mathbb{R}$:

$$d(x, y) := \sup\{\langle x - y, f \rangle \mid f \in \mathcal{D}'_1\} \tag{9}$$

Lemma 1. *Function d is a metric on $\mathcal{D}(E)$.*

Proof. d is non-negative: indeed for all $x \in \mathcal{D}(E)$ and $g \in \mathcal{D}'_1$, $\sup_f \langle x, f \rangle \geq \max(\langle x, g \rangle, \langle x, -g \rangle) = |\langle x, g \rangle|$. Since $x - y \in \mathcal{D}(E)$ whenever $x, y \in \mathcal{D}(E)$, the conclusion follows.

d is symmetric: $d(x, y) = \sup_f \langle x - y, f \rangle = \sup_f \langle y - x, -f \rangle = \sup_{f \in -\mathcal{D}'_1} \langle y - x, f \rangle = \sup_{f \in \mathcal{D}'_1} \langle y - x, f \rangle = d(y, x)$.

d satisfies the triangle inequality: for any $x, y, z \in \mathcal{D}(E)$,

$$d(x, y) = \sup\{\langle x + z - z - y, f \rangle \mid f \in \mathcal{D}'_1\} \leq \sup_{\mathcal{D}'_1}\{\langle x - z, f \rangle\} + \sup_{\mathcal{D}'_1}\{\langle z - y, f \rangle\} = d(x, z) + d(z, y)$$

d separates points: that is, if $d(x, y) = 0$ then $x = y$. We will argue by contradiction. Define function ε by $\varepsilon(t) = x(t) - y(t)$. Assume $x \neq y$ so there exists a $t' \in E$ s.t. $\varepsilon(t') \neq 0$ and without loss of generality we may assume $\varepsilon(t') > 0$ (since $-\varepsilon \in \mathcal{D}(E)$) and that $t' = 0$. Since ε is continuous, there exists a neighborhood I of 0 over which $\varepsilon(t) > 0$. So pick $g \in \mathcal{D}'_1$ s.t. $g(t) > 0$ over I and 0 elsewhere. It then holds that $\langle g, \varepsilon \rangle > 0$, contradicting $d(x, y) = 0$. Therefore $\varepsilon = 0$ and $x = y$. ∎

Metric d takes the distance between signals to be the largest measurement that can be made of their difference; this is consistent with the view that *we have no access to a signal without a measurement device*. The only way to differentiate between signals is to measure a difference between them. (Eq. (2.6) in [3] gives a more widely applicable metric but d above is much more interpretable). We can now proceed with the proof of Theorem 3.

Proof. Let $\mathcal{L}_t(\phi)$ be the set of all x s.t. $(x,t) \models \phi$ and for a subset $S \subset \mathcal{D}(E)$ let $\mathbf{dist}(x,S) = \inf_{y \in S} d(x,y)$. By convention set $\mathbf{dist}(x,\emptyset) = \infty$. Following [9], and given that d is a metric, it suffices to show that the following inequality holds for the base cases $\phi = \top$ and $\phi = p_f$:

$$-\mathbf{dist}(x,\mathcal{L}_t(\phi)) \le \rho_\phi(x)(t) \le \mathbf{dist}(x,\mathcal{D}(E) \setminus \mathcal{L}_t(\phi))$$

The remaining cases then follow by structural induction on ϕ.

$\underline{\phi = \top}$ Then $x \in \mathcal{L}_t(\phi)$ for any x and so $\mathbf{dist}(x,\mathcal{L}_t(\phi)) = 0 \le \infty = \rho_\phi(x)(t) = \mathbf{dist}(x,\emptyset) = \mathbf{dist}(x,\mathcal{D}(E) \setminus \mathcal{L}_t(\phi))$.

$\underline{\phi = p_f}$. Suppose $x \in \mathcal{L}_t(\phi)$. For all $y \in \mathcal{D}(E) \setminus \mathcal{L}_t(\phi)$

$$
\begin{aligned}
d(x,y) &\ge \langle x - y, f(\cdot - t) \rangle \text{ since } f(\cdot - t) \in \mathcal{D}'_1 \\
&= \langle x, f(\cdot - t) \rangle - \langle y, f(\cdot - t) \rangle \\
&\ge \langle x, f(\cdot - t) \rangle \text{ since } \langle y, f(\cdot - t) \rangle < 0 \\
&= \rho_{p_f}(x)(t)
\end{aligned}
$$

Thus, $\mathbf{dist}(x,\mathcal{L}_t(\phi)) = 0 \le \rho_\phi(x)(t) \le \mathbf{dist}(x,\mathcal{D}(E) \setminus \mathcal{L}_t(\phi))$.

Now suppose $x \notin \mathcal{L}_t(\phi)$. As before $\inf_{y \in \mathcal{L}_t(\phi)} d(x,y) \ge \inf_{y \in \mathcal{L}_t(\phi)} \langle y, f(\cdot - t) \rangle - \langle x, f(\cdot - t) \rangle$ so $\mathbf{dist}(x,\mathcal{L}_t(\phi)) \ge -\langle x, f(\cdot - t) \rangle$. Thus, $-\mathbf{dist}(x,\mathcal{L}_t(\phi)) \le \langle x, f(\cdot - t) \rangle = \rho_{p_f}(x)(t) < 0 = \mathbf{dist}(x,\mathcal{D}(E) \setminus \mathcal{L}_t(\phi))$.   ∎

4   Volterra Approximations and Frequency Response of BB-STLFormulas

Having defined the logic BB-STL, we are now in a position to answer the question: what is the frequency content of temporal logic? The strategy will be to show that the robustness of each logical operation $(p_f, \neg, \vee, \diamondsuit_I, \boxminus_I, \mathcal{S}_I)$ can be approximated by a Volterra series, and derive its GFRF. Then using a composition theorem, we can derive the GFRF of entire formulas to deduce which frequencies are given significant weight by the GFRF, and which aren't.

We note at the outset that the robustness operator for $\top$, $\rho_\top$, maps any signal to the improper constant function $t \mapsto +\infty$. Because this function is not in $\mathcal{C}(\mathbb{R},\mathbb{R})$, $\rho_\top$ is not approximable by a finite Volterra series on the basis of Theorem 2. This is not a serious impediment, since it is highly unlikely that an engineer would explicitly include $\top$ in a specification (e.g. $\phi = p \vee \top$), so there is no need to approximate $\rho_\top$ to begin with. As for formulas that accidentally turn out to be tautologies, like $p \vee \neg p$, their STL robustness is not infinite, and neither is their BB-STL robustness.

4.1   Approximability by Volterra Series

We state and prove the main technical result of this paper.

Theorem 4. *For any BB-STL formula ϕ that does not explicitly include $\top$, the robustness operator $\rho_\phi : \mathcal{D}(E) \to \overline{\mathbb{R}}^{\mathbb{R}}$ can be approximated by a finite Volterra series.*

Recall the set K_{M_1,M_2} from Theorem 2, and recall that for a function f, $\|f\|$ is its essential supremum. We will first show that ρ_ϕ is TI and has fading memory. However, the domain of ρ_ϕ is not a set of the form K_{M_1,M_2} so we can't apply Theorem 2 directly. So we show how to roughly decompose $\mathcal{D}(E)$ into sets of the form K_{M_1,M_2} and leverage Theorem 2 to conclude. In all that follows, it is understood that ϕ does not explicitly include $\top$.

Lemma 2. *The operator ρ_ϕ is TI and has fading memory.*

Proof. Time invariance is immediate. To prove fading memory we argue by induction on the structure of ϕ.

Base Cases. Fix an arbitrary p_f. We must exhibit a weight function s.t. for all $\varepsilon > 0$ and $u, v \in \mathcal{D}(E)$, $\sup_{t' \leq 0} |u(t) - v(t)| w(t) < \delta \implies |N_f u(0) - N_f v(0)| = |\int f(\tau)(u(\tau) - v(\tau)) d\tau| < \varepsilon$. Fix $\varepsilon > 0$, and let w be a continuous increasing function from $(-\infty, 0]$ to $(0, 1]$. For every $u, v \in \mathcal{D}(E)$, $g := u - v$ is in $\mathcal{D}(E)$; let C be its compact support. If $\sup_{t' \leq 0} |g(t')| w(t') < \delta$ then

$$\left| \int f(t)g(t)dt \right| = \left| \int_C f(t)g(t)dt \right| \leq \int_{C \cap (-\infty, 0]} |f(t)||g(t)|dt < \delta \int_{C \cap (-\infty, 0]} |f(t)|/w(t)dt$$

The integral is finite and non-zero so choosing $\delta = \varepsilon / (\int |f(t)|/w(t)dt)$ yields the desired result.

Inductive Cases. The case of $\neg \phi$ is immediate.

- For $\phi_1 \vee \phi_2$: by the induction hypothesis there exist weight function w_k for ρ_{ϕ_k}, $k = 1, 2$ s.t. for all $\varepsilon > 0$, $\sup_{t \leq 0} |u(t) - v(t)| w_k(t) < \delta \implies |\rho_{\phi_k}(u)(0) - \rho_{\phi_k}(u)(0)| < \varepsilon$. Then $w = \max\{w_1, w_2\}$ is easily shown to be a weight function for $\rho_{\phi_1 \vee \phi_2}$.
- For $\diamondsuit_I \phi$: By the induction hypothesis, there exists a weight function w s.t. for all $\varepsilon > 0$ and $u, v \in \mathcal{D}(E)$ there exists $\delta > 0$ s.t.

$$\sup_{t \leq 0} |u(t) - v(t)| w(t) < \delta \implies |\rho_\phi(u)(0) - \rho_\phi(v)(0)| < \varepsilon/2 \qquad (10)$$

Fact. If $\sup_{t \leq 0} |u(t) - v(t)| w(t) < \delta$ then $\sup_{\tau \leq 0} |\rho_\phi(u)(\tau) - \rho_\phi(v)(\tau)| \leq \varepsilon/2$.

Indeed, if $\sup_{t \leq 0} |u(t) - v(t)| w(t) < \delta$ then it holds that for all $\tau \geq 0$, $\sup_{t \leq -\tau} |u(t) - v(t)| w(t) < \delta$, which is equivalent (by a change of variables) to $\sup_{t \leq 0} |u(t - \tau) - v(t - \tau)| w(t - \tau) < \delta$. But $w(\cdot - \tau) \leq w$ so

$$\sup_{t \leq 0} |u(t - \tau) - v(t - \tau)| w(t - \tau) < \delta \implies \sup_{t \leq 0} |u(t - \tau) - v(t - \tau)| w(t) < \delta$$

Since $u(\cdot - \tau), v(\cdot - \tau)$ are in $\mathcal{D}(E)$ it follows that $|\rho_\phi(u)(-\tau) - \rho_\phi(v)(-\tau)| < \varepsilon/2$ for all $\tau \geq 0$, and therefore $\sup_{\tau \leq 0} |\rho_\phi(u)(\tau) - \rho_\phi(v)(\tau)| \leq \varepsilon/2$.

Now we claim that w is a weight function for $\rho_{\lozenge_I \phi}$. Indeed $|\rho_{\lozenge_I \phi}(u)(0) - \rho_{\lozenge_I \phi}(v)(0)| = |\max_{t \in -I} \rho_\phi(u)(t) - \max_{t \in -I} \rho_\phi(v)(t)|$. Let $t_u = \mathrm{argmax}_{-I} \rho_\phi(u)(t)$ and $t_v = \mathrm{argmax}_{-I} \rho_\phi(v)(t)$; both exist since I is compact and ρ_ϕ is continuous. Assume the left-hand side of Eq. (10) holds. Then we finally find the string of inequalities

$$-\varepsilon < \varepsilon/2 \leq \rho_\phi(u)(t_v) - \rho_\phi(v)(t_v) \leq \max_{t \in -I} \rho_\phi(u)(t) - \max_{t \in -I} \rho_\phi(v)(t) \leq \rho_\phi(u)(t_u) - \rho_\phi(v)(t_u) \leq \varepsilon/2 < \varepsilon$$

Therefore $|\rho_\phi(u)(0) - \rho_\phi(v)(0)| < \varepsilon$ as desired.

- The case of $\boxminus_I \phi$ is similar.
- For $\psi = \phi_1 \mathcal{S}_I \phi_2$: suppose there exist weight functions w_u and w_v for u and v respectively. Write $\rho_k = \rho_{\phi_k}$, $k = 1, 2$. Set $w = \max\{w_u, w_v\}$: this will be the weight function for ρ_ψ. Given $\varepsilon > 0$, there exists a $\delta > 0$ s.t. $\sup_{t \leq 0} |u(t) - v(t)| w(t) < \delta \implies |\rho_k u(0) - \rho_k v(0)| < \varepsilon$. By the above Fact, it also follows that

$$|\rho_k u(t') - \rho_k v(t')| < \varepsilon \ \forall t' \leq 0, k = 1, 2 \tag{11}$$

We will show that $|\rho_\psi u(0) - \rho_\psi v(0)| < \varepsilon$, where $\rho_\psi u(0) = \max_{t' \in -I} \{\min \{\rho_2 u(t'), \min_{t'' \in (t', 0]} \rho_1 u(t'')\}\}$. Given $t' \leq 0$, define $t_u := \mathrm{argmin}_{(t', 0]} \rho_1 u(t'')$, $t_v := \mathrm{argmin}_{(t', 0]} \rho_1 v(t'')$. The following inequalities are immediate:

$$\rho_1 v(t_v) - \varepsilon \leq \rho_1 v(t_u) - \varepsilon < \rho_1 u(t_u) \leq \rho_1 u(t_v) < \rho_1 v(t_v) + \varepsilon$$

Therefore

$$|\rho_1 u(t_u) - \rho_1 v(t_v)| < \varepsilon \tag{12}$$

From Eqs. (12) and (11) it follows that

$$\forall t' \in -I, \ |\underbrace{\min\{\rho_2 u(t'), \min_{t'' \in (t', 0]} \rho_1 u(t'')\}}_{a(t')} - \underbrace{\min\{\rho_2 v(t'), \min_{t'' \in (t', 0]} \rho_1 v(t'')\}}_{b(t')}| < \varepsilon$$

With $t_a := \mathrm{argmax}_{t' \in -I} a(t')$, $t_b := \mathrm{argmax}_{t' \in -I} b(t')$

$$b(t_b) - \varepsilon \leq b(t_a) - \varepsilon < a(t_a) \leq a(t_b) < b(t_b) + \varepsilon$$

and we get the desired conclusion: $|a(t_a) - b(t_b)| = |\rho_\psi u(0) - \rho_\psi v(0)| < \varepsilon$. ∎

We continue with the main proof. A signal x in $\mathcal{D}(E)$ is infinitely differentiable and compactly supported, so there exist M_1 and M_2 s.t. $x \in K_{M_1, M_2}$. Moreover for every $M_1' \geq M_1$ and $M_2' \geq M_2$, $K_{M_1, M_2} \subseteq K_{M_1', M_2'}$. Thus if we take any ascending sequence $(M_{1,a}, M_{2,a})_{a \in \mathbb{N}}$ with first element $(0, 0)$ and which is unbounded in both dimensions, we have that $\mathcal{D}(E) \subset \cup_{a \in \mathbb{N}} K_{M_{1,a}, M_{2,a}}$. (The lexicographic order is used: $(M_{1,a}, M_{2,a}) \leq (M_{1,a}, M_{2,a})$ iff $M_{1,a} \leq M_{1,a'}$ and $M_{2,a} \leq M_{2,a'}$). For conciseness write $K_a := K_{M_{1,a}, M_{2,a}}$.

Lemma 3. *The restriction of ρ_ϕ to any K_a is an operator over K_a, i.e. ρ_ϕ : $K_a \to K_a$.*

Proof. Take $x \in K_a$, we show that $y = \rho_\phi(x) \in K_a$. For any kernel f and $t \in \mathbb{R}$, Hölder's inequality gives $\langle f(\cdot - t), x \rangle \le \int |f(\tau)| d\tau \cdot \|x\| \le M_{1,a}$, so $\|\rho_{p_f}(x)\| \le M_{1,a}$. Since the robustness of any formula other than $\top$ is obtained by taking max and min of atomic robustness values, $\|\rho_\phi(x)\| \le M_{1,a}$. Moreover for all $t, s \in E$

$$|y(t) - y(s)| = \left| \int f(\tau)[x(\tau + t) - x(\tau + s)] d\tau \right| \le \|f\|_1 \cdot \|x(\cdot + t) - x(\cdot + s)\| \le M_{2,a}|t - s|$$

This shows that $y \in K_a$.   ∎

Lemma 4. *Consider an operator $\mathcal{N} : \mathcal{D}(E) \to \mathbb{R}^{\overline{\mathbb{R}}}$ such that its restriction $\mathcal{N}_a$ to K_a is an operator over K_a. If $\mathcal{N}$ is TI and with fading memory, then it has a finite Volterra series approximation $\widehat{\mathcal{N}}$ over $\mathcal{D}(E)$.*

Proof. It is immediate that if $\mathcal{N}$ is TI and with fading memory, then so is every $\mathcal{N}_a$. Thus, fixing $\varepsilon > 0$, $\mathcal{N}_a$ has a finite Volterra series approximation over K_a by Theorem 2, call it $\widehat{\mathcal{N}}_a$, so that for all $x \in K_a$, $\|\widehat{\mathcal{N}}_a x - \mathcal{N}_a x\| < \varepsilon$.

For every signal $x \in \mathcal{D}(E)$, let x' be its time derivative. Then $x \in K_{\|x\|, \|x'\|}$, and for all $M_1' < M_1$ and $M_2' < M_2$, $x \notin K_{M_1', M_2'}$. (The first part of the last statement is immediate; for the second part, note first that there exists t^* in the support of x s.t. $M_2 = |x'(t^*)|$, so pick b, c s.t. $b \le t^* \le c$ and $x(c) = x(b) + x'(t^*)(c - b)$, or $|x(c) - x(b)| = |x'(t^*)|(c - b) > M_2'(c - b)$). So there exists a unique smallest pair $(M_{1,a}, M_{2,a})$ s.t. $x \in K_a$, namely the smallest pair s.t. $M_{1,a} \ge \|x\|$ and $M_{2,a} \ge \|x'\|$. For a given x let $a(x)$ be the index in $\mathbb{N}$ corresponding to this smallest pair.

Define the operator $\widehat{\mathcal{N}} : \mathcal{D}(E) \to \mathbb{R}^{\overline{\mathbb{R}}}$ by $\widehat{\mathcal{N}}x := \widehat{\mathcal{N}}_{a(x)}x$. Then for all $x \in \mathcal{D}(E)$, $\|\widehat{\mathcal{N}}x - \mathcal{N}x\| = \|\widehat{\mathcal{N}}_{a(x)}x - \mathcal{N}_{a(x)}x\| < \varepsilon$, which establishes that $\widehat{\mathcal{N}}$ is a finite Volterra approximation of $\mathcal{N}$ over $\mathcal{D}(E)$.   ∎

Combining the three lemmas allows us to conclude the main proof. Even though it is only strictly correct to speak of the Volterra kernels of the Volterra series that approximates the robustness operator ρ_ϕ, we will often abuse language and speak directly of the 'Volterra kernels of ϕ'.

4.2   Calculating the Volterra Approximations and Their GFRFs

We seek the Volterra series that approximates ρ_ϕ for a given formula in the sense of Theorem 2. Operator ρ_ϕ is built by composing a few basic operators. The strategy will be to first approximate each basic operator by a Volterra series, then use a composition theorem to compose these into a Volterra series for the entire formula. We exclude the Since operation from the remainder of this discussion because, even though its robustness is approximable by Theorem 4, we don't currently have the tools to compute that approximation. We expand on the technical difficulty of performing that approximation in Sect. 4.3.

Basic Operators. Fix an interval $[a, b] \subset \mathbb{R}_+$, $\varepsilon > 0$ and $f \in \mathcal{D}'_1$, let u, v denote arbitrary signals in $\mathcal{D}(E)$. The basic operators are:

$$\mathcal{N}_f u(t) = \langle f(\cdot - t), u \rangle \qquad \mathcal{N}_- u(t) = -u(t) \qquad \sqcap_{[a,b]} u(t) = \min_{t-b \le t' \le t-a} u(t')$$

$$\sqcup(v, u)(t) = \max\{v(t), u(t)\} \qquad \sqcup_{[a,b]} u(t) = \max_{t-b \le t' \le t-a} u(t') \tag{13}$$

The following relations hold:

$$\rho_{p_f} = \mathcal{N}_f \qquad \rho_{\neg \phi} = \mathcal{N}_- \circ \rho_\phi \qquad \rho_{\boxminus_{[a,b]} \phi} = \sqcap_{[a,b]} \circ \rho_\phi$$

$$\rho_{\phi_1 \wedge \phi_2} = \sqcap(\rho_{\phi_1}, \rho_{\phi_2}) \qquad \rho_{\diamondsuit_{[a,b]} \phi} = \sqcup_{[a,b]} \circ \rho_\phi$$

We approximate each basic operator, on a representative set of signals, using a structure made of delays followed by a read-out polynomial; this structure can then be represented exactly with Volterra series. It is shown in [5] that this structure (delays followed by polynomial) can approximate any discrete-time operator and is a special case of a structure for approximating any continuous-time operator on $\mathcal{C}(\mathbb{R}, \mathbb{R})$.

There are many ways to derive Volterra approximations. Here we give a practical and simple way of computing such an approximation numerically. The first two operators can be represented exactly as Volterra series.

- $\mathcal{N}_f u(t) = \langle f(\cdot - t), u \rangle$. Then $h_0 = 0$, $h_1(t) = f(-t)$, $h_n \equiv 0$ when $n > 1$.
- $\mathcal{N}_- u(t) = -u(t)$. Then $h_0 = 0$, $h_1(t) = -\delta(t)$, $h_n \equiv 0$ when $n > 1$. Note that $\mathcal{N}_-$ is never applied directly to a source signal (i.e. monitored signal x) but only to robustness signals. Robustness signals are produced by previous monitors and their values are stored (perhaps symbolically) in computer memory, so it is possible to access their instantaneous values. So this does not contradict our earlier point about the inability to instantaneously sample an analog *source signal*.
- $\sqcup_{[a,b]} u$. We approximate this operator by a polynomial $P(u(t - t_1), \dots, u(t - t_D))$ for a given choice of polynomial degree d and delays t_j, $a \le t_j \le b$. P is of the form $\sum_r \alpha_r u(t - t_1)^{r_1} \dots u(t - t_D)^{r_D}$ where the sum is over all integer vectors $r = (r_1, \dots, r_D)$ s.t. $0 \le r_j \le d, \sum_j r_j \le d$, and the α_r's are the unknown polynomial coefficients. Then given a set of L signals u_ℓ and the corresponding output signals $\sqcup_{[a,b]} u_\ell$, and given a set $\mathbb{T}$ of sampling times, we setup the linear system in the α_r's:

$$\sum_r \alpha_r u_\ell(t - t_1)^{r_1} \dots u_\ell(t - t_D)^{r_D} = \sqcup_{[a,b]} u_\ell(t), 1 \le \ell \le L, t \in \mathbb{T} \tag{14}$$

A least-squares solution yields the α's. We force $\alpha_0 = 0$ since the $\sqcup$ operator has 0 response to 0 input. Therefore $h_0 = 0$. Given this approximation we seek the kernels h_n s.t.

$$P(u(t - t_1), \dots, u(t - t_D)) = \sum_r \alpha_r u(t - t_1)^{r_1} \dots u(t - t_D)^{r_D} = \sum_{n=1}^{N} \int_{\tau \in \mathbb{R}^n} h_n(\tau) \prod_{j=1}^{n} u(t - t_j) d\tau$$

Define $\Delta_d^D(n) = \{r = (r_1, \ldots, r_D) \in \mathbb{N}^D \mid 0 \le r_j \le d, \sum_j r_j = n\}$ and let $\Delta_d^D = \cup_{0 \le n \le d} \Delta_d^N(n)$. For a given $r \in \Delta_d^D(n)$,

$$u(t - t_1)^{r_1} \ldots u(t - t_D)^{r_D}$$

$$= \int \underbrace{\delta(\tau_1 - t_1) \ldots \delta(\tau_{r_1} - t_1)}_{r_1 \text{ terms}} \underbrace{\delta(\tau_{r_1+1} - t_2) \ldots \delta(\tau_{r_1+r_2} - t_2)}_{r_2 \text{ terms}}$$

$$\ldots \underbrace{\delta(\tau_{n-r_D+1} - t_D) \ldots \delta(\tau_n - t_D)}_{r_D \text{ terms}} \prod_{j=1}^{n} u(t - \tau_j) d\tau$$

Therefore define $h_n^r(\tau_1, \ldots, \tau_n) := \alpha_r \prod_{j=1}^{r_1} \delta(\tau_j - t_1) \ldots \prod_{j=n-r_D+1}^{n} \delta(\tau_j - t_D)$. We can now express

$$P(u(t - t_1), \ldots, u(t - t_D)) = \sum_{r \in \Delta_d^D} \alpha_r u(t - t_1)^{r_1} \ldots u(t - t_D)^{r_D}$$

$$= \sum_{n=1}^{d} \sum_{r \in \Delta_d^D(n)} \int_{\tau \in \mathbb{R}^n} h_n^r(\tau) \prod_{j=1}^{n} u(t - \tau_j) d\tau$$

$$= \sum_{n=1}^{d} \int \left[\sum_{r \in \Delta_d^D(n)} h_n^r(\tau) \right] \prod_{j=1}^{n} u(t - \tau_j) d\tau$$

$$:= \sum_{n=1}^{d} \int h_n(\tau) \prod_{j=1}^{n} u(t - \tau_j) d\tau$$

Therefore $H_0 = 0$ and the nth-order GFRF is

$$H_n(\Omega) = \sum_{r \in \Delta_d^D(n)} \mathcal{F}\{h_n^r\}(\Omega) = \sum_r \alpha_r \exp(-i \cdot t_1 \sum_{j=1}^{r_1} \omega_j) \ldots \exp(-i \cdot t_D \sum_{j=n-r_D+1}^{n} \omega_j) \tag{15}$$

The same approach is used with $\sqcap_{[a,b]}$.

• $\sqcap(u, v)(t) = \min\{u(t), v(t)\}$. Here we must use a separable approximation of the form $\sqcap(u, v) \approx \mathcal{U}u + \mathcal{V}v$. This avoids product terms involving u and v which cause the loss of the nice GFRF representation of Volterra kernels [4]. The Volterra operators $\mathcal{U}$ and $\mathcal{V}$ are obtained, again, by polynomial fitting. Specifically, $\mathcal{U}u(t) = R(u(t))$ for a polynomial R and $\mathcal{V}v(t) = Q(v(t))$ for a polynomial Q. Both polynomials have a 0 constant term since zero inputs produce a zero output from $\sqcap$. Note also that only the present value of the signal, $u(t)$, is used, since it doesn't make sense to use past values $u(t - \tau)$ when approximating the instantaneous min operator. The coefficients of the polynomials are obtained by least-squares as before. Once the coefficients of R and Q are calculated, the following easily established proposition gives the kernels of the equivalent Volterra series.

Proposition 1. *The polynomial operator defined by $Nu(t) = \sum_{0 \leq k \leq d} \alpha_k u(t)^k$ has an exact Volterra representation given by $h_0 = \alpha_0$, $h_n(\tau_1, \ldots, \tau_n) = \alpha_n \delta(\tau_1) \ldots \delta(\tau_n)$, $n \geq 1$. The corresponding GFRFs are $H_0 = 2\pi\alpha_0\delta(\omega)$, $H_n(\boldsymbol{\Omega}) = \alpha_n \; \forall \boldsymbol{\Omega}$.*

This concludes the derivation of Volterra series for the basic operators. The following theorem allows us to calculate the GFRFs of entire formulas. Given $\boldsymbol{\Omega} \in \mathbb{R}^n$ and $\boldsymbol{m} \in \Delta_n^k(n)$, we can divide $\boldsymbol{\Omega}$ into k sub-vectors, $\boldsymbol{\Omega} = (\Theta_1, \Theta_2, \ldots, \Theta_k)$, s.t. sub-vector Θ_j has length m_j. Define the mixing matrix $S^{(k,n)}$ of dimensions k-by-n whose j^{th} row is $(\mathbf{0}_{1\times(m_1+\ldots+m_{j-1})}, \mathbf{1}_{1\times m_j}, \mathbf{0}_{1\times(m_{j+1}+\ldots+m_k)})$, so $S^{(k,n)}\boldsymbol{\Omega} = (\sum_{j=1}^{m_1} \omega_j, \sum_{j=m_1+1}^{m_1+m_2} \omega_j, \ldots, \sum_{j=n-m_k+1}^{n} \omega_j)^T$.

Theorem 5 ([6]). *Let $\mathcal{A}, \mathcal{B}$ be Volterra operators with GFRFs $\{A_n\}_{n=1}^{n_\mathcal{A}}$ and $\{B_n\}_{n=1}^{n_\mathcal{B}}$ respectively. Then the operator $\mathcal{H} := \mathcal{B} \circ \mathcal{A}$ has Volterra GFRFs given by*

$$H_0 = \sum_{k=0}^{n_\mathcal{B}} B_k(0) A_0^k$$

$$H_n(\boldsymbol{\Omega}) = \sum_{k=1}^{n_\mathcal{B}} \sum_{\boldsymbol{m} \in \Delta_n^k(n)} B_k(S^{(k,n)}\boldsymbol{\Omega}) \prod_{j=1}^{k} A_{m_j}(\Theta_j), \quad n \geq 1$$

Thus for instance, to get the GFRF of $\phi = \Diamond_{[0,0.5]} g$ for some atom g, we derive the GFRF $\{B_k\}$ of $\sqcup_{[0,0.5]}$ and $\{A_k\}$ of g, then compute the GFRF of $\mathcal{N}_\phi$ using Theorem 5.

4.3   Why Is Approximating $\phi_1 \, \mathcal{S}_I \, \phi_2$ Different?

For convenience, we write $\psi = \phi_1 \, \mathcal{S}_I \, \phi_2$. The robustness ρ_ψ is an operator on $\mathcal{C}(\mathbb{R}, \mathbb{R})$, and we have shown that it is approximable by a Volterra series. However it is constructed out of operators that change the dimensions of the signals, which adds difficulties to the actual computation of the approximation.

Specifically: fix an interval $[a, b] \subset \mathbb{R}_+$, $\varepsilon > 0$ and $f \in \mathcal{D}_1'$; let u denote an arbitrary signal in $\mathcal{D}(E)$ and let $y \in \mathcal{C}(\mathbb{R}^2, \mathbb{R})$, i.e. a continuous bounded function from $\mathbb{R}^2$ to $\mathbb{R}$. We define three operators: $\sqcup_{2\to1} : \mathcal{C}(\mathbb{R}^2, \mathbb{R}) \to \mathcal{C}(\mathbb{R}, \mathbb{R})$, $\sqcap_{1\to2} : \mathcal{C}(\mathbb{R}, \mathbb{R}) \to \mathcal{C}(\mathbb{R}, \mathbb{R}^2)$, and $\sqcap_{2\to2} : \mathcal{C}(\mathbb{R}^2, \mathbb{R}^2) \to \mathcal{C}(\mathbb{R}^2, \mathbb{R})$. They are:

$$\sqcup_{2\to1}y(t) = \max_{t-b \leq t' \leq t-a} y(t', t) \quad \sqcap_{1\to2}u(t', t) = \min_{t' < t'' \leq t} u(t'') \quad \sqcap_{2\to2}(u, y)(t', t) = \min\{u(t'), y(t', t)\}$$

The following relation holds:

$$\rho_{\phi_1 \, \mathcal{S}_{[a,b]} \, \phi_2} = \sqcup_{2\to1} \circ \sqcap_{2\to2}(\rho_{\phi_2}, \sqcap_{1\to2}\rho_{\phi_1})$$

The approximation of ρ_ψ by Volterra series therefore requires the approximation of the above basic operators, then composing them. Multi-dimensional Volterra series exist (i.e., Volterra operators over $\mathcal{C}(\mathbb{R}^n, \mathbb{R})$), e.g., see [18]. However what we have above are operators that change the dimensions of the signals.

Sandberg [15] provides a generalization of [5] which allows the approximation of certain operators that map $\mathcal{C}(\mathbb{R}^n, \mathbb{R}^m)$ to $\mathcal{C}(\mathbb{R}^m, \mathbb{R})$. However this still falls short of our needs because of the presence of $\sqcap_{1 \to 2}$.

A 'quick-and-dirty' way to produce a Volterra series representation of a *given* formula ψ with Since - that is, with given atoms and structure - is to approximate its input-output relation on a representative set of signals by fitting Volterra kernels. However this requires a new fit every time we change atoms or formula structure. It does not provide a generic approximation that can be composed with others, as we did in Sect. 4.

5   Experiments: Fourier Analysis of Temporal Logic

We implemented the above calculations in a toolbox which we'll make available with the paper. In this section we demonstrate the derivation of Generalized Frequency Response Functions for temporal logic robustness operators. In all experiments, the GFRFs were generated by solving appropriate versions of (14) with degree-4 polynomials and test signals generated as random combinations of sinusoids. Sinusoids are dense in $\mathcal{C}(\mathbb{R}, \mathbb{R})$ so approximating the operators on sinusoids is a sensible thing to do. The approximation error in all cases was in the order of 10^{-12}. That said, our objective here is not to provide the most efficient or the most general approximation scheme - that is for future work.

We reiterate that the Volterra approximations are *not* meant to replace the monitoring algorithms that exist. They are used as *analysis tools* that provide a rigorous quantitative Fourier analysis of temporal logic: one that does not depend on intuition, is automatic, and such that once the GFRFs of a formula are obtained, the formula (and its monitor) are treated as just another signal processing box.

In what follows, $g = G(\mu, s)$ means that g is a Gaussian measurement kernel with mean μ and standard deviation s.

5.1   GFRFs of BB-STL Formulas

- We first consider the spectra of $\Box_{[1,T_2]} \, p_g$ shown in Fig. 3a, with $g = G(0, 0.04)$. Increasing T_2 has a first-order effect (observed in H_1) of distributing the energy more uniformly over the range $[0, 2.5]$ Hz, and suppressing less the higher frequencies. $|H_2|$ on the other hand shows a more complex picture: while there's an increase of magnitude at higher values of f_1 or f_2 (top left and bottom right corners), the increase at higher f_1 *and* f_2 is less marked.
- Consider next the formula $\Diamond_{[0,T]} \, p$ for a fixed atom p, shown Fig. 3b. As T increases, H_1 becomes more low-pass, but H_2 becomes more high-pass! This emphasizes the need to study all orders of the response, not only the linear first-order response.
- We now study the effect of using non-instantaneous measurements. Figure 4a shows the spectra H_1 of $\Diamond_{[0,0.5]} \, p_g$ and $\Box_{[0,0.5]} \, p_g$ where $g = G(0, s)$ for three values of s. As s increases, the Gaussian atom acts more like a low-pass filter

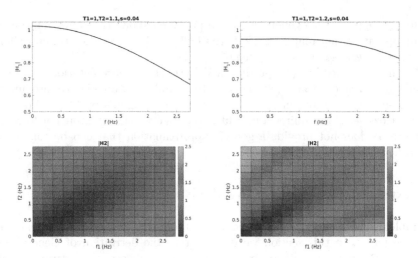

(a) $|H_1|$ and $|H_2|$ for Historically$_{[1,T_2]}p_g$ with $T_2 = 1.1$ (left) and $T_2 = 1.2$ (right). The atom $g = G(0, 0.04)$.

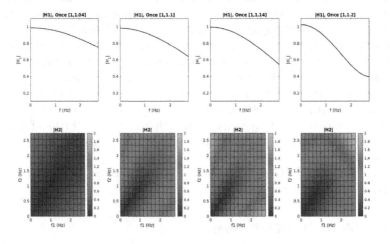

(b) $|H_1|$ and $|H_2|$ for Once$_{[1,T]}p_g$ for four values of $T \in \{1.04, 1.1, 1.14, 1.2\}$. The atom $g = G(0, 0.04)$.

Fig. 3. GFRFs with varying temporal intervals. Color in digital copy.

(the measurement is lower resolution) and the overall formula has a more low-pass nature. By the same token, high-frequency noise is ignored by the formula and does not affect the monitoring verdict. Similarly, the 2nd-order spectra for these two formulas are shown in Fig. 4b with increasing s.

In practice, the filter f used in atomic propositions is imposed by the application and is derived from first-principles modeling of the physics of the system. This Fourier analysis allows us to trace these effects quantitatively.

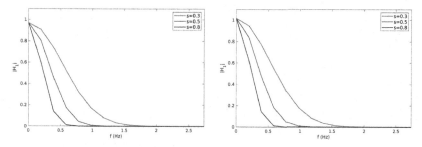

(a) $|H_1|$ of Once$_{[1,1.1]}p_g$ (left) and Historically$_{[0,0.5]}p_g$ with $g = G(0, s)$, $s = 0.3, 0.5, 0.8$.

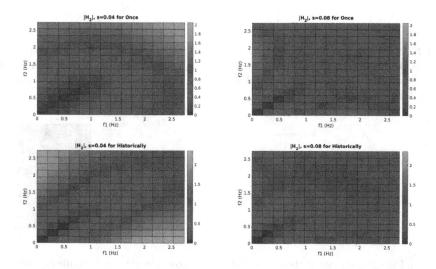

(b) $|H_2|$ of Once$_{[1,1.1]}p_g$ (left) and Historically$_{[1,1.1]}p_g$ (right) with $g = G(0, s)$, $s = 0.04, 0.08$.

Fig. 4. Effect of support size s for the atomic proposition filters. In (a), s is larger than temporal interval width, which is 0.1. In (b) s is much smaller. (Color in digital copy)

- Consider now the more complex formula ϕ_T, which says that a is true, preceded by b T units earlier, preceded by c T units earlier than that. Here a, b and c are atoms with Gaussian filters of various widths.

$$\phi_T = a \wedge (\diamondsuit_{[0,T]}(b \wedge \diamondsuit_{[0,T]} c)) \tag{16}$$

It is not possible to read, from the formula, how the frequency responses of the various sub-monitors (for the sub-formulas) interact or cancel each other out. By contrast, Fig. 5 shows the signal block diagram for computing this formula's Volterra series. This can be read as just another signal processing chain with non-linear filters. On top of each box, we display the GFRF H_1 of the entire

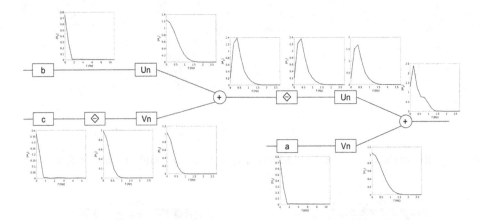

Fig. 5. Block diagram of the Volterra representation of φ_T given in 16. Every displayed $|H_1|$ is the first-order spectrum of the entire composite formula up to that point. Un and Vn are the GFRFs of the separable Volterra operators $\mathcal{U}, \mathcal{V}$ that approximate $\sqcup$ (Sect. 4.2.)

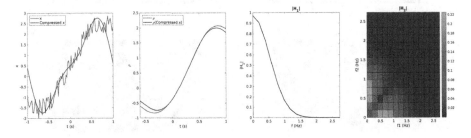

Fig. 6. Filtering signals without accounting for downstream logic monitors leads to incorrect monitoring results. The frequency responses (right two panels) indicate a safe cut-off frequency around 1.5 Hz. If an upstream low-pass filter applies a cut-off of 0.5 Hz (left panel), the robustness signal is significantly changed (second panel). In particular, the truth values differ between red (original) and blue (post-filtering). (Colors in digital copy)

chain up to and including that box. This shows how the relevant frequencies evolve with the addition of each monitoring component).

5.2   Compression's Effect on Monitoring

We now illustrate what happens if attention is not paid to the frequency representation of temporal logic formulas when designing compression or filtering algorithms. In Fig. 2, we The proposed method can be used as a signal processing tool for frequency domain analysis of temporal logic monitors but it is not supposed to replace the monitors themselves. Thus, it is more of an offline analysis tool that can be used to design filters which respect the monitorability requirements.

Had shown how knowledge of the GFRFs allows us to perform monitoring-safe compression: even though the post-compression signal is markedly different from the original x, the monitoring results for the two signals were almost identical.

By contrast, in Fig. 6, we show the same signal but now compressed (via low-pass filtering) without regard to the GFRF or the monitored formula. The resulting monitoring result (in blue) is significantly affected, and the truth value (determined by checking where ρ_ϕ is positive or negative) is modified.

6   Conclusions

We have presented a Fourier analysis of temporal logic using Volterra approximations of the robustness operators. Doing so has necessitated re-defining the semantics of atomic propositions using bounded-bandwidth filters, which led us to introduce the logic Bounded-Bandwidth STL. Using this analysis, it is possible to incorporate temporal logic monitors into signal processing chains as 'just another' signal processing box.

Future work will seek to relax the constraints on the signal space. In particular, we conjecture that it is possible to remove the compact-support requirement. We will also seek more general approximations of the basic operators and extend them to Since. Finally, the frequency representation in this paper presents a unifying formalism which we will leverage for optimal filter design that is monitoring-safe, i.e., that does not remove any signal content that is relevant to the output robustness signal.

Acknowledgments. The authors would like to thank the anonymous reviewers for helpful comments regarding the definition of kernel space.

References

1. Abbas, H., Mangharam, R.: Generalized robust MTL semantics for problems in cardiac electrophysiology. In: 2018 Annual American Control Conference (ACC), pp. 1592–1597 (2018)
2. Abbas, H., Pant, Y.V., Mangharam, R.: Temporal logic robustness for general signal classes. In: Proceedings of the 22nd ACM International Conference on Hybrid Systems: Computation and Control, HSCC 2019, pp. 45–56. Association for Computing Machinery, New York (2019). https://doi.org/10.1145/3302504.3311817
3. Blanchard, P., Brüning, E.: Mathematical Methods in Physics. Progress in Mathematical Physics. Birkhäser, Basel (2003)
4. Boaghe, O.M., Billings, S.A.: Subharmonic oscillation modeling and MISO Volterra series. IEEE Trans. Circ. Syst. I Fundam. Theory Appl. **50**(7), 877–884 (2003)
5. Boyd, S., Chua, L.: Fading memory and the problem of approximating nonlinear operators with Volterra series. IEEE Trans. Circ. Syst. **CAS-32**(11), 1150–1161 (1985)
6. Carassale, L., Kareem, A.: Modeling nonlinear systems by Volterra series. J. Eng. Mech. **136**(6), 801–818 (2010)

7. Donzé, A., Maler, O.: Robust satisfaction of temporal logic over real-valued signals. In: Chatterjee, K., Henzinger, T.A. (eds.) FORMATS 2010. LNCS, vol. 6246, pp. 92–106. Springer, Heidelberg (2010). https://doi.org/10.1007/978-3-642-15297-9_9

8. Donzé, A., Maler, O., Bartocci, E., Nickovic, D., Grosu, R., Smolka, S.: On temporal logic and signal processing. In: Chakraborty, S., Mukund, M. (eds.) ATVA 2012. LNCS, pp. 92–106. Springer, Heidelberg (2012). https://doi.org/10.1007/978-3-642-33386-6_9

9. Fainekos, G., Pappas, G.: Robustness of temporal logic specifications for continuous-time signals. Theor. Comput. Sci. **410**(42), 4262–4291 (2009)

10. Florack, L.: Image Structure. Kluwer Academics, Dordrecht (2013)

11. Jaksić, S., Bartocci, E., Grosu, R., Nicković, D.: An algebraic framework for runtime verification. IEEE Trans. Comput. Aided Des. Integr. Circ. Syst. **37**(11), 2233–2243 (2018)

12. Jing, X., Lang, Z.: Frequency Domain Analysis and Design of Nonlinear Systems Based on Volterra Series Expansion. Springer, Cham (2015). https://doi.org/10.1007/978-3-319-12391-2

13. Maler, O., Nickovic, D.: Monitoring temporal properties of continuous signals. In: Lakhnech, Y., Yovine, S. (eds.) FORMATS/FTRTFT -2004. LNCS, vol. 3253, pp. 152–166. Springer, Heidelberg (2004). https://doi.org/10.1007/978-3-540-30206-3_12

14. Rodionova, A., Bartocci, E., Nickovic, D., Grosu, R.: Temporal logic as filtering. In: Proceedings of the 19th International Conference on Hybrid Systems: Computation and Control, HSCC 2016, pp. 11–20. Association for Computing Machinery, New York (2016). https://doi.org/10.1145/2883817.2883839

15. Sandberg, I.W., Xu, L.: Uniform approximation of multidimensional myopic maps. IEEE Trans. Circ. Syst. I Fundam. Theory Appl. **44**(6), 477–500 (1997)

16. Silvetti, S., Nenzi, L., Bartocci, E., Bortolussi, L.: Signal convolution logic. In: Lahiri, S.K., Wang, C. (eds.) ATVA 2018. LNCS, vol. 11138, pp. 267–283. Springer, Cham (2018). https://doi.org/10.1007/978-3-030-01090-4_16

17. Slepian, D.: On bandwidth. Proc. IEEE **64**, 292–300 (1976)

18. Thurnhofer, S., Mitra, S.K.: A general framework for quadratic Volterra filters for edge enhancement. IEEE Trans. Image Process. **5**(6), 950–963 (1996). https://doi.org/10.1109/83.503911

A Verified Online Monitor for Metric Temporal Logic with Quantitative Semantics

Agnishom Chattopadhyay[✉] and Konstantinos Mamouras

Rice University, Houston, USA
{agnishom,mamouras}@rice.edu

Abstract. We investigate the formalization, using the Coq proof assistant, of a procedure for constructing online monitors from specifications written in past-time metric temporal logic (MTL). We employ an algebraic quantitative semantics that encompasses the Boolean and robustness semantics of MTL and we interpret formulas over a discrete temporal domain. The class of Moore machines, a kind of string transducers, is used as a formal model of online monitors. The main result is that there is a compositional construction from formulas to monitors, so that each monitor computes (in an online fashion) the semantic values of the corresponding formula over the input stream. From our Coq formalization, we extract OCaml code for executable online monitors. We have compared the performance of our monitoring framework with Reelay, a state-of-the-art tool for monitoring temporal properties.

Keywords: Online monitoring · Formal verification · Quantitative semantics

1 Introduction

Runtime verification is a lightweight technique for checking that a system exhibits the desired behavior. It is often performed in an *online* fashion, which means that the execution trace of the system is observed as it is being generated. This trace typically consists of one or more signals and event streams. A *monitor* program runs in parallel with the system, consumes the system trace incrementally, and outputs at every step a value that summarizes the current state of the system. This value can be a Boolean indication of whether an interesting event or pattern has been identified, or it can contain richer quantitative information. There is a substantial amount of existing work on formalisms for specifying monitors, as well as on algorithms for their efficient execution.

The specification of temporal patterns is often driven by logical formalisms. Linear Temporal Logic (LTL) is one such widely utilized formalism which admits efficient algorithms. Since many applications in the domain of cyber-physical systems frequently deal with comparison between numerical signals, Signal Temporal Logic (STL), an extension of LTL with predicates allowing comparison

© Springer Nature Switzerland AG 2020
J. Deshmukh and D. Ničković (Eds.): RV 2020, LNCS 12399, pp. 383–403, 2020.
https://doi.org/10.1007/978-3-030-60508-7_21

with numerical values, is also popular. It is also common to constrain certain temporal behaviors within specified time intervals, which is a capability referred to as a metric extension of temporal logic (MTL).

While temporal logic facilitates the specification of temporal properties, it is equally important to have accompanying algorithms. The notion of a monitor is an algorithm which analyzes given traces for a specific temporal property. In an offline setting, the trace is available in its entirety. In contrast, online monitors are meant to be attached to running systems, so that they may report interesting (or critical) events as they happen, potentially so that a supervisor can act in real time. Thus, they must analyze system traces incrementally (fragment by fragment) as they evolve and this must be done efficiently: each update should be handled quickly.

The standard semantics for temporal logic is qualitative, which means that monitors classify traces only in a binary pass/fail manner. However, this is less than sufficiently informative: some violations can be more serious than others, and on the other hand, some cases of satisfaction could be close to the edge of failure. In some cases, we may be able to apply some corrective actions if we could tell that our system is approaching a potential violation. Indeed, in realistic systems with continuous dynamics, some degree of tolerance must be allowed since every value is accurate only up to the extent of measurement errors. This encourages us to consider quantitative semantics for our formalisms, so that we can quantify how robustly the observed behavior fits the desired specification [18].

The variant of metric temporal logic we consider in this paper is interpreted over a discrete temporal domain. We also consider a past-time only fragment of the logic. In the setting of online monitoring we need to reactively respond to the patterns in what we have seen so far. So, using a past-time fragment makes sense and provides a clean semantics. Online monitoring with future obligations has been considered, but these can be more expensive.

With Coq, an interactive theorem prover, we formalize the semantics of our temporal logic. The implementation of our monitoring algorithms are done within Coq, and a proof of correctness is given. Formal proofs, like the ones described in Coq, are thoroughly rigorous and machine checkable. This gives us confidence in the correctness of our implementations. With the extraction mechanism of Coq, we can obtain executable OCaml code directly from our verified implementation.

As mentioned earlier, a strong motivation for using a quantitative semantics is to quantify how robustly a signal fits a given specification in view of potential perturbations. A very effective way to do so for STL specifications is to interpret formulas over real numbers and interpret the logical connectives $\vee$ and $\wedge$ as max and min respectively [16]. In our work, we use a slightly more general framework, interpreting our formulas over arbitrary bounded distributive lattices. This abstract algebraic framework enables a simpler verification approach and, as we will discuss soon, does not hurt the performance of our algorithms.

In our formalization, we model online monitors as Moore machines. They are abstract machines whose state evolves as fragments of a trace are fed in. Each state of the machine is associated with a value that represents the current output of the monitor. We follow a compositional approach for our implementation and proofs. This is done with the help of combinators, which are constructs that compose Moore machines in different ways (possibly with other data structures) so that their behaviors can be composed or combined. Corresponding to each Boolean or temporal connective in our specification language, we identify a combinator on Moore machines which implements the desired behavior.

We observe that formulas in our temporal logic can be rewritten so that only a few combinators are necessary: (1) combinators which combine the output of Moore machines running in parallel by applying a binary operation on their respective outputs, (2) combinators which compute a running aggregate on the results of a Moore machine, (3) combinators which compute running aggregates on sliding windows, and (4) combinators which withhold the results of a machine until a given number of updates. We can see that most of these can be approached in a straightforward way. Applying a binary operation to the current output values of two running machines can be done with a stateless construction. Computing running aggregates efficiently can be achieved by storing the aggregate of the trace seen so far. In order to withhold the results of a given machine, we can simply store them in a queue of a fixed length. Computing aggregates over sliding windows is slightly trickier. This is usually achieved with an algorithm that maintains monotonic wedges [23]. However, this assumes that the semantic values are totally ordered, which is not necessarily true in our setting of lattices. Instead, we use an algorithm that is inspired from the well-known implementation of a queue data structure using two stacks, popular in functional programming. A variant of this algorithm can be used for computing sliding-window aggregates for any associative operation in a way that every execution step of the monitor needs $O(1)$ amortized time.

Outline of the Paper. In Sect. 2, we first introduce lattices and then present the syntax and semantics of our temporal specification language. In Sect. 3, we give a formal definition of Moore machines, present a collection of Moore combinators, and discuss in detail their implementation. In Sect. 4, we discuss the extraction of executable OCaml code from the Coq scripts and we compare its performance against the Reelay tool [32]. Finally, in Sect. 5, we discuss several different quantitative semantics for Signal Temporal Logic, various algorithmic approaches to online monitoring, and we also give a brief overview of related efforts to produce formally verified monitors.

2   Metric Temporal Logic

In this section, we review Metric Temporal Logic, which will be the formalism that we consider here for specifying quantitative properties. We use bounded distributive lattices as the semantic domain for our logic. While this abstract setting is not usually where Metric Temporal Logic is interpreted, we will see that the standard qualitative (Boolean) and quantitative (robustness) semantics can be obtained simply by choosing the appropriate lattice.

2.1 Lattices

A lattice is a partial order in which every two elements have a least upper bound and a greatest lower bound. We will use an equivalent algebraic definition.

Definition 1. A *lattice* is a set A together with associative and commutative binary operations $\sqcap$ and $\sqcup$, called *meet* and *join* respectively, that satisfy the *absorption laws*, i.e, $x \sqcup (x \sqcap y) = x$ and $x \sqcap (x \sqcup y) = x$ for all $x, y \in A$.

Let A be a lattice. Using the absorption laws it can be shown that $\sqcup$ is idempotent: $x \sqcup x = x \sqcup (x \sqcap (x \sqcup x)) = x$ for every $x \in A$. Similarly, it can also be shown that $\sqcap$ is idempotent. Define the relation $\sqsubseteq$ as follows: $x \sqsubseteq y$ iff $x \sqcup y = y$ for all $x, y \in A$. The relation $\sqsubseteq$ is a partial order. It also holds that $x \sqsubseteq y$ iff $x \sqcap y = x$. For all $x, y \in A$, the element $x \sqcup y$ is the supremum (least upper bound) of $\{x, y\}$ and the element $x \sqcap y$ is the infimum (greatest lower bound) of $\{x, y\}$ w.r.t. the order $\sqsubseteq$.

Definition 2. A lattice A is said to be *bounded* if there exists a *top* element $\top \in$ and a *bottom* element $\bot \in A$ such that $\bot \sqcup x = x$ and $x \sqcap \top = x$ (equivalently, $\bot \sqsubseteq x \sqsubseteq \top$) for every $x \in A$.

Let A be a bounded lattice. It is easy to check that $x \sqcup \top = \top$ and $\bot \sqcap x = \bot$ for every $x \in A$. For a finite subset $X = \{x_1, x_2, \ldots x_n\}$ of a bounded lattice, we write $\bigsqcup X$ for $x_1 \sqcup x_2 \sqcup \cdots \sqcup x_n$ and similarly $\bigsqcap X$ for $x_1 \sqcap x_2 \sqcap \cdots \sqcap x_n$. Moreover, we define $\bigsqcup \emptyset$ to be $\bot$ and $\bigsqcap \emptyset$ to be $\top$. So, $\bigsqcup X$ is the supremum of X and $\bigsqcap X$ is the infimum of X.

Definition 3. A lattice A is said to be *distributive* if $x \sqcap (y \sqcup z) = (x \sqcap y) \sqcup (x \sqcap z)$ and $x \sqcup (y \sqcap z) = (x \sqcup y) \sqcap (x \sqcup z)$ for all $x, y, z \in A$.

Example 4. Consider the two-element set $\mathbb{B} = \{\top, \bot\}$ of Boolean values, where $\top$ represents truth and $\bot$ represents falsity. The set $\mathbb{B}$, together with conjunction as meet and disjunction as join, is a bounded and distributive lattice.

Example 5. The set $\mathbb{R}$ of real numbers, together with min as meet and max as join, is a distributive lattice. However, $(\mathbb{R}, \min, \max)$ is not a bounded lattice. It is commonplace to adjoin the elements ∞ and $-\infty$ to $\mathbb{R}$ so that they serve as the top and bottom element respectively.

2.2 Syntax and Semantics

We fix a set $\mathbb{D}$ of *data items*. A *trace* is a finite sequence over $\mathbb{D}$, and $\mathbb{D}^*$ is the set of all traces. We write ε for the empty trace, and $|w|$ for the length of a trace $w \in \mathbb{D}^*$. For $i \in \mathbb{N}$ and $w \in D^*$ with $i \leq |w|$, we write $w[-i]$ to denote the prefix of w obtained by removing the last i elements of w. In particular, it holds that $w[-0] = w$ and $w[-i] = \varepsilon$ when $i = |w|$. We also fix a bounded distributive lattice $\mathbb{V}$, whose elements are *quantitative truth values* that represent degrees of truth or falsity. Our quantitative semantics will associate a truth value with each formula-trace pair. The set Φ of temporal formulas that we consider are given by the following grammar:

$$\varphi, \psi ::= f : \mathbb{D} \to \mathbb{V} \mid \varphi \vee \psi \mid \varphi \wedge \psi \mid \mathsf{P}_I \varphi \mid \mathsf{H}_I \varphi \mid \varphi \, \mathsf{S}_I \, \psi \mid \varphi \, \overline{\mathsf{S}}_I \, \psi,$$

where I is an interval of the form $[a, b]$ or $[a, \infty)$ with $a, b \in \mathbb{N}$. For every temporal connective $X \in \{\mathsf{P}, \mathsf{H}, \mathsf{S}\}$, we will write X_a as an abbreviation for $X_{[a,a]}$ and X as an abbreviation for $X_{[0,\infty)}$. We interpret formulas from Φ over traces $\mathbb{D}^*$ using the *robustness* interpretation function $\rho : \Phi \times \mathbb{D}^* \to \mathbb{V}$, defined as follows:

$$\rho(f, \varepsilon) = \bot$$
$$\rho(f, w \cdot d) = f(d), \text{ where } d \in \mathbb{D}$$
$$\rho(\varphi \vee \psi, w) = \rho(\varphi, w) \sqcup \rho(\psi, w)$$
$$\rho(\varphi \wedge \psi, w) = \rho(\varphi, w) \sqcap \rho(\psi, w)$$
$$\rho(\mathsf{P}_I \varphi, w) = \bigsqcup_{\substack{i \in I \\ i < |w|}} \rho(\varphi, w[-i])$$
$$\rho(\mathsf{H}_I \varphi, w) = \bigsqcap_{\substack{i \in I \\ i < |w|}} \rho(\varphi, w[-i])$$
$$\rho(\varphi \, \mathsf{S}_I \, \psi, w) = \bigsqcup_{\substack{i \in I \\ i < |w|}} \left(\rho(\psi, w[-i]) \sqcap \bigsqcap_{j < i} \rho(\varphi, w[-j]) \right)$$
$$\rho(\varphi \, \overline{\mathsf{S}}_I \, \psi, w) = \bigsqcap_{\substack{i \in I \\ i < |w|}} \left(\rho(\psi, w[-i]) \sqcup \bigsqcup_{j < i} \rho(\varphi, w[-j]) \right)$$

Notice that $\rho(\mathsf{P}_a \varphi, w) = \bot$ and $\rho(\mathsf{H}_a \varphi, w) = \top$ whenever $a \geq |w|$. Note that the temporal language that we consider does not include negation. However, this does not limit expressiveness as we discuss in the examples below.

Example 6. Extending Example 4, choose $\mathbb{D}$ to be $\mathbb{B}^k$ and set $\mathbb{V}$ to $\mathbb{B}$. The set of functions from $\mathbb{B}^k \to \mathbb{B}$ considered may be restricted to projections $\pi_i(b_1, \dots b_i, \dots b_k) = b_i$ and negated projections $\pi_i(b_1, \dots b_i, \dots b_k) = \overline{b_i}$. This gives us the standard qualitative semantics for metric temporal logic. Formulas with negation can be expressed as equivalent formulas in negation normal form (NNF) in a fairly standard way by pushing negation inside while interchanging operators for their dual operators.

Example 7. We may also express a past time version of STL interpreted over discrete time in this framework. To do so, take $\mathbb{D} = \mathbb{R}^k$. A qualitative semantics is obtained by taking $\mathbb{V}$ to be $\mathbb{B}$ and restricting the functions to comparisons of the form $(r_1, \ldots r_i \ldots r_k) \mapsto r_i \sim c$ where $c \in \mathbb{R}$ and $\sim \in \{\leq, \geq, =\}$. A quantitative semantics can be obtained by taking $\mathbb{V}$ to be $\mathbb{R} \cup \{\infty, -\infty\}$ (as in Example 5) and considering functions of the form $(r_1, \ldots r_i \ldots r_k) \mapsto r_i - c$ or $(r_1, \ldots r_i \ldots r_k) \mapsto c - r_i$. Even in the quantitative setting, STL formulas with negation can be presented in our framework by considering a NNF, again by 'pushing' negation inside while interchanging operators for their dual operators and replacing $r_i - c$ with $c - r_i$.

Since we are interpreting formulas over discrete traces, our logic is essentially equivalent to LTL with a "Previous" operator. In other words, temporal connectives (including S and $\overline{\text{S}}$; see Lemma 13) with bounded intervals can be rewritten in terms of multiple compositions of the Previous operator instead.

3   The Monitoring Problem

Monitoring is analyzing a trace for specific patterns. For quantitative properties, this could be thought of as applying a valuation function on a trace. In an online setting, the trace is supplied to the monitor incrementally. To elaborate, the monitor is fed in fragments of the trace one at a time and the monitor is required to evaluate the quantitative property on the trace prefix seen so far. We intend to discuss a mechanism for monitoring quantitative properties denoted by MTL formulas.

3.1   Moore Machines

We will use Moore machines, a class of sequence transducers, as a formal model of online monitoring algorithms.

Definition 8. Let A and B be sets. A *Moore machine* with input items from A and output values in B is a tuple $(\text{St}, \text{init}, \text{mNext}, \text{mOut})$ where St is a (possibly infinite) set of states, $\text{init} \in \text{St}$ is the initial state, $\text{mNext} : S \times A \to S$ is a transition function which transitions the state of the machine upon seeing an input from A, and $\text{mOut} : S \to B$ associates an output with the current state. We write $\text{Moore}(A, B)$ for the set of all Moore machines with inputs from A and outputs from B.

While this is the standard definition of Moore Machines found in the literature, we use an equivalent, co-inductive definition in our formalization. In the co-inductive view, the states are not explicitly expressed, but described directly in terms of their extensional behavior.

```
CoInductive Moore (A B: Type) := {
    mOut: B;
    mNext: A -> Moore A B;
}.
```

The functions mNext and mOut denote the incremental update and the current output of the machine. More generally, the machine also associates with every trace a value, which can be simply obtained by feeding in the entire trace, element by element. In this sense, a machine denotes a quantitative property, formally captured in the definition of gFinal below.

Definition 9. Let $m \in \mathtt{Moore}(A, B)$. Then, $\mathtt{gNext}(m) : A^* \to \mathtt{Moore}(A, B)$ is defined by $\mathtt{gNext}(m, \varepsilon) = m$ and $\mathtt{gNext}(m, w \cdot a) = \mathtt{mNext}(\mathtt{gNext}(m, w), a)$. $\mathtt{gFinal}(m) : A^* \to B$ is defined as $\mathtt{gFinal}(m, w) = \mathtt{mOut}(\mathtt{gNext}(m, w))$.

For a quantitative property of traces, i.e, a function $f : \mathbb{D}^* \to \mathbb{V}$, we wish to construct a Moore machine that computes f. We restrict our focus to quantitative properties which can be expressed by MTL formulas.

Definition 10. Let $\varphi \in \Phi$ and $m \in \mathtt{Moore}(\mathbb{D}, \mathbb{V})$. We say that the Moore machine m *implements a monitor for* φ if $\mathtt{gFinal}(m, w) = \rho(\varphi, w)$ for all $w \in \mathbb{D}^*$.

Example 11. Following Definition 8, consider the machine $m : \mathtt{Moore}(\mathbb{V}, \mathbb{V})$ with states $\mathbb{V} \times \mathbb{V}$, initial state $(\bot, \bot)$, $\mathtt{mOut}((u, v)) = u$ and $\mathtt{mNext}((u, v), w) = (v, w)$. It holds that $\mathtt{gFinal}(m, \varepsilon) = \mathtt{gFinal}(m, v_1) = \bot$ and $\mathtt{gFinal}(m, v_1 v_2) = v_1$, $\mathtt{gFinal}(m, v_1 v_2 v_3) = v_2$, etc. The machine m implements a monitor for the formula $\mathsf{P}_1(v \mapsto v)$ in the sense of Definition 10.

Stated formally, the monitoring problem is to find a translation $\mathtt{toMonitor} :$ $\Phi \to \mathtt{Moore}(\mathbb{D}, \mathbb{V})$ so that given any $\varphi \in \Phi$, $\mathtt{toMonitor}(\varphi)$ is a monitor for φ.

3.2 Moore Combinators

Combinators are compositional constructs that let one define new machines in terms of existing ones. Our approach towards solving the monitoring problem is to find combinators which correspond to the temporal and Boolean connectives of MTL. With these combinators, a monitor for a given formula can be specified by induction on the structure of the formula.

Proceeding with the idea above, we identify the key constructs which are necessary in achieving the expressive power of MTL. We say that the formulas φ and ψ are *equivalent*, and we write $\varphi \equiv \psi$, if $\rho(\varphi, w) = \rho(\psi, w)$ for all $w \in \mathbb{D}^*$.

Lemma 12. The following identities hold:

$$\mathsf{P}_{[a,b]}\varphi \equiv \mathsf{P}_a \mathsf{P}_{[0,b-a]}\varphi \tag{1}$$

$$\mathsf{H}_{[a,b]}\varphi \equiv \mathsf{H}_a \mathsf{H}_{[0,b-a]}\varphi \tag{2}$$

$$\varphi \, \mathsf{S}_{[a+1,b]} \, \psi \equiv \mathsf{H}_{[0,a]}\varphi \wedge \mathsf{P}_{a+1} \left(\varphi \, \mathsf{S}_{[0,b-a]} \, \psi \right) \tag{3}$$

$$\varphi \, \overline{\mathsf{S}}_{[a+1,b]} \, \psi \equiv \mathsf{P}_{[0,a]}\varphi \vee \mathsf{H}_{a+1} \left(\varphi \, \overline{\mathsf{S}}_{[0,b-a]} \, \psi \right) \tag{4}$$

$$\mathsf{P}_{[a,\infty)}\varphi \equiv \mathsf{P}_a \mathsf{P}_{[0,\infty)}\varphi \tag{5}$$

$$\mathsf{H}_{[a,\infty)}\varphi \equiv \mathsf{H}_a \mathsf{H}_{[0,\infty)}\varphi \tag{6}$$

$$\varphi \, \mathsf{S}_{[a+1,\infty)} \, \psi \equiv \mathsf{H}_{[0,a]}\varphi \wedge \mathsf{P}_{a+1} \left(\varphi \, \mathsf{S}_{[0,\infty)} \, \psi \right) \tag{7}$$

$$\varphi \, \overline{\mathsf{S}}_{[a+1,\infty)} \, \psi \equiv \mathsf{P}_{[0,a]}\varphi \vee \mathsf{H}_{a+1} \left(\varphi \, \overline{\mathsf{S}}_{[0,\infty)} \, \psi \right) \tag{8}$$

The proofs of these identities are straightforward. Proving the identities involving S (or $\overline{\text{S}}$) requires the distributivity axioms, which motivates the need for considering distributive lattices.

Lemma 13. The following identities hold:

$$\varphi \, \text{S}_{[0,a]} \, \psi \equiv (\varphi \, \text{S} \, \psi) \wedge \text{P}_{[0,a]} \psi \tag{9}$$

$$\varphi \, \overline{\text{S}}_{[0,a]} \, \psi \equiv (\varphi \, \overline{\text{S}} \, \psi) \vee \text{H}_{[0,a]} \psi \tag{10}$$

Proof. We will only prove the first identity, since the second one can be proved with analogous arguments. Let $w \in \mathbb{D}^*$ be an arbitrary trace. We define $s_i = \rho(\varphi, w[-i])$ and $t_i = \rho(\psi, w[-i])$ for every $i \in \mathbb{N}$. Then, we have that

$$\rho(\varphi \, \text{S}_{[0,a]} \, \psi, w) = \bigsqcup_{i \leq K} \left(t_i \sqcap \bigsqcap_{j < i} s_j \right)$$

$$\rho(\varphi \, \text{S} \, \psi, w) = \bigsqcup_{i \leq |w|-1} \left(t_i \sqcap \bigsqcap_{j<i} s_j \right) = \rho(\varphi \, \text{S}_{[0,a]} \, \psi, w) \sqcup \bigsqcup_{K < i \leq |w|-1} \left(t_i \sqcap \bigsqcap_{j<i} s_j \right)$$

$$\rho(\text{P}_{[0,a]} \psi, w) = \bigsqcup_{i \leq K} t_i$$

where $K = \min(a, |w| - 1)$. We have to prove that $L = R \sqcap Q$, where $L = \rho(\varphi \, \text{S}_{[0,a]} \, \psi, w)$, $R = \rho(\varphi \, \text{S} \, \psi, w)$ and $Q = \rho(\text{P}_{[0,a]} \psi, w)$. From $K \leq |w| - 1$ we obtain that $L \sqsubseteq R$. It also holds that $L \sqsubseteq Q$ because $t_i \sqcap \bigsqcap_{j<i} s_j \sqsubseteq t_i$ for every $i \leq K$. It follows that $L \sqsubseteq R \sqcap Q$. It remains to show that $R \sqcap Q \sqsubseteq L$. Since

$$R \sqcap Q = \left(L \sqcup \bigsqcup_{K < i \leq |w|-1} \left(t_i \sqcap \bigsqcap_{j<i} s_j \right) \right) \sqcap Q$$

$$= (L \sqcap Q) \sqcup \bigsqcup_{K < i \leq |w|-1} \left(t_i \sqcap \bigsqcap_{j<i} s_j \sqcap Q \right)$$

$$= (L \sqcap Q) \sqcup \bigsqcup_{K < i \leq |w|-1} \bigsqcup_{k \leq K} \left(t_i \sqcap t_k \sqcap \bigsqcap_{j<i} s_j \right),$$

it suffices to establish that $L \sqcap Q \sqsubseteq L$ (which is true) and $t_i \sqcap t_k \sqcap \bigsqcap_{j<i} s_j \sqsubseteq L$ for every i and k with $K < i \leq |w| - 1$ and $k \leq K$. Since $k < i$, we conclude that $t_i \sqcap t_k \sqcap \bigsqcap_{j<i} s_j \sqsubseteq t_k \sqcap \bigsqcap_{j<k} s_j \sqsubseteq L$. $\square$

Remark 14. In the qualitative setting, the identities in Lemma 13 are intuitively clear, but they require a more careful argument in the quantitative setting. They have been used and proven in [15] for the lattice $(\mathbb{R}, \min, \max)$, but the given proof does not generalize to the class of lattices that we consider here. As we can see in the proof of Lemma 13, there is a subtlety in dealing with the terms of $\rho(\varphi \, \text{S} \, \psi, w)$ with index $i = K + 1, \ldots, |w| - 1$.

The first set of identities allows us to express $\text{P}_{[\bullet,\bullet]}$, $\text{S}_{[\bullet,\bullet]}$ in terms of $\text{P}_{[0,\bullet]}$, $\text{S}_{[0,\bullet]}$ and $\text{P}_\bullet$. The second set of identities implies that $\overline{\text{S}}_{[0,\bullet]}$ can be replaced by $\overline{\text{S}}$

$$\frac{f : \mathbb{D} \to \mathbb{V}}{\texttt{mAtomic } f : \texttt{Moore}(\mathbb{D}, \mathbb{V})} \qquad \frac{m : \texttt{Moore}(\mathbb{D}, \mathbb{V}) \quad k : \mathbb{N}}{\texttt{mDelay } k \; m : \texttt{Moore}(\mathbb{D}, \mathbb{V})} \qquad \frac{m : \texttt{Moore}(\mathbb{D}, \mathbb{V}) \quad k : \mathbb{N}}{\overline{\texttt{mDelay }} k \; m : \texttt{Moore}(\mathbb{D}, \mathbb{V})}$$

$$\frac{m_1 : \texttt{Moore}(\mathbb{D}, \mathbb{V}) \qquad m_2 : \texttt{Moore}(\mathbb{D}, \mathbb{V})}{\texttt{mAnd } m_1 \; m_2 : \texttt{Moore}(\mathbb{D}, \mathbb{V})} \qquad \frac{m_1 : \texttt{Moore}(\mathbb{D}, \mathbb{V}) \qquad m_2 : \texttt{Moore}(\mathbb{D}, \mathbb{V})}{\texttt{mOr } m_1 \; m_2 : \texttt{Moore}(\mathbb{D}, \mathbb{V})}$$

$$\frac{m_1 : \texttt{Moore}(\mathbb{D}, \mathbb{V}) \qquad m_2 : \texttt{Moore}(\mathbb{D}, \mathbb{V})}{\texttt{mSince } m_1 \; m_2 : \texttt{Moore}(\mathbb{D}, \mathbb{V})} \qquad \frac{m_1 : \texttt{Moore}(\mathbb{D}, \mathbb{V}) \qquad m_2 : \texttt{Moore}(\mathbb{D}, \mathbb{V})}{\overline{\texttt{mSince}} \; m_1 \; m_2 : \texttt{Moore}(\mathbb{D}, \mathbb{V})}$$

$$\frac{m : \texttt{Moore}(\mathbb{D}, \mathbb{V})}{\texttt{mSometime } m : \texttt{Moore}(\mathbb{D}, \mathbb{V})} \qquad \frac{m : \texttt{Moore}(\mathbb{D}, \mathbb{V})}{\texttt{mAlways } m : \texttt{Moore}(\mathbb{D}, \mathbb{V})}$$

$$\frac{m : \texttt{Moore}(\mathbb{D}, \mathbb{V}) \quad k : \mathbb{N}}{\texttt{mSometimeWithin } k \; m : \texttt{Moore}(\mathbb{D}, \mathbb{V})} \qquad \frac{m : \texttt{Moore}(\mathbb{D}, \mathbb{V}) \quad k : \mathbb{N}}{\texttt{mAlwaysWithin } k \; m : \texttt{Moore}(\mathbb{D}, \mathbb{V})}$$

Fig. 1. Summary of Moore combinators

and $\mathsf{P}_\bullet$. Thus, the only additional constructs required in expressing the bounded temporal operators are $\mathsf{P}_\bullet$ and $\mathsf{P}_{[0,\bullet]}$ (and their duals).

We present in Fig. 1 a summary of the combinators that we will consider. Each combinator can be thought of as the implementation of the corresponding Boolean or temporal connective. The key observation is that this association between combinators on Moore machines and connectives *respect* the implementation relation (Definition 10) between machines and formulas. E.g., if m is a monitor for φ, we expect $\texttt{mSometimeWithin } k \; m$ to be a monitor for $\mathsf{P}_{[0,k]}\varphi$.

We define the translation function $\texttt{toMonitor} : \Phi \to \texttt{Moore}(\mathbb{D}, \mathbb{V})$ as in Fig. 2. We can think that $\texttt{toMonitor}(\varphi)$ is computed by recursively replacing the connectives in φ with Moore combinators. The correctness of $\texttt{toMonitor}$ is a consequence of the correctness of the combinators in the sense described above.

Before we start describing each combinator in detail, we make some remarks about the general organization of our implementation and formal proofs. There is a lot of symmetry among these combinators that can be leveraged for economy of effort. One example is the presence of dual connectives, such as $\vee$ and $\wedge$. This is why in many cases we focus on presenting these combinators in a slightly general way before instantiating them specifically to $\texttt{Moore}(\mathbb{D}, \mathbb{V})$. As discussed before, the correctness for each combinator is phrased in terms of preserving the implementation relation – these theorems are indexed with the suffix _correctness. These theorems are proven via lemmas indexed with the suffix _final which characterize the most recent output of the Moore machine at a fixed point in the computation. The proofs proceed by induction on the trace seen so far. They require additional lemmas that establish invariants about the state of a Moore machine as it evolves during the computation. These latter lemmas are indicated with the suffix _state. These ideas are illustrated in the construction of $\texttt{mAtomic}$ in Fig. 3.

```
Fixpoint toMonitor {A : Type} (f : Formula) : Moore A Val :=
  match f with
  | FAtomic _ g => mAtomic g
  | FDelay _ n g => mDelay n (toMonitor g)
  | FDelayDual _ n g => mDelayDual n (toMonitor g)
  | FAnd _ g h => mAnd (toMonitor g) (toMonitor h)
  | FOr _ g h => mOr (toMonitor g) (toMonitor h)
  | FSometime _ g => mSometime (toMonitor g)
  | FAlways _ g => mAlways (toMonitor g)
  | FSince _ g h => mSince (toMonitor g) (toMonitor h)
  | FSinceDual _ g h => mSinceDual (toMonitor g) (toMonitor h)
  | FSometimeWithin _ hi g => mSometimeWithin hi (toMonitor g)
  | FAlwaysWithin _ hi g => mAlwaysWithin hi (toMonitor g)
  end.

Theorem toMonitor_correctness {A : Type} (f : Formula):
  implements (toMonitor f) f.
```

Fig. 2. The toMonitor function

Atomic Functions. In order to lift functions $f : A \to B$ to Moore(A, B), we define the mLift combinator, as in Fig. 3. Given an $f : A \to B$ and a value init $: B$, it defines a Moore machine which computes f on the latest input and initially emits init. We use the lemma mLift_state to describe the evolution of the machine when an arbitrary stream prefix is fed. Using this, we also prove mLift_final, which describes the final output of the machine after accepting an arbitrary stream prefix. We define mAtomic by instantiating the parameter init of mLift to $\perp$. The Lemma titled mAtomic_correctness establishes that mAtomic correctly translates atomic functions to corresponding monitors.

Pointwise Binary Operations. In Fig. 4, we define the combinator mBinOp that combines the output of two given machines using a binary operation. By plugging in $\sqcup$ and $\sqcap$ as op, we can use mBinOp to implement the $\vee$ and $\wedge$ connectives, respectively. Like in the case of mAtomic, the correctness of this combinator is proven by establishing appropriate lemmas which describe the behavior of mBinOp with gNextand gFinal. These let us prove, in particular, that mAnd and mOr correctly implement formulas involving $\wedge$ and $\vee$, respectively.

Delay Monitors. We view the implementation of P_a and H_a as a mechanism that delays the output of a Moore Machine. For instance, the sequence $\langle \rho(\mathsf{P}_2\varphi, a_1a_2a_3), \rho(\mathsf{P}_2\varphi, a_1a_2a_3a_4) \rangle$ is same as $\langle \rho(\varphi, a_1), \rho(\varphi, a_1a_2) \rangle$. These operators preserve the order of the outputs, but delay them by a given constant.

This can be achieved using a queue maintained at a fixed length. For instance, to implement $\mathsf{P}_a\varphi$, we maintain a queue of length a. Upon being given an input item $a \in \mathbb{D}$, we feed a to toMonitor(φ), enqueue the result and then return what we obtain by dequeuing. This works since the dequeued element was the

```
CoFixpoint mLift {A B: Type} (f : A -> B) (init : B) : Moore A B := {|
   mOut := init;
   mNext (a : A) := mLift f (f a) |}.
Lemma mLift_state {A B : Type}
   (xs : list A) (x : A) (f : A -> B) (init : B) :
     gNext (mLift f init) (xs ++ [x]) = mLift f (f x).
Lemma mLift_final {A B : Type}
   (xs : list A) (x : A) (f : A -> B) (init : B):
     gFinal (mLift f init) (xs ++ [x]) = f x.
Definition mAtomic {A : Type} (f : A -> Val) : Moore A Val :=
   mLift f bottom.
Lemma mAtomic_correctness {A : Type} (f : A -> Val):
   implements (mAtomic f) (FAtomic Val f).
```

Fig. 3. Establishing correctness of mAtomic.

result of toMonitor(φ) a turns ago. The queue needs to be initially filled with a instances of $\bot$ (or $\top$ in the case of H_a) since we have that $\rho(\mathsf{P}_a\varphi, w) = \bot$ (or $\rho(\mathsf{H}_a\varphi, w) = \top$) when $|w| > a$.

Since Coq is based on a functional programming environment, functional lists are the ordered collections that are the easiest for us to reason about and work with. Functional lists are typically implemented via linked lists, which means that in order to access the kth element of the list, one would have to traverse k links and would spend $O(k)$ time. This makes appending to the end of the list expensive. However, obtaining or adding elements at the head (the beginning) of the list is straightforward. Thus, these lists effectively behave as stacks and sometimes we refer to them as such. We use the well-known technique of implementing a queue with two functional lists, which we briefly discuss below.

A queue is represented by two lists front and rear. When an element is enqueued, it is added to the head of the rear list. Thus, the rear list effectively stores the elements of the queue in an order opposite to that in which they were enqueued. When dequeing an element is required, the elements of rear are reversed and placed in the front (thus restoring the order) and the head of front is returned. As long as front is non-empty, subsequent dequeues may be directly handled by returning the head of front.

In our use case, the queue is maintained at a fixed length, say k and every enqueue is followed by a subsequent dequeue. Reversing rear into front takes time $O(k)$. However, we only need to do this every k turns, since front is filled with k items whenever the reversal happens. Thus, every k turns, we do $O(k)$ work and only $O(1)$ work is needed otherwise. This gives us an amortized time complexity of $O(1)$.

We implement this idea in the delayWith combinator in Fig. 5. The key lemma required in proving the correctness of the delayWith combinator shows that the queue maintained always stores the last k-many outputs of the submonitor. To formalize this, we define gCollect : Moore(A, B) $\times\ \mathbb{D}^* \rightarrow \mathbb{V}^*$ as

```
CoFixpoint mBinOp {A B C D: Type} (op : B -> C -> D)
    (m1: Moore A B) (m2 : Moore A C) : Moore A D :=
{|
  mOut := op (mOut m1) (mOut m2);
  mNext (a : A) := mBinOp op (mNext m1 a) (mNext m2 a)
|}.
Definition mAnd {A : Type} (m1 : Moore A Val)
  (m2 : Moore A Val) : Moore A Val := mBinOp meet m1 m2.
Definition mOr {A : Type} (m1 : Moore A Val)
  (m2 : Moore A Val) : Moore A Val := mBinOp join m1 m2.
Lemma mAnd_correctness {A : Type} (m1 m2 : Moore A Val) (f1 f2 : Formula):
  implements m1 f1 -> implements m2 f2
  -> implements (mAnd m1 m2) (FAnd Val f1 f2).
Lemma mOr_correctness {A : Type} (m1 m2 : Moore A Val) (f1 f2 : Formula):
  implements m1 f1 -> implements m2 f2
  -> implements (mOr m1 m2) (FOr Val f1 f2).
```

Fig. 4. The mBinOp combinator

```
  Lemma delayWith_state {A B : Type} (init : B) (inf inb : list B)
      (m : Moore A B) (xs : list A) (x : A):
    forall initSeg, initSeg = [init] ++ inf ++ rev inb ->
    forall k, k = length initSeg ->
    forall str, str = initSeg ++ gCollect m xs ->
    forall lastSeg, lastSeg = lastn k str ->
      exists fr ba ii,
          [ii] ++ fr ++ rev ba = lastSeg /\
          k = length lastSeg /\
          gNext (delayWith init inf inb m) (xs ++ [x])
            = delayWith ii fr ba (gNext m (xs ++ [x])).
```

Fig. 5. Delay monitors.

$$\text{gCollect}(m, a_1 a_2 \cdots a_n) =$$
$$\langle \text{gFinal}(m, \varepsilon), \text{gFinal}(m, a_1), \cdots, \text{gFinal}(m, a_1 a_2 \cdots a_n) \rangle.$$

We may now write the mentioned invariant as in delayWith_state, which is established by induction on the input stream.

Temporal Folds. The unbounded operators P and H can be thought of as a running fold on the input stream, since $\rho(\mathsf{P}\varphi, w \cdot a) = \rho(\mathsf{P}\varphi, w) \sqcup \rho(\varphi, w \cdot a)$. Thus, to evaluate these operators in an online fashion, we only need to store the robustness value for the trace seen so far. For P (resp., H), the robustness of the current trace can then be obtained by computing the join (resp., meet) of the current value and the stored one. In Fig. 6, mAlways (resp., mSometime) computes the robustness values corresponding to the H (resp., P) connectives by computing the meet (resp., join) of the current value with the stored one.

```
CoFixpoint mFoldAux {A : Type} (m : Moore A B)
  (op : B -> B -> B) (st : B) : Moore A B :=
  {| mOut := st;
     mNext (a : A) := mFoldAux (mNext m a) (op st (mNextOut m a)) |}.
Definition mSometime {A : Type} (m : Moore A B) :=
  mFoldAux m meet bottom.
Definition mAlways {A : Type} (m : Moore A B) :=
  mFoldAux m join top.
```

Fig. 6. Temporal Folds

```
CoFixpoint mSinceAux {A : Type}
  (m1 m2 : Moore A Val) (pre : Val) : Moore A Val :=
  {| mOut := pre;
     mNext (a : A) :=
       mSinceAux (mNext m1 a) (mNext m2 a)
       (join (mNextOut m2 a) (meet (mNextOut m1 a) pre)) |}.
Definition mSince {A : Type} (m1 m2 : Moore A Val) :=
  mSinceAux m1 m2 (mOut m2).
```

Fig. 7. Monitoring Since

Using the following identity, we may also view the computation of S as a temporal fold, i.e, the robustness for φ S ψ may be calculated incrementally by only storing the robustness value for the stream prefix so far.

Lemma 15. For all $w \in \mathbb{D}^*$ and $a \in \mathbb{D}$, we have that

$$\rho(\varphi \text{ S } \psi, w \cdot a) = \rho(\psi, w \cdot a) \sqcup (\rho(\varphi \text{ S } \psi, w) \sqcap \rho(\varphi, w \cdot a)).$$

This is a well known equality and can be proved by using distributivity in a straightforward way. A proof of this for the $(\mathbb{R}, \max, \min)$ lattice appears in [13].

Using the equality of Lemma 15, mSince can be implemented as in Fig. 7. The correctness of mSince is established by proving invariants on mSinceAux, which is straightforward once the equality above has been established.

Windowed Temporal Folds. For the operators $P_{[0,a]}$ or $H_{[0,a]}$, the strategy above needs to be modified, since the fold is over a sliding window, rather than the entire trace. For this purpose, we use a queue like data structure (dubbed aggQueue, henceforth) which also maintains sliding window aggregates, in addition. An extended discussion of such a data structure can be found in [8].

Similar to the queues used in the delay monitors, aggQueue consists of two functional lists, the rear into which elements are inserted upon enqueing and the front out of which elements are evicted upon dequeing. The elements of rear and front are pairs: one of them is the enqueued element and the other represents a partial aggregate. For convenience, we denote by contentsff(resp., contentsrr) the enqueued elements currently in front (resp., rear) and by

```
CoFixpoint mWinFoldAux {A : Type} (qq : aggQueue)
  (m : Moore A B) : Moore A B :=
  {| mOut := op (aggOut qq) (mOut m);
     mNext (a : A) :=
         mWinFoldAux (aggDQ (aggEnQ (mOut m) qq)) (mNext m a); |}.
Definition initAggQ (n : nat) : aggQueue :=
     {| front := repeat (unit, unit) (S n)
      ; rear := [] |}.
Definition mWinFold {A : Type} (m : Moore A B) (n : nat) : Moore A B :=
     mWinFoldAux (initAggQ n) m.
Lemma mWinFold_state {A : Type} (m : Moore A B)
  (n : nat) (xs : list A) (x : A) : exists qq,
  gNext (mWinFold m n) (xs ++ [x]) = mWinFoldAux qq (gNext m (xs ++ [x]))
  /\ contentsQ qq = lastn (S n) (repeat unit (S n) ++ gCollect m xs)
  /\ aggsffInv qq
  /\ aggsrrInv qq.
```

Fig. 8. Windowed Temporal Folds

aggsff(resp., aggsrr) the partial aggregates currently in front (resp., rear). The aggregate values and the enqueued items are related in the following manner: (1) The ith-last element of aggsff is the aggregate of the last i elements of contentsff (2) The ith-last element of aggsrr is the aggregate of the last i elements of contentsrr taken in the reverse order. Given these invariants, it is easy to see that the aggregate of the entire queue can be computed as the aggregate of the heads of aggsff and aggsrr.

We maintain these invariants in the following way: Upon enqueue, we simply add the enqueued element to the head of rear along with the aggregate of the element with the head of aggsff. Performing a dequeue is easy when front is non-empty: we simply remove the element at its head. When front is empty, the contents of contentsrr are added to front while recalculating the aggregate, maintaining the invariant above.

Writing op for $\sqcup$ (resp., $\sqcap$) and unit for $\bot$ (resp., $\top$) in Fig. 8, we define the combinator mWinFold. Given a constant k, mWinFold maintains an aggQueue initialized with k instances of $\bot$ (or $\top$). When a new input is available, mWinFold enqueues the result of the corresponding submonitor into queue and dequeues the element which was enqueued k turns ago. The output of mWinFold is simply set to be the aggregate of the elements in the queue. Using a similar argument as before, we can see that the invocations of mNexton mWinFold run in $O(1)$ amortized time. See Fig. 9 for an illustration of the running of mWinFold.

The correctness of the algorithm can be established via mWinFold_state. In essence, it states that the contentsff and contentsrr together store the last k elements of the stream, and that the invariants on aggsff and aggsrr are maintained.

contentsff	aggsff	contentsrr	aggsrr	aggOut
$\langle\bot,\bot,\bot\rangle$	$\langle\bot,\bot,\bot\rangle$	$\langle\rangle$	$\langle\rangle$	$\bot$
$\langle\bot,\bot\rangle$	$\langle\bot,\bot\rangle$	$\langle a\rangle$	$\langle a\rangle$	$\bot\sqcup a$
$\langle\bot\rangle$	$\langle\bot\rangle$	$\langle b,a\rangle$	$\langle ab,a\rangle$	$\bot\sqcup ab$
$\langle\rangle$	$\langle\rangle$	$\langle c,b,a\rangle$	$\langle abc,ab,a\rangle$	$\bot\sqcup abc$
$\langle b,c\rangle$	$\langle bc,c\rangle$	$\langle d\rangle$	$\langle d\rangle$	$bc\sqcup d$
$\langle c\rangle$	$\langle c\rangle$	$\langle e,d\rangle$	$\langle de,d\rangle$	$c\sqcup de$

Fig. 9. A run of `mWinFold` while maintaining a queue of 3 elements. The elements a,b,c,d,e are fed in, incrementally. The binary operation $\sqcup$ has been omitted in this figure except in a few places for the sake of brevity.

Remark 16. The space required by the described algorithm is constant in terms of the size of the input trace but exponential in the size of the constants that appear in the formula. This exponential is unavoidable since computing the value of $\mathsf{P}_a p$ would require storing the last a values of p.

4   Extraction and Experiments

We use Coq's extraction mechanism to produce OCaml code for our `toMonitor` function. For this purpose, we instantiate the lattice $\mathbb{V}$ with the concrete OCaml type `float`.

We extract monitors for formulas involving atomic functions (involving projection and subtraction emulating STL, as explained in Example 5), Boolean operators and other temporal operators. As a measure of performance, we use throughput, which is the number of items that can be processed in a fixed duration. Since P_a and $\mathsf{P}_{[0,a]}$ are the main constructs used to express various other ones, we measure their performance for varying values of a (see Fig. 10). We also measure the throughput for monitors corresponding to similar formulas produced by Reelay [32].

We generate a trace consisting of three random floating point values in each trace item. For the purpose of our tool, we perform experiments on traces of length 20 million as well as 200 million. We observe that this difference on the length of the trace has no significant effect on the throughput. It appears that Reelay has a throughput which is slower by orders of magnitude. For this reason, we perform our experiments on Reelay on smaller traces - of 500 thousand items. The experiment corresponding to each formula was run 10 times and the reported value is their mean. The standard deviation of the results were less than 3% in all cases.

A potential explanation for the comparative worse performance of Reelay is that Reelay stores data values in string-indexed maps. Interval Maps are also used in Reelay's implementation of operators such as $\mathsf{P}_{[a,b]}$. Since our tool does not use any map-like data structure, we do not incur these costs.

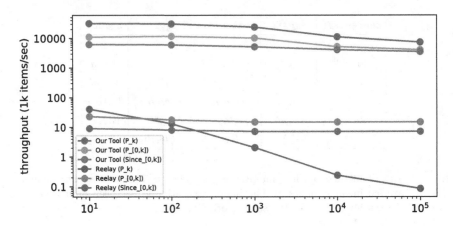

Fig. 10. Throughput for formulas with large constants

In Fig. 11, we use formulas similar to the ones used in the Timescales [31] benchmark. The formulas used in the Timescales benchmark are in propositional MTL, so we define the propositions p, q, r and s as $x > 0.5$, $y > 0.25$, $z > 0.3$ and $z > 0.6$ respectively, where x, y and z are projections of the current trace item. For convenience, also define k and ℓ to be 1000 and 2000 respectively. The formulas F1 through F10 in Fig. 11, in order, are: $\mathsf{H}(\mathsf{P}_{[0,k]}q \rightarrow (\neg p\,\mathsf{S}\,q))$, $\mathsf{H}(r \rightarrow \mathsf{P}_{[0,k]}(\neg p))$, $\mathsf{H}((r \wedge \neg q \wedge \mathsf{P}q) \rightarrow (\neg p\,\mathsf{S}_{[k,\ell]}\,q))$, $\mathsf{H}(\mathsf{P}_{[0,k]}q \rightarrow (p\,\mathsf{S}\,q))$, $\mathsf{H}(r \rightarrow \mathsf{H}_{[0,k]}p)$, $\mathsf{H}((r \wedge \neg q \wedge \mathsf{P}q) \rightarrow (p\mathsf{S}_{[k,\ell]}q))$, $\mathsf{HP}_{[0,k]}p$, $\mathsf{H}((r \wedge \neg q \wedge \mathsf{P}q) \rightarrow (\mathsf{P}_{[0,k]}(p \vee q)\mathsf{S}q))$, $\mathsf{H}((s \rightarrow \mathsf{P}_{k,\ell}p)\wedge\neg(\neg s\mathsf{S}_{[k,\infty)}p))$, and $\mathsf{H}((r\wedge\neg q\wedge \mathsf{P}q) \rightarrow ((s \rightarrow \mathsf{P}_{[k,\ell]}p)\wedge\neg(\neg s\mathsf{S}_{[k,\infty)}$ $p)))$. Implications $\alpha \rightarrow \beta$ were encoded as $\neg\alpha \vee \beta$ and negations were encoded using their negation normal form.

All experiments were run on a computer with Intel Xeon CPU 3.30 GHz with 16 GB memory running Ubuntu 18.04.

5 Related Work

Fainekos and Pappas [18] introduce the notion of robustness for the interpretation of temporal formulas over discrete and continuous time signals. In their setting, signals are functions from a temporal domain to a metric space and the distance function of the metric space is used to endow the space of signals with a metric. The robustness is essentially the largest amount by which a signal can be perturbed while still satisfying the specification. In the same paper, an alternate quantitative semantics is proposed which is defined in an inductive fashion by replacing disjunction with max and conjunction with min. This inductive semantics can be used to under-approximate the robustness value. The framework used in our paper essentially is this under-approximating semantics. This approach is extended by Donzé and Maler [16] to include temporal robustness.

In [21], the authors describe a general algebraic framework for defining robustness based on the monoidal structure of traces using the semiring structure

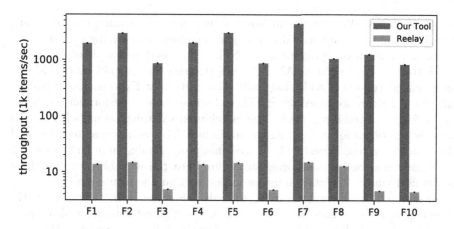

Fig. 11. Throughput for formulas from the Timescales benchmark

on the semantic domain. They suggest the use of symbolic weighted automata for the purpose of monitoring. With this approach, they are able to compute the precise robustness value for a property-signal pair. The construction of a weighted automaton from a temporal formula incurs a doubly exponential blowup, if one assumes a succinct binary representation of the constants appearing in an MTL formula. We consider here a class of lattices, which are also semirings. With our approach, however, we do not calculate the precise robustness value, but an under-approximation in the sense discussed in the previous paragraph. One may also consider a semantics in which disjunction is replaced with $+$ and conjunction with $\times$ from the semiring. With our approach, we would not be able to monitor formulas with this semantics since we make crucial use of the absorption laws in Lemma 13. The most interesting semiring which does not form a lattice which might be relevant in the monitoring of cyber-physical systems is $(\mathbb{R}, \max, +)$.

The distance between two signals can be defined to be the maximum of the distance between the values that the signals take at corresponding points of time. However, other ways to define this distance have been considered. In [20], a quantitative semantics is developed via the notion of weighted edit distance. Averaging temporal operators are proposed in [2] with the goal of introducing an explicit mechanism for temporal robustness. The Skorokhod metric [12] has been suggested as a distance function between continuous signals. In [1], another metric is considered, which compares the value taken by the signal within a neighbourhood of the current time. Another interesting view of temporal logic is in [29], where temporal connectives are viewed as linear time-invariant filters.

Signal Regular Expressions (SREs) [33] are another formalism for describing patterns on signals. They are based on regular expressions, rather than LTL. A robustness semantics for SRE has been proposed in [5] along with an algorithm for offline monitoring. In [4], STL is enriched by considering a more general (and quantitative) interpretation of the Until operator and adding specific aggregation operators. They also give a semantics of their formalism using dual numbers, which are the real numbers with an adjoined element ϵ satisfying $\epsilon^2 = 0$.

In [24], a monitoring algorithm for STL is proposed and implemented in the AMT tool. A later version, AMT 2.0 [28] extends the capabilities of AMT to an extended version of STL along with Timed Regular Expressions. In [15], an efficient algorithm for monitoring STL is discussed whose performance is linear in the length of the input trace. This is achieved by using Lemire's [23] sliding window algorithm for computing the maximum. This is implemented as a part the monitoring tool Breach [14]. A dynamic programming approach is used in [13] to design an online monitoring algorithm. Here, the availability of a predictor is assumed which predicts the future values, so that the future modalities may be interpreted. A different approach towards online monitoring is taken in [17]: they consider robustness intervals, that is, the tightest interval which covers the robustness of all possible extensions of the available trace prefix. There are also monitoring formalisms that are essentially domain-specific languages for processing data streams, such as LOLA [11] and StreamQRE [26]. LOLA has recently been used as a basis for RtLOLA in the StreamLAB framework [19], which adds support for sliding windows and variable-rate streams. A detailed survey on the many extensions to the syntax and semantics of STL along with their monitoring algorithms and applications is presented in [6].

In [10], a framework towards the formalization of runtime verification components are discussed. MonPoly [9] is a tool developed by Basin et al. aimed at monitoring a first order extension of temporal logic. In [30], the authors put forward Verimon, a simplified version of MonPoly which uses the proof assistant Isabelle/HOL to formally prove its correctness. They extend this line of work in Verimon+ [7] which verifies a more efficient version of the monitoring algorithms and uses a dynamic logic, which is an extension of the temporal logic with regular expression-like constructs.

6   Conclusion

We have presented a formalization in the Coq proof assistant of a procedure for constructing online monitors for metric temporal logic with a quantitative semantics. We have extracted verified OCaml code from the Coq formalization. Our experiments show that our formally verified online monitors perform well in comparison to Reelay [32], a state-of-the-art monitoring tool.

The construction of monitors that we presented can be extended and made more compositional by using classes of transducers that can support *dataflow combinators* [22] (serial, parallel and feedback composition), as seen in [25,27]. We leave an exploration of this direction as future work. It is also worth developing a more thorough benchmark suite to compare the presented monitoring framework against the tools Breach [14], S-TaLiRo [3], and StreamLAB [19]. We have extracted OCaml code from a Coq formalization, but a formally verified C implementation would be preferable from a performance standpoint. Another interesting direction is to increase the expressiveness of our specification formalism: one possible candidate is the extension to dynamic logic, as has been done in [7] in a qualitative setting.

References

1. Abbas, H., Mangharam, R.: Generalized robust MTL semantics for problems in cardiac electrophysiology. In: ACC 2018, pp. 1592–1597. IEEE (2018)
2. Akazaki, T., Hasuo, I.: Time robustness in MTL and expressivity in hybrid system falsification. In: Kroening, D., Păsăreanu, C.S. (eds.) CAV 2015. LNCS, vol. 9207, pp. 356–374. Springer, Cham (2015). https://doi.org/10.1007/978-3-319-21668-3_21
3. Annpureddy, Y., Liu, C., Fainekos, G., Sankaranarayanan, S.: S-TaLiRo: a tool for temporal logic falsification for hybrid systems. In: Abdulla, P.A., Leino, K.R.M. (eds.) TACAS 2011. LNCS, vol. 6605, pp. 254–257. Springer, Heidelberg (2011). https://doi.org/10.1007/978-3-642-19835-9_21
4. Bakhirkin, A., Basset, N.: Specification and efficient monitoring beyond STL. In: Vojnar, T., Zhang, L. (eds.) TACAS 2019. LNCS, vol. 11428, pp. 79–97. Springer, Cham (2019). https://doi.org/10.1007/978-3-030-17465-1_5
5. Bakhirkin, A., Ferrère, T., Maler, O., Ulus, D.: On the quantitative semantics of regular expressions over real-valued signals. In: Abate, A., Geeraerts, G. (eds.) FORMATS 2017. LNCS, vol. 10419, pp. 189–206. Springer, Cham (2017). https://doi.org/10.1007/978-3-319-65765-3_11
6. Bartocci, E., et al.: Specification-based monitoring of cyber-physical systems: a survey on theory, tools and applications. In: Bartocci, E., Falcone, Y. (eds.) Lectures on Runtime Verification. LNCS, vol. 10457, pp. 135–175. Springer, Cham (2018). https://doi.org/10.1007/978-3-319-75632-5_5
7. Basin, D., et al.: A formally verified, optimized monitor for metric first-order dynamic logic. In: Peltier, N., Sofronie-Stokkermans, V. (eds.) IJCAR 2020. LNCS (LNAI), vol. 12166, pp. 432–453. Springer, Cham (2020). https://doi.org/10.1007/978-3-030-51074-9_25
8. Basin, D., Klaedtke, F., Zalinescu, E.: Greedily computing associative aggregations on sliding windows. Inf. Process. Lett. **115**(2), 186–192 (2015)
9. Basin, D., Klaedtke, F., Zalinescu, E.: The MonPoly monitoring tool. In: Reger, G., Havelund, K. (eds.) RV-CuBES 2017. Kalpa Publications in Computing, vol. 3, pp. 19–28. EasyChair (2017)
10. Blech, J.O., Falcone, Y., Becker, K.: Towards certified runtime verification. In: Aoki, T., Taguchi, K. (eds.) ICFEM 2012. LNCS, vol. 7635, pp. 494–509. Springer, Heidelberg (2012). https://doi.org/10.1007/978-3-642-34281-3_34
11. D'Angelo, B., et al.: LOLA: runtime monitoring of synchronous systems. In: TIME 2005, pp. 166–174. IEEE (2005)
12. Deshmukh, J.V., Majumdar, R., Prabhu, V.S.: Quantifying conformance using the Skorokhod metric. Formal Methods Syst. Des. **50**(2), 168–206 (2017). https://doi.org/10.1007/s10703-016-0261-8
13. Dokhanchi, A., Hoxha, B., Fainekos, G.: On-line monitoring for temporal logic robustness. In: Bonakdarpour, B., Smolka, S.A. (eds.) RV 2014. LNCS, vol. 8734, pp. 231–246. Springer, Cham (2014). https://doi.org/10.1007/978-3-319-11164-3_19

14. Donzé, A.: Breach, a toolbox for verification and parameter synthesis of hybrid systems. In: Touili, T., Cook, B., Jackson, P. (eds.) CAV 2010. LNCS, vol. 6174, pp. 167–170. Springer, Heidelberg (2010). https://doi.org/10.1007/978-3-642-14295-6_17

15. Donzé, A., Ferrère, T., Maler, O.: Efficient robust monitoring for STL. In: Sharygina, N., Veith, H. (eds.) CAV 2013. LNCS, vol. 8044, pp. 264–279. Springer, Heidelberg (2013). https://doi.org/10.1007/978-3-642-39799-8_19

16. Donzé, A., Maler, O.: Robust satisfaction of temporal logic over real-valued signals. In: Chatterjee, K., Henzinger, T.A. (eds.) FORMATS 2010. LNCS, vol. 6246, pp. 92–106. Springer, Heidelberg (2010). https://doi.org/10.1007/978-3-642-15297-9_9

17. Dreossi, T., Dang, T., Donzé, A., Kapinski, J., Jin, X., Deshmukh, J.V.: Efficient guiding strategies for testing of temporal properties of hybrid systems. In: Havelund, K., Holzmann, G., Joshi, R. (eds.) NFM 2015. LNCS, vol. 9058, pp. 127–142. Springer, Cham (2015). https://doi.org/10.1007/978-3-319-17524-9_10

18. Fainekos, G.E., Pappas, G.J.: Robustness of temporal logic specifications for continuous-time signals. Theor. Comput. Sci. 410(42), 4262–4291 (2009)

19. Faymonville, P., et al.: StreamLAB: stream-based monitoring of cyber-physical systems. In: Dillig, I., Tasiran, S. (eds.) CAV 2019. LNCS, vol. 11561, pp. 421–431. Springer, Cham (2019). https://doi.org/10.1007/978-3-030-25540-4_24

20. Jakšić, S., Bartocci, E., Grosu, R., Nguyen, T., Ničković, D.: Quantitative monitoring of STL with edit distance. Formal Methods Syst. Des. 53(1), 83–112 (2018). https://doi.org/10.1007/s10703-018-0319-x

21. Jakšić, S., Bartocci, E., Grosu, R., Ničković, D.: An algebraic framework for runtime verification. IEEE Trans. Comput. Aided Des. Integr. Circuits Syst. 37(11), 2233–2243 (2018)

22. Kahn, G.: The semantics of a simple language for parallel programming. Inf. Process. 74, 471–475 (1974)

23. Lemire, D.: Streaming maximum-minimum filter using no more than three comparisons per element. Nord. J. Comput. 13(4), 328–339 (2006)

24. Maler, O., Ničković, D.: Monitoring properties of analog and mixed-signal circuits. Int. J. Softw. Tools Technol. Transfer 15(3), 247–268 (2013)

25. Mamouras, K.: Semantic foundations for deterministic dataflow and stream processing. In: Müller, P., et al. (eds.) ESOP 2020. LNCS, vol. 12075, pp. 394–427. Springer, Cham (2020). https://doi.org/10.1007/978-3-030-44914-8_15

26. Mamouras, K., Raghothaman, M., Alur, R., Ives, Z.G., Khanna, S.: StreamQRE: modular specification and efficient evaluation of quantitative queries over streaming data. In: PLDI 2017, pp. 693–708. ACM (2017)

27. Mamouras, K., Wang, Z.: Online signal monitoring with bounded lag (2020). Accepted for publication in the IEEE Transactions on Computer-Aided Design of Integrated Circuits and Systems, ESWEEK-TCAD special issue (EMSOFT 2020)

28. Ničković, D., Lebeltel, O., Maler, O., Ferrère, T., Ulus, D.: AMT 2.0: qualitative and quantitative trace analysis with extended signal temporal logic. In: Beyer, D., Huisman, M. (eds.) TACAS 2018. LNCS, vol. 10806, pp. 303–319. Springer, Cham (2018). https://doi.org/10.1007/978-3-319-89963-3_18

29. Rodionova, A., Bartocci, E., Nickovic, D., Grosu, R.: Temporal logic as filtering. In: International Conference on Hybrid Systems: Computation and Control (HSCC 2016), pp. 11–20. ACM (2016)

30. Schneider, J., Basin, D., Krstić, S., Traytel, D.: A formally verified monitor for metric first-order temporal logic. In: Finkbeiner, B., Mariani, L. (eds.) RV 2019. LNCS, vol. 11757, pp. 310–328. Springer, Cham (2019). https://doi.org/10.1007/978-3-030-32079-9_18

31. Ulus, D.: Timescales: a benchmark generator for MTL monitoring tools. In: Finkbeiner, B., Mariani, L. (eds.) RV 2019. LNCS, vol. 11757, pp. 402–412. Springer, Cham (2019). https://doi.org/10.1007/978-3-030-32079-9_25
32. Ulus, D.: The Reelay monitoring tool (2020). https://doganulus.github.io/reelay/. Accessed 20 Aug 2020
33. Ulus, D., Ferrère, T., Asarin, E., Maler, O.: Timed pattern matching. In: Legay, A., Bozga, M. (eds.) FORMATS 2014. LNCS, vol. 8711, pp. 222–236. Springer, Cham (2014). https://doi.org/10.1007/978-3-319-10512-3_16

TLTk: A Toolbox for Parallel Robustness Computation of Temporal Logic Specifications

Joseph Cralley[1], Ourania Spantidi[1], Bardh Hoxha[2(✉)], and Georgios Fainekos[3]

[1] Southern Illinois University, Carbondale, IL 62901, USA
{jkolecr,ourania.spantidi}@siu.edu
[2] Toyota Research Institute North America, Ann Arbor, MI 48105, USA
bardh.hoxha@toyota.com
[3] Arizona State University, Tempe, AZ 85281, USA
fainekos@asu.edu

Abstract. This paper presents the Temporal Logic Toolkit (TLTk), a modular falsification tool for signal temporal logic specifications developed in Python and C. At the core of the tool, an algorithm for robustness computation is utilized that supports multi-threaded CPU/GPU computation. The tool enables memory-efficient, parallel, robustness computation of system traces. In addition, the python implementation enables the addition and modification of temporal operators for application-specific scenarios. The performance of the tool is evaluated against state-of-the-art robustness computation engines DP-TaLiRo and Breach on a number of benchmark problems.

Keywords: Testing · Temporal logic · Robustness

1 Introduction

The theory of robustness of temporal logics [13] has been utilized in a wide-array of problems, from testing and verification of Cyber-Physical Systems (CPS) to monitoring and planning for autonomous systems [10,13,15,29]. It enables the formulation of the falsification problem [22,25], i.e. the problem of finding system behaviors that do not meet system requirements, as a non-convex, non-linear optimization problem. The falsification process uses a notion of robustness to indicate how well a trajectory satisfies a requirement. This robustness estimate is defined using quantitative semantics of temporal logics such as STL (see [4] for an overview). The robustness indicates by how much a trajectory may be perturbed without changing the Boolean truth value of the specification. In the falsification process, the robustness is used to guide the optimization function to search for regions in the set of inputs and initial conditions of the system in which falsification is more likely.

Falsification, and the related problem of parameter mining [18,19,21], have been used successfully for testing industrial-size CPS. Both of these methods

© Springer Nature Switzerland AG 2020
J. Deshmukh and D. Ničković (Eds.): RV 2020, LNCS 12399, pp. 404–416, 2020.
https://doi.org/10.1007/978-3-030-60508-7_22

have been successfully used in a wide array of applications, from medical device testing [6], engine control testing [17,18,20], Unmanned Aerial Vehicles (UAV) scenario generation [29], to Automated Driving Systems [16,28]. In each optimization loop in the falsification process, the two main computational elements are the system simulator and the robustness computation engine. To improve this process, we introduce TLTk[1], a Python/C toolkit for requirements-based testing of CPS. TLTk is developed with the goal of optimizing the robustness computation engine as much as possible. At the core of the tool, a robustness computation engine that supports multi-threaded CPU and GPU computations is utilized. The memory-efficient algorithm enables robustness computations of large system traces. In addition, the robustness algorithm written in Python/C allows for easy modification/addition of temporal logic operators for application-specific implementations. This is particularly useful in areas such as planning for robotic applications since notions of robustness are usually application-specific.

TLTk supports falsification for STL specifications using only open-source software. Also, we provide a repository through the OS-virtualization engine Docker that allows easy integration with other tools or deployment in large-scale cloud systems like Amazon AWS, Google Cloud or Microsoft Azure. TLTk has been successfully utilized with several benchmark problems from the CPS community. The performance of the tool in comparison to state-of-the-art tools BREACH [9] and DP-TALIRO [11] is presented.

2   Overview and Features

TLTk is an object-oriented toolbox developed in `python3` (front-end) and C (back-end). An overview of the tool is presented in Fig. 1. The toolbox has the following core modules:

1) The **Stochastic Optimizer** module is developed in python and is utilized to generate candidate initial conditions and input signals for the system [1]. Our implementation utilizes global optimization algorithms provided by the SciPy library[2] such as Dual Annealing [30], as well as local optimization algorithms such as Nelder-Mead [24] for refinement. In addition, due to the modular architecture of the tool, the user may develop their own or utilize any other optimization libraries in python to conduct the search.

2) The **System Simulator** module may be a standalone function, an interface for Matlab/Simulink, or other simulators that support python-integration such as SymPy and Mathematica.

3) The **Robustness Computation Engine** module utilizes our C back-end implementation for fast robustness computation. The module utilizes multi-threaded CPU/GPU processing to compute the robustness of a trace with

---

[1] The source code for TLTk is publicly available through the GIT repository: https://bitbucket.org/versyslab/tltk/. Docker image: https://hub.docker.com/r/bardhh/tltk. Python package through PyPi: https://pypi.org/project/tltk-mtl/. User Guide: http://www.bhoxha.com/tltk.

[2] SciPy Optimize: https://docs.scipy.org/doc/scipy/reference/optimize.html.

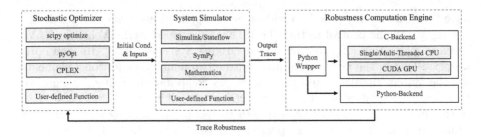

Fig. 1. An overview of TLTK and its major components.

respect to a specification in parallel. A python implementation is also available. Although much slower than the C implementation, the python implementation is developed to make the tool more accessible and also so that modifications to the robustness algorithm can be made easily for utilization in application-specific case studies and even topics such as planning. For example, in [15,23], the authors consider a smooth cumulative robustness, which modifies the semantics of temporal operators to include smoothing functions in order to make it more suitable for planning problems. For specifications with higher dimensional predicates, an optimization problem needs to be solved in order to compute the distance between a point in a trajectory to an unsafe set. Therefore, the back-end robustness calculation module additionally calls the quadratic program solver QuadProg[3]. To setup and run the tool, several options are available:

- *Building from Source* (Linux). This option provides the best performance. However, it is restricted to the Linux OS since we are using OpenMP[4] for parallel computation. The user needs to follow a set of commands provided in the User Guide to install software dependencies and compile the programs.
- *Running through Docker* (Linux, Windows, Mac). Docker enables a single command setup for the tool and all the required dependencies. Currently, GPU functionality is accessible only on Linux hosts[5]. The TLTK docker image can be pulled using the following command: `docker pull bardhh/tltk`.
- *Python API* (Linux). In addition to the previous methods, TLTK is available as a python package and can be installed through the `pip3` Python package installer using the following command: `pip3 install tltk_mtl`. Once the package is installed, it can be imported in any `python3` script and used for robustness computation.

---

[3] QuadProg: https://github.com/rmcgibbo/quadprog.

[4] OpenMP: https://www.openmp.org/.

[5] Nvidia has announced that support for this functionality in Windows OS is under development. https://devblogs.nvidia.com/announcing-cuda-on-windows-subsystem-for-linux-2/.

3 Robustness Computation

First, we review the quantitative semantics of STL specifications that enable us to define the robustness estimate. After that we propose a parallel algorithm for computing the robustness estimate efficiently.

3.1 Quantitative Semantics of STL Specifications

STL is an extension of LTL that enables reasoning over real-time properties of CPS. The syntax of STL is defined as follows:

$$\varphi ::= \top \mid p(x) \geq 0 \mid \neg\varphi \mid \varphi_1 \wedge \varphi_2 \mid \varphi_1 \mathcal{U}_I \varphi_2$$

where $\top$ is *true* and I is a nonsingular interval of positive reals. The eventually operator is defined as $\Diamond\phi \equiv \top \mathcal{U}_I \phi$ and the always operator is defined as $\Box_I \phi \equiv \neg\Diamond_I \neg\phi$. In order to define the quantitative semantics of STL over arbitrary predicates $p(x) \geq 0$, we use a metric d [13] to define the distance of a point $x \in X$ from a set $S \subseteq X$ as follows:

Definition 1 (Signed Distance). *Let $x \in X$ be a point, $S \subseteq X$ be a set and d be a metric on X. Then, we define the Signed Distance from x to S to be*

$$\mathbf{Dist}_d(x, S) := \begin{cases} -\inf\{d(x, y) \mid y \in S\} & \text{if } x \notin S \\ \inf\{d(x, y) \mid y \in X \backslash S\} & \text{if } x \in S \end{cases}$$

The signed distance returns positive values when x is inside set S and negative values when x is outside of set S.

Given a signal x and an STL specification φ, the quantitative semantics of STL enable us to obtain a robustness degree ρ that indicates how far the signal is from satisfying or violating the specification starting from a time instance t. Formally, the robustness of STL specifications is defined as follows:

$$\rho(\top, x, t) := \infty$$
$$\rho(p(x) \geq 0, x, t) := Dist_d(x(t), \{x \mid p(x) \geq 0\})$$
$$\rho(\neg\varphi, x, t) := -\rho(p, x, t)$$
$$\rho(\varphi_1 \wedge \varphi_2, x, t) := \min(\rho(\varphi_1, x, t), \rho(\varphi_2, x, t))$$
$$\rho(\varphi_1 \mathcal{U}_{[a,b]} \varphi_2, x, t) := \sup_{t' \in [t+a, t+b]} \min\left(\rho(\varphi_2, x, t'), \inf_{t'' \in [t, t']} \rho(\varphi_1, x, t'')\right)$$

3.2 Parallel Robustness Computation Algorithm in TLTk

The parallel robustness computation engine builds on the sliding window/dynamic programming algorithm developed in [9,31]. A tabular representation of subformulas of the specification (rows) and the trace samples (columns) of the signal is utilized. In the rows that contain only atomic predicates, quadratic programming is utilized to compute the cells since robustness requires computations of distances between a point and a set [12]. Since the sets defined by the predicates are strictly convex, we can use quadratic programming with low time complexity. This step is simplified when the predicates define a halfspace in $\mathbb{R}$. In this case, the distance may be computed analytically. Following the semantics of the robustness of temporal logic operators, the table can be dynamically collapsed to return a single robustness value for the entire trace.

Consider the specification $\phi = \Box \neg r_1$. The specification states that region r_1 should not be reached. In Fig. 2, an example trace and an illustration of the robustness computation process is presented. The robustness value of the trace with respect to the specification should return the minimum distance ρ^* between the sample point μ^* and the unsafe set r_1. To compute this, the distance of each sample $\mu_0, \mu_1, ..., \mu_i, ..., \mu_n$ to the unsafe set is computed (see Fig. 2 (b)). For each sample, a quadratic program is solved to return the distance to the unsafe set.

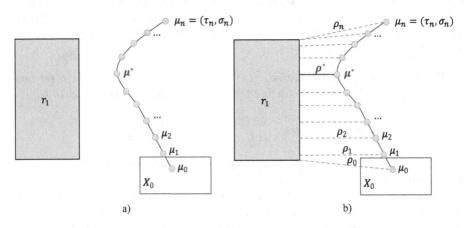

a)   b)

Fig. 2. An example system trajectory is presented. The specification on the system $\phi = \Box \neg r_1$ states that the trajectory should not enter set r_1. For each sample point μ_i the minimum distance ρ_i to the unsafe set r_1 is computed in parallel. The robustness of the trace is ρ^*, which indicates how much disturbance the trace can tolerate before it does not satisfy the requirement $\phi = \Box \neg r_1$ any more.

The worst-case time complexity of the robustness computation algorithm is $\mathcal{O}(|\varphi||\tau|c)$, where $|\varphi|$ is the length of the formula, $|\tau|$ is the number of samples, and c is the number of samples in the longest interval indicated by the timing constraints. We note that each temporal operator has a time interval associated with it and that the sampling rate is not necessarily constant. Even though the worst-case time complexity is the same as in the algorithm presented in [31], the modifications presented in this section significantly improve the running-time of the algorithm. Specifically, performance improvements are achieved due to parallel computation and more efficient memory management.

Parallel Computation: (i) Given a discrete output trace of the system composed of n time-value pairs, the robustness computation requires that for each predicate in the formula, the robustness should be computed n times. This process is parallelized in TLTK with multi-threaded CPU/GPU support. The dynamic programming algorithm generates a table with entries for each subformula and predicate. The bottom rows of the table are reserved for predicates and each distance to the unsafe set is computed in parallel. (ii) Once this is completed, the tree of subformulas is traversed in parallel to return the robustness. Furthermore, for rows with temporal operators that contain timing intervals, the computation of each cell in the table may be computed independently from the results in the adjacent cells, and therefore the entire row may be computed in parallel. The computation of n cells is broken up in n/c groups based on the number of threads c available. For each thread, a consecutive number of cells is computed. In this case, the sliding window algorithm utilizes the results from the adjacent cell to the right to compute the current cell. This reduces the number of operations within a thread by limiting the min/max operations to only new data in the window.

Average Running-time: For time bounded formulas, two improvements are made. (i) A modified binary search algorithm is developed that determines the indices that correspond to the time bounds. For every iteration of the algorithm, the indices are approximated based on the previous indices and then verified. In addition, as the formula is evaluated, the time bound under consideration is restricted to the remaining trace. (ii) For time bounded formulas, there is a sliding window reflecting the time bound of the formula. Since robustness computation is a sequence of min/max operations and most of the data in the current sliding window overlap with the previous window, we only need to consider the changes between the sliding windows to calculate the min/max of the current window.

Memory Management: By dynamically allocating and deallocating memory based on the structure of the formula, TLTK operates with a significantly smaller memory footprint. Initially, a formula φ is decomposed into a tree structure. For example, for $\varphi = \Diamond(\neg r_1 \wedge r_2)$, memory is allocated for predicates r_1 and r_2 and robustness is computed for the two predicates. Instead of allocating a new row for $\neg r_1$, an existing row where r_1 was stored is overwritten with the new values. After, the memory allocated for r_2 is utilized to store the robustness with respect to $\neg r_1 \wedge r_2$. The only additional row added is for the final expression of the eventually operator. This process is illustrated in Fig. 3. The worst case space complexity for the robustness computation is $\mathcal{O}(\beta \times |\tau|)$, where β is the number of predicates in the formula and $|\tau|$ is the number of timestamps. A row is preallocated for each predicate in the formula. We note that if a predicate is repeated in the formula, a memory row is allocated for each repetition. For any number of temporal operators, only one additional row needs to be preallocated. The length of each row is defined by the number of timestamps.

The robustness computation of the Always ($\Box$), Eventually ($\Diamond$), And ($\wedge$), Or ($\vee$), Not ($\neg$) and Until (U) operators is done in parallel in the C backend. The main program and interface of TLTK is implemented in Python. A wrapping function is utilized to ensure the execution of the C code from the

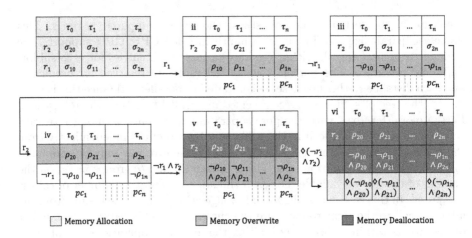

Fig. 3. A sample memory flow for the formula $\phi = \Diamond(\neg r_1 \wedge r_2)$. The initial memory allocation is shown in table (i) on the upper left corner. There are three rows allocated in total: two for the system output signals and one for the timestamps. In the next step, in table (ii), the memory that is allocated for the robustness calculations for r_1 is utilized. Similarly, in the next two steps, in tables $(iii$ and $iv)$, there is a memory overwrite for the formula $\neg r_1$ and robustness calculations for r_2. Next, in table (v), a memory overwrite occurs for the formula $\neg r_1 \wedge r_2$ and a memory deallocation for the r_2 distance row. Finally, in table (vi), there is a new memory allocation for the formula $\Diamond(\neg r_1 \wedge r_2)$, and memory deallocation for $\neg r_1 \wedge r_2$. The number of columns is divided by the number of available processor cores into groups. Each of these groups is processed in parallel.

Python interface. The algorithm and implementation details are presented in the extended technical report [7].

4   Evaluation and Experimental Results

In the following, we evaluate the robustness computation times on various trace sizes and temporal logic specifications. We compare the outcome to the well-known tools DP-TaLiRo [31] and Breach [9]. In more detail, we compare TLTk with Breach and DP-TaLiRo separately so that we may focus in the areas where they have the strongest performance. The comparison with Breach is focused on specifications with single-dimensional predicates, where the robustness of the predicates is computed through a subtraction of samples in a trajectory to the bound of the unsafe set. The comparison with DP-TaLiRo is focused on specifications with multi-dimensional predicates, where the robustness computation for the predicates requires a solution to a quadratic program. Note that Breach does not directly support robustness computations over multidimensional signal predicates. We highlight that in the following results, the TLTk robustness algorithm utilizes parallel processing, while the algorithms in DP-TaLiRo and Breach do not. We have verified the correctness of the robustness computation algorithm for each experimental result and, for ease of exposition, we focus the presentation on the computation time for the tools. The experiments were conducted on a desktop computer with the following specifications: CPU i7-8700K CPU @ 3.70 GHz, GPU GTX 1080Ti, 32 GiB DDR4 RAM and Ubuntu 18.04.3 LTS.

Comparison with Breach (version 1.7)[6]. We present the experimental comparison of TLTk with BREACH in Table 1. We compare the robustness computation of STL formulas with trace lengths ranging from 2^{10} to 2^{29}. The traces are checked against three STL specifications. A performance improvement of at least one order of magnitude can be observed.

Table 1. Comparison of computation times in seconds for TLTk and BREACH with various specifications and trajectory lengths. × indicates out of memory error instances.

2^x	φ_{b1}		φ_{b2}		φ_{b3}	
	TLTK	BREACH	TLTK	BREACH	TLTK	BREACH
10	0.00007	0.00350	0.00009	0.03343	0.00010	0.03588
14	0.00005	0.00935	0.00007	0.00480	0.00022	0.01243
18	0.00057	0.02322	0.00083	0.02862	0.00223	0.10138
22	0.00683	0.30040	0.01305	0.47182	0.03549	1.69170
26	0.10719	5.30410	0.21444	8.58840	0.56538	30.24000
27	0.21375	10.67300	0.42656	17.31700	1.12633	60.25600
28	0.42930	186.82000	0.85081	107.89000	2.24889	×
29	0.85353	×	1.69901	×	4.49088	×

Specification	Predicates
$\phi_{b1} = \neg(\Diamond s_1)$	$s_1 : speed(t) > 160$
$\phi_{b2} = \neg(\Diamond_{[0,1000]}s_1 \wedge \Box_{[100,300]}r_1)$	$r_1 : rpm(t) < 4500$
$\phi_{b3} = \neg(\Diamond_{[0,1000]}s_1 \wedge \Box_{[0,200]}(r_1 \wedge \Box(\Diamond(s_1 \wedge (s_1 \mathcal{U} r_1)))$	

Comparison with DP-TaLiRo (version 1.6)[7]. The experimental comparison of TLTk with DP-TALIRO is presented in Table 2. The comparison is conducted using formulas that are defined for several benchmark problems. Specifically, requirements for the aircraftODE [27] (ϕ_{s1}), Navigation [27] (ϕ_{s2}), Heat Transfer [14] (ϕ_{s6}) and Nonlinear [1] (ϕ_{s3-s5}) Systems. The specifications are defined in Table 3. A performance improvement of at least two orders of magnitude can be observed.

---

[6] BREACH 1.7 downloaded on 01.16.2020 from https://github.com/decyphir/breach.

[7] DP-TALIRO is part of S-TALIRO toolbox version 1.6. The tool was downloaded on 01.16.2020 from https://app.assembla.com/spaces/s-taliro_public/.

Table 2. Comparison of computation times in seconds for TLTk and DP-TaLiRo with various trajectory sizes. Specifications φ_{s1} through φ_{s6} and the predicate definitions can be found in Table 3. Symbol × indicates out of memory instances.

2^x	φ_{s1}		φ_{s2}		φ_{s3}	
	TLTk	DP-TaLiRo	TLTk	DP-TaLiRo	TLTk	DP-TaLiRo
10	0.0023	1.5819	0.0028	1.5995	0.0018	1.8497
12	0.0087	6.3102	0.0106	6.3334	0.0081	7.0429
14	0.0295	25.1800	0.0361	25.3340	0.0252	28.1650
16	0.1118	100.6800	0.1375	101.3300	0.1002	112.6400
18	0.4429	403.1900	0.5334	405.1800	0.4013	450.4800
20	1.7296	1610.3000	2.1250	1621.0000	1.6054	1802.5000
21	3.5078	3222.3000	4.2977	3240.0000	3.2694	3604.3000
22	7.0906	×	8.5688	×	6.4353	×
23	14.0333	×	17.1810	×	13.0045	×
24	28.0057	×	34.2625	×	26.3092	×

2^x	φ_{s4}		φ_{s5}		φ_{s6}	
	TLTk	DP-TaLiRo	TLTk	DP-TaLiRo	TLTk	DP-TaLiRo
10	0.0018	4.3029	0.0022	6.8373	0.0072	5.6698
12	0.0081	17.2180	0.0082	27.4090	0.0211	3.1871
14	0.0257	68.8750	0.0256	109.5900	0.0843	12.7620
16	0.1012	275.4100	0.1021	438.5200	0.3409	51.0760
18	0.4030	1102.0000	0.4097	1753.2000	1.3448	204.0600
20	1.6301	4402.8000	1.6199	7014.8000	5.4648	816.7000
21	3.2396	8805.1000	3.2225	14023.0000	10.9827	1632.2000
22	6.4321	×	6.4926	×	21.8416	×
23	12.8838	×	13.1343	×	43.2679	×
24	25.6910	×	26.0209	×	87.0204	×

5   Related Works

TLTk was inspired by the Matlab toolboxes S-TaLiRo [3,11] and Breach [9]. All three tools provide an automated test-case generation process for finding system behaviors that falsify temporal logic specifications. In addition to falsification, these tools provide methods for requirement mining, conformance testing and real-time monitoring. They provide various optimization algorithms for black-box and grey-box testing. A different approach to falsification is utilized in the tool FalStar [32]. In FalStar, the falsifying system behavior is generated by constructing the input signal incrementally in time. This is particularly useful for reactive specifications. In another tool, **falsify** [2], the program solves the falsification problem through reinforcement learning. The tool attempts to find a falsification by observing the output signal and modifying the input signal during system simulation. A trajectory splicing/multiple shooting approach

Table 3. Specifications and predicates for the Signal Temporal Logic specifications utilized for the comparison between TLTK and S-TALIRO.

MTL Specifications and Predicates	
$\phi_{s1} = \neg(\Box_{[5,150]}r_3 \wedge \Diamond_{[300,400]}r_4)$ $r_3 : A_{s1} * x \leq [250\ {-}240]^T,$ $r_4 : A_{s1} * x \leq [240\ {-}230]^T$	$A_{s1} = \begin{bmatrix} 1 & 0 & 0 \\ -1 & 0 & 0 \end{bmatrix}$
$\phi_{s2} = (\neg p_{11})\mathcal{U}p_{12}$ where $p_{11} : A_{s2} * x \leq [3.8\ {-}3.2\ 0.8\ {-}0.2]^T,$ $p_{12} : A_{s2} * x \leq [3.8\ {-}3.2\ 1.8\ {-}1.2]^T$	$A_{s2} = \begin{bmatrix} 1 & 0 & 0 & 0 \\ -1 & 0 & 0 & 0 \\ 0 & 1 & 0 & 0 \\ 0 & -1 & 0 & 0 \end{bmatrix}$
$\phi_{s3} = \Box(r_7 \wedge \Diamond_{[0,100]}r_8)$ $\phi_{s4} = \neg(\Diamond r_7 \wedge \Box(r_8 \wedge \Box(\Diamond(r_7 \wedge (r_7\mathcal{U}r_8)))))$ $\phi_{s5} = \neg(\Diamond r_7 \wedge \Box(r_8 \wedge \Box(\Diamond(r_7 \wedge (r_7\mathcal{U}r_8)))))\wedge$ $\qquad \Diamond(\Box(r_7 \vee (r_8\mathcal{U}r_7))))$ $r_7 : A_{s345} * x \leq [1.6\ {-}1.4\ 1.1\ {-}0.9]^T,$ $r_8 : A_{s345} * x \leq [1.5\ {-}1.2\ 1.0\ {-}1.0]^T$	$A_{s345} = \begin{bmatrix} -1 & 0 \\ 1 & 0 \\ 0 & -1 \\ 0 & 1 \end{bmatrix}$
$\phi_{s6} = \Box p$ $p : A_{s6} * x \leq$ $\qquad [14.5\ 14.5\ 13.5\ 14\ 13\ 14\ 14\ 13\ 13.5\ 14]^T$	$A_{s6} = I(10)$

is utilized in the tool S3CAM [33], which explores the state-space of CPS and splices trace segments to find a path from one state to another. This approach was later extended to incorporate symbolic reachability techniques in the tool XSPEED [5]. To enable monitoring of temporal logic specifications in robotic systems, in [26], the authors present RTAMT, which offers integration with ROS and supports monitoring of past and future time specifications.

6   Conclusion and Future Work

We have presented TLTK, a tool for falsification and parallel robustness computation of STL specifications. The modular architecture of the tool enables integration with any stochastic optimization algorithm or system simulator available in Python. The experimental results demonstrate that the multi-threaded CPU/GPU robustness engine shows a runtime improvement of at least one order of magnitude in comparison to BREACH and DP-TALIRO.

The robustness computation engine may be improved through syntactic analysis of the specifications to remove potentially redundant subformulas [8], or prioritizing results that imply results for other subformulas. In addition, as part of future work, the GPU algorithm may be improved further. In the current implementation, GPU computations are called for each predicate and temporal operator in the formula. This process causes an overhead when transferring the system trace to the GPU memory for each call. In addition, we plan to add requirement mining functionality as well as integration with ROS. Among our goals is to use the tool for planning and control of robotic systems.

References

1. Abbas, H., Fainekos, G.E., Sankaranarayanan, S., Ivancic, F., Gupta, A.: Probabilistic temporal logic falsification of cyber-physical systems. ACM Trans. Embed. Comput. Syst. **12**(s2), 1–30 (2013)
2. Akazaki, T., Liu, S., Yamagata, Y., Duan, Y., Hao, J.: Falsification of cyber-physical systems using deep reinforcement learning. In: Havelund, K., Peleska, J., Roscoe, B., de Vink, E. (eds.) FM 2018. LNCS, vol. 10951, pp. 456–465. Springer, Cham (2018). https://doi.org/10.1007/978-3-319-95582-7_27
3. Annpureddy, Y., Liu, C., Fainekos, G., Sankaranarayanan, S.: S-TALiRo: a tool for temporal logic falsification for hybrid systems. In: Abdulla, P.A., Leino, K.R.M. (eds.) TACAS 2011. LNCS, vol. 6605, pp. 254–257. Springer, Heidelberg (2011). https://doi.org/10.1007/978-3-642-19835-9_21
4. Bartocci, E., et al.: Specification-based monitoring of cyber-physical systems: a survey on theory, tools and applications. In: Bartocci, E., Falcone, Y. (eds.) Lectures on Runtime Verification. LNCS, vol. 10457, pp. 135–175. Springer, Cham (2018). https://doi.org/10.1007/978-3-319-75632-5_5
5. Bogomolov, S., Frehse, G., Gurung, A., Li, D., Martius, G., Ray, R.: Falsification of hybrid systems using symbolic reachability and trajectory splicing. In: Proceedings of the 22nd ACM International Conference on Hybrid Systems: Computation and Control, pp. 1–10 (2019)
6. Cameron, F., Fainekos, G., Maahs, D.M., Sankaranarayanan, S.: Towards a verified artificial pancreas: challenges and solutions for runtime verification. In: Bartocci, E., Majumdar, R. (eds.) RV 2015. LNCS, vol. 9333, pp. 3–17. Springer, Cham (2015). https://doi.org/10.1007/978-3-319-23820-3_1
7. Cralley, J., Spantidi, O., Hoxha, B., Fainekos, G.: Tltk: toolbox for parallel robustness computation of temporal logic specifications extended version (2020). http://bhoxha.com/papers/TLTk_ExtendedReport.pdf
8. Dokhanchi, A., Hoxha, B., Fainekos, G.: Formal requirement debugging for testing and verification of cyber-physical systems. ACM Trans. Embed. Comput. Syst. (TECS) **17**(2), 34 (2018)
9. Donzé, A.: Breach, a toolbox for verification and parameter synthesis of hybrid systems. In: Touili, T., Cook, B., Jackson, P. (eds.) CAV 2010. LNCS, vol. 6174, pp. 167–170. Springer, Heidelberg (2010). https://doi.org/10.1007/978-3-642-14295-6_17
10. Donzé, A., Ferrère, T., Maler, O.: Efficient robust monitoring for STL. In: Sharygina, N., Veith, H. (eds.) CAV 2013. LNCS, vol. 8044, pp. 264–279. Springer, Heidelberg (2013). https://doi.org/10.1007/978-3-642-39799-8_19
11. Fainekos, G., Hoxha, B., Sankaranarayanan, S.: Robustness of specifications and its applications to falsification, parameter mining, and runtime monitoring with S-TaLiRo. In: Finkbeiner, B., Mariani, L. (eds.) RV 2019. LNCS, vol. 11757, pp. 27–47. Springer, Cham (2019). https://doi.org/10.1007/978-3-030-32079-9_3
12. Fainekos, G.E., Girard, A., Kress-Gazit, H., Pappas, G.J.: Temporal logic motion planning for dynamic robots. Automatica **45**(2), 343–352 (2009)

13. Fainekos, G.E., Pappas, G.J.: Robustness of temporal logic specifications for continuous-time signals. Theoret. Comput. Sci. **410**(42), 4262–4291 (2009)
14. Fehnker, A., Ivančić, F.: Benchmarks for hybrid systems verification. In: Alur, R., Pappas, G.J. (eds.) HSCC 2004. LNCS, vol. 2993, pp. 326–341. Springer, Heidelberg (2004). https://doi.org/10.1007/978-3-540-24743-2_22
15. Haghighi, I., Mehdipour, N., Bartocci, E., Belta, C.: Control from signal temporal logic specifications with smooth cumulative quantitative semantics. arXiv preprint arXiv:1904.11611 (2019)
16. Hekmatnejad, M., Hoxha, B., Fainekos, G.: Search-based test-case generation by monitoring responsibility safety rules. In: 2020 IEEE Intelligent Transportation Systems Conference (ITSC). IEEE (2020)
17. Hoxha, B., Abbas, H., Fainekos, G.: Using s-taliro on industrial size automotive models. In: Proceedings of Applied Verification for Continuous and Hybrid Systems (2014)
18. Hoxha, B., Abbas, H., Fainekos, G.: Benchmarks for temporal logic requirements for automotive systems. In: Workshop on Applied Verification for Continuous and Hybrid Systems (2014)
19. Hoxha, B., Dokhanchi, A., Fainekos, G.: Mining parametric temporal logic properties in model based design for cyber-physical systems. Int. J. Softw. Tools Technol. Transf. **20**, 79–93 (2018). https://doi.org/10.1007/s10009-017-0447-4
20. Jin, X., Deshmukh, J.V., Kapinski, J., Ueda, K., Butts, K.: Powertrain control verification benchmark. In: Proceedings of Hybrid Systems: Computation and Control (2014, to appear)
21. Jin, X., Donzé, A., Deshmukh, J.V., Seshia, S.A.: Mining requirements from closed-loop control models. IEEE Trans. Comput. Aided Des. Integr. Circuits Syst. **34**(11), 1704–1717 (2015)
22. Kapinski, J., Deshmukh, J.V., Jin, X., Ito, H., Butts, K.: Simulation-based approaches for verification of embedded control systems: an overview of traditional and advanced modeling, testing, and verification techniques. IEEE Control Syst. **36**(6), 45–64 (2016)
23. Leung, K., Aréchiga, N., Pavone, M.: Backpropagation for parametric STL. In: 2019 IEEE Intelligent Vehicles Symposium (IV), pp. 185–192. IEEE (2019)
24. Nelder, J.A., Mead, R.: A simplex method for function minimization. Comput. J. **7**(4), 308–313 (1965)
25. Nghiem, T., Sankaranarayanan, S., Fainekos, G.E., Ivancic, F., Gupta, A., Pappas, G.J.: Monte-Carlo techniques for falsification of temporal properties of non-linear hybrid systems. In: Proceedings of the 13th ACM International Conference on Hybrid Systems: Computation and Control, pp. 211–220. ACM Press (2010)
26. Nickovic, D., Yamaguchi, T.: Rtamt: online robustness monitors from STL. arXiv preprint arXiv:2005.11827 (2020)
27. Sankaranarayanan, S., Fainekos, G.: Falsification of temporal properties of hybrid systems using the cross-entropy method. In: ACM International Conference on Hybrid Systems: Computation and Control (2012)
28. Tuncali, C.E., Fainekos, G., Ito, H., Kapinski, J.: Simulation-based adversarial test generation for autonomous vehicles with machine learning components. In: IEEE Intelligent Vehicles Symposium (IV) (2018)
29. Tuncali, C.E., Hoxha, B., Ding, G., Fainekos, G., Sankaranarayanan, S.: Experience report: application of falsification methods on the UxAS system. In: Dutle, A., Muñoz, C., Narkawicz, A. (eds.) NFM 2018. LNCS, vol. 10811, pp. 452–459. Springer, Cham (2018). https://doi.org/10.1007/978-3-319-77935-5_30

30. Xiang, Y., Sun, D., Fan, W., Gong, X.: Generalized simulated annealing algorithm and its application to the Thomson model. Phys. Lett. A **233**(3), 216–220 (1997)
31. Yang, H.: Dynamic programming algorithm for computing temporal logic robustness. Master's thesis, Arizona State University (2013)
32. Zhang, Z., Ernst, G., Sedwards, S., Arcaini, P., Hasuo, I.: Two-layered falsification of hybrid systems guided by Monte Carlo tree search. IEEE Trans. CAD Integr. Circuits Syst. **37**(11), 2894–2905 (2018)
33. Zutshi, A., Deshmukh, J.V., Sankaranarayanan, S., Kapinski, J.: Multiple shooting, cegar-based falsification for hybrid systems. In: Proceedings of the 14th International Conference on Embedded Software, pp. 1–10 (2014)

MoonLight: A Lightweight Tool for Monitoring Spatio-Temporal Properties

Ezio Bartocci[1], Luca Bortolussi[2], Michele Loreti[3], Laura Nenzi[1,2(✉)], and Simone Silvetti[4]

[1] TU Wien, Vienna, Austria
`laura.nenzi@tuwien.ac.at`
[2] DMG, University of Trieste, Trieste, Italy
[3] University of Camerino, Camerino, Italy
[4] Esteco S.p.A., Trieste, Italy

Abstract. We present MOONLIGHT, a tool for monitoring temporal and spatio-temporal properties of mobile and spatially distributed cyber-physical systems (CPS). In the proposed framework, space is represented as a weighted graph, describing the topological configurations in which the single CPS entities (nodes of the graph) are arranged. Both nodes and edges have attributes modelling physical and logical quantities that can change in time. MOONLIGHT is implemented in Java and supports the monitoring of Spatio-Temporal Reach and Escape Logic (STREL) introduced in [6]. MOONLIGHT can be used as a standalone command line tool, as a Java API, or via MATLAB ᵀᴹ interface. We provide here some examples using the MATLAB ᵀᴹ interface and we evaluate the tool performance also by comparing with other tools specialized in monitoring only temporal properties.

1 Introduction

Cyber-physical systems [24] (CPS) are a widespread class of technological arte-facts that include contact tracing devices, self-driving cars, mobile ad-hoc sensor networks and smart cities. CPS are controlled by a computational device and interact within the physical space. As such, they are described by discrete states, controlling actuators, and continuous quantities, measured by sensors, which can both change in time. CPS are arranged in spatial configurations that can be static or dynamic. Their network connectivity can typically change in time.

A fundamental task in engineering CPS is monitoring their behaviors, speci-fied in a suitable formal language, such as Signal Temporal Logic (STL) [18,19]. Monitoring can be performed on a deployed system or on simulations of a model,

This research has been partially supported by the Austrian FWF projects ZK-35 and W1255-N23, by the Italian PRIN project "SEDUCE" n. 2017TWRCNB and by the Italian PRIN project "IT-MaTTerS" n, 2017FTXR7S.

© Springer Nature Switzerland AG 2020
J. Deshmukh and D. Ničković (Eds.): RV 2020, LNCS 12399, pp. 417–428, 2020.
https://doi.org/10.1007/978-3-030-60508-7_23

as typically done in the design phase to test different initial conditions, parameters and inputs [4,7]. Monitoring a trace returns either a Boolean value, witnessing whether the requirement is satisfied or not, or a quantitative value, for instance a real-value indicating how much the specification is satisfied or violated according to a chosen notion of distance [5,10,13,14,25].

Current tools available for monitoring formal specifications are restricted to temporal properties, mostly ignoring the spatial dimension of CPS [4,7].

Our Contribution. We present MOONLIGHT, a lightweight tool for monitoring temporal and spatio-temporal properties of spatially distributed CPS, which can move in space and change their connectivity (mobile CPS). MOONLIGHT is implemented in Java and supports monitoring of Spatio-Temporal Reach and Escape Logic (STREL), a spatio-temporal specification language introduced in [6]. STREL extends STL [18,19] with two main spatial operators *reach* and *escape* from which is possible to derive many other spatial operators (e.g., *everywhere, somewhere* and *surround*). Our implementation is available at: https://github.com/MoonLightSuite/MoonLight. MOONLIGHT can be used: as a standalone command line tool, as a Java API, or via MATLAB ^{TM} interface. In this paper, we describe the usage of MOONLIGHT via MATLAB ^{TM} interface because several CPS models and analysis tools are available for this framework. We refer to the documentation for the other usage possibilities.

MOONLIGHT takes as input a STREL formula and a spatio-temporal trajectory. Space is represented as a weighted graph, describing the topological configurations in which the CPS entities are arranged. Nodes represent single entities. Both nodes and edges have attributes modelling physical and logical quantities that can change in time. Therefore, a spatio-temporal signal, in the most general case, is described by a sequence of such weighted graphs, allowing both spatial arrangement and attributes to change in time. MOONLIGHT monitors such a sequence of graphs with respect to a STREL formula, returning a Boolean or a quantitative verdict, according to the semantic rules of [6].

Related Work. Monitoring tools for CPS are generally agnostic of the spatial configuration of the entities such as sensors and computational units. They are limited to monitor temporal specifications over time series of data. Examples are S-Taliro [2] for Metric Temporal Logic (MTL) [15], R2U2 [20] for Mission Linear Temporal Logic (MLTL) [20], AMT [23] and Breach [9] for Signal Temporal Logic (STL) [18,19], TeSSLa [16] and RTLola [8] for temporal stream-based specification languages and Montre [26] for Timed Regular Expressions (TRE) [3]. However, temporal specification languages are not always expressive enough to capture the rich and complex spatio-temporal patterns that CPS display. For this reason, many researchers have extended temporal specification languages such as STL to express also spatial requirements. Examples include Spatial-Temporal Logic (SpaTeL) [11], the Signal Spatio-Temporal Logic (SSTL) [21], the Spatial Aggregation Signal Temporal Logic (SaSTL) [17] and STREL [6]. Despite many developed prototypes built more for demonstration purposes rather than becoming usable tools, we are aware only about JSSTL [22] as offline monitoring tool for spatio-temporal properties. JSSTL [22] supports SSTL and operates over a *static* topological space, while the tool proposed in this paper can also monitor *dynamical locations*, such as in mobile wireless sensor networks.

2 MoonLight in a Nutshell

The main component of MOONLIGHT is its Java Application Programming Interface (API): a set of specialized classes and interfaces to manage *data domains* and *signals*, to represent *spatial models* that can evolve in time, to *monitor temporal and spatio-temporal properties* and to manage input/output to/from *generic data sources*. Moreover, it also contains a *compiler* that generates the necessary Java classes for monitoring from a MOONLIGHT script. The latter are built and dynamically loaded to enable the monitoring of the specified properties.

MOONLIGHT provides also an interface that enables the integration of its monitoring features in MATLAB^{TM}. We now first introduce a simple running example to guide the reader on how to monitor spatial-temporal properties. Then, we present a MOONLIGHT script together with a gentle introduction of formulas semantics. Finally, we show how MOONLIGHT can be used in the MATLAB^{TM} environment.

2.1 Running Example

A running example is used to describe the behaviour of our tool. We consider a wireless ad-hoc sensor network [1] consisting of three different types of mobile device: *coordinator, router, end-device*. For each network, there is only one coordinator that is responsible to initialize the network. The routers are responsible for passing data on from other devices and they establish a mesh network of intermediate devices to reach more distant ones. The end-devices can only communicate with router or coordinator, and they cannot relay data from other devices. We assume that all the devices are battery-powered and they are equipped with sensors enabling them to measure and collect data from the environment (e.g. pollution, temperature, etc.).

Figure 1 illustrates a network with 10 nodes (1 coordinator (C) in violet, 2 routers (R) in cyan and 7 end devices (E) in yellow). The nodes are distributed in an Euclidean space, i.e. axis represent their coordinates in the space. The edges represent the connectivity graph of the network, expressing the fact that two devices can directly *interact* (i.e. they are within their communication range).

In MOONLIGHT, the space is modelled as a graph, where each node represents a location containing mixed-analog signals while each edge represents a topological relation. Edges are labelled with one or more quantitative attributes describing additional information about the spatial structure. In our example, the sensor network is our graph, each device represents a node/location of the network and contains three signals evolving in time: the type of node (coordinator, router, end-device), the level of battery, and the temperature. The edges are labelled with both their Euclidean distance and with the integer value 1. This last value is used to compute the hop (shortest path) count between two nodes, that is the number of intermediate network nodes through which data must pass between source node and target one.

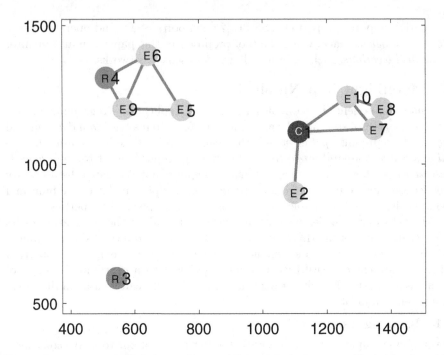

Fig. 1. Sensor network with 1 coordinator (C, in violet), 2 routers (R, in cyan) and 7 end devices (E, in yellow). (Color figure online)

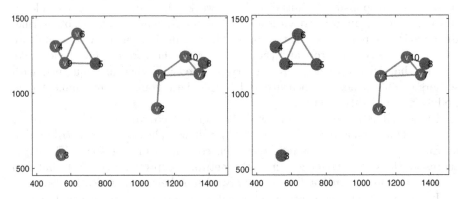

Fig. 2. (**left**) Boolean satisfaction of formula P1, (blue nodes (V) satisfy the formula), red nodes do not satisfy the formula.(**right**) Boolean satisfaction of formula P4, (blue nodes (V) satisfy the formula), red nodes do not satisfy the formula. (Color figure online)

MOONLIGHT evaluates properties specified in the linear-time spatio-temporal logic STREL over spatio-temporal signals, i.e. functions mapping each node and time instant into a vector of values, describing the internal state of each location. In the following, we show how to use the MOONLIGHT scripting language to specify spatio-temporal properties and how to monitor them.

```
1 signal { int nodeType;  real battery;  real temperature; }
2 space { edges { int hop; real dist; } }
3 domain boolean;
4 formula atom = (nodeType==3);
5 formula P1 = atom reach(hop)[0,
     1]{(nodeType==1)|(nodeType==2)};
6 formula Ppar(int k) = atom reach(hop)[0, k] (nodeType== 1);
```

Fig. 3. Example of Moonlight monitor script specification, corresponding to the sensorNetMonitorScript.mls of line 1 in Fig. 5.

2.2 MoonLight Script

A monitor in MOONLIGHT is specified via a MOONLIGHT script. Figure 3 reportes an example that specifies the necessary information to instrument a monitor for our sensor network.

The script (line 1) starts with the definition of the domains of input signal. We recall that STREL is interpreted over spatio-temporal signals. In our scenario, these values are: the type of node, the temperature level and the battery level. As domains, the node type is represented by an integer (int) and the battery and temperature by real values (real). Spatial structures in STREL can change over time. This enables the modelling of the mobile network of sensors as in our example by updating edges and edge labels. The edges can have more than one label with different domains. These are specified in line 2 of our example. In this case we have two labels: hop having type int domain, and dist with type real. Note that, if one is only interested in temporal properties, this part is omitted in the script.

MOONLIGHT, like STREL, supports different semantics for monitoring. A user can specify the desired one by indicating the specific *monitoring domain* (see line 3). Currently, MOONLIGHT supports qualitative (boolean) and quantitative (minmax) semantics of STREL.

After this initial declaration, the script contains the list of formulas that can be monitored (see lines 4–6). Formulas can have parameters that are instantiated when monitoring is performed. A formula can be used within another formula.

The syntax of STREL is summarized in Fig. 4. The atomic expression consists of *Boolean expressions* on signal variables like, for instance, (battery > 0.5) or (nodeType == 2). As expected, the interpretation of atomic formulas depends on the domain of the monitoring.

Formulas are built by using standard Boolean operators (negation !, conjunction &, disjunction |, and implication =>) together with a set of temporal and spatial modalities.

Temporal properties are specified via the standard until and since operators (see e.g. [18,19]) from which we can derive the future eventually and globally operators and the corresponding past variants, once and historically. All these operators may take an interval of the form [a,b], with $\mathbf{a},\mathbf{b} \in \mathbb{R}_{\geq 0}$, to define where the property should be evaluated. The interval can be omitted in case of unbounded temporal operators.

Spatial modalities, instead, are **reach** and **escape** operators, and the derivable operators **somewhere** and **everywhere**. All these operators may be decorated with a *distance interval* [a,b] and a *distance expression*. The distance expression consists of an expression that is used to compute the *length* of an edge. If omitted, the real value 1.0 is used.

```
 1          (atomicExpression)
 2        | ! Formula
 3        | Formula & Formula
 4        | Formula | Formula
 5        | Formula => Formula
 6        | Formula until [a b] Formula
 7        | Formula since [a b] Formula
 8        | eventually [a b] Formula
 9        | globally [a b] Formula
10        | once [a b] Formula
11        | historically [a b] Formula
12        | escape(distanceExpression)[a b] Formula
13        | Formula reach (distanceExpression)[a b] Formula
14        | somewhere(distanceExpression) [a b] Formula
15        | everywhere (distanceExpression) [a b] Formula
16        | {Formula}
```

Fig. 4. STREL syntax.

To describe the spatial operators, we consider some examples. Let us first consider the following property of the script:

P1 = (nodeType==3)reach(hop)[0, 1]{(nodeType==1)|(nodeType==2)}

P1 holds if from a node of type 3 (an *end device*), we can reach a node of type 1 or 2 (a *coordinator* or a *router*), following a path in the spatial graph such that the **hop** distance along this path (i.e. its number of edges) is not bigger than 1. This property specifies that *"end device should be directly connected to a router or the coordinator"*.

The **reach** operator allows us to express properties related to the existence of a path. The other operator of STREL, **escape**, can be used to express the ability of move away from a given point. Let us consider the following property:

P2 = escape(hop)[5,inf] (battery > 0.5)

P2 states that from a given location, we can find a path of (hop) length at least 5 such that all nodes along the path have a battery level greater than 0.5, i.e. that a message will be forwarded along a connection with no risk of power failure.

To specify properties *around* a given location, operators `somewhere` and `everywhere` can be used. For instance, we can consider the following property:

```
P3 = somewhere(dist)[0,250] (battery > 0.5))
```

P3 is satisfied (at a given location) whenever there is a node at a distance between 0 and 250 having a `battery` greater than 0.5. In this formula the distance is computed by summing the value `dist` of traversed edges. The `everywhere` operators works in a similar way, however it requires that its subformula holds in all nodes satisfying the distance constraints.

Note that both `reach` and `escape` are existential operators, as they predicate the existence of a path with certain properties, and all the properties are interpreted at a given location, at a given time. Temporal and spatial operators can be nested as for example:

```
PT1 = (battery <= 0.5)reach(hop)[0, 10] eventually(battery > 0.5)
```

PT1 holds if each node can reach a node in less than 10 hops where the battery is greater than 0.5 in at least one time step in the next 5 time units. We will show a second example later, but for more formal details and examples about STREL, we refer to [6] and the to tool documentation.

2.3 Using MoonLight in Matlab ™

To use MOONLIGHT in MATLAB ™ one has just to run the installation script (named `install.m`) distributed with MOONLIGHT. A detailed description of the installation process is available at the tool web site. After this installation, MOONLIGHT becomes available to be used in the MATLAB ™ environment. In Fig. 5 a simple example is presented showing the main features of this module.

```
1  s = ScriptLoader.loadFromFile("sensorNetMonitorScript");
2  m = s.getMonitor("Ppar");
3  param = 5;
4  br = m.monitor(spatialModel,time,values,param);
5  script.setMinMaxDomain();
6  rr = m.monitor(spatialModel,time,values,param);
```

Fig. 5. Example of MATLAB™ script that uses MOONLIGHT

The function `ScriptLoader.loadFromFile` loads the script. It takes as parameter the file name containing the script to load (see line 1). After this operation is performed, a Java class is generated from the script and dynamically loaded. A reference to this object is returned to be used later. In the provided code, the script of Fig. 3 is loaded from the file `sensorNetMonitorScript`.

After a script is loaded, the *monitors* defined inside can be instantiated. In the example of Fig. 5 the monitor associated with formula named `Ppar` is retrieved (line 2). When we have the monitor we can use it to verify the satisfaction of the property over a given spatio-temporal signal. This is done by invoking the method `monitor` of the just loaded monitor. This function takes the following parameters:

- `spatialModel` is an array of MATLAB ^{TM} graph structures specifying the spatial structure at each point in time; in the sensor network example, for each time step `i`, `spatialModel{i}.Edges` represents the adjacent list of the graph. This input is omitted when purely temporal models are considered.
- `time` is an array of time points at which observations are provided.
- `values` is a map (a cell array), with a cell for each node. In each cell, there is a matrix $n \times m$ where each row represents the values of the signals at the time points specified by `time` (with n equal to the number of time points and m the number of the considered signals); in the sensor network example, each node has a 3 signals representing the node's type, battery, and temperature. We represent different types of nodes using integer numbers, 1, 2, and 3 to represents *coordinator*, *router*, and *end-device* respectively. This input is a simple matrix in case of purely temporal models.
- `param` is used to instantiate the parameter `k` of formula `Ppar`.

The output `br` from line 4 in Fig. 5 is similar to the input signal. It is a map that associates a Boolean-value (for the Boolean semantics) or a real-value signal (for the quantitative semantics) with each node, i.e. the Boolean or quantitative satisfaction at each time in each node. Finally, line 5 shows how to set the quantitative semantics (in the Boolean case: `moonlightScript.setBooleanDomain()`).

In Fig. 2 (left), we can see the Boolean satisfaction at time zero of each node with respect the formula P1 of our script example in Fig. 3. The blue nodes (marked with a V) on the plot of Fig. 2(left) correspond to the nodes that satisfies the property, i.e. the end devices that reach a router or a coordinator with at most 1 hop. Figure 2 (right) shows the satisfaction of formula:

```
P4=(nodeType==3)reach(hop)[0,1]{(nodeType==2)reach(hop)[0,5](nodeType==1)}
```

P4 holds only in the nodes connected directly to the coordinator or to routers that can reach the coordinator through a maximum of four other routers. We can see that nodes 3, 4, 5 and 9 satisfy P1 but not P4. Property `PT2 = globally P4` can be used to check that P4 is true in each time step.

3   Experimental Evaluation

Our experiments were performed on a workstation with an Intel Core i7-5820K (6 cores, 3.30GHz) and 32GB RAM, running Linux Ubuntu 16.04.6 LTS, MATLAB ^{TM} R2020a and OPENJDK 64-Bit Server VM 1.8.0_252.

3.1   Temporal Evaluation: Monitoring Signal Temporal Logic

We consider the *Automatic Transmission* example in [12]. This benchmark consists of a MATLAB ^{TM}/Simulink deterministic model of an automatic transmission controller. The model has two inputs (the throttle and the break) and two outputs: the speed of the engine ω (RPM) and the speed of the vehicle v (mph). We monitor the robustness of four requirements in [12]:

(R1) The engine speed never reaches $\bar{\omega}$: `globally` $(\omega < \bar{\omega})$
(R2) The engine and the vehicle speed never reaches $\bar{\omega}$ and $\bar{v}$ resp.:
`globally` $((\omega < \bar{\omega})$ `&` $(v < \bar{v}))$
(R3) If engine speed is always less than $\bar{\omega}$, then vehicle speed can not exceed $\bar{v}$ in less than T sec.: `!(eventually [0, T]` $(v > \bar{v})$ `& globally` $(\omega < \bar{\omega}))$
(R4) Within T sec. the vehicle speed is above $\bar{v}$ and from that point on the engine speed is always less than $\bar{\omega}$: `eventually [0,T]` $((v \geq \bar{v})$ `& globally` $(\omega < \bar{\omega}))$

We randomly generated 20 different input traces with 6400 samples and another 20 with 12800 samples (0.01 sec. of sampling time). For each input trace, we simulated the model and we monitored the robustness of the four requirements over the outputs by varying the parameters $\bar{v} \in \{120, 160, 170, 200\}$, $\bar{\omega} \in \{4500, 5000, 5200, 5500\}$ and $T \in \{4, 8, 10, 20\}$. For a fixed combination of parameters and output traces, we repeated the monitoring experiment 20 times and we considered the mean of the execution times. In Fig. 6, we compare the performance of our MOONLIGHT monitors with S-TALIRO [2] and BREACH [9] using bloxplots representing the quartiles of the execution times distribution for monitoring each requirement with each tool. The graph shows a good performance of MOONLIGHT with respect to the other tools. However, it is important to note that BREACH considers piece-wise linear signals and computes the interpolation between two consecutive samples when necessary, while our tool and S-TALIRO interpret the signal step-wise.

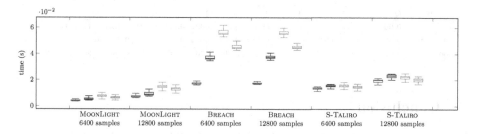

Fig. 6. The comparison of the computational time (in sec.) between MOONLIGHT, BREACH and S-TALIRO for simulation traces with different length. The different colors represent the result for different requirements: (R1), (R2), (R3) and (R4). (Color figure online)

3.2 Spatio-Temporal Evaluation

We evaluate the scalability of the spatial operators in the running example varying the number of nodes of the graph: $N = 10, 100, 1000$. Note that the number of edges is around 1700 for $N = 100$ and 8000 for $N = 1000$. We monitor the Boolean (B) and the quantitative (Q) semantics of the requirements presented in Sect. 2.2, excluding P1. For the spatio-temporal requirements we consider K time step, for $K = 10, 100$. We repeat the monitoring experiments 50 times for each N. Table 1 shows the average execution time. For spatial formulas, we can see that formula (P4) performs better than the other two. (P2) is slower because monitoring algorithms of the reach and somewhere are $O(n^2)$ i.e. linear in the number of edges and quadratic in the number of vertexes, while the one for escape is $O(n^3)$. As expected, the Boolean semantics is faster than the quantitative one: it can reach sooner the fixed point. Formula (P3) is the slowest due to the fact that uses the euclidean distance while formula (P2) and (P4) the lighter hop distance. For spatio-temporal formulas, the reason why (PT1) is much faster than (PT2) is that (PT1) has a temporal subformula, hence the number of time steps can be dramatically reduced before monitoring the spatial part. This does not happen for (PT2), where the operators are inverted. In this case the difference between the two semantics is more evident. For static graphs and properties restricted to everywhere and somewhere spatial modalities, the performances are similar to JSSTL [21,22]. Further experiments can be found in the tool release.

Table 1. The comparison of the computational time (in sec) with respect the number of nodes of the graph N for formulas (P2), (P3), (P4), and with respect N and the number of time steps K for formulas (PT1), and (PT2) for Boolean (B) and quantitative (Q) semantics.

	K = 1						K = 10				K = 100			
	P2		P3		P4		PT1		PT2		PT1		PT2	
N	B	Q	B	Q	B	Q	B	Q	B	Q	B	Q	B	Q
10	0.0031	0.0032	0.0031	0.0029	0.0027	0.0026	0.021	0.021	0.026	0.021	0.0.24	0.17	0.17	0.17
100	0.013	0.020	0.042	0.0419	0.0088	0.0084	0.067	0.081	0.10	0.14	0.76	0.73	1.02	1.5
1000	0.86	4.97	16.91	16.95	0.11	0.12	0.60	0.76	6.18	14.74	6.68	7.29	99.17	276.8

4   Conclusion

MOONLIGHT provides a lightweight and very flexible monitoring tool for temporal and spatio-temporal properties of mobile and spatially arranged CPS. The possibility to use a dedicated MATLAB [TM] interface enables to easily integrate MOONLIGHT as a component in other tool chains implementing more sophisticated computer-aided verification and synthesis techniques such as falsification analysis and parameter synthesis. In the near future, we plan to add also a Python interface and to extend the tool with new functionalities such as the support parallelized and online monitoring.

References

1. Akyildiz, I.F., Su, W., Sankarasubramaniam, Y., Cayirci, E.: A survey on sensor networks. IEEE Commun. Mag. **40**(8), 102–114 (2002). https://doi.org/10.1109/MCOM.2002.1024422
2. Annpureddy, Y., Liu, C., Fainekos, G., Sankaranarayanan, S.: S-TALIRO: a tool for temporal logic falsification for hybrid systems. In: Abdulla, P.A., Leino, K.R.M. (eds.) TACAS 2011. LNCS, vol. 6605, pp. 254–257. Springer, Heidelberg (2011). https://doi.org/10.1007/978-3-642-19835-9_21
3. Asarin, E., Caspi, P., Maler, O.: Timed regular expressions. J. ACM **49**(2), 172–206 (2002). https://doi.org/10.1145/506147.506151
4. Bartocci, E., et al.: Specification-based monitoring of cyber-physical systems: a survey on theory, tools and applications. In: Bartocci, E., Falcone, Y. (eds.) Lectures on Runtime Verification. LNCS, vol. 10457, pp. 135–175. Springer, Cham (2018). https://doi.org/10.1007/978-3-319-75632-5_5
5. Chockler, H., Weissenbacher, G. (eds.): CAV 2018. LNCS, vol. 10981. Springer, Cham (2018). https://doi.org/10.1007/978-3-319-96145-3
6. Bartocci, E., Bortolussi, L., Loreti, M., Nenzi, L.: Monitoring mobile and spatially distributed cyber-physical systems. In: Proc. of MEMOCODE 2017: the 15th ACM-IEEE International Conference on Formal Methods and Models for System Design, pp. 146–155. ACM (2017) https://doi.org/10.1145/3127041.3127050
7. Bartocci, E., Falcone, Y., Francalanza, A., Reger, G.: Introduction to runtime verification. In: Bartocci, E., Falcone, Y. (eds.) Lectures on Runtime Verification. LNCS, vol. 10457, pp. 1–33. Springer, Cham (2018). https://doi.org/10.1007/978-3-319-75632-5_1
8. Baumeister, J., Finkbeiner, B., Schwenger, M., Torfah, H.: FPGA stream-monitoring of real-time properties. ACM Trans. Embedded Comput. Syst. **18**(5), 88:1–88:24 (2019) https://doi.org/10.1145/3358220
9. Donzé, A.: Breach, a toolbox for verification and parameter synthesis of hybrid systems. In: Touili, T., Cook, B., Jackson, P. (eds.) CAV 2010. LNCS, vol. 6174, pp. 167–170. Springer, Heidelberg (2010). https://doi.org/10.1007/978-3-642-14295-6_17
10. Fainekos, G.E., Pappas, G.J.: Robustness of temporal logic specifications for continuous-time signals. Theor. Comput. Sci. **410**(42), 4262–4291 (2009). https://doi.org/10.1016/j.tcs.2009.06.021
11. Haghighi, I., Jones, A., Kong, Z., Bartocci, E., Grosu, R., Belta, C.: SpaTeL: a novel spatial-temporal logic and its applications to networked systems. In: Proc. of HSCC'15: the 18th International Conference on Hybrid Systems: Computation and Control. pp. 189–198. IEEE (2015) https://doi.org/10.1145/2728606.2728633
12. Hoxha, B., Abbas, H., Fainekos, G.E.: Benchmarks for temporal logic requirements for automotive systems. In: Proc. of ARCH@CPSWeek 2014: the 1st and 2nd International Workshop on Applied veRification for Continuous and Hybrid Systems. EPiC Series in Computing, **34**, 25–30 (2015)
13. Jakšić, S., Bartocci, E., Grosu, R., Nguyen, T., Ničković, D.: Quantitative monitoring of STL with edit distance. Formal Methods Syst. Des. **53**(1), 83–112 (2018). https://doi.org/10.1007/s10703-018-0319-x
14. Jaksic, S., Bartocci, E., Grosu, R., Nickovic, D.: An algebraic framework for runtime verification. IEEE Trans. CAD Integr. Circ. Syst. **37**(11), 2233–2243 (2018). https://doi.org/10.1109/TCAD.2018.2858460

15. Koymans, R.: Specifying real-time properties with metric temporal logic. Real-Time Syst. **2**(4), 255–299 (1990). https://doi.org/10.1007/BF01995674

16. Leucker, M., Sánchez, C., Scheffel, T., Schmitz, M., Schramm, A.: Tessla: runtime verification of non-synchronized real-time streams. In: Proc. of SAC 2018: the 33rd Annual ACM Symposium on Applied Computing, pp. 1925–1933. ACM (2018) https://doi.org/10.1145/3167132.3167338

17. Ma, M., Bartocci, E., Lifland, E., Stankovic, J.A., Feng, L.: SaSTL: spatial aggregation signal temporal logic for runtime monitoring in smart cities. In: 11th ACM/IEEE International Conference on Cyber-Physical Systems, ICCPS 2020, Sydney, Australia, April 21–25, 2020, pp. 51–62. IEEE (2020) https://doi.org/10.1109/ICCPS48487.2020.00013

18. Maler, O., Nickovic, D.: Monitoring temporal properties of continuous signals. In: Lakhnech, Y., Yovine, S. (eds.) FORMATS/FTRTFT -2004. LNCS, vol. 3253, pp. 152–166. Springer, Heidelberg (2004). https://doi.org/10.1007/978-3-540-30206-3_12

19. Maler, O., Ničković, D.: Monitoring properties of analog and mixed-signal circuits. STTT **15**(3), 247–268 (2013)

20. Moosbrugger, P., Rozier, K.Y., Schumann, J.: R2U2: monitoring and diagnosis of security threats for unmanned aerial systems. Formal Methods Syst. Des. **51**(1), 31–61 (2017). https://doi.org/10.1007/s10703-017-0275-x

21. Nenzi, L., Bortolussi, L., Ciancia, V., Loreti, M., Massink, M.: Qualitative and quantitative monitoring of spatio-temporal properties with SSTL. Logical Methods in Computer Science, **14**(4) (2018) https://doi.org/10.23638/LMCS-14(4:2)2018

22. Nenzi, L., Bortolussi, L., Loreti, M.: jSSTL - a tool to monitor spatio-temporal properties. In: Proc. of VALUETOOLS 2016: the 10th EAI International Conference on Performance Evaluation Methodologies and Tools, VALUETOOLS 2016, pp. 74–79. ACM (2016) https://doi.org/10.4108/eai.25-10-2016.2266978

23. Beyer, D., Huisman, M. (eds.): TACAS 2018. LNCS, vol. 10806. Springer, Cham (2018). https://doi.org/10.1007/978-3-319-89963-3

24. Ratasich, D., Khalid, F., Geissler, F., Grosu, R., Shafique, M., Bartocci, E.: A roadmap towards resilient internet of things for cyber-physical systems. IEEE Access Early Access, 1–1 (2019) https://doi.org/10.1109/ACCESS.2019.2891969

25. Rodionova, A., Bartocci, E., Ničković, D., Grosu, R.: Temporal logic as filtering. In: Proc. of HSCC 2016, pp. 11–20. ACM (2016) https://doi.org/10.1145/2883817.2883839

26. Majumdar, R., Kunčak, V. (eds.): CAV 2017. LNCS, vol. 10426. Springer, Cham (2017). https://doi.org/10.1007/978-3-319-63387-9

Stream-Based Monitoring

Verified Rust Monitors for Lola Specifications

Bernd Finkbeiner, Stefan Oswald, Noemi Passing,
and Maximilian Schwenger[(✉)]

CISPA Helmholtz Center for Information Security,
66123 Saarbrücken, Germany
{finkbeiner,noemi.passing,maximilian.schwenger}@cispa.saarland,
s.oswald@stud.uni-saarland.de

Abstract. The safety of cyber-physical systems rests on the correctness
of their monitoring mechanisms. This is problematic if the specification
of the monitor is implemented manually or interpreted by unreliable
software. We present a *verifying compiler* that translates specifications
given in the stream-based monitoring language Lola to implementations
in Rust. The generated code contains verification annotations that enable
the Viper toolkit to automatically prove functional correctness, absence
of memory faults, and guaranteed termination. The compiler parallelizes
the evaluation of different streams in the monitor based on a dependency
analysis of the specification. We present encouraging experimental results
obtained with monitor specifications found in the literature. For every
specification, our approach was able to either produce a correctness proof
or to uncover errors in the specification.

1 Introduction

Cyber-physical systems are inherently safety-critical, because failures immediately impact the physical environment. A crucial aspect of the development of such systems is therefore the integration of reliable monitoring mechanisms. A *monitor* is a special system component that typically has broad access to the sensor readings and the resulting control decisions. The monitor assesses the system's health by checking its behavior against a specification. If a violation is detected, the monitor raises an alarm and initiates mitigation protocols such as an emergency landing or a graceful shutdown.

An obvious concern with this approach is that the safety of the system rests on the correctness of the monitor. *Quis custodiet ipsos custodes?* For simple specifications, this is not a serious problem. An LTL [29] specification, for example, can be translated into a finite-state automaton that is proven to correspond to

This work was partially supported by the German Research Foundation (DFG) as part of the Collaborative Research Center "Foundations of Perspicuous Software Systems" (TRR 248, 389792660), and by the European Research Council (ERC) Grant OSARES (No. 683300).

J. Deshmukh and D. Ničković (Eds.): RV 2020, LNCS 12399, pp. 431–450, 2020.
https://doi.org/10.1007/978-3-030-60508-7_24

the semantics of the specification. Implementing such an automaton correctly as a computer program is not difficult. For more expressive specification languages, establishing the correctness of the monitor is much more challenging. Especially problematic is the use of interpreters, which read the specification as input and then rely on complicated and error-prone software to interpret the specification dynamically at runtime [6,12,14–16]. Recently, however, much effort has gone into the development of compilers. Compared to a full-scale interpreter, the code produced by a compiler for a specific specification is fairly simple and well-structured. Some compilers even include special mechanisms that increase the confidence in the monitor. For example, the RTLola compiler [7] generates VHDL code that is annotated with tracing information that relates each line of code back to the specific part of the specification it implements. The Copilot compiler [26] produces a test suite for the generated C code. The framework even includes a bounded model checker, which can check the correctness of the output for input sequences up to a fixed length. However, none of these approaches actually proves the functional correctness of the monitor.

In this paper, we present a *verifying compiler* that translates specifications given in the stream-based monitoring language Lola [13] to implementations in Rust[1]. The generated code is fully annotated with formal function contracts, loop invariants, and inline assertions, so that functional correctness and guaranteed termination can be automatically verified by the Viper [22] toolkit, without any restriction on the length of the input trace. Since the memory requirements of a Lola specification can be computed statically, this yields a formal guarantee that on any platform that satisfies these requirements, the monitor will never crash and will always compute the correct output.

A major practical concern for any compiler is the performance of the generated code. Our Lola-to-Rust compiler produces highly efficient monitor implementations because it parallelizes the code for the evaluation of the specifications. Since Lola is a stream-based specification language, it exhibits a highly modular and memory-local structure, i.e., the computation of a stream writes only in its own local memory, although it may read from the local memory of several other processes. The compiler statically analyzes the dependencies between the streams, resulting in a partial evaluation order. To prove correctness, it is shown that streams that are incomparable with respect to the evaluation order can indeed be evaluated in parallel.

We have used our compiler to build monitors from specifications of varying sizes found in the literature. In our experience, the compiler itself scales very well. The verification in Viper, however, is expensive. It appears that the running times of the underlying SMT solver Z3 [21] vary greatly, even for different runs on the same monitor and specification. Nevertheless, we have been successful in all our benchmarks in the sense that the compiler either generated a verified monitor or uncovered an error in the specification. This is a major step forward towards the *verified monitoring* of real-life safety-critical systems.

---

[1] See https://www.rust-lang.org/.

2 Introduction to Lola

The source language of our verifying compiler is the stream-based monitoring language Lola [13]. A Lola monitor is a reactive component that translates, in an online fashion, input streams into output streams. In each time step, the monitor receives new values for the input streams and produces new values for the output streams in accordance with the specification. In principle, the monitoring can continue forever; if the monitor is terminated, it wraps up the remaining computations, produces a final output, and shuts down. Lola specifications are declarative in the sense that the semantics leaves a lot of implementation freedom: the semantics defines how specific values are combined arithmetically and logically, but the precise evaluation order and the memory management are determined by the implementation.

A Lola specification defines a set of streams. Each stream is an ordered sequence of typed values that is extended throughout the monitor execution. There are three kinds of streams:

Input Streams constitute the interface between the monitor and an external data source, i.e., the system under scrutiny.

Output Streams compute new values based on input streams, other output streams, and constant values. The computed values contain relevant information regarding the performance and health status of the system.

Triggers constitute the interface between the monitor and the user. Trigger values are binary and indicate the violation of a property. In this case, the monitor alerts the user.

Syntactically, a Lola specification is given as a sequence of stream declarations. Input stream declarations are of the form $i_j : T_j$, where i_j is an input stream and T_j is its type. Output stream and trigger declarations are of the form $s_j : T_j = e_j(i_1, \ldots, i_m, s_1, \ldots, s_n)$, where $i_1, \ldots, i_m$ are input streams, $s_1, \ldots, s_n$ are output streams, and the e_j are stream expressions. A stream expression consists of constant values, streams, arithmetic and logic operators $f(e_1, \ldots, e_k)$, if-then-else expressions ite(b, e_1, e_2), and stream accesses $e[k, c]$, where e is a stream, k is the *offset*, and c is the constant *default value*. Stream accesses are either *synchronous*, i.e., a stream accesses the latest value of a stream, or *asynchronous*, i.e., a stream accesses a past or future value of another stream.

The example specification shown in Listing 1.1 monitors the altitude of a drone, detects whether the drone flies below a given minimum altitude or above a given maximum altitude for too long, and raises an alarm if needed. The input stream altitude contains sensor information of the drone. The output stream tooLow checks whether the altitude is lower than the given minimum altitude of 200 in the last, current, and next step, denoted by altitude[-1,0], altitude, and altitude[1,0], respectively. If this is the case, a trigger is raised. Analogously, tooHigh checks whether the altitude is above the given maximum altitude in the last, current, and next step, and a trigger is raised in this case. The evaluations of tooHigh and tooLow try to access the second to last value of altitude as well as the last and the next one. If altitude

```
input altitude: Int32
output tooLow: Bool :=
   altitude[-1,0] < 200 ∧ altitude < 200 ∧ altitude[1,0] < 200
output tooHigh: Bool :=
   altitude[-1,0] > 600 ∧ altitude > 600 ∧ altitude[1,0] > 600
trigger tooLow "Flying below minimum altitude."
trigger tooHigh "Flying above maximum altitude."
```

Listing 1.1. A Lola specification monitoring the altitude of a drone. The output stream tooLow (tooHigh) checks whether the drone flies below (above) a given minimum (maximum) altitude in the last, current, and next step. If this is the case, an alarm is raised.

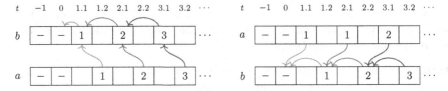

(a) The result of evaluating the output streams respecting the evaluation order.

(b) The result of evaluating the output streams in order of their declaration.

Fig. 1. Two different evaluations of the output streams a and b, where a accesses b synchronously and b accesses its previous value. Both accesses default to 0 and both a and b increase the obtained value by 1.

does not have at least two values, the accesses with offset -1 fail and the default value, in this case 0, is used. If altitude ceases to produce values, the accesses with offset 1 fail. Hence, in contrast to negative offsets, the default value for accesses with positive offset is used at the end of the execution.

The semantics of Lola is defined in terms of *evaluation models*. Intuitively, an evaluation model consists of evaluations of each output stream of the specification. The evaluation is a natural translation of the stream expressions. The full formal definition is given in [13].

Definition 1 (Evaluation Model [13]**).** *Let φ be a Lola specification over input streams $i_1, \ldots, i_\ell$ and output streams $s_1, \ldots, s_n$. The tuple $\langle \sigma_1, \ldots, \sigma_n \rangle$ of streams of length $N + 1$ is called an* evaluation model *if for each equation $s_j = e_j(i_1, \ldots, i_\ell, s_1, \ldots, s_n)$ in φ, $\langle \sigma_1, \ldots, \sigma_n \rangle$ satisfies $\sigma_j(k) = v(e_j)(k)$ for $0 \leq k \leq N$, where $v(e_j)(k)$ evaluates the stream expression e_j at position k.*

Synchronous accesses harbor a pitfall for the monitor realization as illustrated in Fig. 1. Consider the corresponding Lola specification:

```
output a: Int32 := b[ 0, 0] + 1
output b: Int32 := b[-1, 0] + 1
```

Here, a accesses b synchronously, while b accesses its previous value. The evaluation of a tries to access the current value of b and increases the result by one, which yields the next stream value of a. In contrast, the evaluation of b tries to access the last value of b and increases the result by one to determine the next stream value of b. Figure 1a depicts the resulting output. If the monitor evaluates the streams in order of their declaration, however, the resulting output, shown in Fig. 1b, differs from the expected one. The reason is that the *current* value of b changes depending on whether or not b has already been extended when accessing the value. This problem is solved by respecting the evaluation order, a partial order on the output streams. It is induced by the dependency graph of a Lola specification.

Definition 2 (Dependency Graph [13]). *The* dependency graph $D_\varphi = (V, E)$ *of a Lola specification φ is a weighted directed multigraph. Each vertex represents a stream and each edge an access operation. Thus, $s \in V$ iff s is a stream or trigger in φ and $(s_1, n, s_2) \in E$ for $s_1, s_2 \in V$, $n \in \mathbb{N}$ iff the stream expression of s_1 contains an access to s_2 with offset n.*

Based on the dependency graph, d'Angelo et al. define the *shift* of a stream [13]. Intuitively, the shift of s indicates how many steps the evaluation of its expression needs to be delayed. For instance, suppose the delay is $n > 0$. Then the value of s for time t can be computed at time $t + n$.

Definition 3 (Shift [13]). *For a Lola specification φ, the shift $\Delta(s)$ of a stream s is the greatest weight of a path through the dependency graph of φ originating in s: $\Delta(s) = \max(0, \max\{w + \Delta(s') | (s, w, s') \in E\})$.*

The shift allows us to define an order in which streams need to be evaluated. For this, we define the set of synchronized edges E^* where the weight of a synchronized edge $(s, n, s') \in E^*$ indicates when s can access s' successfully with an offset of n. Let $E^* = \{(s, \Delta(s) - w - \Delta(s'), s') \mid (s, w, s') \in E\}$.

Definition 4 (Evaluation Order). *The* evaluation order $\leq_{eo}$ *is a partial order on the output streams of a Lola specification φ. Let $D_\varphi = (V, E)$ be the dependency graph of φ. The evaluation order is the transitive closure of a relation $\prec$ with $s \prec s'$ iff $(s', 0, s) \in E^*$.*

Clearly, we obtain $b \leq_{eo} a$ for the above Lola specification, yielding the expected result depicted in Fig. 1a. For the Lola specification from Listing 1.1, however, the output streams tooLow and tooHigh are incomparable according to the evaluation order. A total evaluation order on the output streams, denoted $\leq_{eo}^+$, is obtained by relating incomparable streams arbitrarily.

Remark 1 (On Asynchronous Accesses and Off-by-one Errors). It is fairly easy to make off-by-one errors in asynchronous stream accesses. When two streams within one layer access each other asynchronously, one of the offsets needs to be decreased by 1, depending on which stream is evaluated first. This cannot be avoided for any $\leq_{eo}^+$. To simplify the presentation, we will ignore this issue in the remainder of the presentation, the correct adjustment of the indices is, however, implemented in the compiler.

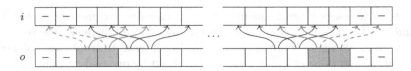

Fig. 2. Illustration of stream accesses in different phases of the execution. An output stream o accesses an input stream i with offsets -2 and $+2$. In the prefix (postfix) of the execution, the past (future) accesses need to be substituted by their default values.

Specifications where the dependency graph has no positive cycles are called *efficiently monitorable*: such specifications can be monitored with constant memory, and an output value can always be produced after a constant delay [13]. All example specifications considered in this paper are efficiently monitorable.

3   From Lola to Rust

The compilation proceeds in two steps. First, the Lola specification is analyzed to determine inter-stream dependencies, the overall memory requirement, and the different phases of the monitoring process. Second, the compiler produces Rust code that implements the specification.

3.1   Specification Analysis

Execution Pre- and Postfix. Refer back to the Lola specification in Listing 1.1. Another beneficial property of the synchronous input model is that, starting from $t = 2$, both stream accesses with offset -1 to altitude will always succeed since the offset refers to the last evaluation of altitude which did already happen at $t \geq 1$. For a more general analysis, suppose an output stream s accesses another stream s' with an offset of n. If n is non-positive, then accesses may fail until $t = \Delta(s) - n - \Delta(s')$, i.e., they will not fail from $\Delta(s) - n - \Delta(s') + 1$ on. If n is strictly positive, however, the evaluation of s needs to be delayed by $\Delta(s) - n$, i.e., until s' received the respective value. By generally delaying the execution of s, all accesses to s' continue to succeed until s' ceases to produce new values. As soon as this is the case, the monitor needs to evaluate s for $\Delta(s) - n$ more times to compensate for the delay. For instance, the evaluations of tooLow and tooHigh both have to be delayed by one step.

This behavior induces the structure of the monitor execution: it starts with a prefix where past accesses always fail, loops in the regular execution where all accesses always succeed, and ends in a postfix where future accesses always fail.

Figure 2 illustrates stream accesses in the different phases. It shows an output stream o that accesses an input stream i with an offset of -2 and 2. In the first two iterations of the monitor execution, i.e., in the prefix, the accesses to the past values will fail, requiring the monitor to use the default values instead. Afterwards, all accesses succeed until the input stream ends. In the last two evaluations, i.e., in the postfix, the future accesses fail and need to be replaced by the default values.

While the shift only concerns time, it can also be used to compute the memory requirement of a stream, i.e., the number of values of a single stream that can be relevant at the same time. If a stream s of type T has a memory requirement $\mu(s) = i$, the monitor needs to reserve $i \cdot \text{size}(T)$ bytes of memory for s.

Definition 5 (Memory Requirement). *The* memory requirement *of a dependency $(s', w, s) \in E$ is determined by the shifts of the streams as well as the weight w of the dependency, i.e., the offset of the stream access: $\Delta(s) - \Delta(s') - w$. The memory requirement of a stream is thus the maximum requirement of any outgoing dependency: $\mu(s) = \max\{\Delta(s) - \Delta(s') - w \mid (s', w, s) \in E\}$.*

Hence, the compilation determines three key values for each specification.

Definition 6 (Memory Consumption, Prefix- and Postfix Length). *Let μ_φ^*, $\eta_\varphi^\leftarrow$, and $\eta_\varphi^\rightarrow$ be the* memory consumption, prefix length *and* postfix length *of φ, respectively, defined as follows:*

$$\mu_\varphi^* = \sum_{s \in \varphi} \{\mu(s) \cdot \text{size}(T_s)\}$$

$$\eta_\varphi^\leftarrow = \max_{s \in \varphi} \{\Delta(s) + \mu(s)\}$$

$$\eta_\varphi^\rightarrow = \max_{s \in \varphi} \{\Delta(s)\}$$

Furthermore, the evaluation order $\leq_{eo}$ of the output streams of a Lola specification induces the so-called *evaluation layers*.

Definition 7 (Evaluation Layer). *Let φ be a Lola specification and let $\leq_{eo}$ be the evaluation order induced by its dependency graph. If $Layer(s) = k$ for an output stream s, then there is a strictly decreasing sequence of k streams with respect to $\leq_{eo}$ starting in s.*

Intuitively, an evaluation layer consists of all streams that are incomparable according to the evaluation order. For the Lola specification from Listing 1.1, for instance, the output streams tooLow and tooHigh are incomparable according to the evaluation order. Thus, they are contained in the same evaluation layer. Evaluation Layers are also used to identify independent streams and thus to enable their concurrent evaluation as described in Sect. 5.

3.2 Code Generation

The monitor code starts with a *prelude* which declares data structures and helper functions. It also contains the main function starting with the static allocation of the working memory. The remainder of the main function is the operative monitoring code consisting of three components: the *execution prefix*, the *monitor loop*, and the *execution postfix*. The general structure is illustrated in Listing 1.2, details follow in the remainder of this section.

```
                                    Prelude
struct Memory { ... }                          fn prefix(mem: &mut Memory) -> bool {
impl Memory { ... }                              if let Some(input) = get_input() {
[[ Evaluation Functions ]]                         mem.add_input(&input);
fn get_input() ->                                    [[ Evaluation Logic ]]
    Option<(T_{s_1},...,T_{s_ℓ})> {              } else {
  [[ Communicate with system ]]                     return true // Jump to Postfix.
}                                                  }
fn emit(output: &(T_{s_1},...,T_{s_n})) {        [[ Repeat η_φ^← times. ]]
  [[ Communicate with system ]]                  false   // Continue with Monitor Loop.
}                                              }
fn main() {                                                        Execution Prefix
  let mut memory = Memory::new();
  let early_exit  = prefix(&mem);              fn postfix(mem &Memory) {
  if !early_exit   {                             [[ Evaluation Logic ]]
    while let Some(input) = get_input() {        [[ Repeat η_φ^→ times. ]]
      mem.add_input(&input1);                  }
      [[ Evaluation Logic ]]                                        Execution Postfix
    }                         Monitor Loop
  }
  postfix(&mem);
}
```

Listing 1.2. Structure of the generated Rust code.

Prelude. The prelude declares several functions required throughout the monitor execution and declares as well as allocates the working memory. The functions consist of two I/O functions and evaluation functions.

The `get_input() -> Option<(T_{s_1},...,T_{s_ℓ})>` function, where $T_{s_1},...,T_{s_ℓ}$ are the types of all input streams, models the receipt of input data. It produces either `None` if the execution of the system under scrutiny terminated, or `Some(v)`, where v is an ℓ-tuple containing the latest input values. Conversely, the function `emit(&(T_{s_{\ell+1}},...,T_{s_k}))` conveys a $(k - \ell)$-tuple of output values to the system.

For each stream, there are evaluation functions in several variants depending on whether they will be called in the prefix, the loop, or the postfix. The implementations differ only in the logic accessing other streams. The Lola semantics dictates that the evaluation needs to check whether the accessed value exists and to substitute it with the respective default value if needed. However, an analysis of the dependency graph reveals statically which accesses will fail. Thus, providing several implementations makes the need for such a check during runtime redundant.

The working memory is a struct aptly named `Memory`. It consists of a static array for each stream in the specification and reads as follows:

```
struct Memory { s_1: [T_{s_1}, μ(s_1)],  ... , s_k: [T_{s_n}, μ(s_n)] }
```

Here, $s_1,...,s_k$ are all input and output streams with types $T_1,...,T_k$. The monitor allocates `Memory` once in its main function, keeps it on the stack, and grants read access to functions evaluating stream expressions.

Execution Prefix. The prefix consists of $\eta_\varphi^←$ conditional blocks, each processing an input event of the system under scrutiny. If the system terminates before the prefix concludes, the function returns true, indicating an early termination, which prompts the main function to initiate the postfix. Otherwise, the input is added to the working memory and, evaluation layer by evaluation layer, each output stream is evaluated in a dedicated function as can be seen in the following code snippet. For this, assume that the specification has λ^* evaluation layers, i.e., $\lambda^* = \max\{x \mid \exists s_1,\ldots,s_x : s_1 \leq_{eo} \cdots \leq_{eo} s_x\}$ Moreover, $\lambda_i = |\{s \mid Layer(s) = i\}|$ denotes the number of streams within evaluation layer $i \leq \lambda^*$. Lastly, let $s_{i,j} \leq_{eo}^+ s_{i,j+1}$ with $Layer(s_{i,j}) = Layer(s_{i,j+1}) = i$.

```
let val_s₁,₁ = eval_pre_1_s₁,₁(&Memory);
...
let val_s₁,λ₁ = eval_pre_1_s₁,λ₁(&Memory);
memory.write_layer_1(val_s₁,₁, ..., val_s₁,λ₁)
...
let val_sλ*,₁ = eval_pre_sλ*,₁(&Memory);
...
let val_sλ*,λλ* = eval_pre_sλ*,λλ*(&Memory);
Memory.write_layer_λ*(val_sλ*,₁, ..., val_sλ*,λλ*);
if val_st₁ == true { emit(mt₁) }
```

Note that, as indicated in the prelude, each conditional block calls a different set of evaluation functions. This allows for a fine-grained treatment of stream accesses, improving the overall performance at the cost of greater code size. Also, the call passes a single argument to the evaluation function: an immutable reference for Memory. As a result, the Rust type system guarantees that the evaluation does not mutate its state. The function returns a value that is committed to Memory after fully evaluating the current layer. The bodies of these functions are straight-forward translations of stream expressions: each arithmetic and logical expression has a counterpart in Rust. Stream lookups access the only argument passed to the function, i.e., a read-only reference to the working memory.

The write_layer_i functions commit computed stream values to Memory. After $\mu(s)$ iterations, the memory evicts the oldest data point for stream s, thus constituting a ring buffer.

Monitor Loop. The main difference between the monitor loop and the prefix is, as the name indicates, that the former consists of a loop. The loop terminates as soon as the system ceases to produce new inputs. At this point, the monitor transitions to the execution postfix.

Within the loop, the monitor proceeds just as in the prefix except that the evaluation functions are agnostic to the current iteration number. In the evaluation, all stream accesses are guaranteed to succeed rendering the evaluation free of conditionals except when the stream expression itself contains one.

Execution Postfix. The structure of the execution postfix closely resembles the prefix except for two differences: The postfix does not check for the presence of new input values and calls a different set of evaluation functions, specifically tailored for the postfix iteration.

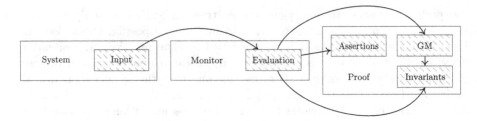

Fig. 3. Information flow between the monitor and the ghost memory.

Code Characteristics. The generated code exhibits two advantageous character-istics. First, the trade-off between an increase in code size by quasi-duplicating the evaluation functions leads to an excellent performance in terms of running time. The functions require few arguments, avoid conditional statements as much as possible, and utilize memory locality. This is further emphasized by the lack of dynamic memory allocation and utilization of native datatypes. Second, the clear code structure, especially with respect to memory accesses, drastically simplifies reasoning about the correctness of the code.

4 Verification

Our goal is to prove that the verdicts produced by the monitor correspond to the formal semantics. The main challenge is that the the evaluation model of the Lola semantics refers to unbounded data sequences, disregarding any memory concerns. The implementation, however, manages the monitoring process with only a finite amount of memory. As a result, the Lola semantics may refer to data values long after they have been discarded in the implementation. Hence, the relation between the memory content and the evaluation model, and thus the correctness of the computation, is no longer apparent.

We solve this problem with the classic proof technique of introducing so-called *ghost memory*. The compilation introduces another data structure named Ghost Memory (GM) which is a wrapper for Rust vectors, i.e., dynamically grow-ing sequences of data. Whenever the monitor receives or computes any data, it commits it to the GM. The GM's size thus obviously exceeds any bound, voiding the memory guarantees. However, the ghost memory's sole purpose is to aid the verification and not the monitor; information flows from the program into the GM and the proof, but remains strictly separated from the monitor execution. This allows for removing the GM after successfully verifying the correctness of the monitor without altering its behavior. Figure 3 illustrates the flow of infor-mation between the monitor and GM. Clearly, the monitor remains unaffected when removing any proof artifacts.

The correctness proof has two major obligations: proving compliance between values in the GM and the working memory, and proving the correctness of the trigger evaluations with respect to the ghost memory. These obligations are encoded as verification annotations, such that the Viper framework verifies them automatically. The compilation generates additional annotations to guide the verification process. Viper annotations fall into the following categories:

Function Contracts. Annotations in front of a function f consist of preconditions and guarantees. Viper imposes constraints on the function caller and the function body itself. Each call to f is replaced by an assertion of the preconditions of f, prompting Viper to prove their validity, and an assumption of the guarantees. In a separate step, Viper assumes the preconditions and verifies that the guarantees hold after executing the function body. Note that the Rust type system already ensures that references passed to the function are accessible and cannot be modified or freed unless they are explicitly declared mutable.

Loop Invariants. Viper analyzes while-loops similarly to functions in three steps. First, the code leading to the loop needs to satisfy the invariants. Second, Viper assumes both the loop invariant and the loop condition to hold and verifies that the invariant again holds after the execution of the body. Lastly, Viper assumes the invariant and the negation of the loop condition to hold for the code after the loop.

Inline Assertions. Both loop invariants and function contracts impose implicit assertions on the code. Viper allows for supplementing them with explicit inline assertions using the Rust assert! macro. Usually, the macro checks an expression during runtime. Viper, however, eliminates the need for this dynamic check as it verifies the correctness statically and transforms it into an assumption for the remainder of the verification. Thus, the assertions serve a similar function as the ghost memory: they are a proof construct and do not influence the monitor per se (cf. Fig. 3).

Annotation Generation. The compilation inserts annotations at several key locations. First, as an example for function annotations, consider a function that retrieves a value of the stream s from the working memory. The function takes the relative index of the retrieved value as single argument, i.e., an index of 1 accesses the second to newest value. The annotation requires that the index must not exceed the memory reserved for s. Syntactically, this results in the following annotation in front of the function head: #[requires="index < $\mu(s)$"]. Moreover, the function needs to guarantee that the return value corresponds to the respective value stored in Memory. This is expressed by the annotation #[ensures="index == i ==> result == self.s[i]"] for each $i \leq \mu(s)$. The remaining function annotations follow a similar pattern, i.e., they require valid arguments, and ensure correct outputs as well as the absence of undesired changes. Note that the ghost memory is essentially a wrapper for Rust vectors as they represent a growing list of values. Thus, functions concerning the ghost memory carry the standard annotation ensuring correctness of the vector as presented in the Viper examples.[2]

---

[2] See e.g. the verified solution for the Knapsack Problem: https://github.com/viperproject/prusti-dev/blob/master/prusti/tests/verify/pass/rosetta/Knapsack_Problem.rs.

Second, the loop has several entry checks that are expressed as inline assertions. These ensure that the iteration count is $\eta_\varphi^\leftarrow$ and that the length of the ghost memory for a stream s is $\eta_\varphi^\leftarrow - \Delta(s)$. This is necessary because the loop invariant asserts equivalence between an excerpt of the ghost memory and the working memory. While the existence of all accessed values in the working memory is guaranteed due to the static allocation, the GM grows dynamically. Hence, the compilation adds the entry checks.

In terms of memory equivalence, it remains to be shown that all values in the working memory correspond to the respective entry in the ghost memory. Formally, let m be the working memory and let g be the ghost memory where index 0 marks the latest value. Furthermore, let η be the current iteration count. Then, the invariant checks:

$$\forall s \colon \forall i \colon (0 \leq i < \mu(s) \implies m_s[i] = g_s[i]). \tag{1}$$

At loop entry, $\mu(s) = \eta_\varphi^\leftarrow - \Delta(s) = \eta - \Delta(s)$ is the number of iterations in which a value for s was computed. In each further iteration of the loop, the invariant checks that the former $\mu(s) - 1$ entries remained the same and that the new values in the ghost memory g and the working memory m are equal. The first of these checks is not strictly necessary for the proof because it immediately follows from the function contracts of the helper functions. However, after completing one loop iteration, Viper deletes prior knowledge about all variables that were mutated in the loop. Further reasoning about these variables is thus solely based on the loop invariants.

To express Eq. (1) in Viper, the compilation needs to statically resolve the universal quantification over the streams. Thus, for each stream s, the compilation generates the annotation `#[invariant="forall i: usize :: (0 <= i && i < $\mu(s)$) ==> mem.get_s(i) == gm.get_s(iter - 1)"]`, where `iter` is a variable denoting the current iteration, `mem` is the working memory, and `gm` is the ghost memory. Viper is able to handle the remaining universal quantification over i. However, the compilation reduces the verification effort further by unrolling it. This is possible since the memory requirement $\mu(s)$ of a stream s is determined statically.

Lastly, the compilation introduces inline assertions after the evaluation of stream expressions, i.e., in the prefix, postfix, and loop body. These annotations show that computed values are correct when assuming that the values retrieved from the working memory are correct as well. This argument is well-founded because the compilation substitutes failing stream accesses by their respective default values. Thus, any value retrieved from `Memory` was computed in an earlier iteration or layer and therefore proven correct by Viper.

It only remains to be shown that the stream expression is properly evaluated. Expressions consist of arithmetic or logical functions, constants, and stream accesses. The former two can be trivially represented in Viper. Since the memory is assumed to be correct and failing accesses are substituted by constants when possible, accesses also translate naturally into Viper.

Conclusion. The validity of the assertions after the evaluation logic shows that newly computed values are correct if the values in the working memory m and the ghost memory g coincide. This fact is guaranteed by the loop invariant. Furthermore, the inductive argument of the loop invariants allows us to conclude that, if m were to never discard values, $m_s[i] = g_s[i]$ for all streams s and $i \leq \eta$. Thus, m is a real subsequence of g, which is a perfect reflection of the evaluation model. As a result, any trigger violation detected by the monitor realization corresponds to a violation in the evaluation model for the same sequence of input values; The realization is verifiably correct.

5   Concurrent Evaluation

Evaluating independent streams concurrently can significantly improve the performance of the monitor. In the following, we devise an analysis of Lola specifications that enables safe parallelization. We observe two characteristics of Lola: the computation of a stream expression can only *read* the memory of other streams, and inter-stream dependencies are determined statically. The evaluation layers are a manifestation of the second observation. They group streams which are incomparable according to the evaluation order. Combined with the first observation, we can conclude that all streams within one layer may be computed in parallel. Thus, the compilation spawns a new thread for each stream within the layer with read access to the global memory. We add annotations to the code that enable Viper to verify that the parallel execution remains correct.

The compilation capitalizes on Rust's concurrency capabilities by evaluating different output streams in parallel. A major advantage of Rust is that its ownership model enforces a strict separation of mutable and immutable data. Any data point has exactly one owner who can transfer ownership for good or let other functions borrow the data. Borrowing data is again either mutable or immutable. If a function mutably borrows data, no other function, including the owner, can read or write this data. Similarly, if a function immutably borrows data, other functions and the owner can only read it. A consequence of this fine-grained access management with static enforcement is that enabling concurrency becomes rather easy when compared to languages like C.

Enabling the concurrent evaluation requires slight changes in the code generation. First, evaluation functions are annotated with #[pure]. This indicates that a function mutates nothing but its local stack portion. For the evaluation logic, the compiler still proceeds layer by layer, opening a *scope* for each of them. In the scope, it generates code following the total evaluation order $\leq_{eo}^+$. However, rather than calling the respective evaluation functions directly, the parallelized version spawns a thread for each stream and starts the evaluation inside it. Assume $s_1, \ldots, s_n$ constitute a single layer of a specification. The evaluation then looks as follows:

```
let (v_1, ..., v_n) = crossbeam::scope(|scope| {
    let handle_s1 = scope.spawn(move |_| {
        eval_s1(&memory)
    });
    ...
```

```
    let handle_sn = scope.spawn(move |_| {
        eval_sn(&memory)
    });
    (handle_s1.join().unwrap(), ..., handle_sn.join().unwrap())
}).unwrap()
```

Note that the code snippet uses the Rust crate crossbeam, a standard concurrency library. A similar result can be achieved without external code by moving the global memory to the heap and using the standard Rust thread logic.[3]

The correctness of this approach is an immediate consequence of the correctness of the evaluation order and memory locality of streams. In particular, the independence of streams within the same evaluation layer and the pureness of the functions are crucial. The latter ensures that the function does not mutate anything outside of its local stack. The former ensures that using pure evaluation functions within the same layer is indeed possible. Thus, the order of execution cannot change the outcome of the function, enabling the concurrent evaluation.

Note that spawning a thread for each stream evaluation is a double-edged sword. While it can drastically reduce the monitor's latency, each spawn induces a constant overhead. Thus, reducing the number of spawns while increasing the parallel computation time maximizes the gain. Consequently, the monitor benefits stronger from the parallel evaluation when its dependency graph is wide, enabling several cores to compute in parallel. Similarly, specifications with large stream expressions benefit from the multi-threading because the share of parallel computations increases. This lowers the relative impact of the constant thread-spawning overhead.

6   Experimental Evaluation

The implementation of the compiler is based on the RTLola[4] framework written in Rust. The code verification uses the Rust-frontend of the Viper framework called Prusti [3]. Prusti translates a Rust program into the Viper intermediate verification language, followed by a translation into an SMT model, which is checked by the Z3 [21] SMT solver. Thus, our toolchain enables completely automatic proof checking.

The experiments were conducted on a machine with a 3.1 GHz Dual-Core Intel i5 processor with 16 GB of RAM. The artifacts for the evaluation are available on github.[5] In all experiments, the compilation itself has a negligible running time of under ten milliseconds and memory consumption of less than 4 MB,

---

[3] On a technical note: Rust's type system requires the programmer to guarantee that the global memory will not be dropped until all threads terminate. Thus, the memory needs to be wrapped into an *Atomically Reference Counted (Arc)* pointer. This has two disadvantages: all accesses to memory require generally slower heap access and the evaluation suffers from the overhead accompanying atomic reference counting.

[4] http://www.rtlola.org/.

[5] https://github.com/reactive-systems/Lola2RustArtifact.

mainly due to the RTLola frontend. As expected, the verification of the annotated rust code using Prusti and the Viper toolkit takes significant time and memory. While the translation into the SMT model is deterministic and can be parallelized, the verification with Z3 exhibits generally high and unpredictable running time.

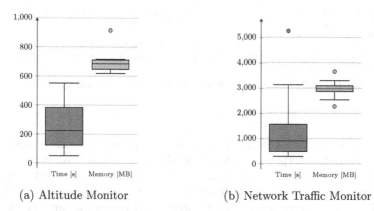

(a) Altitude Monitor   (b) Network Traffic Monitor

Fig. 4. Results of 20 runs in terms of running time (blue, in seconds) and memory consumption (orange, in MB) for the verification of the annotated Rust code of the specification, where the altitude of a drone is monitored (cf. Listing 1.1), and the network traffic monitor specification. (Color figure online)

We discuss the results of compiling and verifying three Lola specification of varying size. The process works flawlessly on two of them while the third one occasionally runs into timeouts and inconclusive verification results.

First, we consider the specification from Listing 1.1, where the altitude of a drone is monitored. The results in terms of both running time and memory consumption for 20 runs are depicted in Fig. 4a. Note that the y-axis displays both the running time in seconds (left plot) and the memory consumption in megabytes (right plot). The plot shows that the running time never exceeds 600 s with a median of 225 s. The memory consumption is significantly more stable ranging between 648 and 711 MB with one outlier (914 MB).

While the first specification was short and illustrative, the second one is more practically relevant. The specification monitors the network traffic of a server based on the source and destination IP of requests, TCP flags, and the length of the payload [7]. The specification counts the number of incoming connections and computes the workload, i.e., the number of bytes received over push requests. If any of these numbers exceeds a threshold, the specification raises an alarm. Moreover, it keeps track of the number of open connections. A trigger indicates when the server attempts to close a connection even though none is open. The full specification can be found in Listing 1.3. Figure 4b depicts the results both in terms of running time and memory consumption for 20 runs. Again, the y-axis represents both running time in seconds and memory consumption in megabytes.

```
input src, dst, length: Int32
input fin: Bool, push: Bool, syn: Bool
constant server: Int32 := ...

output count : Int32 := if count[-1,0] > 201 then 0 else count[-1,0] + 1
output receiver : Int32 := if dst=server then receiver[-2,0] + 2 else
    if count > 200 then 0 else receiver[-1,0]
trigger receiver > 50 "Many incoming connections."

output received : Int32 := if dst=server ∧ push then 0 else length
output workload : Int32 := if count > 200 then workload[-1,0] + 1 else 0
trigger workload > 25 "Workload too high."
output opened : Int32 := opened[-1,0] + int(dst=server ∧ syn)
output closed : Int32 := closed[-1,0] + int(dst=server ∧ fin)
trigger opened - closed < 0 "Closed more connections than have been opened."
```

Listing 1.3. Lola specification for monitoring network traffic

The increase in resource consumption clearly reflects the increase in complexity and size of the input specification. While the longest run took nearly 90 min, most of the runs took less than 25 min with a median of roughly 15 min. Like before, the memory consumption is relatively stable ranging around 3 GB.

Lastly, we considered a Lola specifications that shows the limitations of our approach. It detects different flight phases of a drone and raises an alarm if actual velocity and a reference velocity provided by the flight controller deviate strongly. The specification is based on a Lola specification for flight phase detection shown in Listing 1.4.

After a successful compilation, the verification was able to reveal potential arithmetic errors in the original specification [1]. The errors arose from division in which the denominator was an input stream access. The resulting value is not necessarily non-zero, so Viper reported that the respective annotation cannot be verified. Hence, our approach is able to detect flaws in specifications stemming from implicit assumptions on the system. These assumptions may not hold during runtime, causing the monitor to fail.

Thus, we modified the flight phase detection specification to work without division. Yet, only four of our runs terminated successfully. The running time varies between 6 and 16 min and the memory consumption between 1.38 GB and 1.66 GB. The successful runs show that our approach is able to verify monitor realizations of large and arithmetically challenging Lola specifications. However, two runs did not terminate within three hours. The reason lies within the underlying SMT solver: an unfavorable path choice in the solving procedure can result in extended running times. Additionally, for four runs, the verification reported that some assertions might not hold or crashed internally. While restarting the verification procedure can lead to finding a successful run, the incident shows the reliance of our approach on external tools. Hence, the applicability increases with advances in research on automated proof checking of annotated code. This constitutes another reason for the continued development of valuable tools like Prusti and the Viper framework.

```
input time_s, time_micros, velo_x, velo_y, velo_r_x, velo_r_y: Int32

output time := time_s + time_micros / 1000000
output count := count[-1,0] + 1
output frequency := 1 / (time - time[-1,0])
output freq_sum := frequency + freq_sum[-1,0]
output freq_avg := freq_sum / count
output velo : Int32 := vel_x*vel_x + vel_y*vel_y
output velo_max : Int32 := if res_max[-1,false] then velo
    else max(velo_max[-1,0], velo)
output velo_min : Int32 := if res_max[-1,false] then velo
    else min(velo_min[-1,0], velo)
output res_max: Bool := (velo_max - velo_min) > 1
output unchanged: Int32 := if res_max[-1,false] then 0 else unchanged[-1,0] + 1
output velo_dev : Int32 := velo_r_x - velo_x + velo_r_y - velo_y
output worst_dev: Int32 := if unchanged > 15 then velo_dev else max(velo_dev,
    worst_dev[-1,-10])

trigger freq_avg < 10 "Low input frequency."
trigger velo_dev > 10 "Deviation between velocities too high."
trigger worst_dev > 20 "Worst velocity deviation too high."
```

Listing 1.4. Lola specification for flight phase detection

6.1   Performance of Generated Monitors

As expected, the compiled monitors exhibit superior running time when compared against the RTLola [14] interpreter. The comparison is based on randomly generated input data for the Altimeter[6] and Network Traffic Monitor. For the first specification, the interpreter required 438 ns per event on average out of 10 runs, whereas the compiled version took 6.2 ns. The second, more involved specification shows similar results: 1.535 μs for the interpreter and 63.4 ns for the compiled version.

7   Related Work

The development of a verifying compiler was identified by Tony Hoare as a grand challenge for computing research [18]. Milestone results have been the concept of proof-carrying code (PCC) [23] and the technique of checking the result of each compilation instead of verifying the compiler's source code [24]. PCC architectures [10] and certifying compilers [11] exist for general purpose languages like Java. A variation of the PCC, abstraction-carrying code [2,8] was developed for constraint logic programs, where a fixpoint of an abstract interpretation serves as certificate for invariants. This enables automatic proof generation.

In this paper, we present a verifying compiler for the stream-based monitoring language Lola. Compared to general programming languages, the compilation of monitoring languages is still a young research topic. Some work has focused on compiling specifications immediately into executable code. Rmor [17], for instance, generates constant memory C code.

---

[6] The specification was adapted to be compliant with RTLola: rather than accessing the input with a future offset, the specification used a negative offset of −2.

Similarly, a Copilot [26] specification can be compiled into a constant memory and constant time C realization. The Copilot toolchain [27] enables the verification of the monitor using the CBMC model checker [9]. As opposed to our approach, their verification is limited to the absence of various arithmetic errors, lacking functional correctness. While CBMC can verify arbitrary inline assertions, Copilot does not generate them. Note that, in contrast to Lola, Copilot can express real-time properties.

RTLola [15,32], on the other hand, is a real-time, asynchronous extension of Lola, for which a compilation into the hardware description language VHDL exists [7]. The VHDL code contains traceability annotations [5] and can then be realized on an FPGA. Similarly, Pellizzoni et al. [25] and Schumann et al. [20,31] realize their runtime monitors on FPGAs, yet without verification or traceability.

Rather than using a dedicated specification language, there are several logics for which verified compilers exist. Differential dynamic logic [28], for example, was specifically designed to capture the complex hybrid dynamics of cyberphysical systems. The ModelPlex [19] framework translates such a specification into several verified components monitoring both the environment with respect to the assumed model and the controller decisions. Lastly, there is work on verifying monitors for metric first-order temporal [30] and dynamic logic [4].

8   Conclusion

We have presented a compilation of Lola specifications into Rust code. Using Rust as the compilation target has the advantage that the executables are highly performant and can be used directly on many embedded platforms. The generated code contains annotations that enable the verification of the code using the Viper framework. With the guiding assertions in the code, as well as function contracts and loop invariants, Viper can verify monitors even for large specifications.

Our results are promising and encourage further research in this direction, such as compiling more expressive dialects of Lola such as RTLola [15,32]. RTLola extends Lola with real-time aspects and can handle asynchronous inputs. The added functionality is highly relevant in the design of monitors for cyberphysical systems [6,14]. While generating verifiable RTLola monitors in Rust will require additional effort, such an extension would further improve the practical applicability of our approach.

References

1. Adolf, F.-M., Faymonville, P., Finkbeiner, B., Schirmer, S., Torens, C.: Stream runtime monitoring on UAS. In: Lahiri, S., Reger, G. (eds.) RV 2017. LNCS, vol. 10548, pp. 33–49. Springer, Cham (2017). https://doi.org/10.1007/978-3-319-67531-2_3
2. Albert, E., Puebla, G., Hermenegildo, M.: Abstraction-Carrying Code. In: Baader, F., Voronkov, A. (eds.) LPAR 2005. LNCS (LNAI), vol. 3452, pp. 380–397. Springer, Heidelberg (2005). https://doi.org/10.1007/978-3-540-32275-7_25

3. Astrauskas, V., Müller, P., Poli, F., Summers, A.J.: Leveraging rust types for modular specification and verification. Proc. ACM Program. Lang. **3**(OOPSLA), 147:1–147:30 (2019). https://doi.org/10.1145/3360573

4. Basin, D., et al.: A formally verified, optimized monitor for metric first-order dynamic logic. In: Peltier, N., Sofronie-Stokkermans, V. (eds.) IJCAR 2020. LNCS (LNAI), vol. 12166, pp. 432–453. Springer, Cham (2020). https://doi.org/10.1007/978-3-030-51074-9_25

5. Baumeister: Tracing correctness: a practical Approach to Traceable Runtime Monitoring. Master thesis, Saarland University (2020)

6. Baumeister, J., Finkbeiner, B., Schirmer, S., Schwenger, M., Torens, C.: RTLola cleared for take-off: monitoring autonomous aircraft. In: Lahiri, S.K., Wang, C. (eds.) CAV 2020. LNCS, vol. 12225, pp. 28–39. Springer, Cham (2020). https://doi.org/10.1007/978-3-030-53291-8_3

7. Baumeister, J., Finkbeiner, B., Schwenger, M., Torfah, H.: FPGA stream-monitoring of real-time properties. ACM Trans. Embedded Comput. Syst. **18**(5s), 88:1–88:24 (2019). https://doi.org/10.1145/3358220

8. Besson, F., Jensen, T.P., Pichardie, D.: Proof-carrying code from certified abstract interpretation and fixpoint compression. Theor. Comput. Sci. **364**(3), 273–291 (2006). https://doi.org/10.1016/j.tcs.2006.08.012

9. Clarke, E., Kroening, D., Lerda, F.: A tool for checking ANSI-C programs. In: Jensen, K., Podelski, A. (eds.) TACAS 2004. LNCS, vol. 2988, pp. 168–176. Springer, Heidelberg (2004). https://doi.org/10.1007/978-3-540-24730-2_15

10. Colby, C., Lee, P., Necula, G.C.: A proof-carrying code architecture for java. In: Emerson, E.A., Sistla, A.P. (eds.) CAV 2000. LNCS, vol. 1855, pp. 557–560. Springer, Heidelberg (2000). https://doi.org/10.1007/10722167_44

11. Colby, C., Lee, P., Necula, G.C., Blau, F., Plesko, M., Cline, K.: A certifying compiler for java. In: PLDI 2000, pp. 95–107. ACM (2000). https://doi.org/10.1145/349299.349315

12. Convent, L., Hungerecker, S., Leucker, M., Scheffel, T., Schmitz, M., Thoma, D.: TeSSLa: temporal stream-based specification language. In: Massoni, T., Mousavi, M.R. (eds.) SBMF 2018. LNCS, vol. 11254, pp. 144–162. Springer, Cham (2018). https://doi.org/10.1007/978-3-030-03044-5_10

13. D'Angelo, B., et al.: Lola: runtime monitoring of synchronous systems. In: TIME 2005, pp. 166–174. IEEE Computer Society Press, June 2005

14. Faymonville, P., et al.: StreamLAB: stream-based monitoring of cyber-physical systems. In: Dillig, I., Tasiran, S. (eds.) CAV 2019. LNCS, vol. 11561, pp. 421–431. Springer, Cham (2019). https://doi.org/10.1007/978-3-030-25540-4_24

15. Faymonville, P., Finkbeiner, B., Schwenger, M., Torfah, H.: Real-time Stream-based Monitoring. CoRR abs/1711.03829 (2017). http://arxiv.org/abs/1711.03829

16. Gorostiaga, F., Sánchez, C.: Striver: stream runtime verification for real-time event-streams. In: Colombo, C., Leucker, M. (eds.) RV 2018. LNCS, vol. 11237, pp. 282–298. Springer, Cham (2018). https://doi.org/10.1007/978-3-030-03769-7_16

17. Havelund, K.: Runtime verification of C programs. In: Suzuki, K., Higashino, T., Ulrich, A., Hasegawa, T. (eds.) FATES/TestCom -2008. LNCS, vol. 5047, pp. 7–22. Springer, Heidelberg (2008). https://doi.org/10.1007/978-3-540-68524-1_3

18. Hoare, C.A.R.: The verifying compiler: a grand challenge for computing research. J. ACM **50**(1), 63–69 (2003). https://doi.org/10.1145/602382.602403

19. Mitsch, S., Platzer, A.: Modelplex: verified runtime validation of verified cyber-physical system models. Formal Methods Syst. Des. **49**(1–2), 33–74 (2016). https://doi.org/10.1007/s10703-016-0241-z

20. Moosbrugger, P., Rozier, K.Y., Schumann, J.: R2U2: monitoring and diagnosis of security threats for unmanned aerial systems. Formal Methods Syst. Des. **51**(1), 31–61 (2017). https://doi.org/10.1007/s10703-017-0275-x

21. de Moura, L., Bjørner, N.: Z3: an efficient SMT solver. In: Ramakrishnan, C.R., Rehof, J. (eds.) TACAS 2008. LNCS, vol. 4963, pp. 337–340. Springer, Heidelberg (2008). https://doi.org/10.1007/978-3-540-78800-3_24

22. Müller, P., Schwerhoff, M., Summers, A.J.: Viper: a verification infrastructure for permission-based reasoning. In: Jobstmann, B., Leino, K.R.M. (eds.) VMCAI 2016. LNCS, vol. 9583, pp. 41–62. Springer, Heidelberg (2016). https://doi.org/10.1007/978-3-662-49122-5_2

23. Necula, G.C.: Proof-carrying code. In: POPL 1997, pp. 106–119. ACM Press (1997). https://doi.org/10.1145/263699.263712

24. Necula, G.C., Lee, P.: The design and implementation of a certifying compiler. In: PLDI 1998, pp. 333–344. ACM (1998). https://doi.org/10.1145/277650.277752

25. Pellizzoni, R., Meredith, P.O., Caccamo, M., Rosu, G.: Hardware runtime monitoring for dependable cots-based real-time embedded systems. In: RTSS 2008, pp. 481–491. IEEE Computer Society (2008). https://doi.org/10.1109/RTSS.2008.43

26. Pike, L., Goodloe, A., Morisset, R., Niller, S.: Copilot: a hard real-time runtime monitor. In: Barringer, H., et al. (eds.) RV 2010. LNCS, vol. 6418, pp. 345–359. Springer, Heidelberg (2010). https://doi.org/10.1007/978-3-642-16612-9_26

27. Pike, L., Wegmann, N., Niller, S., Goodloe, A.: Copilot: monitoring embedded systems. Innov. Syst. Softw. Eng. **9**(4), 235–255 (2013). https://doi.org/10.1007/s11334-013-0223-x

28. Platzer, A.: Differential dynamic logic for hybrid systems. J. Autom. Reason. **41**(2), 143–189 (2008). https://doi.org/10.1007/s10817-008-9103-8

29. Pnueli, A.: The temporal logic of programs. In: Annual Symposium on Foundations of Computer Science 1977, pp. 46–57. IEEE Computer Society (1977). https://doi.org/10.1109/SFCS.1977.32

30. Schneider, J., Basin, D., Krstić, S., Traytel, D.: A formally verified monitor for metric first-order temporal logic. In: Finkbeiner, B., Mariani, L. (eds.) RV 2019. LNCS, vol. 11757, pp. 310–328. Springer, Cham (2019). https://doi.org/10.1007/978-3-030-32079-9_18

31. Schumann, J., Moosbrugger, P., Rozier, K.Y.: R2U2: monitoring and diagnosis of security threats for unmanned aerial systems. In: Bartocci, E., Majumdar, R. (eds.) RV 2015. LNCS, vol. 9333, pp. 233–249. Springer, Cham (2015). https://doi.org/10.1007/978-3-319-23820-3_15

32. Schwenger, M.: Let's not Trust Experience Blindly: Formal Monitoring of Humans and other CPS. Master thesis, Saarland University (2019)

Automatic Optimizations
for Stream-Based Monitoring Languages

Jan Baumeister[1]([✉]) [iD], Bernd Finkbeiner[1] [iD], Matthis Kruse[2] [iD],
and Maximilian Schwenger[1] [iD]

[1] CISPA Helmholtz Center for Information Security, Saarland Informatics Campus,
66123 Saarbrücken, Germany
{jan.baumeister,finkbeiner,maximilian.schwenger}@cispa.saarland
[2] Saarland University, Saarland Informatics Campus, 66123 Saarbrücken, Germany
matthis.kruse@cs.uni-saarland.de

Abstract. Runtime monitors that are specified in a stream-based monitoring language tend to be easier to understand, maintain, and reuse than those written in a standard programming language. Because of their formal semantics, such specification languages are also a natural choice for safety-critical applications. Unlike for standard programming languages, there is, however, so far very little support for automatic code optimization. In this paper, we present the first collection of code transformations for the stream-based monitoring language RTLOLA. We show that classic compiler optimizations, such as Sparse Conditional Constant Propagation and Common Subexpression Elimination, can be adapted to monitoring specifications. We also develop new transformations—Pacing Type Refinement and Filter Refinement—which exploit the specific modular structure of RTLOLA as well as the implementation freedom afforded by a declarative specification language. We demonstrate the significant impact of the code transformations on benchmarks from the monitoring of unmanned aircraft systems (UAS).

Keywords: Runtime verification · Stream monitoring · Compiler optimizations · Specification languages

1 Introduction

The spectrum of languages for the development of monitors ranges from standard programming languages, like Java and C++, to formal logics like LTL and its many variations. The advantage of programming languages is the universal expressiveness and the availability of modern compiler technology; programming languages lack, however, the precise semantics and compile-time guarantees

This work was partially supported by the German Research Foundation (DFG) as part of the Collaborative Research Center Foundations of Perspicuous Software Systems (TRR 248, 389792660), and by the European Research Council (ERC) Grant OSARES (No. 683300).

© Springer Nature Switzerland AG 2020
J. Deshmukh and D. Ničković (Eds.): RV 2020, LNCS 12399, pp. 451–461, 2020.
https://doi.org/10.1007/978-3-030-60508-7_25

needed for safety-critical applications. Formal logics, on the other hand, are sufficiently precise, but have limited expressiveness. A good trade-off between the two extremes is provided by stream-based monitoring languages like RTLOLA. Stream-based languages have the expressiveness of a programming language, and, at the same time, the formal semantics and compile-time guarantees of a formal specification language.

For standard programming languages, the development of effective code optimizations is one of the most fundamental research questions. By contrast, there is, so far, very little support for the automatic optimization of monitoring specifications. In this paper, we present the first collection of code transformations for the stream-based monitoring language RTLOLA [7].

Our starting point are compiler optimizations known from imperative programming languages like *Sparse Conditional Constant Propagation* and *Common Subexpression Elimination*. Adapted to stream-based specifications, such transformations allow the user to write code that is easy to read and maintain, without the performance penalty resulting, for example, from unnecessarily recomputing the value of subexpressions.

We also develop optimizations that are specific to stream-based monitoring. Stream-based languages have several features that make them a particularly promising target for code optimization. Stream-based languages are *declarative* in the sense that it is only the correct computation of the trigger conditions that matters for the soundness of the monitor, not the specific order in which intermediate data is produced. This leaves much more freedom for code transformation than in an imperative language. Another feature of stream-based languages that is beneficial for code transformation is that the write-access to memory is inherently *local*: the computation of a stream only writes once in its local memory while potentially reading multiple times from other streams[1]. This means that expressions used for the computation of one stream can be modified without affecting the other streams. Finally, our code optimization exploits the clear *dependency structure* of stream-based specifications, which allows us to efficiently propagate type changes made in one stream to all affected streams in the remainder of the specification. We present two transformations that specifically exploit these advantages. *Pacing Type Refinement* optimizes the points in time when a stream value is calculated, eliminating the computation of stream values that are never used. *Filter Refinement* avoids the unnecessary computation of expressions that appear in the scope of an *if* statement, ensuring that the expression is only evaluated if the condition is actually true.

RTLOLA specifications are used both in interpretation-based monitors [7] and as the source language for compilers, for example to VHDL [3]. Our code transformations are applicable in both approaches, because the transformations are applied already on the level of intermediate representations (AST, IR). In transpilation backends, the optimized code is compiled one more time, and thus

---

[1] This is related to the functional programming paradigm where function calls are *pure*, i.e., free of side effects.

additionally benefits from the standard compiler optimizations for the target platform.

A prime application area for our optimizations is the monitoring of unmanned aircraft systems (UAS) [2]. Monitoring aircraft involves complex computations, such as the crossvalidation of different sensor modules. The performance of the monitor implementation is critical, because the on-board monitor is executed on a platform with limited computing power. Our experience with the code transformations (for details see Sect. 5) is very encouraging.

1.1 Related Work

This paper presents the first collection of code transformations for the stream-based monitoring language RTLOLA. There is, of course, a vast literature on compiler optimization. For an introduction, we refer the reader to the standard textbooks on compiler design and implementation (cf. [1,14,17]). Kildall [13] gives a comprehensive overview on the classic code transformations. The foundation for the code transformations is provided by methods from program analysis such as abstract interpretation [6].

The programming paradigm that most closely resembles stream-based monitoring languages like RTLOLA is *synchronous programming*. Examples of synchronous programming languages are LUSTRE [12], ESTEREL [4], and SIGNAL [9]. These languages are supported by optimization techniques like the annotation-based memory optimization of LUSTRE [10] and the low-level elimination of redundant gates and latches in ESTEREL [15]. There are, however, important differences to the transformations presented in this paper. Our transformations work on the level of intermediate representations, which makes them uniformly applicable to interpretation and compilation. The new *Pacing Type* and *Filter Refinements* furthermore exploit the specific modular structure of RTLOLA as well as the much greater implementation freedom afforded by a declarative specification language.

Our focus on RTLOLA is motivated by recent work on RTLOLA-based monitoring for UAS [2] and other cyber-physical systems [3,7]. It should be possible, however, to develop similar optimizations for other stream-based monitoring languages like TeSSLa [5] and Striver [11].

2   RTLOLA

RTLOLA [7,8] is a runtime monitoring framework. In its core, it takes a specification in the eponymous specification language and analyzes whether and when input data violates the specification. To this end, it interprets sequences of incoming data points as input streams. The RTLOLA stream engine then transforms these values according to stream expressions in the specification to obtain output streams. The specification also contains trigger conditions, i.e., boolean expressions indicating whether a certain property is violated or not. Stream expressions and trigger conditions depend either on input or output stream values.

Consider the following RTLOLA specification.

```
input gps: (Float64, Float64)
output gps_readings: Bool@1Hz := gps.aggregate(over:2s,using:count)
trigger gps_glitch < 10 "GPS sensor frequency < 5Hz"
```

The specification first declares an input stream with the name gps. The output stream gps_readings analyzes the input stream by counting how many readings the monitor received within the last 2s. This computation is a sliding window, so when the gps_readings stream computes a new value at point in time t, RTLOLA takes all data points of the gps stream into account, which were received in the interval $[t - 2s, t]$. The trigger then checks whether the number of GPS readings in such a 2s interval falls below 10. If so, it raises an alarm such that the observed system can react accordingly e.g. by initiating mitigation procedures.

2.1 Type System

Types in RTLOLA are two-dimensional consisting of the value type and the pacing type. The former is drawn from a set of types representable with a static amount of bits. The pacing type consists of two components: an evaluation trigger and a filter condition. The monitor will compute a new value for a stream as soon as the evaluation trigger occurred *unless* the filter condition is false. Let us ignore filter conditions for now. The evaluation trigger can be a real-time frequency as was the case for gps_readings. In this case, the stream is a *periodic* stream. Otherwise, the evaluation trigger is a positive boolean formula φ over the set of input streams, in which case the stream is *event-based*. The reason behind this lies within the input model of RTLOLA. RTLOLA assumes input values to arrive asynchronously, i.e., if a specification declares several input streams $\mathcal{I}$, an incoming data point $\mathcal{I}'$ can cover an arbitrary non-empty subset $\emptyset \neq \mathcal{I}' \subseteq \mathcal{I}$. Only streams in $\mathcal{I}'$ receive a new value. Thus, the monitor evaluates event-based streams with evaluation trigger ι iff $\mathcal{I}' \implies \iota$. I.e., it replaces all occurrence of the input stream name i in ι by true if $\iota \in \mathcal{I}'$ and false otherwise. Consequently, any input stream i has evaluation trigger $\{i\}$ intuitively meaning "i will be extended when the system provides a new value for it." For event-based streams, the evaluation trigger is called the *activation condition*.

Note that the type annotation of gps in the previous example does not contain information about the pacing type at all. In many cases, RTLOLA infers the types of streams automatically based on the stream expression rendering type annotations largely optional. While the type inference for value types is straight-forward because RTLOLA requires input streams to have type annotations, the inference for pacing types is mainly based on stream accesses. There are three kinds of stream accesses: synchronous, asynchronous, and aggregations. If a stream x accesses a stream y synchronously, then the evaluation of x demands the nth-to-latest value of y where n is the *offset* of the access. This ties the evaluation of both streams together, so if y has an evaluation frequency of 5 Hz,

x cannot be evaluated more frequently, nor can x be event-based. Asynchronous accesses refer to the last value of a stream, no matter how old it may be. Here, the pacing of x and y remain decoupled. Aggregating accesses—such as the one in `gps_readings`—decouple the pacing as well.

Lastly, filter conditions are regular RTLOLA expressions. Assume stream x has the evaluation condition π with filter ϕ. Whenever π is true, the monitor evaluates the filter ϕ. Only if the filter is true as well, the monitor evaluates the stream expression and extends x.

2.2 Evaluation

An RTLOLA specification consists of input streams, output streams, and triggers. The monitor for a specification computes a static schedule containing information on which a periodic stream needs to be computed at which point in time. When such a point in time is reached or the monitor receives new input values, it starts an evaluation cycle. Here, the monitor first determines which streams could be affected by checking their frequencies or activation conditions. It then orders them according to an *evaluation order* $\prec$. Following this order, the monitor checks the filter condition of each stream. If it evaluates to true, the monitor extends the stream by evaluating the stream expression to obtain a new value.

This process only works correctly if the evaluation order complies with the *dependency graph* of the specification. The annotated dependency graph is a directed multigraph consisting of one node for each trigger, stream, and filter condition. Each edge in the graph represents a stream access in the specification. For the evaluation order, only synchronous lookups matter: if node s access node s' synchronously, s' needs to be evaluated before s.

After the evaluation, the monitor checks whether a trigger conditions was true. If so, passes the information on to the system under scrutiny. This constitutes the *observable behavior* of the monitor, any other computation is considered internal behavior. Consequently, any computation that does not impact a trigger condition is completely irrelevant.

This is just a rough outline of RTLOLA. For more information refer to [16].

Remark 1 (Transformations Preserve Observable Behavior). The point behind the compiler transformations presented in this paper is to improve the running time and thus decrease the latency between the occurrence and report of a violation. Yet, the correctness, i.e., the observable behavior of the monitor needs to remain unchanged. Thus, the transformations may alter the behavior of the monitor arbitrarily granted the observable behavior remains the same.

3   Classical Compiler Optimizations

In this section, we explain the adaption of classical compiler optimization techniques to the specification language RTLOLA. These techniques focuses on the expression of a stream under consideration of the pacing type. We exemplarily introduce transformations for the *Sparse Conditional Constant Propagation* and the *Common Expression Elimination*.

3.1   Sparse Conditional Constant Propagation

Sparse Conditional Constant Propagation (SCCP) allows the programmer to write maintainable specifications without a performance penalty of constant streams. It inlines them, pre-evaluates constant expressions, and deletes never accessed streams that includes a simple dead-code elimination. This procedure works transitively, i.e., a stream that turns constant due to the inlining will again be subject to the same transformation. Note that evaluating a constant expression might change the activation condition of a stream. Thus, the transformation annotates types explicitly before changing expressions.

3.2   Common Subexpression Elimination

The Common Subexpression Elimination (CSE) identifies subexpressions that appear multiple times and assigns the subexpressions to new streams. These new streams might increase the required memory but save computation time by eliminating repeated computations.

In RTLOLA, finding common subexpressions is simple compared to imperative programing languages for several reasons. First, RTLOLA as a declarative language is agnostic to the syntactic order in which streams are declared; the evaluation order only depends on the dependency graph. Secondly, expression evaluations are *pure*, i.e., free of side effects. As a result, the common subexpression elimination becomes a syntactic task except that it requires access to the inferred types. Here, two subexpressions are only considered common, if their pacing is of the same kind: periodic or event-based. This is necessary because RTLOLA strictly separates the evaluation of expressions with different pacing type kinds.

After identifying a common subexpression, the transformation creates a new stream and replaces occurrences of the expression by stream accesses. The pacing type of the newly created stream is either the disjunction of the activation conditions of accessing streams, or the least common multiple of their evaluation frequencies. The latter case is an over-approximation that introduces additional, irrelevant evaluations of the common subexpression. This might decrease the performance of the monitor, so CSE is only applied if the least common multiple coincides with one of the accessing frequencies. In this case, the transformation is always beneficial.

4   RTLOLA Specific Optimizations

This section introduces transformations around the concept of pacing types. Since these types are specific to the specification language RTLOLA, the transformations are as well. The concepts, however, apply to similar languages as well. We introduce the *Pacing Type Refinement* and the *Filter Refinement* as such transformations.

4.1   Pacing Type Refinement

In this subsection, we describe a transformation refining the pacing type of output streams. Consider the following specification as an example. Note, the inferred pacing types are marked gray, whereas the black ones are annotated explicitly.

```
input alt, lat: Float64
output check_alt @{alt}
  := alt < b₀
output check_lat @{lat}
  := lat ∈ [b₁, b₂]
trigger @{alt ∧ lat}
  ¬(check_alt ∧ check_lat)
```

```
input alt, lat: Float64
output check_alt @{alt ∧ lat}
  := alt < b₀
output check_lat @{alt ∧ lat}
  := lat ∈ [b₁, b₂]
trigger @{alt ∧ lat}
  ¬(check_alt ∧ check_lat)
```

The specification shows a simple geofence, i.e., it checks if the altitude and latitude values are in the specified bounds. Each expression only accesses one input stream, so the specification infers the pacing types @{alt} and @{lat} for the output streams. The trigger then accesses all output stream values and notifies the user if a bound is violated. Transitively, the trigger accesses all input streams, so its inferred pacing type is @{alt ∧ lat}. With this type, the monitor evaluates the trigger iff all input streams receive a new value at the same time. Consequently, whenever an event arrives that does not cover both input streams, the output stream computations are in vain. This justifies refining the pacing types of the output streams to mirror the pacing type of the trigger, which is exactly what the Pacing Type Refinement transformation does.

For event-based streams, the transformation finds the most specific activation condition that does not change the observable behavior. This goal is achieved by annotating a stream with a pacing type that is the disjunction of all pacing types accessing it. For periodic streams, the transformation proceeds similarly. Here, the explicit type annotation is the slowest frequency such that each stream access is still valid, i.e., the least common multiple of each accessing frequency, similar to Sect. 3.2.

Note that the pacing type transformation of a stream s is only possible if all accesses to s are synchronous, i.e., $(s_j^-, 0, s^\top) \in E$. Otherwise, the transformation might change the observable behavior, as illustrated with the following example. Consider a sliding window in a trigger condition targeting a stream $s^\top$. Assume further that the transformation changes the pacing type $s^\top.pt$ from 2 Hz to 1 Hz. As a result, $s^\top$ produces fewer values, changing the result of the sliding window and thus the trigger as well.

The transformation resolves transitive dependencies by applying a fix-point iteration.

4.2   Filter Refinement

RTLOLA is free of side effects and thanks to its evaluation order, it has a static program flow. The static program flow, however, also has a drawback: if a stream

s conditionally accesses a stream s', s' will always be evaluated before the condition is resolved. This problem can be circumvented by integrating the condition occurring in the expression of s into the filter of s'.

Consider the following specifications:

```
input pilots : Float64
input emergency : Bool
output check_1
 @{emergency ∧ pilots}
  := num_pilots > 0

output check_2
 @{emergency ∧ pilots}
  := num_pilots == 2

trigger @{emergency ∧ pilots}
if !emergency then check_1 else
    check_2
```

```
input pilots : Float64
input emergency : Bool
output check_1
 @{emergency ∧ pilots}
 { filter !emergency }
  := pilots > 0
output check_2
 @{emergency ∧ pilots}
 { filter emergency }
  := num_pilots == 2
trigger @{emergency ∧ pilots}
if !emergency then
  check_1.hold(or: true)
else check_2.hold(or: true)
```

Both specifications check the number of pilots in the cockpit. Depending on whether or not the plane is in emergency mode, one or two pilots are adequate. Because of the static evaluation order, the monitor with the specification on the left always computes the values of both output streams. However, the final trigger only uses one of the streams, depending on the emergency input. Thus, the monitor can avoid half of the output computations. The specification on the right show how this can be achieved using Filter Refinement. The transformation adds filters to all streams accessed in the consequence or alternative of a conditional expression. Additionally, it replaces the synchronous lookups to these streams with asynchronous lookups and adds explicit type annotations. The former prevents the type inference from adding the filter to the trigger as well. The latter is necessary because the type of the trigger can no longer be inferred without the synchronous lookups. Similar to previous transformations, Filter Refinement takes direct and transitive dependencies into account.

The algorithm for this transformation consists of four parts: In the first step, it identifies conditional expressions. Afterward, it constructs the filter condition for the synchronously accessed streams based on the condition following four rules. If a stream is accesses in a) the condition, it does not add any filter condition. b) the consequence, it adds a filter containing the if-condition. c) the alternative, it adds a filter containing the negation of the if-condition. d) a nested conditional, it builds the conjunction of the conditions. e) the consequence and the alternative of a nested conditional, it combines the filter conditions with a disjunction. f) the consequence and the alternative of a non-nested conditional, it does not add a filter.

After building the filter conditions for the synchronously accessed streams, the transformation adds the filter to the stream. If the stream already had one, the transformation builds the conjunction of both. It then changes the affected synchronous lookups to asynchronous ones to prevent the type inference from adapting its own filter. This process is repeated until a fix-point is reached. Note that the transformation is only possible for synchronous lookups, otherwise the transformation alters the observable behavior.

5   Evaluation

We evaluate our transformations using the interpreter of the RTLOLA framework [7].[2] We compare the monitor executions with enabled and disabled compiler transformations for a specification checking whether an aircraft remains within a geofence [2]. The traces for the evaluation consists of 10,000 randomly generated events. Each execution was performed ten times on a 2.9 GHz Dual-Core Intel Core i5 processor.

The geofence specification was selected due to its high practical relevance. It checks if the monitored aircraft leaves a polygonal area, i.e., the zone for which the aircraft has a flight permission. If the monitor raises a trigger, the vehicle has to start an emergency landing to prevent further damage. The specification computes the approximated trajectory of the vehicle to decide whether a face of the fence was crossed.

The shape of the fence is determined statically, so the gradient and y-intercept of the faces are constants in the original specification. We generalized the specification slightly for our case study. This makes the specification more maintainable without forsaking performance thanks to the SCCP transformation. In a geofence with five faces, the SCCP propagates and eliminates 48 constants streams. This roughly halves the execution time of the monitor as can be seen in the first graph of Fig. 1.

In the second evaluation, we extended the specification by a third dimension, also taking the altitude of the aircraft into account. The altitude of the aircraft is independent of the longitude and latitude, rendering computations of the output streams unobservable for events not covering all three dimensions. Here, the Pacing Type Refinement places explicit type annotations on 32 streams in the specification with five faces. The new trace contains a new reading for the altitude every 100ms and for the longitude and latitude every 10ms. The impact of the Pacing Type Refinement can be seen in the second graph of Fig. 1: the monitor for the transformed specification is roughly three times faster.

To evaluate the impact of the Filter Refinement, we adapt the specification to perform a violation check for an under-approximation of the geo-fence. The more costly precise geo-fence check is only performed if the under-approximation reports a violation. This specification shows the potential impact of the Filter Refinement transformation, which adds filters to 27 output streams for a geofence with five faces. The first two columns in the third graph of Fig. 1 illustrate the results of the executions with a trace that is most of the time within the under-approximated fence. Surprisingly, the specification after the transformation is about three times slower than the original specification.

---

[2] http://rtlola.org.

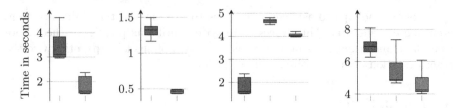

Fig. 1. From left to right, the graphs show the impact of SCCP, Pacing Type Refinement, Filter Refinement without, and with pre-existing filters. Red boxes are the running time before applying the respective transformation, blue after, and green by additionally applying CSE. (Color figure online)

The reason lies within the evaluation process of the monitor. Filters increase the number of nodes in the dependency graph, thus triggering new evaluation steps. In our example, this produces an overhead that is higher than the performance benefits gained by adding filters. The last graph in Fig. 1 shows the results for a specification like that for the same input trace. Here, the transformation reduces the execution time by about 30%.

When now also applying the CSE as well, 27 filter conditions and one if condition can be summarized in a common subexpression. This yields another 5% performance gain as can be seen in the last two graphs in Fig. 1.

6   Conclusion

Since the safety of the monitored system rests on the quality of the monitoring specification, it is crucially important that specifications are easy to understand and maintain. The code transformations presented in this paper contribute towards this goal. By taking care of performance considerations, the transformations help the user to focus on writing clear specifications.

Monitoring languages are, in many ways, similar to programming languages. It is therefore not surprising that classic compiler optimization techniques like Sparse Conditional Constant Propagation and Common Subexpression Elimination are also useful for monitoring. Especially encouraging, however, is the effect of our new Pacing Type and Filter Refinements. In our experiments, the transformations improved the performance of the monitor as much as threefold. This could be a starting point for a new branch of runtime verification research that, similar to the area of compiler optimization in programming language theory, focusses on the automatic transformation and optimization of monitoring specifications.

In future work, our immediate next step is to integrate further common code transformations into our framework. We will also investigate the interplay between the different transformations and develop heuristics that choose the best transformations for a specific specification. A careful understanding of the impact on the monitoring performance is especially needed for transformations that prolong the evaluation order, such as Common Subexpression Elimination and Filter Refinement.

References

1. Aho, A.V., Lam, M.S., Sethi, R., Ullman, J.D.: Compilers: Principles, Techniques, and Tools, 2nd edn. Addison Wesley, Boston (2006)
2. Baumeister, J., Finkbeiner, B., Schirmer, S., Schwenger, M., Torens, C.: RTLola cleared for take-off: monitoring autonomous aircraft. In: Lahiri, S.K., Wang, C. (eds.) CAV 2020. LNCS, vol. 12225, pp. 28–39. Springer, Cham (2020). https://doi.org/10.1007/978-3-030-53291-8_3
3. Baumeister, J., Finkbeiner, B., Schwenger, M., Torfah, H.: FPGA stream-monitoring of real-time properties. ACM Trans. Embed. Comput. Syst. 18(5), 88:1–88:24 (2019). https://doi.org/10.1145/3358220
4. Berry, G.: The foundations of Esterel. In: Proof, Language, and Interaction: Essays in Honour of Robin Milner, pp. 425–454. MIT Press (2000)
5. Convent, L., Hungerecker, S., Leucker, M., Scheffel, T., Schmitz, M., Thoma, D.: TeSSLa: temporal stream-based specification language. In: Massoni, T., Mousavi, M.R. (eds.) SBMF 2018. LNCS, vol. 11254, pp. 144–162. Springer, Cham (2018). https://doi.org/10.1007/978-3-030-03044-5_10
6. Cousot, P., Cousot, R.: Abstract interpretation: a unified lattice model for static analysis of programs by construction or approximation of fixpoints. In: POPL 1977, pp. 238–252. Association for Computing Machinery, New York (1977). https://doi.org/10.1145/512950.512973
7. Faymonville, P., et al.: StreamLAB: stream-based monitoring of cyber-physical systems. In: Dillig, I., Tasiran, S. (eds.) CAV 2019. LNCS, vol. 11561, pp. 421–431. Springer, Cham (2019). https://doi.org/10.1007/978-3-030-25540-4_24
8. Faymonville, P., Finkbeiner, B., Schwenger, M., Torfah, H.: Real-time stream-based monitoring. CoRR abs/1711.03829 (2017). http://arxiv.org/abs/1711.03829
9. Gautier, T., Le Guernic, P., Besnard, L.: SIGNAL: a declarative language for synchronous programming of real-time systems. In: Kahn, G. (ed.) FPCA 1987. LNCS, vol. 274, pp. 257–277. Springer, Heidelberg (1987). https://doi.org/10.1007/3-540-18317-5_15
10. Gérard, L., Guatto, A., Pasteur, C., Pouzet, M.: A modular memory optimization for synchronous data-flow languages: application to arrays in a lustre compiler. SIGPLAN Not. 47(5), 51–60 (2012). https://doi.org/10.1145/2345141.2248426
11. Gorostiaga, F., Sánchez, C.: Striver: stream runtime verification for real-time event-streams. In: Colombo, C., Leucker, M. (eds.) RV 2018. LNCS, vol. 11237, pp. 282–298. Springer, Cham (2018). https://doi.org/10.1007/978-3-030-03769-7_16
12. Halbwachs, N., Caspi, P., Raymond, P., Pilaud, D.: The synchronous data-flow programming language LUSTRE. Proc. of IEEE 79(9), 1305–1320 (1991)
13. Kildall, G.A.: A unified approach to global program optimization. In: POPL 1973, pp. 194–206. Association for Computing Machinery, New York (1973). https://doi.org/10.1145/512927.512945
14. Muchnick, S.S.: Advanced Compiler Design and Implementation. Morgan Kaufmann Publishers Inc., San Francisco (1998)
15. Potop-Butucaru, D.: Fast Redundancy elimination using high-level structural information from Esterel. Technical report RR-4330, INRIA (2001). https://hal.inria.fr/inria-00072257
16. Schwenger, M.: Let's not trust experience blindly: formal monitoring of humans and other CPS. Master thesis, Saarland University (2019)
17. Seidl, H., Wilhelm, R., Hack, S.: Compiler Design - Analysis and Transformation. Springer, Heidelberg (2012). https://doi.org/10.1007/978-3-642-17548-0

Unifying the Time-Event Spectrum for Stream Runtime Verification

Felipe Gorostiaga[1,2,3(✉)], Luis Miguel Danielsson[1,2], and César Sánchez[1(✉)]

[1] IMDEA Software Institute, Madrid, Spain
{felipe.gorostiaga,luismiguel.danielsson,cesar.sanchez}@imdea.org
[2] Universidad Politécnica de Madrid (UPM), Madrid, Spain
[3] CIFASIS, Rosario, Argentina

Abstract. We study the spectra of time-event and of synchronous-asynchronous models of computation for runtime verification, in particular in the context of stream runtime verification (SRV). Most runtime verification formalisms do not involve a notion of time, either by having inputs at all instants (like LTL or Lola) or by reacting to external events in an event-driven fashion (like MOP). Other formalisms consider notions of real-time, ranging from the collection and periodic processing of events to complex computations of the times at which events exist or are produced (like TeSSLa or Striver). Also, some monitoring languages assume that all inputs and outputs change values at once (synchronous), while others allow changes independently (asynchronous).

In this paper we present a unifying view of the event-time and synchronous-asynchronous dimensions in the general setting of SRV. We first prove that the Striver event-based asynchronous language can execute synchronous untimed specifications (written in Lola), and empirically show that this simulation is efficient. We then prove that Lola can simulate real-time Striver monitors under the assumption of the existence of temporal backbones and study two cases: (1) Purely event-driven or when reactions can be precomputed (for example periodic intervals), which results in an efficient simulation but restricted to a fragment. (2) When the time has a minimum quantum: which allows full expressivity but the performance is greatly affected, particularly for sparse input streams.

1 Introduction

Runtime verification (RV) is a dynamic technique for software quality assurance that consists of generating a monitor from a formal specification, that then inspects a single trace of execution of the system under analysis. Stream runtime verification, pioneered by Lola [7], defines monitors by declaring the dependencies

---

This work was funded in part by the Madrid Regional Government under project "S2018/TCS-4339 (BLOQUES-CM)", by Spanish National Project "BOSCO (PGC2018-102210-B-100)", and by FPU Grant FPU18/04362 granted by the Spanish Ministry of Science, Innovation and Universities.

J. Deshmukh and D. Ničković (Eds.): RV 2020, LNCS 12399, pp. 462–481, 2020.
https://doi.org/10.1007/978-3-030-60508-7_26

between output streams of results and input streams of observations. In this paper we study different models of streams and how the corresponding languages compare to each other in terms of expressivity and efficiency.

Motivated by the counterparts in static verification, early approaches for RV specification languages were based on temporal logics [3,9,15], regular expressions [20], timed regular expressions [1], rules [2], or rewriting [18]. SRV is a more expressive formalism that goes beyond Boolean verdicts, like in logical techniques, to allow specifying the collection of statistics and the generation of richer (non-Boolean) verdicts. Examples include counting events, specifying robustness or generating models or quantitative verdicts. See [7,8,12,14] for examples illustrating the expressivity of SRV languages. Some SRV formalisms consider streams to be sequences of raw data (as in LTL propositions), so the data observed in different streams at the same index in their sequences are considered to have occurred at the same time. In this regard, stream sequences are *synchronized* and thus we say that formalisms following this paradigm are *synchronous* SRV formalisms. Examples of synchronous formalisms include Lola [7], LTL, regular-expressions, Mision-time LTL [17], Functional Reactive Programming (FRP) [11] and systems like Copilot [16].

On the other hand, new formalisms have been proposed that consider streams to be sequences of events formed by data values that are time-stamped with the time at which the data is produced (either observed or generated). In this paradigm, streams can be of different length, and the only condition is that the time-stamps are monotonically increasing. As a result, the same position of different streams are not necessarily time-correlated. In this regard, we can say that stream sequences are *asynchronous*, and thus we say that formalisms following this paradigm are *asynchronous* SRV formalisms. Examples of asynchronous SRV formalisms include RTLola [13], Striver [14] and TeSSLa [5].

Synchronous SRV formalisms are best suited for cases when data is periodically gathered for every input stream at the same time from the system under analysis. Asynchronous formalisms are best suited for situations when data on the input streams can be received at unpredictable moments—when something of interest happens—and results can be calculated at any time, not only when an event is observed. By these characteristics, we say that synchronous SRV formalisms are *sample based*, while asynchronous SRV formalisms are *event based*.

In this paper we will use Lola and Striver to show how the semantics of a synchronous SRV formalism can be mimicked by an asynchronous SRV formalism and vice versa. As a corollary, the languages subsumed by each formalism can be automatically translated to the other under the conditions of our results. We also study the impact on efficiency of each approach, and the different alternatives to deal with the loss in performance.

The example specifications and empirical evaluation are based on the real-world data in the dataset Orange4Home [6], which comprises the recording of activities of a single person in an instrumented apartment over the span of four consecutive weeks of work days. This dataset was studied previously in RV using an Execution History Encoding (EHE) in [10].

Contributions and Structure. Section 2 contains the preliminaries. Section 3 contains the main contribution: the comparison of two formalisms from different paradigms, and the proof that they are equally expressive. We also describe different alternatives to translate a Striver specification to Lola, which are empirically evaluated in Sect. 4. Finally, Sect. 5 concludes.

2   Preliminaries

We recall now Stream Runtime Verification (SRV) briefly (see [7] and the tutorial [19]). The fundamental idea of SRV, pioneered by Lola [7] is to cleanly separate the temporal dependencies from the individual operations to be performed at each step, which leads to the generalization of monitoring algorithms for logics to the computation of richer values.

A *value stream* is a sequence of values from a domain[1]. In this paper we use *sequences* to refer to value streams to distinguish them from event streams. We can refer to the value at the n-th position in a sequence z writing $z(n)$. For example, the sequence $co2 = [350, 360, 289, 320, 330]$ contains samples of the level of CO2 in the air (measured in parts-per-million). In this sequence $co2(0) = 350$ and $co2(2) = 289$.

An *event stream* is a succession of events (t, d) where d is a value from a value domain (as in sequences) and t is a time-stamp. Time-stamps are elements of a *temporal domain* (for example $\mathbb{R}, \mathbb{Q}, \mathbb{Z}$), a set whose elements are totally ordered. The interpretation of the time domain is a global clock, which is common to all the streams in a monitor. The time-stamps in the events of a legal event-stream are monotonically increasing. Nothing prevents a temporal domain from being used as a value domain of some stream, and in fact it is common to define streams that compute and store the passage of time. Given an element t in the temporal domain of an event stream r, we use $r(t)$ to refer to the value with time-stamp t in r. For example, the event-stream $tv\_status = \{(1.5, off), (4.0, on), (6.0, off), (7.5, on), (8.0, off)\}$ indicates when a television is turned *on* or *off*. The event $(4.0, on)$ in tv_status or the fact that $tv\_status(4.0) = on$, indicate that the TV is switched *on* at time 4.0. We will use $z, w \ldots$ for sequences and $s, r, \ldots$ for event streams. Also, we use t to denote a value of the time domain, and n to range over sequence indices.

Given a positive number N we use $[N]$ for the set $\{0, \ldots, N-1\}$. Given a sequence z, we also use $[z]$ for the set of indices of the sequence $[z] = \{0 \ldots |z|-1\}$. For example, $[co2] = \{0, 1, 2, 3, 4\}$. Given an event stream s, $dom(s)$ is the set of elements in the temporal domain which have an associated value for s. For example, $dom(tv\_status) = \{1.5, 4.0, 6.0, 7.5, 8.0\}$.

Streams and sequences are typed using arbitrary (interpreted) multi-sorted first-order theories. A type has a collection of symbols used to construct expressions, together with an interpretation of these symbols. The domain of the types is the set of values to be used as data values in sequences and streams, and

---

[1] Even though for past-only specifications the results can be extended to infinite sequences, we use here finite sequences as in [7].

the interpretation of the symbols is used to evaluate ground expressions. A Lola specification describes monitors by declaratively specifying the relation between output sequences (verdicts) and input sequences (observations). Similarly, a Striver specification describes the relation between output event-streams and input event-streams. We describe these formalisms separately.

2.1 Lola

Syntax. Given a set Z of (typed) stream variables, the set of *stream expressions* consists of (1) offsets $v[k, d]$ where v is a stream variable of type D, k is an integer number and d a value from D, and (2) function applications $f(t_1, \ldots, t_n)$ using constructors f from the theories to previously defined terms. Stream variables represent value streams (a.k.a. sequences). The intended meaning of expression $v[-1, false]$ is the value of sequence v in the previous position of the trace (or *false* if there is no such previous position, that is, at the beginning). The particular case for an offset with $k = 0$ requires no default value as the index is guaranteed to be within the range of the sequence. Therefore, we will use $v[now]$ for a 0 offset expression. We assume that all theories have a constructor if $\cdot$ then $\cdot$ else $\cdot$ that given an expression of type Bool and two expressions of type D constructs a term of type D. We use $Term_D(Z)$ for the set of stream expressions of type D constructed from variables from Z (and drop Z if clear from the context).

Definition 1 (Lola Specification). *A Lola specification $\varphi\langle I, O \rangle$ consists of a set $I = \{x_1, \ldots, x_m\}$ of input stream variables, a set $O = \{y_1, \ldots, y_n\}$ of output stream variables, and a set of defining equations, $y_i = e_i(x_1, \ldots, x_m, y_1, \ldots, y_n)$ one per output variable $y_i \in O$, where every e_i is an expression from $Term_D(I \cup O)$, and D is the type of y_i.*

A specification describes the relation between input sequences and output sequences. We will use v for an arbitrary variable (where x_i and y_j refer to input and output stream variables respectively).

Example 1. The specification "*the mean level of CO2 in the air in the last 3 instants*", can be expressed as follows, where denom calculates the number of instants that are taken into account:

```
input   num  co2
output  num  denom := min(3, denom[-1|0]+1)
output  num  mean:=(co2[-2|0]+co2[-1|0]+co2[now])/denom[now]   □
```

Semantics. An input valuation ρ contains one sequence ρ_x of length L for each input stream variable x, of values of the domain of the type of x. Note that $\rho_x(n)$ is the value at position n of sequence ρ_x (with $0 \leq n < L$). We call ρ_x a valuation of x, and ρ_I the collection of valuations of the set of stream variables I. The intended meaning of a Lola specification is to associate sequences to output stream variables (of the same length L) that satisfy the equations in the specification. Formally, this semantics are defined denotationally as follows.

Given a valuation ρ (of all variables in $I \cup O$) the *evaluation* $[\![e]\!]_\rho$ of a term e is a sequence of length L of values of the type of e defined as follows:

- If e is $v[i, c]$ then $[\![v[i, c]]\!]_\rho(j) = [\![v]\!]_\rho(j + i)$ if $0 \leq j + i < L$, and c otherwise.
- If e is $f(e_1, \ldots, e_k)$ then $[\![f(e_1, \ldots, e_k)]\!]_\rho(j) = f([\![e_1]\!]_\rho(j), \ldots, [\![e_k]\!]_\rho(j))$

Note that in particular, $[\![v[now]]\!]_\rho(j) = \rho_v(j)$.

Definition 2 (Evaluation Model). *A valuation* $\rho = (\rho_I, \rho_O)$ *satisfies a* Lola *specification* φ *whenever for every output variable* y_i, $[\![y_i]\!]_\rho = [\![e_i]\!]_\rho$. *In this case we say that* σ *is an evaluation model of* φ *and write* $(\sigma_I, \sigma_O) \vDash \varphi$.

These semantics capture when a candidate valuation is an evaluation model, but the intention of a Lola specification is to compute the unique output sequences given input sequences. A *dependency graph* D_φ of a specification $\varphi\langle I, O\rangle$ is a weighted multi-graph (V, E) whose vertices are the stream variables $V = I \cup O$, and E contains a directed weighted edge $v \xrightarrow{k} y$ whenever $v[k, d]$ is a sub-term in the defining equation of y. If a dependency graph D_φ contains no cycles with 0 weight then the specification is called *well-formed*. Note that well-formedness is equivalent to stating that all cycles in a given maximal strongly connected component (MSCC) M of the dependency graph are positive, or all cycles of M are negative. Well-formedness guarantees that for every ρ_I there is a unique ρ_O such that $(\rho_I, \rho_O) \vDash \varphi$. Essentially, this is because acyclicity guarantees that the value of a sequence at a given position does not depend on itself. A well-formed Lola specification has a unique evaluation model for each input valuation ρ_I and we write $\rho_O = \varphi(\rho_I)$ for this unique output valuation.

Another important concept is the *evaluation graph* which given a length L contains one vertex v_j for every stream variable v and position k. There is an edge from $v_j \to y_{j+k}$ whenever there is an edge $v \xrightarrow{k} y$ in the dependency graph. For example, if the defining equation of y contains $x[-1, d]$ then y_{16} points to x_{15} in all the evaluation graphs with $L \geq 16$. In well-formed specifications there are no cycles in any evaluation graph, which enables us to reason by induction on evaluation graphs. See [7,19] for details of these definitions as well as online and offline monitoring algorithms for Lola specifications.

2.2 Striver

Syntax. The syntax of Striver is:

$$\alpha ::= \{c\} \mid r.\mathbf{ticks} \mid \mathbf{delay}\ \epsilon\ s \mid \alpha \cup \alpha \qquad\qquad (tick\text{-}expr)$$

$$\tau_x ::= x{<}^{\sim}\tau \mid x{<}{<}\tau \mid x{>}^{\sim}\tau \mid x{>}{>}\tau \qquad \tau ::= \mathbf{t} \mid \tau_z\ \text{for}\ z \in Z \qquad (offset\text{-}expr)$$

$$E := d \mid x(\tau_x) \mid \mathbf{f}(E_1, \ldots, E_k) \mid \tau \mid \text{-out} \mid \text{+out} \mid \mathbf{notick} \qquad (value\text{-}expr)$$

There are three kinds of expressions:

- *Ticking Expressions*, which define those instants at which a stream may contain a value. Here $c \in \mathbb{T}$, $\epsilon \in \mathbb{T}^+$ are constants (with $\epsilon \neq 0$), r is a stream variable, and $\cup$ is used for the union of instants.
- *Offset Expressions*: which allow fetching time instants at which streams contain values. The expression t represents the current instant. The expression $x \texttt{<<} \tau$ is used to refer to the previous instant at which x ticked in the past of τ (or $\perp_{\text{-out}}$ if there is not such an instant). The expression $x \texttt{<}\widetilde{}\,\tau$ also considers the present as a candidate instant. Analogously, the intended meaning of $x \texttt{>>} \tau$ is to refer to the next instant strictly in the future of τ at which x ticks (or $\perp_{\text{+out}}$ if there is not such an instant). The expression $x \texttt{>}\widetilde{}\,\tau$ also considers the present as a candidate.
- *Value Expressions*, which compute values. Here, d is a constant of type D, x is a stream variable of type D and f is a function symbol of return type D. Note that in $x(\tau_x)$ the value of stream x is fetched at an offset expression indexed by x, which captures the ticking points of x and guarantees the existence of an event if the point is within the time boundaries. Expressions t and τ_x build expressions of sort $\mathbb{T}_{out}$. The three additional constants -out, +out and **notick** allow reasoning (using equality) about accessing both ends of the streams, or not generating an event at a ticking candidate instant.

We use x(<t,d) and x($\widetilde{}$t,d) as syntactic sugar (mimicking x[-1|d] and x[now] from Lola) as follows

```
x(<t,d) ≝  if x<<t ==-out then d else x(x<<t)
x(~t,d) ≝  if x<~t ==-out then d else x(x<~t)
```

We define the duals x(t>,d) and x(t$\widetilde{}$,d) analogously.

Definition 3 (Striver Specification). *A Striver specification $\psi\langle I, O\rangle$ for input stream variables I and output stream variables O, consists of one value expression V_y and one ticking expression T_y for each $y \in O$ (where V_y is of the same type as y, plus the reserved constant* **notick***).*

As for Lola, Striver specifications are often given programmatically as illustrated in the following example.

Example 2. The property *"count for how long has the tv been on"*, can be expressed as follows, where stream variable tv_on computes the result.

```
input TV_Status tv
ticks tv_on      := tv.ticks
define int tv_on := if tv(<t,off) == on
                    then tv_on(<t,0) + t - tv<<t else 0     □
```

Semantics. The semantics of Striver are again defined denotationally. A valuation σ contains one event-stream σ_x for each stream variable in $x \in \{I \cup O\}$.

The semantics use valuations to evaluate expressions:

- *Ticking Expressions.* The map $[\![.]\!]_\sigma$ assigns a set of instants to each ticking expression:
    - $[\![\{c\}]\!]_\sigma \overset{\text{def}}{=} \{c\}$ and $[\![a_1 \cup \cdots \cup a_k]\!]_\sigma \overset{\text{def}}{=} [\![a_1]\!]_\sigma \cup \cdots \cup [\![a_k]\!]_\sigma$,
    - $[\![r.\textbf{ticks}]\!]_\sigma \overset{\text{def}}{=} dom(\sigma_r)$, and
    - $[\![\textbf{delay } \epsilon \ s]\!]_\sigma$ contains the instants $t + v$ such that $(t, v) \in \sigma_s$, unless $|v| < |\epsilon|$ or $sign(v) \neq sign(\epsilon)$ or there is a $(t', v') \in \sigma_s$ with t' between t and $t + v$.
- *Offset Expressions:* $[\![.]\!]_\sigma$ provides, given an instant t, another instant in a valuation σ. In particular, $[\![\textbf{t}]\!]_\sigma(t) \overset{\text{def}}{=} t$ is the current instant, and
    - $[\![x <\!\!<e]\!]_\sigma$ is the previous instant at which x contains a value strictly before $[\![e]\!]_\sigma(t)$, or $\perp_{\text{-out}}$ if either there is no such instant, or if $[\![e]\!]_\sigma(t) = \perp_{\text{-out}}$. The expression $[\![x <\!\sim e]\!]_\sigma$ is similar but considers $[\![e]\!]_\sigma(t)$ as a candidate, and
    - $[\![x >\!\!>e]\!]_\sigma$ is the dual of $[\![x <\!\!<e]\!]_\sigma$, looking into the future and returning $\perp_{\text{+out}}$ in case it fails. Again, $[\![x >\!\sim e]\!]_\sigma$ is similar to $[\![x >\!\!>e]\!]_\sigma$ but considers the instant $[\![e]\!]_\sigma(t)$ as a candidate.
- *Value Expressions.* The semantics are given in terms of t:
    - $[\![x(e)]\!]_\sigma(t)$ is v for $([\![e]\!]_\sigma(t), v) \in s$, or simply $[\![e]\!]_\sigma(t)$ if it is not an instant,
    - $[\![f(E_1, \ldots, E_k)]\!]_\sigma(t) \overset{\text{def}}{=} f([\![E_1]\!]_\sigma(t), \ldots, [\![E_k]\!]_\sigma(t))$,
    - $[\![\tau_x]\!]_\sigma(t) \overset{\text{def}}{=} [\![\tau_x]\!]_\sigma(t)$, and $[\![c]\!]_\sigma(t) \overset{\text{def}}{=} c$, for the constants in the domain and the reserved constants -out, +out and **notick**.

Evaluating expressions allows defining evaluation models, like in Lola, as those valuations that satisfy all equations (in this case ticking and value equations):

Definition 4 (Evaluation Model). *Given a valuation σ of variables $I \cup O$ the evaluation of the equations for stream $y \in O$ is:*

$$[\![\mathcal{T}_y, V_y]\!]_\sigma \overset{\text{def}}{=} \{(t, d) \mid t \in [\![\mathcal{T}_y]\!]_\sigma \text{ and } d = [\![V_y]\!]_\sigma(t) \text{ and } d \neq \perp_{\text{notick}}\}$$

An evaluation model is a valuation σ such that for every $y \in O$: $\sigma_y = [\![\mathcal{T}_y, V_y]\!]_\sigma$.

Similar definitions of dependency graph and well-formedness as the ones stated above for Lola can be given for Striver specifications. The well-formedness condition for Striver includes the condition for Lola (absence of zero-weight cycles). Additionally, well-formedness for Striver requires that closed paths in a given MSCC do not mix positive and negative edges. That is, cycles in a positive MSCC cannot contain negative edges (and cycles in a negative MSCC cannot contain positive edges). Again, we write $\sigma_O = \psi(\sigma_I)$ for the unique output valuation that corresponds to an input valuation. See [14] for details.

3   Time vs Event-Based Runtime Verification

In this section we study how Lola can simulate Striver and vice versa.

We start by introducing transformations between sequences and streams. Since events happen only at time instants, we reserve a special fresh constant $\bot$ (read as "none") to model the absence of an event in a sequence. We extend every value domain A into $A^{\bot} = A \cup \{\bot\}$. For example, the sequence $[350, \bot, \bot, 360, \bot, 289, 320, 330, 382]$ is a sequence of $\mathbb{Z}^{\bot}$ values. A sequence of $A^{\bot}$ is called a *maybe sequence* of A values.

We say that a set τ of totally ordered elements with a minimum element such that $|\tau| \geq |[z]|$ covers z. When a subset τ of the temporal domain contains the set of time-stamps in a stream s, we say that τ covers s. If τ covers every stream in a valuation σ, we say that τ covers σ and we say that τ is a *temporal backbone* of σ. When ordered, τ can be seen as a sequence of increasing time-stamps.

Definition 5. *Let $\tau = \{t_0, t_1 \ldots\}$ be a temporal backbone that covers an event-stream s of sort A, and let z be a maybe sequence of type A (that is, a sequence of $A^{\bot}$ values). We say that s and z are equivalent for τ (and we write $s \equiv_{\tau} z$) whenever $|z| = |\tau|$, τ covers s and for all $n \in [z]$*

$$z(n) = \begin{cases} s(\tau(n)) & if \ \tau(n) \in dom(s) \\ \bot & otherwise \end{cases}$$

Note that if $s \equiv_{\tau} z$ and $dom(s) = \tau$ then $z(n) \neq \bot$ for any n, this is, z is a value sequence of type A when the backbone contains exactly the time-stamps of the events in s.

We now define two maps that transform sequences into event streams and vice versa. The map *tostream* takes a sequence z and a backbone τ and generates an event stream with underlying time-domain $\mathbb{T} \supseteq \tau$, provided that τ covers z. The map *toseq* takes an event stream s and a backbone τ and produces a sequence, provided that τ covers s. These maps are defined as follows:

$$tostream(z, \tau) \stackrel{\text{def}}{=} \{(\tau(n), z(n)) \mid n \in [z] \text{ and } z(n) \neq \bot\}$$
$$toseq(s, \tau)(n) \stackrel{\text{def}}{=} \begin{cases} s(\tau(n)) & if \ \tau(n) \in dom(s) \\ \bot & \text{otherwise} \end{cases}$$

Example 3. We show the transformations for *co2* and *tv_status* for a backbone $\tau \stackrel{\text{def}}{=} \{1.0, 1.5, 2.0, 2.5, 4.0, 4.5, 6.0, 7.0, 7.1, 7.2, 7.5, 8.0, 9.0\}$:

$$tostream(co2, \tau) \stackrel{\text{def}}{=} \{(1.0, 350), (1.5, 360), (2.0, 289), (2.5, 320), (4.0, 330)\}$$
$$toseq(tv\_status, \tau) \stackrel{\text{def}}{=} [\bot, off, \bot, \bot, on, \bot, off, \bot, \bot, \bot, on, off, \bot] \qquad \square$$

The following lemma relates *tostream* and *toseq*.

Lemma 1. *For every sequence z, event-stream s and backbone τ that covers s:*

- $z \equiv_{[z]} tostream(z, [z])$ and $z = toseq(tostream(z, [z]), [z])$
- $s \equiv_\tau toseq(s, \tau)$ and $s = tostream(toseq(s, \tau), \tau)$.

The previous definitions can be extended to collections of streams and to valuations as follows. Let V be a set of stream variables, σ be a collection of event-streams with one stream σ_v in σ for every $v \in V$, and let τ be a backbone that covers σ. Let ρ be a collection of $A^\perp$, with a sequence ρ_v for each variable v. We say that σ is equivalent to ρ for backbone τ over the streams V, and write $\sigma \equiv_\tau^V \rho$ whenever for all $v \in V$, $\sigma_v \equiv_\tau \rho_v$.

Figure 1 shows the main result proven in the rest of this section.

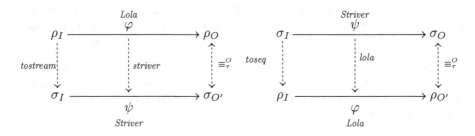

Fig. 1. Commutative diagrams for Theorems 1 and 2.

3.1 From Lola to Striver

We show now how to translate a synchronous specification (written in Lola) into an event-based specification (written in Striver) that generate equivalent outputs from equivalent inputs. Formally, we start from a well-formed Lola specification $\varphi\langle I, O\rangle$ and generate a well-formed Striver specification $\psi\langle I, O'\rangle$ with $O \subseteq O'$ (the equivalence will be restricted to $I \cup O$ as $O' \setminus O$ are auxiliary streams). We will show that for an evaluation model ρ of φ, if we choose $\tau = [\rho]$ (the instants of time $\{0 \ldots |\rho - 1|\}$) as the time backbone, then for every evaluation model of ψ such that $\sigma \equiv_\tau^I \rho$ then $\sigma \equiv_\tau^O \rho$. This is, if the evaluation models coincide in their inputs with respect to the backbone τ, then the evaluation models coincide in the output streams of the Lola specification with respect to τ. We assume that the Lola specification is *flattened*, this is, the specification only contains stream accesses with offsets -1, 0 or 1. This has been proved to be feasible in [7].

Recall that well-formed Lola specifications require that each MSCC of the dependency graph has only positive cycles or only negative cycles. Additionally, well-formed Striver specifications also require that cycles in positive MSCCs have no negative edges and cycles in negative MSCCs have no positive edges. The reason is that in real-time, a single negative edge (corresponding to a future reference fetching an event in the past) can compensate for any number of positive edges and vice versa, and create a zero-weight cycle. Therefore, if we attempt to simply translate a Lola successor access $x[+1|d]$ as a Striver next event access $x(t>, d)$, we may turn a well-formed Lola spec into an illegal Striver spec.

To overcome this issue, the translation proceeds in two stages. First, we translate the initial Lola specification into an equivalent Lola specification that does not contain positive edges in negative MSCCs or negative edges in positive MSCCs. This can be done for every Lola specification. In the second stage, we translate the resulting Lola specification into a Striver specification.

Eliminating Mixed Edges in MSCCs. We show now the translation for removing positive offsets from negative MSCCs. Removing negative offsets from positive MSCCs is dual. We introduce an auxiliary function $exp_M(e, k)$ that expands recursively the offsets within a negative MSCC M by the constant k. The expansion substitutes the definition of the referred stream making all offsets become non-negative:

$$exp_M(x[i|d], k) \stackrel{\text{def}}{=} \begin{cases} x[i + k|d] & \text{if } x \notin M \text{ or } k + i \leq 0 \\ \begin{pmatrix} \text{if } true[k + i|false] \\ \text{then } exp_M(e_x, k + i) \\ \text{else } d \end{pmatrix} & \text{otherwise} \end{cases}$$

$$exp_M(d, i) \stackrel{\text{def}}{=} d$$
$$exp_M(\mathbf{f}(E_1, \ldots, E_l), i) \stackrel{\text{def}}{=} \mathbf{f}(exp_M(E_1, i), \ldots, exp_M(E_l, i))$$

Note that the recursive expansion terminates because each expansion corresponds to following an additional edge and all paths in the negative MSCC eventually either leave the MSCC, or make the path negative. Finally, we rewrite the term of every stream $x = e \in M$ as

$$\text{output } x := exp_M(e_x, 0)$$

Example 4. Take for example the following Lola specification:

```
output x = y[1|999] + 1
output y = x[-2|5] * 2
```

The resulting specification after the expansion is:

```
x = ((if true[1|false] then x[-1|5] * 2) else 999) + 1
y = x[-2|5] * 2
```

The correctness of the translation is provided by the following lemma.

Lemma 2. *Let φ be a Lola spec and φ' be the resulting specification after the defining equation e_x is replaced by $exp_M(e_x, 0)$. Then, φ and φ' are equivalent.*

The proof essentially proceeds by showing that given a candidate valuation $[\![e_x]\!]$, then $[\![e_x]\!] = [\![exp(e_x, 0)]\!]$ by structural induction on the expressions.

The application of exp_M guarantees that, given a well-formed Lola specification φ, the obtained equivalent Lola specification φ' satisfies that every MSCC in its dependency graph contains only positive edges or only negative edges in every cycle.

Translation to Striver . In the second stage of the translation, we define a function *striver* that generates a Striver value expression from the defining expression of a Lola stream.

$$striver(x[-1|d]) \overset{\text{def}}{=} x(\texttt{<t}, d)$$

$$striver(x[now]) \overset{\text{def}}{=} \begin{cases} x(\texttt{~t}) & \text{if } x \text{ belongs to a non-positive MSCC} \\ x(\texttt{t~}) & \text{otherwise} \end{cases}$$

$$striver(x[1|d]) \overset{\text{def}}{=} x(\texttt{t>}, d)$$

$$striver(d) \overset{\text{def}}{=} d$$

$$striver(\mathbf{f}(E_1, \ldots, E_k)) \overset{\text{def}}{=} \mathbf{f}(striver(E_1), \ldots, striver(E_k))$$

For every output stream $x = e_x$ of type A in φ, we define its equivalent in ψ as:

```
ticks x     := r.ticks
define a x :=   striver(e_x)
```

where r is any input stream.

We use $striver(\varphi)$ to refer to the Striver specification resulting by translating all output streams of φ as described above. We prove now that φ and $striver(\varphi)$ are equivalent, so therefore Striver can simulate Lola specifications.

Theorem 1. *Let φ be a well-formed Lola specification and ρ_I a valuation of its inputs of length N. Let $\psi = striver(\varphi)$ be the Striver specification obtained by translating φ and let $\sigma_I = tostream(\rho_I, [N])$. Then, $\psi(\sigma_I) \equiv_{[N]} \varphi(\rho_I)$.*

Proof. Let φ be a Lola specification, and $\psi = striver(\varphi)$ its translation to Striver. Let ρ_I be an input valuation of φ of size N, and let $\tau = 0 \ldots N - 1$, and let $\rho_O = \varphi(\rho_I)$. Let $\sigma_I = tostream(\sigma_I, \tau)$ be the corresponding input valuation for ψ and $\sigma_O = \psi(\sigma_I)$.

If $N = 0$, then $\rho_x = \langle \rangle$ and $\sigma_x = \{\}$ for every stream x in $I \cup O$.

We see now the case of $N > 0$. First, we observe that for the case of specs φ without mixed-edges the dependency graphs of φ and ψ are identical.

We proceed by induction over a topological sort of the acyclic graph of MSCCs in the dependency graphs (the graph of MSCCs). By induction over $0 \ldots N - 1$ for negative MSCCs (and by induction over $N - 1 \ldots 0$ for positive MSCCs). Internally, we reason by induction over a topological sort of the MSCC with $\overset{-}{\rightarrow}$ and $\overset{+}{\rightarrow}$ edges removed.

Let x be a stream variable in a non-positive MSCC, and let $i \in \tau$. We know that $i \in dom(x)$ because $i \in dom(r)$, for any input stream r. Let $v = \rho_x(i)$ be the value at position i in σ_x. We consider the cases separately.

- The definition of x in φ is x=v, and thus the definition of the value of x in ψ is x=v and $\sigma_x(i) = v$, or
- The definition of x in φ is x=y[now]. Then, the corresponding definition of x in ψ is x=y(~t). Since $\rho_y(i) = v$ then also $\sigma_y(i) = v$ (by induction hypothesis), and hence $\sigma_x(i) = v$

- The definition of x in φ is x=y[-1|d], and thus the definition of the value of x in ψ is x=y(<t,d). Then, either:
  - $i = 0$ and $d = v$, and $\sigma_x(i) = v$, or
  - $i > 0$ and $\rho_y(i - 1) = v$, and $\sigma_y(i - 1) = v$ (by induction hypothesis over i), and $\sigma_x(i) = v$.
- The definition of x in φ is x=f(e1,...,ek), and thus the definition of the value of x in ψ is x=f(e1',...,ek'). In this case, we proceed by structural induction over the expression. The leaves fall within one of the previous cases. Since the arguments of every function are the same, they produce the same result. We apply this reasoning until we get to the topmost expression f(e1',...,ek'), where f is applied to the same arguments as in its Lola counterpart expression f(e1,...,ek), and thus the result is v in both cases; and $\sigma'_x(i) = v$.

The proof for positive MSCCs is analogous. □

Example 5. Let φ be the specification from Example 1 and the sequence for *co2* in the preliminaries. The equivalent flattened specification is:

```
input    num  co2
output   num  aux    := co2[-1|0]
output   num  denom  := min(3, denom [-1|0]+1)
output   num  mean  :=(aux[-1|0]+co2[-1|0]+co2[now])/denom[now]
```

The evaluation model for $\rho_{co2} = [350, 360, 289, 320, 330]$ is

$$\rho_{aux} = [\quad 0, 350, 360, 289, 320] \qquad \rho_{denom} = [\,1, 2, 3, 3, 3]$$
$$\rho_{mean} = [\,350, 355, 333, 323, 313]$$

The translated Striver specification is:

```
input  num  co2

ticks aux            := co2.ticks
define num aux       := co2(<t,0)
ticks denom          := co2.ticks
define num denom     := min(3, denom(<t,0)+1)
ticks mean           := co2.ticks
define num mean  :=(aux(<t,0)+co2(<t,0)+co2(~t))/denom(~t)
```

And its evaluation model for $\tau \overset{\text{def}}{=} 0,\ldots,4$ is:

$$\sigma_{co2} = \{(0, 350), (1, 360), (2, 289), (3, 320), (4, 330)\}$$
$$\sigma_{aux} = \{(0, 0), (1, 350), (2, 360), (3, 289), (4, 320)\}$$
$$\sigma_{denom} = \{(0, 1), (1, 2), (2, 3), (3, 3), (4, 3)\}$$
$$\sigma_{mean} = \{(0, 350), (1, 355), (2, 333), (3, 323), (4, 313)\}$$

3.2 Striver to Lola

We show now how to translate a well-formed Striver specification $\psi\langle I, O\rangle$ to an equivalent well-formed Lola specification $\varphi\langle I, O'\rangle$ with the same input I and output stream variables O' (again $O \subseteq O'$ because O' contains some auxiliary stream variables). In this case we do not impose a temporal backbone τ. Instead, we will show the conditions that τ must meet for the translation to be correct. We reserve the word notick in the syntax of Lola to refer to the reserved constant $\bot$. To ease the translation we introduce a new Lola stream variable called *time* and assume that $toseq(\sigma, \tau)$ assigns $time(i) = \tau(i)$ for every instant i in σ.

The main idea of the translation is to create a defining expression for every stream variable $x \in O$ of type A, with ticking expression T_x and value expression V_x, as follows:

```
output A x := if ticks(Tₓ) then value(Vₓ) else notick
```

where $ticks(T_x)$ is a Boolean expression that is true whenever x has a value at the time corresponding to the instant, and $value(V_x)$ is an expression that computes the corresponding value.

We first define *ticks*, which given a *ticking expression* in Striver, returns a Boolean expression in Lola.

$$ticks(\{c\}) \overset{\text{def}}{=} \texttt{time[now]==c}$$

$$ticks(x.\textbf{ticks}) \overset{\text{def}}{=} \texttt{x[now]!=notick}$$

$$ticks(x \cup y) \overset{\text{def}}{=} ticks(x) \texttt{||} ticks(y)$$

$$ticks(\textbf{delay}\ \epsilon\ x) \overset{\text{def}}{=} \begin{cases} \texttt{delay\_eps\_x [-1|noalarm]==time[now]} & \text{if } \epsilon > 0 \\ \texttt{ndelay\_eps\_x [+1|noalarm]==time[now]} & \text{otherwise} \end{cases}$$

where, for each x and ϵ used in an expression $\textbf{delay}\ \epsilon\ x$, we add to $lola(\psi)$ the following stream variable delay_ϵ_x and ndelay_ϵ_x with defining expressions:

```
output Time ∪{noalarm}  delay_ε_x  := if x[now]<ε then noalarm
        else if x[now] == notick then delay_ε_x [-1|noalarm]
        else x[now] + time[now]
output Time ∪{noalarm} ndelay_ε_x  := if x[now]>ε then noalarm
        else if x[now] == notick then ndelay_ε_x [+1|noalarm]
        else x[now] + time[now]
```

Here, noalarm is a fresh value not in $\mathbb{T}$.

We now define the function *value*, which translates Striver value expressions into Lola expressions of the same type. We assume that the Striver specification is *flattened* so it does not contain nested offset expressions.[2]

$$value(x(x \text{ <<t})) \stackrel{\text{def}}{=} \texttt{prev\_x[now]} \qquad\qquad value(d) \stackrel{\text{def}}{=} \texttt{d}$$
$$value(x(x \text{ <\~{}t})) \stackrel{\text{def}}{=} \texttt{preveq\_x[now]} \qquad value(\texttt{-out}) \stackrel{\text{def}}{=} \texttt{-out}$$
$$value(x(x \text{ >>t})) \stackrel{\text{def}}{=} \texttt{succ\_x[now]} \qquad\quad value(\texttt{+out}) \stackrel{\text{def}}{=} \texttt{+out}$$
$$value(x(x \text{ >\~{}t})) \stackrel{\text{def}}{=} \texttt{succeq\_x[now]} \qquad value(\textbf{notick}) \stackrel{\text{def}}{=} \texttt{notick}$$
$$value(\texttt{t}) \stackrel{\text{def}}{=} \texttt{time[now]} \qquad value(\textbf{f}(E_1,\ldots)) \stackrel{\text{def}}{=} \textbf{f}(value(E_1),\ldots)$$

where, for every stream x, we define

```
preveq_x:=if x[now]!=notick then x[now] else preveq_x[-1|-out]
prev_x  :=preveq_x [-1|-out]
succeq_x:=if x[now]!=notick then x[now] else succeq_x[+1|+out]
succ_x  :=succeq_x [+1|+out]
```

Essentially, the new streams `preveq_x` search for the previous value in x that contains an actual value. The other auxiliary streams are analogous. Note that offsets are restricted to values, not times. A specification that contains offset expressions that access time can be translated to an equivalent one accessing values creating a Striver stream `times_of_x`. As a result, we will get a stream `prev_times_of_x`, along with the rest of the auxiliary streams in the translated Lola specification.

We use $lola(\psi)$ for the Lola specification obtained by transforming every output stream variable in ψ as described above. Theorem 2 below captures whether the transformation gives an equivalent Lola specification, which depends on the temporal backbone being covering.

Theorem 2. *Let $\psi\langle I, O\rangle$ be a well-formed Striver specification, σ_I a valuation of the inputs of ψ, τ be a covering temporal backbone, and $\rho_I = toseq(\sigma_I, \tau)$. Let $\varphi = lola(\psi)$. Then, $\psi(\sigma_I) \equiv^O_\tau \varphi(\rho_I)$.*

Proof (sketch). The proof proceeds by complete induction on the evaluation graph of ψ for ρ (which is an acyclic graph). Essentially, if the equivalence does not hold there is a node (corresponding to a stream variable at a concrete position) that is minimal—in the sense that it violates the stated equivalence but all the lower nodes satisfy it—. Since in both cases the value of the node only depends on lower nodes with two expressions that guarantee the same results (given the values on the nodes they depend on), a contradiction is reached. □

Example 6. Let ψ be the specification of Example 2 and the sequence for *tv_status* from Sect. 2 The evaluation model is:

$$\sigma_{tv\_status} = \{(1.5, \textit{off}), (4.0, \textit{on}), (6.0, \textit{off}), (7.5, \textit{on}), (8.0, \textit{off})\}$$
$$\sigma_{tv\_on} = \{(1.5, 0.0), (4.0, 0.0), (6.0, 2.0), (7.5, 0.0), (8.0, 0.5)\}$$

The translated specification is:

---

2 An algorithm to get a flatten specification for a past-only Striver specification has been shown in [14].

```
input   TV_Status tv_status
output  int tv_on :=
  if tv_status[now] != notick then
    if prev_tv_status[now] then
    prev_tv_on[now]+time[now]-prev_times_of_tv_status[now]
    else 0
  else notick
```

Its evaluation model for the covering backbone $\tau = \{1.5, 4.0, 6.0, 7.5, 8.0\}$ is, assuming $\rho_{tv\_status} = [off, on, off, on, off]$:

$$\rho_{tv\_on} = [0.0, 0.0, 2.0, 0.0, 0.5] \quad \rho_{time} = [1.5, 4.0, 6.0, 7.5, 8.0] \qquad \square$$

3.3   Time Backbone Election

The main result of the previous section is Theorem 2, which establishes a translation from Striver to Lola, and a condition under which the translation is correct. Namely, that a temporal backbone is chosen in the translation satisfying that the sequence of times in the backbone contains all the instants where events may happen at runtime. We now describe three cases to compute a temporal backbone that satisfies the conditions of Theorem 2 and later in Sect. 4 evaluate the efficiency of the resulting monitors.

Full Time-Domain. The first obvious choice is to use the minimum granularity of time that the monitoring system considers (this can be one millisecond, one second, etc. depending on the setting). In this case, $\mathbb{T}$ is a finite set (given a starting and finishing time) and choosing $\tau = \mathbb{T}$ guarantees trivially to cover all event-streams of any valuation of the Striver specification. We call the resulting Lola specification the *full-time translation*. As we will see, this approach becomes very inefficient if $|\mathbb{T}| \gg |\bigcup_{x \in I \cup O} dom(x)|$. We use *density* to refer to the ratio of instants at which there are events in a given valuation, and *sparsity* for how close together events are statistically. The less dense a valuation is, the more inefficient $lola(\psi)$ is compared to ψ when a full-time translation is used.

Input Timestamps. Sometimes, it can be guaranteed that a Striver specification is purely event-driven. In other words, all output events of all valuations happen only at instants where there are input-events. The fragment of Striver specifications whose tick operators are restricted to **ticks** and U (i.e. { c } and **delay** are not used) is called *event-driven* and satisfies the following proposition.

Proposition 1. *Let ψ be an event-driven Striver specification, σ_I an input valuation and $\sigma_O = \psi(\sigma_I)$. Then, $\bigcup_{y \in O} dom(y) \subseteq \bigcup_{x \in I} dom(x)$.*

In other words, $\bigcup_{v \in I \cup O} dom(v) = \bigcup_{x \in I} dom(x)$ for event-driven specifications. As a result, we can incrementally define τ as the witnessed input timestamps, and an incremental online Lola engine will be correct. We call the corresponding Lola specification the *event-driven translation*. As we will see, this translation is very efficient regardless of the density or sparsity of the streams observed. However, unfortunately, this choice of backbone only supports a fragment of the Striver language.

Input-Independent Timestamps. A third translation considers the case under which one can statically determine that any valuation will only contain either time instants dictated by the input (event-driven) or a set of instants which may require time calculation but that does not depend on the input.

This happens, for example, when **delay** is used in a controlled way to define periodic clocks (that only depend on themselves in a recursive definition with **delay**), and not depending on instants in the input. Mixing event-driven and periodic clocks allows us to capture the assumptions of the RTLola real-time SRV tool [13]. We call the resulting Lola specification the *isochronous translation*.

4   Empirical Evaluation

In this section we report an empirical evaluation, executed on a MacBook Pro with a Dual Core Intel-i5 at 2.5 GHz with 8 GB of RAM running MacOS Catalina. The Lola monitors are generated using HLola, a Haskell implementation of Lola described in [4] and the Striver monitors are generated using HStriver, a similar infrastructure for Striver[3]. We evaluate empirically the following hypotheses:

- (H1) Lola can be simulated by Striver with little penalty in time.
- (H2) Striver can be simulated by Lola via a full-time translation, but the resource penalty can be very large, particularly for low density inputs.
- (H3) If the Striver specification is purely event-driven then the event-driven translation into Lola can simulate it very efficiently.
- (H4) If the Striver contains only event driven streams or periodic streams, it can also be efficiently simulated via an isochronous translation.
- (H5) In practice, embedded monitoring execution platforms can either enter idle mode immediately after processing an event or remain awake waiting for events to be received shortly. Resources for sparse inputs can be reduced by choosing an optimal patience time before entering idle mode.

To evaluate these hypotheses we have written a number of specifications in HLola and HStriver for properties over the Orange4Home data-set [6]. The translations were computed manually following the algorithms in Sect. 3. Consider for example S1: *"the person does not watch TV for longer than 3 h a day"*, which involves detecting the beginning and end of a TV watching session and computing the total TV watching time during a day. A second specification S2: *"the person does not watch TV more than 30 min more than the daily average in the past"*, requires also computing and maintaining numerical calculations from previous days (note that this specification is not expressible in LTL). This specification also requires events to be generated on the fly at time instants that are neither input-driven nor periodic.

---

[3] Both HLola and HStriver are open source available from http://github.com/imdea-software. All executions in this empirical evaluation are packaged as a docker container downloadable from http://hub.docker.io/imdea-software/rv2020/.

In the first experiment we assess (H1) starting from Lola specifications for S1 and S2, and translating them into Striver. We assume that the events are spaced roughly by one minute during a day and ignore the seconds, which is reasonable in our dataset.

In the second experiment we assess (H2) by re-implemening S1 and S2 in Striver to consider the time of the inputs for their computation. This makes the monitor more precise and allows it to report the excess of TV exactly at the moment the property is violated (at that time no input event occurs in general). The HLola implementation is slightly changed to expect events to be one second apart, making the HLola specification as precise as its HStriver counterpart, but also causing it to be much more inefficient.

In the third experiment we evaluate (H3) running a simpler event-driven Striver Boolean specification S3: *"there is some TV on in the house"* and the numeric S4: *"total TV time when TV is switched-off"*, as well as the Lola equivalent that uses the timestamps of the TV events as a backbone.

In the fourth experiment we evaluate (H4) running a spec S5 that calculates the summary of TV time at the end of every hour.

Table 1. Experiments data

	Event throughput									
	2h38m		9h18m		1d8h46m		11d4h27m		25d2h6m	
	HStriver	HLola	HStriver	HLola	HStriver	HLola	HStriver	HLola	HStriver	HLola
Exp 1	6666	5050	7142	5577	7692	5900	8064	5830	8130	5279
Exp 2	4000	6407	7142	6377	7407	6264	7692	6145	7462	6149
Exp 3	6666	12900	11111	8933	11764	10650	11904	10432	12195	10528
Exp 4	4000	6550	10000	9083	10000	8438	12345	9182	12820	9376

We calculate, for each experiment and a number of running traces, the average number of processed events per second. In each experiment we use a translator that generates the equivalent sequences and event-streams of varying time spans. The summary of the observations can be found in Table 1, Fig. 2, Fig. 3(a) and Fig. 3(b).

The results in Table 1 suggest that the event processing throughput is unaffected by the number of events/instants being processed (all specifications are trace-length independent), as predicted. Also, we observe that the event processing throughput for both HLola and HStriver are similar for the same experiment. Figure 2 shows that the second experiment increases exponentially for Lola with respect to the trace length (note that the y axis has a logarithmic scale), but increases linearly with respect to the trace length in all other cases. The number of events processed by Striver is roughly twice as its Lola counterpart (except in experiment 2), since data from two different origins with the same timestamp accounts for one event in Lola, but Striver processes them separately.

Figure 3(a) reports a variation of experiment 3 where the input sequence is padded with empty data to evaluate the impact on the performance of Lola. For

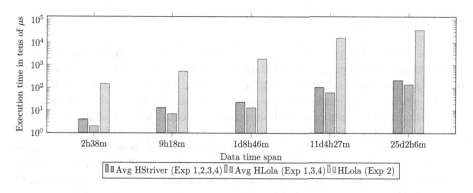

Fig. 2. Execution time

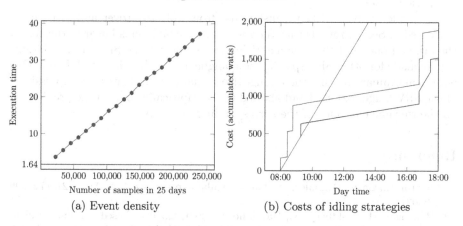

(a) Event density   (b) Costs of idling strategies

Fig. 3. Event density (left) and costs (right).

reference, the blue line at 1.64 indicates the execution time of the corresponding HStriver specification. We can conclude that the execution time increases linearly with respect to the density of the input data, as expected.

Finally, we run an additional experiment to evaluate (H5), with a synthetic cost model that considers the energy of going idle and waking up (Fig. 3(b)). The brown line indicates the accumulated costs of a monitor that never goes idle. The red line represents a monitor that goes idle immediately after processing every event. The jumps in the red line correspond to the times at which an event was received. The blue line corresponds to a monitor that waits for half an hour after the last event processed to go idle. The outcome illustrates that waiting is favourable if the next event comes soon, while sleeping is preferred if the next event takes long to arrive.

5   Conclusions

We have studied the conditions under which synchronous monitoring and fully asynchronous monitoring can simulate each other, particularly in the context of stream runtime verification. Our first result is that every Lola specification can be efficiently simulated by Striver. The second result is the definition of a condition of the temporal backbone under which Lola can simulate Striver, via a general translation, leading to three practical translations: (1) the full-time translation that uses the minimum granularity of time, which is general but inefficient; (2) the event-driven translation, which is efficient but restricted to event-driven Striver specs; and (3) the asynchronous translation, a mixed approach that supports event-driven execution plus simple time-driven events like periodic clocks.

A simple analysis of the translations (from Lola to Striver and vice versa) presented in Sect. 3 reveals that the resulting specification is linear in the size of the original one, and that the algorithm takes linear time. Similar translations can be made for other SRV specification languages like TeSSLa and RTLola. Our empirical evaluation using the Orange4Home dataset illustrates the expressivity of the SRV languages used and allowed us to empirically confirm the predictions on the runtime efficiency of the corresponding monitors.

References

1. Asarin, E., Caspi, P., Maler, O.: Timed regular expressions. J. ACM **49**(2), 172–206 (2002)
2. Barringer, H., Goldberg, A., Havelund, K., Sen, K.: Rule-based runtime verification. In: Steffen, B., Levi, G. (eds.) VMCAI 2004. LNCS, vol. 2937, pp. 44–57. Springer, Heidelberg (2004). https://doi.org/10.1007/978-3-540-24622-0_5
3. Bauer, A., Leucker, M., Schallhart, C.: Runtime verification for LTL and TLTL. ACM Trans. Softw. Eng. Methodol. **20**(4), 14 (2011)
4. Ceresa, M., Gorostiaga, F., Sánchez, C.: Declarative stream runtime verification (hLola) (2020). Under submission
5. Convent, L., Hungerecker, S., Leucker, M., Scheffel, T., Schmitz, M., Thoma, D.: TeSSLa: temporal stream-based specification language. In: Massoni, T., Mousavi, M.R. (eds.) SBMF 2018. LNCS, vol. 11254, pp. 144–162. Springer, Cham (2018). https://doi.org/10.1007/978-3-030-03044-5_10
6. Cumin, J., Lefebvre, G., Ramparany, F., Crowley, J.L.: A dataset of routine daily activities in an instrumented home. In: Ochoa, S.F., Singh, P., Bravo, J. (eds.) UCAmI 2017. LNCS, vol. 10586, pp. 413–425. Springer, Cham (2017). https://doi.org/10.1007/978-3-319-67585-5_43
7. D'Angelo, B.: LOLA: runtime monitoring of synchronous systems. In: Proceedings of the 12th International Symposium of Temporal Representation and Reasoning (TIME 2005), pp. 166–174. IEEE CS Press (2005)
8. Danielsson, L.M., Sánchez, C.: Decentralized stream runtime verification. In: Finkbeiner, B., Mariani, L. (eds.) RV 2019. LNCS, vol. 11757, pp. 185–201. Springer, Cham (2019). https://doi.org/10.1007/978-3-030-32079-9_11

9. Eisner, C., Fisman, D., Havlicek, J., Lustig, Y., McIsaac, A., Van Campenhout, D.: Reasoning with temporal logic on truncated paths. In: Hunt, W.A., Somenzi, F. (eds.) CAV 2003. LNCS, vol. 2725, pp. 27–39. Springer, Heidelberg (2003). https:// doi.org/10.1007/978-3-540-45069-6_3

10. El-Hokayem, A., Falcone, Y.: Bringing runtime verification home. In: Colombo, C., Leucker, M. (eds.) RV 2018. LNCS, vol. 11237, pp. 222–240. Springer, Cham (2018). https://doi.org/10.1007/978-3-030-03769-7_13

11. Elliott, C., Hudak, P.: Functional reactive animation. In: Proceedings of ICFP 2007, pp. 163–173. ACM (1997)

12. Faymonville, P., Finkbeiner, B., Schirmer, S., Torfah, H.: A stream-based specification language for network monitoring. In: Falcone, Y., Sánchez, C. (eds.) RV 2016. LNCS, vol. 10012, pp. 152–168. Springer, Cham (2016). https://doi.org/10.1007/978-3-319-46982-9_10

13. Faymonville, P., Finkbeiner, B., Schwenger, M., Torfah, H.: Real-time stream-based monitoring. CoRR, abs/1711.03829 (2017)

14. Gorostiaga, F., Sánchez, C.: Striver: stream runtime verification for real-time event-streams. In: Colombo, C., Leucker, M. (eds.) RV 2018. LNCS, vol. 11237, pp. 282–298. Springer, Cham (2018). https://doi.org/10.1007/978-3-030-03769-7_16

15. Havelund, K., Roşu, G.: Synthesizing monitors for safety properties. In: Katoen, J.-P., Stevens, P. (eds.) TACAS 2002. LNCS, vol. 2280, pp. 342–356. Springer, Heidelberg (2002). https://doi.org/10.1007/3-540-46002-0_24

16. Pike, L., Goodloe, A., Morisset, R., Niller, S.: Copilot: a hard real-time runtime monitor. In: Barringer, H., et al. (eds.) RV 2010. LNCS, vol. 6418, pp. 345–359. Springer, Heidelberg (2010). https://doi.org/10.1007/978-3-642-16612-9_26

17. Reinbacher, T., Rozier, K.Y., Schumann, J.: Temporal-logic based runtime observer pairs for system health management of real-time systems. In: Ábrahám, E., Havelund, K. (eds.) TACAS 2014. LNCS, vol. 8413, pp. 357–372. Springer, Heidelberg (2014). https://doi.org/10.1007/978-3-642-54862-8_24

18. Roşu, G., Havelund, K.: Rewriting-based techniques for runtime verification. Autom. Softw. Eng. 12(2), 151–197 (2005)

19. Sánchez, C.: Online and offline stream runtime verification of synchronous systems. In: Colombo, C., Leucker, M. (eds.) RV 2018. LNCS, vol. 11237, pp. 138–163. Springer, Cham (2018). https://doi.org/10.1007/978-3-030-03769-7_9

20. Sen, K., Roşu, G.: Generating optimal monitors for extended regular expressions. In: Sokolsky, O., Viswanathan, M. (eds.) Electronic Notes in Theoretical Computer Science, vol. 89. Elsevier (2003)

A Benchmark Generator for Online First-Order Monitoring

Srđan Krstić[(✉)] and Joshua Schneider[(✉)]

Institute of Information Security, Department of Computer Science, ETH Zürich,
Zurich, Switzerland
{srdan.krstic,joshua.schneider}@inf.ethz.ch

Abstract. We present a randomized benchmark generator for attesting the correctness and performance of online first-order monitors. The benchmark generator consists of three components: a stream generator, a stream replayer, and a monitoring oracle. The stream generator produces random event streams that conform to user-defined characteristics such as event frequencies and distributions of the events' parameters. The stream replayer reproduces event streams in real time at a user-defined velocity. By varying the stream characteristics and velocity, one can analyze their impact on the monitor's performance. The monitoring oracle provides the expected result of monitoring the generated streams against metric first-order regular specifications. The specification languages supported by most existing monitors are either a subset of or share a large common fragment with the oracle's language. Thus, we envision that our benchmark generator will be used as a standard correctness and performance testing tool for online monitors.

Keywords: Online monitoring · Temporal logic · Benchmark

1 Introduction

Monitors lie at the core of runtime verification (RV) [4]. Given a sequence of time-stamped events and a specification (i.e., a property formulated in a specification language), a monitor checks that the specification holds at each point in the sequence and otherwise reports the violations. The monitored properties can range from simple state invariants to complex patterns expressing qualitative [14,22] and quantitative [11,18] temporal relations between events. Particularly challenging are first-order [5,8] and aggregation [7,13] properties, which additionally refer to the events' parameters. The implementation of such monitors is a non-trivial task, which can introduce bugs that are difficult to detect. Moreover, the theoretical analysis of a monitor's algorithm often does not provide sufficient insight into its performance. These two reasons motivate thorough, automated testing. In this paper, we present a benchmark generator that *tests the correctness* and *evaluates the performance* of monitors for expressive specification languages.

© Springer Nature Switzerland AG 2020
J. Deshmukh and D. Ničković (Eds.): RV 2020, LNCS 12399, pp. 482–494, 2020.
https://doi.org/10.1007/978-3-030-60508-7_27

We distinguish between *online* and *offline* monitors [16]. Offline monitors read events from a finite event stream (called an *event log*) in an arbitrary fashion, while online monitors must sequentially read from a (potentially unbounded) *event stream*. Due to the nature of streams, each event can be read only once. Hence, an online monitor must keep all relevant events in its memory. Another challenge for online monitors is events arriving out-of-order, which may be caused by unreliable communication channels over which the events are transmitted.

The performance of an online monitor can be assessed in terms of its memory usage and its latency. The latency of processing a single event is the time difference between the moment the event is read and the moment it has been fully processed by the monitor. Latency and memory usage depend on two main factors: the complexity of the monitored specification and the characteristics of the event stream, such as its velocity (i.e., the number of events per second), the distribution of the different event types, and the maximum delay of out-of-order events.

The benchmark generator presented in this paper focuses mainly on the event stream characteristics. They are not only useful for evaluating a monitor's performance, but also for testing its correctness, as streams with specific characteristics can trigger corner cases in the monitoring algorithm. We provide three tools: a stream GENERATOR, a stream REPLAYER, and a monitoring ORACLE.

The GENERATOR randomly generates a stream with user-defined characteristics. The GENERATOR has two modes. In the first mode, it supports arbitrary specifications by generating events independently at random. This mode is useful for the correctness testing of a monitor against a large number of specifications involving different event types. The second mode is restricted to a family of specifications for which a monitor must compute joins over three relations. This is known to be a difficult problem [12,21] and a core task in first-order monitoring. The second mode is thus tailored to the performance evaluation of first-order monitors. For the restricted family of specifications, the GENERATOR uses biased sampling to match the average violation frequency specified by the user.

The REPLAYER feeds the generated stream to an online monitor at a user-defined velocity, which allows for latency measurements under realistic conditions. The REPLAYER can optionally simulate out-of-order streams by exploiting the randomized emission time-stamps that the GENERATOR adds to the stream.

The ORACLE provides the expected correct result (a stream of verdicts) for the generated stream, given a property specified in a monitorable fragment of metric first-order dynamic logic (MFODL) [5]. Since MFODL is very expressive, our benchmark generator can be used to test the correctness of the majority of the existing monitors over a large class of specifications.

The GENERATOR and REPLAYER were originally developed to assess the performance of our online first-order monitor [6,26,28], which is sensitive to the event stream characteristics. Together with the ORACLE, the GENERATOR can be used to test the correctness of monitoring tools, which we have already done [5,29] for a number of existing monitors via differential testing [20]. We summarize these applications of our benchmark in Sect. 4.

An earlier version of this work, called FOStreams, was presented in the benchmark challenge [1] at the RV 2018 conference. Since then, we extended our benchmark generator to 1) generate streams with arbitrary event signatures; 2) use the correct-by-design monitor VERIMON [5,29] as the ORACLE; and 3) generate out-of-order event streams.

Related Work. From 2014 to 2016, the RV community organized an annual tool competition to address a lack of standardized benchmarks in the field [3]. Its goals (among others) were to design and discuss evaluation methods for RV tools and to inspire new efficient implementations of such tools. A follow-up workshop [25], which replaced the competition in 2017, concluded that one of the obstacles in achieving standardized benchmarks is the diversity of the tools' specification languages. Our benchmark generator focuses on the event streams characteristics, which avoids a strong dependence on the specification language. Such a dependence still exists in the ORACLE, but we hope that its highly expressive language allows meaningful testing of the majority of existing tools.

The community continued to collect and curate benchmarks after 2017 [1]. The benchmark by Li and Rozier [19] uses SMT solvers to generate satisfying or violating event streams for propositional monitors. In contrast, our work supports first-order specifications and it relies on an orthogonal approach to stream generation: the ORACLE provides verdicts which are correct by design, while the GENERATOR uses a best-effort strategy to reach the user-defined violation rate. Ulus [30] provides a benchmark generator tailored to propositional monitors and common specification patterns [15] involving parameterized time constraints, whereas we focus on data constraints and the reproduction of real-time streams.

2   The Benchmark Generator

In this section, we first introduce event streams and define the stream characteristics that can be configured in our benchmark generator. We then describe the benchmark generator's three main components.

2.1   Event Streams and Stream Characteristics

An *event* is a tuple of data values that is labeled with an *event type*. The values' domain $\mathbb{D}$ typically includes strings and integers. Every event type R has an associated arity $\alpha(R)$ defining the number of data values for this type. We call $1, \ldots, \alpha(R)$ the *attributes* of the type R. For example, the following line in the /var/log/auth.log file

```
Jul 7 17:14:11 mbp sshd[375]: Accepted publickey for root from 10.11.1.3:5161
```

can be represented by the event login("10.11.1.3", 5161, "mbp", "root", 375, "publickey") with type login and arity $\alpha(\text{login}) = 6$. Every event has an associated time-stamp, modeled as a natural number. The use of naturals is realistic as

Table 1. Summary of stream characteristics for the event stream $(\tau_i, D_i)_{i \in \mathbb{N}}$

Name	Notation	Definition
Index rate	ι_τ	$|\{i \in \mathbb{N} \mid \tau = \tau_i\}|$
Event rate	ε_τ	$|\{e \in D_i \mid \tau = \tau_i\}|$
Relation rate	$\rho_\tau(R)$	$|\{R(d_1, ..., d_{\alpha(R)}) \in D_i \mid \tau = \tau_i\}|$
Relation frequency	$f_\tau(R)$	$\rho_\tau(R)/\varepsilon_\tau$
Data rate	$\delta_\tau(d, R, k)$	$|\{R(d_1, \ldots, d_{\alpha(r)}) \in D_i \mid d_k = d \wedge \tau = \tau_i\}|$
Heavy hitters	$\mathcal{H}_\tau(R, k)$	$\left\{ d \in \mathbb{D} \ \middle| \ \dfrac{\sum_{0 \leq \tau' \leq \tau} \delta_{\tau'}(d, R, k)}{\sum_{0 \leq \tau' \leq \tau} \rho_{\tau'}(R)} > \dfrac{1}{p} \right\}$

time is often recorded in the UNIX format. For example, the event in the above log line has the associated time-stamp 1594142051, which encodes July 7 2020, 17:14:11 in UNIX format, assuming the GMT time zone and a one second time granularity.

We group a finite set of events that happen concurrently (from the event source's point of view) into *databases*. An (*event*) *stream* is thus an infinite sequence $(\tau_i, D_i)_{i \in \mathbb{N}}$ of databases D_i with associated time-stamps τ_i. We distinguish between the time-stamp τ_i and its index in the stream i, also called a *time-point*. Specifically, a stream may have the same time-stamp $\tau_i = \tau_j$ at different indices $i \neq j$, i.e., event sources may record the order of events with higher precision than the time-stamps' granularity. Time-stamps must be non-decreasing $(\forall i.\ \tau_i \leq \tau_{i+1})$ and always eventually strictly increasing $(\forall \tau.\ \exists i.\ \tau < \tau_i)$. The above example can be represented by the tuple $(1594142051, D)$ where D is a singleton database containing the login event.

In the following, we introduce the relevant stream characteristics. Their definitions are summarized in Table 1, where we fix a stream $(\tau_i, D_i)_{i \in \mathbb{N}}$. The *index rate* ι_τ at time τ is the number of time-points in one time unit. The *event rate* ε_τ at time τ is the total number of events in one time unit. The rate of events with type R is called R's *relation rate*. The *relation frequency* of R at τ, denoted by $f_\tau(R)$, is the ratio of R's relation rate and ε_τ. The *data rate* $\delta_\tau(d, R, k)$ of a data value d at time τ with respect to the kth attribute of R is the number of events R that carry the value d in the kth attribute. Finally, we define the sets of *heavy hitters* $\mathcal{H}_\tau(R, k)$. A heavy hitter is a data value that occurs as the kth attribute of R events disproportionately often in the stream prefix up to τ. This characteristic differs from the previous ones in that it is computed over a prefix instead of a single time-stamp. A value is a heavy hitter if its data rate, relative to the corresponding relation rate, exceeds the threshold $1/p$. The parameter $p \in \mathbb{N} - \{0\}$ is typically the monitor's level of parallelism [27].

We exemplify all the stream characteristics using the stream ρ_{ex} depicted in the following figure, which shows the first four time-points as black circles. Databases are drawn above, while time-stamps are the numbers below the circles.

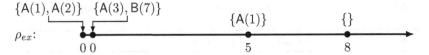

Table 2 lists all the stream characteristics for this stream, where $p = 3$ and $\tau \in \{0, 8\}$. For example, the index rate ι_0 is two because there are two time-points, 0 and 1, with time-stamp 0. Note that two out of the three A events in the time interval $[0, 8]$ carry the data value 1, and $2/3$ is greater than the heavy hitter threshold $1/p = 1/3$. Therefore, the set $\mathcal{H}_8(A, 1)$ contains 1 as the single heavy hitter (as of time-stamp 8) in the first attribute of A events.

2.2   Specification and Oracle

Our benchmark generator can be used with arbitrary specifications. Depending on the benchmark's mode, the generated streams are either compatible with all specifications that use a given *signature*, or they are tailored to a single specification from a fixed family (see Sect. 2.3). A specification's signature describes the finite set of relevant event types together with their arities.

The ORACLE provides the expected output of monitoring any specification expressible in monitorable metric first-order dynamic logic (MFODL) [5] on any *in-order* event stream. MFODL extends MFOTL [8] with regular expressions. The ORACLE is implemented using VERIMON [5], a correct-by-design monitor that has been formally verified in a proof assistant. Its high trustworthiness and expressiveness allows us to attest the correctness of a wide variety of existing monitors [5, 29] by comparing their output to the ORACLE's output.

2.3   Generating Streams

The GENERATOR produces a random but reproducible event stream. Since it generates output as quickly as possible, one must use the REPLAYER (see Sect. 2.4)

Table 2. Stream characteristics of the example stream ρ_{ex}

Name	Examples
Index rate	$\iota_0 = 2,\ \iota_8 = 1$
Event rate	$\varepsilon_0 = 4,\ \varepsilon_8 = 0$
Relation rate	$\rho_0(A) = 3,\ \rho_0(B) = 1,\ \rho_8(A) = \rho_8(B) = 0$
Relation frequency	$f_0(A) = \frac{3}{4},\ f_0(B) = \frac{1}{4},\ f_8(A) = f_8(B) = $ undefined
Data rate	$\delta_0(1, A, 1) = \delta_0(2, A, 1) = \delta_0(3, A, 1) = \delta_0(7, B, 1) = 1$
	$\delta_8(1, A, 1) = \delta_8(2, A, 1) = \delta_8(3, A, 1) = \delta_8(7, B, 1) = 0$
Heavy hitters	$\mathcal{H}_0(A, 1) = \{\},\ \mathcal{H}_0(B, 1) = \mathcal{H}_8(B, 1) = \{7\},\ \mathcal{H}_8(A, 1) = \{1\}$

to simulate a more realistic real-time stream for an online monitor. The GENER-
ATOR can be operated in two different modes, which we detail below.

Mode I (Arbitrary Specifications). When used with arbitrary specifications, the
GENERATOR expects a signature file describing all the event types and their
arities. Users can also configure the event rate, the index rate, and the value
of the first time-stamp. The GENERATOR then creates a random stream with
consecutive time-stamps and constant event and index rates. Event types are
chosen uniformly at random. The GENERATOR maintains a configurable number
of unique most recently sampled data values. It samples from this pool with a
configurable probability, which ensures common data values across events and
thus increases the likelihood of exercising non-trivial computation inside the
monitor. Otherwise, a fresh value is sampled uniformly from the set $\{1, \ldots, 10^9\}$.

Mode II (Temporal Three-Way Conjunctions). The GENERATOR gives more control over the stream generation process for a special family $\mathcal{F}_3$ of specifications,
which we call *temporal three-way conjunctions*. For example, it is possible to
define the expected violation frequency. The family $\mathcal{F}_3$ is inspired by query
patterns that are commonly used in database systems to benchmark the performance of relational joins [12]. Joins are an important operation also for first-order
monitors because (the negations of) many specifications contain conjunctions,
e.g., any specification involving a response constraint [15]. We augment the conjunctions with temporal operators to increase the joins' input size.

A three-way conjunction is a temporal pattern referring to three event types
A, B, and C with integer data values. The specifications differ only in the way
these events are related among each other. They can be formalized using the
parametric MFODL formula $\Box \forall \boldsymbol{v}. \ (\blacklozenge_{[0,w)} A(\boldsymbol{v_A})) \wedge B(\boldsymbol{v_B}) \rightarrow \Box_{[0,w)} \neg C(\boldsymbol{v_C})$, where
is w is a positive integer and $\boldsymbol{v_A}$, $\boldsymbol{v_B}$, and $\boldsymbol{v_C}$ are lists of variables. Informally, the
formula states that whenever there is a B event that was preceded by a matching
A event less than w time units ago, there must *not* be a matching C event within
the next w time units. Two events with different types match if their data values
coincide according to the variables $\boldsymbol{v_A}$, $\boldsymbol{v_B}$, and $\boldsymbol{v_C}$, respectively. For example,
if $\boldsymbol{v_A} = (x, y)$ and $\boldsymbol{v_B} = (y, z)$, then the events A(1, 2) and B(2, 5) match, but
A(1, 2) and B(1, 5) do not.

The variable lists, which must be non-empty, can be chosen freely by the
user. There are three built-in configurations: star ($\boldsymbol{v_A} = (w, x)$, $\boldsymbol{v_B} = (w, y)$,
$\boldsymbol{v_C} = (w, z)$), linear ($\boldsymbol{v_A} = (w, x)$, $\boldsymbol{v_B} = (x, y)$, $\boldsymbol{v_C} = (y, z)$), and triangle ($\boldsymbol{v_A} =
(x, y)$, $\boldsymbol{v_B} = (y, z)$, $\boldsymbol{v_C} = (z, x)$). These configurations are again well-known in
the database literature [12].

For $\mathcal{F}_3$, the events of type A, B and C are generated randomly and independently according to the user-specified relation frequencies $f_\tau(A)$, $f_\tau(B)$, and
$f_\tau(C)$, which are constant with respect to τ. The data values are also chosen
randomly and independently under the following constraints: (1) every A event
must be matched with a B event within the interval w to ensure that the premise
of the specification is satisfied frequently; (2) a user-specified percentage of violations must be generated. Constraint (2) is enforced by generating an appropriate
number of C events matching both a proceeding B event and an A event before

that (both within the appropriate time intervals). The above constraints imply some restrictions on the user-specified frequencies: the sum of all three frequencies must be 1, $f_\tau(A)$ can be at most $f_\tau(B)$, and the frequency of violations can be at most the minimum of $f_\tau(A)$ and $f_\tau(C)$.

By default, values are sampled uniformly from $D = \{1, \ldots, 10^9\}$. It is also possible to select a Zipf distribution per variable, which has the probability mass function $p(x) = (x-s)^{-z} / \sum_{n=1}^{10^9} n^{-z}$ for $x \in \{s+1, s+2, \ldots, s+10^9\}$. The larger the exponent $z > 0$ is, the fewer values have a correspondingly larger relative frequency and are thus more likely to be heavy hitters. The parameter s is the start value, which can be used to further control the specific heavy hitter values. Events that form a violation are always drawn from the uniform distribution to prevent unintended matchings. Likewise, Zipf-distributed values of C events are increased by $1\,000\,000$. Note that there is still a nonzero probability that additional violations occur, even though the set D is large.

Out-of-Order Streams. The GENERATOR optionally attaches an *emission time* to every event. The emission times, which are time differences relative to the start of the stream, may be used to determine the order in which the events are supplied to the monitor. For in-order event streams, the emission times correspond to the events' time-stamps decreased by the value of the first time-stamp in the stream. To create out-of-order streams, the GENERATOR increases each event's emission time by a value sampled from the truncated normal distribution $\mathcal{N}(0, \sigma^2)$ over the interval $[0, \delta_{max}] \cap \mathbb{N}$. Both the *standard deviation* σ and the *maximum delay* δ_{max} are configurable. The GENERATOR also adds watermarks after configurable time-stamp increments called *watermark periods* to the stream. A watermark is a time-stamp which is a strict lower bound on all time-stamps of the events received in the future. They are commonly used in stream processing systems to handle out-of-order events [2].

2.4 Replaying Streams

The time-stamps in an event stream do not necessarily correlate to the (real) times at which the corresponding events are received by an online monitor. Therefore, we distinguish the *ingestion time* of an event from its time-stamp. The *ingestion rate* is the total number of events received by the monitor per unit of (real) time. The REPLAYER tool reproduces an event stream (or log) with an ingestion rate proportional to the stream's event rate. The proportionality constant, called *acceleration*, is chosen by the user. For example, an acceleration of 2 will replay the stream twice as fast. Thus the REPLAYER can be used to generate workloads with different ingestion rates from the same data. This allows for a meaningful performance evaluation as the stream characteristics are retained.

Upon startup, the REPLAYER immediately outputs all events with the smallest time-stamp in its input. The subsequent events with the next time-stamp are delayed proportionally to the difference between the two time-stamps (which are interpreted as seconds), where the delay factor is the inverse of the acceleration parameter. This process is repeated for each unique time-stamp in the stream.

To reproduce streams with out-of-order events, the REPLAYER uses the emission times provided by the GENERATOR instead of the events' time-stamps.

3   Usage Examples

We provide our benchmark generator as a ready-to-use Docker image.[1] The source code is available online.[2] In the following, we assume that Docker version 19.03.8 or higher is installed and configured properly. The components of the benchmark generator can be invoked with the command

```
$ docker run -iv `pwd`:/work infsec/benchmark component [options ...]
```

where *component* is one of `generator`, `replayer`, or `oracle`. The command makes the current working directory available to the Docker container. Hence, one can access all the files below the current directory using relative paths in the components' options. Each component prints detailed usage information if it is invoked with the `--help` option. In the examples below, we omit the Docker part of the invocation and only show the component and its arguments.

Example: Differential Testing with Mode I. We explain the steps needed to test the correctness of a monitor against the ORACLE. An MFODL formula and, if necessary, its translation to the monitor's native language must be provided. Here, we use the MFODL formula $\Box \forall ip, port.\ \mathsf{login}(ip, port) \rightarrow \Diamond_{[0,60]} \mathsf{logout}(ip, port)$, which is loosely inspired by the example from the beginning of Sect. 2.1. In words, every login from some IP address and port combination must be eventually followed by a matching logout within 60 time units. For simplicity, we assume that the time unit is minutes. Note that the interpretation of the time unit is irrelevant for the GENERATOR; the REPLAYER interprets time-stamps in seconds.

We first describe the signature in a text file `ssh.sig` with the content

```
login(ip,port) logout(ip,port)
```

and the specification (without the prefix $\Box \forall$) in a separate file `ssh.spec`:

```
login(ip,port) IMPLIES EVENTUALLY[0,60] logout(ip,port)
```

The syntax for the MFOTL subset is described in [9]. Next, the following command generates a random log for the signature with a length of 300 min.

```
$ generator -sig ssh.sig -i 10 -q 20 -r 0.01 300 > ssh.csv
```

---

[1] https://hub.docker.com/r/infsec/benchmark/ (version 1.2.1).
[2] https://bitbucket.org/krle/scalable-online-monitor.

The GENERATOR prints the events to its standard output. We use a shell redirection to save them in a file. The option -i 10 sets the index rate to 10. Together with the default event rate (option -e), which is also 10, this implies ten databases per minute with one event each. Options -q and -r define the number of the most recently sampled unique data values and the probability to sample a fresh data value. Here we use few values (20) and a low probability (0.01) because otherwise there would be many violations of the specification.

The GENERATOR outputs the CSV format from the first RV competition [3]. For example, the ssh.csv file begins with the line

```
login, tp=0, ts=0, x0=569872521, x1=373321178
```

representing the event login(569872521, 373321178) at time-stamp 0. The random generator's seed is fixed and the output is deterministic. The seed can be customized using the -seed option. Since VERIMON expects a different format for the input event stream, we invoke the REPLAYER to translate the formats:

```
$ replayer -f verimon -a 0 < ssh.csv > ssh.log
```

Note that -a 0 disables the real-time replay and events are emitted as quickly as possible. Finally, the ORACLE provides the reference verdicts:

```
$ oracle -sig ssh.sig -formula ssh.spec < ssh.log
@0. (time point 7): (703748452,559514287)
[...]
```

Each line in the output represents a violation, showing the time-stamp, the time-point, and values of *ip* and *port*. If we now ran another monitoring tool on the same specification and log, we could compare its output to this reference.

Example: Online Performance Measurements with Mode II. Here, we illustrate the generation of a *real-time* stream with out-of-order events for the specification family $\mathcal{F}_3$ (Sect. 2.3). By varying the stream characteristics, one can analyze their impact on the monitor's throughput, latency, and memory usage.

Recall that $\mathcal{F}_3$ is parameterized by three variable lists. One can select either a built-in or a custom variable configuration. The options -S (star), -L (linear), and -T (triangle) select the respective built-in configuration. A custom pattern is supplied as a single argument after the option -P. In this example, we will use the triangle specification, i.e., $\Box \forall x, y, z.\ (\blacklozenge_{[0,w)} A(x,y)) \land B(y,z) \rightarrow \Box_{[0,w)} \neg C(z,x)$.

```
$ generator -T -pA 0.1 -pB 0.5 -z "x=1.5+3,z=2" -e 100
```

The relation frequencies of the three event types are set with -pA and -pB. The frequency of type C is implied by the frequencies of type A and B because their sum is always 1. In the invocation above, the relation frequency of A events is approximately 10 %, that of B events is 50 %, and that of C events is 40 %. To obtain values from a Zipf distribution, the exponent of the distribution can be specified per variable. The exponents of all Zipf-distributed variables are passed as a single argument after option -z. In our case, the values of variables x and z

follow a Zipf distribution with exponents 1.5 and 2. The start value for variable x is 3, while for variable z it is 0 (default). Variable y is distributed uniformly.

We did not specify the frequency of violations (option -x) nor the interval size w (option -w), so they assume their default values of 0.01 and 10, respectively. No log length was specified either, which prompts the GENERATOR to produce an unbounded stream as quickly as possible. We can pipe its output into the REPLAYER to obtain a real-time stream, which can be further sent to the monitor under test:

```
$ generator [...] | replayer | some monitor tool
```

The REPLAYER outputs 100 events per second because the generated stream's event rate is 100 (option -e 100 in the GENERATOR's invocation). With the REPLAYER option -a 2, the stream would be replayed twice as fast at 200 events per second. If a pipeline connects the GENERATOR and the REPLAYER, the former needs to be fast enough for the events to be replayed at the proper time. For higher accelerations or event rates, a finite log should be generated and written to a file from where the REPLAYER can read it.

To obtain an out-of-order stream, we must pass additional options:

```
$ generator [...] -et -md 5 -s 2 -wp 1 | replayer -e
```

The flag -et instructs the GENERATOR to add explicit emission times to the events based on maximum delay (option -md) and standard deviation (option -s). The GENERATOR also outputs watermarks after configurable periods (option -wp), which appear as lines of the form >WATERMARK *time-stamp* < in the stream.

4   Applications

We used previous versions of our benchmark generator to assess the performance of our scalable monitoring framework [28], which relies on first-order (sub)monitors to monitor event streams in parallel. The framework initially supported only MONPOLY [9] as a submonitor, but it was later extended [27] to also support DEJAVU [17]. The framework's performance depends on the stream characteristics shown in Sect. 2.1. We used the GENERATOR in Mode II during the evaluation, which revealed a noticeable impact of the index rate and the specific variable configurations on the monitoring framework's throughput. The framework was later extended to adapt to dynamically changing stream characteristics [26] and to handle multiple event streams with events arriving out-of-order [6]. The evaluation of these extensions was again driven by the GENERATOR and REPLAYER. For example, we could confirm a direct relationship between the monitoring latency and both the maximum delay and the watermark period.

In conjunction with the development of VERIMON [29], the GENERATOR (in Mode I) and the ORACLE were used to perform differential testing of both propositional (AERIAL [10] and HYDRA [23,24]) and first-order monitors (MON-POLY [9] and DEJAVU [17]). Bugs were discovered in each tool [5].

5 Conclusion and Future Work

Online first-order monitors implement complex algorithms, whose correctness is rarely obvious. Furthermore, they require a highly optimized join implementation to achieve competitive performance. We proposed a benchmark generator for evaluating first-order monitors. It consists of three components: a stream generator, stream replayer, and a monitoring oracle. The stream generator and replayer produce random event streams in real time with highly customizable characteristics suitable for evaluating the performance of join implementations in monitors. The monitoring oracle provides the correct monitoring output for monitorable metric first-order regular specifications, which allows for the correctness testing of a large class of first-order monitors.

In the future, we would like to support other event stream formats (e.g., JSON) and additional data value types (e.g., strings). Moreover, the current stream generator determines the time-stamps based on the event rate and log length only. We would like to give the users additional control over the distribution of the time-stamp values. Finally, we plan to improve and publish a version of the generator that provides multiple randomized event streams resembling those obtained from distributed systems [6].

Acknowledgment. We thank Matthieu Gras for his contributions to the stream generator. VERIMON was developed in collaboration with Dmitriy Traytel and Martin Raszyk. This research is supported by the US Air Force grant "Monitoring at Any Cost" (FA9550-17-1-0306) and by the Swiss National Science Foundation grant "Big Data Monitoring" (167162). The authors are listed alphabetically.

References

1. Runtime Verification Benchmark Challenge. https://github.com/runtime-verification/benchmark-challenge-2018 (2018)
2. Akidau, T., et al.: The dataflow model: a practical approach to balancing correctness, latency, and cost in massive-scale, unbounded, out-of-order data processing. Proc. VLDB Endow. **8**(12), 1792–1803 (2015)
3. Bartocci, E., et al.: First international competition on runtime verification: rules, benchmarks, tools, and final results of CRV 2014. Int. J. Softw. Tools Technol. Transf. **21**(1), 31–70 (2019)
4. Bartocci, E., Falcone, Y., Francalanza, A., Reger, G.: Introduction to runtime verification. In: Bartocci, E., Falcone, Y. (eds.) Lectures on Runtime Verification. LNCS, vol. 10457, pp. 1–33. Springer, Cham (2018). https://doi.org/10.1007/978-3-319-75632-5_1
5. Basin, D., et al.: A formally verified, optimized monitor for metric first-order dynamic logic. In: Peltier, N., Sofronie-Stokkermans, V. (eds.) IJCAR 2020. LNCS (LNAI), vol. 12166, pp. 432–453. Springer, Cham (2020). https://doi.org/10.1007/978-3-030-51074-9_25
6. Basin, D., Gras, M., Krstić, S., Schneider, J.: Scalable online monitoring of distributed systems. In: Deshmukh, J., Ničković, D. (eds.) RV 2020. LNCS, vol. 12399, pp. xx–yy. Springer, Cham (2020)

7. Basin, D., Klaedtke, F., Marinovic, S., Zălinescu, E.: Monitoring of temporal first-order properties with aggregations. Formal Methods Syst. Des. **46**(3), 262–285 (2015). https://doi.org/10.1007/s10703-015-0222-7
8. Basin, D., Klaedtke, F., Müller, S., Zălinescu, E.: Monitoring metric first-order temporal properties. J. ACM **62**(2), 15:1–15:45 (2015)
9. Basin, D., Klaedtke, F., Zălinescu, E.: The MonPoly monitoring tool. In: Reger, G., Havelund, K. (eds.) RV-CuBES 2017. Kalpa Publications in Computing, vol. 3, pp. 19–28. EasyChair (2017)
10. Basin, D., Krstić, S., Traytel, D.: AERIAL: almost event-rate independent algorithms for monitoring metric regular properties. In: Reger, G., Havelund, K. (eds.) RV-CuBES 2017. Kalpa Publications in Computing, vol. 3, pp. 29–36. EasyChair (2017)
11. Basin, D., Krstić, S., Traytel, D.: Almost event-rate independent monitoring of metric dynamic logic. In: Lahiri, S., Reger, G. (eds.) RV 2017. LNCS, vol. 10548, pp. 85–102. Springer, Cham (2017). https://doi.org/10.1007/978-3-319-67531-2_6
12. Beame, P., Koutris, P., Suciu, D.: Communication steps for parallel query processing. J. ACM **64**(6), 40:1–40:58 (2017)
13. Bianculli, D., Ghezzi, C., Krstić, S.: Trace checking of metric temporal logic with aggregating modalities using mapreduce. In: Giannakopoulou, D., Salaün, G. (eds.) SEFM 2014. LNCS, vol. 8702, pp. 144–158. Springer, Cham (2014). https://doi.org/10.1007/978-3-319-10431-7_11
14. De Giacomo, G., Vardi, M.Y.: Linear temporal logic and linear dynamic logic on finite traces. In: Rossi, F. (ed.) IJCAI 2013, pp. 854–860. AAAI Press (2013)
15. Dwyer, M.B., Avrunin, G.S., Corbett, J.C.: Patterns in property specifications for finite-state verification. In: Boehm, B.W., Garlan, D., Kramer, J. (eds.) ICSE 1999, pp. 411–420. ACM (1999)
16. Falcone, Y., Krstić, S., Reger, G., Traytel, D.: A taxonomy for classifying runtime verification tools. In: Colombo, C., Leucker, M. (eds.) RV 2018. LNCS, vol. 11237, pp. 241–262. Springer, Cham (2018). https://doi.org/10.1007/978-3-030-03769-7_14
17. Havelund, K., Peled, D., Ulus, D.: First order temporal logic monitoring with BDDs. In: Stewart, D., Weissenbacher, G. (eds.) FMCAD 2017, pp. 116–123. IEEE (2017)
18. Koymans, R.: Specifying real-time properties with metric temporal logic. Real-Time Syst. **2**(4), 255–299 (1990)
19. Li, J., Rozier, K.Y.: MLTL benchmark generation via formula progression. In: Colombo, C., Leucker, M. (eds.) RV 2018. LNCS, vol. 11237, pp. 426–433. Springer, Cham (2018). https://doi.org/10.1007/978-3-030-03769-7_25
20. McKeeman, W.M.: Differential testing for software. Digit. Tech. J. **10**(1), 100–107 (1998)
21. Ngo, H.Q., Porat, E., Ré, C., Rudra, A.: Worst-case optimal join algorithms. J. ACM **65**(3), 16:1–16:40 (2018)
22. Pnueli, A.: The temporal logic of programs. In: FOCS 1977, pp. 46–57. IEEE Computer Society (1977)
23. Raszyk, M., Basin, D., Krstić, S., Traytel, D.: Multi-head monitoring of metric temporal logic. In: Chen, Y.-F., Cheng, C.-H., Esparza, J. (eds.) ATVA 2019. LNCS, vol. 11781, pp. 151–170. Springer, Cham (2019). https://doi.org/10.1007/978-3-030-31784-3_9
24. Raszyk, M., Basin, D., Traytel, D.: Multi-head monitoring of metric dynamic logic. In: Hung, D.V., Sokolsky, O. (eds.) ATVA 2020. LNCS, vol. 12302. Springer, Cham (2020, to appear)

25. Reger, G.: A report of RV-CuBES 2017. In: Reger, G., Havelund, K. (eds.) RV-CuBES 2017. Kalpa Publications in Computing, vol. 3, pp. 1–9. EasyChair (2017)
26. Schneider, J., Basin, D., Brix, F., Krstić, S., Traytel, D.: Adaptive online first-order monitoring. In: Chen, Y.-F., Cheng, C.-H., Esparza, J. (eds.) ATVA 2019. LNCS, vol. 11781, pp. 133–150. Springer, Cham (2019). https://doi.org/10.1007/978-3-030-31784-3_8
27. Schneider, J., Basin, D., Brix, F., Krstić, S., Traytel, D.: Scalable online first-order monitoring. Int. J. Softw. Tools Technol. Transf. (2020)
28. Schneider, J., Basin, D., Brix, F., Krstić, S., Traytel, D.: Scalable online first-order monitoring. In: Colombo, C., Leucker, M. (eds.) RV 2018. LNCS, vol. 11237, pp. 353–371. Springer, Cham (2018). https://doi.org/10.1007/978-3-030-03769-7_20
29. Schneider, J., Basin, D., Krstić, S., Traytel, D.: A formally verified monitor for metric first-order temporal logic. In: Finkbeiner, B., Mariani, L. (eds.) RV 2019. LNCS, vol. 11757, pp. 310–328. Springer, Cham (2019). https://doi.org/10.1007/978-3-030-32079-9_18
30. Ulus, D.: Timescales: a benchmark generator for MTL monitoring tools. In: Finkbeiner, B., Mariani, L. (eds.) RV 2019. LNCS, vol. 11757, pp. 402–412. Springer, Cham (2019). https://doi.org/10.1007/978-3-030-32079-9_25

Runtime Verification for Cyber-Physical Systems

Efficient System Verification
with Multiple Weakly-Hard
Constraints for Runtime Monitoring

Shih-Lun Wu[1], Ching-Yuan Bai[1], Kai-Chieh Chang[1], Yi-Ting Hsieh[1],
Chao Huang[2], Chung-Wei Lin[1]([⊠]), Eunsuk Kang[3], and Qi Zhu[2]

[1] National Taiwan University, Taipei, Taiwan
{b06902080,b05502055,r08922054,b05902031}@ntu.edu.tw,
cwlin@csie.ntu.edu.tw
[2] Northwestern University, Evanston, USA
{chao.huang,qzhu}@northwestern.edu
[3] Carnegie Mellon University, Pittsburgh, USA
eunsukk@andrew.cmu.edu

Abstract. A weakly-hard fault model can be captured by an (m, k) constraint, where $0 \leq m \leq k$, meaning that there are at most m bad events (faults) among any k consecutive events. In this paper, we use a weakly-hard fault model to constrain the occurrences of faults in system inputs. We develop approaches to verify properties for all possible values of (m, k), where k is smaller than or equal to a given K, in an exact and efficient manner. By verifying all possible values of (m, k), we define weakly-hard requirements for the system environment and design a runtime monitor based on counting the number of faults in system inputs. If the system environment satisfies the weakly-hard requirements, the satisfaction of desired properties is guaranteed; otherwise, the runtime monitor can notify the system to switch to a safe mode. Experimental results with a discrete second-order controller demonstrate the efficiency of the proposed approaches.

Keywords: Formal verification · Weakly-hard models

1 Introduction

Weakly-hard models have been studied in a number of works for real-time systems [1–3,5,9,10,12,18,24], mostly from the perspective of scheduling

This work is supported by the Asian Office of Aerospace Research and Development (AOARD), jointly with the Office of Naval Research Global (ONRG), award FA2386-19-1-4037, the Taiwan Ministry of Education (MOE) grants NTU-108V0901 and NTU-107V0901, the Taiwan Ministry of Science and Technology (MOST) grants MOST-109-2636-E-002-022 and MOST-108-2636-E-002-011. It is also supported by the National Science Foundation (NSF) awards CCF-1918140, CNS-1834701, CNS-1801546, and the Office of Naval Research (ONR) grant N00014-19-1-2496.
Shih-Lun Wu and Ching-Yuan Bai contributed equally.

J. Deshmukh and D. Ničković (Eds.): RV 2020, LNCS 12399, pp. 497–516, 2020.
https://doi.org/10.1007/978-3-030-60508-7_28

constraints. In this paper, we use a weakly-hard model to constrain the occurrences of faults, and verify properties of discrete systems under such weakly-hard fault model. In particular, we leverage the (m, k) constraint for fault modeling $(0 \leq m \leq k)$, which specifies that there are at most m bad events (faults) among any k consecutive events. Verifying system properties under this fault model has various applications, such as the ones below:

- In a real-time system, a deadline miss can be considered as a bad event (fault). Our approach can help find the maximum number of deadline misses allowed for ensuring system properties, which can then be used to reduce computation/communication load and maximize resource saving (*e.g.*, CPU or network resource) with a less critical mode of the system.
- In a networked system, a message without authentication can be modeled as a bad event (fault), and again, our approach can be applied to maximize resource saving (*e.g.*, reduce the computation and transmission of message authentication codes) by allowing messages without authentication, while still ensuring system properties. Note that a system that only authenticates partial messages has also been proposed [16].
- In the systems above, a deadline miss (*e.g.*, due to a denial-of-service attack) or a compromised message can be caused by a malicious attacker. From the perspective of the attackers, our approach can be applied to minimize attacking cost while still causing the system to reach a state violating properties.

More generally speaking, our verification approach under the (m, k) weakly-hard fault model provides two important properties for system engineering:

- If the environment and system design (*e.g.*, via scheduling) ensures that the fault occurrences satisfy the (m, k) constraint, the system properties are satisfied.
- If the environment and system design cannot ensure that the fault occurrences always satisfy the (m, k) constraint, a runtime monitor should be developed to monitor the occurrences of faults and adapt the system to a safe (more conservative) mode when the (m, k) constraint is violated.

For example, applications of connected vehicles, such as intersection management and cooperative adaptive cruise control, rely on periodic messages from other vehicles or roadside units. However, a message may be missing due to network faults or even malicious attacks. With the verification results, a connected vehicle can monitor the number of missing messages during runtime. If the corresponding (m, k) constraint is violated, the connected vehicle should switch to a safe mode (*e.g.*, slowing down or stopping immediately). It should be emphasized that, in practice, the cost of a network without missing messages is too high, or even it may not be possible to predict how the environment behaves, so the satisfaction of the (m, k) constraint cannot be guaranteed. Therefore, a runtime monitor for the (m, k) constraint is really desired.

In this paper, given a labelled transition system S, a property P, and a positive integer K, we aim to develop a runtime monitor to verify whether the environment satisfies a subset of the (m, k) constraints, where $1 \leq m \leq k \leq K$ and the subset is sufficient to enforce P, *i.e.*, if the environment satisfies the subset of the (m, k) constraints, it implies that S guarantees to satisfy P; otherwise, S cannot guarantee to satisfy P, which should lead S to switch to a safe mode. Different from some existing runtime-monitoring approaches that do not have the model of S, in this paper the model of S is given, but the satisfaction of an (m, k) constraint can only be verified during runtime.

The runtime monitor relies on a *safety table* which stores the satisfaction condition of the property under each (m, k) constraint. As there are $\frac{K(K+1)}{2}$ constraints in the safety table, a straightforward approach evaluating each (m, k) constraint one by one needs to verify the property $\frac{K(K+1)}{2}$ times, where each individual verification may be expensive to carry out. To remedy this problem, we propose approaches to compute the safety table in a more efficient way. The main contributions include:

- We derive theorems of logical relationships between weakly-hard constraints. Based on the logical relationships, we reduce a safety table to its *satisfaction boundary* and propose approaches which only need to verify the property at most $2K$ times to compute the satisfaction boundary.
- Based on the computed satisfaction boundary, we define weakly-hard requirements for the system environment and design a lightweight runtime monitor monitoring the satisfaction of the weakly-hard requirements.
- We consider a special case of reachability of finite-state machines. We propose a mask-compressing approach which can be plugged into (called by) the proposed approaches above. We further propose a layered Breadth-First Search (BFS) approach which computes the satisfaction boundary for all (m, k) constraints $(1 \leq m \leq k \leq K)$ with the same computational complexity as evaluating a single (m, K) constraint.
- Experiment results with a discrete second-order controller demonstrate the efficiency of the proposed approaches.

The paper is organized as follows. Section 2 provides the problem formulation, and Sect. 3 overviews the proposed approaches. Section 4 describes how we solve the problem for general properties and systems and design a runtime monitor. Section 5 considers the special case of reachability for finite-state machines. Section 6 presents the experimental results. Section 7 reviews the related work, and Sect. 8 concludes the paper.

2   Problem Formulation

In this paper, we consider a labelled transition system $S = \langle Q, \Sigma, R, Q_0 \rangle$ where Q is the set of states, Σ is the set of alphabet, $R \subseteq Q \times \Sigma \times Q$ is the transition relation, and $Q_0 \in Q$ is the set of initial states. Without loss of generality, a subset of alphabet represents input events $\{0, 1\} \subseteq \Sigma$, where 0 and 1 represent a normal and faulty environmental event, respectively. We use $\sigma \in \Sigma = \{0, 1\}^*$ to represent an input trace. We are interested in evaluating whether a property P is satisfied with inputs under the constraints of weakly-hard fault models.

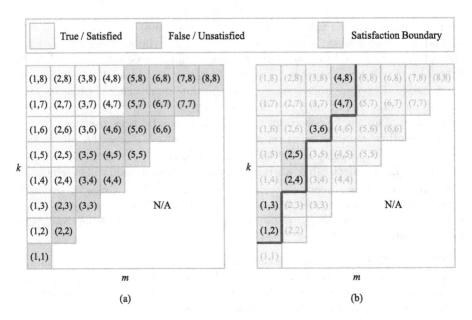

Fig. 1. (a) An example safety table and (b) its satisfaction boundary.

Definition 1. _Weakly-Hard Fault Model_. _A weakly-hard fault model is defined by_ (m, k), _meaning that there are at most m faulty events (denoted as 1's) among any k consecutive events in the input trace. The corresponding constraint is denoted as_ $W(m, k)$.

Based on the definition, an input trace $\sigma \models W(m, k)$ if and only if σ has at most m 1's in any size-k window of σ.

Definition 2. _Weakly-Hard Constraint Set_. _Given_ $K \in \mathbb{Z}^+$, _the weakly-hard constraint set is defined as_ $C(K) := \{W(m, k) \mid 1 \leq m \leq k \leq K\}$.

Given a system S, a property P, and a positive integer K, the goal in this paper is to develop a runtime monitor to verify whether the environment satisfies a subset of $C(K)$, where the subset is sufficient to enforce P, _i.e._, if the environment satisfies the subset of $C(K)$, it implies that S guarantees to satisfy P; otherwise, S cannot guarantee to satisfy P, which should lead S to switch to a safe mode. We do not consider the case of $m = 0$ as, if there is no faulty event, S should be designed to satisfy P, which should be regarded as a design-time problem (although our approach can also fit it).

The runtime monitor relies on a _safety table_, which stores the satisfaction condition of P under each $W(m, k)$ in $C(K)$. A safety table is defined as follows.

Table 1. The proposed approaches, where the monotonic approach (Algorithm 1), the monotonic approach with dynamic upper bound of satisfaction boundary (Algorithm 2), and the lowest-cast-first heuristic (Algorithm 3) decide the order of evaluating the weakly-hard constraints and need to call a verification approach (not covered for general properties and general systems in this paper) for a single (m, k) constraint to complete the verification for multiple (m, k) constraints.

Property & System	Single (m, k) Constraint	Multiple (m, k) Constraints
Reachability & Finite-State Machine	Mask-Compressing (Sect. 5.2)	Layered BFS (Sect. 5.3)
General Property & General System	Not Covered	Algorithms 1, 2, and 3 (Sects. 4.3, 4.5, and 4.6)

Definition 3. _Safety Table_. Given $K \in \mathbb{Z}^+$, a safety table $T \in \{\textit{True}, \textit{False}, N/A\}^{K \times K}$ is defined as

$$T[m, k] = \begin{cases} \textit{True} & \textit{if } m \le k \textit{ and } \forall \sigma \models W(m, k), \ S \models P; \\ \textit{False} & \textit{if } m \le k \textit{ and } \exists \sigma \models W(m, k), \ S \not\models P; \\ N/A & \textit{if } m > k. \end{cases} \tag{1}$$

For $m > k$, $T[m, k]$ is not applicable as the corresponding weakly-hard fault model is undefined. Note the a safety table is computed off-line in design phase, and the satisfaction of P under each $W(m, k)$ in $C(K)$ needs to be stored and accessed during runtime. An example safety table is shown in Fig. 1(a).

3   Overview of Proposed Approaches

We list the proposed approaches in this paper in Table 1. There will be five approaches: the monotonic approach (Algorithm 1) in Sects. 4.3, the monotonic approach with dynamic upper bound of satisfaction boundary (Algorithm 2) in Sects. 4.5, the lowest-cast-first heuristic (Algorithm 3) in Sects. 4.6, the mask-compressing approach in Sects. 5.2, and the layered BFS approach in Sects. 5.3.

The first three approaches are for general properties, general systems, and multiple weakly-hard constraints. They decide the order of evaluating the weakly-hard constraints and need to call a verification approach for a single weakly-hard constraint. Note that the first three approaches assume that one can verify a property P under a single weakly-hard constraint—this paper does not cover how to achieve that, except in the special case of reachability for finite-state machines. The last two approaches are exactly for the special case of reachability for finite-state machines. The mask-compressing approach is for a single weakly-hard constraint, and thus it can be plugged into (called by) the first three approaches, while the layered BFS approach is for multiple weakly-hard constraints.

4 General Approaches and Runtime Monitor Design

In this section, we first define the strength of weakly-hard constraints (Sect. 4.1). We then derive the fundamental theorems of logical relationships between weakly-hard constraints (Sect. 4.2) and propose an algorithm to compute the safety table and its corresponding satisfaction boundary based on these theorems (Sect. 4.3). We further derive advanced theorems of logical relationships between weakly-hard constraints (Sect. 4.4) and propose an improved algorithm (Sect. 4.5) and a lowest-cost-first heuristic (Sect. 4.6) taking all properties into account. Based on the computed safety table and the satisfaction boundary, we can design a runtime monitor (Sect. 4.7).

4.1 Strength of Weakly-Hard Constraint

Definition 4. ***Strength of Weakly-Hard Constraint.*** *Given two two weakly-hard constraints $W(m, k)$ and $W(m', k')$, we define that $W(m, k)$ is stronger than $W(m', k')$, denoted as $W(m, k) \succ W(m', k')$, if and only if any input trace that satisfies $W(m, k)$ also satisfies $W(m', k')$.*

Understanding the logical relationships between constraints allows us to determine the satisfaction of properties under some $W(m, k)$ constraints directly from the known verification results of other $W(m', k')$ constraints. From an algorithm design perspective, exploiting these relationships by evaluating the constraints in a proper order leads to a significant improvement in efficiency.

4.2 Fundamental Theorems

Theorem 1. *For any $m, m', k \in \mathbb{Z}^+, m < m' \le k$, $W(m, k) \succ W(m', k)$.*

Proof. By definition, for any input trace $\sigma \models W(m, k)$, it has at most m 1's in any size-k window of σ. Since $m < m'$, it follows that $\sigma \models W(m', k)$.

Corollary 1. *For any $m, m', k \in \mathbb{Z}^+, m < m' \le k$, if a property P is not satisfied under $W(m, k)$, then P is not satisfied under $W(m', k)$; if a property P is satisfied under $W(m', k)$, then P is satisfied under $W(m, k)$.*

Theorem 2. *For any $m, k, k' \in \mathbb{Z}^+, m \le k' < k$, $W(m, k) \succ W(m, k')$.*

Proof. By definition, for any input trace $\sigma \models W(m, k)$, it has at most m 1's in any size-k window of σ. If we reduce the window size to k', the maximum number of 1's in the window only remains the same or decreases, so it follows that $\sigma \models W(m, k')$.

Corollary 2. *For any $m, k, k' \in \mathbb{Z}^+, m \le k' < k$, if a property P is not satisfied under $W(m, k)$, then P is not satisfied under $W(m, k')$; if a property P is satisfied under $W(m, k')$, then P is satisfied under $W(m, k)$.*

Algorithm 1. Monotonic Approach

1: **procedure** GET_SATISFACTION_BOUNDARY(S, P, K)
2:    $B \leftarrow [\,]$
3:    $m \leftarrow 0$
4:    **for** $k \leftarrow 1$ to K **do**   ▷ Get satisfaction boundary for each k
5:       **while** $m < k$ **do**
6:          **if** $S \not\models P$ under $W(m+1, k)$ **then**
7:             **break**
8:          **end if**
9:          $m \leftarrow m + 1$
10:       **end while**
11:       $B[k] \leftarrow m$
12:    **end for**
13:    **return** B
14: **end procedure**

By Corollary 1, the problem of computing a safety table can be reduced to the problem of computing the *satisfaction boundary* of the safety table. The satisfaction boundary is defined as follows.

Definition 5. *Satisfaction Boundary*. *For each k, the satisfaction boundary $B(k)$ is the maximum m such that $T[m, k]$ (in the safety table) is True.*

The satisfaction boundary of the safety table in Fig. 1(a) is shown in Fig. 1(b). The reduction is crucial because we only need to store the satisfaction boundary rather than the whole safety table for the runtime monitor.

4.3   Monotonic Approach

Corollaries 1 and 2 imply that evaluating constraints in a monotonic manner (*i.e.*, increasing m and increasing k until a given K) can compute the satisfaction boundary without evaluating all constraints in $C(K)$. We assume that we can verify a property P under a single $W(m, k)$—an example of verifying reachability under a single $W(m, k)$ is described in Sect. 5.

We propose Algorithm 1 to compute the satisfaction boundary $B(k)$ for each $k \leq K$. For each $k \leq K$, the algorithm increases m until P is not satisfied and obtains $B(k)$ (Lines 5–11). By Corollary 1, since P is not satisfied under $W(B(k)+1, k)$, P is not satisfied under $W(m, k)$ where $m > B(k)+1$, and thus there is no need to verify P under $W(m, k)$ where $m > B(k)+1$. For example, as shown in Fig. 2(a), if P is not satisfied under $W(3, 4)$, then P is not satisfied under $W(4, 4)$, which does not need to be evaluated. Then, k is increased by 1 (Line 4), and the same procedure repeats and starts with $m = B(k-1)+1$ (not $m = 1$). By Corollary 2, since P is satisfied under $W(B(k-1), k-1)$, P is satisfied under $W(B(k-1), k)$, and thus there is no need to verify P under $W(B(k-1), k)$. For example, as shown in Fig. 2(b), if P is satisfied under $W(3, 4)$, then P is satisfied under $W(3, 5)$ (and $W(3, k)$ where $k \geq 5$), which does not

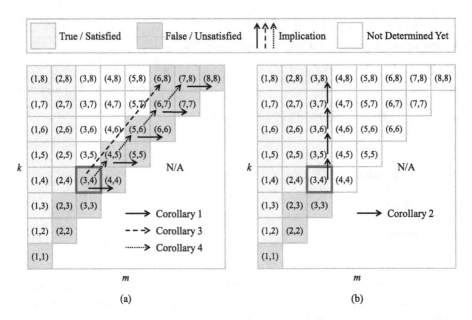

Fig. 2. An illustration of Algorithms 1 (which applies Corollaries 1 and 2 only) and 2 (which applies Corollaries 1, 2, 3, and 4). To have a clear comparison, we focus on the implications of $W(3,4)$ only. (a) If P is not satisfied under $W(3,4)$, then P is not satisfied under $W(4,4)$. Algorithm 2 further implies that P is not satisfied under $W(6,8)$ and $W(m,k)$ where $k \geq 5$ and $m \geq k - 1$. (b) If P is satisfied under $W(3,4)$, then P is satisfied under $W(3,k)$ where $k \geq 5$.

need to be evaluated. The algorithm terminates when $B(k)$ is computed for each $k \leq K$, and the satisfaction boundary is returned (Line 13).

Assuming the complexity of verifying P under a single weakly-hard constraint is $O(X)$, the complexity of Algorithm 1 is $O(2K \cdot X) = O(K \cdot X)$, since both m, k are non-decreasing in the algorithm and bounded above by K. It is a significant improvement over brute-forcing each $W(m,k)$ in $C(K)$, which has the complexity $O(K^2 \cdot X)$.

4.4   Advanced Theorems

Theorem 3. *For any $m, k, x \in \mathbb{Z}^+, m < k, x \geq 2$, $W(m,k) \succ W(xm, xk)$.*

Proof. For any input trace $\sigma \models W(m,k)$ and size-(xk) window of σ, the window can be constructed by x size-k windows, and each of which has at most m 1's. Thus, there are at most xm 1's in the size-(xk) window, and it follows that $\sigma \models W(xm, xk)$.

Corollary 3. *For any $m, k, x \in \mathbb{Z}^+, m < k, x \geq 2$, if a property P is not satisfied under $W(m,k)$, then P is not satisfied under $W(xm, xk)$; if a property P is satisfied under $W(xm, xk)$, then P is satisfied under $W(m,k)$.*

Algorithm 2. Monotonic Approach with Dynamic Upper Bound of Satisfaction Boundary

```
 1: procedure GET_SATISFACTION_BOUNDARY(S, P, K)
 2:     B ← [ ]
 3:     m ← 0
 4:     for k ← 1 to K do                          ▷ Initialize satisfaction boundary
 5:         B[k] = k
 6:     end for
 7:     for k ← 1 to K do                          ▷ Get satisfaction boundary for each k
 8:         while m < B[k] do
 9:             if S ⊭ P under W(m + 1, k) then
10:                 x ← 2
11:                 while x · k ≤ K do             ▷ Corollary 3
12:                     B[xk] ← min(B[xk], x · (m + 1) − 1)
13:                     x ← x + 1
14:                 end while
15:                 x ← 1
16:                 while k + x ≤ K do             ▷ Corollary 4
17:                     B[k + x] ← min(B[k + x], (m + 1) + x − 1)
18:                     x ← x + 1
19:                 end while
20:                 break
21:             end if
22:             m ← m + 1
23:         end while
24:         B[k] ← min(B[k], m)
25:     end for
26:     return B
27: end procedure
```

Theorem 4. *For any* $m, k, x \in \mathbb{Z}^+, m < k$, $W(m, k) \succ W(m + x, k + x)$.

Proof. For any input trace $\sigma \models W(m, k)$ and size-$(k + x)$ window of σ, the window can be constructed by combining two windows of sizes k and x, respectively. Since $\sigma \models W(m, k)$, there are at most m 1's in the size-k window. On the other hand, there are at most x 1's in the size-x window. Thus, there are at most $(m + x)$ 1's in the size-$(k + x)$ window, and it follows that $\sigma \models W(m + x, k + x)$.

Corollary 4. *For any* $m, k, x \in \mathbb{Z}^+, m < k$, *if a property* P *is not satisfied under* $W(m, k)$, *then* P *is not satisfied under* $W(m + x, k + x)$; *if a property* P *is satisfied under* $W(m + x, k + x)$, *then* P *is satisfied under* $W(m, k)$.

4.5 Monotonic Approach with Dynamic Upper Bound of Satisfaction Boundary

Corollaries 3 and 4 imply the satisfaction of a property P beyond the same m or k. Integrating with the previously proposed monotonic approach which

Algorithm 3. Lowest-Cost-First Heuristic

1: **procedure** GET_SAFETY_TABLE(S, P, K)
2:     $T \leftarrow \{\texttt{undefined}\}$ ▷ Initialize as **undefined** for the safety table
3:     **while** T has **undefined** element **do**
4:         Select the lowest-cost **undefined** $W(m, k)$
5:         **if** $S \models P$ under $W(m, k)$ **then**
6:             $T[m, k] \leftarrow$ True
7:         **else**
8:             $T[m, k] \leftarrow$ False
9:         **end if**
10:         Recursively update T by Corollaries 1, 2, 3, and 4
11:     **end while**
12:     **return** T
13: **end procedure**
---

increases m and k, we exploit the corollaries and propose Algorithm 2 to compute the satisfaction boundary $B(k)$ for each $k \leq K$. The main difference between Algorithm 1 and Algorithm 2 is that the former one considers the search range for the satisfaction boundary from an m to k, while the latter one dynamically reduces the search range whenever P is not satisfied under a constraint.

Specifically, suppose the algorithm is in the process of computing $B(k)$, and P is not satisfied under $W(m + 1, k)$ (Line 9). By Corollary 3, P is not satisfied for each $W(x \cdot (m + 1), xk), x \geq 2$, and thus $x \cdot (m + 1) - 1$ is an upper bound of $B(xk)$ (Lines 10–14). Similarly, by Corollary 4, P is not satisfied for each $W((m + 1) + x, k + x), x \in \mathbb{Z}^+$, and thus $(m + 1) + x - 1$ is an upper bound of $B(k + x)$ (Lines 15–19). An example is shown in Fig. 2(a), if P is not satisfied under $W(3, 4)$, then P is not satisfied under $W(4, 4)$, $W(6, 8)$, and $W(m, k)$ where $k \geq 5$ and $m \geq k - 1$, which do not need to be evaluated. If P is satisfied under $W(3, 4)$, then the implication is the same as Algorithm 1, as shown in Fig. 2(b).

4.6   Lowest-Cost-First Heuristic

Since the implications of the theorems do not necessarily restrict the order of evaluating each $W(m, k)$ in $C(K)$, the efficiency can be further improved by a good evaluation order. We suppose that we can estimate the verification (time) cost for each $W(m, k)$ in $C(K)$, e.g., based on the complexity as a function of m and k. Intuitively, evaluating lower-cost constraints which implies more constraints or higher-cost constraints is preferred. We propose Algorithm 3 which iteratively selects a not-yet-evaluated constraint in $C(K)$ by the estimated cost (Line 4), evaluates it (Lines 5–9), and processes all implied constraints after each evaluation (Line 10). The lowest-cost-first heuristic, though not optimal, provides the flexibility of evaluating constraints in $C(K)$ by different orders. The lowest-cost-first heuristic, though not optimal, provides the flexibility of evaluating constraints in orders different from the previous monotonic approaches. System designers can decide the order according to the system features.

Algorithm 4. Runtime Monitoring

```
1:  procedure RUNTIME_MONITORING(K, B[])
2:      for k ← 1 to K do
3:          I[k] ← 0                              ▷ Store the last k-th input
4:          N₁[k] ← 0           ▷ Store the number of 1's among the last k inputs
5:      end for
6:      i ← 0
7:      while 1 do                                ▷ During runtime
8:          x = Get_Input()
9:          for k ← 1 to K do
10:             N₁[k] ← N₁[k] + x − I[(i − k)%K]
11:             if N₁[k] > B[k] then        ▷ Exceed the satisfaction boundary
12:                 Switch to a safe mode
13:             end if
14:         end for
15:         I[i] ← x
16:         i ← (i + 1)%K
17:     end while
18: end procedure
```

4.7   Runtime Monitor Design

Based on the satisfaction boundary computed above, we design a runtime monitor to verify whether the environment satisfies each $W(m, k)$ in $C(K)$. Depending on the satisfaction boundary, we can then determine whether a property P can be guaranteed. If P cannot be guaranteed, we can switch the system to a safe mode. As shown in Algorithm 4, the runtime monitor only needs to store the satisfaction boundary $B[]$, instead of the safety table, in advance, reducing the space complexity from $O(K^2)$ to $O(K)$.

Besides the satisfaction boundary, the runtime monitor only needs two additional arrays, $I[k]$ for the last k-th inputs and $N_1[k]$ for the number of 1's among the last k inputs, where $1 \leq k \leq K$. During runtime (Lines 7–17), the runtime monitor reads an input (Line 8) and, for each k (Line 9), it updates the number of 1's among the last k inputs, $N_1[k]$ (Line 10), and check if it exceeds the satisfaction boundary $B[k]$ (Line 11). If yes, it means that P is not guaranteed to be satisfied, and the system switches to a safe mode (Line 12). The runtime monitor then stores the input (Line 15) and continues monitoring.

5   Reachability Analysis for Finite-State Machines

In this section, we consider a special case of system verification with weakly-hard constraints—reachability analysis for finite-state machines. We first propose a mask-compression approach to verify reachability under a single weakly-hard constraint. The mask-compression approach serves as the example of verifying a property P (reachability) under a single constraint in $C(K)$, and thus it can be plugged into (called by) the approaches in Sect. 4. Then, we propose a layered

BFS approach which computes the safety table in a more efficient way—the layered BFS approach computes the safety table with the same computational complexity as evaluating a single (m, K) constraint.

5.1   Problem Definition

A non-deterministic finite-state machine model S is defined as $\langle Q, \Sigma, \delta, P_r, q_0, F \rangle$ where Q is the finite set of states, $\Sigma = \{0, 1\}$ is the set of input symbols, $\delta \subseteq Q \times \Sigma \times Q$ is the transition table, $P_r : \delta \to (0, 1]$ is the transition probability satisfying

$$\forall (q, x) \in Q \times \Sigma, \quad \sum_{\overline{q} \in Q, (q, x, \overline{q}) \in \delta} P_r(q, x, \overline{q}) = 1, \qquad (2)$$

where q_0 is the initial state, and $F \subseteq Q$ is the finite set of unsafe states. Given a finite-state machine S and a positive integer K, the goal is to determine whether the property P of "never reaching an unsafe state" is satisfied with all possible traces under each $W(m, k)$ in $C(K)$.

5.2   Mask-Compressing Approach

We develop the masking-compressing approach to verify the reachability property P under a single weakly-hard constraint $W(m, k)$. Again, it should be emphasized that the mask-compression approach serves as the example of verifying a property P (reachability) under a single constraint in $C(K)$, and thus it can be plugged into (called by) the approaches in Sect. 4. The mask-compressing approach traverses a finite-state machine with all possible traces that satisfy the weakly-hard constraint. It records the previous $k - 1$ inputs and considers the possibility of the next input. Since there are at most m 1's among any k consecutive inputs, if there have been m 1's among previous $k - 1$ inputs, then the next input must be 0.

Given the previous $k - 1$ inputs, we encode them by compressing them into a $(k - 1)$-bit mask. Formally, given a finite state machine $S = \langle Q, \Sigma, \delta, P_r, q_0, F \rangle$, we define a graph to perform verification for a single weakly-hard constraint $W(m, k)$ as follows:

- The vertex set is the set product of the states of S and the $(k - 1)$-bit mask.
- There is a directed edge from $v_{q, mask}$ to $v_{\overline{q}, \overline{mask}}$ if and only if

$$(q, \; \overline{mask} \; \% \; 2, \; \overline{q}) \in \delta, \qquad (3)$$

$$(mask \cdot 2) \; \% \; 2^{k-1} + \overline{mask} \; \% \; 2 = \overline{mask}, \qquad (4)$$

$$\text{Count1}(mask) + \overline{mask} \; \% \; 2 \leq m, \qquad (5)$$

where Count1() counts the number of 1's in a mask.

Note that Eq. (3) is for the transition in S, Eq. (4) is for the 1-bit "shift" of the mask, and Eq. (5) is for the number of 1's bounded by the weakly-hard fault model. After constructing the graph, we can apply the depth-first search from $v_{q_0,0}$, and P is not satisfied if and only if we can reach a vertex $v_{q,mask}$ where $q \in F$.

The graph has at most $|Q| \cdot 2^k$ vertices and $|\delta| \cdot 2^k$ edges, and thus the complexity is $O(N \cdot 2^k)$, where $N = |Q| + |\delta|$, for the mask-compressing approach verifying the reachability property P under a single $W(m, k)$. When plugging the masking-compressing approach into the approaches in Sect. 4, the complexities are as follows:

- Algorithm 1: $O\left(\sum_{k=1}^{K} \sum_{m=1}^{k} N \cdot 2^k\right)$.
- Algorithm 2: $O\left(\sum_{k=1}^{K} \sum_{m=1}^{B(k)} N \cdot 2^k\right)$.
- Algorithm 3: it depends on the cost estimation and constraint implication.

All of them are bounded by

$$O\left(\sum_{k=1}^{K} k \cdot N \cdot 2^k\right) = O\left((K-1) \cdot N \cdot 2^{K+1} + N\right) = O\left(K \cdot N \cdot 2^K\right). \quad (6)$$

5.3   Layered BFS Approach

The key insight of the layered BFS approach is that multiple weakly-hard constraints $W(m, k)$ with the same k can be verified together within a BFS.

Theorem 5. *For $W(m, k), W(m + 1, k) \in C(K)$, the graph for $W(m, k)$ constructed by the mask-compressing approach is a subgraph of the graph for $W(m + 1, k)$.*

Proof. It is straightforward by Eq. (5).

Theorem 5 implies that evaluating $W(m, k)$ leads to the results for all $W(m', k)$, where $0 \leq m' \leq m$. Thus, only the graph for $W(k, k)$ needs to be traversed. The problem boils down to finding the correct order to perform graph traversal such that all verification results can be collected. Formally, we let E_m and V_m denote the set of edges and vertices of the graph for $W(m, k)$. At the m-th iteration (as a layer), we perform a BFS on the graph $G_m = (V_m, E_m)$. We exploit the previous result of the BFS on $G_{m-1} = (V_{m-1}, E_{m-1})$ and thus avoid redundancy as $G_{m-1} \subseteq G_m$.

Since we aim to expand the smallest graph for $W(1, k)$ incrementally up to $W(k, k)$ in a bottom-up manner, we iteratively allow parts of the graph for $W(k, k)$ to be "visitable" and perform a BFS on visitable vertices. Initially, $E_0 = \emptyset$ and $V_0 = \{v_{q_0,0^k}\}$. At the beginning of the m-th iteration, the layered BFS approach marks each vertex $v_{q,mask}$, where $mask$ satisfies $W(m, k)$, to be visitable. Then, in the same iteration, the layered BFS approach performs a BFS on visitable vertices to find reachable vertices and mark them to be "reachable".

If an unsafe state is reached at the m-th iteration, P is only guaranteed to be satisfied under $W(m', k)$, where $m' < m$.

Since each vertex in the graph for $W(k, k)$ only needs to be traversed once, the complexity for a given k is $O(N \cdot 2^k)$, where $N = |Q| + |\delta|$. The total complexity for all k is

$$O\left(\sum_{k=1}^{K} N \cdot 2^k\right) = O\left(N \cdot 2^{K+1} - N \cdot 2\right) = O(N \cdot 2^K). \tag{7}$$

This shows that the layered BFS approach computes the satisfaction boundary with the same complexity as verifying a single (m, K). Compared with Algorithms 1, 2, and 3 with the complexity $O(K \cdot N \cdot 2^K)$ in Eq. (6), the layered BFS approach is asymptotically K times faster, demonstrating that white or grey box system models allow more efficient verification.

6   Experiment Results

6.1   Setting

The case study is a discrete second-order controller under perturbation attacks. We denote the control value, its first-order derivative, and its second-order derivative at time t as $x(t)$, $\dot{x}(t)$, and $\ddot{x}(t)$, respectively. The objective of the controller is to maintain x at a fixed value (0 in our case), and the attacker attempts to shift x away from the fixed value. The controller is formally defined as $\langle x_{\min}, x_{\max}, \dot{x}_{\min}, \dot{x}_{\max}, \ddot{x}_C, S_{\mathrm{atk}} \rangle$, where

- $[x_{\min}, x_{\max}]$ is the safe range. If x exceeds the range, the safety property is violated.
- $[\dot{x}_{\min}, \dot{x}_{\max}]$ is the physical constraint for the first order derivative of x. If the controller attempts to set $\dot{x}$ to a value larger (smaller) than $\dot{x}_{\max}$ ($\dot{x}_{\min}$), $\dot{x}$ is set to the corresponding limit.
- $\ddot{x}_C$ is the constant magnitude for the second order derivative of x, i.e., $\ddot{x}(t) \in \{-\ddot{x}_C, 0, \ddot{x}_C\}$.
- S_{atk} is the set of possible attack values on x.

Suppose the control value x deviates away from 0, the policy of the controller is to accelerate until $\dot{x}$ reaches the limit ($\dot{x}_{\min}, \dot{x}_{\max}$) and decelerate when the control value x is approaching 0. The timing to start the deceleration is determined such that $\dot{x} = 0$ when $x = 0$, and we denote the value of x at which the deceleration starts as x_{dec}, which is

$$x_{\mathrm{dec}}(t) = \dot{x}(t) \cdot t_{\mathrm{dec}}(t) - \frac{1}{2} \cdot \mathrm{sign}(\dot{x}(t)) \cdot \ddot{x}_C \cdot t_{\mathrm{dec}}(t)^2, \tag{8}$$

where $t_{\mathrm{dec}}(t) = \frac{|\dot{x}(t)|}{\ddot{x}_C}$ is the time required to decelerate $\dot{x}(t)$ to 0. The transition functions of the controller can be expressed as

$$x(t+1) \leftarrow x(t) + \dot{x}(t) + p_{\mathrm{atk}}(t), \tag{9}$$

$$\dot{x}(t+1) \leftarrow \max\left(\min\left(\dot{x}(t)+\ddot{x}(t), \dot{x}_{\max}\right), \dot{x}_{\min}\right), \tag{10}$$

$$\ddot{x}(t+1) \leftarrow -\text{sign}\left(x(t)+p_{\text{atk}}(t)\right) \cdot \text{sign}\left(|x(t)+p_{\text{atk}}(t)| - |x_{\text{dec}}(t)|\right) \cdot \ddot{x}_C, \tag{11}$$

where p_{atk} denotes the perturbation attack. Equation (9) is for the transition of x, where the control value is affected by both the first-order derivative and the perturbation attack. Equation (10) is for the transition of $\dot{x}$, with the updated value clipped to $[\dot{x}_{\min}, \dot{x}_{\max}]$ to satisfy the physical constrain. Equation (11) is for the transition of $\ddot{x}$, where the sign of $\ddot{x}$ is determined by the relative position of x with respect to 0 and whether the system is decelerating as x approaches 0.

For any controller configuration $\langle x_{\min}, x_{\max}, \dot{x}_{\min}, \dot{x}_{\max}, \ddot{x}_C, S_{\text{atk}} \rangle$ we can define a finite state machine $\langle Q, \Sigma, \delta, P_r, q_0, F \rangle$, where

- $Q = \{(x, \dot{x}, \ddot{x}) | x, \dot{x} \in \mathbb{Z}, x \in [x_{\min}, x_{\max}], \dot{x} \in [\dot{x}_{\min}, \dot{x}_{\max}], \ddot{x} \in \{-\ddot{x}_C, 0, \ddot{x}_C\}\} \cup \{q_{\text{unsafe}}\}$.
- $\Sigma = S_{\text{atk}} \cup \{0\}$.
- δ is defined exactly from the transition functions above.
- $P_r((x, \dot{x}, \ddot{x}), p_{\text{atk}}, (x', \dot{x}', \ddot{x}')) = \frac{1}{|S_{\text{atk}}|}$.
- $q_0 = (0, 0, 0)$.
- $F = \{q_{\text{unsafe}}\}$.

q_{unsafe} represents the state where the control value x is out of the range $[x_{\min}, x_{\max}]$. Verifying whether the control value is in the safe range under perturbation attacks is reduced to solving for the reachability of q_{unsafe} for the finite-state machine.

We implemented a brute-force approach which evaluates all constraints in $C(K)$ one by one, the monotonic approach (Algorithm 1), the monotonic approach with dynamic upper bound of satisfaction boundary (Algorithm 2), the lowest-cost-first heuristic (Algorithm 3) which defines the estimated cost for evaluating $W(m, k)$ as $\sum_{i=0}^{m} \binom{k-1}{i}$, and the layered BFS approach. Except the layered BFS approach, the other four approaches call the mask-compressing approach when they need to evaluate a single constraint in $C(K)$. The approaches were implemented in C++ and run in the environment with 2.4GHz Quad-Core Intel Core i5 CPU and 16GB LPDDR3 RAM. Any reported runtime is the average of 5 runs.

6.2   Results

Experiment on $|Q|$. We experimented on how each approach scales with respect to the number of states in the finite-state machine, $|Q|$. To create different numbers of states, we fixed $\dot{x}_{\min} = -4$, $\dot{x}_{\max} = 4$, $\ddot{x}_C = 2$, and $S_{\text{atk}} = \{5\}$ and experimented with $(x_{\min}, x_{\max}) = \{\pm 30, \pm 40, \pm 50, \pm 60, \pm 70, \pm 80, \pm 90, \pm 100\}$, resulting $|Q|$ from 931 to 3,031. A larger safe range $[x_{\min}, x_{\max}]$ of the control value x allows the controller to have a larger margin to recover from attacks. K is set to 20.

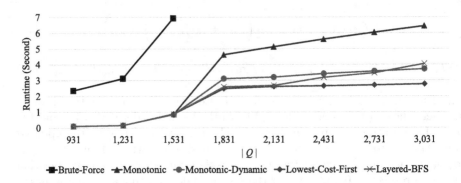

Fig. 3. The runtime over the number of states, $|Q|$ (the out-of-range runtimes of the brute-force approach are 26.972, 29.578, 31.760, 33.975, and 36.047 seconds in an increasing-$|Q|$ order).

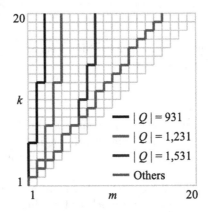

Fig. 4. The computed satisfaction boundaries.

The results are shown in Fig. 3, and the corresponding satisfaction boundaries are illustrated in Fig. 4, where all approaches generate the same satisfaction boundaries. The monotonic approach runs significantly faster than the brute-force approach because the verification results under many weakly-hard constraints are implied by Corollaries 1 and 2. For larger number of states, the runtime differences are even larger, and only the monotonic approach can complete the system verification within reasonable time. We then compare the monotonic approach, the monotonic approach with dynamic upper bound of satisfaction boundary (monotonic-dynamic), and the lowest-cost-first heuristic. The results are aligned with the theoretical expectations. The monotonic-dynamic approach runs strictly faster than the monotonic approach for every setting with the addition implications by Corollaries 3 and 4, and the lowest-cost-first heuristic performs faster than the monotonic-dynamic approach when the number of states is larger. The layered BFS approach runs faster than the monotonic approach,

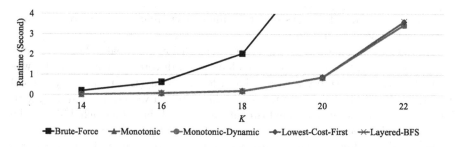

Fig. 5. The runtime over K (the out-of-range runtimes of the brute-force approach are 6.924 and 28.704 seconds in an increasing-K order).

and it has comparable runtime as the monotonic-dynamic approach and the lowest-cost-first heuristic.

Experiment on K. We experimented on how each approach scales with respect to K. We fixed $x_{min} = -50$, $x_{max} = 50$, $\dot{x}_{min} = -4$, $\dot{x}_{max} = 4$, $\ddot{x}_{const} = 2$, and $S_{atk} = \{5\}$. The results are shown in Fig. 5, where we report the results with $K = 14, 16, 18, 20, 22$. Similar to the previous experiment, the proposed approaches outperform the brute-force approach significantly. This is aligned with the theoretical complexity analysis that the brute-force approach needs to evaluate $O(K^2)$ weakly-hard constraints, and the other approaches need to evaluate $O(K)$ weakly-hard constraints only. It should be emphasized that the verification of a property under a single weakly-hard constraint $W(m, k)$ usually needs to store the last k inputs, and thus the complexity is at least $O(2^k)$. If the property is more complicated (*e.g.*, in Linear Temporal Logic), the complexity can be even higher. Therefore, reducing the number of evaluations of weakly-hard constraints is really advantageous to the efficiency of computing the safety table or the satisfaction boundary. It should also be mentioned that the layered BFS approach is especially for the reachability of finite-state machines, and the other proposed approaches are general and compatible with other verification approaches for a single weakly-hard constraint.

7   Related Work

Starting from [10], which is the first work that introduced the notion of (m, k) constraint, weakly-hard systems have been studied from various perspectives in the last two decades. Research interests range from real-time systems [2] to network systems [15]. Most of the works focus on the schedulability analysis for periodic tasks under various assumptions such as bi-modal execution and non-preemptiveness [3,5,17,23], or the temporal behavior analysis of overloaded systems [1,9,11,21,24].

Stable controller synthesis is another important topic in the context of weakly-hard constraints. Based on the extensive studies on the stability under probabilistic deadline misses [20,22], authors in [4] propose a switched controller to stabilize a weakly-hard system with linear dynamic, while a non-switched controller is discussed in [19].

The most related work is the safety verification for weakly-hard systems, where however, only a few prior works have been devoted to this topic. [7] was the first work that attempts to provide a formal analysis for linear dynamical systems with weakly-hard constraints. In this paper, a weakly-hard system with linear dynamic is modeled as a hybrid automaton and then the reachability of the generated hybrid automaton is verified by the tool SpaceEx [8]. [6] transforms the behavior of a linear weakly-hard system into a program, and then uses program verification techniques, such as abstract interpretation and SMT solvers to analyze the safety. In contrast, the infinite-time safety problem of general nonlinear weakly-hard systems is considered in [14]. By modeling a weakly-hard system as a hybrid automaton, which is similar as that in [8], authors in [14] convert the infinite-time safety problem into a finite one and then apply linear programming to obtain a sufficient condition of the initial state to ensure the safety, which is further improved in [13].

The fundamental difference between the above works, and this paper, is that we focus on discrete systems rather than continuous systems. Since a variety of systems are discrete in practice, we believe the study on specific discrete systems is necessary. Benefiting from this, our technique is able to generate sound and complete verification result with respect to the weakly-hard constraints for large scale problems.

8   Conclusion

In this paper, we used a weakly-hard fault model to constrain the occurrences of faults in system inputs. We developed approaches to verify properties for multiple weakly-hard constraints in an exact and efficient manner. By verifying multiple weakly-hard constraints and storing the verification results as a safety table or the corresponding satisfaction boundary, we defined weakly-hard requirements for the system environment and designed a runtime monitor that guarantees desired properties or notifies the system to switch to a safe mode. Experiments with a discrete second-order controller demonstrated the efficiency of the proposed approaches. Future directions include properties in Linear Temporal Logic under weakly-hard constraints, other models of computation under weakly-hard constraints, and system-specific cost estimation for the lowest-cost-first heuristic.

References

1. Ahrendts, L., Quinton, S., Boroske, T., Ernst, R.: Verifying weakly-hard real-time properties of traffic streams in switched networks. In: Euromicro Conference on Real-Time Systems, vol. 106, pp. 15:1–15:22 (2018)
2. Bernat, G., Burns, A., Liamosi, A.: Weakly hard real-time systems. IEEE Trans. Comput. **50**(4), 308–321 (2001)
3. Bernat, G., Cayssials, R.: Guaranteed on-line weakly-hard real-time systems. In: IEEE Real-Time Systems Symposium, pp. 22–35 (2001)

4. Blind, R., Allgöwer, F.: Towards networked control systems with guaranteed stability: using weakly hard real-time constraints to model the loss process. In: IEEE Conference on Decision and Control, pp. 7510–7515. IEEE (2015)
5. Choi, H., Kim, H., Zhu, Q.: Job-class-level fixed priority scheduling of weakly-hard real-time systems. In: IEEE Real-Time Technology and Applications Symposium, pp. 241–253 (2019)
6. Duggirala, P.S., Viswanathan, M.: Analyzing real time linear control systems using software verification. In: IEEE Real-Time Systems Symposium, pp. 216–226. IEEE (2015)
7. Frehse, G., Hamann, A., Quinton, S., Woehrle, M.: Formal analysis of timing effects on closed-loop properties of control software. In: IEEE Real-Time Systems Symposium, pp. 53–62 (2014)
8. Frehse, G., et al.: SpaceEx: scalable verification of hybrid systems. In: Gopalakrishnan, G., Qadeer, S. (eds.) CAV 2011. LNCS, vol. 6806, pp. 379–395. Springer, Heidelberg (2011). https://doi.org/10.1007/978-3-642-22110-1_30
9. Gujarati, A., Nasri, M., Majumdar, R., Brandenburg, B.B.: From iteration to system failure: characterizing the fitness of periodic weakly-hard systems. In: Euromicro Conference on Real-Time Systems, pp. 9:1–9:23 (2019)
10. Hamdaoui, M., Ramanathan, P.: A dynamic priority assignment technique for streams with (m, k)-firm deadlines. IEEE Trans. Comput. **44**(12), 1443–1451 (1995)
11. Hammadeh, Z.A.H., Ernst, R., Quinton, S., Henia, R., Rioux, L.: Bounding deadline misses in weakly-hard real-time systems with task dependencies. In: Design, Automation and Test in Europe Conference, pp. 584–589 (2017)
12. Hammadeh, Z.A.H., Quinton, S., Panunzio, M., Henia, R., Rioux, L., Ernst, R.: Budgeting under-specified tasks for weakly-hard real-time systems. In: Euromicro Conference on Real-Time Systems, vol. 76, pp. 17:1–17:22 (2017)
13. Huang, C., Chang, K.-C., Lin, C.-W., Zhu, Q.: SAW: a tool for safety analysis of weakly-hard systems. In: Lahiri, S.K., Wang, C. (eds.) CAV 2020. LNCS, vol. 12224, pp. 543–555. Springer, Cham (2020). https://doi.org/10.1007/978-3-030-53288-8_26
14. Huang, C., Li, W., Zhu, Q.: Formal verification of weakly-hard systems. In: ACM International Conference on Hybrid Systems: Computation and Control, pp. 197–207 (2019)
15. Huang, C., Wardega, K., Li, W., Zhu, Q.: Exploring weakly-hard paradigm for networked systems. In: Workshop on Design Automation for CPS and IoT, pp. 51–59 (2019)
16. Lesi, V., Jovanov, I., Pajic, M.: Network scheduling for secure cyber-physical systems. In: IEEE Real-Time Systems Symposium, pp. 45–55 (2017)
17. Li, J., Song, Y., Simonot-Lion, F.: Providing real-time applications with graceful degradation of QoS and fault tolerance according to (m, k)-firm model. IEEE Trans. Ind. Inf. **2**(2), 112–119 (2006)
18. Liang, H., Wang, Z., Roy, D., Dey, S., Chakraborty, S., Zhu, Q.: Security-driven codesign with weakly-hard constraints for real-time embedded systems. In: 2019 IEEE 37th International Conference on Computer Design (ICCD), pp. 217–226 (2019)
19. Linsenmayer, S., Allgower, F.: Stabilization of networked control systems with weakly hard real-time dropout description. In: IEEE Conference on Decision and Control, pp. 4765–4770 (2017)
20. Pazzaglia, P., Mandrioli, C., Maggio, M., Cervin, A.: DMAC: deadline-miss-aware control. In: Euromicro Conference on Real-Time Systems, pp. 1:1–1:24 (2019)

21. Quinton, S., Ernst, R.: Generalized weakly-hard constraints. In: Margaria, T., Steffen, B. (eds.) ISoLA 2012. LNCS, vol. 7610, pp. 96–110. Springer, Heidelberg (2012). https://doi.org/10.1007/978-3-642-34032-1_13
22. Schenato, L.: To zero or to hold control inputs with lossy links? IEEE Trans. Autom. Control **54**(5), 1093–1099 (2009)
23. Sun, Y., Natale, M.D.: Weakly hard schedulability analysis for fixed priority scheduling of periodic real-time tasks. ACM Trans. Embed. Comput. Syst. **16**(5s), 171:1–171:19 (2017)
24. Xu, W., Hammadeh, Z.A.H., Kröller, A., Ernst, R., Quinton, S.: Improved deadline miss models for real-time systems using typical worst-case analysis. In: Euromicro Conference on Real-Time Systems, pp. 247–256 (2015)

From Statistical Model Checking to Run-Time Monitoring Using a Bayesian Network Approach

Manfred Jaeger⬤, Kim G. Larsen⬤, and Alessandro Tibo$^{(\boxtimes)}$⬤

Aalborg University, Aalborg, Denmark
{jaeger,kgl,alessandr}@aau.dk

Abstract. We propose a framework for monitoring and updating, at run-time, the probabilities of temporal properties of stochastic timed automata. Our method is based on Bayesian networks and can be useful in various real-time applications, such as flight control systems and cardiac pacemakers. The framework has been implemented by exploiting the statistical model checking engine of UPPAAL-SMC. By run-time monitoring a set of interesting temporal properties of a given stochastic automaton we update their probabilities, modeled through a Bayesian Network. The main advantages of our method are the capacity to discover non-trivial dependencies between properties and to efficiently update probabilities of unobserved properties given real-time observations. We present empirical results on three application scenarios, showing that the query time can keep up with the speed of some realistic real-time applications. We also present experiments demonstrating that the Bayesian Network approach performance-wise enables run-time monitoring while maintaining or even increasing the accuracy of probability estimation compared to statistical model checking.

Keywords: Timed automata · Bayesian networks · Statistical model checking

1 Introduction

Stochastic timed automata are powerful modeling tools for designing and verifying a wide variety of real-time system models, such as real-time monitors for resource management [9], cruise control system [18] in a car, flight control systems [23], and cardiac pacemakers [4,15]. Precise verification of probabilistic properties for such models quickly becomes intractable, and statistical model checking (SMC) (e.g. [2,10,14]) has emerged as a more scalable alternative. However, SMC in many cases will still not be suitable for querying at runtime under real-time constraints, since each probability computation is based on first sampling a number of runs of the stochastic automaton, and the required number of sample runs can become very large when querying probabilities of rare properties. In particular, when we are interested in queries that can be conditioned on

© Springer Nature Switzerland AG 2020
J. Deshmukh and D. Ničković (Eds.): RV 2020, LNCS 12399, pp. 517–535, 2020.
https://doi.org/10.1007/978-3-030-60508-7_30

partial observations of the system behavior, the SMC approach will often not be viable, since the probability estimation then can only be based on the sampled runs that are consistent with the given observations.

In this paper we therefore develop an alternative, model-based approach. We assume that there is a certain number of key system properties of interest. We then construct a Bayesian network model that represents the joint probability distribution for these selected properties, and that can be efficiently queried for probabilities that are conditioned on complex observations. For example, in a model for a production system involving several processes accessing shared resources, the key properties might be when and for how long which process has accessed which resource, and one could be interested in conditional queries for the expected finishing time of the whole production, given that we have observed the resource usage of some processes up to the present point in time.

We use machine learning algorithms to construct Bayesian network models from the same kind of randomly sampled system runs as used by SMC. As we will see, not only does the Bayesian network model then enable much faster, repeated querying for different conditional probabilities, it also turns out to be more data efficient: a Bayesian network learnt from the same amount of random runs often provides more accurate probability values for the queries of interest, than what is obtained by SMC. This is because the Bayesian network also identifies the (conditional) independence structure between the properties, and thereby can provide accurate probability values even for combinations of properties that never occurred once in the sampled run data.

In this paper we focus on application scenarios where the goal is forecasting properties of system runs based on observations made at runtime. For example, we may want to continuously update a probability estimate for the event that a system's battery reaches a critically low level before the current process on the system terminates. Our method can support other types of applications, however. For example, a Bayesian network model learned from a timed automaton model $\mathcal{M}$ could be used for fault-diagnosis of a real-world implementation $\mathcal{S}$. Internal system states that can be observed in simulations of $\mathcal{M}$ may be unobservable in $\mathcal{S}$, and a model learned from traces of $\mathcal{M}$ can therefore be used to infer hidden (failure) system states of $\mathcal{S}$.

The use of Bayesian networks for diagnostics and forecasting of biological and technical systems is, of course, very well established. However, the usual scenario is that the Bayesian network is either manually constructed by experts, or learned from observational data of the same type of system to which it later will be applied. The novelty of our approach lies in the fact that we base the construction of the Bayesian network on a behavioral model (timed automaton) of the system that we later want to diagnose or monitor, and that a Bayesian network modeling and inference approach then becomes a computational alternative to statistical model checking techniques.

Bayesian networks have previously been used as tools in a runtime verification scenario [16]. However, the nature of the Bayesian networks used in [16], their construction and use is very different from what we propose here. The authors of [16] use dynamic Bayesian networks (DBNs) which are obtained by a product construction from a system model given as a Hidden Markov Model (HMM), and a property monitor given as a deterministic finite automaton. The nodes of the DBNs then represent time-indexed internal system and monitor states. This is very different from the nodes in our Bayesian networks, which directly represent properties of interest of entire system traces. Whereas the DBNs of [16] are obtained by a deterministic constructions, ours are learned from simulation data. Finally, the objective of [16] is online monitoring of the current system state. As explained above, our focus is on forecasting future events and properties in the full system run.

We implemented and evaluated our approach based on UPPAAL-SMC [10] as the modeling platform for stochastic timed automata, as the sample generator for random system runs, and as the SMC tool that we compare against.

The paper is organized as follows. In Sect. 2 we formally review some background concepts related to timed automata, statistical model checking, and Bayesian Networks. In Sect. 3 we present the proposed framework. In Sect. 4 we report an experimental evaluation of our method on a real-case scenario, introduced at a first as toy example for a better explanation and then two concreted cases. We also perform a comparison between statistical model checkers and Bayesian Networks in Sect. 5. Finally, in Sect. 6 we draw some conclusions and discuss possible extensions as future work. The code we used for the experiments can be downloaded from https://github.com/alessandro-t/uppaal-bn.

2 Background

In this section we will review the ingredients of our framework: timed automata models, statistical model checking, and Bayesian Networks.

2.1 Timed Automata

Timed Automata are finite automata enriched with real-valued variables called clocks [3]. Clocks measure the progress of time which elapses while an automaton is residing in some location. Transitions between locations can be constrained based on clock values and clocks may be reset on transitions. In the tool UPPAAL [19] the modelling formalism is extended to networks of timed automata, including handshake and broadcast communication primitives, communication over shared variables as well as a C-like imperative programming language which allows transitions to be conditioned on and perform complex updates of discrete structured variables.

Consider the small safety critical Bridge Scenario depicted in Fig. 1. Here a Car needs to cross over bridge, while at the same time a Ship wants to pass under the bridge. However, for the Ship to make the passing safely the bridge needs to be open. Conversely, the bridge needs to be closed in order for the Car to safely cross over the bridge. Obviously, the bridge is only allowed to be opened in case the Car is not on the bridge.

Figure 2 provides a timed automata based model of the Bridge Scenario in UPPAAL. The model consists of two timed automata Car and Ship with their respective clocks x and y used to constrain the timing of their transitions: e.g. the combination of the invariant x<=10 of the location Car.Init and the guard x<=5 implies that the output action carW! will take place after a delay of d time-units with $5 \leq d \leq 10$. When reaching the various locations, both Car and Ship broadcast relevant output actions, Car broadcasts

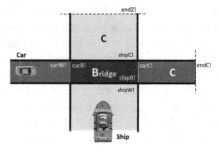

Fig. 1. Safety critical bridge scenario involving a Car and a Ship.

carB! when entering the bridge-location Car.B. The two timed automata synchronize exclusively using the two boolean variables Bcl (indicating that the bridge is closed) and Bus (indicating that the Car is on the bridge). Semantically, a timed automaton describes a timed labelled transition systems, with states being pairs (ℓ, ν), where ℓ is a location and ν is a valuation for the clocks, and with transitions being either delays or discrete actions. In a network of extended timed automata, states are vectors of states – one per component – together with concrete values of discrete variables. E.g. in the Bridge Scenario model of Fig. 2 $[(\text{Car.B}, x = 0), (\text{Ship.W}, y = 11.9), \text{Bus} = 1, \text{Bcl} = 1]$ is a reachable state, witnessed by the following transition sequence:

$$\left[(\text{Car.Init}, x = 0), (\text{Ship.Init}, y = 0), \text{Bus} = 0, \text{Bcl} = 1\right]$$

$$\overset{7.28}{\rightarrow} \overset{\text{carW!}}{\rightarrow} \left[(\text{Car.W}, x = 0), (\text{Ship.W}, y = 7.28), \text{Bus} = 0, \text{Bcl} = 1\right]$$

$$\overset{4.62}{\rightarrow} \overset{\text{carB!}}{\rightarrow} \left[(\text{Car.B}, x = 0), (\text{Ship.W}, y = 11.9), \text{Bus} = 1, \text{Bcl} = 1\right].$$

Given the timed automata model of the Bridge Scenario in Fig. 2, the symbolic verification engine of UPPAAL allows us to verify the crucial safety property A[] !(Car.B and Ship.B), which is a CTL formula expressing that the Ship and the Car cannot be under/at the bridge at the same time. In addition, we may be interested in knowing whether the Car or the Ship may reach their

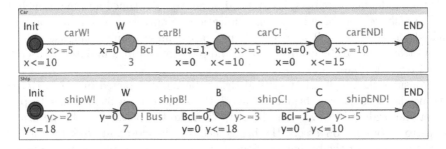

Fig. 2. Timed automata model of the Bridge Scenario of Fig. 1.

respective END-location first. In fact, both outcomes are possible as may be witness by model checking the reachability properties E<> !Car.END and Ship.END and E<> Car.END and !Ship.END.

2.2 Statistical Model Checking

Beyond crucial safety properties, we are often interested in more refined performance analysis of a system. E.g. for the Bridge Scenario, we would be interested in the probabilities that the Car or the Ship finishes first. For such performance queries to be meaningful, we need a *stochastic* semantics of networks of timed automata, where the non-deterministic choices of delays are refined by probability distributions, and where non-deterministic choices between

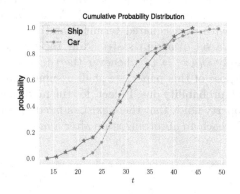

Fig. 3. Cumulative distributions obtained by Pr[<=T](<>Ship.END) and Pr[<=T](<> Car.END)

discrete actions are refined by probabilistic choices. In the branch UPPAAL-SMC, delays of components are by default resolved by a uniform distribution (e.g. in Fig. 2 the delay of Car in Init is uniform between 5 and 10 time-units) or an exponential distribution (e.g. in Fig. 2 the delay of Ship in W is given by an exponential distribution with rate 7). Other distributions may be specified by the user. For composite systems, the choice of which component will perform the next output action (and at which time) is a race between the components settled stochastically by the independent delay distributions of these. We refer the reader to [10–12] for more details on the semantics of stochastic timed automata adopted in UPPAAL-SMC.

Crucially, the stochastic semantics of timed automata offers the basis of a probability measure on measurable sets of runs (obtained from a natural cylinder-construction). In fact, time-bounded reachability, safety properties as well as Metric Interval Temporal Logic (MITL) properties all describe measurable sets of runs [6]. Based on Monte Carlo simulation, the engine of UPPAAL-SMC allows to estimate the probabilities of such (time-bounded) properties by confidence intervals (the user-desired size and confidence of which determines the number of simulations needed). In Fig. 3, we see that the most likely "winner" of the Car and Ship depends highly on the timing bound.

Rather than using MITL or (other logics) for expressing properties of runs, we will use *monitors*, being purely inputting, deterministic timed automata, that are added as extra parallel components to the system. Given a set of (absorbing) accept locations, a monitor M describes all the timed words ϕ_M over the alphabet of the system, that will lead to an accept location. Now, the engine of UPPAAL-SMC allows to estimate $p(\phi_M)$, i.e. the probability that a random run of the system will be accepted by M. In [13] monitors are used to express properties of continuous-time Markov chains. In [1] the logical power of timed automata monitors is characterized.

Monitors M express *logical* properties ϕ_M of runs, i.e. for any given run π, $\phi_M(\pi)$ is either true or false. In this paper, we consider the generalization to *categorical* properties ψ, which for any run π returns a value $\psi(\pi)$ from a finite domain $V = \{v_1, \ldots, v_n\}$. A *categorical monitor* C over V is a monitor, but with n designated terminal and absorbing states $S_a = \{s_1, \ldots s_n\}$ rather than a set of accept states. Now the categorical property ψ_C realized by C is simply $\psi_C(\pi) = v_j$ whenever the run π reaches the terminal state s_j. For the purpose of this paper, we shall assume that monitors reach an absorbing state with probability one. In fact, for the models we use in our examples, the stronger property holds that there exists a fixed upper time bound T, such that monitors will reach an absorbing state after a most T time-units of the underlying system.

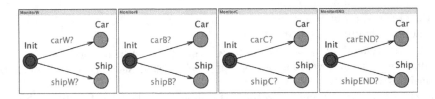

Fig. 4. Monitors from left to right, representing the properties ϕ_W, ϕ_B, ϕ_C, and ϕ_{END}.

For our bridge example, we can consider for $S \in \{W, B, C, END\}$ the categorical properties ϕ_S, all with domain $V = \{Car, Ship\}$, and defined such that $\phi_S(\pi) = Car$ iff in the run π car is first to reach S. Figure 4 shows the monitors for these four properties.

From general stochastic timed automata and the very powerful specification language of monitors, we obtain probabilistic queries $P(\psi_C(\pi) = v_j) =?$ that are undecidable, and therefore outside the reach of exact probabilistic model checking [5]. Approximate estimation techniques like SMC, or the Bayesian network model-based approach we introduce here, therefore are required.

2.3 Bayesian Networks

A (categorical) Bayesian Network is a directed acyclic graph $G = (V, E)$, where each node $v_i \in V$ is associated with a categorical random variables X_i, and edges represent dependencies between the random variables [17]. Let $N := |V|$. G defines the joint probability of the random variables as a product of conditional distributions:

$$p(X_1, \ldots, X_N) := \prod_{i=1}^{N} p(X_i | Parents(X_i)),$$

where $Parents(X_i) = \{X_j | j : (v_j, v_i) \in E\}$. In our application, we need to solve the following computational problems:

Structure Learning. Given a dataset of K observations $(x_1^i, \ldots, x_N^i)$ $(i = 1, \ldots, K)$ of the random variables, learn the edges E of G by optimizing an objective that combines the maximum likelihood criterion with a simplicity objective (sparser structures are preferred). Out of several objective functions that embody similar principles, we choose the Bayesian Information Criterion [21] (BIC) score. The BIC score is asymptotically consistent in the sense that in the large sample limit the BIC-optimal structure will be a minimal structure (in terms of the number of numerical parameters it contains) over which the data generating distribution can be represented [8]. Identifying the BIC-optimal Bayesian network structure is in general NP-hard in the number of variables [7]. On the other hand, it can be shown that, again in the large sample limit, greedy search strategies are sufficient to identify the optimal structure [8]. However, these optimal greedy strategies operate in complex and highly connected search spaces, so that even though the number of search steps they require is polynomial, their overall complexity is not. In all our experiments, we maximize BIC score via greedy Hill Climbing [20], as implemented in the Python library bnlearn [22] for structure learning. We note that even though hill climbing does not necessarily give us the BIC-optimal structure, it will give us in the large sample limit an over-approximation, i.e., a structure that can represent the data-generating distribution, even though not necessarily the sparsest possible such structure. As in our context we are able to generate arbitrary amounts of training data, we can, in principle, approximate the true distribution with arbitrary precision.

Parameter Learning. Once the structure of G is learnt, the parameters of the conditional distributions $p(X_i | Parents(X_i))$ are estimated by maximizing the likelihood. In our case of categorical random variables, and the availability of complete data (the values of all random variables X_i are observed in all of the K samples), this amounts to nothing more than calculating relative frequencies of the value configurations that are needed for a tabular representation of the conditional distributions.

Inference. The learnt Bayesian network is used to compute conditional probability distributions $p(X_i | X_{h_1} = x_{h_1}, \ldots, X_{h_m} = x_{h_m})$ of a query variable X_i given observed values for a subset of the remaining variables. In the worst case, this probabilistic inference is still NP-hard in the size of the Bayesian network. However, several inference techniques exist that often lead to efficient inference in practice. We make use of the Variable Elimination [24] (VE) algorithm, as implemented in the python library bnlearn [22].

3 Methodology

We now describe in detail our approach to combine the power of stochastic timed automata for modeling complex systems with the ability of Bayesian networks for fast and flexible computations of conditional probability distributions.

The fundamental assumption of our approach is that we have at our disposal a stochastic timed automaton, and that we have identified a number of relevant categorical path properties $\phi_1, \ldots, \phi_N$ represented by monitors, such that we need to compute conditional probability distributions involving these properties either over-and-over again, or under real time constraints at run time (or both). In the first case our approach will have an advantage over SMC in terms of amortized time complexity (the time needed to construct the Bayesian network will be more than compensated by much faster computations of query probabilities). In the second case SMC may not be feasible at all because of its inability to meet the time constraints.

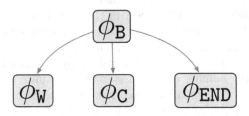

Fig. 5. The Bayesian network learnt from data generated by the model of Fig. 2 and monitors of Fig. 4.

We collect data by running K simulations of the stochastic timed automaton, and recording for each simulation the values returned by the N monitors. This data is collected in a data table D of dimensions $K \times N$, where the ith column then contains values from the domain of ϕ_i.

From D we learn both the structure and the parameters for a Bayesian Networks G, as described in Sect. 2. Figure 5 shows a Bayesian network for the path properties defined by the monitors of Fig. 4 that was learnt from 10,000 random executions of the model shown in Fig. 2. The model learning has identified the ϕ_B property as the central random variable, and correctly shows that given the information which of Car or Ship first passes the bridge, the random variables ϕ_C and ϕ_{END} become independent of ϕ_W.

G can be now used to query the probability distribution of any of the properties, given arbitrary observations of other properties. We illustrate two prototypical query scenarios. The first one is *runtime forecasting*: here we want to continuously update the prediction of a variable as the system run evolves. Figure 6 shows an example where the query random variable is ϕ_{END}, and we update the probability distribution for ϕ_{END} each time the value of one of the other variables becomes known. Figure 7 shows instead the explicit updates of the Bayesian network of Fig. 5 as new properties are observed. We observe that during this particular run of the system the believed probability of the Car being the first at END decreases radically at time-point $t = 10.53$. The second scenario is *diagnostic prediction* for unobservable properties. Even though all the properties in the Bayesian network correspond to monitors in the timed automata model,

Table 1. $p(\phi_W = \text{Car})$ given the four possible combinations for ϕ_C and ϕ_{END}.

	$\phi_{END} = \text{Car}$	$\phi_{END} = \text{Ship}$
$\phi_C = \text{Car}$	0.961	0.5
$\phi_C = \text{Ship}$	0.005	0.005

in the real world some of these properties may not be observable. We can then use the Bayesian network to make predictions about the unobservable properties based on what we could observe. In our example, we may assume that only ϕ_C and ϕ_{END} are observable, due to suitably positioned cameras. We may then be interested in inferring the state of ϕ_W given the available observations. ϕ_W is an interesting property, for example, if one aims to minimize the waiting time of the boat as this latter pollutes more than a car. Table 1 shows the probability values for $\phi_W = \text{Car}$ given the four possible configurations of the observable variables.

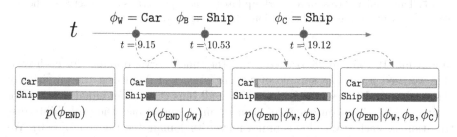

Fig. 6. Evolution of $p(\phi_{END})$ as new properties are observed. Note that right after $t = 9.15$ the Car most likely arrives first to the end. However, at $t = 10.53$ the situation drastically changes due to the observation of $\phi_B = \text{Ship}$.

4   Experiments

We evaluated our method on three different scenarios.

4.1   Bridge Crossing

We consider a more complex set of properties for the Bridge scenario described in Sect. 1. We now define properties $\psi_{Car,S}$, $\psi_{Ship,S}$ for $S \in \{W, B, C, END\}$. Associated with these properties are domains $T_{Car,S}$, $T_{Ship,S}$ that each consist of 8 time intervals.

For example, $T_{Car,B} = \{[0, 5.931], [5.931, 6.601], \ldots, [19.195, 28.614]\}$, and $\psi_{Car,B} = [19.195, 28.614]$ means that the car has arrived at the bridge between

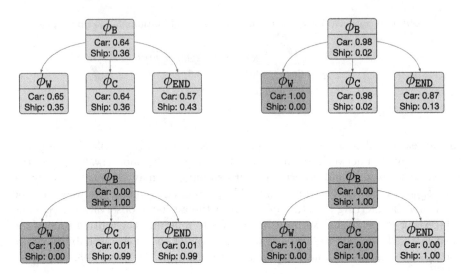

Fig. 7. The explict Bayesian network updates as new properties are observed. The red block represents properties observations. (Color figure online)

time points 19.195 and 28.614. To define the time interval domains for each variable we used a random sample of system runs, and quantized the empirically observed arrival times into 8 bins so that all bins contain an equal numbers of sample points. As a consequence, prior to any observations, the probability distribution for each ψ variable is uniform over its domain (cf. Fig. 9 at $T = 0$). We also retain the property ϕ_{END} with domain $\{\text{Car}, \text{Ship}\}$ as introduced in Sect. 3.

We here consider a runtime forecasting scenario, where we want to maintain a continuously updated prediction for the time $\psi_{\text{Car,END}}$ at which the car reaches its destination. We learnt a Bayesian network for the joint probability distribution of the properties from a dataset of $K = 10,000$ model simulations. The resulting Bayesian Network is depicted in Fig. 8. Figure 9 reports for one particular run the evolution of $p(\psi_{\text{Car,END}})$ as new properties are observed, and hence used as evidence. Here, new evidence is obtained at 4 distinct points in time $T_1, \ldots, T_4$. The figure shows for each of these timepoints the newly acquired observation, and the conditional probability distribution of $p(\psi_{\text{Car,END}})$ given all observations up to that point in time.

Finally, we estimated the time per query by averaging the query time on 10,000 model traces, which results to be 0.08 ± 0.05 s. Those results confirm that the Bayesian Network query can keep up with the speed of this real-time application.

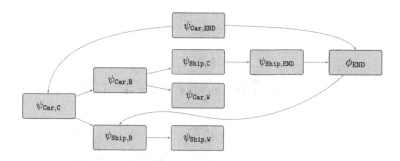

Fig. 8. The Bayesian Network structure for the Bridge Scenario.

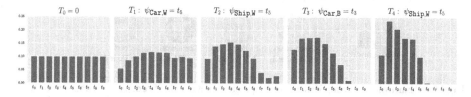

Fig. 9. The evolution of $p(\psi_{Car,END})$ as new properties are observed:

4.2 Job Shop

Three persons Kim, Manfred, and Alessandro, want to read the four sections com, spo, pol, and loc (*Commerce, Sport, Politics,* and *Local news*) of a shared newspaper. Each person can read one section at a time and the sections cannot be shared among the persons. A person must wait until a section becomes available before reading it. Furthermore, each person reads the sections in a given order for a different amount of time. Figure 10 depicts an example of ordered section requests for each person. For each person, we designed a template in UPPAAL-SMC, an example of which is shown in Fig. 11. During each simulation of the model we are interested in several temporal properties. Let $U = \{$Kim, Manfred, Alessandro$\}$ be the set of persons, $S = \{$com, spo, pol, loc$\}$ the set of sections, and $T_U = \{t_0, \dots, t_W\}$ and $T_S = \{t_0, \dots, t_Z\}$ sets of time intervals. We are interested in evaluating the following properties during each simulation of the model

- for each $u \in U$ the property ϕ_u with domain T_U representing the time interval in which u finishes the reading or all sections.
- for each $u \in U$ and $s \in S$ the property $\psi_{u,s}$ with domain T_S representing the time interval in which u finishes to read section s.

We again learnt a Bayesian network for the joint probability distribution of the properties from a dataset of $K = 10,000$ model simulations. The resulting Bayesian Network is depicted in Fig. 12. For this case, the learnt structure shows two main clusters which involves Alessandro and Kim properties. The cluster

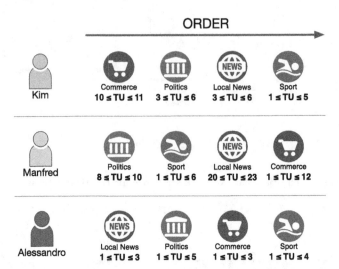

Fig. 10. Example of ordered section requests for Kim, Manfred, and Alessandro. TU represents the time units for which each section is requested by a person, e.g. Kim asks for the com section for at least 10 TU and for at most 11 TU.

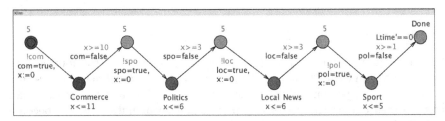

Fig. 11. Uppaal-SMC template for Kim. The green statements represent conditions for executing a transition. The blue statements represent variable updates right after a transition is executed. The purple statements represents invariants. com, pol, loc, and spo are boolean variables representing whether the corresponding section (*Commerce, Sport, Politics,* and *Local news*) is free. x is a clock.

related to Alessandro connects more specific Alessandro properties. A similar behaviour happens for Kim, while the properties related to Manfred are more distributed over the network.

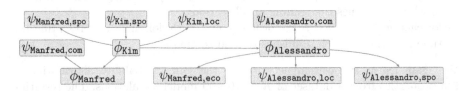

Fig. 12. The Bayesian Network structure for the Job Shop Scenario. Four of the properties are represented by nodes not connected to any other nodes. For the sake of better visualization they are not shown in the figure.

With the trained Bayesian Network we can now infer (on new simulations) probabilities of unobserved properties given the knowledge of real-time observed properties. Figure 13 shows an example of the evolution of $p(\phi_{\text{Kim}})$ as new properties are observed and hence used as evidence. Finally, we report in Fig. 14 the empirical query time distribution on 10,000 model traces, similarly to Sect. 4.1. We point out the fact that the estimated query time distribution has small variance and is concentrated around 0.04 s.

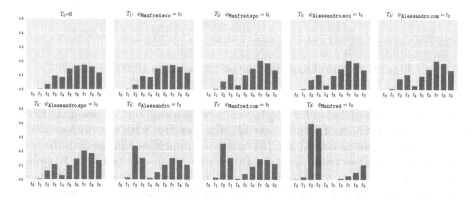

Fig. 13. The evolution of $p(\phi_{\text{Kim}})$ as new properties are observed.

4.3 Process Resource Model

In this section we introduce a general process resource model, which can be seen as a common abstraction of the two previous examples. Here, we assume that we monitor a set of processes which, for being able to complete their execution, have to access a set of resources in a certain order. Each resource can be accessed only by one process at a time and each process can use only one resource at a time. Furthermore, each process cannot reuse the same resource.

We are here interested in studying the scalability of our approach by measuring the execution time for the queries, when the complexity of the system, as given by the number of processes and resources, increases. We consider three different instantiation of the generic system model:

- **System A**: 5 processes and 5 resources;
- **System B**: 10 processes and 10 resources;
- **System C**: 20 processes and 20 resources.

For this scenario we consider two sets of properties: one that contains properties which capture the ending time for each process, and one that contains properties

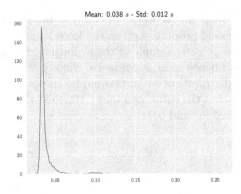

Fig. 14. Empirical time distribution estimated on 10,000 traces.

which capture the duration for which each process uses a certain resource. Each property has a domain of 5 time intervals. For a system with n processes and n resources, this gives us a total of $C(n) := n + n^2$ properties. Similarly to the previous experimental sections, for each of the three systems we trained a Bayesian Network on data from 5,000 sample runs. The learnt models for A, B, C have $C(n)$ nodes, and 14,16 and 22 edges, respectively. This very sparse connectivity is due to the fact that the properties are mostly very weakly dependent, and the BIC score used for training will approximate sufficiently weak dependence by independence assumptions. The computation times for learning the structure of the three Bayesian Networks are 38 s, 373 s, and 1914 s (averaged over 5 different learning runs).[1]

We simulated a runtime forecasting scenario as follows: for each system we generated another 5,000 random runs. For each run, we selected the property whose value was observed last on that run (i.e., the finishing time of the process that finished last on the run) as the query property. Then, similar to what is shown in Figs. 9 and 13, we computed over each run the sequence of conditional probability distributions of the query property, given the incremental observation sequence. Thus, for a system of size n, a total of $5,000 \cdot C(n)$ probability queries conditioned on 0 to $C(n) - 1$ observed properties were computed.

Figure 15 shows the resulting empirical query time distribution for System A, System B, and System C. The results show that here our approach scales very well as the size of the system increases. The almost constant query time here is enabled by the weak dependencies among the properties, and the resulting sparse connectivity of the Bayesian network. Such an independence structure cannot be exploited in a similar manner by SMC, as our following results show.

---

[1] All the experiments ran on an Apple MacBook Pro Mid 2015, 2.5 GHz Quad-Core Intel Core i7, with 16 GB of RAM and only one core has been used.

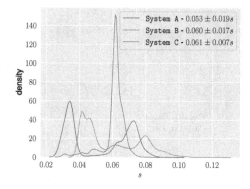

Fig. 15. Distribution of the query time execution for System A, System B, and System C.

We ran the same queries that give the results of Fig. 15 in Uppaal-SMC. Since these are conditional probability queries which are not directly supported by SMC, we calculate a conditional probability $p(A|B)$ as the ratio $p(A,B)/p(B)$, using two separate SMC estimates for $p(A,B)$ and $p(B)$. Uppaal-SMC requires the specification of a confidence parameter ϵ for the width of a confidence interval that will be returned for the query probability. When $[l_{A,B}, u_{A,B}]$ and $[l_B, u_B]$ are the confidence intervals for $p(A,B)$ and $p(B)$, respectively, we compute the confidence interval for $p(A|B)$ as $[\frac{l_{A,B}}{u_B}, \frac{u_{A,B}}{l_B}]$. This can lead to very wide confidence intervals for the conditional, even when $[l_{A,B}, u_{A,B}]$ and $[l_B, u_B]$ have a small width ϵ. Ideally, we would use for this experiment ϵ values such that the confidence intervals for the conditional probabilities become reasonably small, and the accuracy of the SMC estimate matches the accuracy of the Bayesian network values. This is not an easy task, and as the results of the next section will show, would probably require ϵ values that are much smaller than what can feasibly be computed. For the purpose of this runtime comparison we therefore simply consider the three values $\epsilon = 0.1, 0.01, 0.001$, which will only give very rough estimates for conditionals once the probabilities of the conditioning observations become small.

Table 2 shows the average query time for the three models and three ϵ values. We set a timeout at 5 min. We observe that SMC computation here scales neither as a function of the system complexity, nor as a function of the precision parameter ϵ.

Table 2. Average time per query in Uppaal-SMC

ϵ	System A	System B	System C
0.1	0.13 s	0.52 s	3.68 s
0.01	1.60 s	8.22 s	> 5 m
0.001	> 5 m	> 5 m	> 5 m

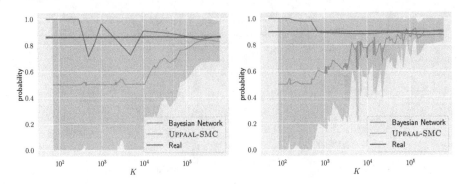

Fig. 16. $p(\phi_{\mathsf{END}} = \mathsf{Car}|\psi_{\mathsf{Car,W}}, \psi_{\mathsf{Ship,W}}, \psi_{\mathsf{Car,B}}, \psi_{\mathsf{Ship,B}})$ estimated with Bayesian Network in blue and Uppaal-SMC in orange. In green the true probability. Left/right: estimated probabilities for the rare/common configuration of observed properties. (Color figure online)

5   Accuracy Analysis

In this section we investigate the accuracy of probabilities calculated with learnt Bayesian networks, and compare against the accuracy that is obtained by SMC using a comparable amount of data.

We return to the Bridge scenario described in Sects. 1 and 4.1. We consider the conditional probability distribution

$$p(\phi_{\mathsf{END}} = \mathsf{Car}|\psi_{\mathsf{Car,W}}, \psi_{\mathsf{Ship,W}}, \psi_{\mathsf{Car,B}}, \psi_{\mathsf{Ship,B}}).$$

For the conditioning variables $\psi_{\mathsf{Car,W}}, \cdots, \psi_{\mathsf{Ship,B}}$ we identify a *rare* and a *common* joint configuration of time-interval values. The rare and common configuration occur 1177, respectively 6147 times in a sample of $1M$ traces.

We estimated the true query probabilities by repeating 10 simulations of 1 M traces each. The mean empirical values of the query probabilities, and the standard deviation over the 10 simulations is shown in Fig. 16 as "Real". The negligible standard deviation shows that we can treat the obtained estimate as the ground truth probability.

We learnt Bayesian networks from K sampled traces for 14 distinct values of K ranging from $K = 50$ to $K = 600,000$. The probabilities obtained from the learnt networks for the two different queries are plotted in Fig. 16 as a function of K. As described in Sect. 4.3, SMC in Uppaal-SMC is not directly controlled by specifying a sample size, but through a confidence parameter ϵ. We ran Uppaal-SMC multiple times, continuously varying ϵ from 0.05 to 0.00005, and computing a confidence interval for the conditional query from the confidence intervals at the specified ϵ level for the two unconditional probabilities. In Fig. 16 the resulting confidence interval is plotted against the size of the sample that was actually required to obtain the confidence intervals at the specified ϵ. The plot also shows the mid-point of the obtained confidence intervals as point estimates for the query probabilities.

There are a number of observations we can make from these plots: first, we see that even for very small ϵ values (i.e., large sample sizes), the width of the SMC confidence interval for the conditional probability decreases only very slowly. This, in particular, indicates that the ϵ values shown in Table 2 are still larger than what would be required to obtain reasonably accurate probability estimates. The point estimates obtained from the Bayesian network converge to the true probability much faster than the SMC point estimates. This is more pronounced in the 'rare' configuration, where SMC is handicapped by the smaller number of samples that will be relevant for the query probability. The Bayesian network estimates are less affected by the rarity of the observed values, since its probabilities are derived from a combination of empirical frequencies, and inferred conditional independence relationships.

6   Conclusions

We have introduced a framework which links statistical model checking with machine learning. We exploited Bayesian Networks to learn dependencies among interesting temporal properties of a stochastic timed automaton. We have identified real-time application scenarios where our approach can be used. In particular, we highlight the advantages of the Bayesian Network approach in comparison with SMC for real-time updating of probabilities of unobserved properties as new property are observed during the evolution of a real-time system. We empirically validated our framework on three real-time scenarios, showing that Bayesian Network inference is able to keep up with the evolution of a real-time system. Furthermore, the estimated probabilities are at least as accurate as what is obtained from UPPAAL-SMC.

It is a interesting subject of future work to extend our approach to learn also a set of interesting properties, rather than defining the properties a priori. This research direction might lead to strengthen the connections between the machine learning and the statistical model checking domains.

References

1. Aceto, L., Bouyer, P., Burgueño, A., Larsen, K.G.: The power of reachability testing for timed automata. In: Arvind, V., Ramanujam, S. (eds.) FSTTCS 1998. LNCS, vol. 1530, pp. 245–256. Springer, Heidelberg (1998). https://doi.org/10.1007/978-3-540-49382-2_22
2. AlTurki, M., Meseguer, J.: PVESTA: a parallel statistical model checking and quantitative analysis tool. In: Corradini, A., Klin, B., Cîrstea, C. (eds.) CALCO 2011. LNCS, vol. 6859, pp. 386–392. Springer, Heidelberg (2011). https://doi.org/10.1007/978-3-642-22944-2_28
3. Alur, R., Dill, D.L.: A theory of timed automata. Theor. Comput. Sci. **126**(2), 183–235 (1994). https://doi.org/10.1016/0304-3975(94)90010-8
4. Alur, R., Giacobbe, M., Henzinger, T.A., Larsen, K.G., Mikučionis, M.: Continuous-time models for system design and analysis. In: Steffen, B., Woeginger, G. (eds.) Computing and Software Science. LNCS, vol. 10000, pp. 452–477. Springer, Cham (2019). https://doi.org/10.1007/978-3-319-91908-9_22

5. Bulychev, P., et al.: UPPAAL-SMC: statistical model checking for priced timed automata. arXiv preprint arXiv:1207.1272 (2012)
6. Bulychev, P., David, A., Larsen, K.G., Legay, A., Li, G., Poulsen, D.B.: Rewrite-based statistical model checking of WMTL. In: Qadeer, S., Tasiran, S. (eds.) RV 2012. LNCS, vol. 7687, pp. 260–275. Springer, Heidelberg (2013). https://doi.org/10.1007/978-3-642-35632-2_25
7. Chickering, D.M., Heckerman, D., Meek, C.: Large-sample learning of Bayesian networks is np-hard. J. Mach. Learn. Res. **5**(Oct), 1287–1330 (2004)
8. Chickering, D.M., Meek, C.: Finding optimal Bayesian networks. In: Proceedings of the Eighteenth Conference on Uncertainty in Artificial Intelligence, pp. 94–102 (2002)
9. David, A., Jensen, P.G., Larsen, K.G., Mikučionis, M., Taankvist, J.H.: UPPAAL STRATEGO. In: Baier, C., Tinelli, C. (eds.) TACAS 2015. LNCS, vol. 9035, pp. 206–211. Springer, Heidelberg (2015). https://doi.org/10.1007/978-3-662-46681-0_16
10. David, A., Larsen, K.G., Legay, A., Mikučionis, M., Poulsen, D.B.: Uppaal SMC tutorial. Int. J. Softw. Tools Technol. Transf. **17**(4), 397–415 (2015). https://doi.org/10.1007/s10009-014-0361-y
11. David, A., et al.: Statistical model checking for networks of priced timed automata. In: Fahrenberg, U., Tripakis, S. (eds.) FORMATS 2011. LNCS, vol. 6919, pp. 80–96. Springer, Heidelberg (2011). https://doi.org/10.1007/978-3-642-24310-3_7
12. David, A., Larsen, K.G., Legay, A., Mikučionis, M., Wang, Z.: Time for statistical model checking of real-time systems. In: Gopalakrishnan, G., Qadeer, S. (eds.) CAV 2011. LNCS, vol. 6806, pp. 349–355. Springer, Heidelberg (2011). https://doi.org/10.1007/978-3-642-22110-1_27
13. Feng, Y., Katoen, J.-P., Li, H., Xia, B., Zhan, N.: Monitoring CTMCs by multi-clock timed automata. In: Chockler, H., Weissenbacher, G. (eds.) CAV 2018. LNCS, vol. 10981, pp. 507–526. Springer, Cham (2018). https://doi.org/10.1007/978-3-319-96145-3_27
14. Jegourel, C., Legay, A., Sedwards, S.: A platform for high performance statistical model checking – PLASMA. In: Flanagan, C., König, B. (eds.) TACAS 2012. LNCS, vol. 7214, pp. 498–503. Springer, Heidelberg (2012). https://doi.org/10.1007/978-3-642-28756-5_37
15. Jiang, Z., Pajic, M., Moarref, S., Alur, R., Mangharam, R.: Modeling and verification of a dual chamber implantable pacemaker. In: Flanagan, C., König, B. (eds.) TACAS 2012. LNCS, vol. 7214, pp. 188–203. Springer, Heidelberg (2012). https://doi.org/10.1007/978-3-642-28756-5_14
16. Kalajdzic, K., Bartocci, E., Smolka, S.A., Stoller, S.D., Grosu, R.: Runtime verification with particle filtering. In: Legay, A., Bensalem, S. (eds.) RV 2013. LNCS, vol. 8174, pp. 149–166. Springer, Heidelberg (2013). https://doi.org/10.1007/978-3-642-40787-1_9
17. Koller, D., Friedman, N.: Probabilistic Graphical Models: Principles and Techniques. MIT Press, Cambridge (2009)
18. Larsen, K.G., Mikučionis, M., Taankvist, J.H.: Safe and optimal adaptive cruise control. In: Meyer, R., Platzer, A., Wehrheim, H. (eds.) Correct System Design. LNCS, vol. 9360, pp. 260–277. Springer, Cham (2015). https://doi.org/10.1007/978-3-319-23506-6_17
19. Larsen, K.G., Pettersson, P., Yi, W.: UPPAAL in a nutshell. Int. J. Softw. Tools Technol. Transf. **1**(1–2), 134–152 (1997). https://doi.org/10.1007/s100090050010
20. Russell, S., Norvig, P.: Artificial Intelligence: A Modern Approach, 3rd edn. Prentice Hall Press, New York (2009)

21. Schwarz, G., et al.: Estimating the dimension of a model. Ann. Stat. **6**(2), 461–464 (1978)
22. Taskesen, E.: bnlearn (2019). https://github.com/erdogant/bnlearn
23. Wu, X., Ling, H., Dong, Y.: On modeling and verifying of application protocols of TTCAN in flight-control system with UPPAAL. In: 2009 International Conference on Embedded Software and Systems, pp. 572–577. IEEE (2009)
24. Zhang, N.L., Poole, D.: A simple approach to Bayesian network computations. In: Proceedings of the Biennial Conference-Canadian Society for Computational Studies of Intelligence, pp. 171–178. Canadian Information Processing Society (1994)

Author Index

Printed in the United States
By Bookmasters